WELFARE BENEFITS AND IMMIGRATION LAW

WELFARE BENEFITS AND IMMIGRATION LAW

Kevin Browne, LLB, Solicitor

Published by
College of Law Publishing,
Braboeuf Manor, Portsmouth Road, St Catherines, Guildford GU3 1HA

© The College of Law 2008

All rights reserved. No part of this publication may be reproduced, stored in a retrieval system, or transmitted in any way or by any means, including photocopying or recording, without the written permission of the copyright holder, application for which should be addressed to the publisher.

British Library Cataloguing-in-Publication Data
A catalogue record for this book is available from the British Library.

ISBN 978 1 905391 51 6

Typeset by Style Photosetting Ltd, Mayfield, East Sussex
Printed in Great Britain by Ashford Colour Press Ltd, Gosport, Hampshire

Preface

This book has been written primarily for use by students studying Welfare Benefits and/or Immigration Law as part of the Legal Practice Course. The author hopes that it will also be of more general use and value to practitioners seeking an introduction to these complex and specialised subjects.

Part I of this book has been written to provide a simple introduction to the social security system in England and Wales. It does not cover all benefits, neither does it cover all the provisions of those benefits within its ambit. In particular, it deals mainly with new claims, and contains little on transitional provisions which may preserve or protect rights to benefits for those claimants who started to receive a benefit before a change in the law which would now disentitle them or require them to be treated differently. In **Chapter 1** the welfare benefits system is outlined. **Chapter 2** then deals with various topics that are common to the non means-tested benefits. In the next seven chapters the benefits are collected together by client group, such as the unemployed, disabled, retired, bereaved etc. **Chapter 10** then considers the inter-relationship of the two areas of law, and in particular the immigration requirements for claiming and exporting a welfare benefit. The Appendices contain practical and, I hope, useful source materials.

Part II of this book is intended to provide a straightforward introduction to the specialist field of immigration and nationality law and practice. In **Chapter 11** the immigration system is introduced. **Chapter 12** deals with British nationality and the right of abode in the UK. **Chapter 13** provides an overview of immigration controls and **Chapter 14** collects together entrants to the UK by immigration category, such as visitor, student, employee etc. **Chapter 15** addresses the question of who is subject to deportation and removal. **Chapter 16** looks at the appeals system. **Chapter 17** provides a brief overview of judicial review proceedings and **Chapter 18** sets out key features to consider when advising.

These two areas of law are always changing. For example, in this edition I have flagged up in welfare benefits two significant changes on the horizon. First, in Autumn 2008 the Government proposes that, for new claimants, Employment and Support Allowance will replace both incapacity benefit, as well as income support paid on the grounds of incapacity (see **4.4.4**). Also, from April 2009 (but in some areas before that), housing benefit for tenants of private landlords will be calculated and paid by local authorities under a new scheme known as local housing allowance. It will be based on local rents (see **9.3.2.6**). In addition to the usual updating, I have also included the Court of Appeal case of *Abdirahman and Ullusow v Secretary of State for Work and Pensions* [2007] EWCA Civ 657 concerning benefit claims by EEA nationals.

As to immigration law, Romania and Bulgaria joined the EU in 2007. Applicants for settlement or naturalisation must pass a 'Life in the UK' test (see **12.2.6.1**). Eligibility for the highly skilled migrants scheme has been revised (see **14.7.2**). The question of whether the permission to marry scheme complies with the European Convention on Human Rights was answered in the negative by the Court of Appeal in *R (Baiai) v Secretary of State for the Home Department* [2007] EWCA Civ 478 (see **14.9.6.1**). The Refugee or Person in Need of International Protection (Qualification) Regulations 2006 (SI 2006/2525) are dealt with in **Chapter 13** and are reproduced in **Appendix 12** to this Part. The House of Lords' decision on reg 6(1)(d) in *K v Secretary of State for the Home Department; Fornah v Secretary of State for the Home Department* [2006] UKHL 45, [2007] 1 All ER 671 is included, as is the Home Office 'New Asylum Model' that was introduced in April 2007 (see **14.17.9**).

KEVIN BROWNE
The College of Law
Store Street

Contents

PREFACE		v
TABLE OF CASES		xiii
TABLE OF STATUTES		xvii
TABLE OF SECONDARY LEGISLATION		xxi
TABLE OF ABBREVIATIONS		xxix

Part I		**WELFARE BENEFITS**	1
Chapter 1		INTRODUCTION TO WELFARE BENEFITS	3
	1.1	The nature of welfare law	3
	1.2	Overview of the benefits system	3
	1.3	Sources of welfare benefits law	6
	1.4	Welfare benefits administration	8
	1.5	Benefits for people entering and leaving the UK	14
	1.6	Welfare law bibliography	14
	1.7	Which benefit? A quick guide	16
	1.8	Fact analysis	17
	1.9	Claimant profiling	18
	1.10	Human rights	18
	1.11	The claimant's 'partner'	19
Chapter 2		INTRODUCTION TO NON MEANS-TESTED BENEFITS	21
	2.1	The scope of this chapter	21
	2.2	National Insurance contributions	22
	2.3	Contribution conditions	27
	2.4	Increases for adult dependants	31
	2.5	Incompatible non means-tested benefits	32
	2.6	Overlapping non means-tested benefits	33
	2.7	Claiming more than one non means-tested benefit: a summary	33
Chapter 3		JOBSEEKER'S ALLOWANCE	35
	3.1	Introduction	35
	3.2	Conditions of entitlement	36
	3.3	Disqualification from benefit	41
	3.4	Amount of contribution-based jobseeker's allowance	44
	3.5	The New Deal	44
	3.6	Contribution-based JSA and other benefits	44
	3.7	Claimant profile: CBJSA	45
Chapter 4		INCAPACITY AND DISABILITY	47
	4.1	Introduction	47
	4.2	Incapacity for work	48
	4.3	Statutory sick pay	52
	4.4	Incapacity benefit	53
	4.5	Non-contributory incapacity benefit: persons incapacitated in youth (SSCBA 1992, s 30A)	55
	4.6	Disability living allowance	56
	4.7	DLA care component	57
	4.8	DLA mobility component	62

	4.9	Attendance allowance (SSCBA 1992, s 64)	66
	4.10	Industrial disablement benefit	66
	4.11	Constant attendance allowance (CAA)	73
	4.12	New Deal for disabled people	73
	4.13	Claimant profiles	74
Chapter 5		RETIREMENT AND BEREAVEMENT	75
	5.1	Introduction	75
	5.2	Retirement benefits	75
	5.3	State pension credit	78
	5.4	Bereavement benefits	81
	5.5	Claimant profiles	83
Chapter 6		MATERNITY, CHILDREN AND CARERS	85
	6.1	Contents of this chapter	85
	6.2	Maternity benefits: an overview	85
	6.3	Statutory maternity pay	86
	6.4	Maternity allowance (SSCBA 1992, s 35)	88
	6.5	Other benefits for pregnant and recently delivered women	89
	6.6	Child benefit (SSCBA 1992, s 143)	89
	6.7	Carer's allowance (SSCBA 1992, s 70)	91
	6.8	Claimant profiles	93
Chapter 7		INTRODUCTION TO THE MEANS-TESTED BENEFITS	95
	7.1	The scope of this chapter	95
	7.2	Resources: capital	96
	7.3	Resources: income	99
	7.4	The family and the benefits household	102
	7.5	Needs: the applicable amount	104
	7.6	Personal allowances	104
	7.7	Premiums	105
	7.8	The comparison	108
	7.9	Common problems of means-tested benefits	108
	7.10	Living together as 'husband and wife' or 'civil partners'	108
	7.11	Overpayment of benefits	111
	7.12	Mechanics of recovery	114
	7.13	Deductions from benefit	114
Chapter 8		INCOME SUPPORT AND INCOME-BASED JOBSEEKER'S ALLOWANCE	117
	8.1	The scope of this chapter	117
	8.2	Income support or jobseeker's allowance?	117
	8.3	Housing costs	120
	8.4	Restrictions on housing costs	122
	8.5	Calculation and payment	123
	8.6	Non-dependants and housing costs	125
	8.7	Worked examples	125
	8.8	Change of circumstances and reviews	128
	8.9	The passport effect	128
	8.10	Hardship payments and urgent cases payments	129
	8.11	Hardship payments (JA Regs 1996, regs 140–146)	129
	8.12	Urgent cases payments	130
	8.13	Passporting	130
	8.14	IS/IBJSA and other benefits	131
	8.15	Claimant profiles	131
Chapter 9		OTHER MEANS-TESTED BENEFITS	133
	9.1	The scope of this chapter	133
	9.2	Local authority benefits: common features	134

9.3	Housing benefit	136
9.4	Council tax benefit	139
9.5	Worked examples	141
9.6	The tax credits	143
9.7	Common features of the two tax credits	143
9.8	Conditions of entitlement for child tax credit	146
9.9	Calculating child tax credit: a summary of the steps	148
9.10	Conditions of entitlement for working tax credit	148
9.11	Tapering when entitled to both credits	156
9.12	Calculating working tax credit: a summary of the steps	157
9.13	Tax credits: worked examples	157
9.14	The tax credits and other benefits	160
9.15	Payment of tax credits	160
9.16	The social fund	160
9.17	Passport benefits	163
9.18	Claimant profiles	165

Chapter 10 BENEFITS AND IMMIGRATION REQUIREMENTS 167

10.1	The scope of this chapter	167
10.2	Potential sources of entitlement to benefits in Great Britain	167
10.3	Immigration status and entitlement to certain non-contributory benefits in Great Britain	169
10.4	Residence requirements and entitlement to benefits in Great Britain and 'exporting' benefits	171
10.5	Northern Ireland and the Common Travel Area	175
10.6	Ordinarily resident	175
10.7	Habitual residence	176
10.8	Immigration law and public funds	181
10.9	Asylum seekers	183
10.10	Urgent cases payments	183
10.11	Social fund payment	183
10.12	EEA nationals claiming benefits	183

Appendices to Part I 185

Appendix 1	Specimen Jobseeker's Agreement	187
Appendix 2	Extracts from the Social Security (Incapacity for Work) (General) Regulations 1995, as amended	191
Appendix 3	Schedule 2 – Prescribed Degrees of Disablement	197
Appendix 4	Working Tax Credit – Disability Which Puts a Person at a Disadvantage in Getting a Job – Part 1 of Schedule 1	201
Appendix 5	Welfare Benefits: Reciprocal Agreements	203

Part II IMMIGRATION AND NATIONALITY 205

Chapter 11 INTRODUCTION TO PART II 207

11.1	The scope of Part II	207
11.2	Sources of immigration law	207
11.3	Institutions	210
11.4	Immigration controls	211

Chapter 12 NATIONALITY AND RIGHT OF ABODE 213

12.1	Introduction	213
12.2	British citizenship	213
12.3	Commonwealth citizens with right of abode	219
12.4	Historical background	220
12.5	Citizens of the European Union	222

x   Welfare Benefits and Immigration Law

Chapter 13	IMMIGRATION STATUS: AN INTRODUCTION	223
13.1	Limited and unlimited leave to enter	223
13.2	Settlement	224
13.3	Immigration controls	226
13.4	Entry clearance	226
13.5	Leave to enter	227
13.6	Variation of leave	230
13.7	EEA nationals	234
13.8	Rights under EC law	235
13.9	The Immigration (European Economic Area) Regulations 2006	236
13.10	Chart cross-referencing key aspects of 2006 Regulations and 2004 Directive	244
13.11	The Common Travel Area	244

Chapter 14	IMMIGRATION STATUS: SPECIAL CATEGORIES	247
14.1	Visitors	247
14.2	Students	251
14.3	Other temporary purposes	256
14.4	Employment, business and independent means	258
14.5	Employment	259
14.6	Businessmen and self-employed persons	266
14.7	Innovators and highly skilled migrants	269
14.8	Investors	273
14.9	Spouses and civil partners	274
14.10	Marriage breakdown	281
14.11	Polygamous marriages or civil partnerships	282
14.12	Spouses or civil partners of persons with limited leave	282
14.13	Fiancé(e)s or proposed civil partners of persons who are settled	282
14.14	Non-marital relationships	283
14.15	Children	285
14.16	Parents and other relatives	290
14.17	Asylum-seekers and refugees	293

Chapter 15	DEPORTATION AND ADMINISTRATIVE REMOVAL	307
15.1	Deportation	307
15.2	Administrative removal	310
15.3	Enforcement action in cases involving spouses	312
15.4	Enforcement action involving children or parents	315

Chapter 16	IMMIGRATION APPEALS	319
16.1	Appeals: the general rule	319
16.2	Decisions against which there is a right of appeal	319
16.3	Grounds of appeal	320
16.4	Appeal rights exercisable in the UK	320
16.5	The 'one stop' process	321
16.6	The appeals system	322
16.7	Pending and abandoned appeals	323
16.8	Ineligible appeals	324
16.9	Visitors or students without entry clearance	324
16.10	Family visitor refused entry clearance	324
16.11	Student	325
16.12	National security and similar matters	325
16.13	'Public good' exclusion	325
16.14	EEA nationals	326
16.15	Asylum appeals: 'third country' removal	326
16.16	Unfounded human rights or asylum claims	326
16.17	Deprivation of citizenship orders	327
16.18	Immigration, Asylum and Nationality Act 2006	327

Chapter 17	JUDICIAL REVIEW		329
	17.1	General	329
	17.2	Availability of judicial review	329
	17.3	Prompt action	330
	17.4	Statutory review under NIAA 2002, s 101	330
	17.5	Habeas corpus	330
Chapter 18	ADVISING THE CLIENT		331
	18.1	Personal details	331
	18.2	Immigration status	331
	18.3	The disputed decision	331
	18.4	Reasons for disputed decision	332
	18.5	Time limits	332
	18.6	Client's objectives	332
	18.7	Available options	332

Appendices to Part II — 335

Appendix 1	Statement of Changes in Immigration Rules 1994 (HC 395)	337
Appendix 2	Commonwealth Citizens	491
Appendix 3	British Overseas Territories	493
Appendix 4	Visa Nationals	495
Appendix 5	The European Union and Associated States	497
Appendix 6	Directive 2004/58/EC	499
Appendix 7	Immigration (European Economic Area) Regulations 2006	513
Appendix 8	Work Permits (UK) Shortage Occupation List May 2007	537
Appendix 9	Extracts from the European Convention on Human Rights	541
Appendix 10	Income Categories: Highly Skilled Migrants	545
Appendix 11	MBA Eligible Programmes	547
Appendix 12	Refugee or Person in Need of International Protection (Qualification) Regulations 2006	549

INDEX — 553

Table of Cases

A

Abdirahman and Ullusow v Secretary of State for Work and Pensions [2007] EWCA Civ 657	v, 178
Adan v Secretary of State for the Home Department [1999] 1 AC 293	295
Ahmed v Secretary of State for Work and Pensions [2005] EWCA Civ 535	227
AI v Secretary of State for the Home Department [2007] EWCA Civ 386	281
Akrich (Case C-109/01) [2003] 3 CMLR 26	240
Alpine Investments BV v Minister van Financiën (Case C-384/93) (1995)	236
Amarjit Kaur (1999) INLP 110	276
Aramide v Secretary of State for the Home Department (2000) LTL, 24 July	307

B

B v Secretary of State for the Home Department [2000] Imm AR 478	244, 308
B v Secretary of State for Work and Pensions [2005] EWCA Civ 929	113
Becerikil v Secretary of State for the Home Department [2006] EWCA Civ 693	295
Begum v Immigration Appeal Tribunal [1994] Imm AR 381	293

C

Canadian Pacific Railway Co v Lockhart [1942] AC 591	67
Carltona Ltd v Commissioner of Works [1943] 2 All ER 560	210
Cockburn v Chief Adjudication Officer; Secretary of State for Social Security v Fairey (also known as Halliday) [1997] 1 WLR 799	57
Collins v Secretary of State for Work and Pensions (2004) The Times, 30 March	180
Collins v Secretary of State for Work and Pensions [2006] EWCA Civ 376	180
Commissioner's Decision 29/00	65
Commissioner's Decision C135/50	69
Commissioner's Decision CA/140/1985	60
Commissioner's Decision CA/281/1989	60
Commissioner's Decision CDLA 8353/95	64
Commissioner's Decision CDLA/042/94	65
Commissioner's Decision CDLA/1148/1997	59
Commissioner's Decision CDLA/1252/1995	61
Commissioner's Decision CDLA/156/1994	64
Commissioner's Decision CDLA/2364/1995	65
Commissioner's Decision CDLA/4125/2000	63
Commissioner's Decision CDLA/4388/1999	63
Commissioner's Decision CDLA/58/1993	59
Commissioner's Decision CDLA/608/1994	63
Commissioner's Decision CIB 1402/96	50
Commissioner's Decision CIB 14534/96	51
Commissioner's Decision CIB 5361/97	50
Commissioner's Decisions CIB/1239/04 and CIB/3397/04	191
Commissioner's Decision CIS 12703/96	177
Commissioner's Decision CIS 4354/1999	10
Commissioner's Decision CIS 600/1995	8
Commissioner's Decision CIS/14850/96	125
Commissioner's Decision CL 182/49	68
Commissioner's Decision CM/158/1994	63
Commissioner's Decision CM/23/1995	63
Commissioner's Decision CM/47/86	63
Commissioner's Decision CS 5/54	51
Commissioner's Decision CSDLA/133/2005	58
Commissioner's Decision CSDLA/29/94	59
Commissioner's Decision CSTC/76/2006	151
Commissioner's Decision R(A)1/83	60
Commissioner's Decision R(A)2/75	60

Commissioner's Decision R(I) 1/88   69
Commissioner's Decision R(I) 7/56   67
Commissioner's Decision R(M) 3/78   63
Commissioner's Decision R(M) 5/86   63
Crake v Supplementary Benefits Commission; Butterworth v Supplementary Benefits Commission [1982] 1 All ER 498   109

D

D v United Kingdom (1997) 24 EHRR 423   302
Desmond (1998) INLP 147   238

E

Eritrea CG [2005] UKIAT 00106   302
Esfandiari v Secretary of State for Work and Pensions [2006] EWCA Civ 282   161

F

Faulkner v Chief Adjudication Officer [1994] PIQR 244   67
Findlay v Matondo [1993] Imm AR 541   316
Flemming v Social Security Commissioners [2002] EWCA Civ 641   92
Frantisek Katrinak v Secretary of State for the Home Department [2001] INLR 499   296

G

Gashi and Nikshiqi v Secretary of State for the Home Department (United Nations High Commissioner for Refugees Intervening) [1997] INLR 96   295

H

Hinchy v Secretary of State for Work and Pensions [2005] UKHL 16, [2005] 1 WLR 967   113
Holub and Holub v Secretary of State for the Home Department [2001] INLR 219   306
Horvath v Secretary of State for the Home Department [2001] 1 AC 489   296
Huang v Secretary of State for the Home Department [2007] UKHL 11   302

I

Inland Revenue Commissioners v Lysaght [1928] AC 234   176
Islam (Shahana) v Secretary of State for the Home Department; R v Immigration Appeal Tribunal and Secretary of State for the Home Department, ex p Syeda Shah [1999] INLR 144   297

J

J (A Minor) (Abduction: Custody Rights), Re [1990] 2 AC 562   177
Januzi v Secretary of State for the Home Department [2006] UKHL 5   299
Jones (Receiver) (on behalf of Wilde) v The Insurance Officer [1972] AC 944   71

K

K v Secretary of State for the Home Department; Fornah v Secretary of State for the Home Department [2006] UKHL 45, [2007] 1 All ER 671   v, 297
Kaba v Secretary of State for the Home Department (Case C-356/98) [2000] All ER (EC) 537   243
Kazantzis v Chief Adjudication Officer (1999) The Times, 30 June   37

L

Levene v Inland Revenue Commissioners [1928] AC 217   175
Loresco (1999) INLP 18   289
Luisi (Graziana) and Carbone (Giuseppe) v Ministero del Tesoro (Joined Cases 286/82 and 26/83) [1984] ECR 377   236

M

Mdawini (1998) INLP 147   253
Megarry v Chief Adjudication Officer (1999) The Times, 11 November   64

Moyna v Secretary of State for Work and Pensions [2003] 4 All ER 162   59

N

N(FC) v Secretary of State for the Home Department [2005] UKHL 31, [2005] 2 WLR 1124   302
Nessa v Chief Adjudication Officer [1999] 1 WLR 1937   178, 292
Nmaju v Entry Clearance Officer (2000) The Times, 6 September   287

O

Oladehinde v Secretary of State for the Home Department; Alexander v Secretary of State for the Home Department [1990] 3 WLR 797   210
Oladunni (15374)   253
Omoruyi v Secretary of State for the Home Department [2001] INLR 33   298

P

Padhu (12318)   295
Parry v Derbyshire Dales District Council [2006] EWHC 988 (Admin)   139

R

R (Baiai) v Secretary of State for the Home Department [2007] EWCA Civ 478   v, 281
R (Graham Ford) v Board of Inland Revenue [2005] EWHC 1109 (Admin)   90
R (Lichfield Securities Ltd) v Lichfield District Council (2001) The Times, 30 March   330
R (Razgar) v Secretary of State for the Home Department [2004] UKHL 27   302
R (Sayania) v Immigration Appeal Tribunal (2001) LTL, 9 April   293
R (Sivakumar) v Secretary of State for the Home Department [2003] 2 All ER 1097   295
R (Ullah) v Special Adjudicator; Do v Secretary of State for the Home Department [2004] UKHL 26   302
R v Barnet London Borough Council, ex p Shah [1983] 2 WLR 16   176
R v Chief Immigration Officer, Gatwick Airport, ex p Kharrazi [1980] 1 WLR 1396   330
R v Immigration Appeal Tribunal and Surinder Singh, ex p Secretary of State for the Home Department [1992] 3 CMLR 358   242
R v Immigration Appeal Tribunal, ex p Jonah [1985] Imm AR 7   299
R v Immigration Appeal Tribunal, ex p Sayana Khatun [1989] Imm AR 482   292
R v Immigration Appeal Tribunal, ex p Wali [1989] Imm AR 86   276
R v Immigration Officer, ex p Chan [1992] 1 WLR 541   310
R v National Insurance Commissioner, ex p Secretary of State for Social Services (Packer's Case) [1981] 1 WLR 1017   57, 60, 61
R v Navabi and Embaye [2005] EWCA Crim 2865   230
R v Secretary of State for the Home Department and Immigration Officer, Waterloo International Station, ex p Canbolat [1997] INLR 198   330
R v Secretary of State for the Home Department, ex p Arman Ali [2000] INLR 89   278
R v Secretary of State for the Home Department, ex p Asif Mahmood Khan [1984] 1 WLR 1337   208
R v Secretary of State for the Home Department, ex p Azad Ullah [2001] INLR 74   215
R v Secretary of State for the Home Department, ex p Bagdanavicius [2005] UKHL 38, [2005] 2 WLR 1359   302
R v Secretary of State for the Home Department, ex p Hosenball [1977] 3 All ER 452   208
R v Secretary of State for the Home Department, ex p Jeyakumaran (Selladurai) [1994] Imm AR 45   295
R v Secretary of State for the Home Department, ex p Khawaja [1984] AC 74   311, 330
R v Secretary of State for the Home Department, ex p Mahmood [2001] INLR 1   314
R v Secretary of State for the Home Department, ex p Muboyayi [1991] 3 WLR 442   330
R v Secretary of State for the Home Department, ex p Patel [1995] Imm AR 223   317
R v Secretary of State for the Home Department, ex p Sivakumaran and conjoined appeals (UN High Commissioner for Refugees Intervening) [1988] 1 All ER 193   294
R v Secretary of State for the Home Department, ex p Swati [1986] 1 All ER 717   329
R v Secretary of State for Work and Pensions, ex p Carson and Reynolds [2005] UKHL 37, [2005] 2 WLR 1369   18
RG (Ethiopia) v Secretary of State for the Home Department [2006] EWCA Civ 339   297

S

Samaroo and Sezek v Secretary of State for the Home Department [2001] UKHRR 1150   307
Secretary of State for Work and Pensions v W [2005] EWCA Civ 570   124

Sepet v Secretary of State for the Home Department [2003] 3 All ER 304 — 298
Sivakumar v Secretary of State for the Home Department [2002] INLR 310 — 298
Smith v Stages [1989] 2 WLR 529 — 68
Soon Ok Ryoo v Secretary of State for the Home Department [1992] Imm AR 59 — 330
Stec v UK, Application No 65731/01 — 18
Sultana (1999) INLP 74 — 277
Suzara Ramos v Immigration Appeal Tribunal [1989] Imm AR 148 — 286
Swaddling v Adjudication Officer [1999] All ER (EC) 217 — 179

T

T v Secretary of State for the Home Department (1996) The Times, 23 May — 300
Thirunavukkarasu v Canada (Minister of Employment and Immigration) (1993) 109 DLR (4th) 682, 687 — 299
Tucker v Secretary of State for Social Security [2001] EWCA Civ 1646 — 19

V

Vaughan v UK, Application No 12639/87 — 19

Table of Statutes

Asylum and Immigration Act 1996 208, 341, 530
  s 8 266
Asylum and Immigration Appeals Act 1993 208, 341, 530
  s 7 305, 467
Asylum and Immigration (Treatment of Claimants, etc) Act 2004 208, 473
  s 2(1) 229
  s 2(4) 229
  s 2(7) 230
  s 2(7)(b) 230
  s 8(1)–(2) 304
  s 10 475
  Sch 3 301, 302
    para 4 475
    para 5(1) 475
    para 9 475
    para 10(1) 475
    para 14 475
    para 15(1) 475
    para 17 475
    Part 2 301, 468, 475
      para 2 301
      para 4 301
      para 5 301
    Parts 3–5 301, 468, 475

British Nationality Act 1948 208, 220, 222
British Nationality Act 1981 208, 213, 214, 217, 218, 220, 221, 222, 225, 344, 345, 347, 364, 376, 379, 387, 390, 400, 408, 455, 530
  s 1(3)–(4) 217, 289
  s 1(7) 217
  s 4 225
  s 4C 214, 217
  s 6 215, 225
  s 30(a) 345
  s 37 491
  s 40 217
  s 40A 322, 327
  s 50(9A) 214
  Sch 3 491
  Sch 6 493
British Nationality (Falkland Islands) Act 1983 493

Child Benefit Act 2005 89
Children Act 1989 316
Civil Partnership Act 2004 20, 341
Consular Fees Act 1980 348

Education Act 1944 357
Education Reform Act 1988
  s 214(2)(c) 341
European Communities Act 1972
  Sch 1 481

Housing Act 1985 277, 289
  Part II 223, 342
  s 326 277
Housing Act 1996
  Part VI 223, 342
  Part VII 223, 342
Housing (Scotland) Act 1987
  Part I 342
  Part II 342
Human Fertilisation and Embryology Act 1990
  s 28 214
Human Rights Act 1998 13, 209, 302, 340, 527
  ss 3–4 209
  s 6 209, 320
  s 10 209

Immigration Act 1971 208, 210, 221, 224, 310, 311, 341, 342, 347, 480, 513, 524, 525, 530
  s 1(3) 244
  s 3 223, 343
  s 3(2) 208, 337, 549
  s 3(3) 230, 348
  s 3(3)(a) 234
  s 3(5)(a) 526
  s 3(5)(b) 307
  s 3(6) 307
  s 3C 230, 485, 486
  s 4 210, 343
  s 5 307, 308, 482, 526, 529, 533
  s 5(1) 319, 530
  s 5(2) 320
  s 6(2) 443, 448
  s 7(1)(b)–(c) 309
  s 7(2) 309
  s 8 342
  s 8(4) 440-1
  s 8(5A) 342
  s 11 432
  s 11(1) 441
  s 24 343
  s 24(1)(a)–(b) 310
  s 33(1) 513
  s 33(2) 226
  s 33(2A) 224
  Sch 2 319, 525
    para 2(1) 227
    para 2A 344
    para 2A(8) 348
    para 8 432, 526, 530
    para 8(2) 529
    para 8c 478
    para 9 432, 530
    para 10 432, 526, 530
    para 10A 432, 526
    para 11 526
    paras 12–14 432

Immigration Act 1971 – *continued*
    paras 16–19 526
    paras 21–24 526
    para 29 529
  Sch 3 309, 526, 529
Immigration Act 1988 208, 341, 342, 480
  s 2(1)(a) 441
  s 7 530
  s 7(1) 235
Immigration and Asylum Act 1999 208, 229, 350, 480, 513
  s 3 485, 486
  s 10 310, 312, 319, 432, 448, 469, 484, 526, 529
  s 10(1)(a) 526, 530
  s 40(1)(b) 530
  s 95 350
  s 108 350
  s 115 169, 170, 171, 173, 174, 175, 181, 182, 183, 343
  s 115(1) 169
  s 115(3) 170, 343
  s 115(4) 343
  s 115(9) 170, 174
Immigration, Asylum and Nationality Act 2006 208, 327
  s 54 300
  s 57 220
  s 64(2) 549
Immigration (Carriers' Liability) Act 1987 299

Jobseekers Act 1995 7, 38, 342
  s 1 36
  s 6 38
  s 7 38, 40
  s 9 36
  s 19 43
  ss 51–53 37

Limitation Act 1980 111

National Assistance Act 1948
  s 29(4)(g) 201
Nationality, Immigration and Asylum Act 2002 208, 214, 319, 480, 513, 527, 529, 530
  Part 3 183
  s 72 300
  s 77 301, 323
  s 78 323, 324
  s 79 324
  s 82 322, 323, 324, 325, 326
  s 82(1) 527, 529, 530, 531
  s 82(2) 319, 530
  s 82(2)(a) 321, 324
  s 82(2)(b) 324
  s 82(2)(c) 320
  s 82(2)(d)–(e) 320, 324
  s 82(2)(f) 320
  s 82(2)(g)–(i) 321
  s 82(2)(j) 320, 321
  s 83(2) 530
  s 84 320
  s 84(1) 529
  s 84(1)(d) 531

Nationality, Immigration and Asylum Act 2002 – *continued*
  s 84(2) 531
  ss 85–87 529
  s 88 324
  s 88A(1) 327
  s 89 324
  s 90 324, 325
  s 91 325
  s 92 320, 324
  s 93 326
  s 94 326
  s 94(4) 326
  s 96 321, 322, 324
  s 96(1)(a) 531
  s 96(2) 531
  ss 97–98 324, 325
  s 99 324
  s 101 330
  ss 102–103 531
  ss 103A–103E 529
  s 104 323
  ss 105–106 529
  s 113 320, 326
  s 120 321
  s 120(2) 531
  s 126 465
  Sch 4 322

Overseas Territories Act 2002 222

Pensions Act 1995 75
Public Health (Control of Disease) Act 1984
  s 38 244, 525

Race Relations Act 1976
  s 19B 320
Rehabilitation of Offenders Act 1974 232

Social Security Act 1998
  schedules 12
Social Security Administration Act 1992 7, 350
  s 2A 9
  s 71 112
  s 71(1) 113
  s 74 114
  s 105 350
  s 106 292
Social Security Administration (Northern Ireland) Act 1992 350
Social Security Contribution and Benefits (Northern Ireland) Act 1992
  Part III 342
  Part VII 342
  Part VIII 342
  Part IX 342
Social Security Contributions and Benefits Act 1992 7, 67
  Part III 342
  Part VII 342
  Part VIII 342
  Part IX 342
  s 1A 65

Social Security Contributions and Benefits Act
1992 – *continued*
  s 2(1) 70
  s 2A 119
  s 30A 54, 55
  s 30A(2A)(d) 174
  s 30B 54
  s 30DD 54
  s 35 88
  s 36 81, 82
  ss 37–39 81
  ss 39A–39B 81
  s 44 75
  s 48BB 77
  s 55 76
  s 64 66
  s 65(4) 11
  s 66(2) 61
  s 70 91
  s 72 57
  s 72(1)(a)(i)–(ii) 59
  s 72(1)(b)(i) 58, 60, 61
  s 72(1)(b)(ii) 60
  s 72(1)(c)(i) 60, 61
  s 72(1)(c)(ii) 61
  s 72(2) 59
  s 72(4)(a) 61
  s 72(6)(a)–(b) 61
  s 73 62
  s 73(1)(a) 63
  s 73(1)(d) 64
  s 73(2)–(3) 64
  s 73(4) 65
  s 76(1) 11
  s 94 66
  s 94(1) 66
  s 94(3) 67
  s 98 67
  s 99 68
  s 100 69
  s 101 70
  s 103(1) 72
  s 103(3) 73
  s 103(6) 73
  ss 108–109 71
  s 130 136
  s 134(1) 8
  s 137 102
  s 143 89
  ss 151–154 52
  s 164 86
  s 171B 48
  s 171C 49
  Sch 6 71
  Sch 10 90
Social Security Contributions (Transfer of Functions, etc) Act 1999 55
Special Immigration Appeals Commission Act 1997 325, 527
  s 2 528, 530
State Pension Credits Act 2002 7, 342
  s 2 78
  s 3 79
Supplementary Benefits Act 1976 109

Tax Credits Act 2002 7, 133, 143, 144, 146
  Part 1 342
  s 7(1)(a) 148
  s 8(1) 147
  s 42 343

Welfare Reform and Pensions Act 1999 7, 77, 119

European primary legislation

EC Treaty 238, 243
  Art 12 180
  Art 17 180, 235
  Art 18 235
  Art 18(1) 235
  Art 38 242
  Art 39 169, 209, 235, 237, 308, 514
  Art 39(2) 180
  Art 39(3) 235
  Art 43 236, 237, 514
  Arts 49–50 236
Treaty on European Union 1992 222

International legislation

Dublin Convention 301
European Convention on Human Rights *v*, 13, 18, 209, 210, 280, 287, 296, 301, 302, 307, 308, 320, 326, 343, 527, 528
  Art 2 295, 302, 541
  Art 3 295, 302, 303, 305, 541
  Art 4 302
  Art 4(1) 295
  Art 5 302, 541
  Art 6 13, 302, 542
  Art 7 295, 302
  Art 8 19, 293, 302, 305, 308, 314, 315, 316, 317, 542
  Art 9 302, 542
  Art 10 542-3
  Art 11 543
  Art 12 281, 543
  Art 14 18, 19, 543
  Art 15 295, 550
  Protocol 1
    Art 1 18, 543
    Art 2 306
Hague Convention 462, 463
  Art 17(c) 462
UN Convention and Protocol relating to the Status of Refugees (Geneva Convention) 293, 294, 295, 299, 301, 302, 303, 304, 307, 320, 327, 468, 469, 474, 476, 478, 483, 484, 527, 528, 549
  Art 1 293
  Art 1(A) 549, 550
  Arts 1D–1E 551
  Art 1F 300, 477, 551
  Art 1F(a) 551
  Art 1F(b)–(c) 300
  Art 33 300
UN Convention on the Rights of the Child 524
Vienna Convention on Diplomatic and Consular Relations 392

Table of Secondary Legislation

Accession (Immigration and Worker Registration)
  Regulations 2004 (SI 2004/1219) 236, 530, 532,
  535-6
  reg 3 531
  reg 6 531
  reg 6(3)(a)–(b) 533
Asylum and Immigration Tribunal (Fast Track
  Procedure) Rules 2005 (SI 2005/560) 323
Asylum and Immigration Tribunal (Procedure)
  Rules 2005 (SI 2005/230) 322, 536

British Nationality (General) Regulations 2003
  (SI 2003/548) 217

Channel Tunnel (International Arrangements)
  Order 1993 (SI 1993/1813) 534
Child Benefit (General) Regulations 1976
  (SI 1976/965) 91
Child Benefit (General) Regulations 2006
  (SI 2006/223) 89, 147
Child Tax Credit Regulations 2002 (SI 2002/2007)
  147
  reg 3 147
Civil Procedure Rules 1998 (SI 1998/3132)
  Part 8 329
  Part 54 329, 330
    r 54.5 329
    r 54.33 322
Council Tax Benefit Regulations 2006 (SI 2006/215)
  Part 11 111
  reg 69(14) 11

Disability Working Allowance (General)
  Regulations 1991 (SI 1991/2887)
  reg 12 63
  reg 12(1)(a)(ii)–(iii) 63
  reg 12(1)(b) 64
  reg 12(2)–(3) 64
  reg 12(4) 63
  reg 12(5)–(6) 64

Housing Benefit Regulations 2006 (SI 2006/213)
  Part 13 111
  reg 83(12) 10
  Sch 1 137, 138
Housing (Northern Ireland) Order 1981
  Part II 342
Housing (Northern Ireland) Order 1988
  Part II 342

Immigration Appeals (Family Visitor) Regulations
  2003 (SI 2003/518) 325
Immigration and Asylum Act 1999 (Part V
  Exemptions: Relevant Employers) Order 2003
  (SI 2003/3214) 535
Immigration (Control on Entry Through the
  Republic of Ireland) Order 1972 (SI 1972/1610)
  245, 345

Immigration (European Economic Area) and
  Accession (Amendment) Regulations 2004
  (SI 2004/1236)
  reg 2 531
Immigration (European Economic Area)
  (Amendment) Regulations 2001 (SI 2001/865)
  531
Immigration (European Economic Area)
  (Amendment) Regulations 2003 (SI 2003/549)
  531
Immigration (European Economic Area)
  (Amendment No. 2) Regulations 2003
  (SI 2003/3188) 531
Immigration (European Economic Area)
  (Amendment) Regulations 2005 (SI 2005/47)
  531
Immigration (European Economic Area)
  (Amendment) (No. 2) Regulations 2005
  (SI 2005/671) 531
Immigration (European Economic Area) Order
  1994 (SI 1994/1895) 424
Immigration (European Economic Area)
  Regulations 2000 (SI 2000/2326) 424, 425, 446,
  531, 532, 533, 534
  reg 21(3)(a)–(b) 533
  reg 26(3) 533
Immigration (European Economic Area)
  Regulations 2006 (SI 2006/1003) 209, 235, 236,
  240, 241, 244, 326, 340, 341, 343, 415, 425, 426,
  446, 513-36
  reg 1 513
  reg 2 238, 244, 513-14
  reg 2(1) 341
  reg 3 241, 244, 514
  reg 4 514-15
  reg 4(4) 237
  reg 5 225, 240, 515-16
  reg 6 237, 241, 285, 516
  reg 6(2)–(3) 238
  reg 7 238, 244, 516-17
  reg 8 239, 244, 517
  reg 9 241, 242, 290, 517-18
  reg 10 241, 244, 518-19
  reg 11 244, 285, 519
  reg 11(1) 236
  reg 11(2) 237
  reg 12 240, 519-20
  reg 13 237, 244, 520
  reg 14 237, 244, 285, 520-1
  reg 15 240, 244, 521
  reg 15(1) 225
  reg 16 240, 243, 521-2
  reg 17 240, 243, 244, 522
  reg 18 241, 243, 244, 523
  reg 19 243, 523-4
  reg 20 524
  reg 21 243, 244, 524-5

Immigration (European Economic Area)
    Regulations 2006 – *continued*
    reg 22 525-6
    regs 23–24 526
    regs 25–26 527
    reg 27 527-8
    reg 28 528
    reg 29 528-9
    regs 30–31 529
    Sch 1 529
    Sch 2
        paras 1–3 530
        para 4 530-1
    Sch 3 531-2
    Sch 4 446, 532-4
        paras 1–2 532
        paras 3–4 533
        para 5 533-4
        para 6 534
    Sch 5 534-6
Immigration (Leave to Enter and Remain) Order 2000 (SI 2000/1161) 344
    art 3 347
    art 13 345, 346, 349
Immigration (Notices) Regulations 2003 (SI 2003/658) 321
Immigration (Procedure for Formation of Civil Partnerships) Regulations 2005 (SI 2005/2917) 281
Immigration (Procedure for Marriage) Regulations 2005 (SI 2005/15) 280
    Sch 2 280
Immigration (Provision of Physical Data) Regulations 2006 (SI 2006/1743) 227
Immigration (Regularisation Period for Overstayers) Regulations 2000 (SI 2000/265) 481
Immigration (Restrictions on Employment) Order 2004 (SI 2004/755) 266, 535
Immigration Rules 208, 209, 210, 223, 224, 225, 226, 228, 229, 237, 239, 243, 247, 250, 251, 252, 253, 254, 256, 258, 259, 262, 266, 269, 273, 274, 275, 276, 278, 281, 283, 285, 286, 290, 292, 293, 305, 309, 312, 320, 331, 332, 337-489
    Part 1 226, 343-51
    Part 2 351-7
    Part 3 231, 357-71
    Part 4 371-9
    Part 5 258, 379-408
    Part 6 258, 408-22
    Part 7 258, 422-41
    Part 8 231, 441-64
    Part 9 464-8
    Part 10 224, 468
    Part 11 293, 348, 468-78
    Part 12 481
    Part 13 481-4
    para 1 340
    para 2 227, 340
    paras 3–5 340
    para 6 224, 259, 275, 276, 286, 340-3
    para 6A 276, 343
    para 6B 181, 182, 343
    paras 7–8 227, 343

Immigration Rules – *continued*
    para 9 227, 343-4
    para 10 227, 344
    paras 10A–10B 344
    para 11 227, 344
    paras 12–14 344
    paras 15–17 345
    paras 17A–17B 345
    para 18 224, 225, 345-6
    para 19 225, 346
    para 19A 346
    para 20 346
    para 20A 346
    paras 21–23 346
    para 23A 346-7
    para 23B 347
    para 24 347
    para 25 227, 347
    para 25A 347
    paras 26–28 347
    paras 29–30 348
    paras 30A–30C 348
    para 31 348
    para 31A 348
    para 32 233, 348
    para 33 349
    para 33A 349
    paras 33B–33F 349
    para 34 350
    para 35 227, 350
    paras 36–37 350
    para 38 350-1
    para 39 351
    para 39A 255, 351
    para 40 248, 351
    para 41 223, 247, 249, 351
    para 42 224, 247, 351
    para 43 351
    paras 44–46 352
    para 46A 248, 352
    paras 46B–46C 352
    paras 46D–46F 353
    paras 47–50 247, 353
    para 51 353-4
    para 52 256, 354
    paras 53–56 354
    para 56A–56C 355
    para 56D 249, 355
    paras 56E–56F 355
    paras 56G–56K 356
    paras 56L–56N 357
    para 57 251, 305, 357
    para 58 224, 251, 358
    para 59 358
    para 60 255, 358
    para 60(i) 231, 256
    para 61 255, 358
    para 62 358
    paras 63–64 359
    para 65 256, 359
    paras 66–67 359
    paras 68–69 360
    para 69A 256, 360

Immigration Rules – *continued*
  paras 69B–69E 360
  para 69F 361
  para 69G 256, 361
  paras 69H–69L 361
  para 69M 361-2
  paras 69N–69O 362
  para 69P 362-3
  paras 69Q–69R 363
  para 70 363-4
  para 71 256, 364
  paras 72–75 364
  paras 75A–75D 365
  paras 75E–75J 366
  para 75K 366-7
  paras 75L–75M 367
  para 76 282, 367-8
  paras 77–78 282, 368
  para 79 368
  para 80 289, 368
  para 81 368-9
  paras 82–86 369
  para 87 370
  para 87A–87E 370
  paras 87F 371
  paras 88–89 371
  para 90 256, 371
  para 91 371
  paras 92–94 372
  para 95 224, 256, 257, 372
  para 96 256, 372
  para 97 373
  paras 101–103 373
  para 104 373-4
  para 105 256, 374
  paras 106–109 374
  para 110 374-5
  para 111 256, 375
  paras 112–115 375
  para 116 376
  para 117 256, 376
  para 118 376
  para 119 376-7
  paras 120–123 377
  paras 124–125 378
  para 126 378-9
  para 127 379
  para 128 263, 265, 379
  para 129 224, 379
  para 130 380
  para 131 265, 266, 380
  para 131A 380
  para 131B 256, 380
  para 131C 380-1
  paras 131D–131G 381
  para 131H 381-2
  para 131I 231
  paras 132–133 382
  para 134 265, 382
  para 135 382
  para 135A 270, 382
  paras 135B–135D 383
  paras 135DA–135DB 383

Immigration Rules – *continued*
  para 135DC 383-4
  paras 135DD–135DH 384
  paras 135E–135F 384
  para 135G 384-5
  paras 135H–135I 385
  para 135J 385-6
  paras 135K–135M 386
  para 135O 386-7
  paras 135P–135T 387
  paras 136–140 388
  paras 141–143 389
  para 143A 389-90
  paras 143B–143C 390
  para 143D 390-1
  para 144 259, 391
  paras 145–146 391
  para 147 261, 391-2
  paras 148–149 392
  para 150 262, 392
  paras 151–154 392
  paras 155–159 393
  paras 159A–159E 394
  paras 159F–159H 395
  paras 160–163 395
  paras 164–169 396
  para 170 396-7
  paras 171–172 397
  para 173 397-8
  para 174 398
  paras 174A–174B 398
  para 175 398
  paras 176–177 399
  para 177A 399
  para 177B 399-400
  paras 177C–177D 400
  para 177E 400-1
  paras 177F–177G 401
  paras 178–179 401
  paras 180–185 402
  para 186 262, 403
  paras 187–191 403
  para 192 262, 403-4
  para 193 404
  para 194 266, 282, 404
  para 195 282, 404
  para 196 282, 404-5
  paras 196A–196C 405
  para 196D 405-6
  paras 196E–196F 406
  para 197 266, 295, 406-7
  para 198 289, 407
  para 199 407
  paras 199A–199C 408
  para 200 408
  para 201 408-9
  paras 202–203 409
  para 204 224, 409
  para 205 409
  para 206 269, 409-10
  paras 206A–206D 410
  para 206E 410-11
  paras 206F–206H 411

Immigration Rules – *continued*
paras 207–208 411
para 209 269, 412
para 210 412
para 210A 269, 412
paras 210B–210D 412
paras 210DA–210DG 413
para 210DH 414
para 210E–210H 414
para 222 414-15
paras 222A–222C 415
para 223 415
para 223A 415
para 224 267, 273, 415-16
paras 225–226 416
para 227 274, 416
para 227A 416
paras 227B–227D 417
paras 228–229 417
para 230 274, 417
para 231 417
para 232 417-18
paras 233–239 418
para 240 282, 419
paras 241–242 282, 419
para 242A 419-20
paras 242B–242E 420
para 242F 421
para 243 421
para 244 289, 421-2
paras 245 422
para 246 282, 316, 422
paras 247–248 316, 423
paras 248A–248B 423
para 248C 424
para 248D 282, 424
paras 248E–248F 424
para 255 424
para 255A 424-5
para 255B 425
paras 257A–257C 425
paras 257D–257E 426
paras 263–265 426
para 266 426-7
paras 266A–266D 427
paras 267–271 427
paras 271–273 428
para 273A 428-9
paras 273B–273D 429
paras 273E–273F 430
para 274 430
para 275 430-1
para 276 431
para 276A 431-2
paras 276A1–276A4 432
para 276AA 438
para 276AB 438-9
paras 276AC–276AE 439
paras 276AF–276AH 440
para 276AI 440-1
para 276B 231, 432-3
paras 276C–276F 433
para 276G 433-4

Immigration Rules – *continued*
paras 276H–276M 434
paras 276N–276Q 435
para 276R 435-6
paras 276S–276V 436
paras 276W–276X 437
paras 276Y–276Z 438
para 277 275, 441
para 278 282, 441
paras 279–280 441
para 281 275, 278, 281, 282, 442
para 281(i)(b) 275, 279
para 282 442-3
para 283 443
para 284 231, 281, 315, 443
para 284(i) 231, 251
paras 285–286 443
para 287 279, 283, 444
para 287(a)(iv)–(v) 280
para 287(b) 279
paras 288–289 445
para 289A 281, 445
para 289AA 282, 445
paras 289B–298C 445
para 290 282, 283, 445-6
para 290A 283, 446
para 291 224, 446
paras 292–295 446
para 295A 239, 283, 285, 447
para 295AA 283, 447
paras 295B–295C 448
para 295D 285, 448
paras 295E–295F 449
para 295G 284, 449
paras 295H–295I 449
paras 295J–295K 285, 450
para 295L 450
para 295M 285, 451
paras 295N–295O 451
para 296 451
para 297 286, 288, 451-2
para 297(i)(f) 288
para 298 286, 452-3
paras 299–300 286, 453
para 301 286, 453-4
paras 302–303 286, 454
para 303A 289, 454
paras 303B–303C 455
paras 303D–303F 455
para 304 289, 455-6
para 305 289, 456
paras 306–308 289, 456
para 309 289, 457
para 309A 290, 457
para 310 290, 457-8
para 311 290, 458-9
paras 312–313 290, 459
para 314 290, 459-60
para 315 290, 460-1
para 316 290, 461
para 316A 290, 461-2
paras 316B–316D 462
paras 316B–316F 290

Immigration Rules – *continued*
  para 316E 462-3
  para 316F 463
  para 317 290, 291, 463
  para 318 289, 290, 292, 293, 464
  para 319 464
  para 320 227, 229, 464-6
  para 320(2) 307
  para 321 227, 229, 466
  para 321A 466
  para 322 230, 466-7
  para 323 234, 467
  para 324 467-8
  paras 325–326 468
  para 327 300, 468
  para 328 468
  para 329 468-9
  paras 330–332 469
  paras 334–336 469
  para 338 469
  para 339A 469-70
  paras 339B–339C 470
  paras 339D–339F 470-1
  para 339G 471-2
  para 339H 472
  paras 339I–339J 304, 472
  para 339K 295, 304, 472
  para 339L 304, 472-3
  paras 339M–339N 304, 473
  para 339O 299, 473
  para 339P 473
  para 339Q 473-4
  para 342 474
  paras 344A–s44B 474
  para 344C 474
  para 345 301, 475
  para 349 475-6
  paras 350–352 476
  para 352A 476
  para 352AA 476-7
  para 352B 477
  para 352BA 477
  para 352C 477
  para 352CA 477
  para 352D 477
  paras 352E–352F 477
  para 352G 478
  para 353 481
  paras 354–355 478
  paras 355A–355B 478
  paras 355C–355G 479
  para 356 479
  para 356A 479-80
  para 356B 480
  paras 357–358 480
  paras 358A–358B 480
  para 359 480
  paras 359A–359C 480
  paras 360-360A 480
  paras 361–363 480-1
  para 363A 481
  para 364 307, 481
  paras 365–368 481-2

Immigration Rules – *continued*
  para 378 482
  para 380 482
  paras 381–382 309, 482
  para 383 483
  para 384 309, 483
  paras 385–389 483
  para 390 310, 483
  para 391 483
  para 392 483
  para 395 483
  para 395A–395B 484
  para 395C 311, 484
  para 395D–395F 484
  Appendix 227
  Appendix 1 343, 359, 484-6, 495
  Appendix 2 224, 486
  Appendix 3 257, 372, 486
  Appendix 4 487
  Appendix 5 488-9
Immigration (Swiss Free Movement of Persons)
  (No 3) Regulations 2002 (SI 2002/1241) 235, 531, 532
Income Support (General) Regulations 1987
  (SI 1987/1967) 97
  reg 4ZA 119
  reg 17 120
  reg 21 179
  regs 45–46 8
  reg 51(6) 96
  reg 70 130
  Sch 3 120, 124
    para 8(1)(a) 124
  Sch 9 8, 99
    paras 19–20 103

Jobseeker's Allowance Regulations 1996
  (SI 1996/207) 38
  regs 5–7 38
  reg 8 38, 39
  regs 9–22 38
  reg 23 41, 42
  reg 25 41
  regs 31–44 36
  reg 72 43
  reg 83 120
  regs 140–145 129
  reg 146 129, 130
  reg 147 130
  Sch 2 120, 124
    para 9(1)(b) 124
    para 9(2)(b) 124
Jobseekers (Northern Ireland) Order 1995
  (SI 1995/2705) 342

National Health Service (Charges to Overseas
  Visitors) Regulations 1989 (SI 1989/306) 223
Nationality, Immigration and Asylum Act 2002
  (Juxtaposed Controls) Order 2003 (SI 2003/2818)
  534-5
Nationality, Immigration and Asylum Act 2002
  (Specification of Particularly Serious Crimes)
  Order 2004 (SI 2004/1910) 300

Refugee or Person in Need of International
    Protection (Qualification) Regulations 2006
    (SI 2006/2525) v, 294
    reg 1 549
    reg 2 469, 470, 549
    reg 3 549
    reg 4 549-50
    reg 5 550
    reg 5(1) 295
    reg 5(2) 294
    reg 6 550-1
    reg 6(1)(b) 298
    reg 6(1)(d) 297
    reg 7 470, 551
    reg 7(2) 300
Rent Officers (Housing Benefit Functions) Order
    1997 (SI 1997/1984) 137

Social Fund Directions 162
    Direction 1 162
    Directions 8-12 162
    Directions 14-23 163
    Directions 25-29 162
Social Security Amendment (Enhanced Disability
    Premium) Regulations 2000 (SI 2000/2629) 106
Social Security (Attendance Allowance and
    Disability Living Allowance) (Amendment)
    (No 2) Regulations 2000 (SI 2000/2313) 59
Social Security (Claims and Payments) Regulations
    1987 (SI 1987/1968)
    reg 19(4) 9, 10
    reg 19(4)(a)-(b) 9, 10
    reg 19(5) 9, 10, 13
    reg 19(7) 9
Social Security (Disability Living Allowance)
    (Amendment) Regulations 2002 (SI 2002/648)
    65
Social Security (Employed Earners' Employments
    for Industrial Injuries Purposes) Regulations 1975
    (SI 1975/467) 70
Social Security (General Benefit) Regulations 1982
    (SI 1982/1408)
    reg 19 73
    Sch 2 72
Social Security (Immigration and Asylum)
    Consequential Amendment Regulations 2000
    (SI 2000/636) 170
    reg 2(1) 170
    reg 2(2) 170, 174
    reg 2(3) 171
Social Security (Incapacity Benefit) Miscellaneous
    Amendments Regulations 2000 (SI 2000/3120)
    54, 56
Social Security (Incapacity for Work) (General)
    Regulations 1995 (SI 1995/311) 51, 191-5
    Part I 191-4
    Part II 194-5
    regs 1-3 191
    reg 4 191-2
    regs 5-7 192
    reg 8 51, 192
    reg 9 192-3
    regs 10-13 193

Social Security (Incapacity for Work) (General)
    Regulations 1995 – *continued*
    reg 14 89, 193-4
    regs 15-16 194
    reg 17 194-5
    reg 18 195
    reg 24 49
    reg 26 50
    reg 26(2)-(3) 50
    Sch 49
    Sch 2 197-9
Social Security (Industrial Injuries) (Prescribed
    Diseases) Regulations 1985 (SI 1985/967)
    reg 4 72
    Sch 1 71-2
Social Security (Persons from Abroad) Amendment
    Regulations 2006 (SI 2006/1026) 177
Special Immigration Appeals Commission
    (Procedure) Rules 2003 (SI 2003/1034) 325
Statement of Changes in Immigration Rules 1994
    (HC 395) *see* Immigration Rules
Statutory Maternity Pay (General) (Amendment)
    Regulations 2005 (SI 2005/729) 87
Statutory Maternity Pay Regulations 1986 (SI 1986/
    1960)
    reg 13 86
Tax Credits (Definition and Calculation of Income)
    Regulations 2002 (SI 2002/2006)
    reg 3 143
    reg 4 144
    reg 5(1) 143
    regs 6-8 144
    regs 10-11 143
    reg 12 143, 144
    regs 13-14 144
    reg 18 144
Tax Credits (Immigration) Regulations 2003 (SI
    2003/653) 171
    reg 3(2) 181
Tax Credits (Income Thresholds and
    Determination of Rates) Regulations 2002 (SI
    2002/2008) 146
Tax Credits (Residence) Regulations 2003 (SI 2003/
    654) 172
Travel Restrictions Order (Prescribed Removal
    Powers) Order 2002 532

Working Tax Credit (Entitlement and Maximum
    Rate) Regulations 2002 (SI 2002/2005)
    reg 4 149
    reg 4(1) 150
    reg 9 150
    reg 9(2) 150
    reg 10 151
    regs 11-13 152
    regs 14-15 153
    reg 17 154
    reg 18 149, 154
    reg 18(3)-(4) 154
    reg 18(5) 155
    reg 18(6)-(8) 154, 155
    Sch 1
        Part 1 150, 201-2

European secondary legislation

Directives
Directive 64/221/EEC 511
Directive 72/194/EEC 511
Directive 73/148/EEC 511
Directive 75/34/EEC 511
Directive 75/35/EEC 511
Directive 90/364/EEC 511
Directive 90/365/EEC 511
Directive 93/96/EEC 511
Directive 2001/55/EC 478
Directive 2001/55/EC art 5 479
Directive 2004/38/EC 209, 235, 244
   Art 2 244
   Art 3 239
   Art 3(2) 244
   Arts 5–7 244
   Art 8(4) 237
   Art 10 244
   Arts 12–13 244
   Arts 16–21 244
   Arts 28–29 244
Directive 2004/58/EC
   Arts 1–3 499
   Arts 4–5 500
   Art 6 500-1
   Art 7 501
   Art 8 501-2
Directive 2004/58/EC – *continued*
   Art 9 502
   Arts 10–11 503
   Art 12 503-4
   Art 13 504
   Art 14 504-5
   Arts 15–16 505
   Art 17 506
   Arts 18–23 507
   Arts 24–26 508
   Art 27 508-9
   Arts 28–29 509
   Art 30 509-10
   Arts 31–33 510
   Arts 34–39 511
   Art 40 511-12
   Arts 41–42 512
Directive 2004/83/EC 294

Regulations
Regulation 1612/68
   Arts 10–11 511
   Art 12 519
Regulation 1408/71 180
   Art 1(h) 179
   Art 10a 179
Regulation 539/2001 500
Regulation 343/2003 301

Table of Abbreviations

AA	attendance allowance
AA Regs 1991	Social Security (Attendance Allowance) Regulations 1991
AIA 1996	Asylum and Immigration Act 1996
AIAA 1993	Asylum and Immigration Appeals Act 1993
AIT	Asylum and Immigration Appeal Tribunal
AI(TC)A 2004	Asylum and Immigration (Treatment of Claimants, etc) Act 2004
BACIFHE	British Accreditation Council for Independent Further and Higher Education
BB	bereavement benefits
BNA 1981	British Nationality Act 1981
BOCs	British overseas citizens
BOTCs	British overseas territories citizens
CA	carer's allowance
CAA	constant attendance allowance
CB	child benefit
CBJSA	contribution-based jobseeker's allowance
CEE	Central and Eastern European
CLS	Community Legal Service
CPAG	Child Poverty Action Group
CP Regs 1987	Social Security (Claims and Payments) Regulations 1987
CPR 1998	Civil Procedure Rules 1998
CSA	Child Support Agency
CTB	council tax benefit
CTB Regs 1992	Council Tax Benefit (General) Regulations 1992
CTB Regs 2006	Council Tax Benefit Regulations 2006
CTC	child tax credit
CUKC	citizen of the UK and colonies
DA Regs 1999	Social Security and Child Support (Decisions and Appeals) Regulations 1999
DfES	Department for Education and Skills
DfWP	Department for Work and Pensions
DLA	disability living allowance
DLA Regs 1991	Social Security (Disability Living Allowance) Regulations 1991
EC	European Community
ECHR	European Convention on Human Rights
ECtHR	European Court of Human Rights
ECJ	European Court of Justice
EEA	European Economic Area
EO	employment officer
EU	European Union
GP	general medical practitioner
HA 1985	Housing Act 1985
HB	housing benefit
HB Regs 2006	Housing Benefit Regulations 2006
HMRC	HM Revenue and Customs
HND	Higher National Diploma
HRA 1998	Human Rights Act 1998
HRP	home responsibilities protection
IA 1971	Immigration Act 1971
IA 1988	Immigration Act 1988
IAA	Immigration Appellate Authority

IAA 1999	Immigration and Asylum Act 1999
IANA 2006	Immigration, Asylum and Nationality Act 2006
IBJSA	income-based jobseeker's allowance
ICA Regs	Social Security (Invalid Care Allowance) Regulations 1976
ICB	incapacity benefit
IDB	industrial disablement benefit
I(EEA) Regs 2006	Immigration (European Economic Area) Regulations 2006
ILPA	Immigration Law Practitioners Association
IND	Immigration and Nationality Directorate
IS	income support
IS Regs 1987	Income Support (General) Regulations 1987
IW Regs 1995	Social Security (Incapacity for Work) (General) Regulations 1995
JA 1995	Jobseekers Act 1995
JA Regs 1996	Jobseeker's Allowance Regulations 1996
JSA	jobseeker's allowance
LAG	Legal Action Group
LEL	lower earnings limit
LSC	Legal Services Commission
MA	maternity allowance
MB	maternity benefits
NHS	National Health Service
NIAA 2002	Nationality, Immigration and Asylum Act 2002
NICs	National Insurance contributions
NINo	National Insurance number
NIRP	National Insurance retirement pension
NVQ	National Vocational Qualification
OB Regs 1979	Social Security (Overlapping Benefits) Regulations 1979
PAQ	Political Asylum Questionnaire
PAYE	pay as you earn
PCT	primary contributions threshold
PD Regs 1985	Social Security (Industrial Injuries) (Prescribed Diseases) Regulations 1985
SAL	Standard Acknowledgement Letter
SERPS	state earnings-related pension scheme
SFD	Social Fund Directions
SIAC	Special Immigration Appeals Commission
SMP	statutory maternity pay
SMP Regs 1986	Statutory Maternity Pay Regulations 1986
SP	State Pension
SSA 1998	Social Security Act 1998
SSAA 1992	Social Security Administration Act 1992
SSCBA 1992	Social Security Contributions and Benefits Act 1992
SS(GB) Regs 1982	Social Security (General Benefit) Regulations 1982
SS(I&A)CA Regs 2000	Social Security (Immigration and Asylum) Consequential Amendments Regulations 2000
SSP	statutory sick pay
UEL	upper earnings limit
UNHCR	United Nations High Commissioner for Refugees
WP (UK)	Work Permits (UK)
WTC	working tax credit

Part I
WELFARE BENEFITS

Chapter 1
Introduction to Welfare Benefits

1.1	The nature of welfare law	3
1.2	Overview of the benefits system	3
1.3	Sources of welfare benefits law	6
1.4	Welfare benefits administration	8
1.5	Benefits for people entering and leaving the UK	14
1.6	Welfare law bibliography	14
1.7	Which benefit? A quick guide	16
1.8	Fact analysis	17
1.9	Claimant profiling	18
1.10	Human rights	18
1.11	The claimant's 'partner'	19

1.1 The nature of welfare law

Welfare benefits law is a complex and rapidly changing area of law, which is often little understood by solicitors. It has evolved piecemeal over a very long period of time. Because of this, the legislation needed to put the schemes in place has also been created piecemeal. This explains the extraordinary diversity of the different benefits, and the arbitrary nature of their rules. The legislation itself is very full: not so much the primary, statute law, but the enormous volume of statutory instruments created under that primary law, where the detail is to be found.

1.2 Overview of the benefits system

1.2.1 The types of benefits

Welfare benefits are traditionally classified as either means-tested or non means-tested. The latter are grouped into three types: contributory, statutory, and other non means-tested. Here, the benefits are grouped in these categories, but generally in the book they are grouped by client group, with appropriate benefits of different types considered together. This should help the reader to grasp the relationship between the different benefits.

At **1.7**, there is a checklist, which can be used to find quickly the benefits appropriate to a particular client's needs. It cross-refers to the detailed discussion of each benefit.

At **1.9** the skill of 'claimant profiling' is outlined. When reading the rest of this book the reader should consider how he will best be able to develop and use that skill.

1.2.2 Contributory benefits

The contributory benefits are dealt with in detail in **Chapters 2 to 5** of the book. In order to qualify for any contributory benefit, the claimant must have paid (or be treated as having paid) National Insurance contributions:

(a) of an appropriate class;
(b) at an appropriate time;
(c) of the appropriate level.

These contribution conditions, which are explained in **Chapter 2**, vary according to the benefit in question.

1.2.2.1 Contribution-based jobseeker's allowance

The contributory form of jobseeker's allowance (see **Chapter 3**) is payable to those who have been employees and become unemployed. It can be paid for a maximum of 26 weeks. It should therefore be thought of as a short-term unemployment benefit.

1.2.2.2 Incapacity benefit

Incapacity benefit (see **4.4**) is payable to people who for medical reasons are incapable of work. The benefit has two components: a short-term element which can be paid for up to one year, and a long-term component which may be paid after one year of incapacity to retirement age.

Note that there is also a limited form of incapacity benefit that does not depend on contributions (see **1.2.4.3** and **4.5**).

1.2.2.3 State Pension

State Pension (see **5.2.1**) is the familiar 'old age pension' to which most people will be entitled once they reach retirement age. It will be paid for the rest of their lives.

1.2.2.4 Bereavement benefits

The bereavement benefits (see **5.4**) are a range of benefits for those whose husbands or wives have died. Uniquely among contributory benefits, entitlement depends not on the claimant's own contributions, but those of the spouse who has died.

1.2.3 Statutory benefits

An employee has no rights at general law to be paid on any day on which he does not work. Until the statutory benefits were introduced, any rights to sick pay and maternity pay were entirely contractual. Now, most employees have the right to statutory sick pay for up to 28 weeks (see **4.3**), and statutory maternity pay (see **6.3**). They will receive these benefits instead of short-term incapacity benefit and maternity allowance.

1.2.4 Other non means-tested benefits

The rest of the benefits in this group are dealt with in **Chapters 4 and 6** of the book. Most of them are for people with disabilities. Their names are a starting point to understanding the purpose of the benefit and are worth committing to memory.

1.2.4.1 Disability living allowance

Disability living allowance (see **4.6** to **4.8**) is the most important benefit for people with disabilities who become disabled while under the age of 65. It is, in fact, two benefits consisting of: the 'care component', for people who need physical help and/or supervision; and the 'mobility component', for people who are either effectively unable to walk, or need guidance or supervision in order to walk out of doors.

1.2.4.2 Attendance allowance

Attendance allowance (see **4.9**) is like the care component of disability living allowance, for those who first become disabled at age 65 or older.

1.2.4.3 Non-contributory incapacity benefit

This version of incapacity benefit is to help young adults aged 16 or over who become incapable of work before reaching 20, or sometimes 25 years of age. See **4.5**.

1.2.4.4 Industrial disablement benefit

This benefit (see **4.10**) is paid to employees who become disabled as a result of an accident at work or from contracting a prescribed industrial disease.

1.2.4.5 Maternity allowance

Maternity allowance (see **6.4**) is a benefit for women who stop working to have a baby, and do not qualify for statutory maternity pay.

1.2.4.6 Carer's allowance

Carer's allowance (see **6.7**) is paid to a volunteer who is effectively working full time to look after a person in receipt of either disability living allowance care component or attendance allowance.

1.2.4.7 Child benefit

Child benefit (see **6.6**) is paid to people with children who are under 16 or up to 19 in certain prescribed circumstances.

1.2.5 Earnings replacement benefits

Some of the above-mentioned non means-tested benefits have been specifically designed to assist people who no longer have earnings because they have become unemployed, incapable of work, pregnant, a full-time carer or have reached retirement age. The exceptions to that principle are widowed parent's allowance and bereavement allowance, which replace the earnings of the deceased spouse.

These so-called 'earnings replacement benefits' are:

(a) contribution-based jobseeker's allowance;
(b) incapacity benefit;
(c) maternity allowance;
(d) carer's allowance;
(e) retirement pension;
(f) widowed parent's allowance and bereavement allowance.

It is important to be able to identify these benefits since, as a general rule, an individual is not entitled to more than one at any time (but see further **2.6**). Moreover, if both members of a couple are each entitled in their own right to such a benefit, the amount of any increase in that benefit may be affected (see **2.4**).

1.2.6 Means-tested benefits

The means-tested benefits require the claimant to undergo a means test as part of the route to qualification. These benefits are described in **Chapters 7 to 9** of the book.

1.2.6.1 Income support

Income support (see **Chapter 8**) is the benefit of last resort for anyone who is not required, under the rules for claiming benefit, to be available for work. That includes the sick, disabled and single parents. It is usually paid to top up other benefits such as sickness and disability benefits, or child tax credit, or on top of part-time earnings (fewer than 16 hours per week). One important feature of the benefit is that it can provide help to owner-occupiers in meeting their housing costs (notably mortgage interest repayments).

1.2.6.2 Income-based jobseeker's allowance

This form of jobseeker's allowance is an identical twin of income support, for those who have to be available for work (see **Chapter 8**).

1.2.6.3 Housing benefit

Housing benefit (see **9.3**) is payable to those who are under a legal liability to pay rent for the dwelling occupied as their home.

1.2.6.4 Council tax benefit

Although called a benefit, council tax benefit (see **9.4**) is actually a rebate against the liability to pay council tax on the occupation of residential property.

1.2.6.5 Pension credit

Although called a credit, this is a benefit designed to ensure that pensioners have a guaranteed level of income (the 'guarantee credit' element) and are not prejudiced, but indeed are rewarded, if they have made some retirement provision in addition to the basic State Pension (the 'savings credit' element). Like income support and income-based jobseeker's allowance, it can provide help to owner-occupiers in meeting their housing costs (see **5.3**).

1.2.6.6 Child tax credit

Although called a tax credit, this is a benefit paid to low-income families with one or more children or qualifying young persons. See **9.8**.

1.2.6.7 Working tax credit

Again, strictly, this is a benefit available to low-paid workers, including those who are disabled. See **9.10**.

1.2.7 Other income-related benefits

In addition to these benefits and credits, there are other payments and benefits in kind which are means-tested. The most important of these are the so-called 'passport benefits', such as free prescriptions and school meals, and the social fund which makes grants and loans towards some one-off expenses. These are both described in **Chapter 9**.

1.3 Sources of welfare benefits law

The law of welfare benefits is unusual in that the same law applies to the whole of Great Britain: not just England and Wales, but Scotland as well. The rest of the UK has separate welfare law systems. We shall see something of the relationship between these systems and the British system in **Chapter 10**. For the rest of this part of the book, we shall be dealing exclusively with British law.

1.3.1 Statute

All welfare law is statutory in origin. The statutes dealing with welfare benefits are principally enabling statutes. Most of the detailed law is contained in statutory instruments (see **1.3.2**).

The principal statutes are set out below.

1.3.1.1 Social Security Contributions and Benefits Act 1992

The Social Security Contributions and Benefits Act 1992 (SSCBA 1992) is the statute that creates the main benefits and deals with the rules for entitlement to them. It has been heavily amended by subsequent legislation.

1.3.1.2 Jobseekers Act 1995

The Jobseekers Act 1995 (JA 1995) created the jobseeker's allowance, which replaced the earlier unemployment benefit in 1996. This is a free-standing Act: it supplements, rather than amends, the SSCBA 1992.

1.3.1.3 Social Security Administration Act 1992

The Social Security Administration Act 1992 (SSAA 1992) is concerned not with benefits but the way the benefits system works. It deals with claims, decision-making, appeals, payment methods and other administrative measures.

1.3.1.4 Welfare Reform and Pensions Act 1999

The title of this Act is self-explanatory! The Act introduced the stakeholder pension schemes (see **5.2.4.2**) and made changes to the regulatory framework for occupational and personal pensions. It also set out the scheme of bereavement benefits (see **5.4**) and made reforms to other benefits.

1.3.1.5 Tax Credits Act 2002 and State Pension Credits Act 2002

These Acts, supplemented in the usual way by numerous statutory instruments, set out the provisions concerning entitlement to these three tax credits.

1.3.2 Statutory instruments

Most welfare benefit law is created by statutory instruments, made under the enabling provisions of one of the Acts listed in the last section. Each of the major benefits (see list at **1.2**) has its own main set of regulations, usually including the word 'general' in the title. Each set of regulations is usually longer than the whole parent statute. There are also regulations to cover transitional provisions, whenever there is one of the frequent changes of law. There are also a large number of regulations to govern the details of administration and payment.

1.3.3 Case law

Where there is complex legislation, there is room for the courts to be asked to interpret it. The review and appeals systems for welfare law are described below (see **1.4.3** and **1.4.4**). Welfare law cases may reach the civil courts at Court of Appeal level, and regularly reach the House of Lords or European Court of Justice. Decisions of the higher courts are binding on the decision-making authorities (see **1.4.4**) in accordance with the usual rules on precedent. In addition, decisions of the second appeal tier, the Social Security Commissioners, are binding on tribunals of first instance and decision-makers as well.

What follows is a typical example of the way the three tiers of authority work together.

Example

Your client, aged 49, wants to claim income support. You are holding £19,000 in your client account, which is due to him following a successful personal injury claim. How does this affect his right to income support?

Section 134(1) of SSCBA 1992 provides that a claimant shall not be entitled to income support if his capital exceeds a 'prescribed amount'. That word 'prescribed' tells us to look in regulations to find what amount has been prescribed.

Regulation 45 of Income Support (General) Regulations 1987 (IS Regs 1987) provides that the prescribed amount is £16,000. But how is that calculated? Calculation of capital is covered by reg 46, which provides for some items which would otherwise be treated as capital to be disregarded. The twelfth item in Sch 9, where these items are listed, reads:

> Where the funds of a trust are derived from a payment made in consequence of any personal injury to the claimant, the value of the trust fund and the value of the right to receive any payment from the trust.

What is the nature of money held by a solicitor on behalf of his client? Does the solicitor hold it on trust for the client, in which case the £19,000 is disregarded? Or is it a simple chose in action like a bank account, in which case it disqualifies him from benefit? In *Commissioner's Decision CIS 600/1995*, the Commissioner held that it was the latter.

Now the picture is complete, and you can give your client the bad news.

1.4 Welfare benefits administration

1.4.1 Making a claim

1.4.1.1 Department for Work and Pensions

The Department for Work and Pensions (DfWP) has the primary responsibility for most of the administration of the benefits system, and most benefits are funded out of its departmental budget. The social security budget is the largest single item of central government expenditure.

1.4.1.2 Jobcentre Plus

The DfWP is responsible for the administration of both forms of jobseeker's allowance. It also works through an executive agency, known as 'Jobcentre Plus', which runs and manages Jobcentres and regional offices. See also **1.4.1.5**.

1.4.1.3 HM Revenue and Customs

HM Revenue and Customs (HMRC) has various roles within the welfare benefits system. It deals with the collection and recording of National Insurance contributions (see **2.2**), and provides information to the DfWP when it needs to check entitlement to contributory benefits. It is responsible for the administration of child benefit (see **6.6**) and the child tax and working tax credits (see **9.6**).

1.4.1.4 Local authorities

As a general rule, local government is responsible for the administration of housing benefit and council tax benefit. The local authorities concerned are those which act as housing authorities: district and borough councils where these still exist, otherwise London boroughs, unitary authorities and metropolitan districts. The councils fund the payments partly out of their own council tax receipts and partly out of support grants from central government.

1.4.1.5 'Work-focused interviews' (SSAA 1992, s 2A)

Currently, the Government is piloting, in some areas of the country, provisions to assist people to find full-time work. This means that some claimants in those areas are required to attend a 'work-focused' interview as a pre-condition to benefit.

Under this pilot scheme, there is a single entry point into the benefit system for those who are capable of work but who are unemployed. Following the initial contact, the claimant is given a personal adviser who conducts a work-focused interview which covers all aspects of looking for a job, including benefits information, job potential and information about services such as childcare.

1.4.2 Backdating

If a claimant wishes to claim a benefit, he must do so on the appropriate form. The claim is made only when the form is received at an office of the appropriate department, accompanied by all the information requested on the form.

If a person lacks the ability to make a claim, the DfWP can authorise a third party, usually a relative or friend, to do so. This person is known as an appointee and he takes on all the rights and obligations of a claimant, for example to appeal a decision and to notify the DfWP of changes in circumstances.

There are strict time limits for claiming benefits. The basic rule is that a benefit must be claimed as soon as the claimant becomes entitled to it. There are only limited powers to backdate a claim before the date on which the appropriate office receives the claim form. Different rules apply to different benefits, as set out below.

1.4.2.1 Child benefit, industrial disablement benefit, State Pensions, bereavement benefits, maternity allowance, incapacity benefit, child tax credit, working tax credit

These benefits can be backdated for up to three months before the date of application. No reason for the late claim is required. The claimant must show that he fulfilled all the conditions of entitlement for the benefit at the date to which he wishes the benefit to be backdated.

1.4.2.2 Income support, jobseeker's allowance

These benefits may be backdated for a maximum of one month before the date of the claim if that is 'consistent with the proper administration of benefit' according to any of the grounds detailed in the Social Security (Claims and Payments) Regulations 1987 (CP Regs 1987), reg 19(7). These include:

(a) the appropriate office where the claimant would be expected to make a claim was closed (eg due to a strike) and alternative arrangements were not available;

(b) the claimant was unable to attend the appropriate office due to difficulties with his normal mode of transport and there was no reasonable alternative available;

(c) there were adverse postal conditions;

(d) during the month before the claim was made the claimant's partner, parent, son, daughter, brother or sister died.

Alternatively, these benefits may be backdated for a maximum of three months before the date of the claim but only if the conditions of CP Regs 1987, reg 19(4)(a),(b) and (5) are met. Regulation 19(4) provides that the prescribed time for claiming the benefit shall be extended, subject to a maximum extension of three months, to the date on which the claim is made, where:

(a) any of the circumstances specified in reg 19(5) applies or has applied to the claimant; and

(b) as a result of that circumstance or those circumstances the claimant could not reasonably have been expected to make the claim earlier.

Hence a two-step test must be carried out. First, as required by reg 19(4)(a), the claimant must establish one or more of the circumstances justifying backdating that are set out in reg 19(5). Secondly, reg 19(4)(b) provides that it must be shown that as a result of any such circumstance the claimant could not reasonably have been expected to make the claim earlier. Note that in *Commissioner's Decision CIS 4354/1999*, Commissioner Mesher held that if a claimant could reasonably have been expected to make a claim even one day earlier than the actual date of the claim, then the second test under reg 19(4)(b) is not met.

Regulation 19(5) provides an exhaustive list of the circumstances referred to in reg 19(4) which are:

(a) the claimant has difficulty communicating because:
 (i) he has learning, language or literacy difficulties; or
 (ii) he is deaf or blind,
 and it was not reasonably practicable for the claimant to obtain assistance from another person to make his claim;

(b) except in the case of a claim for jobseeker's allowance, the claimant was ill or disabled, and it was not reasonably practicable for the claimant to obtain assistance from another person to make his claim;

(c) the claimant was caring for a person who is ill or disabled, and it was not reasonably practicable for the claimant to obtain assistance from another person to make his claim;

(d) the claimant was given information by an officer of the DfWP which led the claimant to believe that a claim for benefit could not succeed;

(e) the claimant was given written advice by a solicitor or other professional adviser, a medical practitioner, a local authority, or a person working in a Citizens' Advice Bureau or a similar advice agency, which led the claimant to believe that a claim for benefit could not succeed;

(f) the claimant or his partner was given written information about his income or capital by his employer or former employer, or by a bank or building society, which led the claimant to believe that a claim for benefit could not succeed;

(g) the claimant was required to deal with a domestic emergency affecting him and it was not reasonably practicable for him to obtain assistance from another person to make his claim; or

(h) the claimant was prevented by adverse weather conditions from attending the appropriate office.

If the reason is not one which is listed, then backdating is impossible, however good and understandable the reason for the delay.

1.4.2.3 Housing benefit and council tax benefit

These benefits can be backdated for a maximum of 52 weeks before the date of the claim provided the claimant 'had continuous good cause for his failure to make a claim' (Housing Benefit Regulations 2006 (HB Regs 2006), reg 83(12) and Council

Tax Benefit Regulations 2006 (CTB Regs 2006), reg 69(14)). The Regulations do not define what is a good cause but circumstances similar to those outlined in **1.4.2.2** would be considered.

1.4.2.4 Disability living allowance and attendance allowance

By ss 65(4) and 76(1) of the SSCBA 1992 neither of these benefits can be backdated.

1.4.2.5 Carer's allowance

As a general rule, this benefit can be backdated for up to three months before the date of application. No reason for the late claim is required. The claimant must show that he fulfilled all the conditions of entitlement for the benefit at the date to which he wishes the benefit to be backdated.

1.4.2.6 Statutory maternity pay

If the employer accepts the claim, he must pay it from the start of the maternity pay period (see **6.3.4**).

1.4.2.7 Statutory sick pay

If the employee gives notice of sickness in time (see **4.3.5**), he must be paid from his first qualifying day. If he is late but gives notice within one month of the time limit, the claim can be backdated to the first qualifying day if there was 'good cause' for the delay (eg the employee had a serious accident or heart attack).

1.4.3 Decision-making, revision and supersession

Every claim for a centrally administered benefit is considered by an officer of the appropriate department, on behalf of the Secretary of State, who will decide whether the claimant is entitled to benefit, and if so, how much. Once the decision has been made, it is sent to the claimant, usually with an explanation. What are his rights if he thinks it is wrong?

1.4.3.1 Written reasons

His first right is to ask for written reasons for the decision, if they are not sent to him at the same time. The request must be made within one month of receipt.

1.4.3.2 Revision

The Secretary of State may revise a decision within one month of notification, on his own initiative or in response to an application by the claimant. No particular grounds are needed for revision.

1.4.3.3 Supersession

A decision may also be superseded at any time, on application or on the Secretary of State's initiative, on certain specified grounds. These are:

(a) that the decision was wrong in law;
(b) that the decision was made in ignorance of, or under a mistake of, a material fact;
(c) that it is a decision against which no appeal lies (see **1.4.4**);
(d) that there has been a change of circumstances since it was made; or
(e) that the decision concerns a sanction for jobseeker's allowance (see **3.3.5**).

If supersession results in more benefit being payable, the extra benefit may be backdated, normally for a month (longer in official error cases). A decision of the Secretary of State may supersede a decision of a tribunal or commissioner, where there are grounds for supersession.

There are similar provisions for revision of decisions for housing benefit and council tax benefit, by the appropriate officer of a local authority.

1.4.4 Appeals and judicial review

The claimant's next step may be to appeal against the decision. His rights of appeal vary according to the benefit in question, and the nature of the disputed decision.

1.4.4.1 Discretionary social fund

Decisions about the discretionary social fund are in the discretion of the Secretary of State. The claimant may ask for revision or supersession, but judicial review is the only route to a challenge through the courts.

1.4.4.2 Benefits and tax credits

The Commissioners for HM Revenue and Customs deal with appeals arising from disputes between employer and employee over statutory sick pay and statutory maternity pay.

For benefits, there is a right of appeal to a tribunal, provided that the disputed decision is one which is appealable. Whether or not a decision is appealable is defined in Schedules to the Social Security Act 1998 (SSA 1998).

The commonest decisions against which there is no right of appeal are:

(a) whether the contribution conditions for a contributory benefit have been met (see **2.3**);

(b) whether and how an overpayment of benefit which is legally recoverable will actually be recovered (see **7.11**);

(c) whether a claim should be backdated for up to one month if it is received within that period after a preliminary enquiry (see **1.4.2**).

The only control over these non-appealable decisions is to ask first for a review, and then, if that is unsuccessful, to seek judicial review. If a claimant wrongly appeals against one of these decisions, the appeal will be struck out, as a tribunal has no jurisdiction.

1.4.5 How to appeal to a tribunal

An appeal must be made in writing, on a prescribed form, and must contain details of the decision appealed against and the grounds for appeal. The appeal must be made within one month of the decision being notified (ie sent, not received). Late appeals can only be admitted in exceptional circumstances.

The Tribunals Service, which administers the tribunal system, is an executive agency of the Department for Constitutional Affairs. The tribunal always includes one lawyer, who may sit alone in cases which do not require any other professional input. The lawyer sits with a doctor if the case involves the question of capacity for work; with two hospital consultants if the case involves the degree of disability following an industrial accident; and with one doctor and a lay member in cases involving disability living allowance and attendance allowance. The lay member in disability cases will either have a disability himself, or will have experience of working with people with disabilities – for example, a social worker, occupational therapist, or advice worker.

Procedure at the tribunals is informal. Appellants are asked beforehand whether they want an oral hearing or the matter to be dealt with on the papers. If they do not opt for an oral hearing, they are not given one, though the tribunal may order an oral hearing if it considers the matter cannot be fairly resolved without oral evidence. The tribunal gives its decision on the day of the hearing, in a short handwritten notice. Either the Secretary of State or the appellant may, within 21 days, ask for a full written statement of the findings of fact and reasons for the decision.

Cases with no realistic prospects of success are weeded out at an early stage, so that they do not waste tribunal time. The commonest ill-founded appeals are against a refusal to backdate an application for benefit where there is no reason within reg 19(5) of CP Regs 1987 (see **1.4.2.2**), or against the amount of a means-tested benefit which has been correctly calculated.

1.4.6 The higher tiers of appeal

1.4.6.1 Social Security Commissioners

Appeals from a tribunal lie to the Social Security Commissioners. A claimant may appeal from the decision of a tribunal only if it was wrong in law. This includes procedural irregularities, such as the failure to make explicit findings of fact, or apparent bias on the part of the tribunal. To appeal, the claimant must obtain a full written statement (see **1.4.5**), and needs leave.

The Commissioner may hold a complete rehearing of the case, make his own findings of fact and substitute his decision for that of the tribunal, or he may quash the decision and remit the case for rehearing by a different tribunal.

1.4.6.2 Court of Appeal and above

Appeals from the Commissioners on points of law lie to the Court of Appeal and then to the House of Lords in the usual fashion. Welfare law cases may also reach the European Court of Justice, since there are many European aspects of social security law (see also Chapter 10).

1.4.6.3 Human Rights Act 1998 and the European Convention on Human Rights

There have been more appeals from the decisions of tribunals as a result of the coming into force of the Human Rights Act 1998 (HRA 1998). This imports into English law the European Convention for the Protection of Human Rights and Fundamental Freedoms 1950, and, specifically, Article 6 which states:

> In the determination of his civil rights and obligations ... everyone is entitled to a fair and public hearing within a reasonable time by an independent and impartial tribunal established by law.

Procedural irregularities and bias will be even more likely to give rise to appeals as a result of this provision.

See further **1.10**.

1.4.7 Getting paid

1.4.7.1 DfWP benefits

Most DfWP benefits used to be paid by an order book, cashed at the Post Office. Forgery of order books is increasingly common and, for security reasons, the DfWP prefers to pay direct into claimants' bank accounts, usually four-weekly. The manner of payment is a non-appealable decision.

1.4.7.2 Mortgage interest

Mortgage interest payments as part of income support or income-based jobseeker's allowance (see **8.3.3**) are paid direct to the lender.

1.4.7.3 Housing benefit and council tax benefit

Council tax benefit, and housing benefit for local authority tenants, take effect as a rebate rather than an actual payment. Rent for private accommodation is paid direct to the landlord.

1.4.7.4 Income-based jobseeker's allowance and social fund payments

The element of jobseeker's allowance which represents anything other than mortgage interest is paid by a fortnightly Girocheque, posted to the claimant, or collected by him if there are problems with post (eg because he is of no fixed abode or he lives in a hostel where Giros are likely to be stolen). The same payment methods are used for social fund payments.

1.5 Benefits for people entering and leaving the UK

This part of the book closes with **Chapter 10**, which covers the rights to benefits of those entering the UK, whether for the first time or returning after a period of absence. In addition, 'exporting' particular benefits is considered. This is the area of law which brings together the two halves of the book, and requires a good understanding of both immigration and welfare law.

1.6 Welfare law bibliography

The following suggestions are offered for a bibliography for welfare law.

1.6.1 Legislation, cases and commentary

Annotated selections of statutes, statutory instruments and case extracts are useful for the study of detailed law. They are essential for the successful preparation of an appeal or other challenge to a decision, whether on the substantive law or procedural grounds. The main selections are Bonner, Hooker and White, *Non Means-Tested Benefits: the Legislation* (Sweet & Maxwell); Mesher and Wood, *Income Related Benefits: the Legislation* (Sweet & Maxwell); Rowland, *Medical and Disability Appeal Tribunals* (Sweet & Maxwell).

The first two are updated annually, the third only when there is a major change in the law. These deal only with the centrally administered benefits.

For locally administered housing benefit and council tax benefit, the Child Poverty Action Group (CPAG) publishes *CPAG's Housing Benefit and Council Tax Benefit: the Legislation* by Findley and Ward.

The DfWP publishes its own handbook for decision-makers (see further at **1.6.3**).

1.6.2 Textbooks and advisers' manuals

The market leader in this subject is the CPAG's *Welfare Benefits and Tax Credits Handbook*. This well-established book has many virtues: it is updated annually to take account of annual changes in the law; it is written in a friendly, direct manner which is addressed to claimants rather than advisers, though with full footnotes and references to original sources; and, not least, it is astonishingly cheap for so authoritative a book. It represents the absolute minimum library for anyone purporting to give advice on welfare law.

The CPAG also publishes an *Immigration and Social Security Handbook* which covers the area of overlap between welfare and immigration law.

The Disability Rights Alliance publishes a large-format *Disability Rights Handbook*. This covers all benefits but naturally concentrates on benefits for the disabled. It is fuller than the CPAG *Handbook* on some subjects of concern to people with disabilities, such as the funding of residential care and war pensions, both of which are outside the scope of this book.

1.6.3 Keeping up to date

Welfare law changes rapidly. Much of the legislation is contained in statutory instruments, which can be changed at very short notice. A means of keeping up to date is thus essential.

Two good journals are CPAG's *Welfare Rights Bulletin*, which updates the *Handbook*, and *Legal Action*, the journal of the Legal Action Group (LAG). Both these journals provide information about new legislation and review recent case law.

There are numerous websites covering various welfare law issues. You might start with those listed in the table below.

Organisation	Website
Department for Work and Pensions including *Decision Maker's Guide*, *Housing Benefit Guidance Manual*, *Social Fund Guide* and *Overpayments Guide*	www.dwp.gov.uk
Government services (includes disability living allowance, attendance allowance and carer's allowance)	www.direct.gov.uk/disability www.direct.gov.uk/carers
Her Majesty's Revenue and Customs including *Tax Credits Manual*, *Tax Credits Guidance Manual* and *Child Benefit Technical Manual*	www.hmrc.gov.uk
Jobcentre Plus	www.jobcentreplus.gov.uk/JCP/index.html

Organisation	Website
Pension Service	www.thepensionservice.gov.uk
Sure Start	www.surestart.gov.uk
Tribunal Service including *Appeals Guide*	www.appeals-service.gov/uk
Citizen's Advice online	www.adviceguide.org.uk
Rightsnet (welfare advice/updating/ courses)	www.rightsnet.org.uk
Child Poverty Action Group (welfare advice/updating/ courses)	www.cpag.org.uk
Dial UK (disability advice)	www.dialuk.info
One parent family advice	www.oneparentfamilies.org.uk
Age Concern	www.ageconcern.org.uk
Disability Alliance	www.disabilityalliance.org
Legal Action Group	www.lag.org.uk
Commissioners' decisions	www.osscsc.gov.uk
Court of Appeal judgments	www.hmcourts-service.gov.uk/cms/civilappeals.htm
House of Lords judgments	www.publications.parliament.uk/pa/ld/ldjudgment.htm
ECJ judgments	www.europa.eu.int/cj/en/transitpage.htm

1.7 Which benefit? A quick guide

Too ill to work, working age:	go to Checklist 1
Physical or mental disability, any age:	go to Checklist 2
Unemployed or working part time:	go to Checklist 3
Low income:	go to Checklist 4

Checklist 1: too ill to work

(a) *Statutory sick pay* for employees for first 28 weeks (**4.3**).

(b) *Incapacity benefit* for others for first 28 weeks and anyone after that subject to contribution conditions (**4.4**).

(c) *Non-contributory incapacity benefit* generally only for those young adults aged 16 and over whose incapacity began before reaching the age of 20 or, exceptionally, 25 (**4.5**).

(d) *Income support* subject to means test (**Chapter 8**)

(e) *Consider also benefits in Checklist 2.*

Checklist 2: physical or mental disability

(a) *Disability living allowance care component* for care or supervision if under 65 at first claim (**4.7**).

(b) *Attendance allowance* for care or supervision if 65 or over at first claim (**4.9**).

(c) *Disability living allowance mobility component* for problems with walking out of doors if at least 3 and under 65 at first claim (**4.8**).

(d) *Industrial disablement benefit* for employees injured or contracting a prescribed disease at work (**4.10**).

(e) *Working tax credit* for employee with a disability (**9.6**).

(f) *Consider also carer's allowance for full-time voluntary carers (6.7) and benefits in Checklists 1 and 3.*

Checklist 3: unemployed or working part time

(a) *Contribution-based jobseeker's allowance* for first 26 weeks subject to contribution conditions and labour market conditions (**Chapter 3**).

(b) *Income-based jobseeker's allowance* subject to means test, labour market conditions and partner's hours of work (**Chapter 8**).

(c) *Income support* if not required to satisfy labour market conditions (eg sick or single parent) subject to means test and partner's hours of work (**Chapter 8**).

(d) *Child tax credit* if responsible for a child or qualifying young person (**9.6**).

(e) *Consider also the benefits in Checklist 4.*

Checklist 4: low income

All these benefits are subject to a means test. Consider first whether any of the benefits in the other three checklists may apply.

(a) *Income support* if not required to satisfy labour market conditions. Can include mortgage interest payments (**Chapter 8**).

(b) *Income-based jobseeker's allowance* as Checklist 3. Can include mortgage interest payments (**Chapter 8**).

(c) *Housing benefit* if there is a legal liability to pay rent (**9.3**).

(d) *Council tax benefit* for residential occupiers of land (**9.4**).

(e) *Pension credit* for a pensioner (**5.3**).

(f) *Working tax credit* for low-paid employee (**9.6**).

(g) *Child tax credit* if responsible for a child or qualifying young person (**9.6**).

(h) *'Passport' benefits* (**9.17**).

(i) *Social fund* (**9.18**).

1.8 Fact analysis

The welfare law adviser must be able to *ask the right questions.* Very often, the client will have a long and complicated story to tell. The adviser must listen carefully, ask probing questions, spot the legal issues that arise in the case and suggest possible courses of action. Look again at the example under **1.3.3**. The right question to ask is: does the £19,000 constitute capital for income support purposes? As we have seen, to be able both to ask and answer that question, the adviser must be aware of the relevant provisions to be found in statute, regulations and case law.

1.9 Claimant profiling

As was stated at **1.8**, a welfare benefits adviser must be able to ask the right questions. This includes being able to identify that a client may be entitled to a whole range of different welfare benefits. I call this skill 'claimant profiling'. It centres on understanding the key conditions of entitlement for each welfare benefit and then asking the right questions in order to determine whether or not the claimant has any entitlement. At the end of each chapter there is set out a short suggested profile of the typical recipient of the benefits discussed.

1.10 Human rights

How does the entitlement to a social security benefit engage rights under the European Convention on Human Rights (ECHR)? The preferred choice of the European Court of Human Rights (ECtHR) in locating a Convention right in cases of economic discrimination by the State has been via Article 1 of the First Protocol. It has long been accepted that State benefits under a contributory scheme are within the article. In the case of *Stec v UK*, Application No 65731/01, the Grand Chamber of the ECtHR (confirmed by the judgment of the Court on 12 April 2006) took the opportunity in its admissibility decision to resolve previous doubts, by holding that non-contributory benefits are to be treated in the same way. The position was explained as follows.

> 54. ... [Article 1 of the First Protocol] does not create a right to acquire property. It places no restriction on the Contracting State's freedom to decide whether or not to have in place any form of social security scheme, or to choose the type or amount of benefits to provide under any such scheme ... If, however, a Contracting State has in force legislation providing for the payment as of right of a welfare benefit — whether conditional or not on the prior payment of contributions — that legislation must be regarded as generating a proprietary interest falling within the ambit of [Article 1 of the First Protocol] for persons satisfying its requirements ...

So it may be possible to argue discrimination in respect of a welfare benefit under Article 14 of the ECHR. As the Grand Chamber stated in *Stec*:

> 55. In cases ... concerning a complaint under Article 14 in conjunction with [Article 1 of the First Protocol] that the applicant has been denied all or part of a particular benefit on a discriminatory ground covered by Article 14, the relevant test is whether, but for the condition of entitlement about which the applicant complains, he or she would have had a right, enforceable under domestic law, to receive the benefit in question ... Although Protocol No 1 does not include the right to receive a social security payment of any kind, if a State does decide to create a benefits scheme, it must do so in a manner which is compatible with Article 14.

However, the chances of succeeding under Article 14 appear to be slim. In the joined appeals of *R v Secretary of State for Work and Pensions, ex p Carson and Reynolds* [2005] UKHL 37, [2005] 2 WLR 1369, Ms Carson had moved to South Africa and received her UK State Pension there, but because there was no reciprocal agreement (see **10.2.2**) with South Africa under which cost of living increases were payable, her UK pension was not increased in line with increases paid to pensioners in the UK. Ms Reynolds was under the age of 25 and for that reason she received a lower rate of jobseeker's allowance than if she had been over the age of 25. Both appellants complained of discrimination.

The House of Lords rejected both claims. Of Ms Carson's claim, Lord Hoffmann said (at paras 18 and 33):

> The denial of a social security benefit to Ms Carson on the ground that she lives abroad cannot possibly be equated with discrimination on grounds of race or sex. It is not a denial of respect for her as an individual. She was under no obligation to move to South Africa. She did so voluntarily and no doubt for good reasons. But in doing so, she put herself outside the primary scope and purpose of the UK social security system . . . What matters in my opinion is that (1) there is no question in this case of discrimination on a ground such as race or gender which denies Ms Carson the right to equal respect (2) in applying a scheme of social security, it is rational and internationally acceptable to distinguish between inhabitants of the UK and persons resident abroad (3) the extent to which the claims, if any, of persons resident abroad should be recognised is a matter for parliamentary decision.

As to Ms Reynolds' claim, Lord Rodger of Earlsferry said (at para 45):

> Ms Reynolds complains of discrimination in terms of Article 14 because, for some of the time when she was under 25 years of age, she received less by way of jobseeker's allowance than people of 25 and over. In other words, she was discriminated against on the ground of her age. There is no doubt that the relevant Regulations, endorsed by Parliament, deliberately gave less to those under 25. But this was not because the policymakers were treating people under 25 years of age as less valuable members of society. Rather, having regard to a number of factors, they judged that the situation of those under 25, as a class, was different from that of people of 25 and over, as a class. For example, in broad terms, those under 25 could be expected to earn less and to have lower living costs. Moreover, paying them a smaller amount of benefit would encourage them to live with others, rather than independently – something that was regarded as desirable in terms of general social policy. The scheme also had certain administrative advantages. In my view, having regard to these and other factors, it was open to ministers and Parliament, in the exercise of a broad political judgment, to differentiate between the two groups and to set different levels of benefit for them. Drawing the bright demarcation line at 25 was simply one part of that exercise. It follows that the difference in treatment of which Ms Reynolds complains easily withstands scrutiny and there is no unlawful discrimination in terms of Article 14.

What about Article 8 of the ECHR? The point was taken in *Carson and Reynolds* but dropped after the High Court stage ([2002] EWHC 426 (Admin) 37). As had been indicated by Maurice Kay J in *Tucker v Secretary of State for Social Security* [2001] EWCA Civ 1646:

> Any attempt to rely upon Article 8 alone to sustain a Convention right to a welfare benefit faces difficulty. The Strasbourg jurisprudence tends not to interpret the obligation on the state to respect family life in such a way as to require financial support.

Thus in 1987, in *Vaughan v UK*, Application No 12639/87, the applicant complained to the Commission that his supplementary benefit had not included a component to cover the travelling cost of contact visits to his home on the part of his children. It was held:

> Insofar as the applicant complains that there has been a violation of his right to respect for family life under Article 8 of the Convention, the Commission considers that the right to respect for family life does not impose an obligation on States to provide financial assistance for the purpose of ensuring that individuals can enjoy family life to the fullest.

1.11 The claimant's 'partner'

Historically, a claimant's partner for welfare benefit purposes has meant his or her spouse or person of the opposite sex with whom he or she is living in a relationship akin to marriage.

The Civil Partnership Act 2004 provides for couples of the same sex to enter into a civil partnership. So now, for welfare benefit purposes, couples in a civil partnership are treated in the same way as married couples. Equally, same-sex couples who are not in a civil partnership but who are living together as if they were civil partners, are treated in the same way as opposite-sex unmarried couples who are living together as husband and wife.

As to the often vexed question of cohabitation, see further **7.10**.

Chapter 2

Introduction to Non Means-Tested Benefits

2.1	The scope of this chapter	21
2.2	National Insurance contributions	22
2.3	Contribution conditions	27
2.4	Increases for adult dependants	31
2.5	Incompatible non means-tested benefits	32
2.6	Overlapping non means-tested benefits	33
2.7	Claiming more than one non means-tested benefit: a summary	33

2.1 The scope of this chapter

2.1.1 Contents of this chapter

This chapter will consider the following topics:

(a) a reminder of the main non means-tested benefits;

(b) National Insurance contributions;

(c) contribution conditions for contributory benefits;

(d) increases for dependent adults;

(e) the incompatible and overlapping benefit rules.

These topics are common to several benefits within this group, and it makes sense to deal with them separately from the basic rules for the benefits themselves.

2.1.2 The non means-tested benefits

The benefits which are commonly called 'non means-tested' are of three types: contributory, non-contributory and statutory. The list that follows cross-refers to the main treatment of each benefit. You may find it helpful to refer to the brief summary of the benefits in **Chapter 1**.

2.1.2.1 Contributory benefits

(a) Contribution-based jobseeker's allowance (**Chapter 3**).

(b) Incapacity benefit (**4.4**).

(c) State Pension (**5.2**).

(d) Bereavement benefits (**5.4**).

2.1.2.2 Non-contributory benefits

(a) Non-contributory incapacity benefit (**4.5**).

(b) Disability living allowance (**4.6** to **4.8**).

(c) Attendance allowance (**4.9**).

(d) Industrial disablement benefit (**4.10**).

(e) Maternity allowance (**6.4**).

(f) Carer's allowance (**6.7**).

(g) Child benefit (**6.6**).

2.1.2.3 Statutory benefits

(a) Statutory sick pay (**4.3**).

(b) Statutory maternity pay (**6.3**).

2.2 National Insurance contributions

2.2.1 What are National Insurance contributions?

Every person in Great Britain is allocated a unique National Insurance number of two letters, six digits and a final letter. The number is used for income tax reference purposes as well as for benefits and contributions. HMRC collects contributions paid by employers and employees, alongside the tax deducted under the Pay As You Earn (PAYE) system for Schedule E income tax. It assesses self-employed people for liability to pay earnings-related contributions on the basis of the information contained in their tax returns. Contributions are paid by reference to the tax year (ie 6 April to 5 April).

2.2.2 The jargon

Before we examine the topic of contributions, we need to define some specialist jargon terms.

2.2.2.1 'Lower earnings limit' (LEL)

The lower earnings limit is a very low level of weekly earnings below which an employee is not involved in the National Insurance system at all. For 2007/08 it was £87.

The LEL is a very important concept. As we will see, it is used as the basic measure for potential entitlement to the contribution-based benefits. However, it is usually National Insurance contributions (NICs) paid in the past which are relevant and so it may be necessary to know the LEL for previous tax years. For example:

Tax year	LEL: £
2006/2007	84
2005/2006	82
2004/2005	79

2.2.2.2 'Primary contributions threshold' (PCT)

Primary Class 1 contributions are paid by employees, by deduction at source from their gross pay by their employers. For 2007/08 the PCT was £100. If an employee earns between the LEL and PCT, he does not pay any Class 1 contributions but he is treated as if he has paid such. That will be important if he later comes to claim a contributory benefit. An employee will pay Class 1 contributions at a prescribed percentage on the amount of his earnings that exceed the PCT up to the upper earnings limit (UEL) (see **2.2.2.4**) and at 1% of earnings above the UEL.

2.2.2.3 'Secondary contribution threshold'

Secondary Class 1 contributions are a tax on employers, payable in respect of their employees. The threshold at which payments start is usually the same as the primary threshold. We shall not be concerned further with secondary contributions, since they do not affect a claimant's right to benefit.

2.2.2.4 'Upper earnings limit'

The UEL is the figure which defines the maximum amount of contributions payable by employees at a prescribed rate depending on whether or not they are part of the additional state pension scheme (see **5.2.3**). Above the UEL, contributions are paid at the flat rate of 1% of earnings. In 2007/08 it was £670.

2.2.2.5 'Earnings factor'

The earnings factor is the total amount of gross earnings on which an employee pays his National Insurance contributions in any tax year. An employee pays a fixed percentage of his gross earnings by way of primary Class 1 contributions. The more he earns, the more he pays. In benefits jargon terms, the higher his earnings, the higher his earnings factor. This can be important in helping him to qualify for contributory benefits if his contribution record has gaps in it. High earnings over a short period of employment can produce as high an earnings factor in a couple of months as low earnings in a complete year.

> **Example**
> (a) Bob is employed for just June, July and August 2007 for the tax year 6 April 2007 to 5 April 2008. He is paid £2,000 each month. He therefore has an earnings factor of £6,000 for that tax year.
> (b) Janet is employed for the whole of the tax year 6 April 2007 to 5 April 2008. She is paid £500 each month. She also has an earnings factor of £6,000.

Self-employed people also have an earnings factor. Each weekly Class 2 NIC payment (see **2.2.3.2**) gives rise to an earnings factor equal to that year's weekly LEL. So, a person who is self-employed for the whole of a tax year (ie 52 weeks) will have an earnings factor of 52 times the LEL for that tax year.

2.2.3 Who is liable to pay compulsory contributions?

Although NICs are a form of tax on earned income, not everyone, even if working for pay, is liable to pay contributions. Every person in the population falls into one of three categories.

(a) Those who are liable to pay compulsory NICs.
(b) Those who are not liable to pay NICs but will not suffer as a result of non-payment.
(c) Those who are not liable to pay NICs but may suffer as a result of non-payment.

Anyone who is aged between 16 and retirement age, and who is working and earning, is prima facie liable to pay contributions in respect of their earnings. How much they pay, and which of the various classes of compulsory NICs, depends on whether they are employed or self-employed, how much they are earning, and some other factors specific to each type of contribution. In reading the following account you may need to refer to the jargon section at **2.2.2**.

2.2.3.1 Employees

Employees pay primary Class 1 contributions on a fixed percentage of all their earnings over the primary contribution threshold. The employer deducts the contributions from the gross pay, together with Schedule E income tax, before payment. The rate of deduction varies according to whether the employee is or is not a member of a private pension scheme (see **5.2**).

If an employee earns between the LEL and PCT, he is deemed to have paid Class 1 NICs on those earnings (see further **2.2.6**).

Class 1 contributions are the only type which can be used as the basis of a claim for all the contributory benefits.

Historically, married women had the right to pay Class 1 contributions at a nominal rate, which did not entitle them to any benefits. However, since 5 April 1977 the only people who still have this right are women who were exercising it in 1977, who are still married to the same man as they were in 1977, and who have been paying contributions at that rate continuously ever since.

2.2.3.2 Self-employed workers

All self-employed people are liable to pay Class 2 contributions on their earnings from self-employment. The contributions are at a very low weekly flat rate which is regarded as producing an earnings factor equivalent to the lower earnings limit. For example, Doris is self-employed for 30 weeks in a tax year. Each week she made a Class 2 NIC payment. Her earnings factor for that tax year was 30 times the LEL.

It is possible for a self-employed person with very low earnings to apply for a certificate of exemption from paying contributions on the grounds of low earnings. This is rarely done, because it jeopardises entitlement to future benefit claims that are described at **2.2.5**.

Class 2 contributions can be used as a basis for a claim for all the contributory benefits except contribution-based jobseeker's allowance.

2.2.3.3 Higher-earning self-employed people

Self-employed people whose profits exceed a level roughly equal to the primary contribution threshold must also pay profit-related Class 4 contributions. This is a fixed percentage of all profits between the Class 4 threshold and a figure equal to the upper earnings limit.

Class 4 contributions are truly income tax under another name. They make no difference whatsoever to entitlement to any benefit.

2.2.4 People who have no need to pay contributions

There are two important groups who are not liable to pay contributions and suffer no detriment whatsoever as a result. This is so, even if they are working and earning in excess of the levels at which contributions are normally compulsory. The first group is children under the age of 16, the second anyone who has reached retirement age (60 for a woman, 65 for a man).

2.2.5 People who may suffer from not paying contributions

Everyone else who is not liable to pay compulsory contributions is theoretically at risk, because they will not have the contribution record needed to claim future benefits. People find themselves in this position for one of two reasons. They may not be working at all, for whatever reason – choice, illness or disability, unemployment, looking after children or invalids – or they may be working, but on earnings so low they are not liable to pay contributions. Some of these people will be given a form of automatic protection: others will have to make their own arrangements.

2.2.5.1 Low-paid employees

An employee may pay no contributions because his earnings are below the primary contribution threshold. Provided he earns at least the lower earnings limit, he is deemed to be paying full Class 1 NICs on an earnings factor equivalent to his actual gross pay. For benefit purposes, these deemed contributions are treated as actual contributions.

2.2.5.2 Contribution Class 1 credits

Contribution Class 1 credits may be awarded to people who do not pay actual contributions and are not deemed to do so. Credits can assist in qualifying for all the contributory benefits. On their own, however, they are not sufficient to enable a person to claim incapacity benefit or contribution-based jobseeker's allowance, which need a minimum number of actual or deemed contributions.

Three classes of people may be awarded contribution Class 1 credits.

(a) Those who are unemployed, registered with the Jobcentre, signing on and complying with the rules for jobseeker's allowance (see **Chapter 3**). This applies whether or not they are actually receiving any benefit.

Example

Mike was a self-employed taxi driver who can no longer drive because he has lost his licence. His wife Jenny works full-time as a teacher. How can Mike protect his contribution record?

Mike cannot claim contribution-based jobseeker's allowance because, being self-employed, he does not have the right contribution record (see **2.3.3**). He cannot claim income-based jobseeker's allowance because his wife is in full-time work (see **Chapter 8**). But, if he fulfils all the other rules for jobseeker's allowance, he will get a Class 1 NIC credit for each week that he signs on.

(b) Those who are incapable of work because of illness, who are not on paid sick leave from an employer, and who are providing evidence of incapacity in the form of medical certificates to the DfWP. Again, this applies whether or not they are entitled to receive any benefit.

Example

Sunita cannot work because she has broken her wrist. She has not worked since her children were born, though they have now left school. Her husband Ajay is a full-time engineer with a good salary. How can she protect her contribution record?

Sunita will not be entitled to incapacity benefit because she will not have paid the right contributions at the right time (see **2.3**). She will not be entitled to income support because of her husband's job (see **Chapter 8**). But if she is providing evidence of incapacity to the DfWP, she will receive a Class 1 NIC credit for each week that she is incapable of work.

(c) A person who is in receipt of carer's allowance (see **6.7**) will also be awarded Class 1 credits for each week the benefit is paid.

Example

Anne starts caring for her elderly mother in the autumn of 2006. She is awarded carer's allowance and receives it for 20 weeks during the tax year 2006/07 and for the entire tax year 2007/08. Anne will have 20 Class 1 NIC credits for 2006/07 and 52 Class 1 NIC credits for 2007/08.

2.2.5.3 Young person's Class 3 credits

A young person, aged at least 16 and under 19, is potentially liable to pay contributions, and would be doing so if he was working. If he stays on at school or college during that period, there may be a period of up to three years of his life when he is not paying contributions, which could affect his future rights to retirement pension (see **2.3.6.1**). As long as his parents are receiving child benefit for him, he will receive Class 3 credits for up to three years. Young person's credits can only assist in qualifying for retirement and bereavement benefits.

2.2.5.4 Home responsibilities protection

A parent of young children who is staying at home to look after those children, or a carer receiving income support, will be awarded 'home responsibilities protection', which was introduced in April 1978. It is awarded automatically to anyone whose records show that they are, throughout a tax year, receiving child benefit for a child under 16, or income support as a carer and are not paying contributions or getting deemed contributions or credits under any of the rules already described. It helps them to qualify for retirement and bereavement benefits only, by reducing the number of years' contributions needed to qualify for full benefits. How this works is explained in detail at **2.3.6.3**.

2.2.5.5 Class 3 (voluntary) contributions

Anyone else who wishes to protect future rights to retirement pension and bereavement benefits must pay voluntary Class 3 contributions. These contributions are paid weekly at a flat rate. Self-employed people with earnings below the small earnings threshold (see **2.2.3.2**) would get a better deal from Class 2 contributions, as these carry the right to incapacity benefit with them, and are much lower.

2.2.6 Contributions and benefits: a summary

If an employee earns less than the LEL, he is not liable to pay Class 1 NICs.

If an employee earns between the LEL and the PCT, he is treated as if he had paid Class 1 NICs on those earnings. These Class 1 contributions are deemed to be paid contributions and so can count towards meeting the first condition to qualify for contribution-based jobseeker's allowance (CBJSA) and incapacity benefit (ICB) (see **2.3.3**).

If an employee earns more than the PCT he pays Class 1 NICs on his earnings.

A self-employed person earning more than the small earnings exemption will pay Class 2 NICs. If he makes a high level of profit he also pays Class 4 NICs, but these are irrelevant when considering any benefit entitlement.

Class 1 credits may assist a person in claiming any contributory benefit (but for CBJSA and ICB can only help meet the second condition: see **2.3.3**).

Class 2 credits may assist a person claiming any contributory benefit apart from CBJSA (and for ICB such can only help meet the second condition: see **2.3.3**).

Class 3 credits can only help a person in claiming bereavement benefits and a retirement pension.

Home responsibilities protection (HRP) must be established for an entire contribution year. Each year of HRP is deducted from the number of years otherwise required to obtain full bereavement benefits or State Pension.

2.3 Contribution conditions

2.3.1 What are contribution conditions?

The right to receive CBJSA, ICB and State Pension Category A depends upon the claimant's contribution record. For each benefit, it is important that the claimant has paid, is deemed to have paid, or is credited with:

(a) the right *number or value* of contributions;
(b) of the right *class*;
(c) at the right *time*.

These rules collectively are called the contribution conditions and they vary with different benefits. The decision whether the contribution conditions are satisfied in any given case is the classic example of a decision against which there is no right of appeal (see **1.4.4**).

Bereavement benefits and certain retirement pensions take account of the record of the deceased spouse.

2.3.2 Terminology

Before we look at the contribution conditions, we need to define some further specialist jargon terms.

2.3.2.1 'Contribution year'

A contribution year is the period of 12 months and is identical to the tax year: 6 April in one year to 5 April in the next.

2.3.2.2 'Benefit year'

The benefit year is the period of 12 months within which the claimant makes a claim for any particular benefit for the first time. It begins on the first Sunday in January (eg the benefit year 2008 begins on 6 January). For CBJSA, the relevant benefit year is that in which the jobseeking period begins. For incapacity benefit, it is the year in which the period of incapacity for work begins.

2.3.2.3 'Working life'

The working life of any individual is from the sixteenth birthday (school leaving age) to retirement age (60 for a woman, 65 for a man). The basic length of the working life is thus 44 years for a woman and 49 for a man, but see **5.2.1.1**.

2.3.3 Contribution-based jobseeker's allowance and incapacity benefit

The contribution conditions for CBJSA and ICB are the most complicated.

2.3.3.1 Contribution-based jobseeker's allowance

The contribution conditions for CBJSA are:

(a) the claimant must have actually paid Class 1 NICs in respect of one of the last two contribution years ending before the beginning of the relevant benefit year and producing an earnings factor of at least 25 times that year's LEL ('the first condition'); *and*
(b) the claimant must have either paid or been credited with Class 1 NICs in each of the last two contribution years ending before the beginning of the relevant benefit year and producing an earnings factor of at least 50 times the LEL each year ('the second condition').

Summary of key points

(a) Only employees may claim CBJSA as only Class 1 NICs count.

(b) The relevant contribution years are the last two years ending before the relevant benefit year starts.

(c) Deemed payments count as actual payments.

(d) Class 1 credits can help meet only the second condition.

Example

Robert is made redundant in June 2008. He signs on and receives CBJSA. His jobseeking period therefore begins in the benefit year 2008. The relevant contribution years to be considered are 6 April 2006–5 April 2007 (that is the contribution year which ends immediately before the relevant benefit year begins) and 6 April 2005–5 April 2006. Let us assume that Robert was employed for both of those years and earned gross £12,000 each year. Does he meet the first condition? Yes, as in fact he paid Class 1 NICs in each year on an earnings factor of £12,000 which exceeds the 2006/07 minimum required of £2,100 (25 × £84) or, in the alternative, the 2005/06 minimum required of £2,050 (25 × £82). Does he also meet the second condition? Yes, given he paid Class 1 NICs in each year on an earnings factor of £12,000 which exceeds the 20065/07 minimum required of £4,200 (50 × £84) and the 2005/06 minimum required of £4,100 (50 × £82).

2.3.3.2 Incapacity benefit

The contribution conditions for incapacity benefit are:

(a) the claimant must have actually paid Class 1 or 2 NICs in respect of one of the last three contribution years ending before the beginning of the relevant benefit year and producing an earnings factor of at least 25 times that year's LEL ('the first condition'); *and*

(b) the claimant must have either paid or been credited with Class 1 or 2 NICs in each of the last two contribution years ending before the beginning of the relevant benefit year and producing an earnings factor of at least 50 times the LEL each year ('the second condition').

Summary of key points

(a) Both employees and the self-employed may claim ICB as Class 1 and 2 NICs count. Class 1 deemed payments count as actual payments.

(b) The relevant contribution years for the first condition are the last three ending before the relevant benefit year starts; whilst the relevant contribution years for the second condition are the last two ending before the relevant benefit year starts.

(c) Class 1 and 2 credits can help meet only the second condition.

Example

Alice becomes incapable of work in June 2008. She claims ICB as she is not employed and so not entitled to SSP. Her period of incapacity for work therefore begins in the benefit year 2008. The relevant contribution years to be considered for the first condition are 6 April 2006–5 April 2007 (that is the contribution year which ends immediately before the relevant benefit year begins); 6 April 2005–5 April 2006 and 6 April 2004–5 April 2005. Let us assume that Alice was self-employed for the whole of 2004/2005 and paid a Class 2 contribution each week, but that in 2005/2006 and 2006/2007 she cared for her aged mother full time and received carer's allowance each week (so each year she was credited with 52 Class 1 NICs). Does she meet the first condition? Yes, as in fact she paid Class 2 NICs in one of the relevant contribution years (ie 2004/2005) on an earnings factor of 52 times the LEL which exceeds the minimum required of 25 times the LEL. Does she also meet the second condition? Yes, given she received Class 1 NIC credits in both relevant contribution years of 2005/06 and 2006/07 on an earnings factor of 52 times the LEL and the minimum required was 50 times the LEL.

2.3.4 Statutory sick pay and qualifying for incapacity benefit

We shall see in **Chapter 4** that most employees cannot claim incapacity benefit for the first 28 weeks of their illness, because they are entitled to statutory sick pay (SSP) instead. If the incapacity lasts more than 28 weeks, employees then claim incapacity benefit. Note that the contribution record used for this claim for incapacity benefit is the one that applied at the time they first became ill and not when their statutory sick pay ended.

2.3.5 Carers

2.3.5.1 Carers and CBJSA

A carer who is looking after a person who is sick or disabled for 35 hours or more a week is likely to be receiving carer's allowance (see **6.7**). He may well be out of the labour market for many years. When his caring responsibilities end with the death, recovery or hospitalisation of the person he has been caring for, he may well wish to return to paid employment. Until he does so, he will sign on to protect his contribution record. But how can he claim CBJSA?

He will have contribution credits with his carer's allowance, and normally credits alone cannot qualify for CBJSA (see **2.3.3.1**). But, by a special concession, a carer may link his claim back to the beginning of the claim for carer's allowance, which is then treated as being the relevant benefit year to consider his contribution record. If at that date, however long ago, he satisfied the conditions for CBJSA, he may claim the benefit now.

2.3.5.2 Carers and ICB

If a person is entitled to carer's allowance before becoming incapable of work, the first contribution condition (see **2.3.3.2**) is modified such that he must have paid the correct amount of Class 1 or 2 NICs for any one contribution year whatsoever during his working life. He can, of course, use any class 1 credits (see **2.2.5.2**) received to meet the second condition.

2.3.6 Retirement and bereavement benefits

To claim either State Pension or bereavement benefits, the claimant needs to show a contribution record for most of the relevant working life. For a claim for State Pension, that is usually the claimant's own working life; for bereavement benefits, the working life in question is that of the spouse who has died. All classes of contributions (except Class 4) and credits count equally for these benefits.

Working life usually means from school-leaving age until retirement age (ie 16 to 60 for women (44 years) and 16 to 65 (49 years) for men), but see **5.2.1.1**. Bereavement benefits may be paid when a husband or wife has died well under retirement age, particularly bereavement allowance (see **5.4.4**). The working life is then from 16 to the date of death.

So what happens if there is a contribution record, but it does not cover the whole of the working life?

2.3.6.1 Total years' contributions necessary for full benefit

It is never necessary to have a record for every year of the working life. In the following table, the first column shows the number of years in the relevant working life, and the second the maximum number of years which can be missed for the claimant still to get the benefit at the full rate.

Working life years	Permissible gap years
1–10	1
11–20	2
21–30	3
31–40	4
41 and over	5

2.3.6.2 State Pension: contribution conditions

For the different types of pensions, see **Chapter 5**.

First, we need to consider who must have paid or been credited with NI contributions. This person is called the 'contributor'. For a category A pension, the contributor is the claimant. However, for a category B pension, the contributor can be the claimant or a spouse, or a deceased spouse's record can be used. Secondly, note that the contribution conditions are:

(a) the contributor must have actually paid in any one contribution year whatsoever before death or pensionable age, Class 1, 2 or 3 NICs producing an earnings factor of at least 52 times that year's LEL ('the first condition'); and

(b) the contributor must have either paid or been credited with Class 1, 2 or 3 NICs for each of the requisite number of years producing an earnings factor of at least 52 times the LEL for each year ('the second condition').

Example

Errol has just retired at the age of 65. He came to England from Trinidad as a spouse 22 years ago and has worked and paid contributions in England ever since. How much pension can he claim?

Errol's working life is 49 years (ie 65 minus 16). His permissible gap is 5 years (see table at **2.3.6.1**) so he would need contributions for 44 years to claim a full pension. He has only 22 years' contributions, so he can only claim a pension at 22/44 or one half of the full normal rate.

2.3.6.3 Home responsibilities protection

Home responsibilities protection (see **2.2.5.4**) works by reducing the total number of years' contributions needed for a full pension.

Example

Judith is 50 years of age and due to retire in 10 years' time. She worked and paid contributions from leaving university at the age of 21 for 8 years before having children. She then did not work for 15 years, and returned to work at the age of 44. She has worked ever since. How much pension can she claim, assuming she continues to work and pay contributions until she retires, aged 60?

Judith's working life will be 44 years (ie 60 minus 16). Normally she would need a contribution record for 39 of them to get a full pension as her permissible gap is 5 years – see table at **2.3.6.1**. The number of years she will have worked will be only 24 (ie 8 years before having children and 16 years before retiring). So at first sight it might seem that she will not get much more than just over half a standard rate pension. However, the 15 years she spent bringing up her children is deducted from the usual target of 39 years to reduce it to 24. As she will have worked and paid contributions for 24 years she will receive her full pension.

2.3.6.4 Bereavement benefits: contribution conditions

The only NIC requirement for a bereavement payment (see **5.4.5**) is that the late spouse must have actually paid in any contribution year whatsoever Class 1, 2 or 3 NICs on an earnings factor of at least 25 times the LEL.

The NIC requirements for a widowed parent's allowance (see **5.4.3**) or a bereavement allowance (see **5.4.4**) are that for each benefit the late spouse must have either:

(a) paid in any contribution year whatsoever Class 1, 2 or 3 NICs on an earnings factor of 52 times the LEL; and

(b) paid Class 1, 2 or 3 NICs or been credited with NICs on an earnings factor of 52 times the LEL for each of the 'requisite number of years' (see the above chart);

or in the alternative he or she died of an industrial injury or disease (see **4.10**).

If the requisite number of years is not met, then the benefit is reduced proportionately. For example, a spouse dies aged 28. That spouse's working life is 12 years (ie 28 (age at death) minus 16 (school leaving age)). The requisite number of years is 12 minus 2 (see table at **2.3.6.1**), ie 10 years. Assume the spouse only paid and/or was credited with the correct number of NICs for eight contribution years. Only eight-tenths or 80% of the benefit is payable. Do not forget that should the spouse have died of an industrial injury or disease then the full benefit is payable.

2.4 Increases for adult dependants

2.4.1 What are increases?

A non means-tested benefit is usually paid at a single flat rate for the claimant alone, irrespective of his family circumstances. However, if he has a partner living in the household, he may be able to claim an additional sum on top of his own benefit. This additional sum is called an increase. The detailed provisions concerning unmarried partners and those living as civil partners are beyond the scope of this book. Note that the term 'dependant' here is somewhat misleading. What it means is that before an increase is payable you must first consider any earnings replacement benefit paid to, or earnings received by, the claimant's partner.

2.4.2 Which non means-tested benefits carry an adult dependant increase?

The following benefits are relevant:

(a) maternity allowance (see **6.4**);
(b) carer's allowance (see **6.7**);
(c) State Pensions (see **5.2**); and
(d) incapacity benefit (see **4.4** and **4.5**). However, the adult dependant increase is claimable only if the adult dependant is over 60 or if under 60 the claimant is entitled to child benefit (see **6.6**).

There are two key questions always to ask.

2.4.2.1 Does the overlapping earnings replacement benefit rule apply?

If the adult dependant for whom the increase is claimable receives an earnings replacement benefit (see **1.2.5**) in their own right then:

(a) if the amount of the increase is the same or less than the amount of the adult dependant's earning replacement benefit, the increase is not payable; but

(b) if the amount of the increase exceeds the amount of the adult dependant earning replacement benefit, the difference is payable.

Example (using 2007/08 figures)

Mrs Morgan receives maternity allowance. Her husband receives contribution-based jobseeker's allowance of £20.00 (he has part-time earnings and receives an occupational pension reducing it to this figure – see **3.4**). Mrs Morgan can claim an increase with her maternity allowance for Mr Morgan. However, Mr Morgan's contribution-based jobseeker's allowance is £20.00 and so only the *difference* between the increase of £37.90 and that contribution-based jobseeker's allowance of £20.00 is paid (ie £17.90). If Mr Morgan's contribution-based jobseeker's allowance had been £37.90 per week or more then no adult dependant increase in his wife's maternity allowance would be payable.

2.4.2.2 Does the adult dependant have earnings?

For incapacity benefit (long-term) and State Pensions, if the amount of the adult dependant's net earnings exceeds a prescribed threshold figure (for 2007/08 it was £59.15 per week), the increase is not payable at all.

Example (using 2007/08 figures)

Mr Jones receives incapacity benefit at the long-term rate. His wife's net earnings are £30 a week. Assume an adult dependant increase is claimable. An incapacity benefit adult dependant increase of £48.65 is payable to Mr Jones as his wife's earnings do not exceed the threshold figure of £59.15.

For incapacity benefit (short-term), maternity allowance and carer's allowance the increase is not payable if the amount of the adult dependant's net earnings equals or exceeds the amount of the increase. If the net earnings are less than the increase, the increase is payable in full.

Example (using 2007/08 figures)

Mrs Richards receives carer's allowance. Her husband's net earnings are £50 per week. No carer's allowance adult dependant increase is payable to Mrs Richards as her husband's earnings exceed the amount of the increase (£29.05).

2.4.3 Summary

When considering if an adult dependant increase is payable ask:

(1) Does the adult dependant for whom the increase is claimable receive an earnings replacement benefit in his or her own right?

(2) Does the adult dependant for whom the increase is claimable have earnings?

2.5 Incompatible non means-tested benefits

As a general rule, a claimant may be entitled to any non means-tested benefit for which he meets the conditions of entitlement. However, the right to one particular non means-tested benefit may prevent the entitlement to another such benefit. These benefits are known as incompatible non means-tested benefits and are set out in the following table.

Benefit claimed	Incompatible with
Incapacity benefit or maternity allowance or State Pension or statutory sick pay or statutory maternity pay	Contribution-based jobseeker's allowance
Incapacity benefit or maternity allowance or statutory sick pay or contribution-based jobseeker's allowance	Statutory maternity pay
Incapacity benefit or statutory sick pay or contribution-based jobseeker's allowance	State Pension
Incapacity benefit or maternity allowance or State Pension or statutory maternity pay or contribution-based jobseeker's allowance	Statutory sick pay
Widowed parent's allowance	Bereavement allowance

2.6 Overlapping non means-tested benefits

As we have seen in **2.5**, whilst as a general rule a claimant may be entitled to any non means-tested benefit for which he meets the conditions of entitlement, some benefits are incompatible. Where non means-tested benefits are compatible (ie can be claimed together), certain provisions, 'the overlapping benefit rules', may affect their rate of pay.

The non means-tested benefits that may be affected by these rules are the so-called earnings replacement benefits (see **1.2.5**). Where a claimant is entitled to claim two or more such benefits, the DfWP makes an adjustment to the rate of pay. If a contributory benefit is payable to the claimant, then that is paid in preference to a non-contributory benefit. However, if the amount of the contributory benefit payable is less than that of the non-contributory benefit, the difference between the two is paid in addition to the contributory benefit. In all other cases the amount of the highest benefit is paid.

There are two non means-tested benefits that have their own unique 'overlapping' rule. The benefits concerned are disability living allowance care component and constant attendance allowance. This is discussed at **4.11**.

The overlapping rules only affect the amount of benefit payable and not the entitlement to it. So, if a claimant meets the conditions of entitlement for both incapacity benefit and carer's allowance, he will be paid incapacity benefit (the contributory benefit which is more than the non-contributory benefit of carer's allowance) but is treated as still entitled to carer's allowance. As a result, he would still receive a carer's premium if entitled to income support (see **7.7.4**).

2.7 Claiming more than one non means-tested benefit: a summary

Subject to the fact that certain non means-tested benefits are incompatible (see **2.5**) or overlap (see **2.6**), a claimant may receive any number of the non means-tested benefits for which he meets the conditions of entitlement. If still on a low income, the claimant may be entitled to one or more means-tested benefits as well.

Examples
(a) Andrew is 30 years of age and he is made redundant. The earnings replacement benefit (see **1.2.5**) he will wish to claim is contribution-based jobseeker's

allowance. He may well not qualify for any other non means-tested benefits. He may therefore need to top up what he receives by also claiming the means-tested version of jobseeker's allowance, namely income-based jobseeker's allowance (see **Chapter 8**).

(b) Brenda is 35 years of age and she has a serious accident at work. As a result, she is incapable of work. Her employer pays her statutory sick pay (see **4.3**) for the first 28 weeks she is off work. Due to her disability she cannot return to work. The earnings replacement benefit she will wish to claim is incapacity benefit (see **4.4**). She may well be entitled to other non means-tested benefits due to her incapacity. If she has care and/or mobility needs she can claim disability living allowance (see **4.6**). As her accident arose out of her employment she may be entitled as well to industrial disablement benefit (see **4.10**). If the amount of her non means-tested benefits is inadequate, she may be able to top it up with the means-tested benefit of income support (see **Chapter 8**).

Chapter 3
Jobseeker's Allowance

3.1	Introduction	35
3.2	Conditions of entitlement	36
3.3	Disqualification from benefit	41
3.4	Amount of contribution-based jobseeker's allowance	44
3.5	The New Deal	44
3.6	Contribution-based JSA and other benefits	44
3.7	Claimant profile: CBJSA	45

3.1 Introduction

3.1.1 What is jobseeker's allowance?

Jobseeker's allowance (JSA) is the latest name for the benefit which until 1996 was called 'unemployment benefit'. However, the change from the passive-sounding 'unemployment benefit' to the active 'jobseeker's allowance' is not just playing with words: it represents a real change in the ethos of the benefit. It is a benefit for people who are actively trying to find work. There are many safeguards to ensure that the benefit is paid only to those who can demonstrate a genuine commitment to find work.

3.1.2 One benefit, two elements

Jobseeker's allowance has two elements. Each should be seen as a separate benefit. The first is contribution-based jobseeker's allowance (CBJSA), which is a contributory, non means-tested earnings replacement benefit (see generally **Chapters 1** and **2**). The second element is income-based jobseeker's allowance (IBJSA), a non-contributory means-tested benefit which is calculated in the same way as income support. This is discussed in **Chapter 8**, where its differences from CBJSA are set out in full.

Here we shall note five points about the similarities and differences, but the rest of the chapter concentrates on CBJSA.

(a) The rules on conditions of entitlement (see **3.2**) and disqualification from benefit (see **3.3**) apply in exactly the same way to both elements.

(b) Entitlement to CBJSA is unaffected by capital or by a partner's income; entitlement to IBJSA may be affected by either.

(c) The CBJSA can be paid only for a maximum of 26 weeks; IBJSA may be paid for many years, until the claimant reaches retirement age.

(d) The CBJSA is available only to those with the appropriate National Insurance contribution record (see **2.3.3.1**); IBJSA depends on a means test.

(e) The IBJSA may be paid if CBJSA is not payable (eg if the contribution conditions are not satisfied), or IBJSA can be paid to top up CBJSA, or IBJSA may be paid after CBJSA runs out at the end of 26 weeks.

3.2 Conditions of entitlement

3.2.1 What are the conditions of entitlement for CBJSA?

To qualify for CBJSA, the claimant must satisfy the contribution conditions (see **2.3.3.1**). He must then satisfy the conditions set out in s 1 of the JA 1995:

(a) he must have signed a jobseeker's agreement;

(b) he must not be in 'remunerative work';

(c) he must be available for work and actively seeking employment (the 'labour market conditions');

(d) he must not be disqualified from benefit for any reason;

(e) he must be capable of work (see **4.2**) and under retirement age (65 for men, 60 for women); and

(f) as a general rule, he must not be under 19 years of age at school, college or on a non-advanced course. There are exceptions which are outside the scope of this book;

(g) he must satisfy the residence requirements (see **Chapter 10**).

3.2.2 Making a claim for jobseeker's allowance

When a person becomes unemployed, his first step should be to visit the nearest Jobcentre Plus to enquire about claiming JSA. The claimant will be given a form to complete, and an appointment with an employment officer (EO) who carries out casework with unemployed claimants.

Among other information needed for processing the claim, the form requires him to suggest the type of work he wants to look for and how he proposes to go about finding it. This information will be used at the interview with the EO, as the starting point for arriving at a jobseeker's agreement (see **3.2.3**).

On receipt of the claim form, the EO may contact the last employer to find more about the circumstances in which the claimant lost his employment, and what payments he received on leaving, since the answers to these enquiries may affect his rights to benefit (see **3.3.3**).

3.2.3 The jobseeker's agreement

The jobseeker's agreement is intended to be a genuine agreement negotiated between the claimant and the Secretary of State, via the EO. It imposes obligations on the claimant in return for the payment of benefit, and provides him with clear guidance on what he must do in order to try to find work.

3.2.3.1 Form and content

The form and content of the agreement are specified in s 9 of the JA 1995, with details in regs 31–44 of the Jobseeker's Allowance Regulations 1996 (SI 1996/207) (JA Regs 1996). A copy of the standard form is reproduced in **Appendix 1** to this part of this book. The agreement must be in writing – in practice, a standard printed form is used, filled in with the appropriate details. It must be signed by the claimant and by the EO on behalf of the Secretary of State. The claimant receives a copy to keep. The agreement is likely to be varied as circumstances change, especially where the claimant remains unemployed for a long time. All variations must also be agreed, reduced into writing, and signed, with a copy given to the claimant.

The agreement contains, among other information:

(a) a list of the types of employment that the claimant is going to look for;
(b) any restrictions on types of employment, hours of work, distance travelled, or expected pay levels, which have been agreed with the EO (see **3.2.7**);
(c) the steps that the claimant will take each week to attempt to find work (see **3.2.8**).

The agreement will also give the claimant the name of the EO who will be his regular contact. Lastly, it must explain his rights to challenge any part of the agreement.

3.2.3.2 Challenging the agreement

The claimant can receive no benefit until he has signed the agreement. If the claimant and the EO cannot agree on any term of the agreement, the claimant has the right to have the disputed term referred to a decision-maker, to decide whether his objections are well founded.

There is an ultimate right of appeal to a tribunal if the claimant is still unhappy after the review, but such appeals are extremely rare. The jobseeker's agreement may be backdated to the date of the first contact if the claimant's objections are accepted. Meanwhile, he has nothing to live on, and may have to apply for hardship payments (see **8.11**).

3.2.4 'Remunerative work' (JA 1995, ss 51–53)

It is easy to understand that a person cannot be entitled to a benefit intended for the unemployed if he is, in fact, working. But what if he is doing only a little part-time work? What if he is doing voluntary work to fill the time while he is unemployed? He is still allowed to claim the benefit (subject to meeting the other conditions) if he is not in 'remunerative work'. The number of hours worked is the starting point for the definition of this term. Work is not 'remunerative work' if it is for an average of less than 16 hours per week, including meal breaks taken at work.

Even if the claimant is working for 16 hours or more per week, it is still not 'remunerative' unless it is done for payment or in the expectation of payment. Voluntary work and hobbies are largely excluded. 'Payment' includes payment in kind if it is given in exchange for work, such as free meals or lodgings. 'Expectation of payment' means more than a mere hope that payment will be made and such expectation must be realistic. For example, a writer who writes a first novel in the hope it will be published will not be considered to be in remunerative work but, if it were a second novel, payment would be a realistic expectation and he will be treated as being in remunerative work.

The regulations are sufficiently wide to allow remunerative work to encompass work done that does not result in payment, as in *Kazantzis v Chief Adjudication Officer* (1999) *The Times*, 30 June. In that case, it was held that the time spent by a taxi driver waiting in the taxi office for customers counted as remunerative work, despite the fact that the taxi driver would not be paid for that time nor did he expect payment for that time. The Court of Appeal decided that the waiting time was an essential part of the employment, just as the time spent by a shopkeeper tidying shelves would be, and therefore the hours spent in such activities should be included in calculating whether a claimant worked 16 hours or more per week.

Certain claimants are deemed not to be in remunerative work despite the number of hours worked. These include charity workers and volunteers; those on training schemes and part-time fire-fighters or auxiliary coastguards or lifeboatmen or members of the territorial army or local authority councillors.

A claimant who is not in remunerative work may still not get benefit. The CBJSA is subject to an earnings rule (see **3.4**): if the claimant is earning as much as he would receive in benefit, he can have no benefit. In addition, he must also satisfy the 'labour market conditions' (see **3.2.5**).

3.2.5 The labour market conditions

The claimant has signed his jobseeker's agreement, and is not in remunerative work. He must now show that he is available for work (JA 1995, s 6) and actively seeking employment (JA 1995, s 7). These two conditions are collectively known as 'the labour market conditions'.

The JA Regs 1996, at regs 5–22, define both conditions in detail, and include extensive deeming provisions, to enable claimants to be treated as available or seeking work when they are not, and vice versa. We shall look at some of these provisions in context.

3.2.6 'Available for work'

'Work', in this context, means work as an employee which it is reasonable for the claimant to do. The claimant will normally be expected to be available to work at least 40 hours per week.

Being available for work usually means 'immediately' available. There should be nothing to prevent the claimant from receiving job offers and acting on them straight away (ie within an hour or two). There are exceptions to this rule, including:

(a) if the claimant provides a paid or unpaid service but is not a volunteer or carer (see below), he is allowed to start work after 24 hours' notice ('services' in this context may include giving someone a regular lift to the shops);

(b) if the claimant is a carer (see **3.2.7.5**) or doing voluntary work, he is allowed to start work after one week's notice ('voluntary work' means work done for a charity or other non-profit making organisation, or for anyone who is not part of the claimant's family, for which no payment is received other than reimbursement of reasonable expenses);

(c) if the claimant is working part time and is required to give notice he will be allowed to work out that notice.

The JA 1995 and the JA Regs 1996 specify the following circumstances in which a person is conclusively deemed to be not available for work.

(a) *If he is incapable of work due to illness or disability.* However, he may be deemed to be capable of work for a period of illness lasting not more than two weeks. This avoids the need to switch benefits for a short-term illness.

(b) *If he is a student on a full-time course.* For students in further education (up to A level), 'full time' is at least 21 hours per week supervised study. There is no definition for higher education (degree level and similar). It is a question of fact, on which the opinion of the teaching institution is persuasive but not conclusive.

(c) *If he is outside Great Britain,* unless the purpose of his absence is to attend a job interview within the EEA (see **10.4.4** and **10.4.9**).

3.2.7 Restricting availability

As a general rule, a claimant may restrict his availability for employment. He may do so by placing restrictions on the nature of the employment for which he is available and the terms or conditions of employment for which he is available (including the rate of remuneration). However, he must show that he has reasonable prospects of securing employment notwithstanding those restrictions (JA Regs 1996, reg 8). We shall now consider particular types of restrictions.

3.2.7.1 Restricting availability during any 'permitted period'

A claimant may be allowed to restrict his availability to his usual employment for a limited period. The permitted period starts on the date of the claim and may last from one week to a maximum of 13 weeks. Whether the claimant is entitled to any permitted period – and, if so, its length – is determined by the EO, who will consider the claimant's usual occupation, his relevant skills or qualifications, the length of any training undertaken for that occupation, his record of employment, whether the employment was continuous, and the availability and location of that type of employment. Generally speaking, the longer the claimant has been working in his usual occupation and the higher the degree of skill, training and qualification, the longer the permitted period will be. If there is little or no skill involved in the job at all, then a permitted period may not be allowed. The claimant's prospects of returning to work will depend on such things as his age, experience, the number and location of vacancies and the number of people who can fill those vacancies. A qualified teacher who has taught for 15 years should be allowed to look for teaching work for the maximum 13 weeks: a labourer who has been a hod carrier on a building site for six months would be lucky to be allowed one week.

3.2.7.2 Restricted level of pay

The claimant may refuse to accept a job during any agreed permitted period which pays below the level of his gross pay which he used to receive, but only if he had been receiving that amount for a long period. The most recent level of pay received will be ignored as the claimant will not be used to receiving it. For example, a claimant spends five years in the same job for which he is paid £20,000 per annum. In the last two months before he is laid off he receives a pay rise of £500 giving him a salary of £20,500. His usual level of pay for the permitted period purposes is £20,000.

Whether or not a permitted period is granted, note that the level of pay cannot be restricted after the initial six-month period of the claim unless such is reasonable because the claimant is disabled (see **3.2.7.6**).

3.2.7.3 Restricting availability by hours of work

As indicated above a claimant must be willing to work at least 40 hours per week. The claimant may choose a pattern of availability as long as it gives him a reasonable prospect of securing employment and it is recorded in his jobseeker's agreement. For example, if a bank clerk restricts his hours of work to between midnight and 8 am on six days a week, it might seriously reduce his prospects of employment unless he can show that work is available with 24-hour telephone or Internet banking. If a claimant is not prepared to work for at least 40 hours per week, he will be unavailable for work and will not receive benefit unless he has caring responsibilities (see **3.2.7.5**), and/or he has physical or mental disabilities (see **3.2.7.6**). Such a claimant must be willing to accept employment of less than 40 hours per benefit week.

3.2.7.4 Religious beliefs and conscientious objections

A claimant may place restrictions on the type of employment he is willing to do because of religious or conscientious objections, which are sincerely held. For example, a claimant may not wish to work on a holy day or a Jewish butcher may wish to work only for a kosher butcher. Again, the restrictions will be acceptable as long as the claimant can show that he has a reasonable prospect of securing employment despite the restrictions.

3.2.7.5 People with caring responsibilities

A person with caring responsibilities may restrict the total number of hours for which he is available for employment to less than 40 hours in any week providing:

(a) in that week he is available for employment for as many hours as his caring responsibilities allow and for the specific hours that those responsibilities allow; and

(b) he has reasonable prospects of securing employment notwithstanding that restriction.

In this context, 'caring responsibilities' means responsibility for caring for a child or for an elderly person or for a person whose physical or mental condition requires him to be cared for, who is either in the same household or a close relative. A close relative here is a spouse or other member of an unmarried couple, parent, step-parent, grandparent, parent-in-law, son, stepson, son-in-law, daughter, stepdaughter, daughter-in-law, brother, sister, grandchild or the spouse of any of the preceding persons or, if that person is one of an unmarried couple, the other member of that couple.

3.2.7.6 People with disabilities

A person who has a disability may not be incapable of work in law (see **4.2.1**), but may be restricted in what they can actually achieve at work. They may restrict their availability for types of work, hours and travelling to any extent which is reasonable in the light of their physical or mental disabilities. It does not matter that this may make it almost impossible to find work.

Thus, an unskilled labourer with lower back pain may refuse any job involving prolonged standing or repeated bending and lifting, or a young woman with chronic fatigue syndrome may need to rest for an hour, two or three times in a working day. This may make them virtually unemployable, but if the restrictions are justified, they must be permitted. A finding that a person is capable of work for incapacity benefit purposes is binding for the purposes of jobseeker's allowance.

3.2.8 'Actively seeking employment'

The jobseeker's agreement also specifies the steps that claimants must take each week in order to find employment. By s 7 of the JA 1995 the claimant will normally be expected to take more than two steps every week. Typical 'steps' include:

(a) visiting Jobcentre Plus at least once a week;
(b) registering with an employment agency;
(c) reading the 'situations vacant' columns of specified local or national newspapers, or trade and professional journals;
(d) telephoning or visiting potential employers;

(e) preparing a CV, learning interview techniques, practising writing application letters;

(f) applying for a certain number of vacancies each week.

A claimant must show that he is actively seeking work within a reasonable daily travelling time of his home and which he is capable of doing. The claimant must take all reasonable steps to give him the best chance of finding work. Whether the steps taken are reasonable will be determined by the EO who will consider such things as the claimant's skills and qualifications, disabilities, the time that has passed since the claimant last worked and the effectiveness of previous steps taken. The steps taken must give the claimant his best chance of securing employment, which means that a step will not count if the claimant has undermined his own chance of being offered the job, for example, by acting abusively towards a prospective employer, or by spoiling an application. Some steps will be more relevant to some claimants than to others. For example, it would be pointless if a highly skilled or qualified person went to the Jobcentre on a daily basis during his permitted period when prospective employers are unlikely to advertise positions there. Equally, it would be pointless for a builder's mate to read the situations vacant column in a computer magazine.

The claimant may be required to keep a diary of his 'steps' to help discussions with his EO.

A claimant can safely ignore a job vacancy which falls outside the terms he has agreed with the EO. But if he refuses or fails to apply for a job which does fall within the agreed parameters he may be penalised by a loss of benefit (see **3.3.5**), especially if he does this more than once.

3.3 Disqualification from benefit

3.3.1 What are the grounds for disqualification?

A claimant may have any benefit refused or withdrawn if it becomes obvious he is not entitled to it. For jobseeker's allowance, leaving aside fraudulent claims, the commonest reasons for disqualification are as follows.

(a) He has not yet signed a jobseeker's agreement (see **3.2.3**).

(b) Doubt has arisen over whether he satisfies the labour market conditions (see **3.2.5–3.2.8**).

(c) He has missed an appointment for signing on or to see an EO.

(d) He has monies from his former employer which are treated as income, so that he is deemed to be in remunerative work.

(e) He is involved in an industrial dispute.

(f) A sanction has been imposed on him because of some aspect of his conduct during or before the start of his claim.

We need now to consider items (c) to (f) of this list.

3.3.2 Missed appointments

Regulation 23 of the JA Regs 1996 provides that a claimant must attend at any appointment notified to him by the Secretary of State. If he fails to do this, then, under reg 25, his benefit will be stopped immediately, unless he attends the Jobcentre within five working days and shows 'good cause' why he failed to attend. Forgetfulness and confusion over the date is not good cause, but other factors such as illness, emergencies and transport problems may be. If the claimant cannot show good cause, he will have to make a new claim to benefit, and will probably lose at least one week's money.

This problem usually arises with claimants who miss their usual signing-on day. Every new claimant for JSA receives a card, which gives him details of the day and time he must attend, every two weeks, at the Jobcentre to sign on. Signing on involves signing a form to confirm that he has attended and that he has notified the Employment Service of any change in his circumstances. The card counts as notification of an appointment within the meaning of reg 23.

Claimants see an EO every 13 weeks. The first interview will coincide with the end of the period of the right to restrict availability to the usual occupation; the second with the expiry of the contribution-based benefit. The interviews are likely to result in changes to the jobseeker's agreement to include new tactics for job hunting, a wider range of types of employment, and possibly to consider retraining. These appointments too are covered by reg 23.

3.3.3 Payments on termination of employment

When an employee leaves employment, he may receive all or any of the following.

(a) Pay for the last period worked before leaving.
(b) A payment to compensate him for loss of earnings, where he is dismissed without notice. This payment may be made voluntarily by his employer, or in a negotiated settlement, or by a court or tribunal in an unfair or wrongful dismissal claim.
(c) A redundancy payment, in a lump sum or instalments.
(d) A cash payment for his accrued rights to paid holiday which he has not taken before leaving.

Of these, items (b) and (d) are treated as pay for the period they cover. The claimant is deemed to be in remunerative work (see **3.2.4**) during that period. Redundancy pay is not income for this purpose, even if paid by instalments.

> **Example**
>
> Karin has been made redundant, without notice. She has a redundancy payment of £4,000, six weeks' pay in lieu of notice and two weeks' pay for her holiday entitlement, which she was due to take next month. The six weeks' pay was paid only after her solicitor threatened to sue the employer. How long will it be before she can receive JSA?
>
> The six weeks' pay is a compensation payment. Karin is treated as being in remunerative work during this period and the two weeks of her holiday pay period. She cannot claim JSA for eight weeks in total. But she should still sign on to get credits for her contribution record.

3.3.4 Industrial disputes

An employee who is out of work because of an industrial dispute at his place of work will not be entitled to benefit, unless he has no interest in the dispute being settled.

> **Example**
>
> Sandie and her brother Alex both work at a car factory. The factory is closed because the assembly workers are on strike for more pay. Alex, who is an assembly worker, cannot receive JSA because he has an interest in the outcome of the dispute. Sandie, who works in the canteen, can receive it because her pay will not be affected by the resolution of the dispute.

3.3.5 Sanctions (JA 1995, s 19)

A sanction denies the claimant JSA temporarily because of some aspect of his conduct. When a claimant is sanctioned, it does not break the claim, but suspends it for the period of the sanction. The period varies according to the type of conduct and its seriousness.

3.3.5.1 Fixed-period sanctions

Fixed-period sanctions are for minor breaches such as:

(a) failure to comply with a specific instruction from an EO (such instructions are called 'jobseeker's directions');

(b) failure to attend on a training course for which the claimant has been enrolled; or

(c) leaving the course before it finishes.

The claimant will escape sanction if he can show 'good cause' for the failure. If there is no good cause, he will be sanctioned for two weeks the first time, four weeks on subsequent occasions. Whether there was good cause is a question of fact, and may be the subject of an appeal to a tribunal.

3.3.5.2 Discretionary period sanctions

For a more serious breach, the period of sanction is in the discretion of the Secretary of State, up to a maximum of 26 weeks. Discretionary period sanctions apply in three main circumstances.

(a) Voluntary unemployment. Employees are expected not to give up a job and throw themselves onto the National Insurance Fund without 'just cause', which means more than 'good cause'. It will include health reasons (including mental health), bullying and harassment, with or without physical assaults, and leaving to go to another job which then falls through. Not liking the job, or feeling 'I could do better than this' is not 'just cause'.

(b) Loss of employment for misconduct. The misconduct must be relevant to the employment, though not necessarily arising from it. It can involve fraud, persistent lateness, malingering, failure to obey reasonable orders and violence, and any act which means the claimant cannot carry out his job.

Example
James, a shop assistant, is convicted and fined for driving while uninsured. His colleague Paula is convicted of stealing from the shop. Both are dismissed. James's crime has no obvious effect on his ability to do his job, and no sanction should be applied. Paula has committed a serious breach of the duty of trust between employer and employee, and will probably be sanctioned for the maximum 26 weeks.

(c) Failing without good cause to apply for or take up a suitable opportunity of employment notified through the Jobcentre. The job must be within the terms of the jobseeker's agreement. The usual reason for refusal is that the pay is very low, although under reg 72 of JA Regs 1996, this is very rarely good cause.

With discretionary sanctions, the claimant may appeal both against the sanction itself and the period. Tribunals have been known to increase the period on appeal.

3.3.5.3 Effect of a sanction

A claimant who is sanctioned cannot receive either form of JSA during the sanction period. The period eats into any award of CBJSA, so that a person who is dismissed for misconduct with a maximum sanction of 26 weeks will never receive any CBJSA at all.

3.3.6 Hardship payments

A person who is disqualified from JSA may literally have nothing to live on. Means-tested hardship payments may be available to the following groups only:

(a) those whose claim has not been decided because they have not yet signed a jobseeker's agreement, or there is doubt about the labour market conditions;

(b) those who have been found not to satisfy the labour market conditions; and

(c) those who have been sanctioned.

Hardship payments are discussed in more detail, including the means test, at **8.11**.

3.4 Amount of contribution-based jobseeker's allowance

The CBJSA is a non means-tested benefit. The amount of capital held by the claimant and any partner is irrelevant. Likewise, the fact that a claimant's partner may be in remunerative work is irrelevant.

The CBJSA is paid at three different rates depending on whether the claimant is aged under 18, between 18 and 24, or 25 and over. It is paid just for the claimant. There is no additional allowance for any partner. If the claimant has a partner who is not in remunerative work, he may be entitled to IBJSA (see **8.2.3**) to top up his CBJSA.

We have seen that a claimant can work part-time. However, his part-time earnings will be taken into account when the benefit is calculated. Only the first £5 is disregarded. Also, if the claimant receives a pension payment under a personal pension or occupational pension scheme which exceeds a prescribed figure (it was £50 in 2007/08), then the excess is taken into account and reduces the amount of the CBJSA.

> **Example (using 2007/08 figures)**
> Fred has claimed CBJSA. He works part-time doing a few gardening jobs and is paid £25 weekly. He also receives an occupational pension of £70 a week. Fred's CBJSA will be the personal rate of pay according to Fred's age *minus* £20 (ie his part-time earnings of £25 after disregarding £5) and *minus* £20 (ie the excess of his occupational pension above £50).

3.5 The New Deal

The New Deal is a series of initiatives taken by the Government designed to reduce the number of benefit claimants by helping people to find work. Everyone on New Deal gets a personal adviser who is their point of contact throughout the programme. There are two types of schemes. The first is for people who would otherwise be claiming benefits as unemployed, which is compulsory for those to whom it applies. The second group of schemes is aimed at people who are not classified as unemployed but are receiving benefits and would like to get back into work. Full details may be found at www.jobcentreplus.gov.uk.

3.6 Contribution-based JSA and other benefits

The CBJSA is treated as income when calculating the child tax credit and working tax credit (see **9.6**).

The CBJSA is treated as income when calculating income-based JSA, income support, housing benefit and council tax benefit (see **7.3**).

The CBJSA is incompatible with (ie it cannot be claimed by an individual with) incapacity benefit, maternity allowance, retirement pension, statutory sick pay and statutory maternity pay (see **2.5**).

The CBJSA is an earnings replacement benefit (see **1.2.5**) and so may affect the entitlement of a spouse to any adult dependant increase in an appropriate benefit (see **2.4**).

The CBJSA and IBJSA can be claimed together. As indicated above, CBJSA will count as income when calculating any entitlement to IBJSA.

3.7 Claimant profile: CBJSA

Contribution-based JSA is a short-term earnings replacement benefit for an employee who has recently lost his job. It is payable only to an employee who has the correct Class 1 national insurance payment history. The claimant must visit Jobcentre Plus and sign a jobseeker's agreement.

Chapter 4
Incapacity and Disability

4.1	Introduction	47
4.2	Incapacity for work	48
4.3	Statutory sick pay	52
4.4	Incapacity benefit	53
4.5	Non-contributory incapacity benefit: persons incapacitated in youth (SSCBA 1992, s 30A)	55
4.6	Disability living allowance	56
4.7	DLA care component	57
4.8	DLA mobility component	62
4.9	Attendance allowance (SSCBA 1992, s 64)	66
4.10	Industrial disablement benefit	66
4.11	Constant attendance allowance (CAA)	73
4.12	New Deal for disabled people	73
4.13	Claimant profiles	74

4.1 Introduction

This chapter considers two groups of benefits intended for those people who are sick or disabled. Benefits law draws a distinction between 'incapacity for work' and 'disability', but in practice, there is some overlap between the two definitions.

4.1.1 Benefits covered by this chapter

4.1.1.1 Incapacity for work

The following are the benefits which may be paid to a person who is incapable of work because of a physical or mental disease or disablement.

(a) Statutory sick pay (SSP), for most employees during the first 28 weeks of incapacity.

(b) Incapacity benefit (ICB), for anyone who meets the contribution conditions, including the self-employed (see **2.3.3.2**), except for those employees initially entitled to SSP. Remember SSP is only payable for 28 weeks, so if a person is still incapable of work he will wish to move on to ICB if he qualifies for it.

(c) Incapacity benefit for a young adult aged 16 or over who does not meet the contribution conditions but has a long-lasting incapacity which began before the age of 20, or sometimes 25. This benefit is known as non-contributory ICB (see **4.5**).

A person who does not qualify for any of these benefits, but who is incapable of work and satisfies the means test, will be entitled to income support (see **Chapter 8**). A person entitled to one of these benefits but otherwise on a low income may also be entitled to income support.

4.1.1.2 Disability

A person who suffers from a disability may receive one or more of the following benefits.

(a) Disability living allowance care component (DLA care), for those under 65 at first claim who need care or supervision.

(b) Disability living allowance mobility component (DLA mobility), for those aged at least 3 and under 65 at first claim, who effectively cannot walk or cannot find their way around out of doors.

(c) Attendance allowance (AA): like DLA care for those aged 65 or over at first claim.

(d) Industrial disablement benefit, for employees who have suffered an accident or contracted an occupational disease in the course of their employment.

4.1.2 Relationship between incapacity and disability

Many people who are incapable of work also have a degree of disability, but the overlap is not complete. Most people who have a spell of incapacity for work do not suffer any permanent disability, because they recover before they have been disabled for the necessary qualifying period. Equally, there are many people who have a degree of permanent disability who remain capable of work.

Examples

Edmund is incapable of work because he has just had an operation on his knee. In two months' time he will be fully recovered and will have no lasting disability.

Firoz also has a knee problem, after a fall at work. He was off work for only a few days, but now he has developed arthritis in the knee which is stiff and can be painful. He can still work, though he has a degree of disability.

Gurmit suffered severe injury to his knee which has left him with a leg which is permanently slightly flexed and very painful. He also has severe back pain from limping. He can hardly walk at all and is unable to bend or kneel. He is both incapable of work and has a permanent disability.

4.2 Incapacity for work

4.2.1 What does 'incapable of work' mean?

Whether a person is or is not incapable of work is a question of fact, based on medical evidence. Before any form of benefit can be paid on the grounds of incapacity, there must be evidence of that incapacity. For the first seven days, a certificate from the claimant ('self-certification') is adequate. After that, the usual form of evidence is a certificate from the claimant's general practitioner, or from a hospital if the claimant has recently been sent home from hospital.

Later on, however, the Secretary of State may require the claimant to attend a medical with an appointed doctor as a condition of continuing to receive benefit.

4.2.2 The 'own occupation' test (SSCBA 1992, s 171B)

4.2.2.1 Incapacity benefit and income support

For incapacity benefit or income support, the test for the first 28 weeks of incapacity is the claimant's ability to carry out his 'own occupation'. An occupation will be regarded as the claimant's 'own occupation' only if he has followed it for more than 8 of the 21 weeks immediately before the start of the period of incapacity. An occupation means paid work of at least 16 hours per week. A GP's certificate is usually accepted as evidence of inability to work.

The 'own occupation' test is described as a test of whether the claimant is incapable by reason of some specific disease or bodily or mental disablement of doing work which he could reasonably be expected to do in the course of the employment in which he was engaged.

4.2.2.2 Statutory sick pay

For statutory sick pay, the test is almost identical, except that it is the ability to carry out the work for which the claimant is employed, irrespective of how long he has been employed (see **4.3**).

4.2.3 The personal capability assessment (SSCBA 1992, s 171C)

Where the 'own occupation' test has never applied, or no longer applies, capacity for work is determined by a personal capability assessment. This assessment is administered by a doctor at a medical, and the GP's certificate is then superseded.

This assessment applies whatever benefits the claimant is receiving. It also applies to those who are not entitled to benefit, but are providing evidence of incapacity so that they can receive incapacity credits to protect their contribution record (see 2.2.5).

The personal capability assessment consists of two separate matters. First, an 'incapacity report' and secondly a 'capability report'. Both reports are compiled by the doctor. At the time of writing, capability reports are being prepared only in certain pilot areas. By reg 24 of Social Security (Incapacity for Work) (General) Regulations 1995 (SI 1995/311) (IW Regs 1995), the incapacity report is designed to determine 'the extent to which a person who has some specific disease or bodily or mental disablement is capable or incapable of performing' a set of prescribed physical and/or mental activities. There are 14 physical activities (from walking on level ground with a walking stick or other aid, if such is normally used, to remaining conscious other than for normal periods of sleep) and four mental activities (completion of tasks, daily living, coping with pressure and interaction with other people).

Each of the activities is divided into a list of 'descriptors' which measure the level of difficulty associated with the task and allocate points accordingly. Details of the descriptors are set out in the Schedule to the IW Regs 1995 (reproduced at **Appendix 2** to this part of this book). Each descriptor carries a score, and the scores from the test are added up to arrive at an overall assessment of capacity for work. To be found incapable of work, the claimant must score at least 15 points for physical descriptors, or 10 for mental descriptors. If both physical and mental descriptors apply, then the combined score must be at least 15: in that case, a score below 6 on mental health descriptors counts as 0, but a score of 6 to 9 inclusive counts as 9.

> Examples
> (a) Ann scores 16 points on the physical descriptors. She is incapable of work as she only needed a score of at least 15 points.
> (b) Bob scores 12 points on the mental descriptors. He is incapable of work as he only needed a score of at least 10 points.
> (c) Cathy scores 12 points on the physical descriptors. She is not incapable of work under a personal capability assessment as she needed a score of at least 15 points.
> (d) David scores 8 points on the mental descriptors. He is not incapable of work under a personal capability assessment as he needed a score of at least 10 points.
> (e) Eric scores 12 points on the physical descriptors and 4 points on the mental descriptors. He is not incapable of work under a personal capability assessment. He does not score enough on each of the physical and mental descriptors to be incapable of work. He needed scores of at least 15 and 10 points respectively. As

he scores less than 6 on the mental descriptors the two scores cannot be added together.

(f) Fred scores 10 points on the physical descriptors and 7 points on the mental descriptors. He is incapable of work under a personal capability assessment. Although he does not score enough on each of the physical and mental descriptors to be incapable of work, since he scores at least 6 points on the mental descriptors, his score for such is deemed to be 9 points and that number of points can be added to his physical disability score of 10 points, giving him a total of 19 points. As the two scores added together exceed 15 points he is incapable of work.

4.2.3.1 Physical activity descriptors

Note that physical activities 1 and 2 in Part I of the assessment (see **Appendix 2**) both concern walking. Regulation 26(2) provides that these activities are, therefore, mutually exclusive and, so where both apply, only the highest descriptor of either activity counts. So, if a person is assessed as being unable to walk more than 200m without stopping or severe discomfort (activity 1 descriptor (d), scoring 7 points) and also unable to walk up and down a flight of 12 stairs without holding on (activity 2 descriptor (d), scoring 3 points) the score would be only 7 rather than 10 points.

How are the physical activities scored? Under Part I, each activity has a number of different descriptors, the first one representing the most severe level of disability and carrying the largest number of points, the bottom one representing 'no problems' and carrying no points, and the ones in between representing a descending scale of severity and appropriate point scores. Only one point score for each physical activity is to be taken, although it is clear from the descriptors themselves and from reg 26 that two or even more descriptors may well be equally applicable to a person for any given activity. Regulation 26(3) deals with this by making it mandatory that:

> In determining a person's score in respect of descriptors specified in Part I where more than one descriptor specified for any activity applies to him, only one descriptor shall be counted and that shall be the descriptor with the highest score in respect of each activity which applies to him.

Hence, as Commissioner Howell said in *Commissioner's Decision CIB 5361/97*:

> Since the descriptors with the highest scores are the ones that appear the furthest up each section of the table, the only valid way to conduct an assessment of a person's physical disability score in accordance with this mandatory requirement of the regulations must therefore be to work down from the top of each section of the table and stop as soon as one comes to a descriptor that applies to him.

4.2.3.2 Mental disability descriptors

As to the mental disabilities listed in Part II, each scoring descriptor counts. So, for example, if a person cannot carry out any of the tasks listed in activity 15, he will score 10 points. However, it is important to remember that these disabilities must arise from a mental disablement. As Commissioner Goodman said in *Commissioner's Decision CIB 1402/96*:

> . . . they must not be mere matters of mood but must relate to a recognisable mental disablement, in the nature of an illness and not shared by healthy members of the population. The generality of such a phrase as 'often sits for hours doing nothing' [15(b)], for example, must be restricted to such a state resulting from a definite mental disability.

4.2.3.3 Variable conditions

What if the claimant's condition fluctuates or there are periods of remission? In *Commissioner's Decision CIB 14534/96*, Commissioners Machin, Sanders and Rowland were addressed by counsel who submitted that the assessment should not be applied to each day in isolation:

> They suggested that material factors to be taken into account, when determining whether a claimant could be regarded as incapable of work throughout a period within which his or her condition varied, were the frequency of 'bad' days, the length of periods of 'bad' days and of intervening periods, the severity of the claimant's disablement on both 'good' and 'bad' days and the unpredictability of 'bad' days ... Although we consider a broad approach to be justified, the words of the legislation cannot be ignored. ... It follows that, in those cases where relevant descriptors are expressed in terms that the claimant 'cannot', rather than 'sometimes cannot', perform the activity, one should not stray too far from an arithmetical approach that considers what the claimant's abilities are 'most of the time' – the phrase used in *C1/95(IB)*. Nevertheless, we agree that all the factors mentioned by counsel ... are relevant when applying the broad approach. Thus, a person whose condition varies from day to day and who would easily satisfy the [assessment] on three days a week and would nearly satisfy it on the other four days might well be considered incapable of work for the whole week.

4.2.4 Deemed capacity for work

4.2.4.1 Effect of actual work

A person is treated as capable of work for any week in which he actually does any work, whether paid or unpaid. If the work is trivial or negligible it will not count. Hence, in *Commissioner's Decision CS 5/54* a man who occasionally helped his wife in her flower shop to cut and pack a few items was held still to be incapable of work. In addition, the following types of work are ignored:

(a) voluntary work, ie work that is not carried out for a close relative (parent, son, daughter, parent-in-law, son- or daughter-in-law, step-parent, stepson or daughter, brother, sister, or the partner or spouse of such relative) and the only payment received is to cover reasonable expenses; or

(b) sitting as a member of an appeal tribunal for not more than one day a week; or

(c) work as a local councillor; or

(d) certain work as prescribed by the IW Regs 1995. Broadly, this allows a claimant to earn up to:

    (i) £20 a week in any kind of work with no time limit; or

    (ii) £81 a week in certain permitted work with no time limit; or

    (iii) £81 a week in any kind of work of less than 16 hours a week for up to 26 weeks (with a further 26 weeks permitted if this could help improve capacity for full-time work).

4.2.4.2 Missed medicals

A claimant who fails to attend at a medical will be deemed capable of work unless he can show good cause for his failure to attend (IW Regs 1995, reg 8).

4.2.4.3 Unemployed claimants and short-term illness

See **3.2.6**, for the provision that a person on jobseeker's allowance may be deemed capable of work for short periods of illness.

4.2.4.4 Pregnant claimants

See **6.5** for the limited circumstances in which a pregnant woman may claim ICB as a result of her pregnancy.

4.2.5 People exempt from the personal capability assessment

Certain claimants are exempt from the assessment and are deemed to be incapable of work. These include:

(a) people receiving disability living allowance care component at the highest rate (see **4.7**);
(b) the terminally ill;
(c) those registered blind; and
(d) people getting industrial disablement benefit (see **4.10**) based on an assessment of at least 80% disablement.

4.2.6 Own occupation test or personal capability assessment: a summary

A claimant will only be subject to the own occupation test for the first 28 weeks of his claim if he can answer yes to all of the following questions:

(a) Has he worked in the 21 weeks before the first day of the period of incapacity that led to the claim?
(b) Did he work 16 hours or more a week?
(c) Did he work 16 hours or more a week for more than 8 weeks during that 21-week period?

A claimant will have to satisfy a personal capability assessment either from the beginning of his claim if the own occupation test does not apply, or from the twenty-ninth week where he has been subject earlier to the own occupation test for statutory sick pay or incapacity benefit purposes.

4.3 Statutory sick pay

4.3.1 General conditions of entitlement

At general law, an employee has no right to be paid if he is not actually working, unless there is an express provision to the contrary in his contract. The right to sick pay is no exception. However, by statute, almost all employees are entitled to receive SSP from their employers for the first 28 weeks of any period of incapacity for work. The contract cannot exclude this right.

4.3.2 Qualifying conditions (SSCBA 1992, ss 151–154)

To qualify for SSP, an employee must:

(a) be earning gross not less than the current lower earnings limit (see **2.2.2.1**);
(b) not be employed on a temporary contract lasting less than three months;
(c) satisfy the own occupation test as applied for SSP purposes (see **4.2.2.2**); and
(d) have been incapacitated for four days.

4.3.3 The earnings condition

For the eight weeks prior to the claim, the employee's normal weekly gross earnings must not be less than the lower earnings limit. If a person has not been employed that long but has received at least one pay packet, his earnings are averaged over the period those wages cover.

4.3.4 Short-term contracts

If a person's contract of employment is for less than three months, he is not entitled to SSP. However, employers cannot use this as a vehicle to avoid liability for the benefit. If a person has actually been continuously employed for more than three months, he cannot be excluded on this basis even if his contract was originally for a short term. Equally, a person employed on a fixed-term contract exceeding three months or permanently can claim even if he has not actually worked for three months under that contract.

4.3.5 Administration and payment

The employee must produce written notification of his incapacity. There is no specified form, but most employers adopt the self-certification scheme used for benefits (see **4.2.1**). Benefit can be paid only for a qualifying day on which the employee would, apart from his incapacity, be at work. It is not payable for the first three qualifying days.

Statutory sick pay paid at a flat rate. It has no increases. It is paid by the employer through the employee's pay packet, net of tax and NICs. It is very commonly, and equally lawfully, paid in one of three ways:

(a) the employee may receive his full normal pay for three or six months, with SSP as part of that pay;

(b) the employee may receive full normal pay for a similar period but with SSP on top, so he is actually better off than when working;

(c) the employee may receive SSP alone.

Once the period of 28 weeks has expired, no further SSP is payable unless the employee works for at least eight weeks continuously. An employee who is still incapable of work after 28 weeks will move on to incapacity benefit (see **4.4**), if he meets the conditions of entitlement.

4.3.6 Statutory sick pay and other benefits

Statutory sick pay counts as income when calculating any entitlement to income support or income-based JSA (see **7.3**).

It counts as income when calculating the working tax credit and child tax credit (see **9.6**) and pension credit (see **5.3**).

It is treated as earnings when calculating any entitlement to housing benefit or council tax benefit and so any appropriate earnings disregard can be made (see **7.3**).

It counts as earnings for carer's allowance (see **6.7**) and increases for adult dependants (see **2.4**).

4.4 Incapacity benefit

4.4.1 Who is entitled to incapacity benefit?

Incapacity benefit is payable to a person who:

(a) is incapable of work according to the own occupation test or personal capability assessment (see **4.2**); and

(b) has the appropriate National Insurance record (see **2.3.3.2**) or qualifies on age (see **4.5**); and

(c) is not entitled to SSP (see **4.3**), either at all or because his period of incapacity has lasted for more than 28 weeks and the entitlement to SSP has expired; and

(d) has provided appropriate evidence of his incapacity (see **4.2.1**).

4.4.2 Administration and payment

Incapacity benefit is payable at three different rates, depending upon the length of time that the claimant has been incapable of work (SSCBA 1992, ss 30A and B).

4.4.2.1 Short-term incapacity benefit

Short-term incapacity benefit is payable during the first 364 days of incapacity. For the first 28 weeks, it is paid at the 'lower short-term rate'. For the next 24 weeks, it is paid at the 'higher short-term rate' which is the same rate of pay as SSP. This makes good sense as a person receiving SSP for 28 weeks will move on to ICB at the higher short-term rate and so continue to receive the same amount. A person who is terminally ill, or receives the highest rate of the disability living allowance care component (see **4.7**) moves straight from the lower, short-term rate after 28 weeks on to the long-term benefit.

As to an increase for an adult dependant see **2.4**.

4.4.2.2 Long-term incapacity benefit

Once the claimant's incapacity for work has lasted for one year (or after 28 weeks if terminally ill or receives disability living allowance, care component at highest rate), he moves onto the long-term form of the benefit, which cannot be paid beyond retirement age. It carries an adult dependant increase (see **2.4**). The claimant may also receive an age-related addition, at a higher rate if his incapacity which led to the claim for ICB (or SSP followed by ICB) began before the age of 35, or at a lower rate if it began between the ages of 35 and 44 inclusive. An age addition is payable only at this rate.

4.4.2.3 Effect of other income (SSCBA 1992, s 30DD)

Incapacity benefit is reduced by 50% of any 'prescribed pension payment' that is received by the claimant which exceeds a specified weekly 'threshold' figure (£85 for 2007/08, ie the benefit is reduced by 50p for every additional £1 of pension income that people receive above the first £85. A prescribed pension payment includes those received under a personal or occupational pension scheme. So, if, for example, the prescribed pension payment is £105, the excess would be £20 and 50% of that excess would be £10.

By the Social Security (Incapacity Benefit) Miscellaneous Amendments Regulations 2000 (SI 2000/3120), the reduction of incapacity benefit for pension payments does not apply to a person who is entitled to the highest rate of the care component of disability living allowance.

4.4.2.4 Linking periods of incapacity

Spells of incapacity separated by periods of fitness for work of not more than eight weeks are treated as the same spell of incapacity. This means that claimants do not have to requalify for the benefit, if they return to work for a period of less than eight weeks. In such circumstances, the claimant will receive ICB at the rate paid before he attempted to return to work.

Example

Ursula is ill with depression for 18 months following the death of her mother. She is receiving long-term incapacity benefit. She attempts to return to work but, after only four weeks, becomes too ill to continue. She claims incapacity benefit again and goes straight back onto the long-term benefit.

4.4.3 Incapacity benefit and other benefits

The lower short-term rate is ignored when calculating any entitlement to child tax credit or working tax credit. However, the higher short-term rate and the long-term rate both count as income for these tax credits (see further **9.6**).

Incapacity benefit is taken into account when assessing entitlement to the pension credit but it is not treated as qualifying income for the savings credit element (see **5.3**).

Incapacity benefit is treated as income when calculating income support, income-based JSA, housing benefit and council tax benefit (see **7.3**).

Incapacity benefit is incompatible with (ie it cannot be claimed by an individual with) contribution-based JSA, retirement pension, statutory sick pay and statutory maternity pay (see **2.5**).

Incapacity benefit is an earnings replacement benefit (see **1.2.5**) and so may affect the entitlement of a spouse to any adult dependant increase in an appropriate benefit (see **2.4**).

4.4.4 Employment and support allowance (ESA)

In autumn 2008, the Government proposes that, for new claimants, ESA will replace incapacity benefit as well as income support paid on the grounds of incapacity. Broadly, the proposals are that when an individual applies for ESA, he will have a work-focused interview and undertake a new-style personal capability assessment. If eligible for the new benefit, he will be paid an 'employment support component', which will be conditional on him preparing a personal action plan that focuses on rehabilitation and work-related activity. The benefit rate will be paid at the current long-term ICB rate. Claimants with the most severe illnesses and disabilities, as identified in the personal capability assessment, will receive the 'support component' of ESA, which will be paid at a higher level than the current equivalent rate. They will not be required to undertake work-related activity, but will be able to engage in it on a voluntary basis. The ESA is not expected to include any age additions or adult dependency payments. For more details, see www.dwp.gov.uk/welfarereform/c2_h.asp.

4.5 Non-contributory incapacity benefit: persons incapacitated in youth (SSCBA 1992, s 30A)

4.5.1 Background

The Social Security Contributions (Transfer of Functions, etc) Act 1999 abolished the benefit known as Severe Disablement Allowance which had generally been available to severely disabled young adults who could not work and had no NIC record to qualify for ICB. The 1999 Act enables young adults who are disabled and cannot work to receive incapacity benefit.

4.5.2 Conditions of entitlement

A claimant must:

(a) be aged 16 or over; but
(b) be under the age of 20 or, in prescribed cases, 25 (see below) on a day which forms part of the period of incapacity for work; and
(c) have been incapable of work under a personal capability assessment throughout a period of 196 consecutive days; and
(d) not be receiving full-time education.

The Social Security (Incapacity Benefit) Miscellaneous Amendments Regulations 2000 (SI 2000/3120) set out the complex and sometimes puzzling qualifying conditions for an applicant whose period of incapacity for work began when aged between 20 and 25. Broadly, these are intended to cover young people who become incapable of work whilst studying and so do not have the appropriate NIC record for the contributory version of ICB. As a general rule, the claimant must have been registered on and attending a course of full-time advanced or secondary education, or vocational or work-based training, for at least three months before he attained the age of 20 years. The course must have ended either immediately before the official date the claim began or within one of the last two contribution years before the benefit year which would have governed a claim for the contributory version of the benefit (see **2.3.2.2**)), whichever is the later.

What is the cut-off date for a claim for this benefit? An article in the CPAG Bulletin (No 161, April 2001) refers to correspondence with the DfWP. The Department's view is that although the 20 and 25 age limits only apply specifically to the beginning of the period of incapacity and not the claim, people cannot claim later in life because they effectively have three months from the end of the 196-day qualifying period in which to make the claim.

4.6 Disability living allowance

4.6.1 Background

Disability living allowance has two components, a care component and a mobility component.

Either component of DLA may be claimed separately, or they may be claimed together. Many claimants are also in receipt of incapacity benefit, but there are also people in receipt of DLA who are in full-time work.

The award can be for an indefinite or fixed period.

4.6.2 DLA and other benefits

Disability living allowance does not count as income when calculating child tax credit and working tax credit (see **9.6**), the pension credit (see **5.3**), income support, income-based JSA, housing benefit and council tax benefit (see **7.3**).

Disability living allowance does not affect the payment of any other non-means tested benefit, except that the DLA care component overlaps with constant attendance allowance (see **2.6** and **4.11**).

A claimant receiving DLA care component at the highest rate is automatically regarded as incapable of work and is exempt from a personal capability assessment (see **4.2.5**).

Someone caring for a recipient of DLA care component at the middle or highest rate may be entitled to carer's allowance (see **6.7**).

4.7 DLA care component

4.7.1 Conditions of entitlement (SSCBA 1992, s 72)

A person is entitled to the care component if he:

(a) is under 65 when first claiming; and
(b) is severely disabled physically or mentally (see **4.7.3**); and
(c) has been so disabled for a continuous period of three months immediately before the claim and is likely to continue to be so throughout the next six months or is terminally ill (see **4.7.4**); and
(d) passes an additional test if under 16 years of age (see **4.7.5**); and
(e) is not subject to immigration control and satisfies the residence conditions (see **Chapter 10**).

4.7.2 Bodily functions

A person may be entitled to DLA care component because he needs help in carrying out his bodily functions (although this is not the only qualifying test). The amount of help that might be needed determines the rate of pay (see **4.7.3**). The interpretation of this term has led to a large amount of case law and so we shall consider that first.

In *R v National Insurance Commissioner, ex p Secretary of State for Social Services (Packer's Case)* [1981] 1 WLR 1017, Lord Denning MR said (at 1022):

> Attention is different from 'activity' or 'attendance'. It connotes something personal to the disabled person. 'Bodily functions' include breathing, hearing, seeing, eating, drinking, walking, sitting, sleeping, getting in or out of bed, dressing, undressing, eliminating waste products – and the like – all of which an ordinary person – who is not suffering from any disability – does for himself. But they do not include cooking, shopping or any of the other things which a wife or daughter does as part of her domestic duties: or generally which one of the household normally does for the rest of the family. It is the words 'in connection with' which give rise to the difficulty. They are very uncertain. Some kinds of attention are closely connected with 'his bodily functions': other kinds are too remote. It is a question of degree upon which different minds may reach different conclusions ... I would hold that ordinary domestic duties such as shopping, cooking meals, making tea or coffee, laying the table or the tray, carrying it into the room, making the bed or filling the hot water bottle, do not qualify as 'attention ... in connection with [the] bodily functions' of the disabled person. But that duties that are out of the ordinary – doing for the disabled person what a normal person would do for himself – such as cutting up food, lifting the cup to the mouth, helping to dress and undress or at the toilet – all do qualify as 'attention ... in connection with [the] bodily functions' of the disabled person.

In 1997, the House of Lords considered this issue when dealing with joint appeals in the cases of *Cockburn v Chief Adjudication Officer; Secretary of State for Social Security v Fairey (also known as Halliday)* [1997] 1 WLR 799. In Mrs Cockburn's case the tribunal had found that

> Mrs Cockburn cannot walk unaided and cannot get out of bed except with difficulty and she cannot dress herself properly without assistance. Mrs Cockburn is incontinent and as a result of this, a lot of washing is generated which Mrs Cockburn is unable to do herself and relies on her daughter.

Lord Clyde commented that attention to be given in connection with a bodily function must be some close and intimate service to the person of the claimant. The service is narrower than that of assistance. Assistance would cover activities done for the person. Attention implies services done to the person. The personal nature of what is comprised in attention prompts the observation made by Dunn LJ in the passage in his judgment in *Packer* [1981] 1 WLR 1017, 1023F that the attention must be a service involving personal contact carried out in the presence of the disabled person. But that should not be understood as being so absolute a requirement as to exclude the changing of bed linen which might be achieved without physical contact between the claimant and the person providing the service. Nor should it be understood to exclude an incidental activity which might occur outwith the presence of the claimant during the course of what is otherwise an attention given to and in the presence of the claimant. But the laundry work in the present case seems to me to fall outwith a service which is directed at the person of the claimant. It involves attention to the linen rather than attention to the claimant.

In Miss Fairey's case, the medical evidence was that she had been 'born deaf, she communicates mainly by signing and also can lip read but not very well, and speaks a little'. She 'may be in trouble if she gets lost and couldn't communicate to find her way. She is difficult to understand and doesn't lip read very well'. She could not hear a fire burning or hear traffic in the street. Physically and mentally she had no other disabilities than those arising from her deafness. Her mother wrote that she had to go out with her daughter as people did not understand what she was saying and she had to interpret for her.

Lord Slynn of Hadley gave the leading judgment in the House of Lords. He observed that:

> There is no issue in Miss Fairey's case as to whether or not she is severely disabled by her deafness. She plainly is; she is not able to hear and that reduces or impedes her ability to speak. Nor is it challenged that, as a result of her disability, some attention throughout the day may be required in connection with her bodily functions. The question is the particular one as to whether such attention given to her '(consisting of the help given by an "interpreter" skilled in the use of sign language) as may enable the claimant to carry out a reasonable degree of social activity' falls within the scope of section 72(1)(b)(i). Is that help capable of being attention in connection with her bodily functions? Although movement of the limbs (including their use for walking and running) is a bodily function, so also in my view is the operation of the senses. The reception of sound, its communication to the brain and the brain's 'instruction' to the limbs or other parts of the body to act or refrain from acting are all as much bodily functions as the movement of the limbs and the actions of the digestive or excretory organs ... Providing someone who can explain or translate normal conversation, or radio or film speech, is different from providing physical guidance by an arm. It seems to me, however, that it is also capable of constituting 'attention'. It is the one, or the principal, way in which messages to the brain normally conveyed through hearing can be conveyed by alternate means. This obviously does not improve natural hearing. Nor does it produce a replacement method of hearing but it provides an alternative way of fulfilling the hearing function.

In *Commissioner's Decision CSDLA/133/2005* a tribunal of three Commissioners stressed that a bodily function primarily refers to the normal action of any organ of the body. For example, one normal function of the lower jaw is to move up and down. As one purpose of the lower jaw moving up and down is to masticate food, it could be said that mastication is a bodily function. But the tribunal stressed that activities such as eating, getting in and out of bed, dressing and undressing are not strictly bodily functions because it cannot properly be said that it is the normal action or purpose of any organ or sets of organs to perform these exercises. These are not functions of organs of the body, but merely things which a body can do if the relevant bodily functions (eg, movement of the lower jaw, arms and legs, etc) are working normally.

According to *CSDLA/133/2005* it is necessary first to identify the specific bodily function or functions that are deficient in a claimant's case and then to assess whether attention is reasonably required in respect of that deficiency. Such attention must, of course, have the active, close, caring and personal characteristics referred to above.

By the Social Security (Attendance Allowance and Disability Living Allowance) (Amendment) (No 2) Regulations 2000 (SI 2000/2313), a person does not satisfy the daytime or night-time attention tests 'unless the attention the severely disabled person requires from another person is required to be given in the physical presence of the severely disabled person'. This overturns such decisions as *Commissioner's Decision CDLA/1148/1997,* where the Commissioner had held that conversations over the telephone could constitute attention.

4.7.3 Degree of severity of disability and rate of pay

4.7.3.1 Lowest rate

(A) A significant portion of the day (s 72(1)(a)(i))

A person is entitled to the lowest rate if 'he requires in connection with his bodily functions [see **4.7.2**] attention from another person for a significant portion of the day (whether during a single period or a number of periods)'.

In *Commissioner's Decision CDLA/58/1993,* the Commissioner did not disagree with the generally held view that attention for a period of one hour or thereabouts is sufficient. He said, in this context, that 'significant' refers to the length, rather than the importance, of the time. Note that, in *Commissioner's Decision CSDLA/ 29/94,* the Commissioner doubted that approach and suggested that attention for less than one hour may be significant depending on the circumstances. So if, for example, the attention required from another person consists of many short periods, the total number of those periods may be significant even if it would not qualify on a pure time test.

(B) The cooking test (s 72(1)(a)(ii))

In the alternative, a person is entitled to the lowest rate if 'he cannot prepare a cooked main meal for himself if he has the ingredients'.

In *Moyna v Secretary of State for Work and Pensions* [2003] 4 All ER 162, the House of Lords held that the purpose of the cooking test is not to ascertain whether a claimant can survive, or enjoy a reasonable diet, without assistance. It is a notional test to calibrate the severity of the disability. It does not matter whether the claimant actually needs to cook. A person who cannot cook for himself is entitled to the benefit whether he solves the problem of eating by obtaining help, buying cooked food, or eating out. The Court of Appeal had been wrong to lay emphasis upon the fact that, unless the claimant in the case could cook more or less every day, she would not enjoy a reasonable quality of life. Moreover, the test says nothing about how often the person should be able to cook. Section 72(2) contemplates a claimant who throughout a nine-month period has a disability which causes him to be unable to cook a main meal. The cooking test involves looking at the whole period and saying whether, in a general sense, the person could fairly be described as a person who is unable to cook a meal. It is an exercise in judgment rather than an arithmetical calculation of frequency.

4.7.3.2 Middle rate

(A) Frequent daytime attention (s 72(1)(b)(i))

A person is entitled to the middle rate if 'he is so severely disabled physically or mentally that, by day, he requires from another person frequent attention throughout the day in connection with his bodily functions' (see **4.7.2**).

If attention to bodily functions for a significant portion of the day is about one hour (see **4.7.3.1(A)**), then how much more attention must be given throughout the day for it to be frequent? A person will have to show a pattern of need over the day (eg with help to get up, get dressed, eat meals, go to the toilet, get undressed, bathe, go to bed, etc). In *Commissioner's Decision CA/281/1989*, it was said that the attention must arise at intervals spread over the day. It therefore is not enough if it is rendered in the morning and evening, however frequent or intense that might be, as it must also be given at least once during the intervening period. In *Commissioner's Decision CA/140/1985*, it was said that a person might qualify even if the spread of need was uneven provided lengthy periods were involved. In *R v National Insurance Commissioner, ex p Secretary of State for Social Services (Packer's Case)* [1981] 1 WLR 1017, Lord Denning MR said (at p 1022) that, 'Frequently connotes several times – not once or twice'.

(B) Continual daytime supervision (s 72(1)(b)(ii))

In the alternative, a person is entitled to the middle rate if 'he is so severely disabled physically or mentally that, by day, he requires from another person continual supervision throughout the day in order to avoid substantial danger to himself or others'.

Continual, rather than continuous, supervision is required. The 'characteristic nature of supervision is overseeing or watching over considered with reference to its frequency or regularity of occurrence' (*Commissioner's Decision R(A)2/75*). But the purpose of this continual supervision must be to avoid a substantial danger to the disabled person or another person. In *Commissioner's Decision R(A)1/83* it was said that:

> What is a substantial danger will, of course, depend upon the facts of each individual case. ... The substantial danger must not be too remote a possibility. The fact that it may take the form of an isolated incident does not in itself constitute remoteness. Moreover, the mere infrequency of a contemplated danger is immaterial. An isolated incident can have catastrophic effects.

(C) Prolonged or repeated night-time attention (s 72(1)(c)(i))

In the alternative, a person is entitled to the middle rate if 'he is so severely disabled physically or mentally that, at night, he requires from another person prolonged or repeated attention in connection with his bodily functions' (see **4.7.2**).

First, we need to consider for these purposes when the day ends and the night begins. In *R v National Insurance Commissioner, ex p Secretary of State for Social Services (Packer's Case)* [1981] 1 WLR 1017, Lord Widgery CJ, sitting in the Court of Appeal said:

> The argument before us has been at one in a number of respects; both [advocates] invite us to regard the night for the purpose of the section as being that period of inactivity, or that principal period of inactivity through which each household goes in the dark hours, and to measure the beginning of the night from the time at which the household, as it were, closed down for the night. I would commend to [tribunals]

dealing with this difficult question in future that they should look at the matter in that way.

Secondly, we need to ask what prolonged or repeated attention means. In *R v National Insurance Commissioner, ex p Secretary of State for Social Services* [1981] 1 WLR 1017, Lord Denning MR said (at 1022) that, 'Prolonged means some little time. Repeated means more than once at any rate'. It is generally accepted that 20 minutes or more is a prolonged period. Note also that the test is repeated, not repeatedly, so twice a night is sufficient.

(D) Night-time watching over (s 72(1)(c)(ii))

In the alternative, a person is entitled to the middle rate if 'he is so severely disabled physically or mentally that, at night, in order to avoid a substantial danger to himself or others he requires another person to be awake for a prolonged period or at frequent intervals for the purpose of watching over him'.

'Prolonged', in this context, probably has the same meaning as in s 72(1)(c)(i) above. 'Frequent intervals' probably constitute more than two occasions following s 72(1)(b)(i) above.

4.7.3.3 Highest rate (s 72(4)(a))

If a person satisfies both a daytime *and* a night-time middle rate care condition (or is terminally ill), he is entitled to payment of the care component at the highest rate.

4.7.4 Terminally ill (s 66(2))

A person is 'terminally ill' at any time if at that time he suffers from a progressive disease and his death in consequence of that disease can reasonably be expected within six months. These claims are normally processed within 10 working days.

4.7.5 Additional test for children under 16

The cooking test does *not* apply to children under 16 years of age (s 72(6)(a)).

If a child is to be entitled to the care component at any rate his needs must be 'substantially in excess of the normal requirements of persons of his age' or substantial needs 'which younger persons in normal physical and mental health may also have but which persons of his age and in normal physical and mental health would not have' (s 72(6)(b)).

4.7.6 Test when needs vary

In *Commissioner's Decision CDLA/1252/1995,* the Commissioner said that if the needs of the disabled person for attention and/or supervision vary over a week, it is necessary to discover if there is such a thing as a 'normal' night (or day). If so, the question is whether the attention or supervision normally given, or on average, satisfies the appropriate test. The Commissioner said:

> For example, I do not consider that the attention requirements would be either prolonged or repeated if, in an average week, a claimant required attention for a short period once a night on six days but required attention three times a night on a single day. On the other hand the attention would satisfy the night-time condition if on average the claimant required attention once a night every other night but required attention three or four times a night on the remaining nights. I think this would be the case even if there were occasional nights when no attention at all was required.

Given the House of Lords decision in *Moyna* (see **4.7.3.1(B)**), the approach should be more general than mathematical.

4.7.7 Summary of key points for DLA care component

The claimant must be under 65 when he first claims and disabled for a continuous period of three months immediately before the claim and likely to continue to be so throughout the next six months (or terminally ill). He must pass an additional test if he is under 16 years of age.

The rate of pay is determined by the degree of disability. The rates for 2007/08 are set out below with a reminder of the qualifying tests:

(a) Lowest rate: £17.10 if the claimant either:
  (i) 'requires in connection with his bodily functions attention from another person for a significant portion of the day (whether during a single period or a number of periods)'; or
  (ii) 'he cannot prepare a cooked main meal for himself if he has the ingredients'.

(b) Middle rate: £43.15 if the claimant is either so severely disabled physically or mentally that:
  (i) 'by day, he requires from another person frequent attention throughout the day in connection with his bodily functions'; or
  (ii) 'by day, he requires from another person continual supervision throughout the day in order to avoid substantial danger to himself or others'; or
  (iii) 'at night, he requires from another person prolonged or repeated attention in connection with his bodily functions'; or
  (iv) 'at night, in order to avoid a substantial danger to himself or others he requires another person to be awake for a prolonged period or at frequent intervals for the purpose of watching over him'.

(c) Highest rate: £64.50 if the claimant satisfies both a day *and* a night-time middle rate test (or is terminally ill).

4.8 DLA mobility component

4.8.1 Conditions of entitlement (SSCBA 1992, s 73)

A person is entitled to the mobility component of DLA if he:

(a) is under 65 when first claims; and
(b) is severely disabled (see **4.8.2**); and
(c) has been so disabled for a continuous period of three months immediately before the claim and is likely to continue to be so throughout the next six months *or* is terminally ill (see **4.7.4**); and
(d) can benefit from enhanced facilities for locomotion (see **4.8.3**);
(e) has attained the relevant age (see **4.8.4**); and
(f) passes an additional test for the lower rate if under 16 years of age (see **4.8.5**); and
(g) is not subject to immigration control and satisfies the residence conditions (see **Chapter 10**).

4.8.2 Degree of severity of disability and rate of pay

4.8.2.1 Higher rate

(A) Unable or virtually unable to walk (s 73(1)(a))

A person is entitled to the higher rate if 'he is suffering from a physical disablement such that he is either unable to walk or virtually unable to walk'. The Disability Working Allowance (General) Regulations 1991 (SI 1991/2887) (DLA Regs 1991), reg 12 provides that a person meets these conditions only if:

(a) his physical condition as a whole is such that, without regard to circumstances peculiar to that person as to the place of residence or as to the place of, or nature of employment—

(i) he is unable to walk (eg paraplegic, tetraplegic etc); or

(ii) his ability to walk out of doors is so limited, as regards the distance over which or the speed at which or the length of time for which or the manner in which he can make progress on foot without severe discomfort, that he is virtually unable to walk; or

(iii) the exertion required to walk would constitute a danger to his life or would be likely to lead to a serious deterioration in his health.

As to reg 12(a)(ii), each of the four factors must be considered. Note that there is no set distance in the regulation. This had led to conflicting cases; for example, in *Commissioner's Decision CM/47/86*, a person who could walk only 50 yards did not qualify, but in *Commissioner's Decision R(M) 5/86*, a person who could only walk the same distance did qualify. As to speed, again there is no guidance in the regulation. The starting point is to consider the disabled person's progress on foot against the average walking speed of an adult, which is approximately 3.4 miles per hour (or 100 yards per minute). The length of time involved takes into account the need to stop and rest. The manner of walking involves looking at the person's balance, gait, incidence of dizziness or falls etc. In *Commissioner's Decision CDLA/608/1994*, the Commissioner said that the test is how far the person can walk before severe discomfort occasioned by going further stops him. In *Commissioner's Decision CDLA/4388/1999*, the Commissioner said that even if a claimant is not virtually unable to walk by reason of limitations on distance, if there were, for example, periods when after walking a moderate distance he could not then walk for some time, it may be that he is virtually unable to walk by reason of limitations on the length of time for which he can walk. Any severe discomfort that might arise after walking has finished is irrelevant.

What does reg 12(a)(iii) mean? In *Commissioner's Decision R(M) 3/78*, it was said that the test may be satisfied if a condition, such as angina, might be induced or precipitated by walking. In *Commissioner's Decision CM/23/1995*, it was suggested that the serious deterioration need not be permanent nor last any great period of time. However, in *Commissioner's Decision CM/158/1994*, the Commissioner imposed a more strenuous test, ie there must be a worsening in the person's health from which he would never recover or only after a significant period (such as 12 months) or medical intervention.

By reg 12(4), a person fails to meet these conditions if he can walk with a prosthesis or artificial aid which he habitually wears or uses, or if he could walk were he to wear or use a suitable prosthesis or artificial aid.

Will a claimant qualify if he suffers from a mental disorder that manifests itself as a physical problem that satisfies the test? Yes, said Commissioner Jacobs in *Commissioner's Decision CDLA/4125/2000*. In that case the claimant's mental condition had caused muscle weakness in her legs such that she could not walk more than 50 yards.

(B) Blind and deaf (s 73(2))

By reg 12(2) and (3), a person is taken to satisfy this condition if he is 100% blind and not less than 80% deaf (on a scale where 100% deaf represents absolute deafness) and 'by reason of the combined effects of the person's blindness and deafness, he is unable, without the assistance of another person, to walk to any intended or required destination whilst out of doors'.

(C) Double amputee (DLA regs 1991, reg 12(1)(b))

In the alternative, a person is entitled to the higher rate if 'he has both legs amputated at levels which are either through or above the ankle, or he has one leg amputated and is without the other leg, or is without both legs to the same extent as if it, or they, had been so amputated'.

It is irrelevant that a person who satisfies this condition might be able to walk with artificial limbs.

(D) Severely mentally impaired with severe behavioural problems and receiving the care component at the highest rate (s 73(3))

By reg 12(5), a person is treated as severely mentally impaired if he 'suffers from a state of arrested development or incomplete physical development of the brain, which results in a severe impairment of intelligence and social functioning'.

Regulation 12(6) provides that a person suffers from severe behavioural problems if he exhibits disruptive behaviour which is '(a) extreme, (b) regularly requires another person to intervene and physically restrain [the disabled person] in order to prevent him causing physical injury to himself or another, or damage to property and (c) is so unpredictable that he requires another person to be present and watching over him whenever he is awake'.

In *Commissioner's Decision CDLA/156/1994*, the claimant was suffering from Alzheimer's disease. The medical evidence satisfied the Commissioner that the claimant's condition had taken effect after the brain had reached its maturity. Accordingly, there could be no question of the claimant's suffering from a state of arrested development or incomplete physical development of the brain. The sufferer in that case was well advanced in years, as indeed are normally all sufferers from Alzheimer's disease.

In *Commissioner's Decision CDLA 8353/95*, the claimant had suffered from schizophrenia since about the age of 16 and she applied for the benefit when she was aged 60. The Commissioner accepted the medical evidence that she suffered from an arrested development of the brain but held that this did not result in severe impairment of intelligence and social functioning.

As to an autistic child, see *Megarry v Chief Adjudication Officer* (1999) *The Times*, 11 November.

4.8.2.2 Lower rate (s 73(1)(d))

A person is entitled to the lower rate if:

> He is able to walk but is so severely disabled physically or mentally that, disregarding any ability he may have to use routes which are familiar to him on his own, he cannot

take advantage of the faculty out of doors without guidance or supervision from another person most of the time.

What constitutes guidance or supervision in this context? In *Commissioner's Decision CDLA/042/94*, the Commissioner expressed the view that 'guidance' could involve physically leading or directing a claimant or oral suggestion or persuasion. In starred *Commissioner's Decision 29/00*, a tribunal of three Commissioners held that mere reassurance cannot constitute supervision. There has to be an element of monitoring or readiness to intervene.

Note that by the Social Security (Disability Living Allowance) (Amendment) Regulations 2002 (SI 2002/648), a person will not meet this test if the reason he does not take advantage of the faculty of walking out of doors unaccompanied is fear or anxiety. However, he will meet the test where the fear or anxiety is a symptom of a mental disability which is so severe as to prevent him from taking advantage of the faculty of walking out of doors unaccompanied.

4.8.3 Benefiting from enhanced facilities for locomotion

A person in a coma or who cannot be moved on medical grounds clearly will not benefit from enhanced facilities for locomotion. But does a claimant have to show that at some point in time, with guidance or supervision, he will actually, rather than theoretically, have an ability to take advantage of the faculty of walking? Unfortunately, there are conflicting views. See *Commissioner's Decisions CDLA/042/94* and *CDLA/2364/1995*.

4.8.4 The relevant age

By s 1A, the minimum age to qualify at the higher rate is three and for the lower rate is five.

4.8.5 Additional test for children under 16

If a child is to be entitled to the mobility component at the lower rate, he must require 'substantially more guidance or supervision from another person than persons of his age in normal physical and mental health would require' or 'persons of his age in normal physical and mental health would not require such guidance or supervision' (s 73(4)).

4.8.6 Summary of key points for DLA mobility component

The claimant must be under 65 when he first claims and have been disabled for a continuous period of three months immediately before the claim and that must be likely to continue to be so throughout the next six months (or he is terminally ill). The claimant must be able to benefit from enhanced facilities for locomotion. He must have attained the relevant age (ie three for the higher rate and five for the lower rate). He must pass an additional test if under 16 years of age.

The rate of pay is determined by the degree of disability. The rates for 2007/08 are set out below with a reminder of the qualifying tests:

(a) higher rate: £45.00 if the claimant is:
    (i) unable or virtually unable to walk; or
    (ii) blind and deaf; or
    (iii) a double amputee; or
    (iv) severely mentally impaired with severe behavioural problems and receiving the care component at the highest rate;

(b) lower rate: £17.10 if 'he is able to walk but is so severely disabled physically or mentally that, disregarding any ability he may have to use routes which are familiar to him on his own, he cannot take advantage of the faculty out of doors without guidance or supervision from another person most of the time'.

4.9 Attendance allowance (SSCBA 1992, s 64)

4.9.1 Differences from DLA care component

Attendance allowance (AA) is very similar to DLA care component. The definitions of attention and supervision are identical. However, there are significant differences, namely:

(a) if the claimant is aged 65 or over at first claim, he must claim AA, not DLA;
(b) the qualifying period before the claim is six months, not three;
(c) AA has only two rates of pay, corresponding to the middle and highest rates of DLA care. The attention and supervision requirements are the same as those rates of DLA. There is no equivalent to the cooking test or the attention for a significant portion of the day test.

4.9.2 AA and other benefits

AA is treated the same as DLA (see **4.6.2**).

4.10 Industrial disablement benefit

4.10.1 What is industrial disablement benefit?

Industrial disablement benefit (IDB), sometimes simply called 'disablement benefit', is the principal remaining component of the industrial injury benefit scheme. The other current component of the scheme is constant attendance allowance (see **4.11**).

The industrial injury scheme provides no-fault compensation to people who have become disabled at work. This may be as a result of an industrial accident (see **4.10.2**) or a prescribed industrial disease (see **4.10.9**).

Industrial disablement benefit is not an earnings replacement benefit. There are no national insurance contribution requirements. It is a non means-tested benefit.

Industrial disablement benefit does not overlap with any other benefit for incapacity or disability. At the lower levels of disability it does not imply incapacity for work, and many claimants can and do work. This has no effect on their IDB. However, constant attendance allowance (CAA) (see **4.11**) does overlap with the DLA care component (see **4.7**).

An award of IDB may be for a limited period or for life depending on the nature of the injury or particular disease. If the former, then the claimant may need to apply for renewal of the benefit at the end of the period.

4.10.2 Industrial accident (SSCBA 1992, s 94)

Section 94(1) provides that industrial injuries benefit shall be payable 'where an employed earner suffers personal injury ... by accident arising out of and in the course of his employment, being employed earner's employment'.

To claim benefit as a result of an industrial accident, the claimant must have suffered:

(a) personal injury;
(b) arising out of and in the course of his employment;
(c) as an employed earner;
(d) by accident;
(e) resulting in a loss of faculty and disablement.

As to the effect of the accident occurring outside Great Britain or the EEA, see **10.4.5**.

4.10.3 Personal injury

Most personal injuries are obvious (eg a broken arm or leg). However, psychological injuries such as post-traumatic stress disorder may also qualify. As the DfWP *Decision Maker's Guide* puts it, the claimant must show that he has suffered a physiological (or, as doctors prefer to call it, a pathological) 'change for the worse affecting the mind or body'. It does not include injury to reputation or to property eg clothing or glasses damaged in the accident, although dislocation of an artificial hip counts according to *Commissioner's Decision R(I) 7/56*.

4.10.4 'Arising out of and in the course of employment'

4.10.4.1 Case-law definition

In *Faulkner v Chief Adjudication Officer* [1994] PIQR 244, Hoffmann LJ said (at 256):

> An office or employment involves a legal relationship: it entails the existence of specific duties on the part of the employee. An act or event happens 'in the course of' employment if it constitutes the discharge of one of those duties or is reasonably incidental thereto: *Smith v Stages* [1989] AC 928. It follows that there are always two separate questions. The first involves deciding what the employee's duties were. As Lord Thankerton crisply put it in *Canadian Pacific Railway Co v Lockhart* [1942] AC 591, 600: 'the first consideration is the ascertainment of what the servant is employed to do.' The second question is whether the act or event was in the discharge of a duty of something reasonably incidental thereto.

4.10.4.2 Statutory deeming provisions

It can often be difficult to determine if an act or event happens in the course of employment. The SSCBA 1992 assists by providing that in certain circumstances an employee is deemed to have sustained an accident in the course of his employment. These are set out below.

(A) Where no evidence is available

By s 94(3), 'an accident arising in the course of an employed earner's employment shall be taken, in the absence of evidence to the contrary, also to have arisen out of that employment'. This provision *only* applies where no facts are known about the accident. For example, the claimant sustains a head injury whilst at work. There are no witnesses as he was working alone at the time. He cannot recall what happened as he lost his memory.

(B) Acting in contravention of regulations etc

By s 98:

> An accident shall be taken to arise out of and in the course of an employed earner's employment, notwithstanding that he is at the time of the accident acting in contravention of any statutory or other regulations applicable to his employment, or of any orders given by or on behalf of his employer, or that he is acting without instructions from his employer, if:
> (a) the accident would have been taken so to have arisen had the act not been done in contravention of any such regulations or orders, or without such instructions, as the case may be; and
> (b) the act is done for the purposes of and in connection with the employer's trade or business.

As the DfWP *Decision Maker's Guide* says, 'this deeming provision is often misunderstood'. It covers an employee who does something he is employed to do, albeit he does it negligently or in breach of regulations or instructions. However, the action must be done for and in connection with his employer's trade or business and not for the claimant's own personal purposes. The claimant must still show that his actions were of a kind that he was employed to do. For example, a miner is injured whilst riding on an underground tram. He falls off and sustains personal injury. Normally, he would not be covered. However, he says he saw the load was moving and he rode with it to stop it falling. As this was done for and in connection with his employer's trade or business he should be covered.

(C) Travelling

By s 99:

> An accident happening while an employed earner is, with the express or implied permission of his employer, travelling as a passenger by any vehicle to or from his place of work shall, notwithstanding that he is under no obligation to his employer to travel by that vehicle, be taken to arise out of and in the course of his employment if:
> (a) the accident would have been taken so to have arisen had he been under such an obligation; and
> (b) at the time of the accident, the vehicle—
>   (i) is being operated by or on behalf of his employer or some other person by whom it is provided in pursuance of arrangements made with his employer; and
>   (ii) is not being operated in the ordinary course of a public transport service.

In this context, 'travelling' has been held to include the act of getting on or off the vehicle and at times when the vehicle is stationary before, during and after a journey. For example, the claimant's employer rents a minibus to collect staff every morning and bring them to the factory. As the minibus is slowly stopping, the claimant gets off, falls and injures himself. This will be an industrial accident arising out of and in the course of his employment as the claimant has merely acted negligently. If the minibus had been going at speed then attempting to get off it in such circumstances would be so rash as to take the act wholly outside the scope of his employment (*Commissioner's Decision CL 182/49*).

What about journeys outside the scope of s 99? Many employees will make their own way to and from work. And what about trips made in the meantime? Lord Lowry, in the House of Lords in the case of *Smith v Stages* [1989] 2 WLR 529 at 551, suggested the following guidelines.

(a) Travelling in the employer's time between workplaces (one of which may be the regular workplace) or in the course of a peripatetic occupation, whether accompanied by goods or tools or simply in order to reach a succession of workplaces (as an inspector of gas meters might do), will be in the course of the employment.

(b) Receipt of wages (though not receipt of a travelling allowance) will indicate that the employee is travelling in the employer's time and for his benefit and is acting in the course of his employment, and in such a case the fact that the employee may have discretion as to the mode and time of travelling will not take the journey out of the course of his employment.

(c) An employee travelling *in the employer's time* from his ordinary residence to a workplace other than his regular workplace or in the course of a peripatetic occupation or to the scene of an emergency (such as a fire, an accident or a mechanical breakdown of plant) will be acting in the course of his employment.

(d) A deviation from or interruption of a journey undertaken in the course of employment (unless the deviation or interruption is merely incidental to the journey) will for the time being (which may include an overnight interruption) take the employee out of the course of his employment.

(e) Return journeys are to be treated on the same footing as outward journeys.

It must be stressed that these are only guidelines and each case will turn on its own unique facts. For example, in *Commissioner's Decision R(I) 1/88*, a claimant had a road accident whilst driving home in his employer's van. It was a Monday evening and he had been working on his employer's site over the weekend. It was held that the accident arose in the course of his employment because he did not have a single place of work; the journey home by van rather than by the usual train was a direct result of his employer requiring him to work that weekend; he was using the van with his employer's consent and was subject to restrictions imposed by his employer as to his route and overnight parking.

(D) Emergencies

By s 100:

> An accident happening to an employed earner in or about any premises at which he is for the time being employed for the purposes of his employer's trade or business shall be taken to arise out of and in the course of his employment if it happens while he is taking steps, on an actual or supposed emergency at those premises, to rescue, succour or protect persons who are, or are thought to be or possibly to be, injured or imperilled, or to avert or minimise serious damage to property.

'Premises' have been given a fairly wide interpretation in this context and include a place where goods are being delivered to, a place being visited to obtain an order and a private house where an employee has been sent to work. However, the emergency must be 'in or about' the relevant premises. If there is, say, a fire in premises adjacent to the employer's property which threatens to spread to that property then an employee giving assistance to put out the fire and being injured as a result may fall within this provision.

What if s 100 does not apply? If the claimant is in the ordinary course of work when the emergency arises and takes action clearly arising from a duty of employment, any personal injury suffered whilst taking that action arises out of and in the course of employment. But if the action taken has nothing to do with any duty the claimant is employed to perform, the action is not in the course of employment (eg a railway worker travelling on a train to work injures himself in an accident caused when helping another passenger to free a stuck window (*Commissioner's Decision C135/50*)). However, a claim may succeed if despite the action being outside the scope of employment it can be said to have been reasonable and sensible to take in the interests of the employer. Moreover, a claimant's action in an emergency need not be essential nor the best course to have taken provided it was reasonable and sensible and not unnecessarily foolhardy in the circumstances.

(E) Misconduct

By s 101:

> An accident ... shall be treated for the purposes of industrial injuries benefit, where it would not apart from this section be so treated, as arising out of an employed earner's employment if—
> (a) the accident arises in the course of employment; and
> (b) the accident is caused—
> (i) by another's misconduct, skylarking or negligence, or
> (ii) by steps taken in consequence of any such misconduct, skylarking or negligence, or
> (iii) by the behaviour or presence of an animal (including a bird, fish or insect),
> or is caused by or consists in the employed earner being struck by any object or by lightning; and
> (c) the employed earner did not directly or indirectly induce or contribute to the happening of the accident by his conduct outside the employment or by any act not incidental to the employment.

The DfWP *Decision Maker's Guide* says:

> This provision would not apply to a person who while at work teases and angers an animal and is attacked by it, unless that is what they are employed to do.

Fortunately, it also says that:

> the decision maker should interpret [the provision] in a broad common-sense way aiming to apply it in employees' favour to accidents at work for which they are the innocent victim of circumstances.

4.10.5 'Employed earner's employment'

An employed earner is 'a person who is gainfully employed in Great Britain either under a contract of service, or in an office (including an elective office) with emoluments chargeable to income tax under Schedule E' (s 2(1)).

In effect, an employed earner is someone who pays Class 1 NICs, or would pay them if his earnings were high enough (see **2.2.3.1**). The Social Security (Employed Earners' Employments for Industrial Injuries Purposes) Regulations 1975 (SI 1975/467) deem a limited number of people to be employed earners (eg apprentices, special constables and taxi drivers). However, they also exclude, for example, an employed earner who is employed by his or her spouse where the employment is either not for the purposes of the spouse's employment or the earnings are normally below the LEL. So a wife employed by her husband to manage his shop would be included.

The largest group of people excluded from the scheme is the self-employed.

4.10.6 'Accident'

An accident has most often been defined as a mishap or untoward event which has neither been planned nor wanted by the employed earner but happens by chance. It covers the obvious, like accidents with machinery, falling off a ladder, being burnt by a blow lamp, etc, but it also includes incidents where the only untoward event is the occurrence of the injury itself, such as heart conditions, hernia, prolapsed intervertebral discs and nervous shock.

Given this definition, a person sustains an accident even if his own negligence or foolhardiness causes it. Equally, an accidental injury may be caused by the deliberate performance of a dangerous act or exposure to a known risk or the deliberate act of another person by, say, a practical joke or assault. However, in these circumstances, as noted above, careful consideration must be given as to whether the accident arose out of and in the course of the claimant's employment.

An injury that arises from a continuous process going on substantially day to day (but not necessarily minute to minute or from hour to hour) where that process produces incapacity gradually over a period of years is not a personal injury caused by an industrial accident. A man who is deafened because he is too near an explosion suffers an accident. But a man who becomes deaf after working for many years in a noisy environment does not suffer personal injury by accident, although he may have a prescribed industrial disease (see **4.10.9**).

The DfWP *Decision Maker's Guide* provides that in deciding whether an injury is due to accident or process it is for the claimant to show that the condition was the result of an accident. It is not enough to show the condition was caused by work. The longer the period over which the events occur (particularly if they are in themselves trivial) the less likely it is that the resultant condition was accidentally caused. Whilst minor, untoward events over a space of hours or several days might be caused by accident, those happening over a period of weeks or months are more likely to be evidence of process.

4.10.7 Accident in Great Britain or EEA

As a general rule, the accident must occur in Great Britain or an EEA country. See further **Chapter 10**.

4.10.8 'Loss of faculty and resulting disablement'

As well as showing that he sustained a personal injury due to an accident arising out of and in the course of his employment, the claimant must also establish that as a consequence he suffered a loss of faculty leading to him being disabled. A loss of faculty was defined in *Jones (Receiver) (on behalf of Wilde) v The Insurance Officer* [1972] AC 944 as damage or impairment of part of the body or mind. So, a person who loses an eye in an industrial accident suffers the loss of sight in that eye. A disability must arise as a result of the loss of faculty. In the example just given this would be partial blindness. By Sch 6, the degree of disablement is assessed by a medical examiner who compares the physical and mental condition of the claimant against that of a person of the same age and sex whose physical and mental condition is normal. No other particular circumstances of the claimant are relevant. See further **4.10.10**.

4.10.9 Prescribed industrial diseases (ss 108 and 109)

A person who is exposed to hazards in the course of his work may contract a disease as a result. This may be the result of a long-term process which would not count as an accident, or sometimes as a result of one unidentifiable occasion. He can claim IDB if the disease is a 'prescribed industrial disease'. There is a list of 66 prescribed diseases set out in Sch 1 to the Social Security (Industrial Injuries)

(Prescribed Diseases) Regulations 1985 (PD Regs 1985), together with the occupations for which they are recognised hazards. The list is constantly updated.

The prescribed diseases are in four categories, labelled A to D:

Category

	A	Conditions due to physical agents (heat, pressure, radiation, noise, vibration): for example heat cataract, writer's cramp, some cancers, deafness, carpal tunnel syndrome.
	B	Conditions due to biological agents (infections): for example leptospirosis, tuberculosis, hepatitis.
	C	Conditions due to chemical agents (including solvents and heavy metals): for example lead poisoning, and assorted skin diseases and cancers.
	D	Miscellaneous conditions. This includes the miners' disease pneumoconiosis, caused by inhaling dust; cancers caused by asbestos, and asthmas caused by allergies.

In each case, the claimant must show that he has the condition and that it arose from a prescribed employment. He may be helped by reg 4 of the PD Regs 1985, which provides a list of circumstances in which causation will be presumed until disproved.

4.10.10 Degree of disability (s 103(1))

All IDB claims are decided on medical grounds, and part of the decision relates to the degree of disability. As seen, the degree of disability is assessed by loss of physical or mental faculty. The result is expressed as a percentage. Certain degrees of disability are prescribed in Sch 2 to the Social Security (General Benefit) Regulations 1982 (SS(GB) Regs 1982); these relate only to physical loss of part of the body. See **Appendix 3** to this part of the book.

If a claimant is unfortunate enough to suffer more than one industrial accident, the percentages of disablement can be added together. If a later relevant accident aggravates an earlier industrial injury, a percentage increase will also be awarded for the effect of the interaction.

What if a disability has more than one cause? The rules for assessment are quite complex. As a general rule, if a disability is congenital or otherwise arose before that sustained in the industrial accident, it is deducted from the total disability. For example, a claimant is born with no little finger on his right hand (for IDB purposes that would be assessed at 7% disablement). At work the claimant's right hand becomes trapped in machinery and has to be amputated. The loss of a hand for IDB purposes is assessed at 60% (although it may in fact be a little more or less than that depending on whether or not the claimant is right-handed) but the claimant's pre-existing non-industrial injury must be taken into account. The assessment will be at 53%, ie 60% less 7% and so paid at 50% (see **4.10.11**).

If a person is described as '100% disabled', he is not necessarily completely helpless. It includes loss of sight sufficient to make the claimant incapable of a job for which eyesight is essential, and loss of a hand and a foot. The lowest level at which benefit is payable for an injury is 14%, which is the amount of disability suffered by the loss of a forefinger or the whole of a big toe. For the prescribed diseases of pneumoconiosis, byssinosis and diffuse mesothelioma, for example, even 1% disability can give rise to a payment of benefit.

4.10.11 Rate of benefit (s 103(3))

Benefit is payable on a sliding scale related directly to the degree of disability. If the claimant is 100% disabled, he receives 100% benefit. Lower degrees of disability are rounded to the nearest 10% (5 or more being rounded up and 4 or less being rounded down), and benefit paid at the resulting rate. The exception to this is that an assessment of 14–19% is always rounded up to 20%.

4.10.12 Waiting period (s 103(6))

There is a waiting period before IDB is payable. Ninety days (excluding Sundays – so, in effect, 15 weeks) must have passed since the date of the accident or the onset of the prescribed disease (save in the case of mesothelioma).

4.10.13 IDB and other benefits

Industrial disablement benefit is not treated as income when calculating child tax credit or working tax credit (see **9.6**).

It is treated as income when calculating income support, income-based JSA, housing benefit and council tax benefit (see **7.3**).

Industrial disablement benefit does not affect the payment of any other non means-tested benefit, except that constant attendance allowance (see **4.11**) overlaps with DLA care component (see **2.6** and **4.6.2**).

4.11 Constant attendance allowance (CAA)

A person who is receiving IDB at *100%* and requires constant attendance as a result of the relevant loss of faculty, may also receive an additional amount of benefit by way of 'constant attendance allowance'. Note that this benefit overlaps with DLA care component (see **4.7**), and some claimants may be better off claiming one rather than the other because of the range of different rates and different tests applied.

The rate of pay of constant attendance allowance depends on the amount of attendance given. The tests set out in the SS(GB) Regs 1982, reg 19 are rather ambiguous. The *exceptional* (highest) rate is payable if the claimant is 'so exceptionally severely disabled as to be entirely, or almost entirely, dependent on such attendance for the necessities of life, and is likely to remain so dependent for a prolonged period and the attendance so required is whole-time'. The *normal* rate is payable if the claimant is 'to a substantial extent dependent on such attendance for the necessities of life and is likely to remain so dependent for a prolonged period'. The *intermediate* rate is payable if 'the extent of such attendance is greater by reason of the [claimant's] exceptionally severe disablement'. The *part-time* (lowest) rate is payable if the claimant is 'to a substantial extent dependent on such attendance for the necessities of life and is likely to remain so dependent for a prolonged period' but 'the attendance so required is part-time only'.

Constant attendance allowance is ignored when calculating any tax credit or other means-tested benefit.

4.12 New Deal for disabled people

The New Deal for disabled people provides one-to-one advice and assistance to help people with disabilities to find work. It is not compulsory and there are no penalties for failing to attend or take part.

4.13 Claimant profiles

4.13.1 Statutory sick pay

This is payable to an employee who is incapable of carrying out the work for which he is employed (the 'own occupation test'). It is payable for a maximum of 28 weeks. If the claimant is still incapable of work he may qualify for the earnings replacement benefit of incapacity benefit (for which he will be subject to a personal capability assessment, unless exempt).

4.13.2 Incapacity benefit

This is an earnings replacement benefit for any worker incapable of work (for which he will be subject to the own occupation test and/or a personal capability assessment, unless exempt) and who has the appropriate history of Class 1 or 2 national insurance payments.

4.13.3 Non-contributory incapacity benefit

This is incapacity benefit for young people who become incapable of work before reaching the age of 20 (or in limited circumstances, 25 years of age).

4.13.4 DLA care component

This is payable to a claimant under 65 who needs help with his bodily functions or supervision to avoid being a danger. The minimum period of need is normally nine months.

4.13.5 DLA mobility component

This is payable to a claimant under 65 whose severe physical or mental disability affects his ability to walk. The minimum period of need is normally nine months.

4.13.6 Attendance allowance

This is payable to a claimant aged 65 or over who needs a substantial amount of help with his bodily functions or supervision to avoid being a danger. The minimum period of need is normally 12 months.

4.13.7 Industrial disablement benefit

This is payable to an employee who has an accident at work that arises out of and in the course of his employment, which results in a loss of faculty and usually at least 14% disablement.

4.13.8 Constant attendance allowance

This is payable to a recipient of IDB at the rate of 100% and who requires care. It is an alternative to the DLA care component.

Chapter 5

Retirement and Bereavement

5.1	Introduction	75
5.2	Retirement benefits	75
5.3	State pension credit	78
5.4	Bereavement benefits	81
5.5	Claimant profiles	83

5.1 Introduction

This chapter is concerned with two groups of benefits: those for people who have reached retirement age, and those for people who have been bereaved by the death of a spouse or civil partner at any age.

These benefits are relatively straightforward in their application. The most complex aspects of State Pension and bereavement benefits are those which are described in **Chapter 2**:

(a) the contribution conditions (see **2.3.6**); and
(b) the availability of an increase (see **2.4**).

It may be helpful to refer to these sections, especially the first, before continuing with this chapter.

In addition, this chapter also deals with the State pension credit.

5.2 Retirement benefits

5.2.1 State Pension (SSCBA 1992, s 44)

The slang name 'old age pension', is actually more accurate than the correct 'State or retirement pension'. What matters is the claimant's age. He does not need to stop work to claim.

There are three conditions for receipt of the benefit. The claimant must:

(a) have reached retirement age;
(b) not have given notice to defer retirement; and
(c) have the appropriate contribution record (see **2.3.6**).

5.2.1.1 Retirement age

At present, 'retirement age' means 65 for a man, and 60 for a woman. The Pensions Act 1995 provides for the ages for both sexes to be equalised at 65 by 2020. The change is due to be phased in incrementally with effect from 6 April 2010, and will not affect any woman who reaches the age of 60 before that date. This is because the Act provides that a woman who was born before 6 April 1950 will reach pensionable age on her sixtieth birthday. A woman born after 5 April 1955 will reach pensionable age on her sixty-fifth birthday. Women born between 6 April 1950 and 5 April 1955 will reach pensionable age between 60 and 65 depending on their birthdates. For example, a woman who was born between 6 December 1950 and 5 January 1951 will reach pensionable age on 6 September

2011 at age 61. A woman born between 6 July 1953 and 5 August 1953 will reach pensionable age on 6 November 2016 when she is 63.

5.2.1.2 Deferring retirement

Under SSCBA 1992, s 55, a claimant may elect to defer his claim for State Pension for up to five years from normal retirement age. He will not be liable to pay any NICs in the meantime but, when he does claim, will receive a higher rate of pension than he would have had if he had claimed at the normal time.

A person who has reached retirement age must claim his pension; it is not paid automatically. As he approaches retirement age, he should receive notification from HMRC of his contribution record and information about the likely rate. He should not assume that he need do nothing more.

5.2.2 Couples and State Pension

Where one or both members of a couple are of pensionable age, there are several different ways in which their combined pension rights could work. The factors going into the equation include:

(a) the increases rules (see **2.4**);
(b) the contribution records of both partners;
(c) their ages; and
(d) whether they are married or in a civil partnership.

A pensioner may receive an adult dependant's increase, under the normal rules, for a partner who is a dependant (whether married or not). If they are both of retirement age, they may each receive a pension on their own contributions (a Category A pension).

There is a special rule for married couples or those in a civil partnership, where both are over retirement age and one has a seriously defective contribution record. This is very common among older married couples, where the wife has not worked since marriage but is too old to have benefited from home responsibilities protection (see **2.2.5.4**). A married person in this situation can claim a pension in her own right, on her husband's contributions (a category B pension: men can claim it too, but this is very rare).

This pension is paid at exactly the same rate as the adult dependant's increase. Since women very often reach 60 before their husbands are 65, this can result in a special application of the overlapping benefit rules, which is illustrated below.

> **Example**
> Eileen and her husband Patrick are both 60. Eileen has a short contribution record since she worked for only nine years after she left school. Since her marriage in 1965, she has not worked, and she has home responsibilities protection for the period from 1978 to 1986, when her last child left school.
>
> Applying the rules for pension entitlement with home responsibilities protection (see **2.3.6.3**), she would need 31 years' contributions for a full category A pension, and she only has 9. She will therefore immediately receive a pension of 9/31 (roughly 30%) of the full State Pension. But when Patrick reaches 65 she could claim a category B pension on his contributions, which would be 60% of the full pension if he has a complete record. This is obviously higher than her own category A pension, so under the overlapping benefit rules she would receive that and forfeit the other.

5.2.3 Additional State Pension scheme

Although the basic State Pension is paid at a flat rate, many pensioners receive much higher payments because they are in the additional State Pension scheme. Any employee who has not joined an occupational pension scheme or taken out a personal pension will be a member of this scheme. This means that he pays his primary Class 1 contributions at a rate slightly higher than those who have contracted out of the scheme (see **2.2.3**). These extra contributions build up an earnings-related element on top of the basic pension.

5.2.4 Other retirement benefits

The State Pension is by no means the only form of pension payable to people who have retired or reached retirement age. Many pensioners receive one of the following, either in addition to or instead of the State Pension.

5.2.4.1 Occupational or personal pension

Employees, particularly at senior level, have long been able to join occupational pension schemes operated by their employers. Self-employed people have also long been able to make personal provision for pensions. Since the 1980s, personal pensions have also been available to employees whose employer had no occupational scheme, or who chose to make their own arrangements.

5.2.4.2 Stakeholder pensions

The new stakeholder pensions were introduced in 2001 by the Welfare Reform and Pensions Act 1999 provide a simple low-cost alternative to occupational pension schemes, particularly suited to people on incomes as low as £6,000 per year.

5.2.4.3 Category D retirement pension

A person who has reached the age of 80 and has no other retirement pension may claim a Category D non-contributory State Pension. This pension can also be paid to a person who has only a very low Category A or B pension, which is below the level of the Category D pension, as an alternative. It is paid at the same rate as the married person's Category B pension (see **5.2.2**).

5.2.5 State Pensions for bereaved persons (SSCBA 1992, s 48BB)

If a person who has been bereaved then reaches retirement age, and is not entitled to a pension on his own contributions, his rights depend on his benefit history.

5.2.5.1 Dependent children

If the claimant was receiving widowed parent's allowance (see **5.4.3**) at the time of reaching retirement age, he will receive a Category B State Pension at the same rate.

5.2.5.2 No dependent children

If the claimant had received widowed parent's allowance in the past, or bereavement allowance (see **5.4.4**), he will receive a Category B State Pension calculated by reference to his spouse's National Insurance record at the date of death. The detailed provisions of the calculation of this pension are beyond the scope of this book.

5.2.5.3 Bereavement after retirement age

If the claimant is bereaved after reaching retirement age, he will receive a full State Pension at the rate his spouse would have received it as a single person.

5.3 State pension credit

5.3.1 Conditions of entitlement

(a) *Age:* to qualify for the pension credit the claimant (man or woman) must have reached 60 years of age. Additionally, the claimant or any partner must be 65 or over in order to qualify for the savings credit element (see **5.3.2.2**).

(b) *Low income:* the credit is a top up for low income pensioners and some reward for making any provision beyond the basic State Pension.

(c) *Immigration requirements:* the claimant must not be subject to immigration control and must satisfy the residence requirements (see **Chapter 10**).

5.3.2 The credit elements

The main element of pension credit is the guarantee credit. It is designed to ensure that pensioners have a minimum standard of living. So the amount of the guarantee credit that is payable is the difference between the weekly needs of the claimant (and any partner) and his (or their joint) income. Factors affecting needs include whether the claimant or any partner suffers from a disability, or has caring responsibilities or incurs eligible housing costs. As to what counts as income see **5.3.4**.

The second potential element of pension credit is the savings credit. This is an additional amount designed to reward those pensioners who have made some provision for their retirement beyond the basic State Pension. It can be paid only if the claimant or any partner is at least 65 years of age. It is subject to a cap and will not be paid if the claimant has too much income.

All the figures below are for 2007/08.

5.3.2.1 Guarantee credit

By s 2 of the State Pension Credit Act 2002, a claimant is entitled to this credit if he has no income, or if his income (see **5.3.3**) does not exceed the appropriate minimum guarantee. The latter is the total of the standard minimum guarantee and such prescribed additional amounts as may be appropriate.

The standard minimum guarantee for a single person is £119.05 per week and for a couple it is £181.70 weekly.

The following additional amounts may be claimed:

(a) Severe disability guarantee: for a single person this is £48.45 per week and for a couple (if both qualify) it is £96.90 weekly. The qualifying conditions for this guarantee are the same as for the severe disability premium for the mainstream means-tested benefits (see **7.7.2**).

(b) Carer guarantee: this is £27.15 per week if the claimant or any partner qualifies, but £54.30 weekly if both qualify. The qualifying conditions for this guarantee are the same as for the carer's premium for the mainstream means-tested benefits (see **7.7.4**).

(c) Eligible housing costs: these are the same as for IS and IBJSA (see **8.3**).

5.3.2.2 The savings credit

By s 3 of the State Pension Credit Act 2002, a claimant is entitled to this credit if his qualifying income (see **5.3.4**) exceeds the savings credit threshold, namely £87.30 per week for a single person and £139.60 weekly for a couple. You will note that the threshold figures are, in fact, the amount of the basic State Pension per person or couple respectively.

The amount of savings credit payable is subject to a cap known as the maximum savings credit. This is 60% of the difference between the standard minimum guarantee (see **5.3.2.1**) and the savings credit threshold. This means that the maximum savings credit is for:

(a) a single person the sum of £19.05 (ie £119.05 – £87.30 = £31.75 × 60%); and
(b) a couple, £25.26 (ie £181.70 – £139.60 = £42.10 × 60%).

The maximum savings credit must be reduced, where appropriate, on a sliding scale of 40% for every £1 of qualifying income above the appropriate guaranteed minimum level. See the third worked example at **5.3.5**.

5.3.3 Income

There is no upper capital limit for the pension credit. As to what constitutes capital, see **7.2**. However, if the claimant has capital above £6,000 he is treated as having a weekly income of £1 for every £500 or part of £500 by which his capital exceeds £6,000. This is known as 'tariff income'. It is similar to that deemed to arise for the four mainstream means-tested benefits (see **7.3.6**).

Income from an occupational or personal pension scheme counts. Child maintenance is ignored. Spousal maintenance counts as income for the guarantee credit only.

The following benefits count as income when calculating pension credit:

(a) contribution-based JSA (see **3.4**);
(b) incapacity benefit (see **4.4**);
(c) maternity allowance (see **6.4**);
(d) carer's allowance (see **6.7**);
(e) bereavement allowance (see **5.4.4**);
(f) State Pensions (see **5.2**);
(g) industrial disablement benefit (see **4.10**);
(h) working tax credit (see **9.6**).

The following benefits are not treated as income but are ignored when calculating pension credit:

(a) child benefit (see **6.6**);
(b) child tax credit (see **9.6**);
(c) disability living allowance and attendance allowance (see **4.7**);
(d) constant attendance allowance (see **4.11**);
(e) widowed parent's allowance (see **5.4.3**).

Note that a bereavement payment is ignored only if the claimant or any partner is aged 60 or over and not claiming IS or IBJSA.

5.3.4 Qualifying income for the savings credit

For the purposes of the savings credit, the position is as described at **5.3.3** above but the following benefits are ignored:

(a) contribution-based JSA;
(b) incapacity benefit;

(c) maternity allowance;
(d) working tax credit.

5.3.5 Worked examples

(1) Gavin and his partner, Annette are both aged 66. Their weekly income consists of £139.60 basic State Pension.

   (a) *Guarantee credit*

   They are entitled to the couple standard minimum guarantee of £181.70. If we deduct their weekly income (£139.60) from this figure, they will receive £42.10 each week.

   (b) *Savings credit*

   As their qualifying income does not exceed the savings threshold (£139.60), none is payable.

(2) Liam is a single man, aged 68. He receives the basic State Pension of £87.30 per week. He has savings of £7,500.

   (a) *Guarantee credit*

   He is entitled to the single standard minimum guarantee of £119.05. If we deduct his weekly income of £90.30 from this figure, he will receive £28.75 each week. Do not forget that his income consists of his State Pension and tariff income on his savings above £6,000 at the rate of £1 for every £500 or part (ie £3 here).

   (b) *Savings credit*

   His total qualifying income is £90.30. As a single man his savings credit threshold is £87.30. So he is entitled to the credit. 60% of the excess (£90.30 – £87.30), namely £3, is £1.80 and so he will receive £1.80 as savings credit in addition to the guarantee credit each week.

(3) Harry and his wife, Irene are both aged 70. Their weekly income consists of £139.60 basic State Pension and £50 personal pension payments.

   (a) *Guarantee credit*

   They are entitled to the couple standard minimum guarantee of £181.70. However, their weekly income (£189.60) exceeds this figure and so none is payable.

   (b) *Savings credit*

   Their total qualifying income of £189.60 exceeds the savings credit threshold of £139.60 and also the standard minimum guarantee of £181.70.

   So they can only receive 60% of the excess between the savings credit threshold of £139.60 and the standard minimum guarantee of £181.70 and this must be reduced by 40% for every £1 of qualifying income above the standard minimum guarantee of £181.70.

   First let us remind ourselves that the maximum savings credit is 60% of the difference between the standard minimum guarantee and the savings credit threshold. This means that the maximum savings credit for Harry and Irene is, as a couple, £25.26 ie (£181.70 – £139.60 = £42.10 × 60%).

   But as their qualifying income exceeds the standard minimum guarantee by £7.90 (£189.60 – £181.70) the maximum savings credit must be reduced by 40% of that excess.

   £7.90 × 40% = £3.16.

   Therefore, Harry and Irene are paid a savings credit of £22.10 per week (£25.26 – £3.16).

5.3.6 Payments of pension credit

The scheme is administered by the DfWP. The benefit is payable weekly. It can be paid by order book, giro or direct credit transfer to a bank, building society or post office account.

5.4 Bereavement benefits

5.4.1 What are bereavement benefits?

Bereavement benefits, which are governed by ss 36–39 of the SSCBA 1992, are those benefits which are paid to a widow or a widower as a result of the death of their spouse or civil partner. In order to claim bereavement benefits, the claimant must have been lawfully married or in a valid civil partnership, at the date of death, to the person who has died.

5.4.2 The benefits: some common factors

The two primary benefits within this group are:

(a) widowed parent's allowance; and
(b) bereavement allowance.

These are National Insurance contributory benefits, but the relevant contribution record is that of the deceased spouse or civil partner, not the claimant. See **2.3.6.4** for the contribution conditions.

Both benefits cease if the claimant remarries, and are suspended during any period in which the claimant cohabits (for the law on cohabitation, see **7.4.2**).

5.4.3 Widowed parent's allowance (SSCBA 1992, s 39A)

To qualify for widowed parent's allowance, the claimant must:

(a) be under retirement age at the date of the spouse's or civil partner's death; and
(b) be caring for a child or qualifying young person for whom either the claimant or the deceased spouse or civil partner was receiving child benefit immediately before their death; or
(c) be pregnant with her husband's child.

The allowance may be paid until child benefit for a qualifying child or young person comes to an end. See further **6.6**. Payment stops when the claimant reaches pension age.

The flat weekly rate of pay is reduced if the deceased spouse or civil partner did not pay sufficient NICs (see **2.3.6.4**).

5.4.4 Bereavement allowance (SSCBA 1992, s 39B)

To qualify for a bereavement allowance, the claimant must:

(a) be under retirement age and over 45 at the date of the death of the spouse or civil partner or when any entitlement to widowed parent's allowance ends; and
(b) not be entitled to widowed parent's allowance.

The flat weekly rate of pay is reduced by 7% for every year or part of a year by which the claimant was under 55 at the time of the claim. It will be further reduced if the deceased spouse or civil partner did not pay sufficient NICs (see **2.3.6.4**).

This allowance is payable for 52 weeks.

5.4.5 Bereavement payment (SSCBA 1992, s 36)

A bereaved person will qualify for a tax-free lump sum bereavement payment of £2,000 if:

(a) the claimant is under retirement age when their spouse or civil partner dies or that person was not on death entitled to a Category A State Pension; and

(b) the deceased spouse or civil partner satisfies the NICs requirements (see **2.3.6.4**).

There is no requirement that the couple had to be cohabiting at the time of the death of the spouse or civil partner. However, if they had separated, no payment can be made if the claimant was cohabiting at the time of their partner's death (see **7.10**).

The claim must be made within 12 months of the death of the spouse or civil partner.

5.4.6 Summary of key points

Client's age and status when spouse or civil partner dies	Benefit(s)
Under 45 with no child/ren or qualifying young person(s)	Bereavement payment only
45 or over, under retirement age, with no child/ren or qualifying young person(s)	Bereavement payment and bereavement allowance
Under retirement age, expecting late husband's child	Bereavement payment and widowed parent's allowance
Under retirement age, with child/ren or qualifying young person(s)	Bereavement payment and widowed parent's allowance

5.4.7 Bereavement benefits and other benefits

Widowed parent's allowance and bereavement allowance are treated as income when calculating entitlement to the child tax credit and working tax credit. A bereavement payment is not treated as income (see **9.6**).

A bereavement payment counts as capital when considering eligibility for and the amount of any tariff income in respect of income support, income-based JSA, housing benefit and council tax benefit (see **7.3**).

Only some of widowed parent's allowance is treated as income when calculating the means-tested benefits. The first £10 is ignored for the purposes of income support and income-based JSA; £15 is ignored when calculating housing benefit and council tax benefit.

Widowed parent's allowance is not treated as income when calculating the pension credit (see **5.3**).

Bereavement allowance is treated as income when calculating income support, income-based JSA, housing benefit, council tax benefit and the pension credit.

Widowed parent's allowance and bereavement allowance are earnings replacement benefits (see **1.2.5**).

5.5 Claimant profiles

5.5.1 State Pension

This earnings replacement benefit is payable to a claimant who has reached retirement age and has the appropriate National Insurance record.

5.5.2 State pension credit

This is payable to a claimant who has reached 60 years of age and who has a low income. Any capital is irrelevant save for any tariff income that it generates.

5.5.3 Widowed parent's allowance

This is an earnings replacement benefit that is payable to a widow or widower who is under retirement age when their spouse or civil partner dies and who is caring for a child or qualifying young person for whom child benefit is paid (or the claimant is a woman who is pregnant with her husband's child).

5.5.4 Bereavement allowance

This is an earnings replacement benefit that is payable to a widow or widower who is over 45 but under retirement age when their spouse or civil partner dies or their entitlement to widowed parent's allowance ends and who is not entitled to widowed parent's allowance.

5.5.5 Bereavement payment

This is an one-off capital payment to a widow or widower or civil partner who is under retirement age when their spouse or civil partner dies and whose spouse or civil partner has the appropriate Class 1, 2 or 3 National Insurance payment history.

Chapter 6
Maternity, Children and Carers

6.1	Contents of this chapter	85
6.2	Maternity benefits: an overview	85
6.3	Statutory maternity pay	86
6.4	Maternity allowance (SSCBA 1992, s 35)	88
6.5	Other benefits for pregnant and recently delivered women	89
6.6	Child benefit (SSCBA 1992, s 143)	89
6.7	Carer's allowance (SSCBA 1992, s 70)	91
6.8	Claimant profiles	93

6.1 Contents of this chapter

This chapter deals with benefits for three groups of claimants who are not covered by the benefits described in earlier chapters: women who give up work to have a baby, people with young children, and carers. The benefits are:

(a) statutory maternity pay (see **6.3**), for most long-term employees who have stopped work to have a baby;

(b) maternity allowance (see **6.4**) for other women with the appropriate work history who have stopped work to have a baby;

(c) Sure Start maternity grant (see **6.5**) for pregnant women on low incomes;

(d) child benefit (see **6.6**) for people looking after a child or a young person aged under 20 in full-time, non-advanced education or Government approved training;

(e) carer's allowance (see **6.7**) for people acting as full-time voluntary carers for people with disabilities.

6.2 Maternity benefits: an overview

6.2.1 What are the maternity benefits?

The maternity benefits are statutory maternity pay (SMP) (see **6.3**) and maternity allowance (MA) (see **6.4**). Maternity allowance can be paid only to a woman who does not qualify for SMP. Most employees will qualify for SMP.

6.2.2 Terminology

The jargon common to maternity benefits is set out below:

(a) 'A week' is a period of seven days, beginning on a Sunday.

(b) 'The expected week of childbirth' is the week in which the pregnant woman's medical advisers have told her that her baby is likely to be born. Neither benefit can be paid more than 11 weeks before the expected week of childbirth. If the baby arrives earlier or later than the expected week of childbirth, this has no effect on the right to benefits. The benefits are payable even if the baby is born dead, provided that the pregnancy has lasted at least 24 weeks.

(c) 'The qualifying week' is the fifteenth week before the beginning of the expected week of childbirth.

(d) 'The maternity allowance threshold' is the minimum average weekly earnings limit which is needed to qualify for maternity allowance. It was £30 a week in 2007/08.

6.2.3 Calculating key dates for SMP and MA

Assume that the claimant's baby is due on Friday, 6 June 2008. The relevant dates are:

(a) her expected week of childbirth starts on the previous Sunday, namely 1 June;

(b) the earliest she can claim is the eleventh week before the expected week of childbirth (ie 16 March 2008);

(c) her qualifying week is the fifteenth week before the expected week of childbirth. It therefore starts on Sunday, 17 February 2008 and ends on Saturday, 23 February 2008.

6.3 Statutory maternity pay

There is no general right for an employee to be paid while she is absent on maternity leave unless there is an express provision to the contrary in her contract. However, many employees have the right to SMP, which is quite independent of their rights in employment law to maternity leave itself, and to return to work after the birth of the baby. The right cannot be excluded by contract, or the rate of payment reduced.

6.3.1 Qualifying conditions (SSCBA 1992, s 164)

To qualify for SMP, the claimant must:

(a) be an employee; and

(b) be employed for at least one day in the qualifying week and have been employed by the same employer for a continuous period of at least 26 weeks ending with employment in at least part of the qualifying week;

(c) earn gross not less than the LEL during a normal working week over the period of eight weeks prior to the qualifying week; and

(d) be pregnant and reached, or had the baby prior to, the start of the eleventh week before the expected week of childbirth; and

(e) given notice (in writing if so requested) to her employer of her intended absence at least 21 days prior to the start of the absence or as soon as is reasonably practicable; and

(f) have stopped work.

6.3.2 The continuous employment rule

The woman must have worked for a continuous period of 26 weeks for the same employer, including at least one day in the qualifying week. Temporary absences from work, such as periods of illness or holiday, count towards the 26 weeks. A strike does not break continuity of employment but it does not count towards the 26 weeks unless the woman can show that at no time did she have a direct interest in the trade dispute (Statutory Maternity Pay Regulations 1986 (SMP Regs 1986) (SI 1986/1960), reg 13).

6.3.3 The earnings condition

Although a claim for SMP does not depend on the woman's National Insurance contribution record, she must have earned a gross weekly average wage of no less than the LEL during the eight-week period before the qualifying week. If the baby is born before the qualifying week, the woman's earnings are averaged over the last eight weeks before the week of birth. What counts as earnings? Any bonuses, overtime and SSP are included but tips and money paid through a profit sharing scheme are excluded.

6.3.4 The maternity pay period

The woman may choose the date upon which to give up work and claim SMP during the maternity pay period as long as it is after the eleventh week before the expected week of childbirth and no later than the week after birth. Once begun, it can continue for up to a maximum of 39 consecutive weeks. The period cannot be extended to take account of a late birth.

6.3.5 The amount of benefit

Although SMP may currently be paid for up to a maximum of 39 consecutive weeks, it is paid at two different rates. For the first six weeks of the claim it is paid at the rate of 90% of the woman's average weekly earnings as calculated in 6.3.3. For the remaining 33 weeks it is paid either at the rate of £112.75 per week (in 2007/08) or it continues at the earnings-related rate if that rate of pay is less than £112.75 per week.

What if the claimant is awarded a pay rise during her maternity leave? By the Statutory Maternity Pay (General) (Amendment) Regulations 2005 (SI 2005/729) the amount of SMP must be recalculated.

6.3.6 Summary of key dates

The diagram below shows the key dates for SMP purposes. The starting point is, of course, the week the baby is due and then looking backwards at earlier weeks to see if the conditions of entitlement have been met. The following abbreviations are used.

(a) EWC: expected week of childbirth;
(b) QW: qualifying week;
(c) SCP: the start of the required 26-week period of continuous employment before, and including at least one day in, the QW.

Week 40 before EWC	Weeks 16 to 39 before EWC	Week 15 before EWC	Weeks 1 to 14 before EWC	Week baby due
SCP		QW		EWC

6.3.7 SMP and other benefits

The first £100 of SMP is ignored when calculating child tax credit or working tax credit and any SMP over £100 is treated as employment income (see 9.6).

Statutory maternity pay is treated as income when calculating income support or income-based JSA. It is treated as earnings when calculating housing benefit or council tax benefit and so any appropriate earnings disregard can be made (see 7.3).

Statutory maternity pay is taken into account when calculating entitlement to the pension credit (see **5.3**).

It is incompatible with, and so cannot be claimed at the same time as, incapacity benefit, maternity allowance, statutory sick pay or contribution-based JSA (see **2.5**).

6.4 Maternity allowance (SSCBA 1992, s 35)

Maternity allowance is an alternative to SMP. It is available to a woman who does not qualify for SMP, perhaps because she has been self-employed or has changed her job during the pregnancy, or given up work just before or during her pregnancy.

6.4.1 Conditions of entitlement for maternity allowance

Maternity allowance is payable if the woman:

(a) has become pregnant and has reached, or given birth before reaching, the start of the eleventh week before the expected week of childbirth; and

(b) she has been engaged in employment as an employed or self-employed earner for any part of a week in respect of at least 26 of the 66 weeks immediately preceding the expected week of childbirth; and

(c) her average weekly earnings are not less than the maternity allowance threshold; and

(d) she is not entitled to statutory maternity pay for the same week in respect of the same pregnancy.

6.4.2 The employment and earnings conditions

The period of employment or self-employment for at least 26 of the 66 weeks immediately preceding the expected week of childbirth need not be continuous.

Maternity allowance is payable provided the woman earned at least the MA threshold (see **6.4.3**), or paid Class 2 NICs for any of the 13 weeks in the 66 weeks immediately preceding the expected week of childbirth.

6.4.3 The maternity allowance threshold

This is the figure set by the Government as the minimum average weekly earnings which must have been received in order to be eligible for MA. For the year 2007/08, it was £30.

6.4.4 Amount of benefit

The weekly rate is the lesser of the fixed standard rate (it was £112.75 in 2007/08) or 90% of the woman's average weekly earnings.

Maternity allowance is payable for a maximum of 39 weeks.

6.4.5 Maternity allowance period

A woman may claim MA at any time between the eleventh week prior to the expected week of childbirth and the week following birth.

6.4.6 MA and other benefits

Maternity allowance is ignored when calculating child tax credit or working tax credit (see **9.6**).

It is treated as income when calculating income support, income-based JSA, housing benefit or council tax benefit (see **7.3**).

It is taken into account when calculating entitlement to the pension credit but ignored when calculating the claimant's qualifying income for the savings credit element (see **5.3**).

It is an earnings replacement benefit (see **1.2.5**) and so may affect the entitlement of a spouse to any adult dependant increase in an appropriate benefit (see **2.4**). It is incompatible with, and so cannot be claimed at the same time as, statutory sick pay or statutory maternity pay or contribution-based JSA (see **2.5**).

6.5 Other benefits for pregnant and recently delivered women

Many women will not be eligible for either SMP or MA because they are not currently employed or do not satisfy the earning conditions. A woman is deemed to be incapable of work for the last four weeks of her pregnancy and for 14 days after the birth of her baby (reg 14 of the IW Regs 1995). This means that she could claim incapacity benefit (see **4.4**) for those weeks provided she satisfies the contribution conditions (see **2.3.3.2**); otherwise she could apply for income support (see **Chapter 7**) on the basis of incapacity for work.

Pregnant women from low-income families may also qualify for a £500 maternity grant under the Sure Start scheme. The claimant or claimant's partner must be receiving either income support or income based jobseeker's allowance (see **Chapter 7**); or working tax credit where a disability or severe disability element is included or child tax credit at a higher rate than the family element (see **Chapter 9**). Payment can be claimed at any time from eleven weeks before the expected week of childbirth until three months after the birth occurs. Note that although called a grant this is a non-repayable lump sum paid out of the social fund (see **9.16**).

6.6 Child benefit (SSCBA 1992, s 143)

6.6.1 What is child benefit?

Child benefit can be paid to any person who has a child or young person in his or her care (note that the great majority of the claimants are women and traditionally payment is made to a child's mother). For full details see the Child Benefit Act 2005 and the Child Benefit (General) Regulations 2006 (SI 2006/223).

Benefit is payable for each 'qualifying child or young person' the claimant is 'responsible for' during a week.

The claimant must not be subject to immigration controls and must meet the residence requirements (see **Chapter 10**).

6.6.2 A qualifying child

A person is treated as a qualifying child for any week in which he is under the age of 16.

6.6.3 Qualifying young person

A qualifying young person is:

(a) a person aged 16 years, from the date on which he attains that age until and including the 31 August which next follows that date; and

(b) a person aged 16 years and over who is undertaking a course of full-time education at a school or college which is not advanced education; or

(c) a person aged 16 years and over who is undertaking approved training that is not provided through a contract of employment.

For the purposes of (b) and (c) above, the person must have commenced the course of full-time education or approved training before reaching the age of 19 and must not have attained the age of 20 years.

What is full-time education? This is a course of at least 12 hours per week during term time that is spent receiving tuition, engaged in practical work or supervised study, or taking examinations.

What is advanced education? This is a course in preparation for a degree, a diploma of higher education, a higher national diploma, or a teaching qualification; or any other course which is of a standard above an ordinary national diploma, a national diploma, a national certificate of Edexcel or a general certificate of education (advanced level).

What is approved training? In England the Government schemes covered are 'Entry to Employment' and 'Programme Led Pathways into Apprenticeships'; whilst in Wales they are 'Skillbuild', 'Skillbuild+' and 'Foundation Modern Apprenticeships'.

6.6.4 Responsibility for a qualifying child or young person

A person is responsible for a child or young person who is part of his benefits household in the week of the claim, or if he contributes to the weekly cost of supporting the child or young person at a rate not less than that payable for child benefit.

6.6.5 Competing claims (SSCBA 1992, Sch 10)

Only one person may receive child benefit for any one child. If the parents of the child are living in the same household, the benefit will usually be paid to the mother. If a child spends equal time in two households because his parents are living apart, they must decide who will have the benefit. There is no provision in social security law to split child benefit in these circumstances. What if there is more than one child and their care is shared between the separated parents? See *R (Graham Ford) v Board of Inland Revenue* [2005] EWHC 1109 (Admin).

6.6.6 Administration and payment

There are two possible levels of payment of child benefit.

(a) For the only or eldest qualifying child or young person a higher rate is paid. If the eldest qualifying child or young person is one of twins, the higher rate is paid for the elder twin. If a new family unit is formed by a couple, both of whom already have qualifying children or young persons from previous relationships, then it will become payable for the qualifying child or young person who is the eldest overall.

(b) For all subsequent qualifying children or young persons a standard rate applies.

6.6.7 Child benefit and other benefits

Child benefit is ignored when calculating entitlement to the child tax credit and working tax credit (see **9.6**).

Child benefit is ignored when calculating entitlement to income support and income-based JSA (see **7.3**).

Child benefit is treated as income when calculating entitlement to housing benefit and council tax benefit (see **7.3**).

Child benefit is not payable if the child in question receives non-contributory incapacity benefit (see **4.5**).

6.7 Carer's allowance (SSCBA 1992, s 70)

6.7.1 What is carer's allowance?

Carer's allowance (CA) is not a benefit for people suffering from incapacity or disability. It is paid to people who are not professional carers, but are spending a significant amount of their time without payment attending to the needs of a person who is seriously disabled. Although CA is classified as a non means-tested benefit, the claimant's earnings can disqualify him from receiving it (see **6.7.6**). Carer's allowance carries an adult dependant increase (see **2.4**). It is an earnings replacement benefit (see **1.2.5**).

To qualify for CA, the claimant must:

(a)   be 16 years of age or over; and
(b)   be regularly and substantially engaged in caring for a severely disabled person; and
(c)   not be in full-time education;
(d)   not be gainfully employed; and
(e)   not be subject to immigration controls and must meet the residence requirements (see **Chapter 10**).

6.7.2 Age requirement

The minimum age to qualify is 16. There is no maximum age.

6.7.3 Regularly and substantially engaged in caring

To satisfy this condition, the claimant must spend at least 35 hours per week in caring for the disabled person. A 'caring week' is a period of seven days beginning with a Sunday. However, the care may be given over a shorter period, for example, seven hours per day during a five-day period, or 17.5 hours per day over a weekend. The carer, however, must be engaged for 35 hours in *every* week for which the claim is made so that any average amount of hours over a number of weeks will not satisfy the condition.

There is no legal definition of 'caring'. DfWP guidance is that it is reasonable to expect that the carer and severely disabled person are together for most of the time. However, this is not limited to the time that constitutes attention to bodily functions (see **4.7.2**) for the purposes of DLA or AA. There may be occasions when the carer spends some time apart from the severely disabled person, for example preparing for and clearing up after their stay. Any reasonable time spent in these ways can be counted as a period of caring for CA purposes.

If two people care regularly and substantially for the same severely disabled person, only one of them will be entitled to receive CA.

Most claimants are close relatives of the person they are caring for, and live in the same accommodation. There is, however, no reason why a friend or neighbour should not claim this benefit.

6.7.4 Severely disabled person

This is a person who is receiving either attendance allowance (see **4.9**) or the care component of disability living allowance (see **4.7**) at the highest or middle rates or constant attendance allowance in respect of industrial disablement benefit (see **4.11**).

6.7.5 Full-time education

A person is treated as receiving full-time education for any period during which he attends a course of education at a university, college, school or other educational establishment for 21 hours or more a week.

In calculating the hours of attendance, there is included the time spent receiving instruction or tuition, undertaking supervised study, examination or practical work or taking part in any exercise, experiment or project for which provision is made in the curriculum of the course: see *Flemming v Social Security Commissioners* [2002] EWCA Civ 641.

6.7.6 Gainfully employed

If the carer earns net more than the LEL (see **2.2.2.1**) per week, he is gainfully employed and will not be entitled to CA. Voluntary work or an occupational pension will not make the claimant fall foul of the earnings rule.

6.7.7 Administration and payment

Carer's allowance is paid at a flat rate, subject to the availability of an adult dependant increase (see **2.4**).

An award of CA can be made for a fixed period or indefinitely. It will usually last for the same duration as the severely disabled person's benefit (see **6.7.4**).

6.7.8 CA and other benefits

A person entitled to CA may also be entitled to income support, housing benefit and council tax benefit with a carer's premium (see **7.7.4**). However, note that if the disabled person is also entitled to income support, housing benefit or council tax benefit, then he will not be able to claim the severe disability premium if his carer receives CA. Therefore, a check should be made to see whether it is more advantageous for the carer to forgo any entitlement to CA where the disabled person is entitled to the severe disability premium.

Carer's allowance is treated as income when calculating child tax credit and working tax credit (see **9.6**), income support, income-based JSA, housing benefit and council tax benefit (see **7.3**).

It is taken into account when calculating entitlement to the pension credit and when calculating the claimant's qualifying income for the savings credit element (see **5.3**).

It is an earnings replacement benefit (see **1.2.5**) and so may affect the entitlement of a spouse to any adult dependant increase in an appropriate benefit (see **2.4**).

6.8 Claimant profiles

6.8.1 Statutory maternity pay

Paid by employers to an employee who has been with that employer throughout her pregnancy.

6.8.2 Maternity allowance

This is an earnings replacement benefit that is paid by the DfWP to a short-term employee or self-employed woman.

6.8.3 Child benefit

Paid to a person who is responsible for a qualifying child or young person.

6.8.4 Carer's allowance

This is an earnings replacement benefit that is paid to someone who cares for at least 35 hours every week for a severely disabled person. The claimant must not be in full-time education or in remunerative employment.

Chapter 7
Introduction to the Means-Tested Benefits

7.1	The scope of this chapter	95
7.2	Resources: capital	96
7.3	Resources: income	99
7.4	The family and the benefits household	102
7.5	Needs: the applicable amount	104
7.6	Personal allowances	104
7.7	Premiums	105
7.8	The comparison	108
7.9	Common problems of means-tested benefits	108
7.10	Living together as 'husband and wife' or 'civil partners'	108
7.11	Overpayment of benefits	111
7.12	Mechanics of recovery	114
7.13	Deductions from benefit	114

7.1 The scope of this chapter

7.1.1 Contents of this chapter

In this chapter, we shall consider the following topics:

(a) a reminder of the main means-tested benefits;
(b) the meaning of the expression 'means test';
(c) capital and income;
(d) the family and the household;
(e) the applicable amount;
(f) cohabitation;
(g) overpayments of benefit and their recovery.

Most of these topics are common to all the means-tested benefits and it is more sensible to consider them together. Variations applicable to the individual benefits are considered in the main discussion of the benefits in **Chapters 8** and **9**.

7.1.2 The benefits discussed in this chapter

There are four principal means-tested benefits, which form natural pairs. Within each pair, the method of calculation is identical, or nearly so. In **Chapters 8** and **9**, the benefits are grouped together in those pairs. Collectively, in this chapter, the benefits are described as 'the four benefits' or 'all four benefits'.

7.1.2.1 Income support and income-based jobseeker's allowance (Chapter 8)

Income support (IS) and income-based jobseeker's allowance (IBJSA) are the ultimate top-up benefits for anyone who has a very low income, from whatever source, and is not in remunerative work. These are the benefits which are meant when people talk about 'being on social security'. It is only with these benefits that an owner-occupier may get assistance with his housing costs.

7.1.2.2 Local authority benefits (Chapter 9)

The local authority benefits are housing benefit (HB) and council tax benefit (CTB). Housing benefit gives help to those under a legal liability to pay rent for the place they occupy (but do not own) as their home; CTB reduces the amount that the occupiers of residential property pay in local taxes.

7.1.3 What is the means test?

In order to qualify for any of the four benefits, the claimant must satisfy a means test, in addition to satisfying any qualifying conditions specific to the benefit he wishes to claim. The means test is an arithmetical calculation which compares the claimant's means, or resources, with a specified level of need. The resulting figure shows whether the client is entitled to benefit on the basis of the means test, and if so how much benefit he will receive.

The details of how the means test is carried out differ according to which benefit is being claimed. There are, however, a number of common factors which we shall deal with here. We shall consider the factors specific to each benefit as a preliminary to discussing the other aspects of that benefit in the appropriate chapter.

7.2 Resources: capital

7.2.1 What is capital?

For all four benefits, there are three types of capital which may be taken into account.

7.2.1.1 Actual capital

Any form of asset or investment is capable of being capital for benefit purposes. This includes savings, lump sum or one-off payments, shares, life insurance policies, real property and trust monies. Even the rights to capital are regarded as capital because such rights can be sold (eg endowment policies) or enforced (eg by legal action).

For benefit purposes, only capital in which the person has a beneficial interest can be included in the calculation. If a person is the legal owner of a capital resource, an assumption will be made that he is also the beneficial owner unless he can prove to the contrary. Beneficial ownership may arise in a variety of circumstances wherein the person is not the legal owner. For example, he has invested in a limited company; his solicitor holds personal injury damages; he is a beneficiary in an estate still in probate or he has an interest in a trust fund.

7.2.1.2 Income which is treated as capital

Certain types of income are treated as capital. These include an advance of earnings or a loan from an employer; income tax refunds and irregular (one-off) charitable payments. However, these do not count if the claimant is involved in returning to work after a trade dispute.

7.2.1.3 Notional capital

This is capital in which the claimant has a beneficial interest but which is not in his possession at the date of the claim (Income Support (General) Regulations 1987 (SI 1987/1967) (IS Regs 1987), reg 51(6)). It most often arises in the following circumstances:

(a) Where the claimant has deliberately deprived himself of the capital resource in order either to claim a benefit or a greater amount of benefit. This is largely a matter of common sense. Using capital to pay debts or to buy personal possessions will often be regarded as deprivation of capital, but the DfWP will still have to show that it was the claimant's intent in doing so to secure the benefit or more of it. If it is found that the claimant has deprived himself of capital then the value of the capital or whatever it purchased will be counted as notional capital. For example, if the claimant buys a car in order to reduce his capital so that he will be eligible for benefits, then the value of the car will be considered as notional capital.

The onus of proving that a claimant has deliberately deprived himself of capital to improve his benefits position is on the DfWP. It does not have to show that the claimant's or his partner's sole or predominant purpose was to get benefit or to get more benefit but must show that it was a significant one. The following factors will be taken into consideration:

(i) the mental capabilities of the claimant and/or his partner at the time of disposing of the capital;

(ii) the options open to the claimant and/or his partner. If there was a choice as to how the capital should be used, then it is more likely that it will be considered as having been spent in order to get benefit. If money is spent extravagantly (eg on an expensive holiday); or to pay off a debt early; or simply given away then the amount in question will be notional capital included in the benefit calculation. If, on the other hand, the money was used to pay for necessities of life such as food or fuel, or immediately repayable debts, then it will probably not be considered as notional capital;

(iii) the knowledge of the claimant and/or his partner. If they did not know that the amount of capital they owned would affect their benefit entitlement then they would not be considered to have deliberately deprived themselves of capital in order to gain benefit. The amount of knowledge they are deemed to have will depend on their familiarity with the benefits system, the contents of any forms they may have been given when applying for benefit and their general standard of education.

A claimant who has received a personal injury payment which is put into a discretionary trust on his behalf will not be considered as having notional capital.

(b) What about the situation where a claimant is able to get capital if he were to apply for it? This is known as 'capital which is available on application' and includes money which may be owed to the claimant and/or his partner in the form of say an unclaimed win on the national lottery or premium bonds or a returnable deposit.

(c) There may be capital in which the claimant has a beneficial interest and this has been paid to a third party or the claimant may have received money on behalf of a third party. Where money is paid to a third party (eg a household utility supplier or a bank or building society) on behalf of the claimant or a member of his benefits household (excluding payments made by certain specified trust funds), then that may be treated as notional capital in the possession of the claimant. It counts as capital if the payment is to cover certain of the claimant's or his family's normal living expenses. Under the IS Regs 1987 these include such items as food, household fuel, ordinary clothing and footwear. As to the last two items, school uniforms and sportswear are excluded. Payments for other kinds of expenses (eg a television licence fee) do not count. Conversely, where the claimant or a member of his benefits household receives money on behalf of a third party but retains this or uses it for his own purposes, this will count as capital.

7.2.2 Capital that is disregarded

Not all capital will be included when calculating the amount of capital held by the claimant. Certain types of capital can be disregarded for an indefinite period of time; other types will be disregarded for two years; others for one year and still others for six months. The onus is on the claimant to show that the capital should be disregarded.

Capital which is disregarded indefinitely includes:

(a) the surrender value of any life assurance policy or endowment policy or annuity;

(b) business assets of a self-employed earner whilst he continues in self-employment;

(c) the dwelling which is occupied as the claimant's home (this includes any garage, garden, outbuildings and land, together with any premises not occupied as a home which it is impracticable or unreasonable to sell separately);

(d) all personal possessions such as jewellery, cars, furniture, etc;

(e) the value of the right to an occupational pension;

(f) personal injury damages held in a trust fund or a fund administered by the court;

(g) the value of a personal pension;

(h) social fund payments;

(i) most charitable trust lump sum payments;

(j) money deposited with a housing association by tenants as a condition of occupying the home.

Capital which can be disregarded for up to two years includes certain specified trust fund payments which are beyond the scope of this book.

Capital which can be disregarded for one year includes arrears of the majority of benefits.

Capital disregarded for six months includes:

(a) loans or gifts made for the express purpose of essential repairs and improvements to the claimant's home;

(b) grants made to local authority tenants for the purchase, repair or alteration of a home;

(c) proceeds of sale of a home if a replacement home is to be purchased;

(d) insurance payments or compensation paid for the replacement or repair of the home or personal possessions.

There is a discretionary extension of time available for all these matters.

7.2.3 Value of the capital

The value of actual capital will be determined by the DfWP. Each type of asset will be valued according to a set of rules specific to it but generally speaking the current market value is used (ie the price that a willing buyer would pay a willing seller in that market on the date of the claim). Ten per cent of the proceeds will be deducted from the capital to cover the relevant costs of the sale. Stocks and shares will first be valued by looking at the figures given in most of the daily newspapers. If the value is close to the capital limit, then a complicated calculation using the figures given by the Stock Exchange Daily Official List is used. Shares in a private company need to be valued by an expert.

7.2.4 Capital limits

For each benefit, there is an upper and a lower capital limit. The upper limit is the amount of capital which acts as an absolute bar to receiving the benefit. The lower limit is an amount which is completely disregarded and has no effect whatever on the amount of benefit. Between the limits, the capital is deemed to produce income in a way which is described under the heading 'tariff income' at **7.3.6**.

The lower limit for the four benefits is £6,000.

The upper limit for the four benefits is £16,000.

7.2.5 The diminishing notional capital rule

The amount of notional capital is calculated in the same way as actual capital and the same disregards apply (see above). It is then added to actual capital and any income which is treated as capital to determine eligibility for the four benefits. If, as a result, the maximum is exceeded (see above), the claimant will not be entitled to the benefit. In the alternative, if the capital adds up to more than the lower capital limit then the tariff income rule (see **7.3.6**) applies and the claimant's benefit will reduce by £1 for every £250 or part that is above £6,000. However, if the notional capital figure affects the claimant's entitlement to the benefit, the diminishing notional capital rule comes to his aid by reducing the value of the notional capital to which he is presumed to have access. The amount of notional capital is reduced gradually by the extra the claimant would have received in benefits each week if the notional capital had not been included in his capital figure. As soon as the capital figure drops beneath the maximum the claimant will be eligible for the benefit. Where a claimant is receiving benefit at a reduced rate because of the tariff income rule, then the benefit will increase as the notional capital figure decreases.

> **Example**
>
> Humphrey is 38 years of age and he has no actual capital or income that is treated as capital but he is found to have notional capital of £7,000 and that yields a tariff income of £4 and so reduces his weekly benefit by £4. If his benefit were otherwise, say £56.20 a week, he will be paid only £52.20 per week as a result. The notional capital which he is deemed to have will decrease by £4 each week until the notional capital reaches £6,750 (after approximately 62 weeks) when the tariff income will fall to £3 a week and so on.

7.3 Resources: income

7.3.1 What is income?

For all four benefits, income from all sources has to be taken into account. Some income may be disregarded (see, for example, Sch 9 to the IS Regs 1987 for a list). The principal types of reckonable income that a claimant may have are:

(a) earnings from employment (see **7.3.2**) or self-employment (see **7.3.3**);
(b) maintenance (see **7.3.4**);

(c) other benefits and pensions (see **7.3.5**);
(d) other income, eg from boarders or lodgers (see **7.4**); and
(e) tariff income (see **7.3.6**).

Each of the types of income has its own rules, some of which are the same for all four benefits. Here we shall consider the rules which are common to all or most of the benefits, and leave the rules which are specific to one pair of benefits to the later chapters. Rules which apply to one of a pair of benefits usually apply to the other as well.

7.3.2 Earnings from employment and earnings disregard

Earnings from employment are taken net of tax and National Insurance contributions, and half of any contribution to a pension scheme. There are complex provisions for working out earnings that fluctuate from week to week. Usually, some sort of average over a period of several weeks is used. There is a system of disregards for the first slice of net earnings, varying from £5 to a maximum of £25 per week.

7.3.3 Earnings from self-employment and earnings disregard

Earnings from self-employment are based on profits after tax, National Insurance contributions, half of pension contributions, and allowable expenses. These expenses are the same that would be allowed for tax purposes. The same system of disregards applies as with earnings from employment. Earnings from self-employment are normally calculated from the annual profits of the business. There is a system of disregards for the first slice of net earnings, varying from £5 to a maximum of £25 per week.

7.3.4 Maintenance

As a general rule, £10 of maintenance paid in respect of a child of the family is ignored when calculating entitlement to IS or IBJSA.

For HB and CTB purposes, if the claimant is either a lone parent or has a partner and child, then provided the claimant (and any partner) is aged under 60 or claiming IS or IBJSA, then £15 of any child maintenance payments is ignored.

Spousal maintenance counts as income for the four benefits.

7.3.5 Other benefits and pensions

Other social security benefits and occupational or personal pensions usually count as income in full, without any disregards. However, here the differences between the pairs of benefits are most marked.

With all four benefits, the following always count in full as income:

(a) the contributory benefits but, as to widowed parent's allowance, see **5.4.6**;
(b) carer's allowance;
(c) industrial disablement benefit;
(d) all private and occupational pensions;
(e) maternity allowance.

The following never count as income:

(a) disability living allowance and attendance allowance;
(b) IS and IBJSA for HB and CTB.

This leaves the following benefits, which are treated differently for different benefits.

(a) *Working tax credit:* whilst this counts as income for all four benefits, note that when calculating entitlement to housing benefit and council tax benefit any 30-hour element of working tax credit and/or relevant child care costs up to a maximum permitted figure (see **9.10.2.2**) may be ignored.

(b) *Child tax credit and child benefit:* these are ignored when calculating entitlement to income support and income-based JSA but taken into account as income when calculating entitlement to housing benefit and council tax benefit.

(c) *SSP and SMP:* these are treated as income when calculating income support or income-based JSA. SSP and SMP are treated as earnings when calculating housing benefit or council tax benefit so any appropriate earnings disregard can be made. Note that if the claimant of housing benefit or council tax benefit or any partner is aged 60 or over and not claiming IS or IBJSA, then SSP and SMP are ignored.

7.3.6 Tariff income

For all the four benefits, capital between the upper and lower limits is deemed to produce 'tariff income'. This is a complete fantasy: many forms of capital produce no income at all, while those that do rarely produce it at the level that is assumed for tariff income. Any actual income that an investment does produce is completely disregarded.

To calculate tariff income, the amount up to the lower capital limit (see **7.2.4**) is deducted from all relevant capital.

For all four benefits the general rule is that the claimant is assumed to have an income of £1 for every £250, or part of £250, by which capital exceeds £6,000 (up to the maximum of £16,000).

For HB and CTB purposes, if the claimant and any partner are aged 60 or over and not claiming IS or IBJSA the following tariff income rules apply instead:

(a) if the guarantee credit element of pension credit (see **5.3**) is being paid then all capital is ignored;

(b) otherwise, the lower limit is £6,000 but the claimant is assumed to have an income of £1 for every £500, or part of £500, by which capital exceeds £6,000 (up to the maximum of £16,000).

Examples

(1) Enrico is 45 years of age and his capital consists of some shares in a private company, which are valued by the DfWP at £6,186. How much tariff income will they be deemed to produce?

Deduct the first £6,000 to leave £186. This is 'part of £250' so is deemed to be producing £1 per week. The total tariff income is therefore £1 per week.

(2) Florence is 55 years of age. She applies for IS as she has become incapable of work. Her partner is on a low income and not in remunerative work. They have savings of £9,645. What is her tariff income?

Deduct the first £6,000 to leave £3,645. £3,000 would produce a tariff income of £12 and the next £250 another £1 and the next £250 a further £1, leaving just £145. This is 'part of £250' and so is deemed to produce another £1 tariff income per week. So her total weekly tariff income is £15.

7.4 The family and the benefits household

7.4.1 What does 'family' mean in benefits law?

The members of the claimant's family are those people for whom he may be able to claim additional benefit, and whose resources may affect the amount of benefit he can claim (SSCBA 1992, s 137).

7.4.2 The claimant's partner

The first member of the claimant's family is his 'partner'. This means either:

(a) a husband or wife, or any person of the opposite sex with whom he is 'living together as husband and wife'; or
(b) a couple of the same sex in a civil partnership or who are living together as if they were civil partners.

The question of whether two people are indeed living in such a relationship is considered at **7.10**.

7.4.3 Children of the family

The children of the family are any children or qualifying young persons for whom the claimant or his partner is receiving child benefit (see **6.6**).

For IS and IBJSA purposes, the existence of children or qualifying young persons in the benefits household does not play any part in the calculation. A check needs to be made to see if the claimant is entitled to child tax credit (see **9.6**). For HB and CTB purposes, the existence of children or qualifying young persons in the benefits household does play a part in the calculation.

7.4.4 The claimant's benefits household

When considering how much of a means-tested benefit a claimant may be entitled to, it is best to work out first who makes up his benefits household as this will determine what personal allowances and premiums can be claimed for IS, IBJSA, HB and CTB and housing costs for IS and IBJSA.

The claimant's benefits household may consist of the claimant, his or her partner and for HB and CTB purposes the children or young persons of the family, as defined above. Anyone else sharing the accommodation will have a different status that may well affect the amount of benefit payable (see **7.4.6**).

7.4.5 Aggregation of resources

The resources of one claimant and any partner are generally aggregated for means-tested benefit purposes, and treated as the resources of the claimant. Capital and income belonging to the claimant's partner are treated exactly as if they were capital or income of the claimant.

But what about the resources of a dependent child or young person for HB and CTB purposes? The rules are:

(a) If the claimant or any partner is aged 60 or over and not claiming IS or IBJSA, the child will form part of the benefits household regardless of the amount of capital held by that child. All appropriate allowances and premiums are payable, except that the lone parent rate of family premium is not payable if the child has more than £3,000.

(b) If the claimant and any partner are both aged under 60 or claiming IS or IBJSA, then if a child has capital exceeding £3,000 that child is ignored when calculating the applicable amount, except that any standard family premium or its lone parent rate is still payable.

7.4.6 What about people who are not in the claimant's benefits household?

Other people besides the claimant's family may share the family home. They are likely to have an effect on his benefit, because of the contributions that they make or are treated as making to household expenses.

There are three mutually exclusive categories of people who may share the family home: non-dependants, boarders, and subtenants (lodgers). They are not members of the claimant's family and their resources are never aggregated with that of the claimant.

7.4.7 Non-dependants

A non-dependant is an adult who lives with the claimant on an informal basis. Most non-dependants are relatives, such as grown-up children or elderly parents.

Any actual payments that a non-dependant makes towards his keep are disregarded in full. However, if the claimant is receiving HB or CTB, or help with housing costs under IS or IBJSA, his benefit will usually be reduced to reflect the expected contribution from the non-dependant. The deductions vary from benefit to benefit and with the gross earnings of the non-dependant. Examples of non-dependant deductions are shown at **8.7.2** and **9.5.3**.

7.4.8 Subtenants (lodgers)

A subtenant need not have a formal lease, but lives within the claimant's home under a contract, paying rent or a licence fee. Normally, only £4 of the payment can be disregarded, but £19.45 (the figure for 2007/08) is disregarded if the charge covers heating costs. The balance counts as income (IS Regs 1987, Sch 9, para 19).

> Example
>
> John lives with his partner, Catherine and their child, Thomas, aged 4. They recently found a lodger, Robert, for their spare room after placing an advertisement in the local newspaper. John's benefits household consists of himself, Catherine and Thomas. Robert is a subtenant (lodger). Assume he pays rent of £50 a week. How much of that would be treated as John's income?
>
> £46.00, if the rent did not include heating costs, but £30.55 if it did.

7.4.9 Boarders

The difference between boarders and subtenants is that a boarder is provided with regular meals. Here, the disregard is more generous: the first £20 of the weekly payment, plus 50% of the remainder is disregarded (IS Regs 1987, Sch 9, para 20). The balance counts as income. This rule applies for each boarder.

> Example
>
> Bryan lives with his partner, Anne and their children, Wayne, aged 14, and Chris, aged 9. They recently found a boarder, Janet, for their spare room after placing an advertisement in the window of a local shop. Janet is provided with an evening meal. Bryan's benefits household consists of himself, Anne, Wayne and Chris. Janet is a boarder. Assume her rent is £90 a week. How much of that would be treated as Bryan's income?

First, ignore £20, so that reduces the sum to £70. Secondly, ignore one half (ie £35), and so the balance of £35 is taken into account as income.

7.5 Needs: the applicable amount

7.5.1 What is the applicable amount?

Once the claimant's resources have been worked out, they must be compared with his needs. For all the benefits, the figure that is used in the needs side of the equation is called the 'applicable amount', because this is the amount of income which is applicable in each benefit to a person in the claimant's circumstances.

For IS and IBJSA, the applicable amount is the income which the Government says the claimant and any partner need to live on. Prescribed rates apply according to the status of the claimant eg single, disabled, etc. There are no elements for children as these form part of the child tax credit (see **9.6**) and a check should be made to see if that is payable.

For HB and CTB the applicable amount is the income the claimant's benefits household (ie including any partner and/or children or qualifying young persons) needs to meet such liability according to the Government's prescribed rates. Also, for HB and CTB the calculation has an additional element. It is necessary first to work out the maximum amount of benefit the claimant could get. If income exceeds the applicable amount, a prescribed percentage of the excess is then deducted from the maximum benefit to find out how much the claimant will actually get. This is called 'tapering', and is illustrated in Chapter 9.

7.5.2 How is the applicable amount calculated?

The applicable amount has two principal elements, common to all four of these benefits, which are called 'allowances' and 'premiums'. For IS and IBJSA only, a third element goes into the calculation if the claimant is an owner-occupier and responsible, for example, for paying a mortgage on his home. This is explained at **8.3**. Here we shall confine ourselves to the common elements.

7.6 Personal allowances

The first element of the applicable amount is any personal allowances that reflect the composition of the claimant's benefits household: whether he is single or living with a partner, and for HB and CTB purposes whether he has qualifying children and/or young children and the ages of those children.

The personal allowances are categorised by age and by whether the claimant has a partner and, for HB and CTB purposes, any qualifying children or young persons. The child tax credit (see **9.8**) has replaced the child allowances for IS and IBJSA.

The categories are as follows:

(a) single person aged 16 to 17;
(b) single person aged 18 to 24;
(c) single person aged 25 and over;
(d) single person for HB or CTB only, aged 60 to 64 and not claiming IS or IBJSA;
(e) single person for HB or CTB only, aged 65 or over and not claiming IS or IBJSA;
(f) lone parent aged under 18;
(g) lone parent aged over 18;

(h) couple, where both aged under 18;
(i) couple, where both or one aged over 18;
(j) couple for HB or CTB only, where one or both are aged 60 to 64 and not claiming IS or IBJSA;
(k) couple for HB or CTB only, where one or both are aged 65 or over and not claiming IS or IBJSA;
(l) child under 16 (note that a child is not treated as being aged 16 until the first Monday in September of the year in which he is 16 (see **7.4.3**));
(m) qualifying young person over 16.

At the very least, every claimant's applicable amount includes an allowance for himself. A single claimant with no children or young persons, in good health and under 60, has an applicable amount made up of his personal allowance only, according to his age.

7.7 Premiums

Many claimants also qualify for premiums in addition to their allowances. Premiums reflect special circumstances, which indicate that the claimant, or a member of his benefits household, if any, need a higher income than other people.

7.7.1 Standard rate family premium (HB and CTB only)

This will be paid if the claimant's benefits household includes at least one qualifying child or young person for child benefit purposes (see **6.6**). It is paid at a flat rate regardless of the number of qualifying children or young persons. It is still paid, even if there is only one qualifying child or young person. It is paid at a higher rate if at least one qualifying child is under one year old.

7.7.2 Severe disability premium (IS, IBJSA, HB, CTB)

Single claimants and lone parents are entitled to this premium at the lower single rate if:

(a) the claimant is in receipt of a 'qualifying benefit' ie attendance allowance; or DLA care component at the middle or highest rate; and
(b) no non-dependant (see **7.4.7**) aged 18 or over normally resides with the claimant; and
(c) carer's allowance is not payable to anyone for caring for the claimant.

Members of a couple are entitled to the higher couple rate if:

(a) each of them is in receipt of a 'qualifying benefit'; and
(b) no non-dependant (see **7.4.7**) aged 18 or over normally resides with them, and
(c) carer's allowance is not payable in respect of both of them.

Note that provided (a) and (b) above for a couple are met, then the lower single rate is payable where carer's allowance is payable for one of the couple.

7.7.3 Disabled child premium (HB and CTB only)

This will be paid for each qualifying child or young person in the claimant's benefits household who receives disability living allowance (either component at any rate of pay) or is registered blind.

7.7.4 Carer's premium (IS, IBJSA, HB and CTB)

This will be paid if the claimant or any partner are receiving or are treated as being entitled to carer's allowance. A double premium is payable if both the claimant and his partner qualify for the premium.

In what circumstances will the claimant or any partner be 'treated as being entitled to carer's allowance'? It must be remembered that carer's allowance is an earnings replacement benefit (see **1.2.5**). Where the claimant or a partner are entitled in their own right to another earnings replacement benefit, both benefits cannot be paid due to the overlapping benefits rule (see **2.6**). If the claimant or partner, as the case may be, elects to receive the other earnings replacement benefit instead of carer's allowance, he or she will still be treated as being entitled to carer's allowance and so will be entitled to carer's premium.

Example

Jo is entitled to carer's allowance as a result of caring for her husband. She is awarded income support which includes the carer's premium. She becomes incapable of work and fulfils the qualifying conditions for incapacity benefit. However, she still struggles to do her caring duties and remains entitled to carer's allowance. Although she meets the qualifying conditions for both benefits she will be paid for only one and she should elect incapacity benefit as it is paid at a higher rate. She is said to have an 'underlying entitlement' to carer's allowance and as such is treated as entitled to it and so will continue to receive the carer's premium as part of her income support.

7.7.5 Enhanced disability premium (IS, IBJSA, HB, CTB)

The Social Security Amendment (Enhanced Disability Premium) Regulations 2000 (SI 2000/2629) introduced this premium. The qualifying conditions are:

(a) the highest rate of DLA care component must be paid to the claimant, his or her partner or, for HB and CTB, any child dependant or young person in the claimant's benefits household; and

(b) if it is the claimant or a partner who receives the DLA, he or she must be under 60 years of age.

Note that for HB and CTB purposes, if the claimant or any partner is aged 60 or over and not claiming IS or IBJSA, this premium cannot be paid for the claimant or any partner. The pensioner premium will be payable instead (see **7.7.8**).

It is payable at three rates: for a single claimant or qualifying child, or a couple where one or both qualify.

7.7.6 Lone parent family premium increase (HB and CTB only)

Prior to 6 April 1998, a higher rate of the family premium was payable to a lone parent. Some claimants remain entitled to this additional amount. The regulations are complex but as a general rule the increase is payable if the claimant was entitled as a lone parent to the premium on 5 April 1998 and has continued since to be a lone parent.

The premium is not payable if the claimant or any partner is aged 60 or over.

It should be remembered that this premium cannot be claimed along with those that follow below.

7.7.7 Disability premium (IS, IBJSA, HB, CTB)

The circumstances in which this premium is payable depend upon whether or not the claimant has a partner. The premium is payable only where the claimant or any partner is under 60 and satisfies the qualifying conditions.

The qualifying conditions for the premium are that the claimant or any partner receives disability living allowance (either component at any rate of pay), or incapacity benefit at either the long-term rate or the special short-term rate payable to a terminally ill person, or is registered blind.

If the claimant has a partner, it is paid at the couple rate, provided one of them meets the qualifying conditions.

For HB and CTB purposes, this premium is not payable if the claimant or any partner is aged 60 or over and not claiming IS or IBJSA.

7.7.8 Pensioner premium (IS, IBJSA, HB, CTB)

Age is the only qualifying condition for this premium, which is paid, for IS and IBJSA, if the claimant or any partner is aged 60 or over. For HB and CTB purposes, this premium is payable only if the claimant or any partner is aged 60 or over and claiming IS or IBJSA. There are two rates, one for single people and one for couples, where one or both of them is aged 60 or over.

7.7.9 Enhanced pensioner premium (IS, IBJSA, HB, CTB)

Age is the only qualifying condition for this premium which will be paid, for IS and IBJSA, if the claimant or partner is between the ages of 75 and 79 inclusive. For HB and CTB purposes, this premium is payable only if the claimant or any partner is aged 75 to 79 and claiming IS or IBJSA. There are two rates, one for single people and one for couples where either or both qualify.

7.7.10 Higher pensioner premium (IS, IBJSA, HB, CTB)

The premium is payable if:

(a) the HB or CTB claimant or any partner are aged 80 or over; or
(b) the claimant was receiving a disability premium for at least eight weeks prior to his sixtieth birthday and has been receiving the premium ever since; or
(c) the HB or CTB claimant or any partner are aged between 60 and 79 and at least one of them is either registered blind or in receipt of disability living allowance (either component at any rate of pay); or incapacity benefit at either the long-term rate or special short-term rate payable to a terminally ill person.

There are two rates, one for single people and one for couples where either or both qualify.

7.7.11 Which premiums can be claimed together?

Of the premiums listed above, 7.7.1 to 7.7.5 inclusive can be claimed at the same time.

> **Example**
> A HB or CTB benefits household which consists of the claimant, his partner and a disabled qualifying child or young person who is cared for by the claimant will be able to claim the standard rate family premium but in addition to that may also be entitled to a disabled child's premium and a carer's premium.

However, only one of the premiums listed in **7.7.6** to **7.7.10** inclusive can be claimed at the same time, the highest in value being paid.

> **Example**
> A HB or CTB benefits household which consists of a disabled claimant who is also a lone parent will be able to claim the standard rate family premium but, in addition to that, the claimant may also be entitled to the lone parent family premium increase and to a disability premium. However, the lone parent family premium increase and a disability premium cannot be paid at the same time. If entitled to the disability premium, the claimant would receive that as it is paid at a higher rate than the lone parent family premium increase.

7.7.12 Premiums: a summary

For IS and IBJSA purposes, none of the premiums concerning children or young persons are relevant. These form part of child tax credit.

For HB and CTB purposes, all the premiums should be considered if the claimant and any partner are aged under 60 or if over 60 and claiming IS or IBJSA. However, if the claimant and any partner are aged 60 or over and are not claiming IS or IBJSA then only the family, disabled child, enhanced disability, severe disability and carer's premium can potentially be claimed.

7.8 The comparison

The last stage in the means test is a comparison of the applicable amount, as calculated, with the claimant's income, as calculated. This is the most important difference between IS and IBJSA on the one hand and the other two benefits. For IS and IBJSA, the comparison is extremely simple. If the claimant's income is less than the applicable amount, he receives benefit to top up the income to the level of the applicable amount. If his income equals or exceeds the applicable amount, he gets nothing.

With the other benefits there is another layer of calculation, and it is possible for a claimant to receive benefit even if his income is higher than the applicable amount. For details of how this last stage in the calculation works, see **Chapter 9**.

7.9 Common problems of means-tested benefits

Means-tested benefits are particularly likely to cause problems for claimants. The means test itself is so complicated that it is very easy for a mistake to be made. Claimants do not understand the law and frequently fail to pass on information which affects their right to benefit.

The problems covered in this section usually arise from unreported changes in the claimant's circumstances. The failure to report may be deliberate (and thus fraudulent), but is more often merely negligent, ignorant or misinformed. The consequence for the claimant may well depend on establishing which of these it is.

7.10 Living together as 'husband and wife' or 'civil partners'

To ensure fair treatment between those couples who are married or in a civil partnership and those who are not, couples who are living together as 'husband and wife' or 'civil partners' are treated for welfare benefit purposes in the same way as a married couple or a same-sex couple in a civil partnership.

The expression living together as 'husband and wife' or 'civil partners' is benefits jargon for the cohabitation of an opposite-sex or same-sex couple. We have already seen, at **7.4.5**, that when such a couple are living together their assets are aggregated.

If a person who is claiming a means-tested benefit starts to live with a partner, their entitlement to benefit will change. For all the benefits the applicable amount for a couple is less than the total for two single people. If the new partner is in remunerative work, the claimant's rights to IS and IBJSA will cease immediately (see **8.2.1**).

7.10.1 The *Crake* guidelines

It is often very difficult to decide whether two people are living together as husband and wife or civil partners. The question is one of fact, not of law. There is an almost infinite range of possibilities, from true cohabitation to friends who just happen to share a house or flat. The crucial test is whether they live in the same household rather than in the same home. They may live in the same home without living together as husband and wife or civil partners but if they live in the same household, then they may well be considered as living together as husband and wife or civil partners. To avoid being considered as such, the two people must show that they live in entirely separate households within the home. Independent financial, eating and cooking arrangements and exclusive occupation of an area within the home are evidence of separate households.

Difficulties may arise where there has been a previous relationship between the two people, such as a divorced couple, both of whom continue to live in the marital home. This may happen while one awaits new accommodation or, perhaps, through sheer obstinacy. When confronted with a situation in which two people may be living together as husband and wife or civil partner, the DfWP and appeal tribunals use guidelines approved by Woolf J in *Crake v Supplementary Benefits Commission; Butterworth v Supplementary Benefits Commission* [1982] 1 All ER 498 at 502 to make the determination. This case involved the judicial review of two tribunal decisions made under the old Supplementary Benefits Act 1976. In the first, Mrs Crake had claimed Supplementary Benefit (the forerunner of IS) for herself and her two children whilst living in the home of Mr Watts following the breakdown of her marriage. She claimed that she was his housekeeper and that she received no money for the services she provided as they were done in exchange for board and lodging. She further claimed that they led entirely independent lives and that Mr Watts could not support her and her two children. Her claim for Supplementary Benefit was rejected on the grounds that she and Mr Watts were living in the same household as husband and wife: 'There were no exceptional circumstances to justify not aggregating requirements and resources'. The court held that, although the Tribunal had failed to give adequate reasons for its decision (the reason for the judicial review), it had considered the case on its merits and had taken into account the correct issues to determine the matter.

In the second case, the court upheld Mrs Butterworth's appeal. She had been badly injured in a road traffic accident and needed assistance in the house. She lived alone and was initially helped by her daughter-in-law until she was unable to assist. The daughter-in-law arranged for Mr Jones to come and live in Mrs Butterworth's house to assist her whilst she recuperated. There had been a relationship between Mrs Butterworth and Mr Jones in the past. Both she and Mr Jones had their own bedrooms with locks on the doors. Despite the fact that the tribunal accepted Mrs Butterworth's description of the situation, it still rejected her claim on the grounds that she was living with Mr Jones as husband and wife in the same household. It had come to this conclusion for two reasons: first, because he was 'performing the same duties and providing the same care and attention as a husband would give to his wife' and, secondly, because he and Mrs Butterworth were not maintaining entirely separate households within the same accommodation. The court held that neither of these facts were sufficient to establish that Mrs Butterworth and Mr Jones were living in the same household as husband and wife because they could not outweigh the fact that neither party intended to live as husband and wife.

No single factor can determine the issue as to whether two people are living together as husband and wife or civil partner and the authority making the decision should consider evidence relating to the existence of financial support; a sexual relationship; membership of the same household; stability in the relationship; any children of the relationship and the public image presented by the two people.

7.10.1.1 Financial support

Financial support is indicated by the pooling of resources; joint purchases, the responsibility of each person for payment of bills or the actual support by one of the other.

7.10.1.2 Sexual relationship

If a sexual relationship exists, then it is more likely that two people are living as husband and wife or civil partners but it is not conclusive evidence. Equally the non-existence of a sexual relationship is not conclusive evidence that the two people are not living together as husband and wife or civil partners.

7.10.1.3 Membership of the same household

Two people cannot be considered to be living together as man and wife or civil partners unless they occupy the same household. The terms 'household' and 'home' are not the same. The reason for sharing the same home and the circumstances which exist whilst they do so are of utmost importance when deciding the question of whether they are members of the same household.

7.10.1.4 Stability of the relationship

The activities undertaken by the two people together or for one another such as cooking, cleaning, caring for children, decorating and gardening may be indicative of a stable relationship. The amount of time the two people have been together is not regarded as conclusive evidence of stability. A lack of commitment and refusal to accept responsibility for jointly required activities might show a lack of stability.

7.10.1.5 Children of the relationship

Where there are children or young persons in the household who are the children of both the man and the woman, or where each person takes on the role of step-parent to the other's children, this will be regarded as strong evidence that the two people live together as husband and wife or civil partners.

7.10.1.6 Public image

The question here is how a couple are seen in their business and/or private lives. If the two people have given others the impression of being husband and wife or civil partners, by perhaps one taking the other's surname, then this is indicative of living together as husband and wife or civil partners.

7.11 Overpayment of benefits

Overpayments may arise with any benefit, where either a claimant has received a benefit to which he was not entitled at all, or has received more than he should have received. Because of the complexity of the means test, overpayment problems are most common with the four benefits.

Overpayments become a problem only if the paying department tries to make the claimant repay the money that has been wrongly paid to him. By definition, a person who is properly in receipt of a means-tested benefit, even if he has been receiving too much, has few spare resources to repay an overpayment. Overpayments can run for many years before they are discovered and repayment demanded. They may run into four or even five figures: the largest repayment demand the writer has ever seen was over £32,000. The Limitation Act 1980 does not apply to recovery of overpaid benefits, and it is common for overpayments only to come to light many years after they occurred.

7.11.1 How do overpayments arise?

Most overpayments of any benefit arise for one reason only: the paying department acts in ignorance of some circumstance of the claimant which affects his right to benefit. The technical term for such a circumstance is 'material fact'.

For the four benefits, typical examples of material facts might be:

(a) capital assets owned by the claimant or his family;
(b) benefits or earnings received by other members of the claimant's family;
(c) children leaving school and young persons ceasing to qualify for child benefit;
(d) pay increases or changes in working hours leading to increased earnings.

Some of these facts may have been in existence throughout the period of claim, while others may represent changes since the claim began. What is most important is why the paying authority acted in ignorance of the material fact, since that affects their right to recover.

7.11.2 Local authority benefits (HB and CTB)

7.11.2.1 No automatic right of recovery

Recovery of overpayments of HB and CTB is covered by Pt 13 of the HB Regs 2006 and Pt 11 of the CTB Regs 2006 respectively. The principle is that overpayments are recoverable, unless the claimant could not reasonably have been expected to recognise that he was being overpaid. This is so, even if the cause of the overpayment was 'official error', an administrative mistake for which the claimant was not in any way responsible.

This appears harsh, but in practice it is likely that a claimant would be able to succeed in arguing that he had done nothing wrong, had not misled the local authority in any way, and had no way of knowing that he was getting too much benefit. If he notified them of an important change in his circumstances, and his benefit did not change at all, he might have difficulty with this argument. However, an unrelated change in the amount of his benefit might mislead him into thinking that the right adjustment had been made.

7.11.2.2 Automatic right of recovery

Local authorities are supposed to process applications for HB for private tenants within two weeks, but rarely do. Any delay in paying benefit may put the tenant at risk of repossession, so, if there is a delay, the local authority must make interim payments. When the application is eventually processed, the amount paid in interim payments may prove to be too much. The excess is always recoverable.

7.11.3 Social security benefits and tax credits

The law on recovery of overpayments of all social security benefits and the two tax credits is contained in SSAA 1992, s 71. Here the presumption is that the overpayment is not recoverable unless it results from either misrepresentation of, or failure to disclose, a material fact. Causation is an essential part of this presumption. Unless there has been a failure to disclose or a misrepresentation, s 71 does not provide a remedy. Parliament did not provide a statutory right to repayment if the payment was due to an administrative error. The implications for the claimant are different depending on which of the two causes is alleged.

7.11.3.1 Misrepresentation

This means a statement of fact which is false, including innocent misrepresentation, for example, because the fact was not known to the claimant. A claimant risks making a misrepresentation whenever he signs a document that includes a declaration that he has declared all material facts. Such declarations are routinely found:

(a) on all claim forms for any benefit;
(b) on the orders in a payment book, which he signs when he cashes them; and
(c) on the form he signs every time he signs on at the Jobcentre.

A misrepresentation can be either an act or omission by the claimant. A misrepresentation may occur, therefore, where a statement written by a claimant is incorrect or incomplete; where information supplied orally by the claimant is incorrect or incomplete; where someone else has written a statement based on incomplete or incorrect information supplied by the claimant; or where part of a form is left blank.

There are few defences to an allegation of misrepresentation. A claimant may argue that he did not know the fact and that he had signed a declaration which included the words 'known to me' or similar wording. This is rare, although some older claim forms had this form of wording, such as the old postal claim forms, which read: 'Declaration: as far as I know, the information on this form is true and complete'. If, on the other hand, the form read: 'Declaration: the information on this form is true and complete', then the claimant's knowledge of a material fact is irrelevant. If a man were to declare that he had no sources of income while, unbeknownst to him, his wife had earnings of her own, then he would still have made a misrepresentation. The only defence to this type of misrepresentation is non est factum (ie 'it is not my deed'). This defence will apply if the claimant did not know what he was signing. A claimant may have made a representation if he has signed a form which has been filled in by someone else. The only defence to misrepresentation in this instance would be if the claimant is blind, illiterate or lacks an understanding of the form because of poor education, illness or inborn incapacity. To rely upon this defence, however, the claimant must show that he made some attempt to understand what he had signed. If that person merely signs the form without thought, then he will be considered as having made a misrepresentation.

Some payments are made without any declaration. An example is a giro cheque in excess of £250. It is the act of trying to cash the giro cheque which amounts to the misrepresentation. For a giro cheque of less than £250, the claimant signs a declaration stating: 'I acknowledge receipt of the above sum to which I am entitled' and so a misrepresentation occurs only if the claimant is not entitled to benefit.

It is possible to raise a defence based on causation; that the misrepresentation did not cause the overpayment because the fact had been disclosed separately to the paying authority, outside the signed document (see below).

7.11.3.2 Failure to disclose

Claimants are under a continuing duty to disclose any material facts that are known to them, or that they ought to have known had they made reasonable enquiries, which might affect their claims. Further, the claimant is attributed to have knowledge of the types of circumstances which might affect his claim because of the warning notices on forms, etc, but also because such knowledge is within the public domain. It is not sufficient for a claimant to say that he did not realise the fact was material.

Does the disclosure have to be 'reasonably expected'? Is the meaning of 'failed to disclose' in s 71(1) qualified in favour of claimants who did not appreciate that they had an obligation to disclose a material fact once it became known? 'No', held the Court of Appeal in *B v Secretary of State for Work and Pensions* [2005] EWCA Civ 929. The appellant, B, appealed against the decision of the social security commissioners allowing the Secretary of State to recover an overpayment of child benefit. B suffered from severe learning disabilities. She received child benefit for her three children but they were taken into care. The DfWP was not informed of this fact and continued to pay B child-related benefits. The Secretary of State sought to recover the overpaid benefits on the basis that B was required to disclose the fact that her children were no longer living with her. It was argued for B that she was unable to understand that the placing of her children in care was a material fact that she needed to disclose. The Court of Appeal held that on the face of the legislation, a claimant was under a legal obligation to report more than she could reasonably be expected to report. There was no allowance in the legislation for the moral argument against fixing B with the financial consequences of not reporting something which she did not appreciate she needed to report. It was irrelevant that B did not understand the materiality of the fact.

If one Government department knows that a claimant is no longer entitled to a particular benefit, is it still a material non-disclosure if the claimant fails to inform another department of that fact? 'Yes', held the House of Lords in *Hinchy v Secretary of State for Work and Pensions* [2005] UKHL 16, [2005] 1 WLR 967.

Again, the Secretary of State must prove that the failure to disclose caused the overpayment to be made.

7.11.3.3 Proof

If an overpayment decision is taken to appeal, all elements of the burden of proof are on the Secretary of State: that there was an overpayment, that it is recoverable because it resulted from one of the specified causes, and how much was overpaid. The DfWP loses many cases on appeal because some element of this proof is missing.

A tribunal can decide, on the balance of probabilities, only whether the overpayment is recoverable, and has no power over the terms on which a recoverable benefit is recovered. However, it is always worth appealing an overpayment decision: if the calculation is complex, it may not be correct, and the DfWP may not discharge all elements of the burden of proof.

7.11.4 Automatic right of recovery (IS, IBJSA, SPC)

The SSAA 1992, s 74 gives an automatic right of recovery if a claimant is overpaid income support, income based JSA or State pension credit on receiving arrears of another benefit to which he is entitled. Sometimes a claimant will be paid too much income support, income based JSA or State pension credit because money that is due to him (and which constitutes income when calculating any such benefit) is late in being paid and so the benefit is paid in full rather than taking the money due into account. Section 74 therefore seeks to avoid duplication of payment. When the income that affects the amount of income support, income based JSA or State pension credit is finally paid (and very often this may be another benefit or maintenance: see 5.3.3, 7.3.4 and 7.3.5), repayment of the overpayment will normally be requested.

7.12 Mechanics of recovery

7.12.1 How are overpayments recovered?

Even where recovery is possible, it is always in the discretion of the paying department. It may see little point in pursuing recovery, or compassionate grounds for not doing so. If it decides to recover, the commonest method is by deduction from current benefits. Most benefits may be used for this purpose, but there are ceilings on maximum deductions, especially where no fraud has been proved.

If the claimant is no longer on benefits, the overpayment decision is treated as a judgment debt and can be enforced through the civil courts.

7.12.2 From whom may the overpayment be recovered?

The overpayment will usually be recovered from the claimant himself, but may be recovered from anyone else who is responsible for causing it. This may be a person who has stolen a benefit order book or Girocheque and misrepresented himself as the payee on cashing it. More often, the problem arises if someone has been appointed to deal with the affairs of a person with diminished mental capacity, and misrepresents the claimant's affairs. Exceptionally, if the appointee has acted culpably, he may be made personally liable to repay the overpayment.

There are special rules allowing the recovery of overpaid mortgage interest from the lender, and HB from the landlord.

7.13 Deductions from benefit

We have already seen two types of deduction from benefits, where part of a claimant's benefit is withheld. The first is where the benefit is being paid direct to the ultimate intended recipient: the mortgage lender or the landlord. The second is to pay a liability of the claimant: repayment of an overpayment of benefit.

There are other repayments which may also be made from benefits, especially income support and income-based jobseeker's allowance. They fall into one or other of the two categories.

(a) Payment to intended recipient: payments may be made by deduction to gas and electricity suppliers, if the claimant has got into debt and needs the fuel supply to continue. In return, the fuel company agrees not to disconnect the service. Deductions cover arrears and current needs.

(b) Payment of liabilities: as well as payment of arrears of fuel charges, deductions may be made for:
 (i) arrears of council tax and water charges;
 (ii) child support maintenance;
 (iii) magistrates' court fines, costs and compensation orders; and
 (iv) repayment of social fund loans (see **9.16.5**).

Chapter 8
Income Support and Income-Based Jobseeker's Allowance

8.1	The scope of this chapter	117
8.2	Income support or jobseeker's allowance?	117
8.3	Housing costs	120
8.4	Restrictions on housing costs	122
8.5	Calculation and payment	123
8.6	Non-dependants and housing costs	125
8.7	Worked examples	125
8.8	Change of circumstances and reviews	128
8.9	The passport effect	128
8.10	Hardship payments and urgent cases payments	129
8.11	Hardship payments (JA Regs 1996, regs 140–146)	129
8.12	Urgent cases payments	130
8.13	Passporting	130
8.14	IS/IBJSA and other benefits	131
8.15	Claimant profiles	131

8.1 The scope of this chapter

This chapter is concerned with the two most important means-tested benefits, income support (IS) and income-based jobseeker's allowance (IBJSA). The two form a natural pair because the means test for both benefits is identical. Jobseeker's allowance (JSA) was first introduced in October 1996, and the income-based form of the benefit replaced IS for one category of claimants, the unemployed.

The chapter covers the following topics:

(a) determining whether a claimant receives IS or IBJSA;
(b) common factors of the qualifying conditions;
(c) relationship of IBJSA to contribution-based JSA;
(d) housing costs;
(e) worked examples of calculations of entitlement to benefit;
(f) hardship and urgent cases payments;
(g) passports to other benefits.

8.2 Income support or jobseeker's allowance?

8.2.1 Conditions of entitlement

Almost any person who satisfies the means test, because his capital and income fall below the prescribed limits, is potentially able to claim either IS or IBJSA. They may be claimed as the claimant's sole source of income, or as a top-up to other benefits, part-time earnings, maintenance or other income. But it is impossible for one person to be entitled to both at once: the statutory conditions of entitlement are mutually exclusive. So which does the claimant claim?

A person will qualify for IBJSA if:

(a) he passes the means test;
(b) his capital when aggregated with that of any partner does not exceed £16,000;
(c) he is not receiving IS;
(d) any partner is not receiving IS or IBJSA already;
(e) he is not a young person for whom someone else already claims IS or IBJSA for him as part of their benefits household;
(f) he is aged 18 or over (some 16- and 17-year-olds may get IBJSA in exceptional circumstances but they are outside the scope of this book);
(g) he is below pensionable age;
(h) he is not in full-time education (some students may get IBJSA in exceptional circumstances but they are outside the scope of this book);
(i) he and any partner are not in remunerative work;
(j) he has signed a jobseeker's agreement;
(k) he meets the labour market conditions;
(l) he is not disqualified from the benefit for any reason;
(m) he is capable of work;
(n) he is not subject to immigration control and is habitually resident (see **Chapter 10**).

As to conditions (a) and (b), see **Chapter 7**, and in respect of conditions (h) to (l), see **Chapter 3**. However, note that, for IBJSA, 'remunerative work', in respect of the claimant, means he or she must not be working 16 hours or more a week and, as to any partner, he or she must not be working 24 hours or more a week. As to condition (g), as a man's pensionable age is currently 65, a man aged between 60 and 65 can choose to claim either the pension credit (see **5.3**) or IBJSA. A woman aged 60 or more cannot claim IBJSA and must claim the pension credit.

A person will qualify for IS if:

(a) he passes the means test;
(b) his capital when aggregated with that of any partner does not exceed £16,000;
(c) he and any partner are not in remunerative work;
(d) he is not receiving IBJSA or CBJSA;
(e) any partner is not receiving IBJSA or pension credit;
(f) he is at least 16 years of age;
(g) as a general rule he is not studying full time (but see **8.2.2**);
(h) he is in a prescribed category of permitted claimants (see **8.2.2**);
(i) he is not subject to immigration control and is habitually resident (see **Chapter 10**).

As to conditions (a) and (b), see **Chapter 7**. In respect of condition (c), note that, for IS, 'remunerative work', in respect of the claimant, means he or she must not be working 16 hours or more a week and, as to any partner, he or she must not be working 24 hours or more a week. As to condition (e), note that a claimant's partner may receive CBJSA but that will be taken into account when calculating the amount of income support (see **7.3.5**).

8.2.2 Who may claim income support? (IS Regs 1987, reg 4ZA)

Only certain people are entitled to claim income support. The most important categories are as follows.

(a) Any person who is a single parent, with qualifying children under the age of 16, but not older than that.

(b) Any person who receives or would be entitled to claim carer's allowance.

(c) Any person who is incapable of work because of illness or disability, and, for example, receives statutory sick pay, or satisfies the own occupation test or personal capability assessment for incapacity benefit purposes (see **4.2** and **4.3**).

(d) Some disabled people in work whose earning capacity is reduced by at least 25% because of their disability.

(e) Full-time students who are deaf or entitled to a disability premium.

If neither the claimant nor his partner falls into any of the prescribed categories, he must claim IBJSA and be subject to the standard JSA regime (see **Chapter 3**).

8.2.3 Relationship between the two forms of JSA

An unemployed person will claim IBJSA for one or more of the following three reasons:

(a) he does not have the contribution record necessary to claim CBJSA; or

(b) he has been unemployed for more than 26 weeks, and his entitlement to CBJSA has expired; or

(c) his income from all sources, including any CBJSA, is below his applicable amount.

The following conditions described in Chapter 3 for the award of jobseeker's allowance apply to IBJSA as well as CBJSA:

(a) that the claimant has entered into a jobseeker's agreement (see **3.2.3**);

(b) that he is not in remunerative work (see **3.2.4**);

(c) that he is available for work and actively seeking employment, with full-time students excluded on the grounds of non-availability (see **3.2.5** to **3.2.8**);

(d) that he is not disqualified from benefit for any reason (see **3.3**); and

(e) that he is capable of work and under retirement age.

Sanctions, as described at **3.3.5**, apply to IBJSA as well as CBJSA. Sanctions may last for up to 26 weeks, which could mean that the claimant is faced with the possibility of no income at all for that period. Some claimants who are barred from claiming any form of JSA will be able to claim hardship payments, at a lower level than IBJSA in its normal form (see **8.11**).

8.2.4 Joint claims for income-based jobseeker's allowance

If both members of a couple are not in remunerative employment, and they have no qualifying children for child benefit purposes, they must make their claim for IBJSA jointly (SSCBA 1992, s 2A, inserted by the Welfare Reform and Pensions Act 1999). This means that it is not possible for one member of the couple to claim IBJSA for them as a couple, and the other to make no effort to find work. There are complex rules to deal with disqualification from benefit for industrial disputes or sanctions applicable to one member of a joint-claim couple. Effectively in each case the other is allowed to claim as a single person.

8.3 Housing costs

8.3.1 Meaning of 'housing costs'

As well as allowances and premiums, there is a third element which may be included in the applicable amount for IS and IBJSA only, for the claimant's housing costs. The law governing housing costs is contained in reg 17 of and Sch 3 to the IS Regs 1987, and in reg 83 of and Sch 2 to the JA Regs 1996. The wording for both benefits is identical.

The housing costs element of IS or IBJSA is payable only with respect to owner-occupied accommodation. Where a claimant is a tenant who rents his accommodation, he will not receive assistance as part of IS or IBJSA entitlement to pay the rent and any associated charges, but he must make a separate application to his local authority for housing benefit (see **Chapter 9**).

The usual types of housing costs included as part of IS or IBJSA are:

(a) interest on mortgages and other loans used to buy a home;
(b) interest on loans used to fund certain repairs and improvements or to pay a service charge on a leasehold property in respect of repairs and improvements;
(c) ground rent and certain qualifying service charges in respect of a leasehold property (the so-called 'other housing costs').

8.3.2 Who is entitled to claim assistance with housing costs?

The Regulations provide that a claimant is entitled to assistance only with housing costs which 'he or, where he is a member of a family, he or any member of that family, is ... liable to meet in respect of the dwelling occupied as the home'. This means that, as a general rule:

(a) a person is liable to meet housing costs where the liability falls upon him or his partner. If the claimant or any partner share the liability with anyone else they may be able to get assistance with their share;
(b) housing costs are payable only for the home in which the claimant normally lives.

8.3.3 Mortgage and loan payments

Mortgage payments may comprise two elements, the capital and the interest of a loan, which is normally secured against a property. However, there is no requirement for the loan to be secured to qualify for assistance. It is possible, for example, for a claimant who lives in a mobile home to claim for interest in respect of a hire-purchase agreement if it was used to fund the purchase of his home.

The claimant will be entitled only to assistance to pay the interest element of his mortgage. There are different types of mortgages which affect this. The most common are endowment mortgages and repayment mortgages. If a person takes out an endowment mortgage then he will need to make interest payments each month on the entire capital sum throughout the duration of the mortgage. In addition to the interest payments, he must pay the premiums on an endowment policy, which is a method of investment. When the endowment policy matures, there should be sufficient money to repay the capital. As we have seen, the benefits legislation disregards the value of the endowment policy when considering the amount of the claimant's capital (see **7.2.2**). A repayment mortgage operates differently. The person makes one payment per month which is divided between interest and capital. This means that the outstanding capital is reduced each year.

Income support and IBJSA allowable housing costs will not cover any capital repayment, nor any endowment policy premiums. The claimant should do his best to continue to pay these from available resources, but few claimants can afford to do so. Most mortgagees, however, will come to an arrangement with the claimant in respect of the capital and endowment policy instalments, particularly since the mortgage interest payments are made directly to them by the DfWP and therefore become a regular source of repayment.

So what types of mortgages and loans qualify? The conditions are that the mortgage or loan must have been taken out:

(a) to buy the home in which the claimant normally lives. If any part of the loan was taken out for any other purpose, that part will not qualify (see the example in **8.4**); or

(b) to buy an additional interest in that home (eg to buy out an ex-partner's share or to purchase the freehold on a leasehold property); or

(c) to repay a loan which itself would have qualified.

8.3.4 Loans for repairs and improvements

A loan qualifies for assistance where it is taken out, with or without security, for and used for the purpose of:

(a) carrying out repairs and improvements to the dwelling occupied as the home; or

(b) paying any service charge imposed to meet the cost of repairs and improvements to the dwelling occupied as the home; or

(c) paying off another loan to the extent that it would have qualified had it not been paid off.

What are qualifying 'repairs and improvements'? These are any of the following measures undertaken with a view to maintaining the fitness of the dwelling for human habitation or, where the dwelling forms part of a building, any part of the building containing that dwelling:

(a) Provision of a fixed bath, shower, wash basin, sink or lavatory, and necessary associated plumbing, including the provision of hot water not connected to a central heating system.

(b) Repairs to existing heating systems.

(c) Damp-proof measures.

(d) Provision of any of the following:
  (i) ventilation and natural lighting;
  (ii) draining facilities;
  (iii) facilities for preparing and cooking food;
  (iv) insulation of the dwelling occupied as the home;
  (v) electric lighting and sockets;
  (vi) storage facilities for fuel or refuse.

(e) Repairs of unsafe structural defects.

(f) Adapting a dwelling for the special needs of a disabled person.

(g) The provision of separate sleeping accommodation for children of different sexes aged 10 or over who are part of the same family as the claimant.

Note that the provision of any of the above matters, like a fixed bath in (a), may include its repair or replacement.

Where a loan is applied only in part for any of the above purposes, only that portion of the loan which is actually applied for that purpose qualifies for assistance.

8.3.5 Assistance with 'other housing costs'

Allowable housing costs include the normally weekly charge for ground rent under a long lease (ie of more than 21 years) and certain service charges payable in respect of leasehold property (eg buildings insurance payable under the terms of the lease). If the charge relates to a repair or improvement, as defined above, the claimant is expected to take out a loan to meet the cost (and can then claim assistance with the interest repayments). Certain charges are expressly excluded, for example:

(a) charges in respect of day-to-day living expenses including, in particular, any provision of laundry services (other than the provision of premises or equipment to enable a person to do his own laundry);

(b) leisure items such as sports facilities (except a children's play area);

(c) the cleaning of rooms and windows except the exterior of any windows in accommodation where neither the claimant nor any member of his household is able to clean those windows and those in communal areas.

8.4 Restrictions on housing costs

Example

You take instructions from David and learn that he and his wife bought a one-bedroom flat in 1992 while they were both working. They purchased the home for £70,000 and paid a deposit of £5,000 out of their own savings. They took out an endowment mortgage of £80,000, partly to fund the balance of the purchase price of £65,000, but the rest was to fund the purchase of a car costing £15,000. They make payments of £600 per month in interest and pay £75 per month for the endowment policy. In 1998, they took out a second mortgage, this time a repayment mortgage of £15,000 to fund an extension to their home in preparation for the arrival of their first child. They pay a single amount of £150 per month, £25 in respect of the repayment element of the mortgage and £125 in respect of the interest payments.

At the time David claims IBJSA, the amount outstanding on the first mortgage is £80,000 (it has yet to decrease because the endowment policy has not matured). There is £12,500 outstanding on the second mortgage.

What is David's entitlement with regards to housing costs?

There are two loans relating to the home but only the first mortgage is definitely a qualifying loan to the extent that he and his partner who are liable for it used it to finance the purchase of the property. They used £65,000 towards the house purchase, therefore, only £65,000 qualifies for assistance. The contractual interest they pay is irrelevant and the mortgagee will receive the prescribed rate of interest calculated on the outstanding capital (see **8.5.5**). David and his wife will have to meet any shortfall in interest payments and the cost of the endowment policy premiums themselves or come to some arrangement with the mortgagee. The second mortgage will not qualify unless they can show the extension was necessary to maintain the home's fitness for human habitation because of the arrival of the baby. This argument may not succeed if it is felt that the accommodation was already adequate for two adults and a child. If it does succeed, David could claim payment of the prescribed interest on the outstanding part of the loan but he and his wife would need to fund the capital repayments themselves.

8.4.1 Is there a maximum amount on qualifying loans?

There are different maximum limits which depend on the date the claim for IS or IBJSA was made. Since 9 April 1995, the maximum amount on which housing costs will be paid is £100,000.

8.4.2 Excessive housing costs

Where a claimant's housing costs are considered to be excessive, assistance will be restricted to the costs of suitable and available alternative accommodation. Housing costs will be considered to be excessive if the home is larger than required or its location is more expensive than other locations or where the costs are higher than those for suitable and available alternative accommodation. In other words, a claimant living in a luxury home is expected to move or pay the difference between his contractual housing costs and those allowable. When applying the restriction, however, account will be taken of other non-financial factors such as the age and health of the benefits household, the employment prospects of the claimant, interruptions to children's education, negative equity, the ability to sell the home and any inability to raise new funds.

8.4.3 What is the effect of a claimant taking out a loan or increasing it whilst in receipt of IS or IBJSA?

The answer is that, generally, no assistance is given for the increased amount. There are two main exceptions to that rule.

(a) If the loan, or increased amount, is used to buy a home which is better suited to the needs of a disabled person than the previous property. A disabled person in this context is someone for whom any of the following premiums are payable: disabled child, disability, enhanced pensioner or higher pensioner.

(b) If the claimant has a boy and a girl aged 10 or over and the loan was increased to move to a home where they could have separate bedrooms.

8.5 Calculation and payment

The law on interest payments changed substantially on 1 October 1995. A loan taken out before that date is known as 'existing housing costs': if it was taken out on or after that date, it is 'new housing costs'. There is an important difference in the way the two are treated.

8.5.1 Existing housing costs

If the claimant's loan is classified as 'existing housing costs', he is not eligible for any assistance with housing costs as part of his applicable amount for the first 8 weeks after his claim. He is then eligible for 50% of his maximum allowable housing costs for 18 weeks. Only after a total of 26 weeks are his maximum allowable housing costs paid in full. This is often called the '26 weeks rule'. For an exception to it, see **8.5.4**.

8.5.2 New housing costs

If the loan is classified as 'new housing costs', the claimant is expected to have taken out insurance to cover himself for the first 39 weeks of his period of claim. Only after 39 weeks will he receive any help with housing costs. These are then paid in full as part of the applicable amount. This is often called the '39 weeks rule'.

8.5.3 New housing costs which are treated as existing housing costs

In certain prescribed circumstances (see IS Regs 1987, Sch 3 and JA Regs 1996, Sch 2) new housing costs are treated as existing housing costs (ie the claimant is subject to the more generous 26 weeks rule (see **8.5.1**) rather than having to wait 39 weeks for housing costs to form part of his applicable amount). The main exceptions are:

(a) the claimant is a carer receiving carer's allowance; or

(b) the claimant is caring for someone receiving attendance allowance or disability living allowance care component at the middle or highest rate; or

(c) the claimant claims the benefit as a lone parent because of either the death of his partner or due to being 'abandoned'. In *Secretary of State for Work and Pensions v W* [2005] EWCA Civ 570 the Court of Appeal held that 'abandonment' has the same meaning as 'desertion' in matrimonial law. Desertion requires both physical separation and an intention on the part of the deserting party to desert the other party.

For a general exception to the 39 weeks rule, see **8.5.4**.

8.5.4 An exception to both rules

The distinction between existing or new housing costs does not apply to a claimant of IS whose partner is aged 60 or over, nor to an IBJSA claimant where he or his partner is aged 60 or over. In those circumstances the claimant will qualify for maximum housing costs as part of his applicable amount immediately: (IS Regs 1987, Sch 3, para 8(1)(a); JA Regs 1996, Sch 2, para 9(1)(b) and (2)(b)).

8.5.5 Prescribed interest rate

A standard prescribed rate is used for all loans, rather than the actual contractual rate. The prescribed rate is based on the Bank of England base rate plus 1.58% from dates determined by the Secretary of State.

To calculate the amount payable:

(a) calculate the allowable capital after any restrictions;

(b) multiply that capital by the prescribed rate to find the annual rate;

(c) divide by 52 to find the weekly rate; and

(d) round up to the next whole penny.

The claimant's actual interest payments are simply irrelevant.

All housing costs are paid direct to the lender, to avoid any risk of the claimant being tempted to use the money for other purposes. Because of the restrictions and delays in paying full benefit, most claimants get into arrears with their payments when they are on benefits. Advisers should keep the lender fully informed of what is happening to avert any attempt to get possession. Lenders can usually be persuaded to accept whatever the DfWP pays in full satisfaction of the borrower's liability, at least for the short term, as long as they are kept fully informed.

8.5.6 Summary: mortgage interest

When checking whether a loan under which the client pays interest will form part of the client's applicable amount as allowable housing, and if so, how much, you should ask the following questions.

(a) Is it all a qualifying loan?
(b) Is it subject to the £100,000 cap?
(c) Is it excessive?
(d) Was it taken out when the applicant was already on IS or IBJSA?
(e) Was the loan taken out on or before 1 October 1995? Does the loan constitute existing or new housing costs? If new, is there any exception making it existing? In either case will the allowable housing costs immediately form part of the applicable amount because the claimant or partner is aged 60 or over?
(f) What is the prescribed mortgage interest rate?
(g) Will any non-dependant deduction have to be made?

8.6 Non-dependants and housing costs

Generally, the resources of a person who is not a member of the claimant's family are irrelevant to the claimant's right to benefits. The exception is if that person is a non-dependant (see **7.4**), usually an adult relative who is sharing the accommodation and making an informal contribution to the cost of his keep. If there is a non-dependant and the claimant is receiving housing costs, the maximum allowable housing costs will usually have to be reduced to take account of the contribution the non-dependant is expected to make. There is no effect at all if the claimant is not receiving housing costs. Moreover, if the non-dependant does pay anything towards his keep, that is disregarded.

If there is a non-dependant sharing the claimant's accommodation, the maximum allowable housing costs will be reduced by a prescribed amount determined by the gross earnings of the non-dependant. However, deductions from allowable housing costs will not be made in respect of non-dependants if:

(a) the claimant or his partner is blind or receiving attendance allowance or the care component of disability living allowance;
(b) the non-dependant is a full-time student in a period of study or not in remunerative work during the recognised summer vacation relevant to their course;
(c) the non-dependant is not normally resident with the claimant (see *Commissioner's Decision CIS/14850/96*);
(d) the non-dependant is a person aged 16 to 17;
(e) the non-dependant is a person who is aged 18 to 24 who is receiving IS or IBJSA in his own right,
(f) the non-dependant is a co-owner or joint tenant.

8.7 Worked examples

8.7.1 Purpose of this section

To understand how to calculate means-tested benefits, it is useful to have some examples. We shall therefore look at two short case studies. These examples are worked using the benefit rates in force for the period 6 April 2007 to 5 April 2008.

Before presenting each calculation, we shall analyse the key facts of each case study.

8.7.2 Married jobseeker with capital, a mortgage and a non-dependant sharing the accomodation

8.7.2.1 Facts

Mark (aged 49) was made redundant last month. He is married to Janet (aged 42). They have one child, Laura, who is 19 and earns £120 per week gross. They live in a house which they bought in 1994 with the help of a £75,000 endowment mortgage. Laura gives her mother £30 per week for her keep. Mark receives CBJSA. The couple have savings of £7,680 including what is left over from his redundancy payment. Assume a standard mortgage interest rate of 5%. How much IBJSA should he receive now?

8.7.2.2 Analysis

Step 1: calculate the applicable amount

(a) The couple allowance for a couple with both members at least 18.

Note: only this allowance will form the applicable amount for the first eight weeks of the claim as during that time no allowable housing costs are payable (see immediately below). Once allowable housing costs are payable then such will be added to this amount.

(b) Interest on his mortgage. The original loan was £75,000, and as it is an endowment mortgage no capital will have been repaid, so that will remain the figure to use in the calculation. A check should be made to ensure it is a qualifying loan and that it is not excessive. It does not exceed £100,000. Find the weekly rate at a prescribed rate of 5%. The mortgage was taken out in 1994 so this is 'existing housing costs'. As neither Mark nor Janet are aged 60 or over, the '26 weeks rule' applies and nothing will be paid by way of allowable housing costs for the first eight weeks of the claim, then only 50% of such can be paid from the ninth to the twenty-sixth week and the full amount is payable after 26 weeks. However, both of those amounts that are payable will be reduced because there is a non-dependant, Laura, sharing the accommodation. The amount of the deduction will be determined by her gross earnings. The £30 she pays towards her keep is disregarded.

Step 2: calculate Mark's income from all sources

(a) CBJSA at the standard flat rate for a person of at least 25. This will end after 26 weeks and so his income will be reduced by that amount.

(b) Tariff income on savings of £7,680. Deduct the first £6,000 and calculate £1 for each £250 or part of £250.

Step 3: calculate the benefit payable by deducting the income from the applicable amount

The calculation

Step 1: calculate applicable amount	£	£	£
Couple allowance			92.80
Housing costs (£75,000 × 5% ÷ 52) (72.12)	(72.12)		
at 50% from 9th to 26th week, rounded up to next penny		36.06	
Less deduction for non-dependant with gross earnings of £120		17.00	19.06

Housing costs at 100% after 26 weeks	72.12	
Less non-dependant deduction	17.00	55.12

Applicable amount	
For first 8 weeks	92.80
For next 18 weeks	111.86
After 26 weeks	147.92

Step 2: calculate income from all sources

CBJSA	59.15	
Tariff income on £7,680	7.00	
Income		66.15

Step 3: deduct income from applicable amount

Applicable amount for first eight weeks	92.10
Deduct income	66.15
Amount of benefit payable	25.95
Applicable amount from 9th to 26th week	111.86
Deduct income	66.15
Amount of benefit payable	45.71
Applicable amount after 26 weeks	147.92
Deduct income (CBJSA no longer received)	7.00
Amount of benefit payable	140.92

8.7.3 Income support for incapacitated claimant; several premiums

8.7.3.1 Facts

Elon has been incapable of work for two years following a road accident when he was 36. He receives long-term incapacity benefit and DLA care component at the higher rate. He is married to Sharon (aged 33) and she looks after him and receives carer's allowance. They live in a ground-floor maisonette rented from the local council, and have no savings. How much IS can Elon claim?

8.7.3.2 Analysis

Elon is entitled to claim IS because he is incapable of work.

Step 1: calculate the applicable amount

(a) Couple allowance at the rate applicable to a couple aged at least 18.
(b) Disability premium at the couple rate because he is under 60, in receipt of long-term incapacity benefit, and living with a partner, Sharon.
(c) Enhanced disability premium at the couple rate, as he is under 60 and receiving DLA care component at the highest rate and living with a partner, Sharon.

Step 2: calculate Elon's income from all sources

(a) His long-term incapacity benefit. He will receive an age-related addition with his incapacity benefit because his incapacity began under the age of 45. He will not receive an adult dependant increase for Sharon because she is receiving an earnings replacement benefit and the amount of the increase is the same as the carer's allowance.
(b) His DLA is not taken into account as income.

Step 3: calculate the benefit payable by deducting the income from the applicable amount.

Step 1: calculate applicable amount	£	£
Couple allowance	92.80	
Carer's premium	27.15	
Disability premium (couple rate)	36.00	
Enhanced disability premium (couple rate)	17.75	
Applicable amount		173.70
Step 2: calculate income from all sources		
Long-term incapacity benefit	81.35	
Age-related addition (lower rate)	8.55	
Carer's allowance	48.65	
Income		138.55
Step 3: calculate amount of benefit payable		
Applicable amount less		173.70
Income		138.55
Benefit payable		35.15

8.8 Change of circumstances and reviews

A claimant must report any material change in his circumstances that might affect his entitlement to, or the amount of, his benefit. Any failure to report may lead to an overpayment (see **7.11**). A decision-maker considers the facts and makes a new decision on the claim – this is known as 'supersession' (see **1.4.3.3**). Provided the report was made within one month of the change in circumstances, the new decision takes effect from the payment week in which the change occurred.

8.9 The passport effect

8.9.1 What is the passport effect?

Both IS and IBJSA provide a basic subsistence-level income. A person whose income is at this level has no spare income left over to pay for anything other than the basic necessities of life.

We shall see at **9.16** that there are a number of means-tested benefits outside the social security system, for which people on low incomes qualify. These include free prescriptions, eye tests and dental treatment. Entitlement to public funding is also dependent upon resources. Most people have to undergo a means test in order to ascertain their entitlement to these extra benefits, but a person who is in receipt of IS or IBJSA will be able to claim many of them without further means testing. These benefits are called 'passport benefits' because the entitlement to IS or IBJSA is an automatic passport to them.

One benefit is available only to families in receipt of IS or IBJSA. That is the right to free school meals. For a family struggling to bring up several children on a very low income, free school meals can be of great value.

8.9.2 Rent and council tax

The housing costs which can be paid as part of IS or IBJSA are limited to the interest on qualifying loans and leaseholders' service charges and ground rents.

Tenants must rely on housing benefit to cover the cost of their rent, and all householders must pay council tax or receive council tax benefit.

In **Chapter 9**, we shall look at the means test for these two benefits, which is more generous than the IS/IBJSA means test. This means that a person who qualifies for IS or IBJSA will automatically qualify for the maximum amount of housing benefit or council tax benefit that could be paid, subject only to deductions for non-dependants. All the local authority needs is a certificate from the DfWP or the Jobcentre that the claimant is receiving one of these benefits, and he will immediately be awarded the maximum amount of housing benefit or council tax benefit.

8.10 Hardship payments and urgent cases payments

8.10.1 What are hardship and urgent cases payments?

A person who is not entitled to IS or IBJSA under the normal rules may be able to make a successful claim under either the hardship or the urgent cases rules, if they have no other means of support.

The test is more realistic than the standard means test. Tariff income is ignored, as are some forms of income which the claimant may be treated as possessing, even though he does not. For both IS and IBJSA, the claimant is usually treated as receiving income which is due to him, even though he may never receive it. This does not apply to payments due from an employer on redundancy. For hardship payments and urgent cases, only resources actually available to the claimant go into the calculation.

8.11 Hardship payments (JA Regs 1996, regs 140–146)

Your client is unemployed and has made a claim for jobseeker's allowance, but has not received it yet, or it has been stopped. He has no income and he and his family have nothing to live on. What is he to do?

8.11.1 Who may claim hardship payments?

He may be able to make an immediate claim for hardship payments, but only if his failure to receive benefit is for one of the following reasons.

(a) He has not signed a jobseeker's agreement (see **3.2.3**), or the Secretary of State has decided the agreement is not valid.

(b) There is a problem with the labour market conditions (see **3.2.5** to **3.2.8**): either the Secretary of State has not yet decided whether the claimant satisfies them, or has decided that he does not, or has suspended payment of benefit because the matter is in doubt.

(c) He has been sanctioned (see **3.3.5**).

If the failure is for some other reason, such as disputes about his capital, his partner's working hours or whether he is involved in industrial action, there is no right to claim hardship payments.

No hardship payment can be made if the claimant's partner would be entitled to claim IS, because of age or incapacity.

8.11.2 Assessment of hardship

When the claimant has applied for hardship payments, the Secretary of State will decide whether he and his family will be in hardship if no payment is made. The following factors must be taken into account:

(a) whether any member of the family is sick or disabled;

(b) all actual resources available to the family; and

(c) whether there is a substantial risk that the family will be without essentials, such as food, clothes, heating and accommodation, if no payment is made.

This list is not exhaustive.

8.11.3 Effect of being in a 'vulnerable group'

If the claimant is in a vulnerable group, he will be able to receive hardship payments immediately. Those who are not in a vulnerable group will have to wait two weeks for any payment. The claimant is in a vulnerable group if:

(a) his family includes a qualifying child or a sick or disabled member, and that family member (not the claimant) would suffer hardship if no payment was made; or

(b) the claimant or his partner is a carer and could not go on caring without a payment.

The amount of a hardship payment is calculated in the normal way, but the applicable amount is reduced by 40% of the single person's allowance, or 20% if any member of the family is pregnant or seriously ill.

8.12 Urgent cases payments

8.12.1 Eligibility

Urgent cases payment may be paid as part of income support (IS Regs 1987, reg 70) or IBJSA (JA Regs 1996, regs 146 and 147). They are most likely to be paid to people who have been admitted to the UK with a condition against resorting to public funds (see **10.3.1**). Members of this group are allowed to claim if a source of income on which they were relying has temporarily ceased.

Similarly, a British resident may be debarred from claiming benefit under the normal rules because he is treated as having income that he does not in fact have, such as rent from a tenant. In these circumstances, he may be able to claim urgent cases payments.

8.12.2 Calculation of benefit

Urgent cases payments are more generous than hardship payments. Although some forms of capital disregard applicable to standard IS or IBJSA are not available, the usual capital limits still apply. The applicable amount is reduced by 10% of the personal allowance for the claimant himself if he is single, or 10% of the couple allowance if he has a partner.

8.13 Passporting

Hardship payments are part of IBJSA and urgent cases payments are part of IS or IBJSA as appropriate. All the consequences described at **8.9** therefore apply just as if the claimant was receiving the standard benefit.

8.14 IS/IBJSA and other benefits

Working tax credit counts as income when calculating either of these benefits (see 9.6). Child tax credit is ignored.

A person entitled to either of these benefits is immediately entitled to the maximum amount of housing benefit and council tax benefit that can be paid (see **Chapter 9**).

As to which non-means tested benefits are ignored or taken into account when calculating either of these benefits see **7.3.5**.

8.15 Claimant profiles

8.15.1 Income-based JSA

This is payable to a person capable of and available for work but who is not in remunerative work. The claimant must sign a jobseeker's agreement and have a low income with a limited amount of capital.

8.15.2 Income support

This is payable to a person who does not have to be available for work, who is not in remunerative work and who has a limited amount of capital.

Chapter 9
Other Means-Tested Benefits

9.1	The scope of this chapter	133
9.2	Local authority benefits: common features	134
9.3	Housing benefit	136
9.4	Council tax benefit	139
9.5	Worked examples	141
9.6	The tax credits	143
9.7	Common features of the two tax credits	143
9.8	Conditions of entitlement for child tax credit	146
9.9	Calculating child tax credit: a summary of the steps	148
9.10	Conditions of entitlement for working tax credit	148
9.11	Tapering when entitled to both credits	156
9.12	Calculating working tax credit: a summary of the steps	157
9.13	Tax credits: worked examples	157
9.14	The tax credits and other benefits	160
9.15	Payment of tax credits	160
9.16	The social fund	160
9.17	Passport benefits	163
9.18	Claimant profiles	165

9.1 The scope of this chapter

In this chapter, we are mainly concerned with the means-tested benefits, except for IS and IBJSA which were covered in **Chapter 8**. These are:

(a) the local authority benefits, housing benefit (HB) and council tax benefit (CTB);

(b) working tax credit and child tax credit;

(c) the social fund; and

(d) passport benefits.

9.1.1 Local authority benefits

There are two local authority-administered benefits, HB and CTB. Housing benefit covers those housing costs which are irrelevant to IS and IBJSA, ie a tenant's rent and a licensee's licence fees in all their variety; CTB is to help with paying council tax.

9.1.2 The tax credits

Working tax credits and child tax credits were introduced in April 2003 following the Tax Credits Act 2002. The Government said that the tax credits were to

> separate support for adults in a family from support for the children, and for the first time integrate all income-related support for children, to provide a clearer focus on the two aims of: supporting families and tackling poverty through the Child Tax Credit and making work pay through the Working Tax Credit. The Child Tax Credit will create a single, seamless support system for families with children, irrespective of the work status of the adults in the household ... The Working Tax Credit will tackle poor work incentives and persistent poverty among working people.

(See the Treasury paper, *The Child and Working Tax Credits: The Modernisation of Britain's Tax and Benefits System, Number Ten*.)

9.1.3 Other means-tested benefits

We shall conclude the chapter by looking briefly at the social fund, which makes means-tested grants and loans for various purposes, and at the National Health Service benefits, which may be provided free or at very low cost to people on low incomes.

9.2 Local authority benefits: common features

9.2.1 Administration

The two local authority benefits have many features in common, not least that they are administered at local level by the local housing authority: district or borough council, unitary authority, or London borough.

9.2.2 Non-dependants

If the claimant has a non-dependant sharing his accommodation, this may affect his entitlement to both benefits. The figures used differ for the two benefits: HB uses the same deductions as IS/IBJSA, but the deductions for CTB are lower because the weekly amount of council tax is itself much lower.

For both benefits, any non-dependant deduction that is to be made occurs when calculating the maximum benefit. However, no non-dependant deduction is made in the following circumstances:

(a) if the claimant or any partner is registered blind or receives AA, CAA for IDB purposes or the care component of DLA (at any rate of pay);

(b) if the non-dependant is any of the following: a full-time student during his period of study (or the summer vacation, unless he is in full-time work); a person under 18; or a person under 25 receiving IS or IBJSA. Note that, for CTB purposes only, no non-dependant deduction is made if:

  (i) the non-dependant is a full-time student even if he is in full-time work during the summer vacation; or

  (ii) the non-dependant is aged 25 or over but in receipt of IS or IBJSA.

9.2.3 Income

The calculation of the claimant's income is identical for the two benefits. See **Chapter 7** for a reminder of the basic means test, and the special rules for these two benefits. The major differences from the income calculation for IS/IBJSA are:

(a) earnings disregards tend to be higher;

(b) there is a disregard for the first £15 of maintenance;

(c) the treatment of maternity benefits and SSP is more generous;

(d) there is an earnings disregard for the costs of qualifying childcare. The qualifying conditions are:

  (i) the claimant must be either:

   (A) a lone parent; or

   (B) a member of a couple where both work at least 16 hours a week or one of them works at least 16 hours a week and the other is either (1) 'incapacitated', ie in receipt of any of the following benefits: the higher rate of short-term ICB or long-term rate ICB; AA; DLA (either component at any rate of pay); HB or CTB that includes a disability premium or higher pensioner premium based on disability; HB or CTB that includes a disregard for childcare costs; or (2) a hospital in-patient; or (3) in prison;

and

(ii) the care must be provided for a child in the claimant's benefits household who is under the qualifying age, ie from birth up to but not including the first Monday in September that follows the child's fifteenth birthday (or sixteenth birthday if the child receives DLA (either component at any rate of pay) or is registered blind);

and

(iii) each child of qualifying age must be receiving 'relevant childcare', ie care provided by any of the following: a registered childminder in the childminder's home; a registered childcare provider such as a nursery, playscheme or after school club; an out of hours club on school premises run by a school or local authority.

If the claimant qualifies, the childcare costs will be disregarded from his and any partner's earnings up to a prescribed maximum amount. In 2006/07 this was £175 for one child of qualifying age receiving relevant childcare and £300 for two or more qualifying children each receiving relevant childcare.

Examples

Bruce pays £160 a week for his four-year-old daughter to attend a nursery. As that does not exceed the prescribed maximum of £175, the whole £160 will be disregarded from his and any partner's earnings.

Claire pays £385 a week in total for her three qualifying children who each receive relevant childcare. The amount exceeds the maximum of £300 and so Claire is limited to that, namely £300 will be disregarded from her and any partner's earnings.

Note that special rules apply to recipients of the pension credit (see generally **5.3**) where the claimant or any partner is aged 60 or over and not claiming IS or IBJSA. In outline these mean that, if the guarantee credit element is being paid, then all income is ignored. However, where only the savings credit element is being paid, then income for the purposes of HB and CTB is the income figure used by the DfWP to assess the pension credit plus the amount of the savings credit element, any child benefit, any child tax credit and any partner's income not taken into account for the pension credit.

9.2.4 Applicable amount

The applicable amount is calculated using allowances and premiums (see **Chapter 7**).

9.2.5 Tapering

For all the means-tested benefits, the final stage of the means test involves a comparison between the claimant's income and his applicable amount. For all except IS and IBJSA, the calculation also involves a third figure, the 'maximum benefit'. For HB, the maximum benefit is the 'allowable rent' (see **9.3.2.5**); and for CTB it is the amount of council tax payable (see **9.4.4**), subject to any deduction for non-dependants.

If the claimant's income does not exceed his applicable amount, he will receive the maximum benefit. If the income does exceed the applicable amount, the maximum benefit is reduced by a fixed percentage of the excess income. This process is called 'tapering', and we shall meet it again when we consider tax credits. For HB the percentage used for tapering is 65%, and it is 20% for CTB.

9.2.6 Claimants receiving IS or IBJSA or the guarantee credit element of pension credit

For both benefits, there is no need to carry out a full means test calculation if the claimant is in receipt of IS or IBJSA or the guarantee credit element of pension credit. He will automatically receive the maximum amount of benefit, subject to any non-dependant deduction(s).

9.3 Housing benefit

9.3.1 Who is entitled to housing benefit?

Housing benefit may be paid to a person who has a legal liability to pay rent for the place where he lives (ie his 'dwelling') (SSCBA 1992, s 130). The term 'dwelling' includes caravans, mobile homes and crofts and any land for which the occupier must pay rent so that he may occupy the dwelling. The mooring fees for houseboats will be eligible under the same conditions.

To be eligible for HB, the claimant (or any partner) must be liable to pay the rent for accommodation that is normally occupied as a home. The term 'rent' is used loosely to cover:

(a) rent paid by private tenants of residential property to their landlords;

(b) rent paid by local authority tenants to the local authority;

(c) licence fees paid by boarders and lodgers to the person in whose household they live (see **7.4.8** and **7.4.9**);

(d) service charges paid by tenants to private landlords or local authorities for such things as cleaning and maintaining common parts of the building;

(e) charges for hostels and bed-and-breakfast accommodation.

It does not include:

(a) ground rent or service charges for people with long leases. These may be paid as part of IS or IBJSA (see **8.3**);

(b) payments made under an informal arrangement by a non-dependant (see **7.4.7**);

(c) payments for anything other than the accommodation itself – food, heating, lighting, hot water and so on (see **9.3.2**).

To be eligible for HB, the claimant must be liable to pay the rent for accommodation that is normally occupied as a home or any partner must be so liable. If a couple is jointly liable for rent, only one can claim. 'Liable', in this context, means an agreement that is legally enforceable. In certain limited circumstances, a person who is not legally liable to pay rent is treated as liable to pay it for HB purposes (eg the claimant's former partner is liable to make the payments on the dwelling but is not doing so, and the claimant is paying the rent in order to remain living in that property as a home).

An agreement that is not on a commercial basis does not give rise to a liability to pay rent. So, for example, an adult child who continues to live with his parents whilst in full-time work is not their tenant or lodger but for benefit purposes is treated as their non-dependant (see **7.4.7**).

9.3.2 Restrictions on amount of housing benefit

Some tenants may find that their entitlement to HB is 'capped' in one of four ways. For the first three, the capping applies to tenants of private landlords and does not apply to local authority tenants, or those who rent from housing associations. Housing associations provide low-cost housing, often in association with local authorities. Some of them specialise in housing particular vulnerable groups such as the elderly or single homeless people with psychiatric disorders. The rents of both housing associations and local authorities are much lower than private sector rents.

9.3.2.1 People under 25

A single person under the age of 25 can normally only receive as a maximum the average local cost of shared accommodation. This could be a shared flat or house, or a bedsitter. This limitation does not apply to single parents, the disabled, or anyone who is particularly vulnerable for any reason.

9.3.2.2 Relevant rent

The 'relevant rent' is the rent which is appropriate for the housing needs of the claimant's family. If the rented property is bigger or more expensive than the claimant needs, the rent will be capped accordingly.

9.3.2.3 Reference rent

The reference rent is the average local rent for properties of the type in which the claimant is living. This produces a cap on the rent if it is high in comparison with similar property in the area.

When considering a claim for HB, the local authority rent officer must determine whether the rent is reasonable with respect to the type of property being rented and the claimant's needs. The requirements of a family are prescribed under the Rent Officers (Housing Benefit Functions) Order 1997 (SI 1997/1984), which allows one bedroom or a room suitable for living in for each of the following categories:

(a) a married or unmarried couple;
(b) a person who is not a child;
(c) two children of the same sex;
(d) two children under 10 (regardless of sex);
(e) one child alone.

The number of rooms suitable for living in allowed, in addition to bedrooms, in a property is:

(a) one room, if there are less than four people;
(b) two rooms, if there are more than three and less than seven people;
(c) three, in any other case.

The amount of rent payable will then be compared with the 'local reference rent'. The local reference rent or, where young people are concerned, the so-called single room rent (see above), is the mean between the highest and lowest rent that the local authority has deemed to be reasonable in respect of comparable accommodation in their area. The maximum rent that may be claimed is generally capped at this level.

9.3.2.4 Eligible rent

This is the only restriction that applies to all tenants. The 'eligible rent' is that part of the contractual payment which covers the housing element and includes most service charges. However, Sch 1 to the HB Regs 2006 provides that the following service charges are ineligible, namely those that are in respect of day-to-day living expenses including, in particular, all provision of meals (including the preparation of meals or provision of unprepared food); laundry (other than the provision of premises or equipment to enable a person to do his own laundry); leisure items, such as either sports facilities (except a children's play area), or television rental, television subscription charges and licence fees; cleaning of rooms and windows (except the exterior of any windows in accommodation where neither the claimant nor any member of his household is able to clean those windows himself) and in communal areas; and transport. Also excluded are charges in respect of the acquisition of furniture or household equipment, the use of such furniture or equipment where that furniture or household equipment will become the property of the claimant by virtue of an agreement with the landlord, charges in respect of the provision of an emergency alarm system.

Where a charge for meals is ineligible to be met by housing benefit, the amount that is ineligible in respect of each week is that specified in the HB Regs 2006 and not the claimant's tenancy agreement. As to any other ineligible service charge, such as fuel costs, if this is not separated from or separately identified within other payments made by the claimant under his tenancy agreement, the local authority 'apportion such charge as is fairly attributable to the provision of that service having regard to the cost of comparable services' (Sch 1).

If the local authority considers that the amount of any ineligible service charge which is separately identified within other payments made by the occupier in respect of the dwelling is unreasonably low having regard to the service provided, it will substitute a sum for the charge in question which, it considers, represents the value of the services concerned and the amount so substituted is ineligible to be met by housing benefit. Further, if the local authority considers that the amount of an eligible service charge is excessive in relation to the service provided for the claimant or his family, having regard to the cost of comparable services, it will deduct from that charge the excess and the amount so deducted is ineligible to be met by housing benefit.

9.3.2.5 Allowable rent

The lowest of the claimant's relevant rent, reference rent and eligible rent is his 'allowable rent', the figure that represents his maximum benefit in the means test calculation after any non-dependant deductions (see **9.2.2**).

9.3.2.6 Local housing allowance (LHA)

From April 2009 (but in some areas before that) housing benefit for tenants of private landlords will be calculated and paid by local authorities under a new scheme known as LHA, which will be based on local rents. For more details see www.dwp.gov.uk/lifeevent/benefits/lha.asp.

9.3.3 Administration and payment

The claimant must claim his benefit from the local authority in the area where he lives. The local authority is under a duty to process the claim within 14 days. If there is going to be a delay in processing the claim, the local authority must make interim payments of benefit to avoid the risk that the landlord will try to repossess the claimant's home.

If the landlord is the local authority itself, no actual payments of benefit are made. The benefit takes effect as a rebate, a reduction of the amount of rent which is payable. If the landlord is a housing association or private landlord, the rent is usually paid direct to avoid possible misuse by the claimant.

Worked examples of HB calculations are given at **9.5**.

9.3.4 Calculating the benefit

There are four steps to be taken when calculating HB.

Step 1: work out the maximum housing benefit that the claimant is entitled to (ie the allowable rent less any non-dependant deduction(s)). If the claimant is receiving IS or IBJSA or the guarantee credit element of pension credit, no further calculation is necessary.

Step 2: calculate the claimant's applicable amount (ie aggregate the allowances and any premiums to which he is entitled for his benefits household).

Step 3: calculate the claimant's income for the purposes of HB from all relevant sources.

Step 4: determine whether the claimant is entitled to HB and, if so, how much. Do this by comparing the income and the applicable amount. If the income is the same or less than the applicable amount, then the maximum HB calculated at Step 1 is payable. If the income is more than the applicable amount, then the maximum HB is tapered downwards (ie 65% of the income that exceeds the applicable amount is deducted from the maximum HB and the resulting figure is the claimant's entitlement).

9.4 Council tax benefit

9.4.1 Who is eligible for council tax benefit?

Council tax is a local tax paid by most residents to their local authority for such local services as rubbish collection, street lighting, leisure facilities, education, social services and policing. Council tax is paid once per household, the amount varying according to the area in which the householder resides and the value of the property in which he lives. Properties were 'banded' on a national basis in 1992 according to their value at that date. It does not matter if house values have increased or decreased since that date, the house remains in the same Band, although there are limited rights of appeal for new owners of property. The Bands range from A to H. Properties in Band A have the lowest value at below £40,000, whilst properties in Band H have the highest in value at over £320,000. Using its annual budget as a basis, the local authority determines the amount of tax to be paid by the householders in each Band.

To be eligible for CTB, the claimant must be liable to pay the tax on a property which is his sole or main residence: see *Parry v Derbyshire Dales District Council* [2006] EWHC 988 (Admin). Unlike HB, it does not have to be a property normally occupied as a home (see **9.3.1**).

9.4.2 Exempt persons

Some occupiers of residential property are not liable to pay council tax. The most important groups are:

(a) full-time students and some trainees, including anyone under 20 in non-advanced education;

(b) people who do not live in their own accommodation: boarders and lodgers, people in residential care.

9.4.3 Special categories

If the householder is a single occupier or a lone parent, he pays only 75% of the normal amount of tax for the valuation band. If there are two or more non-exempt occupiers (see above), they will pay 100% of the normal tax. A house which has been specially adapted for the needs of a disabled person is placed in the valuation Band below the one into which it would otherwise fall.

9.4.4 The amount of benefit

The administration and payment of the benefit are similar to HB (see **9.3.3**).

Council tax benefit has two forms. The first is calculated in the same way as HB, using allowances and premiums, and the maximum benefit figure subject to any non-dependant deductions, all based on the claimant's personal circumstances. The second form is the 'second adult rebate', which is peculiar in that the claimant's financial circumstances are totally irrelevant to the calculation.

Second adult rebate is an alternative to standard CTB. It may be claimed by a single person who has living in his household a non-dependant on a low income. A non-dependant who is not exempt (ie not a full-time student, in practice) would be expected to contribute to the claimant's liability to pay council tax. The householder is not entitled to the single occupier discount if he has a non-dependant living with him who is not exempt.

The second adult rebate is calculated on the income of the non-dependant. The claimant's capital and income are totally irrelevant. The maximum rebate is 25%, which produces the same tax liability as the single occupier discount. There are smaller rebates for non-dependants with higher incomes.

Some householders who qualify for CTB under the normal rules are better off on second adult rebate. Local authorities must always carry out comparative calculations and award whichever is the more advantageous.

9.4.5 Calculating the benefit

There are five steps to be taken when calculating CTB.

Step 1: calculate the maximum CTB, having regard to the single occupier rate and any non-dependant deduction(s), if appropriate. If the claimant is in receipt of IS, or IBJSA or the guarantee credit element of pension credit, he will be entitled to this maximum and no further calculation needs be done.

Step 2: calculate the applicable amount which is made up of the personal allowances and any premiums to which the claimant is entitled for his benefits household.

Step 3: calculate the claimant's income for CTB purposes from all sources.

Step 4: determine whether the claimant is entitled to CTB and, if so, how much. Do this by comparing the income and the applicable amount. If the income is the same or less than the applicable amount, then the maximum CTB calculated at Step 1 is payable. If the income is more than the applicable amount, then the maximum CTB is tapered downward by 20% of the income that exceeds the applicable amount. The resulting figure is the claimant's entitlement.

Step 5: there is, however, a further step to be taken if the claimant is entitled to the second adult rebate. A comparison should be made between the CTB entitlement calculated under the above four Steps and the council tax payable if the second adult rebate is applicable.

9.5 Worked examples

9.5.1 Introduction

We shall now look at two short case studies, which illustrate the calculation of the local authority benefits. These examples are worked using the benefit rates in force for the period 6 April 2006 to 5 April 2007.

Before presenting each calculation, we shall analyse the key facts of each case study.

9.5.2 Tapering

9.5.2.1 Facts

James had a car crash two years ago when he was 48 years of age. He receives long-term incapacity benefit, DLA care component at the middle rate and DLA mobility component at the lower rate. His partner, Eileen, aged 47, gave up work and looks after him. She receives carer's allowance. They have savings of £14,000. They live in a housing association flat for which they pay £75 per week. How much HB should they be receiving?

9.5.2.2 Analysis

Step 1: calculate maximum HB

Their allowable rent is the full rent they pay. It is a housing association flat, so the restrictions do not apply, and there is no indication that they are paying for anything except housing and probably service charges. They have no non-dependants living in their flat with them.

Step 2: calculate applicable amount

Their applicable amount is:

(a) allowance at the standard rate for a couple over 18;
(b) the carer's premium is payable as Eileen receives carer's allowance;
(c) the disability premium is payable as James receives DLA and as he has a partner it is paid at the couple rate.

Step 3: calculate income from all sources

James and Eileen's income from all sources is:

(a) Eileen's carer's allowance;
(b) James's long-term incapacity benefit;
(c) tariff income on £8,000 (ie after ignoring £6,000) at the rate of £1 for every £250 or part;
(d) James's DLA is ignored.

The calculation

£   £

Step 1: calculate maximum housing benefit
    Allowable rent   75.00

Step 2: calculate applicable amount

Couple allowance	92.80	
Disability premium (couple rate)	36.00	
Carer's premium	27.15	155.95

Step 3: calculate income from all sources

James's ICB	81.35	
Eileen's CA	48.65	
Tariff income	32.00	162.00

Income (£162.00) exceeds applicable amount (£155.95) by £6.05, so maximum benefit is not payable

Maximum benefit	75.00	
less 65% of excess (£6.05)	3.93	
Benefit payable		71.07

9.5.3 Non-dependant in house: claimant in receipt of IBJSA

9.5.3.1 Facts

Chris (aged 35) is unemployed and claiming IBJSA. He lives in a three-bedroomed local authority house with his wife, Karen (aged 30). Their rent is £95 per week. The house is in Band D for council tax purposes, which in their area is £658 per year. Karen's younger sister Martina lives with them. Martina is 22 and works as a waitress, earning £180 gross per week.

How much HB and CTB will they receive?

9.5.3.2 Analysis

(a) Because Chris is in receipt of IBJSA, we know that he will automatically receive the maximum amount of HB and CTB, subject only to any restrictions and the effect of any non-dependants in the household. We do not therefore need to know anything about his resources and do not need to work out his applicable amount.

(b) The house is a council house, so there will be no capping of the amount payable. It is unlikely that the payment covers anything except accommodation, so the eligible and allowable rents are the same as the actual rent. Also, the benefit will be a rebate, not an actual payment.

(c) Both Chris and Karen are liable to pay council tax, so there is no single householder discount and no possibility of second adult rebate.

(d) Martina is a non-dependant who has earnings which will affect both benefits.

The calculation

	£	£
Housing benefit		
Maximum benefit = allowable rent	95.00	
Non-dependant deduction (earnings £180 pw)	23.35	
Rent rebate		71.65
Council tax benefit		
Maximum benefit = £658 ÷ 52	12.66	
Non-dependant (as above)	4.60	
Council tax rebate		8.06

The effect of this is that Chris and Karen will actually have to pay to the local authority each week a total of the two deductions for Martina, ie £27.95. They can reasonably expect her to contribute at least as much as this each week, in addition to paying a fair share of the grocery and fuel bills.

9.6 The tax credits

9.6.1 What are the tax credits?

As we saw at **9.1.2**, the aim of the child tax credit is to encompass all income-related support for children and the goal of the working tax credit is to make work pay. So how are these ideals to be achieved? First, child tax credit now contains all the premiums relating to children that used to be claimable with IS or IBJSA (and indeed remain part of a HB or CTB calculation where the benefits household includes at least one qualifying child). Claimants who receive IS or IBJSA automatically receive the maximum amount of child tax credit. The only other child-centred benefit is, of course, child benefit (see **6.6**). Secondly, tax credits are subject to an income only test. There is no upper capital limit. Finally, the category of potential claimants for working tax credit is far wider than any earlier version of this benefit.

Although called credits, these tax credits are 'payable' so that claimants receive them even if they have no income tax or National Insurance contributions to pay.

9.7 Common features of the two tax credits

9.7.1 Age

The claimant must be aged 16 or over or, if under 16, have a partner who least 16.

There is no maximum age.

9.7.2 Immigration requirements

The claimant must not be subject to immigration control and must meet residence requirements (see **Chapter 10**).

9.7.3 Income: an overview

To qualify for either tax credit the claimant and any partner must have a sufficiently low annual income. It is based over a full tax year from 6 April to 5 April. The income of a child or qualifying young person is ignored. If the claimant was part of a couple in the previous tax year but is now single or a lone parent, only the claimant's income counts. So what counts as income? At the start of a claim, it is calculated by reference to income for the previous tax year. For claims for later tax years the award is based initially on income from the previous tax year.

Regulation 3 of the Tax Credits (Definition and Calculation of Income) Regulations 2002 (SI 2002/2006) states that

> the manner in which income of a claimant or, in the case of a joint claim, the aggregate income of the claimants, is to be calculated for a tax year for the purposes of the [2002] Act is as follows.
> *Step One:* calculate and then add together—
> (a) the pension income (as defined in regulation 5(1)),
> (b) the investment income (as defined in regulation 10),
> (c) the property income (as defined in regulation 11),

(d) the foreign income (as defined in regulation 12) and
(e) the notional income (as defined in regulation 13)
of the claimant, or, in the case of a joint claim, of the claimants.

If the result of this step is £300 or less, it is treated as nil. If the result of this step is more than £300, only the excess is taken into account in the following steps.

Step Two: calculate and then add together—
(a) the employment income (as defined in regulation 4),
(b) the social security income (as defined in regulation 7),
(c) the student income (as defined in regulation 8) and
(d) the miscellaneous income (as defined in regulation 18)
of the claimant, or in the case of a joint claim, of the claimants.

Step Three

Add together the results of Steps One and Two.

Step Four

Calculate the trading income (as defined in regulation 6) of the claimant, or in the case of a joint claim, of the claimants.

Add the result of this step to that produced by Step Three, unless there has been a trading loss in the year.

If there has been a trading loss in the year, subtract the amount of that loss from the result of Step Three.

Subject to certain qualifications, the result of Step Four is the income of the claimant, or, in the case of a joint claim, of the claimants, for the purposes of the Act.

9.7.4 Income: the detail

We have set out below some examples of the most common type of income that is taken into account.

9.7.4.1 Pension income

This includes State Pension (see **5.2.1**), any adult dependant increase (see **2.4**), any additional State Pension (see **5.2.3**), personal and occupational pensions, and widowed parent's allowance (see **5.4.3**).

9.7.4.2 Investment income

This includes, before tax is deducted, any interest on money invested (eg in a bank or building society), dividends from UK company shares and income from government stocks and bonds.

9.7.4.3 Property income

This basically means rental income after the expenses incurred in running the property (eg repairs). However, if the claimant rents out property as a business that should be included as income from self-employment (see **9.7.4.5**). Note that where the claimant rents out a furnished room in his own home to a boarder or subtenant then up to £4,250 of the annual rent is exempt from tax. Anything above that figure will count.

9.7.4.4 Notional income

The rules are very similar to those relating to notional capital for the four means-tested benefits (see **7.2.1.3**). So if a claimant has deprived himself of income for the purpose of securing entitlement to, or increasing the amount of, a tax credit, he is treated as having that income. Equally, if income would become available to a claimant upon the making of an application for that income he is treated as having that income.

9.7.4.5 Employment income

The gross earnings of an employee count, including any bonuses, overtime etc. However, any contributions made to a personal or occupational pension approved by HMRC can be deducted.

Any statutory sick pay (see **4.3**) that is paid is included. Only statutory maternity pay (see **6.3**) exceeding £100 counts.

9.7.4.6 Social security income

The following benefits count:

(a)   bereavement allowance (see **5.4.4**);
(b)   carer's allowance (see **6.7**);
(c)   contribution-based JSA (see **3.4**);
(d)   short-term higher rate incapacity benefit and long-term rate incapacity benefit (see **4.4.2.1** and **4.4.2.2**); and
(e)   any increase (see **2.4**) paid for an adult dependant with any of these.

The following benefits do not count:

(a)   attendance allowance (see **4.9**);
(b)   bereavement payment (see **5.4.5**);
(c)   child benefit (see **6.6**);
(d)   council tax benefit (see **9.4**);
(e)   disability living allowance (see **4.6**);
(f)   housing benefit (see **9.3**);
(g)   income support (see **8.2**);
(h)   income-based JSA (see **8.2**);
(i)   industrial disablement benefit (see **4.10**);
(j)   maternity allowance (see **6.4**);
(k)   short-term lower rate incapacity benefit (see **4.4.2.1**);
(l)   social fund payment (see **9.16**); and
(m)   any adult dependant increase (see **2.4**) that may be payable with any of these.

Note that widowed parent's allowance is treated as pension income (see **9.7.4.1**).

9.7.4.7 Trading income

This is the taxable profit made by a self-employed person from a trade, profession or vocation. If the claimant is a partner in a business it is the taxable profits from his share that counts.

9.7.5 Income: an example

9.7.5.1 Facts

Ivan and Lucy claim tax credits in April 2008. HMRC assesses their claim based on their joint income for the previous tax year 6 April 2007 to 5 April 2008. For that tax year, Ivan was employed and earned £25,950 gross (after taking into account contributions to an approved occupational pension deducted by his employer).

Lucy received an occupational pension of £750, disability living allowance care component at the lowest rate, industrial disablement benefit (at 30%) and long-term incapacity benefit including the lower rate age addition of £4,674.80. They received gross dividends on their UK company shareholdings of £360.

9.7.5.2 Analysis

Following the five stages outlined at **9.7.3**, their annual income is:

Step One: calculate and then add together:

(a) the pension income, namely Lucy's occupational pension of £750;

(b) the investment income, namely the dividends on the shares: £360.

As the result of this step is more than £300, only the excess of £810 is taken into account in the following steps.

Step Two: calculate and then add together—

(a) the employment income, namely Ivan's earnings of £25,950;

(b) the social security income, namely Lucy's long-term incapacity benefit of £4,674.80 (her disability living allowance and industrial disablement benefit do not count).

The total for this step is £30,624.80

Step Three

Add together the results of Steps One and Two, ie £810 + £30,624.80 = £31,434.80.

Step Four

Neither had a trading income.

So £31,434.80 is the income of Ivan and Lucy for the purposes of the 2002 Act.

9.7.6 Notifying changes in income

Increases in income of £25,000 or less between the current tax year and the previous tax year do not affect an award and there is no need to tell HMRC. Larger increases, or decreases of any size, affect an award and it is best to notify HMRC immediately so the credit(s) can be recalculated and the risk of an overpayment or underpayment minimised.

At the end of the tax year, HMRC finalises the assessment.

9.7.7 Entitlement over a tax year

Tax credits are calculated by reference to a maximum annual amount. So if a claim is made at the beginning of a tax year, the award is made for a whole year. Otherwise, only the appropriate proportion of the annual award is payable. A formula for calculating the latter can be found in the Tax Credits (Income Thresholds and Determination of Rates) Regulations 2002 (SI 2002/2008).

9.8 Conditions of entitlement for child tax credit

To qualify for child tax credit the claimant must:

(a) be aged 16 or over (or if under 16 have a partner aged at least 16);

(b) be responsible for at least one dependent child or qualifying young person;

(c) have a sufficiently low income;

(d) not be subject to immigration control and meet residence requirements (see **Chapter 10**).

9.8.1 A child or qualifying young person

Section 8(1) of the Tax Credits Act 2002 provides that 'the entitlement of the person or persons by whom a claim for child tax credit has been made is dependent on him, or either or both of them, being responsible for one or more children or qualifying young persons'.

The definitions of a child and qualifying young person are exactly the same as under the Child Benefit (General) Regulations 2006 (see **6.6.2** and **6.6.3**).

9.8.2 Being responsible for the child or qualifying young person

The most common way of establishing responsibility is set out in reg 3 of the Child Tax Credit Reglations 2002 (SI 2002/2007), namely 'a person is treated as responsible for a child or qualifying young person who is normally living with him'. Whilst reg 3 describes this as the 'normally living with test' it does not set out how the test is to be met. Common sense suggests that this is describing a situation where the child lives with the claimant under the same roof. Should a child reside part of the week with one parent (or adult, say grandparent) and the rest with another adult, there are two potential conflicting claims which the parties must resolve, otherwise HMRC will.

9.8.3 The elements making up maximum child tax credit

The maximum rate at which a claimant may be entitled to child tax credit is the aggregate of:

(a) the family element of child tax credit; and
(b) an individual element of child tax credit, in respect of each child or qualifying young person.

All the figures that follow are for 2007/08.

The family element of child tax credit is made up as follows:

(a) in a case where any child is under the age of one year it is £1,090 a year; but
(b) in any other case it is £545.

Note that only one amount forms the family element. So a family that includes two children aged six months and three years of age gets £1,090, whilst a family that includes three children aged two, four and five years gets £545.

The individual element of child tax credit for any child or qualifying young person may be made up as follows:

(a) where the child or qualifying young person is disabled it is £4,285; or
(b) where the child or qualifying young person is severely disabled it is £5,265; or
(c) in the case of any other child or qualifying young person it is £1,845pa.

The disability element is payable for any child or qualifying young person who receives DLA (either component at any rate of pay: see **4.7** and **4.8**), or is registered blind.

The severe disability element is payable for any child or qualifying young person who receives the highest rate of DLA care component (see **4.7.3.3**).

9.8.4 Examples of maximum child tax credit

(1) Ann is a single parent. She has two children, Bob aged 6 months and Dan aged 5. She receives DLA care at the lowest rate for Dan. The annual elements used when calculating Ann's maximum child tax credit are:

Family element: £1,090
Child element for Bob: £1,845
Disabled Child element for Dan: £4,285

(2) Brenda and Mike have three children, Alice aged 13, Clive aged 15 and Derek aged 18. Derek is doing his 'A' levels at the local College (non-advanced education and he is a qualifying young person). The annual elements used when calculating their maximum child tax credit are:

Family element: £545
Child element for Alice: £1,845
Child element for Clive: £1,845
Child element for Derek: £1,845

9.8.5 Will the maximum child tax credit be paid?

If the claimant is entitled to IS or IBJSA, he will receive the maximum child tax credit consisting of the family and child elements as described at **9.8.3** and illustrated at **9.8.4**.

If the claimant is not receiving IS or IBJSA, his income (see **9.7.3**) must be compared with a prescribed figure called 'the income threshold' (TCA 2002, s 7(1)(a)). If the claimant is also entitled to working tax credit (see **9.10**), the annual threshold figure is £5,220. If the claimant is not entitled to working tax credit the figure is £14,495.

If the claimant's income is *the same as or less* than the income threshold, the maximum child tax credit is payable.

If the claimant's income is *more* than the income threshold, the maximum child tax credit is not payable. Instead, it will be tapered, that is reduced, by 37% of the excess income (see further **9.11**).

9.9 Calculating child tax credit: a summary of the steps

If the claimant is entitled to IS or IBJSA, he will receive the maximum child tax credit. This is made up of the family and child elements as described at **9.8.3** and illustrated at **9.8.4**.

If the claimant is not receiving IS or IBJSA, the following steps must be taken:

Step 1: calculate the maximum child tax credit

Step 2: calculate relevant income (see **9.7.3**).

Step 3: compare income with the annual threshold (see **9.8.5**).

Step 4: if the claimant's income is the same or less than the income threshold, the maximum child tax credit is payable.

If the claimant's income is more than the income threshold, the maximum child tax credit is not payable. Instead, it will be tapered, that is reduced, by 37% of the excess income. See the worked examples at **9.13**.

9.10 Conditions of entitlement for working tax credit

To qualify for working tax credit the claimant must:

(a) be aged 16 or over (or if under 16 have a partner aged at least 16);

(b) be in qualifying remunerative work;
(c) have a sufficiently low income;
(d) not be subject to immigration control and meet residence requirements (see **Chapter 10**).

9.10.1 Qualifying remunerative work

By reg 4 of the Working Tax Credit (Entitlement and Maximum Rate) Regulations 2002 (SI 2002/2005), a person must be treated as engaged in qualifying remunerative work if, but only if, he satisfies all of the following conditions.

9.10.1.1 First condition

The person:

(a) is working at the date of the claim; or
(b) has an offer of work which he has accepted at the date of the claim and the work is expected to commence within seven days of the making of the claim.

In relation to a case falling within (b), references in the second, third and fourth conditions (see **9.10.1.2**, **9.10.1.3** and **9.10.1.4**) to work which the person undertakes are to be construed as references to the work which the person will undertake when it commences. In such a case the person is only treated as being in qualifying remunerative work when he actually begins that work.

9.10.1.2 Second condition

The person:

(a) is aged at least 16 and undertakes work for not less than 16 hours per week if:
　(i) there is a child or qualifying young person for whom he or his partner is responsible (see **9.8.1**); or
　(ii) he has a physical or mental disability which puts him at a disadvantage in getting a job (see **9.10.2.1**); or
(b) satisfies the conditions in reg 18 ie is entitled to a 50-plus element (see **9.10.2.7**); or
(c) is aged at least 25 and undertakes not less than 30 hours work per week in any other case.

9.10.1.3 Third condition

The work which the person undertakes is expected to continue for at least four weeks after the making of the claim or, in a case falling within (b) of the first condition (see **9.10.1.1**), after the work starts.

9.10.1.4 Fourth condition

The work is done for payment or in expectation of payment.

The number of hours for which a person undertakes qualifying remunerative work is:

(a) in the case of an apprentice, employee or office-holder the number of hours of such work which he normally performs:
　(i) under the contract of service or of apprenticeship under which he is employed; or
　(ii) in the office in which he is employed;

(b) in the case of an agency worker, the number of hours in respect of which remuneration is normally paid to him by an employment agency with whom he has a contract of employment; or

(c) in the case of a person who is self-employed, the number of hours he normally performs for payment or in expectation of payment.

This is subject to the following qualification. In reckoning the number of hours of qualifying remunerative work which a person normally undertakes the following are disregarded:

(a) any period of customary or paid holiday; and

(b) any time allowed for meals or refreshment, unless the person is, or expects to be, paid earnings in respect of that time.

What about a claimant on maternity leave? For the purposes of the second and fourth conditions (see **9.10.1.2** and **9.10.1.4**) in reg 4(1) a woman is treated as engaged in qualifying remunerative work for the requisite number of hours during any period for which maternity allowance or statutory maternity pay is paid to her; if she was so engaged (under a contract of service or a contract for services) immediately before the time when that payment began.

What about a claimant on SSP? For the purposes of the second and third conditions (see **9.10.1.2** and **9.10.1.3**) in reg 4(1), a person is treated as engaged in qualifying remunerative work for the requisite number of hours during any period for which statutory sick pay is paid to him, if he was so engaged immediately before that payment began.

Note that a person who is self-employed is treated as engaged in qualifying remunerative work for the requisite number of hours during any period for which he would have been entitled to statutory sick pay but for the fact that the work he performed in the week immediately before the period began, although done for payment or in expectation of payment, was not performed under a contract of service.

9.10.2 The elements making up maximum working tax credit

If the claimant satisfies the conditions of entitlement (see **9.10**), he will be entitled to the basic element. It was £1,620 in 2005/06.

In addition, the following elements may be included if the qualifying conditions are met.

9.10.2.1 Disability element

By reg 9, the determination of the maximum rate must include the disability element, if any person in respect of whom the claim is made:

(a) undertakes qualifying remunerative work for at least 16 hours per week; and

(b) satisfies para (2); and

(c) has any of the disabilities listed in Pt 1 of Sch 1 (see **Appendix 4**).

A person satisfies para (2) in any of the Cases listed in reg 9. These include:

Case A

For at least one day in the 182 days immediately preceding the making of the claim the claimant, or, in the case of a joint claim, at least one of the claimants, must have been in receipt of the higher rate of short-term incapacity benefit or long-term incapacity benefit.

Case B

For at least one day in the 182 days immediately preceding the making of the claim the applicable amount for the claimant, or, in the case of a joint claim, at least one of the claimants, must have included as part of income support, income-based JSA, housing benefit or council tax benefit a higher pensioner or disability premium (see **7.7**).

Case C

At the date of the claim there is payable to the claimant, or in the case of a joint claim, to at least one of the claimants, disability living allowance (either component at any rate of pay) or attendance allowance (at any rate of pay).

Evidence of how the disability affects the claimant or co-claimant may be provided by his doctor, occupational therapist, community nurse or the like.

A claimant or co-claimant must meet conditions (a), (b) and (c) in his own right for a disability element to be payable. So, if both members of a couple satisfy conditions (a), (b) and (c) then two disability elements are payable. See *Commissioner's Decision CSTC/76/2006*.

Example 1

Alan works 20 hours a week (condition (a) met). He receives DLA care component at the lowest rate (condition (b) met). People who know him well have difficulty in understanding what he says (condition (c) met – see disability 13).

Example 2

Bryan works 16 hours a week and his civil partner, Clive, works 20 hours a week (each meet condition (a)). Bryan receives DLA care component at the middle rate and Clive receives DLA mobility component at the higer rate (each meets condition (b)). Bryan cannot, due to lack of manual dexterity, pick up with his left hand a coin of less than 2.5 cm, and Clive will lose his balance when standing unless he continually holds onto something (each meets condition (c) – see disabilities 6 and 1 respectively).

9.10.2.2 30-hour element

By reg 10, the determination of the maximum rate must include a 30-hour element if the claimant, or in the case of a joint claim, at least one of the claimants, is engaged in qualifying remunerative work for at least 30 hours per week.

The determination of the maximum rate must also include the 30-hour element if:

(a) the claim is a joint claim;
(b) at least one of the claimants is responsible for one or more children or qualifying young people (see **9.8.1**);
(c) the aggregate number of hours for which the couple engage in qualifying remunerative work is at least 30 hours per week; and
(d) at least one member of the couple engages in qualifying remunerative work for at least 16 hours per week.

Examples

(1) Bob, a single claimant, works full time 30 hours a week (qualifying remunerative work).
(2) Carol and Mike are joint claimants. Carol works 35 hours a week (qualifying remunerative work). Mike works part time for 10 hours (so on his own Mike would not qualify for this element).

152   Welfare Benefits and Immigration Law

(3) Debra and John are joint claimants. Their two children aged six and eight live with them (and so they are responsible for two children). Debra works 16 hours each week (qualifying remunerative work) and John works part time for 14 hours. Between them they work 30 hours a week and so qualify for the 30-hour element.

Note that in example (3), even if both Debra and John had each worked 30 hours or more a week they would still only receive one 30-hour element.

9.10.2.3 A second adult element

By reg 11, the determination of the maximum rate must include the second adult element if the claim is a joint claim unless:

(a) one of the claimants is aged 50 or over; and
(b) the 50-plus element is payable (see **9.10.2.7**); and
(c) neither of the claimants is engaged in qualifying remunerative work for at least 30 hours per week. However, this condition does not apply if at least one of the claimants is responsible for a child or a qualifying young person; or is entitled to the disability element (see **9.10.2.1**).

Examples
(1) Alice, aged 40 and her civil partner, Lucy aged 45, apply jointly.
(2) Claire, aged 51 and her partner, Dan aged 47, apply jointly. Claire is not entitled to the 50-plus element.
(3) Eileen, aged 46 and her partner, Fred, aged 50, apply jointly. Fred is entitled to the 50-plus element but the couple are responsible for their 13-year-old grandson who is living with them. Or, alternatively, assume Eileen was entitled to the disability element.

9.10.2.4 A lone parent element

By reg 12, the determination of the maximum rate must include the lone parent element if:

(a) the claim is a single claim; and
(b) the claimant is responsible for one or more children or qualifying young people (see **9.8.1**).

9.10.2.5 A child care element

By reg 13, the determination of the maximum rate must include a child care element where that person, or in the case of a joint claim at least one of those persons, is incurring relevant child care charges and:

(a) is a person, not being a member of a married or unmarried couple or civil partnership, engaged in remunerative work; or
(b) is a member or are members of a married or unmarried couple or civil partnership where:
   (i) both are engaged in remunerative work; or
   (ii) one member is engaged in remunerative work and the other is incapacitated.

Note that for the purposes of this regulation a person is a child until the last day of the week in which falls the first day of September following that child's fifteenth birthday or sixteenth birthday if the child is disabled. A child is disabled for these purposes if he receives disability living allowance (either component at any rate of pay) or is registered blind.

So what are relevant child care charges? By reg 14, 'child care' means care provided for a child in England and Wales (there are different rules for other parts of the UK):

(a) by a registered child minder or child care provider (such as an approved nanny or au pair), nursery or child care scheme;

(b) in schools or establishments which are exempted from registration;

(c) in respect of any period on or before the day preceding the first Tuesday in September following his twelfth birthday, where the care is provided out of school hours, by a school on school premises or by a local authority; or

(d) in respect of a child aged seven or over, that provided by a child care provider approved by an accredited organisation. This may include a childminder (not in the claimant's home) and organisations such as school breakfast clubs, after-school clubs and school holiday clubs.

Relevant child care charges are calculated on an average weekly charge basis in accordance with reg 15. The annual amount of the element therefore depends on whether the charges are paid weekly or monthly and whether the amount fluctuates over a year. So if charges are incurred every week for the same amount, simply multiply by 52. If charges are incurred weekly but vary over time, add together the charges in the 52 weeks before the claim and divide by 52. If charges are not incurred every week, simply add those together that are incurred in the year and divide by 52. For example, where a child attends an after-school club, he will do so during term time only (in the region of 40 weeks). If charges are paid monthly for a fixed monthly amount, multiply that amount by 12 and divide the result by 52. If charges are for variable monthly amounts, aggregate the charges for the previous 12 months and divide the total by 52.

> **Examples**
>
> (1) Amanda pays £50 a week for relevant child care during the school terms (40 weeks). She incurs no relevant charges during school holidays. Her average weekly child care costs are £50 multiplied by 40 divided by 52 = £38.46.
>
> (2) Brian pays £40 a week relevant child care costs during school terms (40 weeks) and during school holidays (12 weeks) he pays £140 a week. His average weekly child care costs are £40 multiplied by 40 (£1,600) plus £140 multiplied by 12 (£1,680) = £3,280 divided by 52 = £63.08.
>
> (3) Claire has paid relevant child care costs over the last 12 months as follows: April, £190; May, October and December, £210; July and August, £290; the other six months at £170. Her average weekly costs are £190 plus £210 multiplied by 3 (£630) plus £290 multiplied by 2 (£580) plus £170 multiplied by 6 (£1,020) = £2,420 divided by 52 = £46.54.

If the claimant's average relevant weekly child care costs fall or rise by £10 or more a week, he should inform HMRC.

If the claimant is entitled to the child care element, it will be paid at the rate of 80% (ie 80 pence for every £1 actually paid) but limited to a maximum, namely:

(a) £175 per week, where the claimant's family includes only one child in respect of whom relevant child care charges are paid; and

(b) £300 per week where the claimant's family includes more than one child in respect of whom relevant child care charges are paid.

This means that the most a claimant can receive for this element is £140 for one child or £240 for two or more children for any week that relevant child care costs are actually incurred.

To summarise, the key questions to answer are as follows:

(a) Are relevant child care costs being incurred? If so, go to question (b).

(b) What is the average weekly charge? Work out the annual charge if the costs are not incurred for all 52 weeks in the year. Ascertain these figures and go to question (c).

(c) Does the average weekly charge incurred exceed the maximum? If not, go to question (d). If so, go to question (e).

(d) What is the annual allowable child care element (ascertain it by multiplying the annual charges incurred by 80%).

(e) What is the annual allowable child care element (ascertain it by multiplying the maximum annual charges incurred by 80%).

See the worked example at **9.13.3**.

In what circumstances is the member of a joint claim said to be 'incapacitated'? This is where:

(a) housing benefit or council tax benefit is payable to the claimant or partner and the applicable amount includes a disability premium or a higher pensioner premium by virtue of incapacity; or

(b) short-term higher rate incapacity benefit or long-term incapacity benefit is payable to that person; or

(c) attendance allowance (at any rate of pay) or disability living allowance (either component at any rate of pay) is payable to that person; or

(d) industrial disablement benefit with constant attendance allowance (at any rate of pay) is payable to that person.

9.10.2.6 A severe disability element

By reg 17, the determination of the maximum rate must include the severe disability element if the claimant, or, in the case of a joint claim, one of the claimants receives disability living allowance care component payable at the highest rate, or attendance allowance payable at the higher rate.

Note that if both members of a couple satisfy a condition then two severe disability elements are payable.

9.10.2.7 A 50-plus element

By reg 18, the determination of the maximum rate must include the 50-plus element if:

(a) in the case of a single claim, the claimant satisfies para (3); or

(b) in the case of a joint claim, at least one of the claimants satisfies that paragraph.

A claimant satisfies para (3) if:

(a) he is aged at least 50;

(b) he started work within the preceding three months; and

(c) he undertakes qualifying remunerative work for at least 16 hours per week; and

(d) he satisfies any of the conditions set out in paras (4) or (6) or (7) or (8).

The condition in para (4) is that for a period of at least six months immediately before his starting work for consecutive periods, amounting in the aggregate to at least six months, the last of which ends immediately before his starting work, para (5) is satisfied.

Paragraph (5) is satisfied while the claimant is receiving:

(a) income support; or
(b) a jobseeker's allowance; or
(c) incapacity benefit.

Examples

(1) Ethel is 52 years of age. For the last year she has received income support. Today she takes up a full-time job of 25 hours a week.

(2) Sam is 53 years of age. Over the last twelve months he has received three months worth of incapacity benefit and six months worth of contribution-based JSA. For the last two months he has received income-based JSA. He is about to take up full-time work of 30 hours a week.

The condition under para (6) is that for at least six months immediately prior to his starting work another person was receiving an increase in their income support, jobseeker's allowance or incapacity benefit in respect of the claimant, as a dependant of the other person.

The condition under para (7) is that for at least six months immediately prior to his starting work he satisfied the conditions entitling him to be credited with national insurance contributions or earnings (see **2.2.5**).

The condition under para (8) is that:

(a) for a period immediately prior to his starting work another person was receiving an increase in their income support, jobseeker's allowance or incapacity benefit in respect of the claimant, as a dependant of the other person; and
(b) for a period immediately before this, the claimant or any partner was receiving carer's allowance, bereavement allowance, or widowed parent's allowance; and
(c) these two periods add up to at least six months.

Note that this element is only payable for a 12-month period starting from when the claimant returns to work. It can be paid for one continuous period of 12 months; or for periods amounting in aggregate to 12 months if the gap between any consecutive pair of those periods is not more than 26 weeks.

The rate of pay of this element depends on the amount of qualifying remunerative work undertaken. It is paid at a lower rate if the work is for 16 to 29 hours a week but at a higher rate where the work is for 30 hours or more a week. As to the latter, a 30-hour element (see **9.10.2.2**) will also be payable.

If joint claimants each meet the qualifying criteria, then two 50-plus elements are payable at the appropriate rate.

9.10.3 The annual amount of each element

For 2007/08 the rate of each element was as follows:

Basic element: £1,730
Disability element: £2,310
30-hour element: £705
Second adult element: £1,700

Lone parent element: £1,700

Severe disability element: £980

50-plus element: £1,185 if any claimant normally undertakes qualifying remunerative work of at least 16 hours but less than 30 hours per week but £1,770 if any claimant normally undertakes qualifying remunerative work of at least 30 hours per week.

9.10.4 Examples of maximum working tax credit

(1) Arthur, aged 52 and his partner, Belinda, aged 47, both work 35 hours a week. Arthur started his job one month ago. Immediately before that he received contribution-based JSA for six months. Their maximum working tax credit will include the following annual elements:

(a) basic element;

(b) second adult element (although Arthur is over 50 and eligible for the 50-plus element he and indeed Belinda are working for at least 30 hours a week);

(c) 30-hour element (only one such element is payable even though both are working at least 30 hours a week);

(d) 50-plus element at the higher rate (Arthur is over 50, started full-time work of at least 16 hours a week work in the last three months and immediately before that received jobseeker's allowance for at least six months. It is paid at the higher rate as he is working for at least 30 hours a week).

(2) Viv is aged 26. She is a single parent. Her daughter is aged eight. She pays £10 a week for her daughter to attend the school's breakfast club on the mornings that she works. Viv works 25 hours a week. Viv receives disability living allowance mobility component at the lower rate. When standing she cannot keep her balance and continually holds onto something. Her maximum working tax credit will include the following annual elements:

(a) basic element;

(b) disability element (she is working at least 16 hours a week, she has a disability that puts her at a disadvantage in getting a job and she receives disability living allowance);

(c) lone parent element (she is a single parent);

(d) child care charges (more details are needed to work out the annual element).

Note that since Viv is responsible for a child, she may also qualify for child tax credit (see **9.8**).

9.10.5 Will the maximum working tax credit be paid?

The maximum credit will be paid only if the claimant's income (see **9.7.3**) does not exceed the annual threshold. For 2007/08 that was £5,220.

If the claimant's income is *the same as or less* than the income threshold, the maximum working tax credit is payable.

If the claimant's income is more than the income threshold, the maximum working tax credit is not payable. Instead, it will be tapered, that is reduced, by 37% of the excess income (see further **9.11**).

Note that the different elements are tapered away in a set order. First, reduce all the elements apart from any child care element. Only if that reduces those elements to nil must you then reduce the child care element. See the examples at **9.13**.

9.11 Tapering when entitled to both credits

As we saw at **9.8.5** and **9.10.5**, when calculating entitlement to either tax credit, you apply the appropriate annual income threshold.

If the annual income exceeds the threshold, the maximum credit must be reduced by 37% of the excess.

Where a claimant is entitled to both credits, the different elements are tapered away in the following set order:

(a) first, reduce all the elements of working tax credit, apart from any child care element;
(b) secondly, reduce any child care element of working tax credit;
(c) thirdly, reduce the child elements of child tax credit;
(d) finally, note that the family element of child tax credit is not reduced unless the claimant has an annual income in excess of £50,000. If so, the family element is reduced by 6.67% of the excess (namely at the rate of £1 for every £15 of income exceeding £50,000).

Example:

Assume a claimant qualifies for both tax credits but as he has a high income all elements, apart from the family element, have been reduced to nil. If his income were say £55,000pa then his family element would have to be reduced by £333.50 (ie £5,000 × 6.67%).

See further the worked examples at **9.13**.

9.12 Calculating working tax credit: a summary of the steps

Step 1: calculate the maximum working tax credit.

Step 2: calculate relevant income (see **9.7.3**).

Step 3: compare income with the annual threshold (see **9.10.5**).

Step 4: if the claimant's income is the same or less than the income threshold, the maximum working tax credit is payable.

If the claimant's income is more than the income threshold, the maximum working tax credit is not payable. Instead, it will be tapered, that is reduced, by 37% of the excess income (see the worked examples at **9.13**).

9.13 Tax credits: worked examples

9.13.1 Claimant entitled to child tax credit only

Jan, aged 20, is a single parent. She has two children, Amanda, aged nine months and Keith aged three. She receives disability living allowance care component at the middle rate for Keith. Jan is receiving income support and as a result she is entitled to maximum child tax credit. This will consist of the following annual elements.

Family: £1,090 (as she is responsible for a child under one year of age).
Child element for Amanda: £1,845.
Disabled child element for Keith: £4,285 (as he is in receipt of disability living allowance).
Total: £7,220pa or £138.85 per week.

9.13.2 Claimant entitled to working tax credit only

Elizabeth, aged 25, works 35 hours a week. She earned £8,000 gross in the last tax year. Her partner, Lionel, aged 35 has been permanently disabled for the last five years. He receives long-term incapacity benefit (with higher rate age addition) of

£98.45 per week or £5,119.40 per annum. He also receives disability living allowance care component at the middle rate and disability living allowance mobility component at the lower rate. The couple received interest on their building society account for the last tax year of £37.

Step 1: maximum working tax credit

This will consist of the following annual elements:

>Basic element: £1,730.
>30-hour element: £705.
>Second adult element: £1,700.
>Total: £4,135.

Step 2: income from all relevant sources

As the investment income (£37 interest on savings) does not exceed £300, it is ignored.

Elizabeth's employment income is £8,000.

Lionel's long-term incapacity benefit is social security income of £5,119.40.

Total: £13,119.40.

Lionel's disability living allowance does not count.

Step 3: compare income with annual threshold

>Income: £13,119.40
>Threshold: £5,220,
>Excess: £7,899.40.

As income exceeds annual threshold, proceed to Step 4.

Step 4: reduce maximum by excess

Maximum credit must be reduced by 37% of the excess, namely:

>£7,899.40 × 37% = £2,922.78

>Maximum credit: £4,135
>Less tapered excess: £2,922.78
>Credit payable is: £1,212.22 or £23.31 per week.

9.13.3 Claimant entitled to child tax credit and working tax credit

Gareth is aged 35. He is a single parent. His wife died two years ago. For the last tax year he received weekly widowed parent's allowance of £87.30 or £4,539.60 a year and child benefit. His son, Jack, is aged 9. Ever since his wife died, Gareth pays £60 a week for Jack to attend the after-school club. He attends each school week, totalling 40 weeks a year. Gareth is self-employed. His taxable profit for last year was £17,000. He has no savings and no other sources of income.

Step 1: maximum tax credits entitlement

Child tax credit:

>His maximum child tax credit will include the following annual elements:
>Family element: £545
>Child element for Jack: £1,845.

Working tax credit:

As to the child care costs, let us answer the questions at **9.10.2.5**:

(a) Are relevant child care costs being incurred by Gareth for his 9-year-old child, Jack? Yes, as Jack is over 7 and the care is at his after-school club.

(b) What is the average weekly charge? He spends £60 for 40 weeks, ie £2,400 pa or £46.15 (£2,400 ÷ 52).

(c) Does the average weekly charge exceed the maximum? The weekly amount of £46.15 does not exceed the maximum for one child of £175.

(d) So we ascertain the annual allowable child care element by multiplying the allowable annual charge by 80%, ie £2,400 × 80% = £1,920.

His maximum working tax credit will include the following annual elements:

Basic element: £1,730
Lone parent element: £1,700
Child care charges: £1,920 (ie £60 × 40 × 80%)

Total maximum credits: £7,740

Step 2: income from all relevant sources

Pension income ie widowed parent's allowance of £4,539.60 exceeds £300 and so the balance of £4,239.60 counts.

Employment income is £17,000.
Total: £21,239.60
Child benefit is ignored.

Step 3: compare income with annual threshold

Income: £21,239.60
Threshold: £5,220
Excess: £16,019.60.

As income exceeds annual threshold, proceed to Step 4.

Step 4: reduce maximum by excess

Maximum credit must be tapered by 37% of the excess, namely:

£16,019.60 × 37% = £5,927.25.

First, the elements of working tax credit apart from his child care costs must be reduced, ie £3,430 (basic element: £1,730 and lone parent element: £1,700) is reduced by the excess to nil. That leaves a tapered excess of £2,497.25 still to be made.

Secondly, the child care costs of £1,920 are reduced by the excess to nil. That leaves a tapered excess of £577.25 still to be made.

Thirdly, the child element of child tax credit of £1,845 is reduced by the remaining tapered excess of £577.25 to £1,267.75.

He will receive the family element in full.

So he will receive an annual child tax credit totalling £1,812.75 (or £34.86 per week). This is made up of £1,267.75 child element and £545 family element. His income is too large to receive any working tax credit.

9.14 The tax credits and other benefits

Child tax credit does not count as income when calculating income support or income-based JSA (see **7.3**) or pension credit (see **5.3**).

Child tax credit does count as income when calculating housing benefit or council tax benefit (see **9.2**).

Working tax credit counts as income when calculating income support and income-based JSA.

Whilst working tax credit counts as income when calculating housing benefit and council tax benefit there are two points to note. First, if any 30-hour element (see **9.10.2.2**) is payable, that is ignored. Secondly, if any child care costs (see **9.10.2.5**) are payable, these are ignored subject to a weekly maximum of £140 for one child or £240 for two or more children.

Working tax credit is taken into account when assessing eligibility for the pension credit but it is ignored when calculating any savings credit.

Some non-means tested benefits are treated as income when calculating entitlement to a tax credit whilst others are not (see **9.7.4**).

9.15 Payment of tax credits

Payments of child tax credit are usually made each week or month, whichever is more convenient for the claimant. It is usually paid directly to the bank, building society or post office account of the child's main carer.

Payments of working tax credit are usually made each week or month, whichever is more convenient for the claimant, directly to their bank, building society or post office account. However, if the award includes a child care element, that part is paid directly to the main carer of the child.

9.16 The social fund

9.16.1 What is the social fund?

The social fund makes grants and loans to assist with expenses that are not covered by other means-tested benefits. It has two elements, the regulated social fund and the discretionary social fund.

9.16.2 The regulated social fund

The regulated social fund makes outright payments, as of right, to any claimant who satisfies the criteria. There is a right of appeal to an appeal tribunal against an adverse decision. The regulated social fund includes the sure start maternity grant (see **6.5**), funeral costs and cold weather payments.

9.16.3 Funeral payments

9.16.3.1 Who may claim?

A claimant may receive a funeral payment if:

(a) he is responsible for arranging a funeral to be held in the UK (or in certain cases an EEA State); and

(b) he is in receipt of a 'qualifying benefit' (IS, IBJSA, HB, CTB, child tax credit at the maximum rate or any rate greater than the appropriate family element, working tax credit that includes a disability or severe disability element); and

(c) it is reasonable for him to take responsibility for arranging the funeral because there is no closer relative of the deceased who could have taken responsibility and would not qualify for a social fund payment; and

(d) he makes a claim within three months of the funeral taking place.

The resources of the person who has died are largely irrelevant.

Is the requirement that the funeral must be held in the UK (or in certain cases an EEA State) compatible with the ECHR? Yes, held the Court of Appeal in *Esfandiari v Secretary of State for Work and Pensions* [2006] EWCA Civ 282.

9.16.3.2 Amount of the payment

The maximum payment is made up of:

(a) the necessary cost of a burial (including a burial plot) or cremation;

(b) the cost of transporting the body to a funeral director's premises, if this is over 50 miles;

(c) the cost of a hearse and one car for mourners on the day of the funeral;

(d) the cost of one return journey for the responsible person to arrange or attend the funeral; and

(e) a maximum of £600 for all other expenses.

This low limit is well below the typical cost of a funeral. It creates problems if the claimant does not know about it before contracting with the funeral director. Most appeals to tribunals about the social fund are trying to get more money to meet a funeral bill, but they are usually doomed to failure.

9.16.3.3 Resources taken into account

The payment is reduced by:

(a) any assets of the deceased which are readily accessible without probate;

(b) payments from pre-paid funeral plans.

The costs of a funeral are the first charge on the estate of anyone who has died. The social fund has first charge on any assets that only become available after probate, to recoup the payment.

9.16.4 Cold weather payments

Cold weather payments are paid as an automatic addition to IS or IBJSA if:

(a) the claimant has a child under the age of five; or

(b) the claimant's applicable amount includes any of the disability or pensioner premiums, including the disabled child premium; and, in either case

(c) a 'period of cold weather' has been forecast or recorded in his home area.

9.16.4.1 Period of cold weather

A period of cold weather is a period of seven or more consecutive days when the average daily temperature is recorded as freezing (0° Celsius) or below. Weather records are collated at 72 centres across the country to allow for local variations in temperature. It is unusual for cold weather payments to cause problems.

9.16.4.2 Winter fuel payments

In recent winters, the Government has announced one-off additional payments to help with winter heating bills for all people on income support, and pensioners. This scheme is not part of the social fund and is dealt with on a year-by-year basis.

9.16.5 The discretionary social fund

Payments from the discretionary social fund are indeed discretionary, which means that there is no right of appeal against refusal. Claimants may always ask for a review, especially if it appears that there is evidence to support the application which has been overlooked. The details of the administration of this fund are not in legislation but Social Fund Directions (SFD). These directions define the circumstances in which social fund payments may be made, but leave it to the discretion of the Department whether to make a payment in any case.

There are two forms of social fund payments, grants and loans. Grants are outright payments which are not repayable. Loans are repayable, by weekly deduction from other benefits. A loan may be refused if it is unlikely that the claimant will be able to repay it. This could be because of the amount borrowed, or because of other deductions from benefit (see **7.13**).

9.16.5.1 Community care grants (SFD 25–29)

To be eligible for a community care grant, the claimant must be in receipt of either IS or IBJSA and need the grant for one of the following reasons:

(a) to re-establish himself in the community after a long spell in institutional or residential care. This includes prisons, youth custody, hospitals, residential care homes and special schools. These grants would include help with the costs of removals, essential furniture and clothing;

(b) to enable him to live in the community without having to go into residential care. The commonest use for these grants is to make alterations to a disabled claimant's home, or buy him aids to make life easier;

(c) to ease 'exceptional pressure on families'. This includes helping people to move away from or otherwise cope with the breakdown of a non-marital relationship (especially if there is domestic violence), or the stresses of caring for a very seriously disabled or disturbed family member;

(d) to pay some travelling costs, for example to visit relatives in hospital or attend a family funeral.

The claim must be for at least £30, except for the travelling costs which have no lower limit. Capital of £500 or more reduces the payment pound for pound.

9.16.5.2 Budgeting loans (SFD 1 and 8–12)

A claimant receiving IS or IBJSA is supposed to be able to put aside small sums regularly for predictable future bills. But a claimant may face the need to make a large payment for which it would not be reasonable to expect him to budget in this way. This could include essential items of furniture, essential household repairs and maintenance, and purchase of fuel such as oil or coal, which has to be bought in bulk. A budgeting loan is one way of meeting such payments.

To qualify for a loan, the claimant must have been in receipt of IS or IBJSA for at least 26 weeks. The maximum loan is £1,000, but the DfWP may be unwilling to lend so much because claimants may have difficulty in repaying it.

9.16.5.3 Crisis loans (SFD 14–23)

Crisis loans may be paid to someone who has suffered a crisis or disaster, has no resources to meet his immediate needs and is facing the serious risk of damage to his health or safety. A domestic flood or fire will always qualify, as will being penniless while waiting for first wages from a new job, or being stranded away from home with no money and no transport.

A second form of crisis loan may be made to a person who is receiving a community care grant, to help him pay rent in advance to a private landlord (advance rent is not covered by HB).

9.17 Passport benefits

9.17.1 What are passport benefits?

The term 'passport benefits' is used to describe a collection of more or less means-tested benefits which are outside the social security system. Most of them are connected with the National Health Service and are collectively called 'NHS benefits'. The word 'passport' is used because a person who is receiving some of the main means-tested benefits is often automatically entitled to the NHS benefits. In other words, the social security benefit is a passport to them, just as it may be to CTB or HB (see **9.17.2**).

9.17.2 Who is entitled to NHS benefits?

Although the rules of entitlement vary with the benefits, there are four main qualifying groups of people who will be entitled to most of them.

(a) Anyone who is receiving IS or IBJSA or if the claimant's gross annual income is no more than £14,200 and he receives child tax credit only or both tax credits or working tax credit only but with a disability element, and any member of their families.

(b) Other people on low incomes, subject to undergoing a means test.

(c) Children under 16, and anyone under 19 who is in full-time education.

(d) War pensioners disabled as a result of military service (including peace-time service), if they need the benefit because of their disability.

For the rest of this section, these four groups will be described as 'the qualifying groups'.

9.17.3 The benefits and those entitled to them

9.17.3.1 Free prescriptions

All the qualifying groups are exempt from paying prescription charges, as are the following:

(a) hospital in-patients;
(b) women who are pregnant or have had a baby within the last 12 months;
(c) some people with chronic illnesses, or who are so disabled that they cannot leave the house alone; and
(d) any person of State Pension age.

A person who wishes to claim free prescriptions from a chemist will have to produce evidence of his entitlement.

9.17.3.2 Free dental treatment

Members of all the qualifying groups are entitled to free dental treatment and dentures, as are women who are pregnant or have had a baby in the last 12 months. In addition, anyone under 18 is entitled to free treatment only. People whose income is low, but not low enough to have free treatment, may be entitled to reduced charges.

These rights may be difficult to enforce. They apply only to dentists who work for the National Health Service, who can be hard to find.

9.17.3.3 Sight tests and glasses

Members of the qualifying groups are entitled to free sight tests, as are the following:

(a) anyone registered blind or partially sighted;

(b) anyone aged 60 or over;

(c) anyone suffering from diabetes or glaucoma, and anyone aged at least 40 who has a close relative with glaucoma; and

(d) anyone who has in the past needed exceptionally complex lenses (this does not mean bifocals or varifocals).

The prescribing oculist who carries out the examination will issue a voucher to cover some or all of the cost of glasses or contact lenses if the patient:

(a) is in one of the qualifying groups; or

(b) needs frequent changes of prescription; or

(c) needs particularly complex lenses; and, in any case

(d) there is a reason why new glasses are needed, for example because the prescription has changed, the patient has not needed glasses before, the glasses have worn out, or (exceptionally) the glasses have been lost or damaged.

9.17.3.4 Fares to hospital

Members of all the qualifying groups except the fourth may be entitled to help from the hospital with the cost of transport to and from hospital. This usually means public transport or private car, and covers only the patient's costs, although taxi fares and the cost of a companion may be allowed, where appropriate.

War pensioners do not need this benefit, as there is a parallel provision within the war pensions system.

9.17.4 Free milk and school meals

9.17.4.1 Free milk and vitamins

Free tokens to buy one pint of milk per day, for each qualifying person, are given to:

(a) children who are too disabled to go to school; and

(b) pregnant women and children under five in families receiving IS or IBJSA.

Pregnant and nursing women and children under five in families receiving IS or IBJSA are also entitled to free vitamin tablets or drops.

Free milk and vitamins are also available to children under five who are members of a family of someone who receives child tax credit and has an annual taxable income of no more than £14,495.

Any person who is attending a maternity or childcare clinic is entitled to buy dried milk and vitamins at reduced prices.

9.17.4.2 Free school meals

All State schools must provide children with a midday meal, though it need not be suitable as the main meal of the day. They must generally charge for the meals, but must provide them free to children from families in receipt of IS or IBJSA only. This can be a valuable right to a family with several children of school age.

9.18 Claimant profiles

9.18.1 Housing benefit

This is payable to a claimant liable to pay rent for his home and who is on a low income with a limited amount of capital.

9.18.2 Council tax benefit

This is payable to a claimant liable to pay council tax and who is on a low income with a limited amount of capital.

9.18.3 Child tax credit

This is payable to a claimant responsible for a child or qualifying young person and who is on a low income.

9.18.4 Working tax credit

This is payable to a claimant who is in qualifying remunerative work but on a low income.

Chapter 10
Benefits and Immigration Requirements

10.1	The scope of this chapter	167
10.2	Potential sources of entitlement to benefits in Great Britain	167
10.3	Immigration status and entitlement to certain non-contributory benefits in Great Britain	169
10.4	Residence requirements and entitlement to benefits in Great Britain and 'exporting' benefits	171
10.5	Northern Ireland and the Common Travel Area	175
10.6	Ordinarily resident	175
10.7	Habitual residence	176
10.8	Immigration law and public funds	181
10.9	Asylum seekers	183
10.10	Urgent cases payments	183
10.11	Social fund payment	183
10.12	EEA nationals claiming benefits	183

10.1 The scope of this chapter

So far, in this part of the book, we have been considering the basic rules of entitlement to benefit only as they apply to people who have been living and working in Great Britain for several years. We have not considered the rules relating to residence and presence in Great Britain, and their effect on people who have only recently come into the country. Nor have we considered what benefit rights can be taken or acquired abroad. This chapter is concerned with those rules, which form an area of overlap between the law of welfare benefits and immigration law.

For most benefits, entitlement is directly linked to the claimant's nationality and immigration status within the UK generally, and Great Britain specifically (ie England, Scotland and Wales). The reason for this focus on Great Britain is that, as we saw at **1.3**, welfare law is the law of Great Britain. This contrasts with immigration law, which is the law of the UK as a whole (ie including Northern Ireland).

In order to decide on a claimant's entitlement to benefits, it is necessary to have a good understanding of immigration law. All potential sources of entitlement need to be considered. Two key questions should be asked: first, does the claimant's immigration status disqualify him from a benefit; and secondly, are any residence requirements met? The claimant's nationality and current immigration status are always good starting points from which to analyse his rights in welfare law.

10.2 Potential sources of entitlement to benefits in Great Britain

10.2.1 Introduction

A person who has recently arrived in the UK may have rights to welfare benefits arising from several different sources. Some of these rights run in parallel, while others may confer rights completely independent of any other source of rights.

The sources of rights are:

(a) domestic legislation, covering Great Britain alone or including the rest of the UK;
(b) EC legislation and international conventions to which the UK is a signatory;
(c) reciprocal agreements between the British Government and governments of other countries (see **10.2.2**);
(d) the law of the country from which the claimant has arrived.

Of these, the last is outside the scope of this book.

10.2.2 Reciprocal agreements

The governments of several countries have entered into reciprocal agreements with the UK Government, for the payment of social security benefits. By these agreements the nationals of the other countries may be able to claim a benefit, whilst living in the reciprocal agreement country, from that country's government. In some circumstances an agreement may help a UK national continue to receive a benefit whilst living in the reciprocal agreement country. In limited circumstances an agreement may provide that presence and residence in a reciprocal agreement country constitutes such in Great Britain for the purposes of claiming the benefit here.

The countries with which the UK Government has reciprocal agreements are Barbados, Bermuda, Bosnia-Herzegovina, Canada, Croatia, Guernsey, Isle of Man, Israel, Jamaica, Jersey, Macedonia, Mauritius, New Zealand, The Philippines, Serbia and Montenegro, Turkey and the USA.

The scope of the agreements varies widely and should always be checked carefully. Benefit coverage is outlined in a chart at **Appendix 5** to this Part of this book. However, the following features are common:

(a) means-tested benefits are always excluded;
(b) benefits for the unemployed can never be claimed outside the country where contributions were paid;
(c) retirement and bereavement benefits are always covered in some way.

Rights to benefits for sickness, disability and children are variable. The DfWP has a range of leaflets which explain the agreements.

Example

(1) Alice is entitled to long-term incapacity benefit. She decides to go and live permanently in Jamaica. As her absence is not temporary she would usually be disqualified from the benefit (see **10.4.7**). However, under the provisions of the UK–Jamaica agreement, payment of her long-term incapacity benefit may continue.

(2) Bob is entitled to State Pension. He decides to go and live permanently in Barbados. Under UK law his pension would be frozen at the rate paid when he left the UK. However, under the provisions of the UK–Barbados agreement, it will not be frozen.

(3) Claire is entitled to CBJSA. If she is absent from the UK in the Isle of Man, it can still be paid to her under that agreement. In respect of the other agreements that cover CBJSA, periods of residence in the reciprocal agreement country by a UK national only count as periods for which national insurance contributions are deemed to be paid.

There are also reciprocal agreements with most EEA countries (and Switzerland). However, a member of an EEA Member State will be able to rely on a reciprocal agreement only if he has no rights to benefit in EC law. Whether he has will depend in part upon his reasons for going to another Member State and the date upon which his rights arose.

10.2.3 Contributory benefits and the EC

Contributory benefits are not affected by a claimant's immigration status.

The right of free movement of labour, under Article 39 EC, would be of reduced value if citizens of Member States had to start afresh to build up contribution records every time they exercised this right. EC law requires the mutual recognition of NICs, so that a claimant can use contributions paid in one Member State to help satisfy the contribution conditions for a benefit claimed in another.

The basic principle is that the claimant must claim the benefit of the Member State in which he last worked and paid NICs, and comply with the laws of that State. There is an exception if the claimant remained 'resident' in one State while working in another. This will only happen if his work was of a temporary nature, whether as an employee or self-employed.

> Example 1
> Dieter has just arrived in Great Britain for the first time from Germany, where he has paid contributions for six years. He has no work. Can he claim contribution-based JSA?
> No. He last paid contributions in Germany, so can only claim German unemployment benefits. But they can be paid to him in Great Britain.
>
> Example 2
> Marie-Claire has been working in London for six months, paying Class 1 contributions. Before that she lived and worked for many years in Brussels. She has just been made redundant. Can she claim contribution-based JSA?
> Yes. She last paid contributions in Great Britain. She can use contributions paid in Belgium to help her qualify for CBJSA.
>
> Example 3
> Sai-ling has just returned home to Edinburgh after spending three months in Seville learning Spanish and doing various temporary jobs for which she paid contributions. She broke her arm the day after she got back. Can she claim short-term ICB?
> Provided she has the necessary contribution record, yes. She last paid contributions in Spain, but the nature of her work was not such as to prevent her from remaining resident in Great Britain during her absence.

10.3 Immigration status and entitlement to certain non-contributory benefits in Great Britain

10.3.1 The general s 115 exclusionary rule

A person to whom s 115(1) of the Immigration and Asylum Act 1999 (IAA 1999) applies is not entitled to:

(a) income-based jobseeker's allowance;
(b) attendance allowance;
(c) carer's allowance;
(d) disability living allowance;
(e) income support;

(f) working tax credit;
(g) child tax credit;
(h) a social fund payment;
(i) child benefit;
(j) housing benefit;
(k) council tax benefit;
(l) State pension credit,

while he is a person to whom this section applies.

Subsection (3) of s 115 provides that:

> This section applies to a *person subject to immigration control* unless he falls within such category or description, or satisfies such conditions, as may be prescribed. (emphasis added)

Regulations under s 115(3) may provide for a person to be treated for prescribed purposes only as not being a person to whom s 115 applies (see **10.3.2**).

Subsection (9) of s 115 defines 'a person subject to immigration control' as meaning:

> a person who is not a national of an EEA State and who—
> (a) requires leave to enter or remain in the United Kingdom but does not have it [eg an illegal entrant or overstayer];
> (b) has leave to enter or remain in the United Kingdom which is subject to a condition that he does not have recourse to public funds [see **10.8**];
> (c) has leave to enter or remain in the United Kingdom given as a result of a maintenance undertaking [defined by subsection 10 as 'a written undertaking given by another person in pursuance of the immigration rules to be responsible for that person's maintenance and accommodation' (and see **13.4.2**)]; or
> (d) has leave to enter or remain in the United Kingdom only because he has appealed a decision to vary or refuse to vary that leave [see **Chapter 16**].

10.3.2 Exceptions to the general s 115 exclusionary rule

The Social Security (Immigration and Asylum) Consequential Amendments Regulations 2000 (SS(I&A)CA Regs 2000) (SI 2000/636) provide that certain categories of persons are not treated as being subject to s 115. In respect of IBJSA, IS, a social fund payment, HB and CTB, reg 2(1) provides that the following people are entitled to claim the benefit:

(a) persons with limited leave whose funds from abroad have been temporarily interrupted provided there is a reasonable expectation that the supply of those funds will be resumed;
(b) sponsored immigrants whose sponsor has died before completing five years residence;
(c) sponsored immigrants who have been in the UK for at least five years, beginning on the date of entry or the date on which the undertaking was given, if later;
(d) nationals of Turkey who are lawfully present in the UK.

By reg 2(2), the categories of persons entitled to claim AA, CA, DLA, a social fund payment and child benefit are:

(a) a member of the family of a national of an EEA country (it is unclear who is covered by this provision given that family members of qualifying EEA nationals do not need leave to enter the UK and so cannot be excluded by s 115);

(b) a person who is legally working and living in Great Britain and is a national of a State with which the EU has made an agreement relating to equal treatment (namely Turkey, Morocco, Algeria and Tunisia) and any members of their family living with them;

(c) a sponsored immigrant regardless of the length of stay in the UK.

By reg 2(3), the categories of persons entitled to claim AA, DLA and child benefit are nationals of a country where there is a reciprocal agreement (see **10.2.2**) in force in respect of the benefit.

The Tax Credits (Immigration) Regulations 2003 (SI 2003/653) provide that no person is entitled to child tax credit or working tax credit while he is a person subject to immigration control, except in five prescribed cases. In summary these are:

> *Case 1:* (a) The claimant has been given leave to enter, or remain in, the UK upon the written undertaking of another person to be responsible for his maintenance and accommodation; and (b) he has been resident in the UK for a period of at least five years commencing on or after the date of his entry into the UK, or the date on which the undertaking was given in respect of him, whichever is the later.
>
> *Case 2:* The claimant is a person who falls within Case 1(a) and he has been resident in the UK for less than the five years mentioned in Case 1(b) but the person giving the undertaking has died.
>
> *Case 3:* The claimant has limited leave to enter or remain in the UK; his funds from abroad have been temporarily interrupted but there is a reasonable expectation that his supply of funds will be resumed. Note that the period (or aggregate of periods) for which this Case applies must not exceed 42 days during any single period of limited leave (including any extension to that period).
>
> *Case 4:* Where the claim is for working tax credit, that the claimant is a national of Turkey (see above) and he is lawfully present in the UK.
>
> *Case 5:* Where the claim is for child tax credit, that the claimant is a person who is lawfully working in the UK and a national of a State with which the EU has made an agreement relating to equal treatment and their family members (see above).

10.4 Residence requirements and entitlement to benefits in Great Britain and 'exporting' benefits

It is obvious from **10.3** that you must first check that a person is not excluded from a benefit due to his immigration status. However, even if a claim can be made it is then important to check that any residence requirements are met.

10.4.1 Attendance allowance, disability living allowance and carer's allowance

To qualify for any such benefit, the claimant must:

(a) be ordinarily resident (see **10.6**) in Great Britain; and

(b) be present in Great Britain; and

(c) have been present in Great Britain for a total of 26 weeks, in the last 12 months (unless claiming DLA or AA on the basis that he is terminally ill).

For AA and DLA, claimants who are absent from Great Britain on any day during the claim are treated as being present if the absence is for a temporary purpose and lasts no longer than 26 weeks; or the absence is for the specific purpose of being treated for a pre-existing incapacity or a disabling condition as certified by the Secretary of State.

For CA, claimants who are absent from Great Britain on any day during the claim are treated as being present if the absence is for a temporary purpose and lasts no longer than four weeks, or for an indefinite period if the temporary absence is for the specific purpose of caring for a severely disabled person who himself is absent from Great Britain.

UK law does not allow claimants to go abroad permanently to live and still receive such a benefit. The reciprocal agreements that cover the benefit do not help claimants to export it. A person residing permanently in another EEA country may be able to claim the equivalent benefit there.

10.4.2 Child benefit

As a general rule, to qualify for this benefit:

(a) the qualifying child or young person and claimant must be in Great Britain; and

(b) the qualifying child or young person and claimant must be ordinarily resident (see **10.6**) in Great Britain; and

(c) the qualifying child or young person and claimant must have a legal right to reside in the UK under either domestic or EC law.

As a general rule, a child or young person is treated as present if the absence is for a temporary purpose and lasts no longer than for 12 weeks; or, if longer, the child or young person is abroad receiving full-time education in an EEA State or Switzerland at a recognised educational establishment or for the purpose of treatment for a pre-existing illness or disability.

Claimants who are absent from Great Britain are treated as being present if the absence is for a temporary purpose and lasts no longer than for eight weeks.

Under EEA law, this benefit constitutes a 'family benefit or allowance'. The payment of such is generally the responsibility of the EEA country in which an employed or self-employed person is insured (or an unemployed person is drawing an unemployment benefit) even though the person's family may be living in another EEA country.

There are various reciprocal agreements which enable residence and/or presence in other countries to be treated for child benefit purposes as constituting such in Great Britain. The extent to which reciprocity exists varies, according to the particular agreement.

10.4.3 Working tax credit and child tax credit

By the Tax Credits (Residence) Regulations 2003 (SI 2003/654) (as amended) a claimant must be ordinarily resident (see **10.6**) in the UK and have a legal right to reside in the UK under either domestic or EC law.

Each tax credit can be paid during a period of absence from the UK of the claimant:

(a) for up to eight weeks of any period of absence; or

(b) for up to 12 weeks of any period of absence where that period of absence, or any extension to that period of absence, is in connection with:

   (i) the treatment of the claimant's illness or physical or mental disability;

   (ii) the treatment of his partner's illness or physical or mental disability;

(iii) the death of a person who, immediately prior to the date of death, was his partner;

(iv) the death, or the treatment of the illness or physical or mental disability, of a child or qualifying young person for whom either he or his partner is, or both of them are, responsible; or

(v) the death, or the treatment of the illness or physical or mental disability, of his or his partner's brother, sister, ancestor or lineal descendant.

Note that a person is treated as temporarily absent from the UK only if at the beginning of the period of absence his absence was unlikely to exceed 52 weeks.

What if the claimant is eligible for tax credits but his partner is excluded by s 115? See **10.8.4**.

10.4.4 Income support, income-based jobseeker's allowance, housing benefit and council tax benefit

To qualify for any such benefit, the person must be, or must be treated as being, habitually resident (see **10.7**) in the Common Travel Area (see **10.5**). To be treated as habitually resident the claimant must have a legal right to reside in the UK under either domestic or EC law (see **10.7**).

For IS purposes, the benefit can usually be paid for the first four weeks of temporary absence. This is extended to eight weeks if the claimant is accompanying a qualifying child abroad for the purposes of medical treatment.

For JSA purposes, it is a fundamental condition of entitlement that the person is in Great Britain so as to be available for work. However, it can be paid during an absence from Great Britain:

(a) for up to four weeks if the claimant has a partner who is either disabled, or aged 60 or over, and a premium (see **7.7**) is payable as a result;

(b) for up to eight weeks (as per IS above);

(c) for up to seven days if the claimant is attending a job interview;

(d) for up to three months if the claimant is looking for work in another EEA country.

For HB and CTB purposes, the benefit can be paid during a temporary absence of no longer than 13 weeks (or 52 weeks if the claimant is abroad for the purposes of medical treatment).

None of these benefits is within the scope of either EC law or any of the reciprocal agreements.

What if the claimant is eligible for IS or IBJSA but his partner is excluded by s 115? See **10.8.3**.

10.4.5 Industrial disablement benefit

A claimant does not have to satisfy any residence conditions to claim the benefit. However, it may not be payable if the accident occurred or the prescribed disease was contracted outside Great Britain or the EEA.

If a person sustains an industrial accident or contracts a prescribed disease outside Great Britain or the EEA but, during his absence, he has paid Class 1 contributions (or Class 2 as a volunteer development worker), the benefit can be claimed on returning to Great Britain.

A claimant who sustains an industrial accident or contracts a prescribed disease in a country with a reciprocal agreement may qualify under the terms of that agreement.

A person is not disqualified from receiving the benefit whilst absent from Great Britain. It can usually be permanently exported to another EEA country or one with a reciprocal agreement.

10.4.6 Statutory sick pay and statutory maternity pay

There are no presence or residence requirements for these benefits which can be continued to be paid whilst the claimant is abroad so long as the normal conditions of entitlement are met.

10.4.7 Incapacity benefit

A person does not have to satisfy any residence or presence conditions to become entitled to incapacity benefit. However, a person may be disqualified for receiving the benefit whilst absent from Great Britain. A person is not disqualified if his absence is in another EEA country, or a country with which the UK has a social security agreement which provides for the continued payment of the benefit, or if the absence lasts no longer than for 26 weeks and is for the specific purpose of being treated for a pre-existing incapacity as certified by the Secretary of State.

Note that, to satisfy the National Insurance conditions (see **Chapter 2**) for the contributory version of the benefit, the claimant may be able to rely on EC provisions (see **10.2**) or a reciprocal agreement with another country (see **10.2.2**).

10.4.8 Non-contributory incapacity benefit

Section 30A(2A)(d) of the SSCBA 1992 imposes residence and presence requirements for this version of ICB (see generally **4.5**), namely that the claimant:

(a) is ordinarily resident in Great Britain; and
(b) is present in Great Britain; and
(c) has been present in Great Britain for a period of, or for periods amounting in aggregate to, not less than 26 weeks in the 52 weeks immediately preceding the 'relevant day' (ie the day in respect of which the claimant is entitled to claim incapacity benefit and which falls on any day immediately after a period of 196 consecutive days of incapacity for work and which forms part of a period of incapacity for work); and
(d) is not a person subject to immigration control within the meaning of s 115(9) of the IAA 1999. However, note that claimants who fall within the exception to s 115 by SS(I&A)CA Regs 2000, reg 2(2) (see **10.3.2**) can claim.

A claimant is deemed to satisfy the residence or presence requirements on any subsequent day of incapacity for work that falls within the same period of incapacity where the conditions are satisfied on the first relevant day.

10.4.9 Contribution-based jobseeker's allowance

For JSA purposes, it is a fundamental condition of entitlement that the person is in Great Britain so as to be available for work. However, it can be paid during an absence from Great Britain:

(a) for up to four weeks if the claimant has a partner who is either disabled, or aged 60 or over, and a premium (see **7.7**) is payable as a result;
(b) for up to eight weeks (as per IS above);

(c) for up to seven days if the claimant is attending a job interview;

(d) for up to three months if the claimant is looking for work in another EEA country.

For the unique position of a work permit holder who ceases employment, see **10.8.6.2**.

In addition, as a general rule, a person remains entitled to the benefit whilst absent from Great Britain in another EEA country for up to three months, provided he has registered with the employment services of that country within seven days.

Note that, to satisfy the national insurance conditions for CBJSA (see **Chapter 2**), the claimant may be able to rely on EC provisions (see **10.2.3**). However, any reciprocal agreement with another country cannot affect the entitlement to British CBJSA as it is a benefit for the unemployed (see **10.2.2**).

10.5 Northern Ireland and the Common Travel Area

We have already noted that the law of social security is the law of Great Britain. What is the position of a person who arrives in Great Britain from Northern Ireland or the Common Travel Area (see **13.11**)? The answer depends more on the type of benefit being claimed than the place of origin of the claimant.

10.5.1 Means-tested benefits

If the claimant has been habitually resident within any part of the UK or the Common Travel Area, and is not a person subject to immigration control under s 115 of the IAA 1999, he can claim means-tested benefits on the same basis as any British resident who has no restrictions on his leave to be in the UK.

10.5.2 Contributory benefits

(a) Contributions paid by a person from Northern Ireland can be used to claim any contributory benefit in Great Britain, including CBJSA.

(b) People from the Channel Islands and the Isle of Man depend on reciprocal agreements which effectively give them full rights to claim all British benefits except CBJSA, relying on their contribution records at home.

(c) Citizens of the Republic of Ireland can rely on EC law rights (see **10.2.3**).

Note that the Channel Islands and the Isle of Man have an anomalous status within the UK; their citizens are British citizens but not EU nationals, as these islands do not belong to the EU. People from the islands therefore do not have special rights in EC law.

10.5.3 Non-contributory, non means-tested benefits

A combination of EC law, domestic British law and the reciprocal agreements between them gives people from Northern Ireland and the Common Travel Area the same right to non-contributory, non means-tested benefits as British residents.

10.6 Ordinarily resident

The words 'ordinary residence' were considered by the House of Lords in two tax cases reported in 1928. In each, the House sought the natural and ordinary meaning of the words. In *Levene v Inland Revenue Commissioners* [1928] AC 217 at

225, Viscount Cave LC said, 'I think that [ordinary residence] connotes residence in a place with some degree of continuity and apart from accidental or temporary absences'. In *Inland Revenue Commissioners v Lysaght* [1928] AC 234 at 243, Viscount Sumner said, 'I think the converse to "ordinarily" is "extraordinarily" and that part of the regular order of a man's life, adopted voluntarily and for settled purposes, is not "extraordinary"'.

In *R v Barnet London Borough Council, ex p Shah* [1983] 2 WLR 16, Lord Scarman said (at 28):

> There are two, and no more than two, respects in which the mind of the [claimant] is important in determining ordinary residence. The residence must be voluntarily adopted. Enforced presence by reason of kidnapping or imprisonment, or a Robinson Crusoe existence on a desert island with no opportunity of escape, may be so overwhelming a factor as to negative the will to be where one is. And there must be a degree of settled purpose. The purpose may be one; or there may be several. It may be specific or general. All the law requires is that there is a settled purpose. This is not to say that the [claimant] intends to stay where he is indefinitely; indeed his purpose, while settled, may be for a limited period. Education, business or profession, employment, health, family, or merely love of the place spring to mind as common reasons for a choice of regular abode. And there may well be many others. All that is necessary is that the purpose of living where one does has a sufficient degree of continuity to be properly described as settled.

10.7 Habitual residence

10.7.1 The test

For IS, IBJSA, HB and CTB, the test is 'habitual residence'. The question is whether the claimant is habitually resident within the Common Travel Area, not just Great Britain or even the UK. This extension to the rest of the Common Travel Area means that residents of the Republic of Ireland, the Channel Islands and the Isle of Man can claim these benefits on the same basis as British residents.

The habitual residence test is itself made up of three tests, namely:

(a) that the UK is the claimant's so-called 'centre of interest';
(b) that residence has been for an appreciable period of time with a settled intent; and
(c) that the claimant has a right to reside in the UK under domestic or EC law.

10.7.1.1 Centre of interest

'Habitual residence' is more than just 'residence'; it is a complex question of fact. It is often paraphrased as indicating the claimant's 'centre of interest'. The DfWP's standard questionnaire for recent arrivals includes the following:

(a) Does the claimant have another home elsewhere?
(b) Where are the members of his immediate family living?
(c) Where are his personal possessions?
(d) Does he have a bank account, utility accounts and so on within Great Britain?
(e) Community ties: is he registered with a local doctor? Where do his children go to school? Does he belong to a local church/mosque/temple?
(f) How is he proposing to support himself?

The DfWP *Decision Maker's Guide* says:

People who maintain their centre of interest in the United Kingdom, for example a home, a job, friends, membership of clubs, are likely to be habitually resident in the United Kingdom. People who have retained their centre of interest in another country and have no particular ties here are unlikely to be habitually resident in the United Kingdom.

In *Commissioner's Decision CIS 12703/96*, the claimant arrived from Bangladesh. She had never been in the UK before and was living with relatives. One factor taken into account was, as Commissioner Henty stated, 'her husband and children, to be presumed to be her centre of interest, remained resident in Bangladesh'.

10.7.1.2 Appreciable period and settled intent

Lord Brandon in *Re J (A Minor) (Abduction: Custody Rights)* [1990] 2 AC 562 at 578–9 said:

> It follows, I think, that the expression [habitually resident] is not to be treated as a term of art with some special meaning, but as rather to be understood according to the ordinary natural meaning of the two words which it contained. The second point is that the question whether a person is or is not habitually resident in a specified country is a question of fact to be decided by reference to all the circumstances of any particular case. The third point is that there is a significant difference between a person ceasing to be habitually resident in country A, and his subsequently becoming habitually resident in country B. A person may cease to be habitually resident in country A in a single day if he or she leaves it with a settled intention not to return to it but to take up long-term residence in country B instead. Such a person cannot, however, become habitually resident in country B in a single day. An appreciable period of time and a settled intention will be necessary to enable him or her to become so. During that appreciable period of time the person will have ceased to be habitually resident in country A but not yet have become habitually resident in country B.

10.7.1.3 The right to reside test

The Social Security (Persons from Abroad) Amendment Regulations 2006 (SI 2006/1026) provide that no person is treated as habitually resident in the Common Travel Area unless he has a right to reside in the UK under domestic or EC law. As to the latter, see **10.7.2**.

10.7.2 EEA nationals and their family members

An EEA national and his family members are entitled to reside in the UK for a period not exceeding three months (see **13.9.3**), where the only condition is that the EEA national and any family member must not become an unreasonable burden on the social assistance system of the UK. This includes economically inactive people, who are not required to be self-sufficient during this period. Claimants who have a right to reside solely on this basis will not satisfy the right to reside aspect of the habitual residence test (see **10.7.1.3**).

After three months, an EEA national and his family members may reside in the UK if the EEA national is a qualified person (see **13.9.5**). EEA workers and self-employed persons satisfy the right to reside test. What about the other categories?

Those EEA jobseekers who have registered with Jobcentre Plus and have claimed JSA will have a right to reside for an initial period of six months, and for longer if they are genuinely seeking work and have a reasonable chance of securing employment.

An EEA national who has the right to reside as a jobseeker will not satisfy the right to reside aspect of the habitual residence test for IS. Such a right to reside will satisfy the test for IBJSA.

Those EEA nationals who are in the UK as students or self-sufficient persons have a right to reside. However, they risk losing their right of residence if they become an unreasonable burden on the social assistance system of the UK.

The above was confirmed by the Court of Appeal in *Abdirahman and Ullusow v Secretary of State for Work and Pensions* [2007] EWCA Civ 657. As neither EEA national claimant was a worker or otherwise economically self-sufficient, their claims for any one of these benefits were rejected on the basis that they did not have a right to reside in the UK under EC law.

Family members (see **13.9.6**) of an EEA worker, a self-employed person, student or self-sufficient person satisfy the right to reside test. More distant relatives, known as extended family members (see **13.9.6**), satisfy the right to reside test if they have been issued with a family permit, registration certificate or residence card (see **13.9.13**).

Family members of an EEA national who has the right to reside as a jobseeker will not satisfy the right to reside aspect of the habitual residence test for IS. Such a right to reside will satisfy the test for IBJSA.

10.7.3 Other exempt categories

People granted refugee status (see **14.17**) or humanitarian protection (see **14.17.13**) are treated as being habitually resident.

10.7.4 First-time entrants

If a British citizen, a Commonwealth citizen with the right of abode or a person granted entry clearance for the purposes of settlement has never lived in the Common Travel Area before, he will need to establish habitual residence before being entitled to the benefit.

In the case of *Nessa v Chief Adjudication Officer* [1999] 1 WLR 1937, Mrs Nessa arrived at Heathrow on 22 August 1994. She was then aged 55 and she had lived all her life in Bangladesh. She had a right of abode in the UK. In Bangladesh, she had lived in the house of her husband's father with her husband's other wife and the children of both wives. On arrival, she planned to live at the home of her husband's brother in England. Her three children, all adults, wanted to come to join her. She applied for income support. Her application was dated 2 September 1994. It was refused as the decision-maker found she was 'not habitually resident in the United Kingdom' as 'Customer has never lived in the UK. Husband died in UK 1.5.75. All other family ties and home in Bangladesh'.

Lord Slynn of Hadley said:

> If Parliament had intended that a person seeking to enter the United Kingdom or such a person declaring his intention to settle here is to have Income Support on arrival, it could have said so. It seems to me impossible to accept the argument at one time advanced that a person who has never been here before who says on landing, 'I intend to settle in the United Kingdom' and who is fully believed is automatically a person who is habitually resident here. Nor is it enough to say I am going to live at X or with Y. He must show residence in fact for a period which shows that the residence has become 'habitual' and, as I see it, will or is likely to continue to be habitual.

I do not consider that when he spoke of residence for an appreciable period, Lord Brandon [see **10.7.1.2**] meant more than this. It is a question of fact to be decided on the date where the determination has to be made on the circumstances of each case whether and when that habitual residence had been established. Bringing possessions, doing everything necessary to establish residence before coming, having a right of abode, seeking to bring family, 'durable ties' with the country of residence or intended residence, and many other factors have to be taken into account.

The requisite period is not a fixed period. It may be longer where there are doubts. It may be short (as the House accepted in *In re S (A Minor) (Custody: Habitual Residence)* [1998] AC 750, my speech at p 763A; and *Re F (A Minor) (Child Abduction)* [1994] 1 FLR 548, 555 where Butler-Sloss, LJ said 'A month can be ... an appreciable period of time.')

10.7.5 Returning 'residents'

What if a British citizen, a Commonwealth citizen with the right of abode or a person with settled status has lived in the Common Travel Area before and is now returning? In Case C–90/97 *Swaddling v Adjudication Officer* [1999] All ER (EC) 217, the ECJ had to consider the position of a British citizen who had spent much of his adult life working in France. Between 1980 and 1994, Mr Swaddling had worked for various employers mainly in France but occasionally in the UK. In 1994, his French employer's business collapsed and in January 1995, after an unsuccessful attempt to find work in France, Mr Swaddling returned to the UK to live with his brother. Mr Swaddling declared that he no longer wished to take a job which entailed spending long periods of time abroad and on 9 January he applied for income support. The application was refused on the grounds that Mr Swaddling did not meet the habitual residence requirement prescribed by reg 21 of the IS Regs 1987. However, the Social Security Appeal Tribunal allowed Mr Swaddling's appeal on the ground that he had shown the necessary intention to establish habitual residence in the UK as of 9 January. On a further appeal, the Social Security Commissioner considered that, for the purposes of the national legislation, 'habitual residence' presupposed an appreciable period of residence (such as eight weeks) in the UK in addition to the settled intention of residing there. However, the Commissioner stayed the proceedings and referred to the European Court of Justice (ECJ) for a preliminary ruling the question whether, in the circumstances, the imposition of a condition of habitual residence, involving the existence of an appreciable period of residence, was compatible with Community law.

The ECJ held that under Articles 1(h) and 10a of Council Regulation 1408/71 on the application of social security schemes to employed persons, to self-employed persons and to members of their families moving within the Community, payment of income support was conditional on the claimant being resident in the territory of the Member State under whose legislation he was claiming and having the habitual centre of his interests there. In determining whether that was the case, account had to be taken of the person's family situation, the reasons which had led him to move, the length and continuity of his residence, and his intention as it appeared in all the circumstances. However, the length of residence in the Member State in which payment of the benefit was sought could not be regarded as an intrinsic element of the concept of residence within the meaning of art 10a. In particular, when, as in the instant case, an employed person, on returning to his State of origin after exercising his right to freedom of movement, had made it clear at the time of applying for income support that he intended to remain in his State of origin where his close relatives lived, he did not fail to satisfy the Article 10a residence condition merely because the period of residence completed there was too short. It followed that in such circumstances, the application of the rule at issue was precluded by Regulation 1408/71.

Whilst the *Swaddling* case concerned EC law, the Government issued a press release on 14 June 1999 saying:

> People returning to the UK from living abroad are to get fairer access to benefits – but tough action to prevent 'benefit tourism' will continue.

Social Security Minister Angela Eagle said:

> We have accepted a recent judgment of the European Court of Justice which has made it clear that people returning to the UK from an EU member state and re-establishing their ties here should be treated as habitually resident immediately upon their return.

The DfWP has issued guidance (Memo DMG Vol 2 01/02) as to the application of EC law in this area. It stresses that a claimant who was previously habitually resident in the Common Travel Area and moved to live and work in another EU State and returns to resume the previous habitual residence is habitually resident immediately on arrival in the Common Travel Area. In deciding whether the claimant is resuming previous residence a decision-maker should take into account the length and continuity of the previous residence in the Common Travel Area, his employment history in the EU State and whether the claimant has maintained sufficient links with the previous residence to be said to be resuming it rather than commencing a new period of residence. The guidance also gives the following example. The claimant, a UK national, lived and worked in the UK before moving to Germany where he worked for several years. He was made redundant and having failed to find work in Germany for three months returned to the UK where he had his family and friends. On claiming IBJSA, he stated that his intention was to find work and remain permanently in the UK. JSA was awarded because he was resuming a previous habitual residence.

Is the habitual residence test compatible with EC law? In Case C-138/02 *Collins v Secretary of State for Work and Pensions* (2004) *The Times*, 30 March, the ECJ held that the right to equal treatment laid down in Article 39(2) EC, read in conjunction with Articles 12 EC and 17 EC, does not preclude national legislation which makes entitlement to a jobseeker's allowance conditional on a residence requirement, in so far as that requirement may be justified on the basis of objective considerations that are independent of the nationality of the persons concerned and proportionate to the legitimate aim of the national provisions. When the case returned to the domestic courts, the Court of Appeal held that the habitual residence test is compatible with EC law: see *Collins v Secretary of State for Work and Pensions* [2006] EWCA Civ 376.

What if EC law does not apply? The DfWP also issued its own guidance (AM(AOG) 109), which includes the following:

> A JSA (IB) or IS claimant of any nationality who was previously habitually resident in the UK, Republic of Ireland, Channel Islands or Isle of Man and moved and lived in another country and returns to resume the previous residence is habitually resident immediately on arrival in the UK, Republic of Ireland, Channel Islands or Isle of Man. In deciding habitual residence questions [decision-makers] should take account of the length and continuity of the previous residence in the UK, Republic of Ireland, Channel Islands or Isle of Man and whether the claimant has sufficient links with that previous residence to be regarded as picking up the pieces of their old life ... a claimant who is temporarily absent from the UK may in any case retain habitual residence in the UK.

The DfWP guidance (Memo DMG Vol 2 01/02) accepts that there may be special cases where a person is resuming a previous habitual residence following a period living abroad. It states that if a person abandons their life in the other country in circumstances which make the decision irrevocable and returns to take up residence previously held in the UK they may be habitually resident immediately on their return. The following example is given. A woman who lived with her partner, an Australian national, in Canada for several years returned to the UK where she had previously lived and worked until she was 27 years old. She stated that following her partner's imprisonment, it was necessary for her to remove the two children of the family from any influence he might try to exert. Before embarking on the journey to rejoin her parents in Wales she had arranged for the future schooling of her children and had obtained a firm offer of employment. She had left nothing behind in Canada and intended to bring up the children in her parents' household.

10.8 Immigration law and public funds

10.8.1 Immigration rules

A person who has limited leave to enter the UK will be placed under a prohibition on 'resorting to public funds' as part of the conditions attached to their leave to enter (see **13.1.1**). The various categories of entrants subject to this condition are covered in detail in **Chapter 14**. They include students, work permit holders, fiancé(e)s, spouses in their two-year probationary period, business persons and sponsored immigrants under a written undertaking.

10.8.2 Public funds

As we have seen at **10.3**, a person with limited leave is not entitled to certain benefits and perhaps, not surprisingly, these constitute 'public funds'.

Note that by Immigration Rules, para 6B, a person is not regarded as having recourse to public funds if he is entitled to such as a member of an exempt group: see **10.3.2**.

10.8.3 Claims by a couple for IS or IBJSA

Where one partner is eligible to claim but the other is excluded by s 115, the qualifying partner should apply but the excluded partner will be deemed to have a *nil* applicable amount. This means that the claimant is therefore awarded a single person's allowance according to his or her age. Any premiums appropriate to the claimant (but not the excluded partner) are payable. Any allowable housing costs will form part of the applicable amount in the usual way. Moreover, the capital and income of both partners is also aggregated in the usual way.

10.8.4 Claims by a couple for tax credits

Regulation 3(2) of the Tax Credits (Immigration) Regulations 2003 (SI 2003/653) provides that where one member of a couple is a person subject to immigration control, but the other member is not, or that person is within any one of the five prescribed cases (see **10.3.2**), then:

(a) the calculation of the amount of tax credit (including any second adult element or other element in respect of, or determined by reference to, that person);

(b) the method of making (or proceeding with) a joint claim by the couple; and

(c) the method of payment of the tax credit;

is to be determined in the same way as if that person were not subject to immigration control.

Note that where the other member is within prescribed case 4 or 5 (see **10.3.2**), the above applies only to the appropriate tax credit to which he is entitled.

Also note that by Immigration Rules, para 6B, the member of the couple who is subject to immigration controls will not be regarded as resorting to public funds.

10.8.5 Not 'public funds'

The benefits which do not count as 'public funds', and which can theoretically be claimed by a person with limited leave, are:

(a) statutory sick pay and statutory maternity pay;

(b) all the contributory benefits; and

(c) industrial disablement benefit.

10.8.6 Practical problems of claiming benefits which are not public funds

Even if a benefit is not public funds, few new arrivals are likely to be eligible. There are a number of reasons for this, as outlined below.

10.8.6.1 Contributory benefits

Few people who have recently arrived in Great Britain will have the appropriate National Insurance contribution record to claim any contributory benefit (see **Chapter 2**).

10.8.6.2 Contribution-based jobseeker's allowance

A work permit employee could easily satisfy the contribution conditions for CBJSA if he has worked in Great Britain for three years or more. But his employment is dependent on his employer obtaining a work permit for him. Can he be said to be 'available for work' (see **3.2.6** and **3.2.7**) in these circumstances? According to the DfWP *Decision Maker's Guide*, the answer is no.

10.8.6.3 Statutory sick pay, statutory maternity pay and industrial disablement benefit

The right to SSP, SMP or disablement benefit depends upon status as an employee. If the claimant is prohibited from working by the terms of his leave to enter, there is a risk that a claim for any of these benefits will lead to the Home Office becoming aware that the claimant is working unlawfully.

If a person has entered the UK in a category which allows him to work, there is no reason whatever why he should not claim any of the benefits in this group, provided that he satisfies the other qualifying conditions.

The entry categories most likely to be able to claim benefits successfully are detailed in **Chapter 14**. These are:

(a) all the above-mentioned benefits: permit-free employment (Commonwealth citizens with UK ancestry);

(b) all the above-mentioned benefits except contribution-based jobseeker's allowance: work permit holders;

(c) the above-mentioned non-contributory benefits: spouses in the two-year probationary period (before acquiring settled status);

(d) industrial disablement benefit only: students and working holidaymakers who are doing permitted work.

10.9 Asylum seekers

Section 115 of the IAA 1999 excludes asylum seekers from the main benefits. Part 3 of the Nationality, Immigration and Asylum Act 2002 laid down a blueprint for giving financial support to asylum seekers.

10.10 Urgent cases payments

As we saw at **10.3**, persons with limited leave whose funds from abroad have been temporarily interrupted can claim income support provided there is a reasonable expectation that the supply of those funds will be resumed. In fact, the claim is for an urgent case payment(s) in the short term. See further **8.12**.

10.11 Social fund payment

As we saw at **10.3**, a social fund payment can be sought by the following: a person with limited leave whose funds from abroad have been temporarily interrupted provided there is a reasonable expectation that the supply of those funds will be resumed; nationals of Turkey who are lawfully present in the UK; a member of the family of a national of an EEA country; a person who is legally working and living in Great Britain and is a national of a State with which the EU has made an agreement relating to equal treatment (namely Turkey, Morocco, Algeria and Tunisia) and any members of their family living with them; and a sponsored immigrant regardless of the length of stay in the UK.

See further **9.15**.

10.12 EEA nationals claiming benefits

As we have seen, EEA nationals are not excluded from benefits. But can claiming benefits affect their right of residence in the UK? That right derives after three months from having a qualifying status, ie a jobseeker, a worker, a self-employed person, a self-sufficient person or a student (see **13.9.5**).

An EEA jobseeker who has registered with Jobcentre Plus and has claimed JSA will have a right to reside for an initial period of six months, and for longer if he is genuinely seeking work and has a reasonable chance of securing employment. If the Home Office considers that he no longer satisfies those requirements, it may seek to remove him: see **13.9.14**. EEA nationals who are in the UK as students or self-sufficient persons have a right to reside. However, they risk losing their right of residence if they become an unreasonable burden on the social assistance system of the UK. Workers and self-employed EEA nationals retain their qualifying status if they temporarily cease economic activity due to involuntary redundancy or illness. In those circumstances, resorting to public funds would be acceptable.

APPENDICES TO PART I

		Page
Appendix 1	Specimen Jobseeker's Agreement	187
Appendix 2	Extracts from the Social Security (Incapacity for Work) (General) Regulations 1995, as amended	191
Appendix 3	Schedule 2 – Prescribed Degrees of Disablement	197
Appendix 4	Working Tax Credit – Disability Which Puts a Person at a Disadvantage in Getting a Job – Part 1 of Schedule 1	201
Appendix 5	Welfare Benefits: Reciprocal Agreements	203

Appendix 1

Specimen Jobseeker's Agreement

Jobseeker's **Allowance**   *Jobseeker's*   **Agreement**

Jobseeker's Agreement
This Jobseeker's Agreement sets out
- when I can work
- the types of work I am willing to do
- what I am going to do to find work and increase my chances of finding work.

I, or an Employment Services adviser, can ask for it to be changed at any time. If we cannot agree about changing the Agreement, an independent adjudication officer will be asked to look at it. If I am not satisfied with their decision, I can have it looked at by another adjudication officer. If I am still not satisfied, I can appeal to an independent tribunal.

Availability of work
I understand I must
- be available for work
- (unless the limitation is for health reasons) have a reasonable chance of getting work if I limit
    - the kind of work I am willing to do
    - the rate of pay I will accept
    - where I am willing to work
    - the hours I am willing to work
- be capable of work.

Permitted period
*I know I can limit myself to accepting work in my usual job and at my usual wages from / / to / / After this I will be interviewed about broadening my availability and job search.

Actively seeking work
I understand that I must actively seek work. I will be asked regularly to show what I have done to find work. I have been advised to keep a record of what I do to find work.

Jobseeker's Allowance
I understand my allowance may be affected if I
- do not do enough to find work
- am not available for work
- reduce my chances of getting work, or
- become incapable of work.

If this happens, I will be told and my case may be sent to an independent adjudication officer for a decision. If I am not satisfied with the decision, I can appeal to an independent tribunal. I understand that this is general information and not a full statement of the law.

* The adviser had read this Agreement to me.

Jobseeker's signature		Adviser's signature	
Date	/ /	Date	/ /
		Adviser's name	
		Telephone number	
(* Please delete as appropriate)		TAM date	/ /

ES 3

Name		

The types of job I am looking for			
I am willing and able to start work	* immediately within 48 hours other within 24 hours after giving a weeks notice		
I want to limit the days and hours I am available for work	* No Yes		
	Earliest start time	**Latest** finish time	**Most hours** I can work
I am available for work these days and these hours Monday			
Tuesday			
Wednesday			
Thursday			
Friday			
Saturday			
Sunday			
		Most hours I can work each week	
Other agreed restrictions on my availability and/or agreed restrictions on types of work			

Specimen Jobseeker's Agreement 189

| NI Number | | Claim file/cycle | |

What I will do to identify and apply for jobs

* Write to at least ☐ employers a week

* Phone at least ☐ employers a week

Visit at least ☐ employers a week

Contact the Jobcentre at least ☐ times a week

* Ask family, friends and people I have worked with before

* Look in these newspapers and trade papers   How often I will look

Other activities including any steps to improve my chances of finding a job

Our commitment to you

Jobseeker's Charter
If you are out of work and looking for a job, we want to offer you the best possible service.
Our jobseeker's Charter sets out the standards of service we aim to provide. It also tells you how to complain if you are not satisfied. You can get a copy of the Charter from your Jobcentre.

What you can expect from us
You can expect us to
- wear a name badge and give our name when we answer the phone and write
- be polite, considerate, open and honest
- respect your privacy. In most cases we can provide a private room for sensitive interviews
- apologise if we get things wrong, explain what happened and put things right promptly
- deliver our services fairly and to the same high standards regardless of race, sex, disability or religion.

Your views
We regularly ask people what they think of our service and we publish the results. We welcome your comments at any time. If you want to comment or complain, ask for a copy of our leaflet.

Jobs
The vacancies we display should be up to date and available. We will not display vacancies which discriminate unlawfully because of race, sex, disability or religion. We encourage people of all ages to apply for the vacancies we display.

Information
We will give you advice about employment opportunities, training and setting up your own business.
Health problems and disabilities
If you have a health problem or disability which affects the type of work you can do we will tell you about the special help available.

Interviews
You will be asked to attend the office regularly. Each time we will
- talk about your search for work
- make sure your Agreement is up to date
- see what other help we can give you.

If possible you will be seen by the same person or someone from the same team.

Jobseeker's Allowance
If you are entitled to Jobseeker's Allowance we will aim to get the right money to you in time.

Other benefits
We will give you information about other benefits you may be entitled to.
You may get benefit even when you start work, for example, Family Credit.

More about our services
You will find out more information about our services in the leaflet '*Just the job*'

Appendix 2

Extracts from the Social Security (Incapacity for Work) (General) Regulations 1995, as amended

Disabilities which may make a person incapable of work

Part I: Physical disabilities

NB: Only the higher score for physical activities 1 and 2 counts towards the total.

1. Walking on level ground with a walking stick or other aid if such aid is normally used.

(a)	Cannot walk at all	15
(b)	Cannot walk more than a few steps without stopping or severe discomfort	15
(c)	Cannot walk more than 50 m without stopping or severe discomfort	15
(d)	Cannot walk more than 200 m without stopping or severe discomfort	7
(e)	Cannot walk more than 400 m without stopping or severe discomfort	3
(f)	Cannot walk more than 800 m without stopping or severe discomfort	0
(g)	No walking problem	0

2. Walking up and down stairs.

(a)	Cannot walk up and down one stair	15
(b)	Cannot walk up and down a flight of 12 stairs	15
(c)	Cannot walk up and down a flight of 12 stairs without holding on and taking a rest	7
(d)	Cannot walk up and down a flight of 12 stairs without holding on	3
(e)	Can only walk up and down a flight of 12 stairs if goes sideways or one step at a time	3
(f)	No problem in walking up and down stairs	0

3. Sitting in an upright chair with a back, but no arms.

(a)	Cannot sit comfortably	15
(b)	Cannot sit comfortably for more than 10 minutes without having to move from the chair*	15
(c)	Cannot sit comfortably for more than 30 minutes without having to move from the chair*	7
(d)	Cannot sit comfortably for more than 1 hour without having to move from the chair*	3
(e)	Cannot sit comfortably for more than 2 hours without having to move from the chair*	0
(f)	No problem with sitting	0

[* because the degree of discomfort makes it impossible to continue sitting – see *Commissioner's Decisions CIB/1239/04 and CIB/3397/04*]

4. Standing without the support of another person or the use of an aid except a walking stick.

(a)	Cannot stand unassisted	15

(b)	Cannot stand for more than a minute before needing to sit down	15
(c)	Cannot stand for more than 10 minutes before needing to sit down	15
(d)	Cannot stand for more than 30 minutes before needing to sit down	7
(e)	Cannot stand for more than 10 minutes before needing to move around	7
(f)	Cannot stand for more than 30 minutes before needing to move around	3
(g)	No problem standing	0
5.	Rising from sitting in an upright chair with a back but no arms without the help of another person.	
(a)	Cannot rise from sitting to standing	15
(b)	Cannot rise from sitting to standing without holding onto something	7
(c)	Sometimes cannot rise from sitting to standing without holding onto something	3
(d)	No problem with rising from sitting to standing	0
6.	Bending and kneeling.	
(a)	Cannot bend to touch his knees and straighten up again	15
(b)	Cannot either bend or kneel, or bend and kneel, as if to pick up a piece of paper from the floor and straighten up again	15
(c)	Sometimes cannot either bend or kneel, or bend and kneel, as if to pick up a piece of paper from the floor and straighten up again	3
(d)	No problem with bending or kneeling	0
7.	Manual dexterity.	
(a)	Cannot turn the pages of a book with either hand	15
(b)	Cannot turn a sink tap or the control knobs of a cooker with either hand	15
(c)	Cannot pick up a coin which is 2.5 cm or less in diameter with either hand	15
(d)	Cannot use a pen or pencil	15
(e)	Cannot tie a bow in laces or string	10
(f)	Cannot turn a sink tap or the control knobs of a cooker with one hand, but can with the other	6
(g)	Cannot pick up a coin which is 2.5 cm or less in diameter with one hand, but can with the other	6
(h)	No problem with manual dexterity	0
8.	Lifting and carrying by the use of upper body and arms (excluding all other activities specified in Part I of this Schedule).	
(a)	Cannot pick up a paper-back book with either hand	15
(b)	Cannot pick up and carry a 0.5 litre carton of milk with either hand	15
(c)	Cannot pick up and pour from a full saucepan or kettle of 1.7 litre capacity with either hand	15
(d)	Cannot pick up and carry a 2.5 kg bag of potatoes with either hand	8
(e)	Cannot pick up and carry a 0.5 litre carton of milk with one hand, but can with the other	6
(f)	Cannot pick up and carry a 2.5 kg bag of potatoes with one hand, but can with the other	0
(g)	No problem with lifting and carrying	0
9.	Reaching.	
(a)	Cannot raise either arm as if to put something in the top pocket of a coat or jacket	15
(b)	Cannot raise either arm to his head as if to put on a hat	15

(c)	Cannot put either arm behind back as if to put on a coat or jacket	15
(d)	Cannot raise either arm above his head as if to reach for something	15
(e)	Cannot raise one arm to his head as if to put on a hat, but can with the other	6
(f)	Cannot raise one arm above his head as if to reach for something, but can with the other	0
(g)	No problem with reaching	0

10. Speech.

(a)	Cannot speak	15
(b)	Speech cannot be understood by family and friends	15
(c)	Speech cannot be understood by strangers	15
(d)	Strangers have great difficulty understanding speech	10
(e)	Strangers have some difficulty understanding speech	8
(f)	No problems with speech	0

11. Hearing with a hearing aid or other aid if normally worn.

(a)	Cannot hear sounds at all	15
(b)	Cannot hear well enough to follow a television programme with the volume turned up	15
(c)	Cannot hear well enough to understand someone talking in a loud voice in a quiet room	15
(d)	Cannot hear well enough to understand someone talking in a normal voice in a quiet room	10
(e)	Cannot hear well enough to understand someone talking in a normal voice on a busy street	8
(f)	No problem with hearing	0

12. Vision in normal daylight or bright electric light with glasses or other aid to vision if such is normally worn.

(a)	Cannot tell light from dark	15
(b)	Cannot see the shape of furniture in the room	15
(c)	Cannot see well enough to read 16 point print at a distance greater than 20 cm	15
(d)	Cannot see well enough to recognise a friend across the room at a distance of at least 5 m	12
(e)	Cannot see well enough to recognise a friend across the road at a distance of at least 15 m	8
(f)	No problem with vision	0

13. Continence other than enuresis (bed-wetting).

(a)	No voluntary control over bowels	15
(b)	No voluntary control over bladder	15
(c)	Loses control of bowels at least once a week	15
(d)	Loses control of bowels at least once a month	15
(e)	Loses control of bowels occasionally	9
(f)	Loses control of bladder at least once a month	3
(g)	Loses control of bladder occasionally	0
(h)	No problem with continence	0

14. Remaining conscious other than for normal periods of sleep.

(a)	Has an involuntary episode of lost or altered consciousness at least once a day	15

(b)	Has an involuntary episode of lost or altered consciousness at least once a week	15
(c)	Has an involuntary episode of lost or altered consciousness at least once a month	15
(d)	Has had an involuntary episode of lost or altered consciousness at least twice in the 6 months before the day in respect to which it falls to be determined whether he is incapable of work for the purposes of entitlement to any benefit, allowance or advantage	12
(e)	Has had an involuntary episode of lost or altered consciousness once in the 6 months before the day in respect to which it falls to be determined whether he is incapable of work for the purposes of entitlement to any benefit, allowance or advantage	8
(f)	Has had an involuntary episode of lost or altered consciousness once in the 3 years before the day in respect to which it falls to be determined whether he is incapable of work for the purposes of entitlement to any benefit, allowance or advantage	0
(g)	Has no problems with consciousness	0

Part II: Mental disabilities

Note: For a mental descriptor to apply, it must arise from a mental disablement, not from a physical problem [all qualifying descriptors may be added together].

15.	Completion of tasks.	
(a)	Cannot answer the telephone and reliably take a message	2
(b)	Often sits for hours doing nothing	2
(c)	Cannot concentrate to read a magazine article or follow a radio programme	1
(d)	Cannot use a telephone book or directory to find a number	1
(e)	Mental condition prevents him from undertaking leisure activities previously enjoyed	1
(f)	Overlooks or forgets the risks posed by domestic appliances or other hazards due to poor concentration	1
(g)	Agitation, confusion or forgetfulness has resulted in potentially dangerous accidents in the 3 months before the day in respect to which it falls to be determined whether he is incapable of work for the purposes of entitlement to any benefit, allowance or advantage	1
(h)	Concentration can only be sustained by prompting	1
16.	Daily living.	
(a)	Needs encouragement to get up and dress	2
(b)	Needs alcohol before midday	2
(c)	Is frequently distressed at some time of the day due to fluctuation of mood	1
(d)	Does not care about his appearance or living conditions	1
(e)	Sleep problems interfere with his daytime activities	1
17.	Coping with pressure.	
(a)	Mental stress was a factor in making him stop work	2
(b)	Frequently feels scared or panicky for no obvious reason	2
(c)	Avoids carrying out routine tasks because he is convinced they will prove too tiring or stressful	1
(d)	Is unable to cope with changes in daily routine	1
(e)	Frequently finds that there are so many things to do that he gives up because of fatigue, apathy or disinterest	1

(f)	Is scared or anxious that work would bring back or worsen his illness	1
18.	Interaction with other people.	
(a)	Cannot look after himself without help from others	2
(b)	Gets upset by ordinary events and it results in disruptive behavioural problems	2
(c)	Mental problems impair ability to communicate with other people	2
(d)	Gets irritated by things that would not have bothered him before he became ill	1
(e)	Prefers to be left alone for 6 hours or more each day	1
(f)	Is too frightened to go out alone	1

Appendix 3

Schedule 2 – Prescribed Degrees of Disablement

	Description of injury	Regulation 11 Degree of disablement per cent
1	Loss of both hands or amputation at higher sites	100
2	Loss of a hand and a foot	100
3	Double amputation through leg or thigh, or amputation through leg or thigh on one side and loss of other foot	100
4	Loss of sight to such an extent as to render the claimant unable to perform any work for which eyesight is essential	100
5	Very severe facial disfiguration	100
6	Absolute deafness	100
7	Forequarter or hindquarter amputation	100

Amputation cases – upper limbs (either arm)

8	Amputation through shoulder joint	90
9	Amputation below shoulder with stump less than 20.5 centimetres from tip of acromion	80
10	Amputation from 20.5 centimetres from tip of acromion to less than 11.5 centimetres below tip of olecranon	70
11	Loss of a hand or of the thumb and four fingers of one hand or amputation from 11.5 centimetres below tip of olecranon	60
12	Loss of thumb	30
13	Loss of thumb and its metacarpal bone	40
14	Loss of four fingers of one hand	50
15	Loss of three fingers of one hand	30
16	Loss of two fingers of one hand	20
17	Loss of terminal phalanx of thumb	20

Amputation cases – lower limbs

18	Amputation of both feet resulting in end-bearing stumps	90
19	Amputation through both feet proximal to the metatarsophalangeal joint	80
20	Loss of all toes of both feet through the metatarsophalangeal joint	40
21	Loss of all toes of both feet proximal to the proximal inter-phalangeal joint	30
22	Loss of all toes of both feet distal to the proximal inter-phalangeal joint	20
23	Amputation at hip	90
24	Amputation below hip with stump not exceeding 13 centimetres in length measured from tip of great trochanter	80

25	Amputation below hip and above knee with stump exceeding 13 centimetres in length measured from tip of great trochanter, or at knee not resulting in end-bearing stump	70
26	Amputation at knee resulting in end-bearing stump or below knee with stump not exceeding 9 centimetres	60
27	Amputation below knee with stump exceeding 9 centimetres but not exceeding 13 centimetres	50
28	Amputation below knee with stump exceeding 13 centimetres	40
29	Amputation of one foot resulting in end-bearing stump	30
30	Amputation through one foot proximal to the metatarsophalangeal joint	30
31	Loss of all toes of one foot through the metatarsophalangeal joint	20

Other injuries

32	Loss of one eye, without complications, the other being normal	40
33	Loss of vision of one eye, without complications or disfigurement of eyeball, the other being normal	30

Loss of:

A. *Fingers of right or left hand*

Index finger –

34	Whole	14
35	Two phalanges	11
36	One phalanx	9
37	Guillotine amputation of tip without loss of bone	5

Middle finger –

38	Whole	12
39	Two phalanges	9
40	One phalanx	7
41	Guillotine amputation of tip without loss of bone	4

Ring or little finger –

42	Whole	7
43	Two phalanges	6
44	One phalanx	5
45	Guillotine of tip without loss of bone	2

B. *Toes of right or left foot*

14 Great toe –

46	Through metatarsophalangeal joint	14
47	Part, with some loss of bone	3

Any other toe –

48	Through metatarsophalangeal joint	3
49	Part, with some loss of bone	1

Two toes of one foot, excluding great toe –

50	Through metatarsophalangeal joint	5
51	Part, with some loss of bone	2

Three toes of one foot, excluding great toe –

52	Through metatarsophalangeal joint	6
53	Part, with some loss of bone	3

Four toes of one foot, excluding great toe –

54	Through metatarsophalangeal joint	9
55	Part, with some loss of bone	3

Note: for any injury not covered by these Regulations, a government-appointed doctor will examine the claimant and make an assessment of the degree of disablement as a percentage.

Appendix 4

Working Tax Credit – Disability Which Puts a Person at a Disadvantage in Getting a Job – Part 1 of Schedule 1

1. When standing he cannot keep his balance unless he continually holds onto something.
2. Using any crutches, walking frame, walking stick, prosthesis or similar walking aid which he habitually uses, he cannot walk a continuous distance of 100 metres along level ground without stopping or without suffering severe pain.
3. He can use neither of his hands behind his back as in the process of putting on a jacket or of tucking a shirt into trousers.
4. He can extend neither of his arms in front of him so as to shake hands with another person without difficulty.
5. He can put neither of his hands up to his head without difficulty so as to put on a hat.
6. Due to lack of manual dexterity he cannot [with one hand, pick up] a coin which is not more than 2½ centimetres in diameter.
7. He is not able to use his hands or arms to pick up a full jug of 1 litre capacity and pour from it into a cup, without difficulty.
8. He can turn neither of his hands sideways through 180 degrees.
9. He is registered as blind or registered as partially sighted in a register compiled by a local authority under section 29(4)(g) of the National Assistance Act 1948 (welfare services) or, in Scotland, has been certified as blind or as partially sighted and in consequence registered as blind or partially sighted in a register maintained by or on behalf of a regional or island council.
10. He cannot see to read 16 point print at a distance greater than 20 centimetres, if appropriate, wearing the glasses he normally uses.
11. He cannot hear a telephone ring when he is in the same room as the telephone, if appropriate, using a hearing aid he normally uses.
12. In a quiet room he has difficulty in hearing what someone talking in a loud voice at a distance of 2 metres says, if appropriate, using a hearing aid he normally uses.
13. People who know him well have difficulty in understanding what he says.
14. When a person he knows well speaks to him, he has difficulty in understanding what that person says.
15. At least once a year during waking hours he is in a coma or has a fit in which he loses consciousness.
16. He has a mental illness for which he receives regular treatment under the supervision of a medically qualified person.
17. Due to mental disability he is often confused or forgetful.
18. He cannot do the simplest addition and subtraction.
19. Due to mental disability he strikes people or damages property or is unable to form normal social relationships.
20. He cannot normally sustain an 8 hour working day or a 5 day working week due to a medical condition or intermittent or continuous severe pain. [Note that HMRC state that a person should not fail the test simply because the job exceeds 8 hours per day or 5 days per week. The test is whether a person is disadvantaged in getting a job in the open market. A person may work more than 8 hours per day or 5 days per week if the job has been adapted to suit his needs.]
21. For initial claims only, as a result of an illness or accident, he is undergoing a period of habilation or rehabilitation. [The habilation and rehabilitation criteria apply only

to initial claims, ie a claim for the disability element by someone who has not qualified for it in the two years immediately preceding the claim. Guidance from HMRC states that rehabilitation is helping somebody to do something again which they could do before the illness or accident. Habilitation means enabling them to do something they have not done before. Rehabilitation following illness or injury may involve making a person fully effective throughout the working day. The person may be too weak, or recovering from a psychiatric illness, to work a full day. Time off for physiotherapy or some other form of treatment may be needed. The person may take longer, or need extra, rest periods, or have to avoid stress. Part-time working may be appropriate. Habilitation could be training a person who cannot do his previous job because of an accident or illness, to be able to do a different job. A person who has never worked before can receive habilitation following illness or injury.]

Appendix 5

Welfare Benefits: Reciprocal Agreements

	AA	BB	CA	CB	DLA	ICB: ST	ICB: LT	IDB	JSA	MB	SP
Barbados		X		X		X	X	X		X	X
Bermuda		X						X			X
Bosnia-Herzegovina		X		X		X	X	X	X	X	X
Canada				X					X		X
Croatia		X		X		X	X	X	X	X	X
Guernsey	X	X		X	X	X	X	X	X	X	X
Isle of Man	X	X	X	X	X	X	X	X	X	X	X
Israel		X		X		X	X	X		X	X
Jamaica		X					X	X			
Jersey	X	X		X	X	X	X	X		X	X
Macedonia		X		X		X	X	X	X	X	X
Mauritius		X		X				X			X
New Zealand		X		X		X			X		X
Philippines		X						X			
Serbia and Montenegro		X		X		X	X	X	X	X	X
Turkey		X				X	X	X		X	X
USA		X				X	X				X

Part II
IMMIGRATION AND NATIONALITY

Chapter 11
Introduction to Part II

11.1	The scope of Part II	207
11.2	Sources of immigration law	207
11.3	Institutions	210
11.4	Immigration controls	211

11.1 The scope of Part II

As stated in the Preface, Part II of this book provides an introduction to immigration and nationality law and practice.

This is a public law subject, dealing with relations between the State and the individual, concerned fundamentally with the exercise of discretion by officials. A thorough grounding in the principles of public law will be an advantage.

It is, however, easy to understand the practical problems which arise in this area of the law, as it concerns the individual's ability to live, work and enjoy family life in the country of his or her choice. In practice, it involves a great deal of client contact, argument with officials, advocacy in tribunals and familiarity with a wide range of legal sources. It therefore calls upon the full range of legal skills.

11.2 Sources of immigration law

11.2.1 Practitioner texts

The practitioner in immigration law relies heavily on a limited number of secondary sources. These include:

(a) *Macdonald's Immigration Law and Practice* (Butterworths): the leading practitioner text;

(b) *Butterworths Immigration Law Service*: in the form of a loose-leaf encyclopaedia, particularly useful as a source for Home Office practices;

(c) *Tolley's Immigration and Nationality Law and Practice:* a quarterly journal;

(d) *Immigration, Nationality and Refugee Law Handbook* (Joint Council for the Welfare of Immigrants): an invaluable practical guide (*JCWI Handbook*);

(e) Fransman, *British Nationality Law* (Butterworths);

(f) Webb and Grant, *Immigration and Asylum Emergency Procedures* (Legal Action Group).

11.2.2 Websites

There are many useful websites, most of which have links to other, related sites. You might start with the following:

Home Office, Border and Immigration Agency: www.ind.homeoffice.gov.uk
UK Visas government unit: www.ukvisas.gov.uk
Work Permits (UK): www.workingintheuk.gov.uk
Identity and Passport Service: www.ips.gov.uk
European Union on-line: www.europa.eu.int

Asylum and Immigration Tribunal: www.ait.gov.uk
Immigration Advisory Service: www.iasuk.org
European Court of Human Rights: www.echr.coe.int
Joint Council for the Welfare of Immigrants: www.jcwi.org.uk
Refugee Council: www.refugeecouncil.org.uk
UNHCR UN Refugee Agency: www.unhcr.ch/cgi-bin/texis/utx/home
Electronic Immigration Network: www.ein.org.uk

11.2.3 Legislation

The basic principles of immigration law are contained in the Immigration Act 1971 (IA 1971) as amended by subsequent legislation including, the Immigration Act 1988; the Asylum and Immigration Appeals Act 1993 (AIAA 1993); the Asylum and Immigration Act 1996 (AIA 1996); the Immigration and Asylum Act 1999 (IAA 1999); the Nationality, Immigration and Asylum Act 2002 (NIAA 2002); Asylum and Immigration (Treatment of Claimants, etc) Act 2004 (AI(TC)A 2004) and the Immigration, Asylum and Nationality Act 2006 (IANA 2006). Nationality law is dealt with in the British Nationality Acts 1948 and 1981 (as amended).

A considerable number of statutory instruments have been made under those Acts. For a fuller list, see the practitioner works referred to in **11.2.1**.

11.2.4 The Immigration Rules

The Immigration Rules have a peculiar legal status. They are made under statute (IA 1971, s 3(2)), but are not delegated legislation. This is because the section describes them as rules laid down by the Home Secretary as to the practice to be followed in administration of the IA 1971. The Immigration Rules structure the discretion given by the IA 1971 to grant leave to enter, to vary leave, or to make a deportation order. They bind immigration officers, but not the Home Secretary who, in the exercise of his discretion, may, in appropriate circumstances, depart from the Rules he has laid down, for instance granting leave to remain in the UK when the Rules would require refusal. They are, therefore, not rules of law in the strict sense (*R v Secretary of State for the Home Department, ex p Hosenball* [1977] 3 All ER 452).

Nevertheless, a lawyer can base his advice on the Rules because they are normally followed by the immigration authorities, and because failure to apply them may give grounds for appeal or judicial review (see **Chapters 15** and **16**).

The current Rules are cited as the Statement of Changes in Immigration Rules 1994 (HC 395). As the Rules are not delegated legislation, they are cited as a House of Commons Paper and not as a statutory instrument. Later amendments to the Rules are cited similarly. A copy of the current Rules appears in **Appendix 1** to this Part of the book.

11.2.5 Home Office practices

Since the Home Office has considerable discretion not governed by the Rules, it is inevitable that informal practices evolve in order to ensure that comparable cases are treated in like ways. An example is the concession for visitors who wish to enter or remain to care for a sick relative (see **14.1.6**). These practices are not generally binding although, under the administrative law doctrine of legitimate expectation, a decision which disregards them may be quashed as unreasonable (*R v Secretary of State for the Home Department, ex p Asif Mahmood Khan* [1984] 1 WLR 1337).

The Home Office has made public some of the internal instructions to staff on the handling of immigration cases. These are available via the Internet on the home page of the Immigration and Nationality Directorate (see **11.2.2**).

11.2.6 Case law

Immigration cases have in recent years formed the largest single category of applications to the High Court for judicial review. In addition, cases may reach the higher courts by way of appeal. These cases may be reported in the standard series of law reports, but may also be found in the specialist Immigration and Nationality Law Reports (INLR), published six times a year by Jordans, and the Immigration Appeal Reports (Imm LR), published quarterly by The Stationery Office.

11.2.7 EC law

Nationals of EU Member States have special rights under EC law (eg under Article 39 EC (freedom of movement of workers)). These rights are set out in detail in EC Regulations and Directives. The rights often have direct effect and so override conflicting provisions of UK immigration law. The UK Government will try to ensure that legislation and the Immigration Rules give effect to EC law, but be aware that UK provisions may be open to challenge.

In addition, there is a considerable body of case law of the ECJ on the meaning and effect of Treaty provisions and legislation. This is binding on UK courts. Directives, Regulations, EC judgments etc can be found on the European Union on-line website at www.europa.eu.int.

Probably the most significant EC Directive is Directive 2004/38/EC of the European Parliament and Council. A copy appears at **Appendix 6** to this Part. This sets out the terms and limits of the right of free movement. It has been implemented into domestic law by the I(EEA) Regs 2006 (see **13.9**). There is a chart at **13.10** which sets out where the 2006 Regs implement the 2004 Directive.

11.2.8 The European Convention on Human Rights and the Human Rights Act 1998

The Human Rights Act 1998 (HRA 1998) interprets, rather than incorporates, the ECHR. Although the legislation requires UK courts to apply Acts of Parliament even if they are incompatible with the Convention, it contains a number of measures which will enable practitioners to rely on the Convention in immigration cases. In outline these are as follows.

Section 3 requires UK courts to try to interpret an Act of Parliament in a way which is compatible with listed Convention rights, whether or not the Act is ambiguous.

Section 4 enables the courts to make a declaration that an Act is incompatible with Convention rights. The court must still apply the Act in the case before it, but s 10 enables the Government to introduce fast-track delegated legislation to alter the law.

Section 6 is probably the most far-reaching provision. It states that it is unlawful for public authorities (such as the Home Office) to act in a way which infringes Convention rights, unless required to do so by Act of Parliament. So, when exercising a discretion, the Home Secretary must take Convention rights into account and, if statute permits it, he must avoid decisions which infringe them. As the Immigration Rules themselves are made in the exercise of a discretion, both the Rules and decisions made under them are open to challenge if they infringe Convention rights.

The provisions listed as giving rise to Convention rights and most relevant in immigration cases are set out in **Appendix 9** to this Part of the book.

11.3 Institutions

11.3.1 The Home Office

Under the IA 1971, the Home Secretary has overall responsibility for the administration of immigration control. The Act designates him as the person who makes the Immigration Rules, appoints immigration officers, and takes specific decisions such as the decision to deport. The law generally recognises that, in practice, he acts through his civil servants (*Carltona Ltd v Commissioner of Works* [1943] 2 All ER 560). However, there is a division of functions under s 4 of the IA 1971. The immigration service is specifically made responsible for granting leave to enter the UK, whilst the Home Office in general deals with the subsequent variation of leave.

11.3.2 The immigration service

The immigration service consists of immigration officers, chief immigration officers and inspectors appointed by the Home Secretary. As explained in **11.3.1**, they are responsible for control on entry to the UK. They operate from the various ports of entry (including airports). Division of functions between the immigration service and the Home Office in general is not always clear-cut, as the Home Secretary may validly delegate some functions (eg the decision to deport overstayers) to the immigration service (*Oladehinde v Secretary of State for the Home Department; Alexander v Secretary of State for the Home Department* [1990] 3 WLR 797).

11.3.3 Border and Immigration Agency (BIA)

The BIA of the Home Office is the Government executive agency which deals with citizenship and immigration matters, including asylum claims.

11.3.4 The Identity and Passport Service

This is another executive agency of the Home Office. It provides passport services and (in the future, as part of the National Identity Scheme) ID cards for British and Irish nationals resident in the UK. Foreign nationals resident in the UK will also be included by linking the scheme to biometric immigration documents.

11.3.5 UKvisas

UKvisas is a joint Home Office and Foreign and Commonwealth Office Directorate. It operates visa offices, manned by entry clearance officers, in 160 locations throughout the world. The largest handles 300,000 applications a year; the smallest fewer than 10.

11.3.6 The Asylum and Immigration Appeal Tribunal (AIT)

Many, but not all, of the decisions made by an official in an immigration context are appealable to the AIT. A party can apply to the High Court for an order requiring the AIT to reconsider its decision. If the High Court considers that the AIT may have made an error of law, it will order the case to be reconsidered by the

Tribunal. Any further appeal on a point of law is to the Court of Appeal. See further **Chapter 16**.

11.4 Immigration controls

Immigration controls are dealt with in detail in **Chapter 13**. However, it is important to grasp the following points at this stage. As a general rule, immigration controls may exist at three particular points in time, namely:

(a) before a person travels to the UK. This is known as entry clearance and most persons, apart from some people who wish to enter for less than six months, must obtain it;

(b) on arrival in the UK at the port of entry. This is known as leave to enter the UK. All people who are subject to immigration controls must obtain permission to enter the UK when first arriving;

(c) after arrival, if an extension of the initial limited time granted for the stay is required.

A 'visa national' is a person who always needs entry clearance in advance of travelling to the UK for whatever purpose. The entry clearance document he needs to obtain from the British High Commission or embassy in his own country before travelling is a visa, and this will state the purpose of the entry to the UK, for example as a visitor or student, etc. Most visas appear as a stamp in the person's passport. A list of countries whose nationals must obtain visas appears at **Appendix 4** to this Part of the book.

Upon arriving at a UK port of entry, a visa national requires leave to enter the UK, that is, he must convince the immigration officer that entry is pursuant to the terms of his visa. If leave is given, a stamp to that effect is put in his passport.

Example

Kim is Chinese. He is a visa national. He wishes to come to the UK for a holiday. If he is to be given leave to enter the UK, he must, as a general rule:

(a) obtain a visa in China before travelling; and

(b) on arrival in the UK, convince the immigration officer that he is entering as a genuine visitor.

A non-visa national is a person who is not on the visa list. He does not require entry clearance in advance of travelling to the UK for short-term purposes, ie a stay of up to six months in the UK, such as a visitor (see **14.1**). However, he will require it for long-term purposes (ie a stay of more than six months), for example as a businessman or if he wishes to stay permanently in the UK. The entry clearance document he needs to obtain from the British High Commission or embassy in his own country before travelling is an entry certificate. This will state the purpose of the entry to the UK, for example, 'settlement as spouse', and usually appears as a stamp in the person's passport.

Upon arriving at a UK port of entry, a non-visa national will require leave to enter the UK, ie he must convince the immigration officer that entry is pursuant to the Immigration Rules.

Example

Bob is an American. He is a non-visa national. He wishes to come to the UK for a holiday (ie for up to six months). He does not have to obtain an entry certificate in America before travelling but, on arrival, he must convince the immigration officer that he is entering as a genuine visitor, if he is to be given leave to enter. But if Bob wanted to enter and stay for more than six months, he would need to obtain an entry certificate before travelling to the UK.

A person with 'settled status' (also known as unconditional leave, permanent stay, permanent residence, indefinite leave and settlement) does not have the right of abode in the UK and so, in theory, can be removed or deported (see **Chapter 15**). This is a person who is legally in the UK without any conditions or restrictions being placed on his residence. Hence, it is not limited in time. If a person with settled status leaves the UK, he will be subject to immigration control on return, ie he will need leave to enter the UK on the basis that he is returning to reside again (see **13.2.1**).

Summary: who does what?

- Entry clearance officer – visas and entry certificates;
- Immigration officer – leave to enter the UK;
- Home Office – extension of stay in UK, including switching of category.

Chapter 12

Nationality and Right of Abode

12.1	Introduction	213
12.2	British citizenship	213
12.3	Commonwealth citizens with right of abode	219
12.4	Historical background	220
12.5	Citizens of the European Union	222

12.1 Introduction

The law relating to nationality or citizenship forms the background to immigration law because a person's right to live in the country of his choice often depends on his nationality. This is true in UK law, in that a British citizen has a right to live in the UK.

There are two categories of people who have a statutory 'right of abode in the UK': all British citizens (see **12.2**) and certain Commonwealth citizens (see **12.3**). A person with the right of abode can freely enter the UK (ie he is not subject to immigration controls (see **11.4** and **Chapter 13**)). Moreover, he cannot be excluded from the UK (ie he cannot be removed or deported (see **Chapter 15**)). Nationals of the EEA do not have the right of abode, although they have a right of entry to and residence in the UK (see **13.7**).

12.2 British citizenship

British nationality law has changed considerably over the last century. For an historical analysis, see **12.4**. The British Nationality Act 1981 (BNA 1981) was implemented on 1 January 1983, thereby creating the nationality of British citizenship. The starting points for determining whether a person is a British citizen or not is to ask two questions:

(a) was he born before 1983 or after 1982; and
(b) was he born in the UK or elsewhere?

12.2.1 People born in the UK before 1983

A person is a British citizen if, before 1983, he was born in the UK.

12.2.2 People born outside the UK before 1983

A person is a British citizen if, before 1983, he was born outside the UK and:

(a) his father was born in the UK; or
(b) his father was naturalised or registered (see **12.2.6** and **12.2.7**) as a British citizen in the UK before the child's birth (if a father becomes British after the child's birth, this does not retrospectively make the child British); and
(c) his parents were married, or subsequently marry in a country where that marriage operates to legitimise the child.

So, before 1983, a father could pass on his British citizenship acquired in the UK only to his legitimate child. An illegitimate child could not 'inherit' British citizenship through his father.

Before 1983, a mother could not pass on her citizenship to any child born outside the UK. In those circumstances, the Home Office allowed for the child to be registered as British, and this is now possible pursuant to BNA 1981, s 4C (see **12.2.7**).

12.2.3 People born in the UK after 1982

A person is a British citizen if, after 1982, he was born in the UK and at the time of his birth either of his parents was:

(a) a British citizen; or

(b) settled in the UK. (As to settled status, see **13.2.1**. Note that for these purposes a Commonwealth citizen with the right of abode (see **12.3**) is treated as 'settled'.)

Note that until the NIAA 2002 came into force on 1 July 2006, a 'parent' in this context did not include a father of a child who was not married to the child's mother. However, the BNA 1981, as amended by the NIAA 2002, provides at s 50(9A) that from 1 July 2006 a child's father is:

(a) the husband, at the time of the child's birth, of the woman who gives birth to the child; or

(b) where a person is treated as the father of the child under s 28 of the Human Fertilisation and Embryology Act 1990, that person; or

(c) where neither paragraph (a) nor (b) applies, any person who is proven to be the father by the production of either a birth certificate identifying him as such, and issued by the competent registration authority within 12 months of the birth of the child to which it relates, or such other evidence (eg a DNA test report or court order) as may satisfy the Secretary of State on this point.

This means that subject to satisfying (c) above, an illegitimate person born in the UK on or after 1 July 2006 is a British citizen if his father was either a British citizen or settled at that time.

12.2.4 People born outside the UK after 1982

A person is a British citizen if, after 1982, he is born outside the UK, and:

(a) his father or mother was born in the UK; or

(b) his father or mother was naturalised or registered (see **12.2.6** and **12.2.7**) as a British citizen in the UK before the child's birth (if either parent becomes British after the child's birth, this does not retrospectively make the child British).

As noted at **12.2.3**, until the NIAA 2002 came into force on 1 July 2006, a 'parent' in this context did not include a father of a child who was not married to the child's mother.

This means that subject to satisfying condition (c) of s 50(9A) of the BNA 1981 (**12.2.3**), an illegitimate person born outside the UK on or after 1 July 2006 is a British citizen if his father was either born in the UK, or registered or naturalised as a British citizen before the child's birth.

12.2.5 British citizenship by descent or otherwise

A person who acquires British citizenship by birth in the UK (see **12.2.1** and **12.2.3**), or by naturalisation in the UK (see **12.2.6**) is classified as a *British citizen otherwise than by descent*. This means he can automatically pass on British citizenship to a child born outside the UK in the circumstances described above.

Where a person is born outside the UK (see **12.2.2** and **12.2.4**) and acquires British citizenship only because one or both of his parents is a British citizen, he is classified as a *British citizen by descent*. This means that he cannot automatically pass on British citizenship to any child who is also born abroad. However, some second-generation children can be registered abroad at the British consulate as British citizens (by descent) if this occurs within a year of birth and:

(a) one of the parents is a British citizen by descent; and

(b) the British parent has a parent who is or was British otherwise than by descent; and

(c) the British parent had at some time before the child's birth lived in the UK for a continuous period of three years, not being absent for more than 270 days in that period.

What if (a) and (b) are met but not (c)? It will be possible to register the child in the UK as a British citizen if during his childhood his father and mother come and live in the UK with him for a continuous period of three years and are not absent during that time for more than 270 days. Note that the requirement is that both parents live in the UK unless one of them is dead or the couple have divorced. Further note that such a child is treated as a British citizen otherwise than by descent.

> **Example**
>
> James was born in Germany in 1970. His father, Larry, was born in London, England in 1940. Larry had married James's mother in 1965. In 1990, James married Steffi, a German national. In 1999, their son, Thomas was born in Germany.
>
> Larry was born before 1983 in the UK and is therefore a British citizen otherwise than by descent. His son, James, was born outside the UK before 1983 and is therefore British by descent. Thomas can only be registered as a British citizen if James has lived in the UK at some time for a continuous period of three years before Thomas's birth.
>
> What if James has not lived in the UK for the requisite period before Thomas's birth? If James, Steffi and Thomas all come to live in the UK whilst Thomas is still a child and do so for a continuous period of three years, Thomas will have a right to register as a British citizen and will, in fact, be treated as a British citizen otherwise than by descent.

Can a British citizen by descent apply for naturalisation as a British citizen (see **12.2.6**) in order that his children born abroad automatically become British citizens? 'No', said the Court of Appeal in the case of *R v Secretary of State for the Home Department, ex p Azad Ullah* [2001] INLR 74.

12.2.6 Naturalisation

Under s 6 of the BNA 1981, the Home Secretary has a discretion to grant a certificate of naturalisation to any person who is not a British citizen. The requirements are slightly different, depending on whether or not the applicant is married to or in a civil partnership with a British citizen at the time the application is made. Broadly, those requirements are as follows.

12.2.6.1 If the applicant is neither married to nor in a civil partnership with a British citizen

The applicant:

(a) must have been living in the UK legally for five years continuously;

(b) must have been physically present in the UK on the date five years before the application;

(c) must not have been absent for more than 450 days in total, and not more than 90 days in the year immediately before the application;

(d) must have been settled (see **13.2.1**) for at least one year before the application;

(e) must show a sufficient knowledge of English, Welsh or Scottish Gaelic. The applicant must file a certificate showing that he has attained a qualification in English for Speakers of Other Languages (ESOL) skills for life Entry 3 approved by the Qualifications and Curriculum Authority, or written confirmation from a person designated under regulations that he has an alternative qualification which shows that he can speak English to at least ESOL Entry 3 standard for the purpose of naturalisation. The language requirement alternatively may be met by having a sufficient knowledge of the Welsh or Scottish Gaelic language instead of English. The Home Office may dispense with the requirement if it decides that because of the applicant's age or health it would be unreasonable to expect him to fulfil it;

(f) must show a sufficient knowledge about life in the UK. A formal test must be taken, which consists of a number of questions based on the information contained in the Government handbook, *Life in the United Kingdom: A Journey to Citizenship*. For further details, see www.lifeintheuktest.gov.uk. The Home Office may dispense with this if it decides that because of the applicant's age or health it would be unreasonable to expect him to fulfil it;

(g) must show good character. The application form requires all previous convictions, save those that are spent, to be revealed;

(h) must show an intention to live in the UK.

12.2.6.2 If the applicant is married to or in a civil partnership with a British citizen

The applicant:

(a) must have been living in the UK legally for three years continuously;

(b) must have been physically present in the UK on the date three years before the application;

(c) must not have been absent for more than 270 days in total, and not more than 90 days in the year immediately before the application;

(d) must show sufficient knowledge of English, Welsh or Scottish Gaelic. The Home Office may dispense with the test as at **12.2.6.1** (item (e));

(e) must show a sufficient knowledge about life in the UK. The Home Office may dispense with this as at **12.2.6.1** (item (f));

(f) must be settled at the time of the application;

(g) must show good character.

The Home Office has indicated that it will normally disregard 30 days over the 270 or 450 absent days limit provided all the other requirements are met. If the absences are greater than that, the test applied is whether the applicant has 'thrown in his lot with the UK ... what we are looking for is that the applicant has established his or her home, family and a substantial part of their estate here, that there has been compensating prior residence and that absences were due to the nature of the person's career'. Also, the Home Office expects the applicant to be resident in the UK for tax purposes.

12.2.6.3 EEA nationals

Certain EEA nationals are treated as settled for the purposes of naturalisation. See **13.2.3**.

12.2.7 Registration

A child has a right to register as a British citizen, pursuant to s 1(3) and (4) of the BNA 1981, if he was born in the UK after 1982 and, after his birth:

(a) one of his parents becomes settled in the UK (see **13.2.1**); or
(b) he remains in the UK for the first 10 years of his life and is not absent for more than 90 days during that period. By s 1(7), a longer period of absence may be acceptable.

Such a person is a British citizen otherwise than by descent (see **12.2.5**).

As we saw at **12.2.2**, a British mother could not before 1983 transmit her citizenship to her child born outside the UK. However, by concession, the Home Office did allow such a child to be registered as British provided the application was made before the child reached 18. What if no such registration occurred, given that the concession, by its very nature, expired at the end of 2000? Section 4C of the BNA 1981 now gives a right to such a person born after 7 February 1961 and before 1 January 1983 to apply to register as a British citizen. Such a person is a British citizen by descent (see **12.2.5**). An applicant under s 4C has to satisfy the Secretary of State that he is of good character before being registered.

12.2.8 Formalities for registration and naturalisation

These are governed by the BNA 1981 and the British Nationality (General) Regulations 2003 (SI 2003/548). In particular, applicants of full age are required to make an oath of allegiance and pledge. The latter states that the person will respect the rights and freedoms of the UK and will uphold its democratic values, observe its laws and fulfil the duties and obligations of citizenship.

12.2.9 Deprivation of citizenship

This is governed by s 40 of the BNA 1981 and the British Nationality (General) Regulations 2003 (SI 2003/548). The Secretary of State may by order deprive a person of his British citizenship status if he is satisfied that it would be conducive to the public good.

The Secretary of State may also by order deprive a person of his British citizenship status where it was obtained by registration or naturalisation, if he is satisfied that such was obtained by means of fraud, false representation or concealment of a material fact.

The Secretary of State may not make either of the above orders if it would make a person stateless.

Before making a deprivation order the Secretary of State must give the person concerned written notice specifying that a decision has been made to make the order and the reasons for it. The notice must also advise the person of his right to appeal (see **Chapter 16**).

12.2.10 British citizenship: a summary

The BNA 1981 sets out some basic rules for determining who is a British citizen. The following series of questions can be used to work out if a person may be a British citizen. However, remember that nationality law can be complex, and you will not always be able to work out if a person is a British citizen or not without detailed research of the law and facts.

Q1. When was the person born?
   (a) Before [1st January] 1983: go to Q2.
   (b) After [31st December] 1982: go to Q9.

Q2. Where was the person born?
   (a) In the UK: he is a British citizen otherwise than by descent (see **12.2.1**).
   (b) Outside the UK: go to Q3.

Q3. Was the person's father born [or registered/naturalised before he was born] in the UK?
   (a) Yes: go to Q4.
   (b) No: go to Q5.

Q4. Was the person's father married to their mother? [If after the child's birth, did that marriage legitimise the child?]
   (a) Yes: he is a British citizen by descent (see **12.2.2**).
   (b) No: go to Q5.

Q5. Was the person's mother born [or registered/naturalised before he was born] in the UK?
   (a) Yes: go to Q6.
   (b) No: go to Q7.

Q6. Did the person's mother register him as a British citizen?
   (a) Yes: he is a British citizen by descent (see **12.2.7**).
   (b) No: go to Q7.

Q7. Has the person registered as a British citizen? [This applies only if born after 7 February 1961].
   (a) Yes: he is a British citizen by descent (see **12.2.7**).
   (b) No: go to Q8.

Q8. Has the person naturalised in the UK as a British citizen?
   (a) Yes: he is a British citizen otherwise than by descent (see **12.2.6**).
   (b) No: he is not a British citizen under these rules but a detailed analysis of law and facts is required.

Q9. Was the person born in the UK?
   (a) Yes: go to Q10.
   (b) No: go to Q13.

Q10. Was either of the person's parents a British citizen or settled in the UK when he was born?
   (a) Yes: he is a British citizen otherwise than by descent (see **12.2.4**).
   (b) No: go to Q11.

Q11. Did either of the person's parents subsequently become settled in the UK?
   (a) Yes: he can apply to register as a British citizen otherwise than by descent (see **12.2.7**).
   (b) No: go to Q12.

Q12. Has the person remained in the UK for the first 10 years of his life and not been absent for more than 90 days?
  (a) Yes: he is a British citizen otherwise than by descent (see **12.2.7**).
  (b) No: he is not a British citizen under these rules but a detailed analysis of law and facts is required.

Q13. Was one of the person's parents born [or registered/naturalised before he was born] in the UK?
  (a) Yes: he is a British citizen by descent (see **12.2.4**).
  (b) No: go to Q14.

Q14. Was one of the person's parents a British citizen by descent?
  (a) Yes: consider if registration as a British citizen is possible (see **12.2.5**).
  (b) No: he is not a British citizen under these rules but a detailed analysis of law and facts is required.

Note: a parent in this context includes the father of an illegitimate child born on or after 1 July 2006 if certain conditions are met (see **12.2.3** and **12.2.4**).

12.3 Commonwealth citizens with right of abode

There are two categories of Commonwealth citizens who have the right of abode in the UK, ie the right to enter the UK without being subject to immigration controls (see **11.4** and **Chapter 13**). There is a list of Commonwealth countries in **Appendix 2** to this Part of the book.

12.3.1 Parental link

The first category concerns those Commonwealth citizens with a 'parental link' to the UK. The requirements are that:

(a) the person was a Commonwealth citizen on 31 December 1982, and continues to be such; and

(b) either parent was born in the UK.

Example

Bill was born in New Zealand in 1979. His mother, Ada, was born in London, England. His father was a citizen of New Zealand. Assuming that Bill is a citizen of New Zealand under that country's nationality laws and so remained, Bill was a Commonwealth citizen on 31 December 1982. Bill cannot be a British citizen by descent as his father was not British and, before 1983, mothers could not pass on their citizenship (see **12.2.2**). However, as a Commonwealth citizen, he has the right of abode in the UK by virtue of his mother's birth in the UK. Query if Ada registered him as British in these circumstances before he reached 18 or, if she failed to do so, whether he can now apply (see **12.2.7**).

12.3.2 Acquired by marriage

The second category concerns those Commonwealth citizen women who acquired the right of abode by marriage. The requirements are that:

(a) the woman was a Commonwealth citizen on 31 December 1982 and continues to be such; and

(b) on or before 31 December 1982, she married a man who was either:
  (i) born, registered or naturalised in the UK, or
  (ii) was a Commonwealth citizen with a right of abode.

Note that any subsequent divorce or the death of the husband does not affect her status.

> **Example**
>
> Anna was a citizen of Barbados on 31 December 1982 and continues to be such. In 1980 she married Frank. He had been born in the UK in 1960. Anna acquired the right of abode in the UK by marrying Frank.

12.3.3 Certificate of entitlement

A Commonwealth citizen with the right of abode will travel under his or her own country's passport. Before travelling to the UK for the first time, he or she should apply to the British High Commission for a certificate showing that right of abode.

To get the certificate in the first category, the applicant will need to produce the appropriate parent's birth certificate. To get it in the second category, the applicant will need to produce the couple's marriage certificate as well as evidence that her husband was either:

(a) British by birth (eg his birth certificate, etc); or
(b) a Commonwealth citizen with his own right of abode (eg his parent's birth certificate etc).

12.3.4 Excluded Commonwealth nationals

It is important to note that, as Cameroon, Mozambique, Namibia, Pakistan and South Africa were not members of the Commonwealth on 31 December 1982, nationals of those countries cannot take advantage of the above provisions.

12.3.5 Deprivation of right of abode

Section 57 of IANA 2006 gives the Secretary of State power to remove this right of abode if it is conducive to the public good to remove or exclude the Commonwealth citizen from the UK. There is a similar power for deprivation of British citizenship (see **12.2.9**).

There is a right of appeal to the AIT or, if issues of national security arise, to the Special Immigration Appeals Commission (see **Chapter 16**).

12.4 Historical background

One of the difficulties in understanding the law in this area is that a person's citizenship may change over time. Someone born in the UK in 1940 would have had the status of 'British subject' at common law. Under the British Nationality Act 1948, he would have become a citizen of the UK and colonies (CUKC). Under the BNA 1981, he would become a British citizen. The problem is that his current citizenship status is defined in the legislation in terms of his earlier status. Thus, it is necessary to know a little of the history of citizenship law – in particular, three major developments, illustrated in the diagram below.

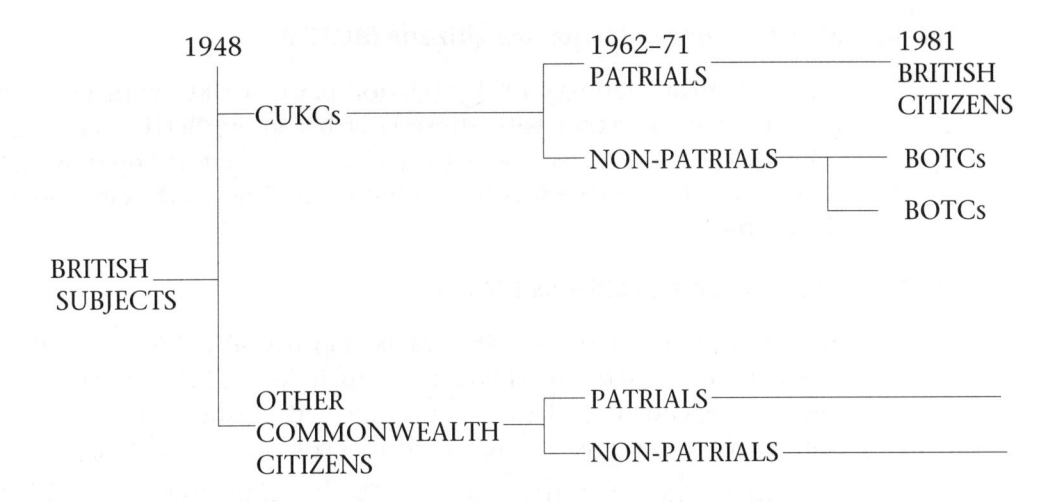

```
                    1948                    1962-71              1981
                                        ┌── PATRIALS ──────── BRITISH
                  ┌── CUKCs ────────────┤                      CITIZENS
                  │                     │
                  │                     └── NON-PATRIALS ──┬── BOTCs
                  │                                        │
BRITISH ──────────┤                                        └── BOTCs
SUBJECTS          │
                  │
                  │    OTHER              ┌── PATRIALS ─────────────────
                  └── COMMONWEALTH ───────┤
                       CITIZENS           └── NON-PATRIALS ─────────────
```

The terms used in the diagram have the following broad meanings.

12.4.1 British subjects

Before 1948, anyone who owed allegiance to the Crown, regardless of the Crown territory in which he was born.

12.4.2 CUKCs

After 1948, anyone connected with the UK or a Crown colony (such as Hong Kong).

12.4.3 Commonwealth citizens

After 1948, anyone having citizenship of an independent Commonwealth country, according to the law of that country. Independent Commonwealth countries included the former Dominions (eg Canada, Australia, New Zealand) and also former colonies (eg Jamaica) when they gained independence. On independence, existing citizens who were CUKCs might lose that status by becoming citizens of the newly independent Commonwealth country. The current list of countries whose citizens are Commonwealth citizens is given in **Appendix 2** to this Part of the book. In addition, anyone who has British citizenship, British overseas territories citizenship or British overseas citizenship (see **12.4.5** to **12.4.7** below) is also a Commonwealth citizen.

12.4.4 Patrials

Anyone who under the IA 1971 had the right of abode in the UK. Until 1962, Commonwealth citizens and CUKCs could enter the UK freely. From that year, controls were introduced which were finally enacted in the 1971 Act. The controls extended to both CUKCs and Commonwealth citizens, but CUKCs and Commonwealth citizens who had a close connection with the UK were recognised as 'patrials', having the right of abode.

12.4.5 British citizens

Anyone who at 1 January 1983 was a CUKC with right of abode in the UK, and anyone who acquired British citizenship after that date (eg by birth in the UK, see **12.2.1**). British citizenship and the following categories of citizenship were created by BNA 1981.

12.4.6 British overseas territories citizens (BOTCs)

Anyone who at 1 January 1983 was a non-patrial CUKC, with a close connection with a colony, together with those later becoming BOTCs (eg by birth in the colony). The list of British overseas territories is given in **Appendix 3** to this Part of the book. By the Overseas Territories Act 2002, all BOTCs were granted British citizenship.

12.4.7 British overseas citizens (BOCs)

Anyone who at 1 January 1983 was a non-patrial CUKC, but without a close connection with a colony. This category included CUKCs living in a colony which gained independence, who did not acquire citizenship of the newly independent country (eg those of Asian origin in former colonies in East Africa).

This list is not exhaustive. There are other minor categories such as British protected persons, British nationals (overseas) and British subjects under the 1981 Act.

The following other major categories of citizens were unaffected by these changes in UK law.

12.4.8 Irish citizens

Citizens of the Republic of Ireland. They were not Commonwealth citizens under the British Nationality Act 1948. They are not subject to immigration controls (see **13.11**, Common Travel Area), but may be liable to deportation (see **Chapter 15**).

12.4.9 Aliens

Broadly, anyone who does not fall into the above categories. Citizens of countries outside the Commonwealth such as the USA, Brazil, France (but see **12.5** and **13.7** as to EEA nationals). Immigration controls were introduced for aliens in 1905. They do not have the right of abode. However, UK law does permit dual nationality, so that someone who lacks the right of abode as an alien, may nevertheless have it if he can also claim British citizenship.

12.5 Citizens of the European Union

Under the Treaty on European Union 1992, all citizens of Member States of the European Union (including the UK) acquire citizenship of the Union. However, this adds little to the rights of freedom of movement conferred by EC law. These rights have now been extended to all nationals of Member States in the EEA and Switzerland (see **13.7**).

Chapter 13
Immigration Status: An Introduction

13.1	Limited and unlimited leave to enter	223
13.2	Settlement	224
13.3	Immigration controls	226
13.4	Entry clearance	226
13.5	Leave to enter	227
13.6	Variation of leave	230
13.7	EEA nationals	234
13.8	Rights under EC law	235
13.9	The Immigration (European Economic Area) Regulations 2006	236
13.10	Chart cross-referencing key aspects of 2006 Regulations and 2004 Directive	244
13.11	The Common Travel Area	244

13.1 Limited and unlimited leave to enter

Under s 3 of the IA 1971, a person without 'right of abode' (see **12.1**) may enter the UK only if given leave to enter. Leave may be unlimited or limited, and is given in accordance with the Immigration Rules. The power to give leave is exercisable by immigration officers (see **11.4**).

If unlimited leave is given, the entrant may remain in the UK for an indefinite period (see **13.2**). If leave is limited, the period of stay will be specified, and conditions may be attached.

13.1.1 Requirements and conditions

To obtain entry clearance, where necessary, and leave to enter or remain in the UK, an applicant must satisfy the entry clearance officer, immigration officer and Home Office (see **11.4**), as appropriate, that he meets the requirements as set out in the appropriate paragraph of the Immigration Rules. For example, to obtain a visitor visa the applicant must satisfy the entry clearance officer that he meets all the requirements of para 41 and then do the same with the Immigration Officer on arrival in the UK.

After entering the UK an entrant does not commit a criminal offence by failing to meet any of the requirements. However, it may result in a refusal by the Home Office of any request to extend leave (see **13.6**), or may lead to the leave itself being curtailed (see **13.6.7**).

Conditions may be attached to a person's limited leave to enter or remain in the UK. All entrants with limited leave are subject to the condition not to have recourse to public funds. Public funds include housing under the homeless persons legislation (eg Pts VI or VII of the Housing Act 1996 and under Pt II of the Housing Act 1985), attendance allowance, carer's allowance, disability living allowance, income support, council tax benefit, housing benefit, a social fund payment, child benefit, income based jobseeker's allowance, state pension credit, child tax credit and working tax credit. Note that NHS treatment is not public funds. In certain limited circumstances a charge can be imposed under the National Health Service (Charges to Overseas Visitors) Regs 1989 (SI 1989/306).

Note also that education for a child at a local authority maintained school is not public funds.

See further **Chapter 10** and para 6 of the Immigration Rules.

It is also a condition of leave of entry to the UK for many nationals that they register with the police. See Part 10 of and Appendix 2 to the Immigration Rules.

For some entrants their limited leave will be subject to a condition restricting their ability to take employment. As defined by para 6 of the Immigration Rules, this includes 'paid and unpaid employment, self employment and engaging in business or any professional activity.' The condition can be found in the appropriate paragraph of the Immigration Rules under which leave of entry is granted. So, for example, a visitor cannot work at all (para 42 and see **14.1.1**), a fiancé(e) cannot work at all (para 291 and see **14.13**), a student can work only within prescribed guidelines (para 58 and see **14.2.1.5**), a working holidaymaker is limited to working no more than 12 months during the stay and prohibited from engaging in business or providing services as a professional sportsperson (para 95 and see **14.3.2**), a work permit holder can take up only the approved employment specified in the permit (para 129 and see **14.5.4**) and a business person can work only in the approved business (para 204 and see **14.6**).

Any one or more of these three possible conditions will usually be part of the leave of entry stamp on the passport. Breach of a condition is a criminal offence and may lead to removal from the UK (see **15.1**).

> **Example**
> Andrew is admitted to the UK as a student with 12 months' leave, subject to conditions restricting his employment and not to have recourse to public funds. After three months he gives up the course on which he was enrolled. Has he broken a condition of leave?
> No. On entry he would have been required under the Rules to show that he intended to follow his course, but no condition to that effect would have been attached to his leave. Obviously it is unlikely that Andrew will, on expiry of his 12 months' leave, obtain an extension of stay as a student. It is possible that his leave may be curtailed (see **13.6.7**).

13.2 Settlement

A person who has been given unlimited leave may acquire 'settled' status, which is almost as secure as having the 'right of abode' itself, save that this person may be deported.

A person is settled according to the definition in s 33(2A) of the IA 1971 if he is ordinarily resident in the UK without being subject under the immigration laws to any restriction on the period for which he may remain. The status will be acquired by a person given unlimited leave who satisfies the 'ordinary residence' test (see **13.2.5**). A person who has been given indefinite leave to remain in the UK would not be 'settled' in the UK under the IA 1971, if he has emigrated to another country and is no longer ordinarily resident in the UK.

13.2.1 Nature of settled status

A person who is settled in the UK has, subject to the Immigration Rules, the right to continue to live in the UK. Unlike a person with right of abode, he may be deported (see **Chapter 15**). If he leaves the UK and returns within two years, his leave will continue (see **13.5.6**), leave to enter has to be given again and his settled status in effect confirmed. This is usually automatic under para 18 of the Rules, dealing with 'returning residents', provided that the entrant satisfies the immigration officer that he had indefinite leave to enter or remain in the UK when he last left, that he has not been away for longer than two years, and that he now seeks admission for the purpose of settlement. If a person is returning periodically only for a limited period simply to show residence in the UK within two years of each departure, then eventually he or she is likely to be denied the benefit of para 18 of the Immigration Rules.

What if a person with settled status does not return to the UK within two years of last leaving it? This is dealt with in para 19 of the Immigration Rules where consideration is given to such factors as:

(a) the length of the original residence in the UK;
(b) the time the applicant has been outside the UK;
(c) the reason for the delay beyond the two years – was it through his own wish or no fault of his own or could he reasonably have been expected to return within two years?
(d) why did he go abroad when he did and what were his intentions?
(e) the nature of his family ties here – how close are they, and to what extent has he maintained them in his absence?
(f) whether he has a home in the UK and, if admitted, would resume his residency.

Lastly, acquisition of settled status may be a step towards registration or naturalisation as a British citizen, with right of abode (BNA 1981, ss 4 and 6; see **12.2.6**).

13.2.2 'Settled' in the Immigration Rules

Note that the Immigration Rules use the term 'settled' to cover British citizens and Commonwealth citizens who have the right of abode, as well as those people who have indefinite leave. So the Rules applying to 'the spouse of a person settled in the UK' will apply also to the spouse of a British citizen or a Commonwealth citizen with the right of abode (see **14.9**).

13.2.3 EEA nationals

Nationals of the EEA do not need leave to enter or remain while exercising rights in EC law (see **13.7.2**). Does this mean that while in the UK they have no restriction on the period for which they can remain and are therefore 'settled' under UK immigration law? The answer is, 'No'. However, by reg 15(1) of the I(EEA) Regs 2006 (see **13.9.9** and **Appendix 7**), EEA nationals acquire the right to reside in the UK permanently where, as a general rule, they have resided in the UK in accordance with the Regulations for a continuous period of five years. In limited circumstances, the right to reside in the UK permanently may be acquired more quickly, eg under reg 15(1) by a worker or self-employed person who has ceased activity as defined in reg 5. People falling within reg 15(1) are treated as settled for the purposes of applying for naturalisation (see **12.2.6**).

13.2.4 Acquisition of settled status

Under the Immigration Rules some categories of entrants are admitted for immediate settlement, whilst others are given limited leave with a view to future settlement (eg spouses and civil partners two years after entry). Other categories (eg work permit holders, businessmen, EEA nationals) become eligible to apply five years after entry (see **14.5.4.3**, **14.6.1** and **13.9.9**). However, in some cases where the purpose of the initial entry was inconsistent with the desire to settle, the entrant will be expected to leave at the end of his permitted stay. These categories include visitors, students, and persons entering for short-term employment (see **Chapter 14**). Where someone has been resident in the UK for a long period, it may be possible to obtain settled status (see **13.6.5**).

Any adult, aged between 18 and 65, who has entered the UK with limited leave and subsequently wishes to apply for settled status, must satisfy the usual language and 'life in the UK' tests that apply to applicants for naturalisation (see **12.2.6.1(e)** and **(f)**).

13.2.5 Ordinary residence

This is a condition of settled status. It has a quite distinct meaning. Case law from various fields suggests that a person can be 'ordinarily resident' without having the right, or the intention, to reside here permanently. All that is necessary is that a person resides in a place with a 'settled purpose' (eg to undertake a course of education). It is possible to have ordinary residence in more than one place at the same time. A person may be ordinarily resident in the UK even though temporarily absent (eg on holiday). Generally, however, for purposes other than exemption from deportation, a person cannot be so resident at a time when he is in breach of immigration laws (eg overstaying) (see the IA 1971, s 33(2)).

> Examples
> (1) Erasmus is a student who has been in the UK for the last 8 years, periodically renewing his 12-month leave to remain.
>
> He is 'ordinarily resident' in the UK, but not 'settled' as he is subject to limited leave.
>
> (2) Farooq was given indefinite leave to remain in the UK 10 years ago, but emigrated 6 years ago. He is now here for a holiday, having been admitted as a visitor.
>
> He is not 'ordinarily resident'. Nor is he 'settled' as his indefinite leave to remain was not renewed on his return to the UK.
>
> (3) As (2), but Farooq has been admitted as a student, with 12 months' leave.
>
> He is 'ordinarily resident', but not 'settled'.

13.3 Immigration controls

The immigration adviser may have to assist a client with problems at various stages of immigration control. He may be seeking entry clearance, leave of entry, or variation of leave. In each case, the position will be governed by the Immigration Rules. Part 1 of the Rules deals with general provisions, and the remaining Parts deal with special rules affecting different categories of entrants (see **Chapter 14**). Remember, however, that the Home Secretary may, in exceptional cases, exercise his discretion to act outside the Rules (see **11.2.4**). This is often in response to an intervention by a Member of Parliament, who may have been briefed by the adviser.

13.4 Entry clearance

13.4.1 The general rule

The entry clearance procedure is, in effect, a form of pre-entry control, in which a UK official known as a visa or entry clearance officer acts as an immigration officer, applying the Immigration Rules, but usually in the country in which the entrant is living before travel to the UK.

The form of clearance depends on the nationality of the entrant. The Appendix to the Immigration Rules specifies countries whose nationals (known as 'visa nationals') require entry clearance in the form of a visa (usually stamped on the passport). A list of these countries is given in **Appendix 4** to this Part of the book. In the case of some 'non-visa nationals', entry clearance is required for a stay of more than six months (see **12.1**). In this case, the entry clearance is shown by a different stamp, known as an entry certificate (see para 25 of the Immigration Rules).

An applicant for entry clearance as a visitor must apply to a particular designated post. However, any other type of application must be made to the appropriate designated post in the country or territory where the applicant is living.

Under the Immigration (Provision of Physical Data) Regulations 2006 (SI 2006/1743), an applicant for entry clearance may be required to provide a record of his fingerprints or a photograph of his face.

If entry clearance is required, an entrant who fails to obtain it will be refused leave to enter (see para 320).

If entry clearance has been obtained, leave to enter will be refused only on grounds specified in para 321 (see **13.5.7**).

13.4.2 Financial undertakings

Often entry clearance is sought for the purposes of immediate or ultimate settlement (eg child joining parent in UK, or grandparent joining grandchild in UK or spouse joining partner in UK, etc). The person based in the UK is usually known as 'the sponsor'. See Immigration Rules, para 2. This does not necessarily mean that that person has signed a written agreement with the DfWP to be financially responsible for the entrant. As para 35 of the Immigration Rules states, 'A sponsor of a person ... may be asked to give an undertaking in writing to be responsible for that person's maintenance and accommodation'. Only if such a written undertaking is given can the DfWP seek to recover any benefits paid. Guidance from the BIA is that written undertakings will normally be required only from the sponsors of elderly dependent relatives. As to what constitutes a written undertaking, see *Ahmed v Secretary of State for Work and Pensions* [2005] EWCA Civ 535.

Note that a person entering the UK to settle who is the subject of a written undertaking from a sponsor will not have access to mainstream welfare benefits (see **10.3.1**).

13.5 Leave to enter

13.5.1 The general rule

Leave to enter is dealt with in paras 7–11 of the Immigration Rules. Everyone must, on arrival in the UK, produce a passport or other document establishing his nationality and identity. On examination by an immigration officer, the entrant must furnish such information as may be required to enable the officer to decide whether he requires leave to enter, whether leave should be given, and the terms of leave. It is para 2(1) of Sch 2 to the IA 1971 which gives an immigration officer the power to examine any person who arrives in the UK and sets out the purpose for which such an examination is conducted, namely to determine whether:

(a) he is or is not a British citizen; and, if not,

(b) if he may or may not enter the UK without leave; and, if not,
(c) if he has been given leave which is still in force, or should be given leave and for what period or on what conditions (if any), or should be refused leave.

If it is concluded that a person is a British citizen, the immigration officer takes no further action. If he is not a British citizen, however, he will be examined to determine whether or not he requires permission to enter the UK. This permission is called leave to enter. If a person qualifies for leave to enter then the immigration officer will go on to decide the length of the leave and any conditions, such as permission to work, which will apply. Finally, if a person does not qualify for leave to enter then the immigration officer may refuse leave to enter.

These controls do not, however, apply to persons arriving from another part of the Common Travel Area (see **13.11**).

13.5.2 Documentary evidence

Documentary evidence to be produced to an immigration officer may include:

(a) a UK passport: required to be produced by a British citizen as evidence of his right of abode;
(b) a certificate of entitlement issued by the UK Government: evidence of right of abode which may be produced as an alternative to (a) above (by a Commonwealth citizen who has the right of abode, see **12.3**);
(c) entry clearance in the form of a visa or entry certificate;
(d) a non-UK passport or identity card: identity cards can be used as a substitute for a passport by EEA nationals.

13.5.3 Grant of leave under the general rule

The immigration officer grants leave by written notice, usually in the form of a stamp on the entrant's passport. The stamp gives the date and port of entry, the time limit of the leave, and any conditions imposed, but does not indicate the Rule under which leave has been granted.

After admission, any extension of the time limit, or variation of conditions, is dealt with by an application to the Home Office (see **13.6.2**).

13.5.4 Temporary admission

If a decision on whether to grant leave cannot be reached quickly, the immigration officer will usually issue a notice of temporary admission (in Form IS96). This tells the entrant that he is liable to detention, but may physically enter the UK, without having leave to enter. He may be directed to reside at a particular place, and is asked to report back to an immigration officer at a specified time. He may not take employment.

As an alternative to temporary admission, the entrant can be detained, but may apply to an Immigration Judge for bail if he remains detained seven days after his arrival in the UK.

13.5.5 Travel outside the UK by people with settled status

Someone who is settled in the UK may usually rely on leave being given as a 'returning resident' (see **13.2.1**) and visa nationals will not in this case require a visa to return to the UK.

13.5.6 Leave under the IAA 1999

The IAA 1999 provides for greater flexibility in the way permission to enter the UK and to remain may be granted. Instead of leave to enter always having to be given in writing at a port of entry, the IAA 1999 allows for additional ways of giving leave to enter to be specified (eg that a visa or other entry clearance is to be treated as leave to enter). This means that holders of visas, for example, will be able to pass through the port control with only a quick check on identity and on the rightful ownership of the travel document and entry clearance, unless there is a need to examine for, among other matters, change of circumstances.

13.5.7 Refusal of leave

Detailed provisions in the Immigration Rules cover the requirements for admission of particular categories of entrant (see **Chapter 14**). Anyone who does not meet the requirements for the relevant category is refused leave to enter. Even if a person does formally qualify, leave may be refused on general grounds set out in para 320, for example, if he has previously been in breach of the terms of leave, or if a previous leave to enter has been obtained by deception. Where entry clearance has been given, para 321 cuts down the general grounds for refusal. In this case, leave can be refused only on the grounds of:

(a) false representations or non-disclosure of material fact;

(b) a change in relevant circumstances before admission;

(c) various public interest considerations, including medical reasons, the fact that the entrant is subject to a deportation order, or a criminal record.

The authority of a Chief Immigration Officer is required for refusal. The entrant should be given a notice informing him of the decision and of the reasons for refusal. This will state his rights of appeal (see **Chapter 16**).

After refusal of leave to enter, the immigration officer will usually give directions for removal of the entrant as soon as possible. The entrant will be liable to detention, subject to grant of bail. Temporary admission may be granted, particularly where the entrant is exercising a right of appeal from within the UK.

So, when does limited leave expire? If it was granted for a specific period, it expires at the end of that period. So if leave was granted on 2 January for six months, it expires at 23.59 on 2 July (the first day does not count). If leave is granted until a specific date, say 1 November, it expires at 23.59 on 1 November (ie the last moment of the last day of that leave).

A valid application (see **13.6**) for a variation of leave is considered by the Home Office to be 'in time' if it is posted before the applicant's leave expires. For these purposes, the BIA considers the postmark on the envelope containing the application as evidence of the date of posting and the envelope is retained on the applicant's file.

13.5.8 Entry without a passport

By s 2(1) of the Asylum and Immigration (Treatment of Claimants, etc) Act 2004 (AI (TC)A 2004), a person commits an offence if, when seeking leave either to enter or remain in the UK or asylum, he does not have with him a passport (or similar immigration document) which is in force and satisfactorily establishes his identity and nationality or citizenship. By s 2(4) various defences may be raised, such as proving a reasonable excuse for not being in possession of the required document. The defendant has the legal burden of proving the defence on the balance of probabilities: see *R v Navabi and Embaye* [2005] EWCA Crim 2865.

However, note that by s 2(7) the fact that a document was deliberately destroyed or disposed of is not such a reasonable excuse unless it is shown that the destruction or disposal was for a reasonable cause, or that it was beyond the control of the person charged with the offence. So what is a 'reasonable cause'? By s 2(7)(b) this does not include the purpose of (i) delaying the handling or resolution of a claim or application or the taking of a decision, (ii) increasing the chances of success of a claim or application, or (iii) complying with instructions or advice given by a person who offers advice about, or facilitates, immigration into the UK, unless in the circumstances of the case it is unreasonable to expect non-compliance with the instructions or advice.

As to an asylum claim, see **14.17**.

13.6 Variation of leave

13.6.1 General

The general framework is laid down by s 3(3) of the IA 1971 which provides that limited leave may be varied, whether by restricting, enlarging, or removing the time limit, or by adding, varying, or removing conditions. If the time limit is removed, the leave becomes indefinite and any conditions cease to have effect. Indefinite leave cannot be varied.

13.6.2 Application for variation

Application for variation is made to the Home Office. Immigration officers have no powers to deal with variations. Application should be made before expiry of the time limit on leave, because overstaying is a criminal offence, and may result in refusal of the application to extend leave.

By s 3C of the IA 1971, when a person applies for variation of his leave before that leave expires, but it then expires before a decision is taken, the leave is automatically extended to the point at which the appropriate period for appealing a refusal expires (see **Chapter 16**). This will protect the immigration status of that person and prevent him from becoming an overstayer. All conditions attached to the leave will still apply. So if a person who entered the UK as a fiancé(e) subsequently applies to stay as a spouse following the marriage, until the variation is granted by the Home Office, the applicant cannot work (see **14.13**). A person will not be able to submit further applications during the leave as extended under this section, although he would be able to vary his original application: this is to ensure that all issues raised are covered by one decision and consequently one appeal (see further **Chapter 16**).

13.6.3 General considerations

As with the initial leave to enter, applications to vary are governed by rules relating to particular categories of applicant (see **Chapter 14**). General considerations are dealt with in para 322 of the Immigration Rules; the Home Office has a discretion to refuse applications on specified grounds. Leave may be curtailed, or an application to vary leave refused, on the basis of false representations, or non-disclosure of material facts, breach of conditions attached to leave, or recourse to public funds for maintenance or accommodation, undesirable character, conduct or associations, or danger to national security. An application to vary may, in addition, be refused on a number of other grounds, for example, if a person has failed to honour any undertaking as to the duration and purpose of his stay, or where there has been delay in producing documents or evidence in support of his application.

An applicant who wishes to extend his stay in the UK in his existing category or to switch to a new category must have 'effective' or 'valid' limited leave. For example, under para 284(i) of the Immigration Rules, an extension of stay as a spouse (see **14.9.6.3**) requires that the applicant *has* limited leave to remain in the UK and by para 131(i) an extension of stay as a work permit holder (see **14.5.4**) requires that that applicant entered the UK with a *valid* work permit. So, if the Home Office finds that the original leave was obtained by deception, it may determine that the applicant is an illegal entrant (see **15.2.2**) and as such without effective or valid limited leave. In those circumstances the applicant may be subject to administrative removal (see **Chapter 15**).

13.6.4 Switching categories

In many cases, an entrant will apply to vary his leave by switching from one category of entry to another. For example, someone who has entered as a student (Part 3 of the Immigration Rules) may wish to remain as the spouse of someone living in the UK (Part 8). In every case, it will be necessary to check the detailed provisions of the Rules relating to the new category. For example, para 60(i) provides that only a very limited number of people may switch to being a student.

On the other hand, if a person with limited leave marries someone settled in the UK, para 284 does not prevent him (unless he is a visitor) obtaining an extension as a spouse solely on the ground that he failed to obtain entry clearance in that capacity – even though a spouse or fiancé(e) would usually have to obtain entry clearance before coming to the UK.

Is there any danger in applying to switch categories? The danger is that the Home Office may refuse the application and curtail the existing leave (see **13.6.7**).

13.6.5 The long-residence rules

Even where the requirements of the Immigration Rules for a switch to settled status are not met, it may be possible to obtain indefinite leave by virtue of long residence in the UK. Pursuant to Immigration Rules, para 276B, it is Home Office practice to consider this in cases where the applicant has been continuously resident in the UK for 10 years. The residence must have been lawful and continuous. In addition, where the applicant has been in the UK continuously for 14 years or more, indefinite leave may be granted even though the residence has been unlawful for the whole, or part of the period.

How is the 10- or 14-year period calculated? Continuity of residence is not broken by a small number of short absences abroad of up to six months at any one time during the relevant period. Short absences cannot be said to disrupt or sever ties with the UK. These absences should normally be ignored, unless the trips are frequent. In such cases, the reasons for the frequent trips are requested by the BIA, which will be concerned that the applicant may have a business abroad or might be maintaining family ties abroad. In some cases, a lengthier absence may still not sever the ties to the UK. In each case the strength of the ties to the UK, the reason for, and effect of, the absence are taken into account. However, continuity of residence is considered by the BIA as being broken if:

(a) the applicant has been removed or deported (see **Chapter 15**) or has left the UK having been refused leave to enter or remain here; or

(b) the applicant has left the UK and, on doing so, evidenced a clear intention not to return; or

(c) he has left the UK in circumstances in which he could have had no reasonable expectation at the time of leaving that he would lawfully be able to return; or

(d) he has been convicted of an offence and was sentenced to a period of imprisonment or was directed to be detained in an institution other than a prison (including, in particular, a hospital or an institution for young offenders), provided that the sentence in question was not a suspended sentence; or

(e) he has spent a total of more than 18 months absent from the UK during the period in question.

What factors does the Home Office consider? The public interest is the key concern, namely that there are no reasons why it would be undesirable for the applicant to be given indefinite leave to remain on the ground of long residence, taking into account the applicant's age; strength of connections in the UK; his personal history, including character, conduct, associations and employment record; his domestic circumstances; any previous criminal record and the nature of any offence of which he has been convicted; any compassionate circumstances and any representations received on his behalf.

Indefinite leave to remain is normally granted in the absence of any strong countervailing factors. These include deliberate and blatant attempts to evade or circumvent the control, for example, by using forged documents; absconding and contracting a marriage of convenience. Criminal offences which are spent under the Rehabilitation of Offenders Act 1974 and behaviour which happened five years or more ago are not normally sufficient to outweigh positive ties with the UK. If the continuous residence is in excess of 14 years, indefinite leave is invariably granted unless the countervailing factors are exceptionally serious.

> Example
>
> Vijay, a citizen of India, has studied in the UK since he was sent to an English public school at the age of 13. He is now 23, has obtained a degree at an English university, and is enrolled on a postgraduate vocational course. His parents are now dead and he would like to remain in the UK rather than return to India.
>
> Apart from occasional visits home he has been resident in the UK with leave as a student, periodically renewed. When he was 21 he failed to apply for an extension of stay in time, but the Home Office allowed him to remain to continue his studies. It is now more than 10 years since he first arrived in the UK. On his next application for an extension, will he be given indefinite leave?
>
> As Vijay was an overstayer for a period he has not had 10 years' continuous lawful residence in the UK, and is therefore ineligible under the 10-year provision. He must wait nearly 4 years to qualify under the 14-year provision. (He must be able to obtain extensions, or somehow remain without deliberately evading immigration control.)

13.6.6 Procedure for variation

The Home Office will ask to see the applicant's passport and other relevant documentary evidence, and may ask him to attend for interview. If the application to vary is granted, an entry will normally be made in his passport and the decision will also be notified by letter. If the application is refused, the decision is notified by letter, explaining rights of appeal.

A fee is usually payable on lodging applications for an extension of stay in the UK or settlement.

All applications to vary leave (other than asylum applications or applications under EC law) must be on a prescribed Home Office form, including:

FLR(IED): application for an extension of stay in UK for work permit employment or approved training or work experience or as a highly skilled migrant.

FLR(M): application for an extension of stay in UK as the spouse, civil partner or unmarried partner of a person present and settled here.

FLR(O): application for extension of stay in UK if applying in certain categories, such as visitor, person with UK ancestry and any other purpose or reason not covered by other application forms.

FLR(S): application for an extension of stay in UK as a student, student nurse, to resit an examination or to write up a thesis.

SET(M): application for indefinite leave to remain in UK as the spouse, civil partner or unmarried partner of a person who is present and settled here.

SET(O): application for indefinite leave to remain in UK on completion of five years of continuous leave to remain in UK in categories such as work permit holder, highly skilled migrant and person with UK ancestry. The form is also used to apply for indefinite leave to remain in one of the following categories: long residence in UK, victim of domestic violence and any other purpose or reason not covered by other application forms.

SET(F): application for indefinite leave to remain in UK as a family member (other than husband or wife or unmarried partner) of a person present and settled in UK, ie a child under 18 of a parent, parents or relative present and settled in UK and the parent, grandparent or other dependent relative of a person present and settled in UK.

BUS: application for an extension of stay or for indefinite leave to remain in UK as a business person, sole representative, retired person of independent means, investor or innovator.

EEA1: application for a registration certificate by an EEA national.

EEA2: application for a residence card by a non-EEA family member of an EEA national.

EEA3: application for permanent residence by an EEA national.

EEA4: application for permanent residence by a non-EEA family member of an EEA national.

When should an application be made? The answer is not more than two months before the applicant's leave expires. Any earlier than that and it may be difficult, if not impossible, for the applicant to produce satisfactory evidence that he will indeed qualify for further leave to remain after his present leave expires.

If an applicant chooses the wrong form, the application is not valid. In addition, each form specifies the documents which must accompany the application and an application will not be valid if they are not sent. See para 32 of the Immigration Rules. If any documents are not available at the time of making the application, it appears the BIA may accept a good reason as to why such cannot be provided at that stage. The Home Office will return an invalid application, but only the new application counts in deciding whether the application was made in time. So, the immigration adviser must take great care to select the correct form.

13.6.7 Curtailment of existing leave

If a person enters the UK in one category and before his limited leave expires he applies to switch to another category, there is a danger not only that the application might be refused but also that the existing leave might be curtailed (or the applicant removed from the UK).

Example

Bob enters the UK as a student with 12 months' limited leave. After three months he applies to remain in the UK as the spouse of a British citizen. The suspicion may well be that he never intended to leave the UK because he always intended to marry. Not only might his leave be curtailed but alternatively he may be removed from the UK as an illegal entrant (see **Chapter 15**).

The power to curtail a person's leave is contained in s 3(3)(a) of the IA 1971. It may be used when a person has failed to comply with certain requirements of the Immigration Rules or has lost the justification for his presence here, eg a work permit holder's job ends. It is only available when a person has limited leave. Guidance from the BIA is that curtailment should not normally be used unless the person has at least six months' leave outstanding.

Paragraph 323 of the Immigration Rules allows curtailment, for example, if:

(a) false representations have been made or material facts not disclosed in order to obtain leave to enter or a previous variation of leave;

(b) the person has failed to comply with any conditions attached to his leave;

(c) the person has failed to maintain and accommodate himself and any dependants without recourse to public funds;

(d) the person ceases to meet the requirements of the Rules under which that leave was granted.

As curtailment is a matter of Home Office discretion it is not automatic. The burden of proof rests with the Secretary of State. Very often a person will be removed rather than his leave curtailed, eg where a person has failed to disclose relevant facts or has made false representations in order to obtain leave, consideration may be given to curtailing any subsisting leave but it is more usual to proceed directly to administrative removal (see **Chapter 15**) or in the case of leave to enter, removal for illegal entry (also **Chapter 15**). Equally, although leave may be curtailed where a person fails to observe the conditions of his leave to enter or remain, normally the Home Office proceeds direct to administrative removal for breach of conditions (see **Chapter 15**). Curtailment therefore is only normally considered where the person's actions are not so serious as to merit enforcement action, but where it would be inappropriate to let him remain for the duration of his leave.

See also **14.17.12**.

13.7 EEA nationals

13.7.1 Who are EEA nationals?

'EEA nationals' are nationals of the Member States of the European Union together with Iceland, Liechtenstein and Norway (which are parties to the European Economic Area Agreement). See **Appendix 5** to this Part for the full list of relevant countries.

Note that by an Agreement on the Free Movement of Persons made between the EC and the Swiss Confederation (Cm 4904), Swiss nationals and their family members were from 1 June 2002 given broadly similar rights of entry to and residence in the UK as are enjoyed by EEA nationals. See the Immigration (Swiss Free Movement of Persons) (No 3) Regulations 2002 (SI 2002/1241).

Nationals of Cyprus, the Czech Republic, Estonia, Hungary, Latvia, Lithuania, Malta, Poland, Slovakia and Slovenia became members of the EU on 1 May 2004 (the so-called 'Accession States'). However, until 30 April 2009 a national of the Czech Republic, Estonia, Hungary, Latvia, Lithuania, Poland, Slovakia and Slovenia is usually required to register as a worker in the UK (see **13.8.1.1**).

Romania and Bulgaria joined the EU in 2007.

13.7.2 What is their immigration status?

Nationals of the EEA have a hybrid status. They do not have the right of abode possessed by British citizens but, unlike other aliens, they do not require leave to enter or remain while exercising rights in EC law (s 7(1) of the IA 1988). Paragraph **13.8** outlines their rights in EC law. These have been implemented in UK law by the I(EEA) Regs 2006, considered in detail in **13.9**.

13.8 Rights under EC law

Article 17 EC states that:

> Citizenship of the Union is hereby established. Every person holding the nationality of a Member State shall be a citizen of the Union. Citizenship of the Union shall complement and not replace national citizenship. Citizens of the Union shall enjoy the rights conferred by this Treaty and shall be subject to the duties imposed thereby.

Article 18(1) EC provides that:

> every citizen of the Union is to have the right to move and reside freely within the territory of the Member States, subject to the limitations and conditions laid down in the EC Treaty and by the measures adopted to give it effect.

It can be seen that Article 18 EC provides for a right of residence and movement of EEA nationals throughout the EU. Directive 2004/38/EC of the European Parliament and Council of 29 April 2004 sets out the terms and limits of this right of movement. It is a consolidation and modernisation of existing EC secondary legislation in this area. It has been implemented into domestic law by the I(EEA) Regs 2006 (see **13.9**). This book will look at the detail of the 2006 Regs. There is a chart at **13.10** which sets out where the 2006 Regs implement the 2004 Directive. A copy of the Directive is set out in **Appendix 6** to this Part.

A fuller treatment of this topic is found in Part III of ***Legal Foundations***. The following is a summary of the main principles.

13.8.1 The right of free movement

13.8.1.1 Workers

Article 39 EC requires free movement for workers within the Community. Article 39(3) EC provides that this entails the right to:

(a) accept offers of employment;
(b) move freely within the EU for this purpose;
(c) stay in a Member State for employment;

(d) remain after employment, subject to conditions.

Out of the 10 Accession States (see **13.7.1**) that joined the EU in May 2004, nationals of the Czech Republic, Estonia, Hungary, Latvia, Lithuania, Poland, Slovakia and Slovenia are usually required to register as a worker in the UK under the Accession (Immigration and Worker Registration) Regulations 2004 (SI 2004/1219). Broadly, those subject to registration are not allowed to enter the UK to look for work (although a national may enter as a self-sufficient person whilst looking for work). The national is treated as a worker for EEA purposes only during the period in which he is working for an authorised employer. Similar provisions apply to nationals of Bulgaria and Romania.

13.8.1.2 Business and the self-employed

Article 43 EC requires abolition of restrictions on the freedom of establishment of EU nationals. This freedom includes the right to pursue activities as self-employed persons, and to set up and manage undertakings such as companies or firms.

13.8.1.3 Services

Article 49 EC requires abolition of the restrictions on freedom to provide services within the Community in respect of nationals of Member States who are established in a State of the Community other than that of the person for whom the services are intended.

Article 50 EC states that the provider of a service (including industrial, commercial, craft, and professional activities) may temporarily pursue his activity in a State where the service is provided. Permanent provision of the service would involve 'establishment'.

Freedom of movement extends not only to the providers, but also to the recipients of services. In Joined Cases 286/82 and 26/83 *Luisi (Graziana) and Carbone (Giuseppe) v Ministero del Tesoro* [1984] ECR 377, the ECJ held that this covered tourists, and those who travel for medical treatment, education or business.

Does the EEA national have to travel to another EEA country and provide services there? 'No', held the ECJ in Case C-384/93 *Alpine Investments BV v Minister van Financiën* (1995). The ECJ held that offers to provide services over the telephone to potential recipients established in other Member States is sufficient. On a proper construction, Article 49 applies to services which a provider supplies, without moving from the Member State in which he is established, to recipients established in other Member States.

13.9 The Immigration (European Economic Area) Regulations 2006

As stated in **13.7.2**, the I(EEA) Regs 2006 enact EC law rights of free movement in UK law. A copy can be found at **Appendix 7** to this Part of the book. The immigration adviser can refer directly to the I(EEA) Regs 2006 but should be aware that, in the event that they fail to give effect to EC law, EC law will prevail. In addition, EC case law may affect the interpretation of the Regulations.

All references in this section are to the I(EEA) Regs 2006 unless otherwise stated.

13.9.1 Right of admission for EEA nationals (reg 11(1))

An EEA national must be admitted to the UK if he produces on arrival a valid national identity card or passport issued by an EEA State.

13.9.2 Right of admission for family members of EEA nationals (reg 11(2))

A person who is not an EEA national must be admitted to the UK if he is a family member of an EEA national and he produces on arrival a valid passport or an EEA family permit (see **13.9.7**), a residence card (see **13.9.8**) or a permanent residence card (see **13.9.10**).

The family member may be travelling with the EEA national to the UK, or joining the EEA national who is already in the UK. If the family member is travelling independently of the EEA national and not joining him in the UK then the Immigration Rules apply.

13.9.3 Initial right of residence for three months (reg 13)

An EEA national and his family member(s) are entitled to reside in the UK for a period not exceeding three months. The only condition is that the EEA national and any family member must not become an unreasonable burden on the social assistance system of the UK.

As to the right to claim any welfare benefits during this period, see **10.7.2**.

13.9.4 Residence beyond three months (reg 14)

An EEA national is entitled to reside in the UK for a period exceeding three months if he is a qualified person. Indeed, he has the right to reside in the UK for as long as he remains a qualified person. His family member(s) have the same right.

It is important to appreciate that the family member's right to reside is dependent upon the EEA national having a right to reside. The problem that arises if the EEA national dies or leaves the UK, etc is considered at **13.9.11**.

As to the right to claim any welfare benefits during this period, see **10.7.2**.

13.9.5 Who is a qualified person? (reg 6)

A qualified person is an EEA national who is in the UK in any of the following categories:

(a) a jobseeker;
(b) a worker (see Article 39 of the EC Treaty (see **13.8.1.1**));
(c) a self-employed person (see Article 43 of the EC Treaty (see **13.8.1.2**));
(d) a self-sufficient person; or
(e) a student.

A 'jobseeker' is an EEA national who enters the UK in order to look for employment. He must be able to provide evidence that he is seeking employment and that he has a genuine chance of securing employment.

A 'self-sufficient person' is an EEA national who has (i) sufficient resources not to become a burden on the social assistance system of the UK during his period of residence; and (ii) comprehensive sickness insurance cover in the UK. Guidance from the BIA is that a retired person would be self-sufficient if he could demonstrate that he was in receipt of a pension and/or had sufficient funds or income from investments not to become a burden on the UK's social assistance system.

Is a set amount of money required to demonstrate self-sufficiency? Directive 2004/58 EC, Article 8(4) prohibits this. However, reg 4(4) provides that a person's resources are regarded as sufficient if they exceed the maximum level of resources which a UK national and his family members may possess if he is to become eligible for social assistance under the UK benefit system.

A 'student' means an EEA national who:

(a) is enrolled at a private or public establishment, included on the Department for Education and Skills' Register of Education and Training Providers or financed from public funds, for the principal purpose of following a course of study, including vocational training;

(b) has comprehensive sickness insurance cover in the UK; and

(c) assures the Secretary of State, by means of a declaration, or by such equivalent means as the person may choose, that he has sufficient resources not to become a burden on the social assistance system of the UK during his period of residence.

Note that by reg 6(2) and (3) a person who is not currently working may be still treated as a worker or as self-employed if, for example, he is temporarily unable to work as the result of an illness or accident.

13.9.6 Who is a family member of an EEA national?

Under reg 7, as a general rule, the following are family members of an EEA national:

(a) his spouse or his civil partner;

(b) direct descendants (children, grandchildren, etc) of him, his spouse or his civil partner who are—

 (i) under 21, or

 (ii) dependants of him, his spouse or his civil partner;

(c) dependent direct relatives in his ascending line (parents, grandparents, etc) or that of his spouse or his civil partner.

A spouse or civil partner ((a) above) will not cease to be a family member in the event of marital breakdown or separation as long as the EEA national continues to exercise Treaty rights. The right of residence will continue until any divorce is finalised by decree absolute, or until a civil partnership is dissolved.

Note that by reg 2 a 'spouse' does not include a party to a marriage of convenience; and a 'civil partner' does not include a party to a civil partnership of convenience. Earlier Home Office guidance D2/93 suggested that where a marriage of convenience was suspected and the couple did not intend to live together, the Home Office might seek removal. The replacement guidance D3/96 says that the matter should be referred to the Home Office EC Group, whether the marriage is before or after any enforcement action (see **Chapter 15**). The case of *Desmond* (1998) INLP 147 is said to be one of a series where a Chinese person had married an Irish national who was exercising Treaty rights in the UK. It was contended that a residence permit should be issued to the non-EEA spouse simply on production of the couple's passports and marriage certificate. The couple had been advised, although it is unclear by whom, not to attend a Home Office interview nor to produce any evidence of cohabitation. The Tribunal held that the Home Office was entitled to investigate whether the marriage was genuine; but the burden was on it to show that it was a sham, and here the Home Office had not made all reasonable enquiries. Specifically, while a visit to the wife's long-term address had revealed no evidence of male occupation, no visit had been made to the husband's address to check whether it showed signs of female occupation.

As to (b) above, 'children' include step-children, and adopted children provided that the adoption is recognised by the UK (see **14.15.9**).

Whilst the above is the general rule, there is a major exception. Once a student has been residing in the UK for a period of three months, his family members are limited to (i) his spouse or his civil partner, and (ii) his dependent children or those of his civil partner.

What about direct descendants (children, etc) aged 21 or over, or direct relatives in the ascending line (parents, etc) who cannot show dependency? What about other relatives, such as brothers and sisters, uncles and aunts, cousins, etc? These may fall within reg 8, which deals with 'extended family members'. These are any of the following:

(a) a person who is a relative of an EEA national, his spouse or his civil partner and—

  (i) who is residing in an EEA State in which the EEA national also resides and who is either dependent upon the EEA national or a member of his household, or

  (ii) who satisfied the condition in para (i) and is accompanying the EEA national to the UK or wishes to join him here, or

  (iii) who satisfied the condition in para (i), has joined the EEA national in the UK and continues to be either dependent upon him or a member of his household

(b) a person who is a relative of an EEA national, or his spouse or his civil partner and, on serious health grounds, who strictly requires the personal care of the EEA national, his spouse or his civil partner;

(c) a person who is a relative of an EEA national and who would meet the requirements in the Immigration Rules (other than those relating to entry clearance) for indefinite leave to enter or remain in the UK as a dependent relative of the EEA national were the EEA national a person present and settled in the UK;

(d) a person who is the partner of an EEA national (other than a civil partner) and who can prove to the decision maker that he is in a durable relationship with the EEA national. The BIA advises that the test it imposes is similar to that in Immigration Rules, para 295A (see **14.14**).

Some of the above categories have a test of dependency on the EEA national. Guidance from the BIA is that the dependency may be one of choice rather than necessity, but the definition of 'dependency' includes only financial dependency and not emotional dependency. Financial dependency might be shown by the family member being unemployed.

Guidance from the BIA is that Directive 2004/38 refers in Article 3 only to facilitating the entry and residence of extended family members. When deciding whether to issue a residence card, the BIA must assess whether refusal would deter the EEA national from exercising his EC Treaty rights or would create an effective obstacle to the exercise of those rights. An example is given that it might be appropriate to issue a residence card where the family member was very elderly or incapacitated. In assessing such a case the BIA state that it would be important to consider whether there were relatives to care for the person in the home country.

In considering cases under reg 8, the BIA normally refuses those who have, for example, their own family unit (unless there are sufficient compassionate circumstances), or who have lived in a third country whilst the EEA national has resided in another Member State prior to entering the UK, or who lived as part of the EEA national's household many years ago.

13.9.7 Does a family member need a travel document? (reg 12)

To be admitted to the UK, a family member should apply to an entry clearance officer for a travel document known as a family permit before travelling to the UK. It is required only where the family member is not an EEA national. In order to obtain the permit the family member will have to produce documentation demonstrating the relationship with the EEA national (eg marriage certificate, etc) and that he is lawfully resident in the EEA State (see *Akrich* (Case C-109/01) [2003] 3 CMLR 26).

13.9.8 How can an EEA national or family member confirm their right of residence?

Under regs 16 and 17, an EEA national or a non-EEA family member entitled to residence can apply to the Secretary of State for a residence certificate or residence card respectively. A residence certificate or card is normally valid for five years.

A family member may find it useful to obtain a residence certificate, particularly when applying for employment, as it confirms his entitlement to take employment in the UK. Also, if he leaves the UK, it will prove his right of re-entry (otherwise he will need to obtain a family permit: see **13.9.7**).

13.9.9 Permanent right of residence in UK (reg 15)

The following persons can acquire the right to reside in the UK permanently:

(a) an EEA national who has resided in the UK in accordance with the 2006 Regs for a continuous period of five years;

(b) a family member of an EEA national (who is not himself an EEA national) who has resided in the UK with the EEA national in accordance with the 2006 Regs for a continuous period of five years;

(c) a worker or self-employed person who has ceased activity;

(d) the family member of a worker or self-employed person who has ceased activity;

(e) a person who was the family member of a worker or self-employed person where—

(i) the worker or self-employed person has died,

(ii) the family member resided with him immediately before his death, and

(iii) the worker or self-employed person had resided continuously in the UK for at least the two years immediately before his death, or the death was the result of an accident at work or an occupational disease;

(f) a person who—

(i) has resided in the UK in accordance with the 2006 Regs for a continuous period of five years; and

(ii) was, at the end of that period, a family member who has retained the right of residence.

Note that as to (c) above (a worker or self-employed person who has ceased activity) this category of person is defined by reg 5. So, for example, it includes a worker or self-employed person who has to stop work as a result of a permanent incapacity and who had resided in the UK continuously for more than two years prior to his work ending.

Some of the above categories are based on a period of continuous residence in the UK. What about any periods of absence? Regulation 3 provides that continuity of residence is not affected by:

(a) periods of absence from the UK which do not exceed six months in total in any year;

(b) periods of absence from the UK on military service; or

(c) any one absence from the UK not exceeding 12 months for an important reason, such as pregnancy and childbirth, serious illness, study or vocational training, or an overseas posting.

Can the right of permanent residence be lost once acquired? Yes, but only through absence from the UK for a period exceeding two consecutive years.

13.9.10 How can an EEA national or family member confirm his permanent residence?

Under reg 18, an EEA national or non-EEA family member entitled to permanent residence can apply to the Secretary of State for a document certifying permanent residence or a permanent residence card respectively.

A document certifying permanent residence does not have an expiry date. A permanent residence card is valid for 10 years and is renewable.

13.9.11 What is the status of a family member who has not acquired permanent residence on the death or departure from the UK of the qualified person, or the termination of marriage or civil partnership?

Until a family member acquires his own right of permanent residence he is in a vulnerable position: What if the qualified person dies or leaves the UK? If his right of residence is dependent on marriage to, or on a civil partnership with, a qualified person, what is his immigration status when that relationship formally ends?

The answer is to be found in reg 10, which allows certain family members to retain the right of residence. This includes, for example, a person who:

(a) is a family member of a qualified person when the qualified person dies;

(b) resided in the UK in accordance with the 2006 Regs for at least the year immediately before the death of the qualified person; and

(c) if he had been an EEA national himself, would qualify as a worker, a self-employed person or a self-sufficient person as defined by reg 6, or who is the family member of a person who was a worker, a self-employed person or a self-sufficient person as defined by reg 6.

The BIA guidance is that it will normally revoke, or refuse to issue or renew, a residence card where a family member's marriage to, or civil partnership with, a qualified person terminates, or there is evidence that the EEA national has left the UK, unless the family member has retained the right of residence under reg 10.

13.9.12 British citizens who exercise EC Treaty rights and then return to the UK (reg 9)

If a British citizen travels to another EEA country to work or otherwise exercise Treaty rights, he is entitled to be accompanied by his family. Equally, if a British citizen travels to the UK from an EEA country after exercising Treaty rights there, his family may accompany him. So, for example, the Indian spouse of a British citizen who has worked in another EEA country may take advantage of Article 38 EC, acquiring rights of residence in the UK itself beyond those given by UK immigration law – see *R v Immigration Appeal Tribunal and Surinder Singh, ex p Secretary of State for the Home Department* [1992] 3 CMLR 358.

Mr Singh, an Indian national, married a British citizen in the UK in 1982. At no time did the authorities allege that the marriage was a sham. It appears that Mr Singh was lawfully in the UK, but his immigration status is not clear from the case report. In 1983 Mr and Mrs Singh went to Germany where they were both employed for two years. At the end of 1985 the couple returned to the UK to open a business. The ECJ held that the provisions of the Council Regulations and Directives on freedom of movement within the Community for employed and self-employed persons provide that Member States must grant the spouse and children of such a person rights of residence equivalent to those granted to the person himself. A national of a Member State might be deterred from leaving his country of origin in order to pursue an activity as an employed or self-employed person as envisaged by the Treaty in the territory of another Member State if, on returning to the Member State of which he is a national in order to pursue an activity there as an employed or self-employed person, the conditions of his entry and residence were not at least equivalent to those which he would enjoy under the Treaty or secondary law in the territory of another Member State. He would in particular be deterred from so doing if his spouse and children were not also permitted to enter and reside in the territory of his Member State of origin under conditions at least equivalent to those granted them by Community law in the territory of another Member State.

Regulation 9 is said to give effect to the *Surinder Singh* judgment.

Where a UK national is residing in an EEA State as a worker or self-employed person, or was so residing before returning to the UK, he is entitled to be accompanied by his family members (spouse, civil partner, partner in a durable relationship, child under 21, etc: see **13.9.6**).

The BIA advises that the UK national must either have been employed in an EEA State other than on a transient or casual basis, or have established himself there as a self-employed person. As a rule of thumb it is said that the UK national should have carried out such an activity for at least six months. It might be less if he was required to return to the UK earlier for a good reason, eg health grounds.

If the family member of the UK national is his spouse or civil partner, the marriage or civil partnership must take place, and the parties must have been living together in an EEA State, before the UK national returns to the UK.

As generally is the case, the family member will have a right to enter the UK with the British citizen under reg 9 only if lawfully in an EEA State (see *Akrich* at **13.9.7**).

The family member will be entitled to a family permit, residence card and permanent residence under the same conditions as any family member.

If the family member of the UK national is his spouse or civil partner, he has the choice of entry under EC law or domestic law (see **14.9**). If he chooses EC law and is successful, he will be issued with a family permit and a residence card. He may qualify for permanent residence after five years. Compare this to domestic law, where settled status can be acquired after two years (see **14.9.5**).

The BIA's policy is that if a spouse or civil partner enters the UK under EC law then he can avail himself of the Immigration Rules only if he leaves the UK and applies for entry clearance under the Immigration Rules as the spouse or civil partner of a British citizen (see **14.9**).

Is it discrimination under EC law that the spouse of an EEA national has to wait five years (rather than two years as applies under UK domestic law – see **14.9**) to potentially gain settled status? The ECJ answered that question in the negative when considering the point in the case of Case C–356/98 *Kaba v Secretary of State for the Home Department* [2000] All ER (EC) 537. The ECJ held that there was no discrimination contrary to Community law.

13.9.13 Summary of key terms

'Qualified person'	An EEA national who is exercising Treaty rights as a jobseeker; worker; self-employed person; a self-sufficient person or student.
'Family permit'	A form of entry clearance issued to a non-EEA national who is the family member of an EEA national.
'Registration certificate'	This is issued to an EEA national who is exercising Treaty rights (reg 16).
'Residence card'	This is issued to a non-EEA national who is the family member of a qualified person (reg 17).
'A document certifying permanent residence'	This is issued to an EEA national who has been residing in the UK for at least five years exercising Treaty rights (reg 18).
'A permanent residence card'	This is issued to a non-EEA national who is the family member of a qualified person, when he has resided for at least five years with a qualified person, who, during those five years has exercised Treaty rights (reg 18).

13.9.14 Excluding and removing an EEA national from the UK

Regulation 19 of the I(EEA) Regs 2006 provides for the exclusion and removal of an EEA national or his family member who has ceased to qualify, or whose removal is justified on the grounds of public policy pursuant to reg 21.

For a person to be excluded or removed on public policy grounds under reg 21, he must present a serious threat to the fundamental interests of society by his personal conduct. Guidance from the BIA provides that previous criminal convictions are not in themselves sufficient grounds, unless the offence(s) are particularly serious (eg rape, murder, drug smuggling) or it is likely that the person would reoffend. A person charged with minor customs offences is not refused admission on that basis alone, whereas a person who is the leader of an extreme political party might present such a threat. Facilitation of illegal entry may, in itself, be sufficient grounds to refuse admission to EEA nationals. National security can also fall under this heading.

Public security under reg 21 does not necessarily equate with national security. Public security may also be a matter of personal security within society. Certain medical conditions (eg drug addiction or profound mental disturbance) may pose a threat to public policy or public security. These conditions might provide reasons for exclusion on public policy or public security grounds, but not on public health grounds.

As to public health, only a disease that has epidemic potential as defined by the World Health Organisation, or a disease to which s 38 of the Public Health (Control of Disease) Act 1984 applies (detention in hospital of a person with a notifiable disease), will constitute a ground for a decision to exclude or remove. However, if the person concerned is in the UK, any disease occurring after the initial three-month period does not count.

See further the case of *B v Secretary of State for the Home Department* [2000] Imm AR 478 detailed at **15.1.3**.

13.10 Chart cross-referencing key aspects of 2006 Regulations and 2004 Directive

Coverage	2006 Regulations	2004 Directive
Definitions	reg 2 'EEA national'	Art 2 'Union citizen'
	reg 7 'family member'	Art 2
	reg 8 'extended family member'	Art 3(2)
Right of entry	reg 11	Art 5
Initial right of residence up to 3 months	reg 13	Art 6
Right of residence for more than 3 months	reg 14	Art 7
Issue of residence cards	reg 17	Art 10
Retention of right of residence by family members on death or departure of qualified person	reg 10	Art 12
Retention of right of residence by family members on formal ending of marriage or registered civil partnership with qualified person	reg 10	Art 13
Right of permanent residence	reg 15	Arts 16, 17 and 18
A document certifying permanent residence	reg 18	Art 19
A permanent residence card	reg 18	Art 20
Continuity of residence	reg 3	Art 21
Protection against expulsion	reg 21	Art 28
Public health	reg 21	Art 29

13.11 The Common Travel Area

The Common Travel Area consists of the UK, Ireland, the Channel Islands and the Isle of Man. The basic principle, set out in s 1(3) of the IA 1971, is that persons arriving on local journeys to the UK from elsewhere in the Common Travel Area are not subject to immigration control, and no leave to enter is required. Control operates only on initial entry to the Area from outside. This is subject to some exceptions, for example under the Immigration (Control on Entry through the Republic of Ireland) Order 1972 (SI 1972/1610). This subjects some persons to immigration control (such as visa nationals without a visa for entry to the UK). If such persons enter the UK, for example, from Ireland, they are illegal entrants, even though they have never been examined by the immigration service. The 1972 Order also imposes conditions in other cases (eg where a person who is not Irish, and does not have the right of abode in the UK, travels to the UK from outside the Area, via the Republic). Usually such persons will have deemed leave to enter for three months, with a prohibition on employment and business for non-EEA nationals. As the person will not have passed through immigration control, there will be no indication of these conditions on his passport.

Chapter 14
Immigration Status: Special Categories

14.1	Visitors	247
14.2	Students	251
14.3	Other temporary purposes	256
14.4	Employment, business and independent means	258
14.5	Employment	259
14.6	Businessmen and self-employed persons	266
14.7	Innovators and highly skilled migrants	269
14.8	Investors	273
14.9	Spouses and civil partners	274
14.10	Marriage breakdown	281
14.11	Polygamous marriages or civil partnerships	282
14.12	Spouses or civil partners of persons with limited leave	282
14.13	Fiancé(e)s or proposed civil partners of persons who are settled	282
14.14	Non-marital relationships	283
14.15	Children	285
14.16	Parents and other relatives	290
14.17	Asylum-seekers and refugees	293

14.1 Visitors

14.1.1 Introduction – who is a 'visitor'?

The term 'visitor' is not defined in the Immigration Rules, except to make it clear that it includes 'business visitors'. A person will be a visitor if he is coming to the UK for less than six months, and is not seeking entry for any other purpose within the Rules. Typically, a visitor will be coming to the UK for a holiday, to visit relatives or friends, or to transact business. Visitors in transit to another country are dealt with under separate rules (paras 47–50), under which they may be admitted for a period not exceeding 48 hours.

Except in the case of visa nationals, no entry clearance is required for a short-term visit to the UK. It will, however, reduce problems on entry, for those who are not simply tourists, if entry clearance is obtained in advance.

Provided that there is no general reason for refusal of entry (see **13.5.7**), leave will normally be granted under para 42 of the Immigration Rules, usually with a time limit of six months. However, the immigration officer must be satisfied that requirements set out in para 41 are met, ie that the visitor:

(a) is genuinely seeking entry for the stated period of his visit;
(b) intends to leave thereafter;
(c) does not intend to take employment in the UK;
(d) does not intend to produce goods or provide services in the UK;
(e) does not intend to study at a maintained school;
(f) will maintain and accommodate himself and any dependants adequately without recourse to public funds or taking employment; or will, with dependants, be maintained and accommodated adequately by relatives or friends;
(g) can meet the cost of leaving the UK;

(h) is not a child under the age of 18. As to entry by a child as a visitor, see the Immigration Rules, para 46A.

Guidance from the BIA provides that

> the examination of visitors should be aimed at identifying promptly, with a minimum of questioning, those passengers who clearly meet the requirements of the Rules. Immediately it becomes apparent that a passenger qualifies for leave to enter as a visitor, the examination should be concluded and the passenger given leave to enter.

The key points the immigration officer is looking for during his examination are:

(a) that the passenger is giving a true account of what he intends to do during his stay in the UK;

(b) the length of time he will stay here;

(c) that he does not intend undertaking any activity which is not allowed by the Rules relating to visitors during his stay; and

(d) that there are sufficient funds available to finance the passenger's stay (and that of any dependants) and his onward or return journey.

As to the last point, BIA guidance states, 'a visitor's proposed purpose in coming to the UK must bear some reasonable relationship to his financial means and his family, social and economic background'.

Conditions will be imposed prohibiting employment and recourse to public funds (see **13.1.1**), but a visitor is free to transact business (without setting up a business) during the visit.

> **Example**
>
> Ada is a non-visa national. She does not hold an entry certificate. At the point of entry, she informs an immigration officer that she is visiting her sister in the UK for six months. When questioned, she discloses:
>
> (a) that she has just lost her job in Jamaica;
> (b) that her sister has just obtained a job;
> (c) that she has agreed to look after her sister's children; and
> (d) that she has only £100 cash with her.
>
> The immigration officer may claim that the childminding arrangement may prevent her leaving after six months (see requirements (a) and (b)), that she intends to take employment as a childminder (see requirement (c)), and that she has insufficient cash to support herself and meet the cost of her return to Jamaica (see requirements (f) and (g)). It would help her case (on (f) and (g)) if she had a letter from her sister promising to provide meals and accommodation, and a return ticket.

Family members of visitors must meet the requirements of the visitor rules in their own right. There are no special rules applying to them, as there are for other categories.

14.1.2 Business visitor

A person who enters the UK to transact business is classified as a 'visitor' rather than as someone entering for employment or as a businessman. Paragraph 40 of the Rules says that this would include 'attending meetings and briefings, fact finding, negotiating or making contracts with UK businesses to buy or sell goods or services'. The activity must not amount to productive work or otherwise constitute employment for which a work permit would be required. The salary must be paid from abroad. In addition, people may be admitted as business visitors if they are, for example, delivering goods from abroad (eg lorry drivers), installing machinery from a foreign manufacturer, or attending a conference as a guest speaker.

> **Example 1**
>
> Bill wishes to come to the UK from the USA to help install a business software product purchased by a UK company from the USA.
>
> He can be admitted as a business visitor.
>
> **Example 2**
>
> Samir is a farmer in Morocco. He wishes to drive to the UK and sell his produce from the lorry, in the UK.
>
> He is unlikely to be given a visa to enter as a business visitor. Delivery of goods is permissible, but direct sale of goods to the public would amount to engaging in a business. It would be acceptable for him to visit the UK to negotiate a contract for supply of the produce to a UK retailer.

14.1.3 The six-month time limit

There is no restriction on the number of visits a person may make to the UK nor any requirement that a specified time must elapse between successive visits. The fact that a person has made a series of visits with only brief intervals between them does not, in the absence of any other relevant factors, constitute sufficient ground for refusal of leave to enter. It is reasonable, however, for the immigration officer to consider the stated purpose of the visit in the light of the length of time that has elapsed since previous visits. Guidance from the BIA is that a visitor should not, for example, normally spend more than 6 out of any 12 months in the UK.

Occasionally, a business visitor may require to stay for a period of weeks or even months in the UK (eg where machinery is being installed or faults being diagnosed and corrected). The immigration officer must be satisfied, however, that a person's presence here on business for more than 6 out of any 12 months does not mean that he is basing himself in the UK and holding down a specific post which constitutes employment requiring a work permit.

Leave to remain beyond the six-month maximum period is granted in only the most exceptional compassionate circumstances, such as the illness of a close relative (see **14.1.6**).

14.1.4 Marriage and civil partnership visits

What if a person wishes to enter the UK to marry or enter into a civil partnership with, someone here but the couple do not intend to remain in the UK after the marriage or civil partnership has been entered into? By para 56D of the Immigration Rules a person can seek entry clearance and leave to enter the UK as a visitor for such a purpose provided he meets the requirements set out in para 41 for entry as a visitor; can show that he intends to give notice of marriage, or civil partnership, in the UK within the period for which entry is sought; and can produce satisfactory evidence, if required to do so, of the arrangements for giving notice of marriage or civil partnership, or for the ceremony to take place, in the UK during the period for which entry is sought.

Any leave granted will not exceed six months and is subject to conditions prohibiting employment and recourse to public funds (see **13.1.1**).

A person granted leave in this category will not require Home Office permission to marry or form a civil partnership (see **14.9.6**).

If the couple wish to remain in the UK afterwards the applicant should apply for entry clearance as a fiancé(e) or proposed civil partner (see **14.13**).

14.1.5 Extensions

Having entered as a visitor, a person is normally expected to leave when the visit is concluded. It is possible for a visitor granted leave of less than six months to apply for an extension of the visit (to a maximum of six months), but there must be a good reason for the change of plan. An extension of a visit beyond six months would require an exceptional exercise of discretion by the Home Office.

> **Example**
> Carol entered the UK with six months' leave, to visit her mother. Her mother has fallen ill and Carol wishes to remain (beyond six months) until she has recovered.
>
> She can apply for an extension, outside the Rules. If she applies before her existing leave expires, she receives the normal automatic extension of her leave (see **13.6.2**). However, if refused she has no right of appeal (see **16.8**). The fact that she has tried to remain for more than six months may jeopardise future visits.

14.1.6 Visitors and carers

There is no provision in the Immigration Rules for leave to enter or remain to be granted solely to allow a person to care for a friend or relative in the UK. Applications for leave to enter as a carer may be refused on the ground that there is no provision for this in the Immigration Rules. However, where an applicant wishes to care for a friend or relative for a short period, the application may be considered under the requirements of the rules relating to visitors. Applications from persons already in the UK in a temporary capacity seeking leave to remain to care for a sick relative or friend who is suffering from a terminal illness, such as cancer or AIDS, or who is mentally or physically disabled are dealt with outside the Immigration Rules under the Secretary of State's discretion. If leave to remain is granted, it is made clear to the applicant that it is only a temporary capacity and that, once alternative arrangements have been made or if the patient should die, then the 'carer' is expected to return home. An extension of stay on this basis will not lead to settlement.

Where the application is to care for a sick or disabled relative, leave for three months is usually granted. Where it is decided to grant leave for three months exceptionally, outside the Rules, the applicant is informed that leave has been granted on the strict understanding that, during this period, arrangements must be made for the future care of the patient by a person who does not require leave to remain outside the Immigration Rules. However, applications for leave to remain in order to care for a sick or disabled friend are normally refused save in an emergency (eg the patient has suddenly fallen ill and there is insufficient time to arrange permanent care or there is nobody else in the UK to whom the patient can turn). In those circumstances, leave to remain may be granted for a period of three months. An extension of further leave will not be given unless there are wholly exceptional circumstances.

When the BIA is considering whether a period of leave should be granted, it takes into account the following:

(a) the type of illness/condition (this should be supported by a doctor's letter); and

(b) the type of care required; and

(c) the care which is available (eg from the social services or other relatives/friends); and

(d) the long-term prognosis.

In cases where there are sufficient exceptional compassionate circumstances to continue the exercise of discretion, leave to remain may be granted for up to 12 months.

The patient may be entitled to the care component of disability living allowance or attendance allowance from which he can choose to pay for a person to care for him. The benefit is paid to the patient rather than the carer and therefore the carer is not considered to be in receipt of public funds. If the patient claims other benefits and uses these to support and accommodate the carer, provided the patient is not claiming any extra benefit for the carer this again is not considered as recourse to public funds unless the carer claims benefits in his own right. See further **Chapter 10**.

14.1.7 Switching to another category

Visitors will not normally be permitted to remain in another category. However, the Rules do permit applications to remain as a close relative of someone settled in the UK (see **14.15** and **14.16**) or as the spouse of someone who has limited leave (see **14.9**). Note in particular that a visitor is prohibited from switching to a spouse under para 284(i) of the Immigration Rules.

14.2 Students

14.2.1 Entry

Entry clearance is not generally required where an entrant seeks admission to pursue a course of study, except in the case of visa nationals or specified nationals whose course exceeds six months. However, it is often advisable to obtain it in advance.

Leave to enter may be given under para 58 of the Immigration Rules if the requirements set out in para 57 are met.

14.2.1.1 The student has been accepted for a place at an institution specified in the rules

Higher education covers all post-school courses above GCE A-level standard. These courses are available at universities, colleges, institutions of higher education (some wholly concerned with teacher training) and some institutions of further education. Further education is for people over 16 taking courses at various levels up to the standard required for entry to higher education. Publicly funded institutions within the further and higher education sector receive funds through the Further or Higher Education Funding Councils. There is a wide range of private institutions which provide courses of further and higher education (which do not receive funds through the Further or Higher Education Funding Councils). All institutions must be on the Government register of education providers. Leave to study will not be granted to a student wishing to attend a college not on the register.

14.2.1.2 The student is able and intends to follow a full-time course of a type specified

A person who has been accepted for a course at a reputable educational establishment may, on arrival, appear to the immigration officer to lack a knowledge of basic subjects, including English language, which would enable him to follow the course. However, as the BIA guidance states:

> The immigration officer should avoid giving the impression that he is setting an educational test. In such a case, therefore, he should explain his doubts to the principal of the establishment. In some cases, the establishment may be aware of the situation and have made arrangements to bring the student up to standard before commencement of the course. Where this is not the case the principal should be asked to arrange to assess the student himself before a decision can be made as to whether or not the passenger may be given leave to enter. If the assessment is that the passenger is not able to follow the course, he should be refused leave to enter.

A student should provide an up-to-date letter from his college containing the following information:

(a) the type of course;
(b) what qualifications it will lead to;
(c) the duration of the course;
(d) whether or not the course is full time;
(e) the cost of the course;
(f) whether the fees have been paid either in part or in full;
(g) the level or stage reached (if continuing a course).

When considering an application for leave to enter or remain to undertake a course which is not due to commence for several months, the immigration officer will ask for the reason for the delay. Where there is a good reason (eg a student's present course finishes at the end of the academic year but he has an unconditional offer for a course starting in October), leave to remain is granted to cover the period of enrolment, provided all the normal requirements are also met. An application for leave to remain to undertake a course which is not due to commence for four months or more from a person not currently engaged in full-time studies is normally refused without further enquiry.

What is a full-time course? Students following a recognised degree course at a publicly funded institution of further or higher education, or a course at an independent fee-paying school, need only demonstrate that the course is full time. This also applies to those following a degree course at a bona fide private education institution where the degree will be awarded by a recognised university, including the Open University. All other students must demonstrate that they meet the requirement to spend at least 15 hours per week in organised daytime study. Occasionally, because of the nature of exam syllabuses, some students may be obliged to enrol on two or more part-time courses; others may do so as a means of saving money on fees. This is acceptable to the BIA, provided that the courses involve attendance at a single institution for a minimum of 15 hours' organised daytime study per week and the subjects are directly related. However, evening and weekend courses do not meet the requirements of the Rules and no account is taken of any classes which commence at 6 pm or later, or any classes attended at the weekend. Where a class starts during the afternoon and continues after 6 pm, this may be acceptable to the BIA provided a substantial part of the class takes place during the daytime.

14.2.1.3 The student, if under 16, is enrolled (full time) at an independent fee-paying school

Children from overseas may join independent schools. There are over 2,000 independent fee-charging primary and secondary schools in the UK, some of which are known as 'public schools'. All independent schools with five pupils or more have to be registered with the DfES and are open to the Department's inspection. A school not registered as an independent school may not be regarded as such for the purposes of the Immigration Rules even if it has fewer than five pupils. In addition, schools providing boarding accommodation for 50 children or fewer are required to register with the local Social Services Department.

14.2.1.4 The student intends to leave the UK at end of studies

The immigration officer must be satisfied that a person seeking leave to enter as a student is genuinely intending to study here and to leave at the end of his studies. Where there is cause for doubt in this respect or where his intentions are not clear, the immigration officer will question the student fully in order to clarify matters and assess his credibility.

Full account is taken of all information obtained, including the cost of the studies and the availability of suitable courses in the passenger's country of residence. Guidance from the BIA is that the immigration officer should consider whether the enterprise on which the student is about to embark is reasonable to a person of his family, social and economic background. To this end, it may be appropriate to ask about his job opportunities in his country and the material benefits to be gained from the course and to weigh this against the cost of the course which may represent the expenditure of a large sum of money to a person or family of low income.

How can this intention be shown? In the case of *Mdawini* (1998) INLP 147, a student nurse said that she would return to her home in Zimbabwe unless the political situation there deteriorated. That qualified intention was said to satisfy the Rule. However, compare this with *Oladunni* (15374), where the student's answer, 'I don't know what the future holds', did not meet the Rule.

14.2.1.5 The student does not intend to engage in business or take employment, except part-time or vacation work undertaken with the prior consent of the DfEE

Although a student will normally be granted leave that permits part-time and vacation work (see below), his prospective earnings are not taken into account when assessing the adequacy of the funds available for support and accommodation of the student and any dependants. However, if the part-time work is guaranteed at a publicly funded institution of further or higher education at which the student is studying, such earnings may be taken into account when assessing the student's financial means. Equally, the potential earnings of any spouse of a student are not taken into account unless he or she is already in employment.

What about working after entry as a student? Students studying at UK institutions and who are not nationals of an EEA country are no longer required to obtain permission from the Jobcentre to take spare time and vacation work. Similarly, they are able to do work placements which are part of a 'sandwich course' or to undertake internship placements without the need to obtain permission.

Under the BIA guidelines, students do not need to obtain permission before they can work. The conditions covering the hours and type of work they may do are:

(a) the student should not work for more than 20 hours per week during term-time, except where the placement is a necessary part of his studies with the agreement of the education institution;

(b) the student should not engage in business, self-employment or the provision of services as a professional sportsman or entertainer;

(c) the student should not pursue a career by filling a permanent full-time vacancy.

This policy applies to people admitted to the UK as students for more than six months. Their passport stamp will continue to state that they can work only with permission from the Secretary of State for Employment. Under the guidelines, this approval, subject to the conditions above, is automatically deemed to have been given. The above arrangements do not apply to students on courses of six months or less, whose leave of entry prohibits employment. However, if short-term students indicate that they want to take part-time work, the Immigration Officer will grant entry on the above conditions, assuming that they meet the normal requirements of the student rules.

14.2.1.6 The student is able to meet the cost of his course and accommodation and maintenance for himself and his dependants without taking employment or engaging in business or having recourse to public funds

A student arriving for the first time may well not have a UK bank account and so will need to produce other evidence of his ability to finance his stay (eg cash, travellers' cheques, a banker's draft or a satisfactory sponsorship letter). If the applicant is dependent on funds from abroad, he will be asked to prove that the funds are transferable, as certain countries operate strict exchange controls.

Students sponsored by their home Government, the British Council or any international organisation need only provide evidence of the award and its duration. For these purposes, 'sponsored' means wholly supported by an award which covers both fees and maintenance. Such students are not normally given leave to enter or remain beyond the period of sponsorship. Discretion, however, may be exercised if a sponsored student who otherwise qualifies for leave can show that the sponsoring body has agreed to his remaining in the UK for further studies not covered by the award.

It is not a requirement of the Immigration Rules that a student should pay his fees for his course before leave to enter or remain may be granted. A student need only demonstrate that he can meet the cost. Where a student produces a letter from a publicly funded institution of further or higher education stating that financial requirements have been satisfied, no further enquiries into the payment of fees are usually necessary. In fact, some institutions make provisions for certain students to stagger the payment of fees over the academic year whilst others allow students to defer payment and some even waive the fees altogether.

14.2.2 Length of leave

Time limits depend on the length of the course. Students on courses of one year or more that finish in the summer should be granted leave until 31 October following the end of the course. If the course does not follow the standard autumn to summer pattern, an additional two months is normally added to the end of the course date. Recourse to public funds is prohibited (see **Chapter 10**).

14.2.3 Family members

Family members of students (but not prospective students) may be admitted for the same period as the student (see **14.12** and **14.15.6**).

14.2.4 Extensions and switching

Once admitted as a student, a person may apply for an extension of his stay as a student under para 61 of the Immigration Rules. In addition to the requirements applying on entry, there are conditions which, under para 60, include the following.

(a) Satisfactory evidence of regular attendance and progress. The BIA guidance is that caseworkers should always obtain an attendance record after a student has been here for three years; or if an English language student has been studying for 12 months and requests leave to remain to continue English studies. The BIA recognises that there is a clear link between a student's attendance and the progress he is likely to make on a course. Also, poor attendance may signify that a student cannot support himself without working or that his intentions are not to study at all. The caseworker will therefore make enquiries in relation to funds and progress whenever attendance checks are made.

(b) That any extension will not result in the student having spent more than two years on short courses below degree level. The BIA guidance states that this provision is not intended to prevent a person from taking short courses which form part of a planned course with a defined educational objective but enquiries as to a student's educational plans should be considered where:

   (i) a student has enrolled on a new course which bears no relation to previous studies; or

   (ii) a student is re-enrolling on the same or similar course without apparently making progress; or

   (iii) a student breaks off mid-course for no good reason and then seeks to commence another course; or

   (iv) there is any reason to suspect that a student is making his studies an excuse for remaining in the UK for some other purpose.

(c) Of course, the authorities will want assurance that the student and any dependants will not resort to public funds. By now, the student is likely to have a UK bank or building society account. The BIA will expect it to be in the name of the student or his sponsor. The statement should show that there are sufficient funds present in the account on a regular basis and should normally indicate the receipt of funds from abroad along with regular withdrawals from the account. If the account does not appear to be used, this may indicate that a student is living on funds from another source. Letters or receipts, which simply show the balance in the account on a particular day, are not sufficient for BIA purposes. Statements apparently should cover a period of approximately three months.

(d) Enquiries as to a student's intentions are not usually made on an application for an extension except in cases where there is reason to believe that the applicant does not intend to go home (eg after an unsuccessful asylum application; or the applicant was previously refused in another capacity; or the applicant appears to be moving from course to course without any intention of bringing his studies to a close; or the applicant has applied for British citizenship). Any student who expresses the wish to remain in the UK beyond his studies should not be refused without the BIA caseworker giving him the opportunity to clarify his intentions.

Note that by para 39A of the Immigration Rules an application for a variation of leave to enter or remain made by a student who is sponsored by a government or international sponsorship agency may be refused if the sponsor has not given written consent to the proposed variation.

A student may apply to remain as a trainee (see **14.3.1**) or, if a degree graduate, for employment with a work permit (see **14.5.4**). Student nurses, postgraduate doctors and dentists may also qualify for work permit employment under para 131B. In addition, the provisions for resitting examinations (para 69A) and writing up a thesis (para 69G) are to be noted. Otherwise, he is expected to leave the UK on expiry of his leave as a student.

Very few people are allowed to switch into the student category. Paragraph 60(i) of the Immigration Rules requires that such persons must last have been admitted to the UK with entry clearance as a student, or a prospective student, or a student nurse, or a person re-sitting an examination, or a person writing up a thesis, or a students' union sabbatical officer, or an overseas qualified nurse or midwife, or a postgraduate doctor or dentist, or a person taking a PLAB Test, or a person undertaking a clinical attachment or dental observer post.

14.2.5 EEA students

EEA nationals have rights of free movement for the purpose of study if:

(a) they have enrolled at a recognised educational establishment for a vocational course (this is widely construed and would cover degree courses which might facilitate future employment);

(b) they have sufficient resources to avoid becoming a charge on public funds;

(c) they are covered by all-risks sickness insurance.

14.2.6 International Graduates Scheme (IGS)

The aim of this scheme is to encourage non-EEA national graduates of UK universities to pursue careers in the UK. To be granted leave to work in the UK for 12 months under the scheme, an applicant must have successfully completed a recognised degree course, Masters course, PhD, postgraduate certificate or diploma at a UK institution of higher or further education and intend to work during the period of leave granted under the scheme. In the usual way the applicant must be able to maintain and accommodate himself and any dependants without recourse to public funds. In addition the applicant must intend to leave the UK at the end of his stay.

An applicant may either switch in-country from student status, or return to the UK from abroad no later than one year after he has completed his course. Entry clearance is mandatory for those returning to the UK under the scheme.

An IGS participant is eligible to switch in-country into employment and the self-employment categories of work permit employment (see **14.5.4**), innovator or highly skilled migrant programme (see **14.7**) or businessman (see **14.6**), provided he meets the requirements of the category in the usual way.

14.3 Other temporary purposes

The Immigration Rules deal specifically with visitors admitted for private medical treatment (para 52), student nurses (para 65), doctors and dentists seeking postgraduate training (para 71), 'au-pairs' (para 90), working holidaymakers (para 96, see **14.3.2**), seasonal agricultural workers (para 105), teachers and language assistants on exchange schemes (para 111), and approved training or work experience (para 117, see **14.3.1**).

Immigration Status: Special Categories   257

14.3.1 Trainees

Trainees differ from students in that they are not enrolled with an educational institution; training is in employment only (eg trainee solicitors). Their UK-based employers must apply to the BIA under the Training and Work Experience Scheme (TWES). The purpose of the TWES is to allow individuals to gain skills and experience through work-based learning, which builds on their previous education and training, and which they intend to use on their return overseas. Hence, a TWES permit is granted on the understanding that the person intends to leave the UK at the end of the agreed period (a maximum of five years) to use his new skills and experience. It is important to note that an individual who holds a TWES permit is not allowed to transfer to work permit employment. For further details, see www.workingintheuk.gov.uk/working_in_the_uk/en/homepage.html.

14.3.2 Working holidaymakers

Young tourists who wish to make an extended visit to the UK, 'paying their way' by working, may take advantage of the working holidaymaker rules. However, only Commonwealth citizens qualify.

The requirements for leave to enter under para 95 are as follows.

(a) The applicant is a Commonwealth citizen of a country listed in Appendix 3 to the Immigration Rules, or a British Overseas Citizen; a British Overseas Territories Citizen; or a British National (Overseas) (see **12.4**).

(b) The applicant is aged between 17 and 30, or was so aged at the date of his application for leave to enter.

(c) The applicant is unmarried and is not a civil partner (or the spouse or civil partner is taking a working holiday too). The BIA guidance is that a working holidaymaker should normally be single, widowed or divorced. If an applicant is not single, particular attention will be paid to any family commitments. A prospective working holidaymaker who is married or in a civil partnership can qualify for entry clearance only if he and his spouse or civil partner intend coming on a working holiday together and both qualify in their own right.

(d) The applicant has the means to pay for his return or onward journey. A working holidaymaker must have the cost of the outward fare to the UK. The requirement to have the means to pay for the return or onward journey is flexibly applied by an immigration officer where there is a reasonable expectation that the necessary funds will be earned before the expiry of the two-year period.

(e) The applicant is able and intends to maintain and accommodate himself without recourse to public funds. This provision is interpreted by the BIA as meaning that a working holidaymaker must have the means to support himself for at least the first two months after arrival without recourse to public funds or for at least one month if he has a job arranged in advance.

(f) The applicant is intending only to take employment incidental to a holiday, and not to engage in business, or to provide services as a professional sportsperson, and in any event not to work for more than 12 months during his stay. The BIA guidance is that the applicant must intend to work; he cannot come for just a two-year visit, although the holiday should be the primary reason for entry. Whilst 12 months maximum can be spent working, at least 12 months should be spent holidaying. The BIA suggests that some self-employment is possible provided it is clearly temporary in nature and so should not involve investment in premises, expensive equipment or the employment of staff.

(g) The applicant does not have dependent children any of whom are five years of age or over, or who will reach five years of age before the applicant completes his working holiday.

(h) The applicant must intend to leave the UK at the end of the working holiday. The BIA guidance is that an entry clearance officer should be satisfied at the time the application is made that the applicant intends to return home at the end of his working holiday. The entry clearance officer will make enquiries in order to be satisfied that a prospective working holidaymaker, whilst not settled down in his own country, nevertheless has sufficient ties and prospects there as to be likely to return after his permitted stay in the category. As the BIA accepts, in the course of a two-year stay plans may change, and a working holidaymaker may decide to apply for an extension of stay in another category. In such circumstances, an application for leave to remain in another capacity may be granted provided that the requirements of the Immigration Rules are met. It is important to note that working holidaymakers are permitted under the Immigration Rules to switch into work permit employment (see **14.5.4**) after they have spent more than 12 months in the UK in this category in total.

(i) The applicant has not spent time in the UK on a previous working holidaymaker entry clearance. Entry in this category can therefore occur only once in a person's lifetime.

(j) The applicant holds a valid entry clearance as a working holidaymaker granted for a limited period not exceeding two years. This is required whether or not he is a visa national.

A person who is admitted in this category may be given leave to remain for up to two years. What conditions are imposed on that leave? Like all entrants with limited leave it will be a condition not to have recourse to public funds (see **13.1.1**). But in addition the entrant will be subject to a work restriction limiting work to a total of 12 months during the stay and prohibiting him from engaging in business or providing services as a professional sportsperson. If he meets the work permit criteria (see **14.5.4**), switching is allowed into that category after 12 months.

14.4 Employment, business and independent means

14.4.1 Introduction

Whereas entry under the heads considered in the last section will rarely lead to settlement, entry for employment, business or as a person of independent means can do so. Parts 5–7 of the Immigration Rules deal with entry in these categories, although different principles apply to EEA nationals (see **13.7** and **13.8**).

Note that the employment and business rules are relevant only if someone is actually entering for employment, or to engage in business. It is possible for someone to enter in another capacity in which no prohibition upon employment is imposed, in which case he will be able to take a job, or engage in business, without having to meet the requirements of the employment and business rules. The following categories of entrants are in this position:

(a) anyone admitted for settlement;

(b) anyone given 24 months' limited leave with a view to settlement (eg spouses of persons settled in the UK);

(c) anyone admitted as a refugee, or given humanitarian protection (see **14.17**);

(d) anyone subject only to a restriction on employment (eg students, working holidaymakers);

(e) anyone admitted, without a prohibition on employment, as the dependant of someone with limited leave (eg the spouse of an employee with a work permit).

A condition prohibiting employment (imposed by means of a passport stamp) normally extends to paid or unpaid employment, self-employment, and engaging in business or any professional activity (Immigration Rules, para 6).

> **Example**
>
> Adam has been admitted to the UK as a work permit employee. His wife, Eve, is prepared to give up her job abroad to follow him, but only if she can look for employment in the UK. Is this possible, or will she too need a work permit?
>
> She can seek leave to enter as a spouse for the same period as Adam. She will not be prohibited from taking employment, and so can work without a work permit (see **14.12**).

14.5 Employment

Entry to seek or take employment is generally permitted only if the entrant has a work permit issued by the BIA. However, in some cases, no permit is required.

14.5.1 Permit-free employment

Under the Rules, the following categories of entrants are permit-free, in most cases because the employee has an employer based abroad:

(a) representatives of overseas newspapers, news agencies and broadcasting organisations (outside the scope of this book);

(b) sole representatives of overseas firms (see **14.5.2**);

(c) private servants in diplomatic households and domestic workers in private households (outside the scope of this book);

(d) overseas government employees (outside the scope of this book);

(e) ministers of religion, missionaries and members of religious orders (outside the scope of this book);

(f) airport-based ground staff of overseas-owned airlines (outside the scope of this book);

(g) persons (Commonwealth citizens) with UK ancestry (see **14.5.3**).

14.5.2 Sole representatives of overseas firms

Paragraph 144 of the Immigration Rules provides for the admission of a representative of an overseas firm which has no branch, subsidiary, or other representation in the UK. Entry clearance is mandatory for persons who wish to enter the UK in this category. Where a branch, subsidiary, or other representation already exists, staff will require work permits (see **14.5.4**). Where two representatives are coming to the UK, they cannot both be treated as permit-free. One may be treated as a sole representative and, after arrival, he should make a work permit application for the other. It should be noted that permit-free status does not extend to a secretary or personal assistant accompanying a sole representative. Such persons require a work permit if they wish to enter the UK in that capacity.

The overseas firm must be a genuine commercial enterprise. This is judged in the round, taking into account the length of time that the company has been established, its turnover, profitability, the number of employees, etc. It must be the intention that the business remains centred abroad. This does not mean, however, that an otherwise sound application is refused because of evidence of an intention to make the branch in the UK flourish so vigorously that it might, at some time in the longer term, overshadow the overseas parent company. Companies which have been trading for less than 12 months are required to justify the need to establish an overseas branch here.

The overseas parent company must be sending the sole representative to the UK in order that he establishes a commercial presence for the company here in the form either of a registered branch or of a wholly-owned subsidiary. A 'branch' is a part of a company which is organised so as to conduct business on behalf of the company. This means that a person is able to deal directly with the branch in the UK, instead of the company overseas. The company setting up a branch in the UK must apply to register with Companies House within one month of having opened the branch. A wholly-owned subsidiary is a separate corporate body and is not subject to these registration requirements, being treated in the same way as any other company incorporated in the UK.

The sole representative must have been recruited outside the UK and joined the parent company abroad. The BIA guidance is that 'he is likely to be someone who has been employed by the parent company for some time and holds a senior position there'. If the sole representative is not an existing employee, or has been employed for a short time only, then he must be able to demonstrate a good track record in the same or in a closely related field, in order to show that the reasons for his appointment are compelling. Sole representatives must, in the first instance, be employed by the overseas firm direct (although they may later be employed by the UK subsidiary). Agents who are hired to market the company's product in the UK are normally self-employed and provide their services for a fee. Such people cannot therefore qualify as sole representatives. Nor can sales representatives or others, such as buyers, who fulfil a single function only. However, senior sales staff who have other responsibilities, such as marketing and distribution, are not debarred from qualifying as sole representatives.

Sole representatives may be offered a remuneration package consisting of a basic salary and commission. This is acceptable to the BIA as long as the salary element is sufficient to support the applicant and his family without recourse to public funds.

The applicant is required to provide a document detailing the terms and conditions of his employment. The importance of the position should be reflected in the salary and other benefits. The BIA expects a sole representative to be vested with the authority to take the majority of decisions locally, but accepts that it is unreasonable to expect him to take unilateral decisions on all matters.

Sole representatives are required to work full time as such, but this is not linked to a set number of hours per week. The main consideration is that the parent firm should be paying a 'full-time' salary sufficient for the sole representative to support and accommodate himself and any dependants without taking other work or resorting to public funds.

Sole representatives are expected to base themselves in the UK and to spend a minimum of nine months of the year here. However, applications may be approved from those who intend to spend less time in the UK, provided that the additional absences are essential to the running of the UK business, for example, if the UK office is to be the centre of European operations. Applicants who intend to spend less than four months of the year in the UK are unlikely to satisfy the BIA that they are making genuine efforts to establish a commercial presence in the UK. Such persons should be advised to apply instead as business visitors (see **14.1.2**).

Majority shareholders in the parent company are not eligible for entry as sole representatives. When the sole representative is a major shareholder in the parent company, the BIA guidance provides that care must be taken to establish that the arrangement is not one devised simply to circumvent the more rigorous requirements of the business rules. As a rule of thumb, shareholdings in excess of 30% should attract detailed scrutiny. If it is evident that the applicant, as well as being a major shareholder, is also the driving force behind the parent company such that his presence in the UK is likely to mean that the centre of operations has shifted to this country, the application should be refused. The factors to be weighed in deciding this include:

(a) the size of the applicant's shareholding;
(b) his position within the firm;
(c) the number of senior employees who will remain abroad; and
(d) the extent to which the company's success seems linked to the applicant's specific talents and performance.

The BIA requires the following documents to support the application:

(a) a full description of the company's activities with details of the company's assets and accounts, including full details of the company share distribution for the previous year;
(b) confirmation that the overseas company will establish a wholly-owned subsidiary or register a branch in the UK;
(c) the applicant's job description, salary and contract of employment;
(d) confirmation that the applicant is fully familiar with the company's activities and that he has full powers to negotiate and take operational decisions without reference to the parent company;
(e) a notarised statement from the company that the applicant will be its sole representative and that it has no other branch, subsidiary, or representative in the UK;
(f) a notarised statement confirming that the company's operations will remain centred overseas;
(g) a notarised statement that the applicant will not engage in business of his own, neither will he represent any other company's interest.

Leave is initially given for two years. Towards the end of that time an application can be made to the Home Office for a three-year extension of stay (Immigration Rules, para 147). The application should be supported by the following evidence:

(a) a letter from the parent company stating that it wishes to continue to employ the applicant as previously;
(b) evidence in the form of accounts of the business generated (this form can be flexible according to the nature of the company's business);

(c) evidence of the salary paid to the applicant in the first two years of operation and the terms on which the salary will be paid in future;

(d) evidence that he has established and is in charge of a registered branch or wholly-owned subsidiary of the overseas parent company.

When a sole representative has remained in the UK for five years in this capacity, he may be eligible to apply for settlement under the Immigration Rules, para 150.

14.5.3 Persons (Commonwealth citizens) with UK ancestry

The requirements for leave to enter under para 186 of the Immigration Rules include the following.

(a) The entrant is a Commonwealth citizen.

(b) The entrant is aged 17 or over.

(c) The entrant is able to provide proof that one of his grandparents was born in the UK. Proof will normally take the form of the relevant grandparent's birth and marriage certificates, as well as the birth and marriage certificates of the mother or father descended from that grandparent and the applicant's own birth certificate.

(d) The entrant is able to work and intends to take or seek employment in the UK. It should be noted that this Rule relates to taking employment in the UK and not entry in order to study or visit. Applicants must be able to show that they have employment in the UK or genuinely intend to seek employment and are able to do so. An ability and intention to seek employment must be realistic in the circumstances. When assessing this, the BIA considers the applicant's age and health (ie does he have any medical problems which may prevent him from taking employment?). The applicant need only demonstrate that he is able to work and genuinely intends to seek employment but, if there is reason to believe that there is little realistic prospect of his obtaining employment and that he may have recourse to public funds, then the application is refused.

(e) The entrant will be able to maintain and accommodate himself and any dependants adequately without recourse to public funds.

(f) The entrant holds a valid UK entry clearance in this capacity. This is required whether or not he is a visa national.

An applicant who has been adopted, or whose parents were adopted, can qualify if:

(a) he has been adopted by someone who has a UK-born parent; or

(b) one of his parents was adopted by a person born in the UK; or

(c) his natural grandparents were born in the UK.

There is no claim to UK ancestry through step-parents.

The entrant may be given up to five years' leave, after which he may apply for settlement (see para 192). The key requirement is for the applicant to show that he has resided in the UK continuously in this capacity for five years. There is no requirement that any employment taken must be continuous. The Rules only require the applicant either to continue in employment, or to seek further employment. If an applicant is in employment, the BIA requires a letter from his current employer confirming that the job will continue. If, however, the applicant is not employed at the time of application, the BIA will request evidence of his employment record throughout the five years, and evidence of any attempts he has made to find employment. If it is clear that the applicant has not been in employment for any length of time over the five years he will be asked to provide reasons for failing to obtain employment. Unless there is a very good reason for this, the application will be refused. Enquiries will also be made as to how the applicant has supported himself without a regular income.

A person cannot switch into this category after entering the UK.

> **Example 1**
>
> Bill is a citizen of Canada who has been offered a job for 12 months, advising a UK law college which is developing a new course. The college thinks it might be difficult to obtain a work permit for him and asks whether there is any easier way of bringing him to the UK.
>
> Ask Bill whether he has a UK-born grandparent. If he can prove it, no work permit is needed.
>
> **Example 2**
>
> Carla is a citizen of Argentina. She wishes to enter the UK and get a job as a translator. She thinks that she is unlikely to qualify for a work permit, but reveals that her grandmother was born in Wales in 1924. As she is not a Commonwealth citizen, she does not qualify for permit-free employment as a person with UK ancestry.

14.5.4 Work permit employment

Work Permits (UK) (WP (UK)) is the Home Office department responsible for issuing work permits. These are issued pursuant to para 128 of the Immigration Rules, which provides that the applicant must:

(a) hold a valid Home Office work permit; and

(b) not be of an age which puts him outside the limits for employment; and

(c) be capable of undertaking the employment specified in the work permit; and

(d) not intend to take employment except as specified in the work permit; and

(e) be able to maintain and accommodate himself and any dependants adequately without recourse to public funds; and

(f) in the case of a person in possession of a work permit which is valid for a period of 12 months or less, intend to leave the UK at the end of his approved employment.

The work permit arrangements allow employers based in the UK to employ people who are not EEA nationals and who are not otherwise entitled to work here. The scheme aims to ensure that recruitment is primarily from within the EEA. As a result, there are two types of work permits. The first, called a 'Tier 1' permit, is granted in very limited circumstances without the job having previously been advertised in the EEA. The second, 'Tier 2' permit, is subject to what is known as the EEA or resident labour market test and requires that the post must first be advertised in the EEA.

The scheme is outlined in guidance notes published by the IND and available on its website (see **11.2.2**).

A work permit is issued to a specific overseas national for a specific job with a specified UK-based employer. The permit belongs to the employer and not the employee.

In order to meet the qualification and skills criteria to obtain a work permit, an overseas national must have either:

(a) a UK-equivalent degree level qualification; or

(b) a Higher National Diploma (HND) level occupational qualification which entitles a person to do a specific job (eg medical laboratory technician); or

(c) a general HND level qualification plus one year's work experience doing the type of job for which the permit is sought; or

(d) high level or specialist skills acquired through doing the type of job for which the permit is sought for at least three years. This type of job should be at NVQ level 3 or above. Those who would qualify include, for example, head or second chefs; specialist chefs with skills in preparing ethnic cuisine; and those with occupational skills and language or cultural skills that are not readily available in the EEA.

For some professions where the employee needs to be registered with the appropriate UK professional organisation (eg General Medical Council, Royal College of Veterinary Surgeons), WP (UK) will accept registration as proof that the individual meets the criteria.

No permits are granted for unskilled jobs at manual, craft, clerical, secretarial or similar levels, or for resident domestic work.

14.5.4.1 Applying for a work permit

Work Permits (UK) needs to consider the identity of the UK-based employer, the nature of the job, and the identity of the employee.

If an employer has not applied for a work permit before, WP (UK) will need documentation showing that the applicant is a UK trading company (eg latest audited accounts and annual report), or professional partnership (eg evidence of registration with the relevant professional body).

Other evidence is provided via Form WP1. The employer must sign a declaration that no UK resident or EEA national will be displaced or excluded as a result of the employment of the overseas national. It is necessary to complete sections in the form designed to show that there is no suitably qualified resident or EEA labour available to do the job. In four cases (Tier 1 applications), it is not necessary to provide evidence of this, and it is sufficient to complete Part 1 of the form, establishing that the job is in one of the relevant categories. These four cases are as follows:

(a) a senior post in an international company, which requires an existing employee to transfer from abroad;

(b) a post at senior board level;

(c) a new post essential to an inward investment project bringing jobs and capital to the UK;

(d) occupations in which personnel are widely acknowledged as being in short supply within the UK and the EEA. Work Permits (UK) publishes a list of these occupations on its website. The list at the time of writing appears as **Appendix 8** to this Part of the book.

In all other cases, it will be necessary to complete Part 2 of the form, which requires detailed evidence of need to recruit from outside the EEA. The employer must show why he is unable to use an existing employee to do the job, and why he needs to employ the overseas national, and must provide evidence to show what action he has taken to train or recruit UK or other EEA workers to fill the post. Relevant evidence, including copies of the employee's qualifications, references, and of all advertising to fill the post, should be sent to WP (UK) with the application form. In certain limited circumstances, WP (UK) may be prepared to waive the advertising requirements (eg if the employment skills are rare and highly specialised).

Examples

(1) Kim is a senior executive working for a Korean car company. His company wishes to second him to its British-based subsidiary to supervise the establishment of a new factory in Great Britain.

(2) Pak is a chef who specialises in Korean cooking. A restaurant in London wishes to offer him the post of head chef.

(3) Sun is a systems analyst, who is an expert in the computer system to be used at Kim's factory. Kim wants to employ him in Great Britain to supervise the setting up of the system. The occupation is not on the short supply list.

(4) Silva works as a cashier in a bank in Damascus. She can speak and, unusually, write a number of Middle Eastern languages which she uses in her work. The London branch of the bank wish to employ her as a cashier and she will spend at least 60% of her time speaking and writing to customers in their own language.

Which sections of the form should be completed?

For Kim, the British-based company would complete only Part 1 of the form.

For Pak, the employer would also complete Part 2.

Work Permits (UK) would require Part 2 to be completed for Sun. He could qualify as a Tier 1 applicant only on the basis of an occupation which is in short supply. However, although his specific combination of skills might be rare, his occupation as such is not in short supply in the UK or EEA. As the post in question clearly requires a highly qualified technician with specialised skills, it meets the work permit skills criteria. The company should, however, advertise the post in a UK national newspaper or a trade journal (in each case available in EEA countries).

For Silva, the bank in London should apply for a Tier 2 work permit if Silva has the necessary experience and her language skills are not readily available in the EEA.

Where the employee is an entertainer or sportsperson, there are separate schemes and different forms must be used.

14.5.4.2 Requirements for entry

Work Permits (UK) will send the original permit to the employer or its advisers who must then forward it to the overseas national. If the employee is a non-visa national, the original work permit serves as entry clearance, but if he is a visa national he must also obtain a visa. In either case, the employee may also be interviewed at the port of entry to check whether the requirements of the Rules are met (para 128). However, provided that the employee holds the permit, is genuinely entering to do the job specified, and can meet the usual accommodation and maintenance condition, he should have little difficulty obtaining leave.

Leave to enter will be granted subject to conditions preventing him from changing his job without the consent of the BIA and prohibiting recourse to public funds.

14.5.4.3 Period of work permit

A work permit is issued for the expected duration of the job, up to a maximum of five years in Tier 1 or 2 cases. If it is initially granted for less than five years, an extension may be sought (see Immigration Rules, para 131). After five years of holding a work permit, the employee may apply for settlement (para 134), and provided that is granted, no further work permit is needed.

If the employee's job ends within his period of leave, the employer should inform the Home Office. The BIA guidance is that as the person no longer meets the requirements of the Immigration Rules under which he was admitted, action may be taken to curtail his leave (see **13.6.7**). If the person has found alternative employment, the BIA may consider a work permit application from the new employer, but it will not grant further leave to remain in the UK unless it is satisfied that the individual took steps to find new employment as quickly as possible.

14.5.4.4 Extensions and switching

Some matters are dealt with by WP (UK) alone, whilst others require Home Office decisions too. For example, if the worker, within his original period of leave, wishes to change jobs, either working for the same employer, or for a new employer, the employer obtains consent from WP (UK) alone. If the original period of leave is about to expire, it will be necessary to obtain both an extension of the work permit from WP (UK), and leave to remain from the Home Office. The application for both is made via WP (UK). Work Permits (UK) will need evidence that employment of the overseas national remains necessary, and it may be difficult to persuade WP (UK) where the job has lasted longer than originally envisaged. If the work permit has been extended, the Home Office will grant an extension of stay (for the period stated above), provided that the requirements of the Rules (eg as to accommodation and maintenance) are still met (para 131).

Under the Rules, it is not generally possible to switch into the work permit category, as the requirement that a work permit should have been obtained before entry. Leave to remain for work permit employment can, however, be granted outside the Rules. However, trainees (see **14.3.1**), students (see **14.2.4**), working holidaymakers (see **14.3.2**), innovators and highly skilled migrants (see **14.7**) may in certain circumstances be allowed to switch to work permit employment.

14.5.4.5 Family members

The spouse and children under 18 of the worker will normally be admitted for the same period as the worker, but will need entry clearance even if they are non-visa nationals (see further, Immigration Rules, paras 194 and 197 and also **14.12**). They can work without the need to hold their own permits.

14.5.4.6 Illegal working

Under s 8 of the AIA 1996 it is an offence to employ someone who either does not have a current and valid permission to be in the UK, or who is in breach of his permission as a result of taking the job in question. This makes it very important for employers to check the immigration status of workers from abroad, by asking for appropriate documentary evidence as prescribed by the Immigration (Restrictions on Employment) Order 2004 (SI 2004/755).

14.6 Businessmen and self-employed persons

14.6.1 Requirements

The Rules permit entry in order to join or take over an existing business or to set up a new one. Business is defined as an enterprise as a sole trader, a partnership or a company registered in the UK. The requirements of para 201 of the Immigration Rules include the following.

(a) The entrant must invest £200,000 of his own money. How can applicants make such an investment? The BIA guidance is that it can be done by a direct cash investment, share capital, or a combination of the two, the proportion of which does not matter. The following, however, are not acceptable to the BIA:

   (i) a director's loan, unless it is unsecured and in favour of third-party creditors;

   (ii) an investment from or through an off-shore company, even where the investor is the sole beneficial owner of the off-shore company.

   The money must be the applicant's own money and not from another source, however close that source might be. A gift of money and/or shares in the business is acceptable only where the BIA is satisfied that the gift was genuine. A gift, for example from a business associate or other person who has a commercial relationship with the applicant, is not acceptable, since the BIA would not be satisfied that the arrangement did not amount to disguised employment. A copy of an irrevocable Deed of Gift will be requested to ensure that the money is under the applicant's own control.

   Money for investment in the business over and above the minimum £200,000 may be raised by way of bank or other loans or grants generally available to the public, say, under a government enterprise scheme. If the applicant proposes to buy premises which include residential accommodation for himself and his family, the value of this part of the property is deducted from the business investment.

(b) The entrant must be able to maintain and accommodate himself and his dependants, without recourse to employment or public funds, in the period before his business produces an income.

(c) The entrant must be actively involved, full time, in the business. This requirement is to ensure that he is economically active as a businessman and not using his investment as a means of establishing himself in the UK for some other purpose. An applicant who does not wish to work full time but has a large sum of money to invest in the UK should apply for entry clearance as an investor under para 224 of the Rules (see **14.8**).

(d) The entrant must invest an amount proportional to his interest in the business (see immediately below).

(e) The entrant must have an equal or controlling interest in the business (without any 'disguised employment'). The applicant's level of financial investment must be proportional to his role in the business and he must have either a controlling or equal interest in the business (ie he should have more than a 50% interest or be one of a number of partners or directors with equal interest). The BIA gives the following examples:

   (i) A person who has a majority or equal financial interest in a business but who nevertheless clearly has no major say in running the business or setting its policy will not have an interest in the business proportional to his investment.

   (ii) A person holding a 5% share in a firm in which the other directors each held 20% or more would not have an equal or controlling interest in the business unless the voting rights were weighted. Whether or not the voting rights were weighted, he would fall to be regarded as not having made an investment equal to his interest in the business and would require a work permit. Where, however, such an applicant falls for refusal on these grounds but he more than meets the investment

and employment requirements and his expertise and voting rights give him an authoritative voice in the business, discretion may be exercised.
(f) The entrant must be able to bear his share of the liabilities.
(g) The entrant must demonstrate a genuine need for his investment and services in the UK.
(h) The entrant must have a sufficient share of the profits to maintain and accommodate himself and his dependants as in (b) above.
(i) The entrant must not intend to seek additional employment in the UK.
(j) The entrant must hold an entry clearance in this capacity. This is required whether or not she is a visa national.

A detailed business plan showing the object of the business, the investment and employment involved and financial projections should be submitted. The plan should include the following minimum information:

(a) evidence that the applicant has not less than £200,000 of his own money under his control and disposable in the UK to be invested in the business;
(b) the object of the business;
(c) how many full-time jobs the business will create for people already settled in the UK (employees' likely pay, hours and duties should be described);
(d) the projected opening balance sheet following the start of the business. This should contain the following details:
   (i) the financial outlay;
   (ii) any loan to the company (this must be unsecured and fully subordinated to third-party creditors);
   (iii) assets, fixed and tangible;
   (iv) stock, which should be described;
   (v) the number and value of paid-up shares.
(e) projected trading and profit/loss account;
(f) overhead expenses; this should detail the following:
   (i) establishment expenses;
   (ii) administration expenses (under this heading individual salaries of staff including the applicant should be given);
   (iii) other expenses and depreciation.

An applicant must be able to justify projected figures given above, if so requested by the BIA (eg with evidence of market research).

If the entrant is joining or taking over an existing business, he will also have to provide a written statement of the terms, and audited accounts of the business. If establishing a new business, he will have to show that he will be bringing into the UK enough of his own money to do so.

In each case, he must show that at least two new full-time jobs will be created. The business plan should show details of two new full-time jobs to be created within the first 24 months. These must be substantive posts and not short-term posts for trainees. Where there is an existing business, the business plan should show details to confirm that the new full-time jobs are not to be at the expense of existing part-time jobs and that overall 'man hours' of employment among the staff are to be increased. If the applicant is joining or taking over an existing business, full details of existing employees must also be provided.

The applicant must show that at least £200,000 of his own money is to be fully used in the business. Unless there are uncertainties about the bona fides of the applicant, the BIA normally concentrates on evidence of funds and the requirement to provide employment. If an investor can produce the sum required from his own funds there is a strong presumption that he expects the business to succeed, especially if additional funds are being provided by a bank, etc. The applicant will, however, be asked to justify the basis of his financial projections, if necessary, with details of any market research he has undertaken.

> Example
>
> Lee is a citizen of China who owns a successful car sales business in Hong Kong. He wishes to acquire settled status in the UK and, in order to do so, is prepared to invest over £200,000 in acquiring a similar business in the UK. He would have to employ a local manager to run the business as he would need to spend at least half his time running the Hong Kong business.
>
> Lee would not qualify under the Rules as he would not be actively involved, full time, in running the UK business.

14.6.2 Entry, extensions, and switching

The entrant is admitted initially for a period of 24 months, with a condition restricting his freedom to take employment and prohibiting recourse to public funds. An application for an extension of three years can be made under para 206 of the Immigration Rules. This enables the Home Office to check whether the entry requirements are still being met. As with employees, settlement is possible after five years in the UK (para 209).

Under para 206, switching to these categories by someone who entered in another capacity is limited to work permit holders (see **14.5.4**), innovators and highly skilled migrants (see **14.7**), students (see **14.2**) and working holidaymakers (see **14.3.2**). An extension to remain in business can be granted only to someone who entered the UK with an entry clearance in that capacity.

14.7 Innovators and highly skilled migrants

14.7.1 Innovators

This scheme allows individuals to set up a business in the UK. It is designed to attract and select entrepreneurs whose business proposals will lead to exceptional economic benefits to the UK. It is open to people who have plans to set up businesses, especially in the areas of science and technology, including e-commerce. The applicant has to show that he has entrepreneurial ability, technical skills and a good business plan which will develop e-commerce or other new technologies in the UK.

By para 210A of the Immigration Rules the requirements to be met by a person seeking leave to enter as an innovator are that the applicant:

> (i) is approved by the Home Office as a person who meets the criteria specified by the Secretary of State for entry under the innovator scheme at the time that approval is sought under that scheme ...

The criteria for the scheme consist of a points system. To qualify, the applicant must score a minimum number of points in three different areas and reach an overall score of 100 points. The individual scoring areas are as follows.

(a) *Personal characteristics*

Work and business experience.

Proven entrepreneurial ability.

Educational qualifications (mainly in technology, science and business).

Personal references.

(b) *Business plan: general*

A realistic business plan.

Plans for creating a management team.

(c) *Business plan: economic benefits*

The skilled jobs that will be created.

The number of jobs that will be created.

New and creative aspects of the proposals (eg will it introduce a new technology, process or product to the UK or to the business area?).

How much will be spent on research and development.

For full details see the application form.

The applicant should send in support such documents as a current curriculum vitae; certificates of any formal qualifications; a formal business plan; registered accounts and trading records of his business; references from any previous employer; intellectual property rights; financial references, guarantees and forecasts; technical references; commercial references; evidence of market research carried out; a marketing plan and evidence of the shares he will have in the proposed UK registered company (see (iii) below).

> (ii) intends to set up a business that will create full-time paid employment for at least two persons already settled in the UK;
>
> (iii) intends to maintain a minimum 5% shareholding of the equity capital in that business, once it has been set up, throughout the period of his stay as an innovator;
>
> (iv) will be able to maintain and accommodate himself and any dependants adequately without recourse to public funds or to other employment ...

The applicant must demonstrate that he has sufficient capital or initial funding in place or agreed in principle for at least the first six months and that he will be able to maintain and accommodate himself and any dependants without recourse to other employment or public funds until the business provides him with a sufficient income.

> (v) holds a valid United Kingdom entry clearance for entry in this capacity.

If successful, the applicant will be given leave for a period not exceeding 24 months. Thereafter an extension can be sought for three years and ultimately after five years settlement may be granted.

Who can switch into this category? Only students (see **14.2**), working holidaymakers (see **14.3.2**), highly skilled migrants (see **14.7.2**) and business people (see **14.6**).

14.7.2 Highly skilled migrant programme (HSMP)

This scheme is designed to allow individuals with exceptional skills to seek entry or stay to work in the UK without having a prior offer of employment, or to take up self-employment opportunities.

By para 135A of the Immigration Rules, the requirements to be met by a person seeking leave to enter as a highly skilled migrant are that the applicant:

(i) must produce a valid document issued by the Home Office confirming that he or she meets, at the time of the issue of that document, the criteria specified by the Secretary of State for entry to the UK under the Highly Skilled Migrant programme.

The criteria consist of a points-based system of qualification and an English language requirement. Points are available in the following areas:

(a) *Qualifications*

50 points for those holding a PhD; or

35 points for those with a Master's degree such as an LLM; or

30 points for those with a graduate degree such as BA or BSc.

An applicant who is a graduate of an eligible MBA (Masters in Business Administration) programme is awarded 75 points. The eligible programmes are in **Appendix 11** to this Part of the book.

Examples

Alan is a scientist. He has a BSc, MSc and a PhD. He will be awarded 50 points, as only the highest scoring qualification counts.

Michael is a management consultant. He has a MBA from University College Cork, Ireland. As that is not an eligible MBA, he scores 35 points.

Zelda is an entrepreneur. She has a MBA from the London Business School, UK. As this is an eligible MBA, she scores 75 points.

(b) *Previous earnings*

Points here depend on the gross earnings before tax over a total period of up to 12 months out of the 15 months immediately prior to the application. Any allowances paid are taken into account only if they are declared on pay slips. If the applicant works for a company and receives part of his pay as dividends, again these count only if they have been lawfully declared as earnings.

Not all income counts. Unearned income such as dividends from investments (unless, as above, it is in a company in which the applicant is active in day-today management), property rental income and interest on savings is not considered.

It is the country where the applicant has been residing and working over the relevant period that determines the appropriate income band. There are five income bands as set out in **Appendix 10** to this Part of the book.

Example

For the last 12 months Henry has worked in Andorra and earned £30,000 gross. Andorra is in Band A. Henry has earned more than £29,000 but less than £32,000 and so scores 30 points.

(c) *UK experience*

A maximum of 5 points can be scored in this area. The 5 points are awarded either if the applicant successfully scored points under the previous earnings category where the earnings were in the UK, or if the applicant studied and graduated at Bachelors degree level or higher in full-time higher education in the UK, or at a UK-based overseas educational institution, for at least one full academic year.

(d) *The age assessment*

The BIA guidance is that this assessment is intended to recognise that it is more difficult for a highly skilled young graduate to score maximum points in the previous earnings category, compared to an older counterpart with the same level of skills. Furthermore, there is a greater potential for young, highly skilled individuals to be active in the labour market for longer than their older counterparts. The age assessment involves the awarding of points depending on age.

Points can be claimed as follows: aged 27 or under is 20 points; aged 28 or 29 is 10 points; aged 30 or 31 is 5 points. Those aged 32 and over when the application is received score no points.

Example

Nazim will shortly reach his 28th birthday. In order successfully to claim 20 points for being in the 27 or under age category, he must ensure that his application reaches the BIA by the last working day before his 28th birthday. If it reaches the BIA after that date, he will be awarded only 10 points, as he will fall within the 28 and 29 years of age category.

In addition to scoring at least 75 points in the above areas or having an eligible MBA, the applicant must meet the English language requirement. Why? The BIA policy is that lack of English is considered a significant barrier to taking employment as a highly skilled migrant. In order to qualify for the HSMP, an applicant must have a good knowledge of English and provide the appropriate evidence to support this. Only two types of evidence will count. The applicant must provide either an IELTS (International English Language Testing System) Test Report Form, issued in the two years prior to the date that the application is received by the BIA, at Band 6 or above; or evidence that the applicant holds a Bachelors degree that was taught in English and is of an equivalent level to a UK Bachelors degree. Note that the fact that any Masters degree or PhD was taught in English is irrelevant.

> (ii) intends to make the UK his main home ...

The BIA requires the applicant to provide a written undertaking to this effect.

> (iii) is able to maintain and accommodate himself and any dependants adequately without recourse to public funds ...

What capital is available to the applicant? Is his assessment of his potential living costs realistic and in line with his past living expenses? Are his plans to find work in the UK realistic? The BIA guidance is that those who have firm or tentative job offers or contracts need to demonstrate a smaller cash reserve as they will start earning almost immediately. The BIA also takes the view that language and qualification barriers can impact on maintenance and accommodation such that care should be taken to ensure that those who are likely to spend some of their initial time in the UK acclimatising to the working environment will have the ability to finance any period of extended job search.

The applicant should produce in support documents such as UK bank statements in his name, or overseas bank statements with confirmation that funds can be transferred to the UK if appropriate; evidence of personal assets in the UK and overseas generating an income disposable in the UK; a firm job offer, confirmed job interviews or acceptance onto employment agency books; prospective contracts of employment or accepted freelance bids; a breakdown of projected expenditure and income in the first 24 months in the UK; evidence of appropriate accommodation etc.

The application is made in two stages. First, the applicant must obtain approval from WP (UK) under the scheme. The application forms are on its website (see **11.2.2**). Then the applicant must obtain entry clearance (or further leave to remain, if already in the UK in another category that permits switching).

If successful, the applicant will be given leave for a period not exceeding 24 months. Thereafter an extension can be sought for three years and, ultimately after five years, settlement may be granted.

Who can switch into this category? Only students (see **14.2**), working holidaymakers (see **14.3.2**), work permit holders (see **14.5.4**) and innovators (see **14.7.1**).

14.8 Investors

The applicant must be able to show evidence of money of his own, under his control and disposable in the UK, of no less than £1 million. Alternatively, the applicant must be able to provide evidence of a personal net worth of no less than £2 million. The £1 million sum for investment will be acceptable by way of a loan by a financial institution that is regulated by the Financial Services Authority. See para 224 of the Immigration Rules.

The applicant must be able to transfer and dispose of the money freely and no other person must have a controlling interest. The only exception to this which is allowed by the BIA is funds jointly held by an applicant and his spouse. These are acceptable, provided that the applicant and his spouse together have unrestricted right to transfer and dispose of them and both are coming to the UK. If the applicant is applying on the basis of a personal net worth of no less than £2 million, he may use loaned money (up to £1 million) to present as his investment funds. Examples of satisfactory evidence of capital include a portfolio of investments held as certified by a stockbroker or accountant, or letters from a bank confirming that the investor (or his or her spouse) has a certain sum on deposit and, if necessary, that such investments or deposits have been held since a certain date. If loaned funds are being used, evidence should also be presented to show that the loan has been provided by an authorised financial institution.

All of the £1 million capital required to qualify must be freely transferable to the UK and convertible to sterling. Many countries have strict currency control and, if there is any doubt about the applicant's ability to transfer money here, the applicant will be asked to produce specific evidence on this point (eg a letter from his bank manager or the authorities of the country concerned).

The sum of at least £1 million may include investments, as well as convertible currency. Major assets in the UK, such as unmortgaged property, may also be taken into account, provided that they do not make up more than £250,000 of the total sum required. Personal effects, such as jewellery or antique furniture, are not to be taken into account, unless it is clear that such items are held for investment purposes. A painting of substantial and durable value, for example, is acceptable.

The applicant must intend to invest £750,000 in the UK by way of one or more of the forms of investment specified in the Rules. The £750,000 must not be invested through an off-shore company or trust. This is to ensure, among other things, maximum tax benefit to the UK. The Inland Revenue has advised the BIA that it is not possible to draw up a comprehensive list of methods which might be used for tax avoidance but, as a general rule, only investments made in the applicant's own name are acceptable. It should be noted that the applicant is, of course, free to invest any additional capital in whatever way he chooses.

The restrictions on the type of investment permitted are designed to channel funds into investments which help to stimulate growth in the UK in the most direct way possible. Investment in property management and property holding

274   Welfare Benefits and Immigration Law

may not be taken into account. There is no objection, however, to investment in companies primarily involved in construction.

The applicant must intend to make the UK his main home. This does not mean that the applicant cannot spend time abroad or have residences overseas, or that he must intend to live in the UK for the rest of his life. However, the application will be refused if it appears that the applicant intends to maintain his main home abroad and make only short visits to the UK. In such a case, it would be more appropriate for him to be considered as a visitor.

Given the financial requirements, the applicant's ability to support himself and his dependants should not be in doubt. However, the application will be refused if there is reason to believe that the applicant intends to take employment other than self-employment or engage in business.

Initial leave will be for two years. Provided there is evidence that the applicant has invested £750,000 and kept the investment, any reduction in the current value of his investment by way of stocks and shareholdings due to fluctuations in share prices need not lead to a refusal of further leave to remain for three years provided the applicant still has £1 million overall (see Immigration Rules, para 227). The value of the applicant's own home and assets in the UK held for investment purposes may be taken into account, subject to a limit of £250,000. The value of all other investments in the UK and money on deposit in the UK which are not personal possessions can be taken fully into account. Ultimately, settlement may be granted after five years under para 230.

Who can switch into this category? Only work permit holders (see **14.5.4**), innovators and highly skilled migrants (see **14.7**) and business people (see **14.6**).

14.9 Spouses and civil partners

14.9.1 Introduction

The Immigration Rules relating to family, marriage and civil partnerships deal with a range of possibilities. A person may seek entry to the UK as the spouse or civil partner of someone who has the right of abode, or of someone who is settled, or entering for settlement, or of someone with limited leave (eg as a businessman). A fiancé(e) or proposed civil partner may seek entry in order to marry or enter into a civil partnership. A person who has entered the UK with limited leave may wish to settle here on marriage to, or having entered into a civil partnership with, a British citizen, or to someone who is already settled. This section covers some of the many permutations.

14.9.2 Exempt groups

The Rules do not apply to those who do not need leave, or are seeking entry other than as a spouse or civil partner, for example:

(a)   persons who already have the right of abode;
(b)   EEA citizens and family members entering by virtue of EC law (see **13.7**);
(c)   persons who are entering in another category under the Rules (eg visitors, etc).

Example 1
Ben is a citizen of Canada. He was born there in 1972. Ben's father is Canadian but his mother was born in the UK and she is British.

Ben is a Commonwealth citizen with right of abode, and can enter the UK without the need to comply with the spouse or civil partner rules (he needs a 'certificate of entitlement'). See **12.3**. A check should be made to see if he is registered as a British citizen. See **12.2.7**.

Example 2

Vlad is a citizen of Russia who is married to Maria, a citizen of Austria.

As an EEA national, Maria can enter the UK, and Vlad may enter as her spouse, without the need to comply with the spouse rules. See **13.9.2**.

Example 3

Carla is a citizen of the Philippines. She married Denis, a British citizen, whilst he was on holiday there, but has not yet agreed to join him in the UK. She has applied for a visa to enter the UK as a visitor, to see whether she would wish to live in the UK.

In principle, Carla could obtain a visitor visa, but would need to satisfy the entry clearance officer that she did intend to return after her visit.

14.9.3 Spouses or civil partners of persons who are settled

Paragraph 281 of the Immigration Rules applies to a person seeking entry as the spouse of someone already present and settled in the UK or of someone entering for settlement at the same time. A British citizen or a Commonwealth citizen with the right of abode will be 'settled' for this purpose. If successful the applicant is granted limited leave for two years subject to a condition not to have recourse to public funds (see **13.1.1** and see further below).

Paragraph 6 of the Immigration Rules defines 'present and settled' as meaning that the person concerned is settled in the UK, and, at the time that an application under these Rules is made, is physically present here or is coming here with or to join the applicant and intends to make the UK their home with the applicant if their application is successful.

Further, para 281(i)(b) applies to a person seeking entry as the spouse or civil partner of someone who has a right of abode in the UK or settled status and who is on the same occasion seeking admission to the UK for the purposes of settlement where the parties were married or formed a civil partnership at least four years ago and since then they have been living together outside the UK. Note that such a couple may be granted entry for immediate settlement in the UK (see **14.9.5**).

Note that by para 277 of the Immigration Rules both the spouse or civil partner seeking entry and the spouse or civil partner in the UK must be at least 18 years of age on the date of arrival in the UK.

The spouse or civil partner, whether or not he is a visa national, must have an entry clearance granted for entry as a spouse or civil partner. Entry clearance will be refused unless the entry clearance officer is satisfied, under para 281, that:

(a) each of the parties has the intention of living permanently with the other as his or her spouse or civil partner and the marriage or civil partnership is subsisting; and

(b) the parties to the marriage or civil partnership have met; and

(c) there will be adequate accommodation for the parties and their dependants without recourse to public funds in accommodation of their own or which they occupy exclusively; and

(d) the parties will be able to maintain themselves and their dependants adequately without recourse to public funds.

Example 1: Intention to live together

Paragraph 6 of the Immigration Rules defines 'intention to live permanently with the other' as 'an intention to live together, evidenced by a clear commitment from both parties that they will live together permanently in the UK immediately following the outcome of the application in question or as soon as circumstances permit thereafter'.

Anne is a British citizen. She enters into a civil partnership with Jamila, a citizen of Nigeria, in order to enable her to settle in the UK without having to apply for refugee status. Anne has no intention of continuing the relationship with Jamila once she has obtained settlement.

The Home Office may contest an application by Jamila on the grounds that the parties do not intend to live permanently with each other.

Example 2: Intention and intervening devotion

Sumeina is a British citizen. Her father arranged her marriage to Khalid, a citizen of Pakistan, by correspondence with his father, on the basis that the couple were first cousins, between whom marriage is customary. She travelled to Pakistan to marry him, and then returned to the UK. He later applied for a visa to enter the UK as her spouse. He has admitted that he lacks the means to support her in Pakistan, and she has made it clear that she is not prepared to emigrate to Pakistan.

The Home Office may argue that both parties lack the intent to live permanently with each other, as their intent is conditional on Khalid gaining entry to the UK, and that the marriage is not yet 'subsisting'.

However, it may be perfectly reasonable for Sumeina as a British citizen to insist on continuing to live in the UK (see *R v Immigration Appeal Tribunal, ex p Wali* [1989] Imm AR 86). The fact that material considerations outweigh emotional ones at this stage need not mean that the marriage is a sham, particularly in the context of an arranged marriage.

If a couple live separately after the marriage or civil partnership, that might be said to show a lack of intent to live together. Very often, a couple will seek to rebut that by producing details of letters sent and telephone calls made during this period to illustrate their 'intervening devotion'. In the case of *Amarjit Kaur* (1999) INLP 110, the adjudicator had found the appellant's 'overriding wish was to marry someone from abroad. The letters and phone calls were evidence, not of intervening devotion, but merely of intervening contact'. No further evidence of letters or phone calls was produced to the Tribunal, and although the sponsor had visited his wife in India, the appeal was dismissed. The adjudicator had taken a dim view of the fact that the sponsor was a divorcée 20 years older than the appellant, who had turned down Indian-based suitors in order to marry him. The Tribunal did not demur from that.

The question whether parties intend to live together is basically one of fact and decisions will depend on the credibility of evidence, and in particular whether the parties to the marriage have contradicted themselves.

Example 3: Public funds

Deirdre is a British citizen who is living in homeless persons' accommodation. She marries Samir, who requires leave to enter the UK as her spouse. Samir has an offer of a good job in the UK. Will Deirdre's reliance on public funds result in a refusal of Samir's application for a visa?

No – because Samir's presence in the UK would not create 'additional' reliance on public funds, ie no additional accommodation is required. See para 6A of the Immigration Rules.

Example 4: Accommodation

Fatima is settled in the UK. She marries Farooq who requires leave to enter as a spouse. Initially, they will live with Fatima's parents in their house with their own bedroom, but sharing the rest of the property. Will the accommodation requirement of the Rules be met?

According to BIA guidance, accommodation can be shared with other members of a family, provided that at least part of the accommodation is for the exclusive use of the sponsor and his dependants. The unit of accommodation may be as small as a separate bedroom but must be owned or legally occupied by the sponsor and its occupation must not contravene public health regulations and must not cause overcrowding as defined in the Housing Act (HA) 1985 (see below).

The couple will have to provide evidence that the property is either owned or rented by themselves. This may be in the form of a letter from the building society, a copy of the property deeds and, in the case of rented accommodation, a rent book and lease agreement. Where the accommodation is rented from a local authority or housing association, correspondence from the landlord is normally regarded as genuine and sufficient. The BIA suggests that greater care needs to be taken where there is purportedly private tenancy. If there are any aspects of the case which raise substantial doubts it might seek corroborative evidence of residence.

If the accommodation is not 'owned', in the sense that the sponsor is not the head of the household but is for instance a son or daughter of the family, the Rules require there to be adequate accommodation which the couple and any dependants will occupy themselves for their exclusive use. This need not be a separate house or self-contained flat but where it is as little as one bedroom of their own, enquiries are usually made about the number of rooms, the number of occupants in the house and whether this is intended to be only a short-term arrangement.

In the case of *Sultana* (1999) INLP 74, the Tribunal held that a report from the local council stating that the matrimonial home would not become statutorily overcrowded if the appellant was admitted, although it would be congested, satisfied the test. It should be noted that, over recent years, Tribunals have made it clear that parties are not required to obtain such reports from local councils or surveyors in every case. Indeed, the BIA guidance is that whilst the applicant or sponsor will be asked to provide evidence that the accommodation provided will be adequate, that may take the form of a letter from a housing authority, a building society or an accurate description of the premises.

The HA 1985 contains two statutory definitions of overcrowding in dwelling-houses. A house is overcrowded if either two persons of 10 years old or more of the opposite sex (other than husband and wife) have to sleep in the same room, or if the number sleeping in the house exceeds that permitted in the HA 1985. The HA 1985 specifies the numbers permitted for a given number of rooms or given floor area. The BIA adopts the so-called room number yardstick. Account is only taken of rooms with a floor area larger than 50 sq feet and rooms that are 'available as sleeping accomodation if it is of a type normally used in the locality as a living room or as a bedroom' (s 326). Using the above-noted yardstick, the following table provides guidance as to the acceptable, for BIA purposes, number of persons occupying a house with a stated number of rooms available as sleeping accommodation.

Number of rooms	Permitted number of persons
1	2
2	3
3	5
4	7.5
5	10
*	with an additional 2 persons for each room in excess of 5.

NOTE: a child under the age of 1 does not count as a person. A child aged 1 or over but under 10 years will count as only half a person. A child aged 10 0or over counts as one person.

Also note that these guidelines on overcrowding are used by the BIA and Tribunals when considering other categories of entrants, for example children joining parents (see **14.15**).

Example 5: Maintenance

Assume in Example 4 above that Fatima and Farooq would be financially dependent on her parents for some time after Farooq's entry to the UK. Would that meet para 281 of the Immigration Rules?

There is much controversy as to whether or not long-term support for a couple from third parties is permissible. The BIA guidance is that:

> a couple who are unable to produce sufficient evidence to meet the maintenance requirement, may provide an undertaking from members of their families that they will support the couple until they are able to support themselves from their own resources. This is not acceptable as the Rules require the couple to be able to support themselves and any dependants from their own resources. Nevertheless, such an arrangement may be accepted exceptionally if it is clear that it would only be in effect for a limited period and the couple have a realistic prospect of supporting themselves thereafter.

However, Sir Andrew Collins sitting in the High Court, fuelled this debate further when he held in the case of *R v Secretary of State for the Home Department, ex p Arman Ali* [2000] INLR 89, that long-term third-party financial support can be acceptable, provided it could be proven. However, he did indicate that it would be rare for applicants to be able to do so.

He said:

> If a rich relation, or a benefactor is willing and able to maintain a family in this country so that there is no need to have recourse to public funds, I see no reason in principle why that family should be kept apart ... I am satisfied that *Najmun Neesa* (IAT 11545) was wrong insofar as it decided that there could be no long-term maintenance by third parties to meet the requirements of the Rules ... I do not doubt that it will be rare for applicants to be able to satisfy an Entry Clearance Officer, the Secretary of State or an adjudicator that long term maintenance by a third party will be provided so that there will be no recourse to public funds. But whether or not such long term support will be provided is a question of fact to be determined on the evidence.

Apart from the vexed question of third-party support, what pointers can be found in the BIA guidance? To be satisfied that the couple will be able to maintain themselves and any dependants adequately without recourse to public funds, the BIA will need to see evidence of:

(a) sufficient independent means; or

(b) employment for one or both of the parties; or

(c) sufficient prospects of employment for one or both the parties.

When conducting an interview, the following areas of questioning in relation to maintenance may be put by the authorities:

(a) the applicant's present employment;

(b) the applicant's educational achievement;

(c) other skills or qualifications the applicant may have acquired that would assist in getting established in the UK;

(d) similar information about the sponsor;

(e) what plans the applicant may have for obtaining employment in the UK;

(f) what arrangements have been or could be made to obtain employment by the applicant, sponsor or friend or relatives in the UK;

(g) what other support is available to the couple from friends or relatives in the UK.

All the evidence in the form of oral answers, papers and any evidence gathered from this country are assessed in the light of the context of the employment situation where the couple intend to make their home. A judgment is then made on whether the BIA can be satisfied that the couple has a reasonable prospect of being able to maintain themselves and any dependants without recourse to public funds by asking the following questions.

(a) Have the applicant and/or sponsor demonstrated relevant skills/qualifications or a reasonable prospect of employment?

(b) Have the applicant and/or sponsor provided evidence that he has a job waiting for him in the UK?

(c) Where the applicant has made no arrangements for employment, what are the prospects in the light of his background?

Finally, it should be noted that the parties will always greatly assist their case if they produce a schedule of income and outgoings, of assets and liabilities. This is especially true at any appeal hearing.

14.9.4 Grant of leave to enter

If a person is granted leave to enter as the spouse or civil partner of someone settled in the UK, the leave will be for an initial period of 24 months, often called the 'probationary period'. After 24 months, indefinite leave may be granted (see below).

The spouse or civil partner may obtain employment within the initial 24-month probationary period.

You will recall that there is a second type of applicant, namely a spouse or civil partner falling under para 281(i)(b) of the Immigration Rules (see **14.9.3**). As the couple have already been married or in a civil partnership for at least four years, the applicant may be granted indefinite leave to enter the UK and so will have no probationary period to serve.

14.9.5 Grant of settled status

Shortly before the 24-month probationary period expires, an application should be made, under para 287 of the Immigration Rules and on the prescribed form (see **13.6.6**), for indefinite leave to remain. The BIA guidance is that detailed enquiries are normally made only where doubts exist as to whether the relationship is genuine and subsisting, for example:

(a) where there is an allegation or other information suggesting that the marriage or civil partnership may not be genuine or the couple are not living together;

(b) where an applicant switched into marriage or civil partnership whilst here as a working holidaymaker or student, or a combination of these categories, or has an outstanding asylum application and whose record was less than satisfactory.

What if the marriage or civil partnership ends during the probationary period due to the death of the sponsor? An application for settlement can still be made pursuant to para 287(b).

What if the marriage or civil partnership has ended during the probationary period because of the sponsor's desertion? The normal expectation is that the spouse or civil partner should return to his home country. An application made in these circumstances is normally refused. However, sympathetic consideration may be given to such applications but will only be granted where there are exceptional compassionate circumstances over and above the desertion of the spouse. Consideration is given to such factors as the applicant's circumstances in the UK and his home country; and the presence of children from the relationship, especially if the children have the right of abode in the UK.

Must the applicant have been present in the UK throughout the probationary period? There is no specific requirement in the Immigration Rules that the entire probationary period must be spent in the UK. For example, where an applicant has spent a limited period outside of the UK in connection with his employment, this should not count against him. However, if he has spent the majority of the period overseas, there may be reason to doubt that all the requirements of the Rules have been met. Each case must be judged on its merits, taking into account reasons for travel, length of absences and whether the applicant and sponsor travelled and lived together during the time spent outside the UK. These factors will need to be considered against the requirements of the Rules.

On completion of the probationary period, applicants are required to provide full details of how they have maintained and accommodated themselves when completing the prescribed application form to apply for settlement. Paragraph 287(a)(iv) and (v) require that the couple should be able to maintain and accommodate themselves and any dependants without recourse to (additional) public funds. However, if a person has, through no fault of his or her own, had to have strictly temporary assistance from public funds, BIA guidance is that he should not be refused on this basis.

14.9.6 Switching

14.9.6.1 Permission to marry

As from 1 February 2005, people who are subject to immigration control (ie who require leave to enter or remain in the UK) who wish to marry in the UK need permission to do so. They must either:

(a) hold entry clearance as a fiancé(e) (see **14.13**) or marriage visitor (see **14.1.4**); or

(b) be a person with settled status in the UK (see **13.2**); or

(c) hold a Home Office certificate of approval.

To qualify for the certificate of approval from the Home Office, the applicant must have been granted leave to enter or remain for more than six months from the date that he was admitted into the UK and three months of that leave must still remain. So a person will not qualify if he was granted six months' or less leave to enter or remain in the UK, or has less than three months' leave remaining, or does not have valid leave to remain in the UK. In those circumstances the applicant must return to his own country or the country of normal residence and apply for entry clearance as a fiancé(e) or a marriage visitor.

The formal requirements are set out in the Immigration (Procedure for Marriage) Regulations 2005 (SI 2005/15). To obtain a certificate of approval an applicant must supply the information required by the Home Office set out in Sch 2, which includes his name, date of birth, nationality, full postal address, passport or travel document number, Home Office reference number, current immigration status and the date on which current leave to enter or remain in the UK was granted.

Note that people who are subject to immigration control are also required to give notice to marry to a registrar at one of a number of designated register offices throughout the UK. The certificate of approval is not a grant of further leave to remain in the UK. The certificate only allows the applicant to give notice to marry to a registrar at a designated register office.

Does the permission to marry scheme comply with the ECHR? At the time of writing (July 2007), the Court of Appeal has considered the scheme to be unlawful: see *R (Baiai) v Secretary of State for the Home Department* [2007] EWCA Civ 478. Article 12 of the ECHR provides that 'Men and women of marriageable age have the right to marry and to found a family, according to the national laws governing the exercise of this right.' The Court held that the scheme operated in a disproportionate manner, effectively as a statutory presumption that a marriage involving a person with less than six months' leave to stay was not a genuine marriage. The Secretary of State has sought to appeal the decision.

14.9.6.2 Permission to enter into a civil partnership.

The Immigration (Procedure for Formation of Civil Partnerships) Regulations 2005 (SI 2005/2917) provide similar permission and notice requirements to those applying to spouses (see **14.9.6.1**) where one or both parties are subject to immigration controls.

14.9.6.3 Applying to switch categories

If a person with limited leave marries or enters into a civil partnership with a person who is settled here, he or she may seek an extension of stay under para 284 unless he or she is a visitor. This imposes similar conditions to para 281, but in addition, the Home Office must be satisfied that the applicant is not remaining in breach of the immigration laws, or liable to be deported. There is no requirement in this case to obtain entry clearance as a spouse or civil partner, since obviously the parties may have become acquainted only after the non-settled party entered. However, evidence of 'queue-jumping' (ie entering without revealing the intention to marry or enter into a civil partnership, thus bypassing the requirement to obtain entry clearance as a fiancé(e) or proposed civil partner), may be used to establish that the applicant does not have effective limited leave (see **13.6.3** and **15.2.2**).

If an extension is granted to remain as the spouse or civil partner of someone settled in the UK, the initial period of leave will be 24 months (as for someone who enters as a spouse).

If an EEA national marries or enters into a civil partnership with a British citizen or a settled person, he can apply under the Immigration Rules for leave to remain. Why might an EEA national take this step? The most common reason is to obtain permanent residence within two years rather than five years (see **13.9.9** and **14.9.5**) in order to apply for British citizenship (by naturalisation: compare **12.2.6.2** and **12.2.6.1**) at an earlier stage.

14.10 Marriage breakdown

A person who marries or enters into a civil partnership with someone settled in the UK is in a vulnerable position until he or she obtains settled status. If there are problems in the marriage or civil partnership during the initial 24-month probationary period of leave, the non-settled spouse or civil partner may be faced with the threat of removal if the marriage or civil partnership breaks down. Settled status will not be granted unless the marriage or civil partnership is subsisting. Once the initial period of leave expires, the non-settled spouse or civil partner will become an overstayer, liable to removal. This is not inevitable, as the Home Office should consider compassionate circumstances, for example where children would be left behind in the UK (see **15.1.4**). In addition, by para 289A of the Immigration Rules, the Home Office may grant settled status where the applicant is a victim of domestic violence (see *AI v Secretary of State for the Home Department* [2007] EWCA Civ 386).

Once settled status has been granted, breakdown of a relationship cannot affect immigration status.

It is possible for a divorced or separated parent who lacks settled status to apply to enter the UK for up to 12 months, to exercise rights of contact (access) to a child resident in the UK (para 246) and thereafter to seek indefinite leave to remain (para 248D).

14.11 Polygamous marriages or civil partnerships

See para 278 of the Rules and the practitioners' texts referred to at **11.2.1**.

14.12 Spouses or civil partners of persons with limited leave

There are separate provisions applying to spouses and civil partners of persons in each category of limited leave, other than those such as visitors, where the spouse or civil partner would be expected to obtain leave in his or her own right.

Paragraphs 76–78 deal with spouses and civil partners of students. The requirements (abbreviated) are as follows:

(a) the parties must intend to live together;
(b) they must have adequate accommodation and maintenance without recourse to public funds;
(c) the applicant must not intend to take employment unless permitted and must intend to leave the UK when leave expires.

The spouse or civil partner will be prohibited from taking employment unless granted leave of 12 months or more. The length of the spouse's or civil partner's leave will depend on that of the student.

Paragraphs 194–196 deal with spouses and civil partner of employees, and paras 240–242 with spouses and civil partners of businessmen. The requirements are similar to those for spouses and civil partners of students, except that accommodation must be occupied exclusively and entry clearance must have been obtained in the capacity of spouse or civil partner.

In each case, the provisions apply both to leave to enter, and to leave to remain. In particular, someone who seeks an extension as a spouse or civil partner of an employee or businessman must have obtained entry clearance in that capacity.

14.13 Fiancé(e)s or proposed civil partners of persons who are settled

Note that by para 289AA of the Immigration Rules, both the applicant and the party in the UK must be at least 18 years of age.

Paragraph 290 applies conditions similar to those in para 281 to persons seeking admission in order to marry or enter into a civil partnership with a person present and settled in the UK. However, two main points should be considered.

(a) The fiancé(e) or proposed civil partner will be prohibited from taking employment until granted 24 months' leave following the marriage or civil partnership (see **14.9.4**).
(b) It is unreasonable to require a fiancé(e) or proposed civil partner overseas to be as clear as a spouse or civil partner may be about the couple's future accommodation.

The maintenance test in most cases is based on the sponsor's income and/or employment and the applicant's employment prospects. There will also be cases where a friend or relative in the UK may offer assistance until the marriage or civil partnership takes place and the applicant is free to take employment. An applicant may have a specific job waiting for him, although where he is relying on this job offer to meet the maintenance requirement of the Rules, the BIA will take care to ensure that the job offer is genuine and will be held open for him until such time as he is free to take employment.

Accommodation for the couple will often be prospective rather than available on arrival. The test used by the BIA is whether there is a reasonable prospect that adequate accommodation will be available after the marriage or civil partnership has taken place. This requirement will, of course, have to be satisfied on application for leave to remain on the basis of the marriage or civil partnership (see above). In the period before the marriage or civil partnership takes place, temporary accommodation provided by relatives or friends is acceptable.

Can the fiancé(e) or proposed civil partner of an EEA national who is exercising Treaty rights in the UK make use of para 290? Yes, since para 290A of the Immigration Rules provides that an EEA national who has been issued with a registration certificate valid for five years is regarded as present and settled in the UK even if that EEA national has not been granted permanent residence.

Can a person in the UK already switch to this status? There is no provision in the Immigration Rules for a person admitted in another temporary capacity to be granted leave to remain as a fiancé(e) or proposed civil partner, and such applications are normally refused. However, where the BIA is satisfied that there are exceptional compassionate circumstances, such as the serious terminal illness of one of the parties to the relationship, further leave to remain may be granted exceptionally outside the Rules. The maintenance and accommodation requirements must be met if an extension is granted exceptionally. Whether a case can be considered to have exceptional compassionate circumstances is assessed according to the individual circumstances of the case. However, the inconvenience or the expense of having to travel home to obtain a visa is not sufficient reason to grant outside the Rules.

Example

Ghulam has obtained entry clearance in order to marry someone settled in the UK. When will he be able to take a job, and when will he himself obtain settled status?

Ghulam will not be able to take a job until he has obtained an extension to remain in the UK as a spouse, after his marriage. This will give him leave to remain for a further 24 months. He will not be given settled status until he has remained in the UK as a spouse for 24 months (para 287).

14.14 Non-marital relationships

Paragraph 295A of the Immigration Rules deals with partners in stable relationships, whether a heterosexual or homosexual relationship. Note that by para 295AA of the Immigration Rules, both the partner seeking entry to the UK and the partner in the UK must be at least 18 years of age.

In effect, such partners will be treated as spouses or civil partners for the purpose of applications to enter or remain for settlement. The special additional conditions are that:

(a) any previous marriage, civil partnership or similar relationship of either party must have broken down permanently;

(b) the parties have been living together in a relationship akin to marriage which has subsisted for two years or more; and

(c) the relationship is subsisting and the couple intend to live together permanently.

Each of the parties is required to provide information regarding any previous marital, civil partnership or similar relationship they have had. They are asked to specify how long ago the previous relationship was terminated, by divorce, dissolution or separation.

According to BIA guidance, 'living together', should be applied fairly tightly, in that the BIA expects a couple to show evidence of cohabitation for the preceding two-year period. Short breaks apart would be acceptable for good reasons, such as work commitments, or looking after a relative which takes one partner away for a period of up to six months where it was not possible for the other partner to accompany and it can be seen that the relationship continued throughout that period by visits, letters, etc. 'Akin to marriage' is said to be a relationship that is similar in its nature to a marriage which would include both common-law and same-sex relationships. In order to demonstrate a two-year relationship, evidence of cohabitation is needed. In order to show a relationship akin to marriage, the BIA looks for evidence of a committed relationship. The following type of evidence is useful in this respect:

(a) joint commitments (such as joint bank accounts, investments, rent agreements, mortgage, death benefit, etc);

(b) if there are children of the relationship, a record of their birth entry;

(c) correspondence which links them to the same address;

(d) any official records of their address (eg doctor's records, DfWP record, national insurance record, etc);

(e) any other evidence that adequately demonstrates their commitment to each other.

It is not necessary to provide all of the above, but BIA caseworkers are instructed to look for conclusive evidence of the relationship.

A successful applicant will be given leave (to enter or remain) for an initial period of 24 months. He may then apply for indefinite leave after completing a period of 24 months as an unmarried partner, provided the relationship is still subsisting etc (see para 295G).

Note that like spouses and civil partners (see **14.9.3**), if the couple are living outside the UK and have already been in a relationship akin to marriage for at least four years, the applicant may be granted indefinite leave to enter the UK and so will have no probationary period to serve.

Examples

(1) David is a British citizen. He has worked abroad for some years and for the past two years has been living abroad with John, who is a US citizen. David now wishes to return to the UK and John wishes to return with him. If John is admitted he intends to live with David permanently.

John is within para 295A and should be given entry clearance and 24 months' leave to enter.

(2) May is a British citizen who lives in the UK. At university she met June who was a US citizen admitted to the UK with limited leave as a student. They have lived together in a committed relationship for more than two years, June overstaying

her leave to remain with May. She wishes to apply for an extension of leave as May's partner.

June is not within para 295D. As with spouses, it is a requirement that the applicant has effective limited leave and should not have remained in breach of immigration law.

(3) Edward is a British citizen. He is married to Deirdre who is also a British citizen. They have children. For the past six years, Edward has been working abroad, and for the past four years he has been living with Rashida who is a citizen of India. On visits home, he stayed with his wife and family. He now wishes to return to the UK and set up home with Rashida, if she can be admitted for settlement. Deirdre has said that she will divorce him if this happens.

Rashida is within para 295A in that she and Edward have lived together for at least two years. However, an entry clearance officer may refuse Rashida a visa if he is not satisfied that Edward's relationship with Deirdre has broken down permanently.

(4) Anna is a British citizen. At university she met Bill who is a US citizen. They have been living together for two years in the UK, Bill having obtained extensions to his limited leave as a student. They do not wish to marry, but intend to have children and live together permanently. Bill now wishes to apply to remain in the UK as Anna's partner.

Bill is within para 295D and may apply.

The Immigration Rules (paras 295J and 295K) also deal with applications to enter or remain in the UK by unmarried partners of persons with only limited leave. Subject to similar conditions to those at **14.12**, such applicants can be treated in the same way as spouses. Equally, there is a similar provision (para 295M) should the sponsor die during the 24-month probationary period.

14.15 Children

14.15.1 Introduction

This section deals with the Immigration Rules applying to children (under 18) who apply to enter or remain in the UK with their parents, one or both of whom may be settled, or in the UK with limited leave. These Rules will not apply to the following:

(a) children who have the right of abode (see **Chapter 12**);

(b) children who have rights of residence, as the family members of EEA nationals (see **13.8.1.4**);

(c) children who are entering in their own right under other provisions of the Rules (eg as visitors or students etc).

Example 1

Eva is a German citizen, aged 17. Her father, also German, is working in the UK. She is entitled to enter the UK in her own right (I(EEA) Regs 2006, reg 11). Whether she has any right of residence beyond three months (reg 14) depends on establishing a qualifying status under reg 6. In the alternative she can enter and reside as the family member of an EEA national. The Immigration Rules do not apply.

Example 2

Abdul is a citizen of Saudi Arabia, aged 17. His father has 12 months' leave to enter as a work permit holder. Abdul has obtained a place at a college in the UK.

He should apply for leave to enter the UK as a student, rather than as the child of a person with limited leave, so that his period of leave will not have to depend on that of his father.

14.15.2 Children entering for settlement

Under paras 297–303 of the Immigration Rules, children under 18 may be admitted for settlement where both parents are already present and settled in the UK, or the child is entering for settlement with them. Parents who are British or Commonwealth citizens with the right of abode are 'settled' for this purpose.

The term 'parent', for the purposes of the Immigration Rules, is defined in para 6 and includes:

(a) the step-father of a child whose father is dead, and the reference to 'step-father' includes a relationship arising through civil partnership;

(b) the step-mother of a child whose mother is dead, and the reference to 'step-mother' includes a relationship arising through civil partnership;

(c) the father, as well as the mother, of an illegitimate child (where he is proved to be the father);

(d) an adoptive parent (provided that the child was legally adopted in a country whose adoption orders are recognised by the UK – see **14.15.9**).

If only one of his parents is settled in the UK, the child may be admitted for settlement with that parent alone only if that parent has the sole responsibility for the child's upbringing (see **14.15.3**), or where there are serious and compelling considerations which make exclusion undesirable and arrangements have been made to care for the child in the UK (see **14.15.4**). As to the remaining requirements, see **14.5.5**.

14.15.3 Sole responsibility

Where a child's parents are not married, or his parents' marriage subsists but they do not live together, or where the parents' marriage has been dissolved, a child may qualify to join or remain with one parent, provided that parent has had 'sole responsibility' for the child's upbringing. According to BIA guidance, the phrase 'sole responsibility' is intended to reflect a situation where parental responsibility of a child, to all intents and purposes, rests chiefly with one parent. Such a situation is in contrast to the ordinary family unit where responsibility for a child's upbringing is shared between the two parents (although not necessarily equally).

In *Suzara Ramos v Immigration Appeal Tribunal* [1989] Imm AR 148, the Court of Appeal (per Dillon LJ) held that:

> ... the words 'sole responsibility' have to carry some form of qualification in that the rule envisages that a parent who is settled in the United Kingdom will or may have had the sole responsibility for the child's upbringing in another country. Obviously there are matters of day-to-day decision in the upbringing of a child which are bound to be decided on the spot by whoever is looking after the child in the absence of the parent settled here, such as getting the child to school safely and on time, or putting the child to bed, or seeing what it has for breakfast, or that it cleans its teeth, or has enough clothing, and so forth. ... The question must be a broad question.
>
> Direction and control of upbringing are ... factors which are part of the total pattern of facts on which the adjudicator had to make his decision. Another matter was of course the extent of contact that the mother had had with the child since the mother went to the United Kingdom ...

A parent claiming to have had 'sole responsibility' for a child must satisfactorily demonstrate that he has, for a period of time, been the chief person exercising parental responsibility. For such an assertion to be accepted by the BIA, it must be shown that he has had, and still has, the ultimate responsibility for the major decisions relating to the child's upbringing, and provides the child with the majority of the financial and emotional support he requires. It must also be shown that he has had and continues to have care and control of the child. In the case of *Nmaju v Entry Clearance Officer* (2000) *The Times*, 6 September, the Court of Appeal held that this requirement could be satisfied even where the parent in question had exercised sole responsibility only for a short period of time (namely about two and a half months on the facts). The court said that the question posed by the rules was: had the parent settled in the UK sole responsibility for the upbringing of the child? In this case the Tribunal had found that the mother had had sole responsibility for the upbringing of the appellants. Having concluded that, the Tribunal was not at liberty under the rules to find that the appellants did not qualify for entry merely because that sole responsibility had not been assumed for a period of in excess of much over two months.

In *Nmaju* the Court of Appeal indicated that:

> While legal responsibility under the appropriate legal system will be a relevant consideration, it will not be a conclusive one. One must also look at what has actually been done in relation to the child's upbringing by whom and whether it has been done under the direction of the parent settled here (per Schiemann LJ).

Where the child and parent are separated, the physical day-to-day care of the child must be entrusted to others, and it is expected that where the child is being looked after by relatives, they should be the relatives of the parent claiming 'sole responsibility' rather than those of the other parent. Should this be the case, the parent claiming 'sole responsibility' must still be able to show that he has retained the ultimate responsibility for the child's upbringing and provides the majority of the emotional and financial support needed. If it is established that the child is being cared for by the relatives of the father but it is the mother who has applied for the child to join her in this country (or vice versa), the application is normally refused.

14.15.4 Serious and compelling reasons

Guidance from the BIA states that:

> the objective of this provision is to allow a child to join a parent or relative in this country only where that child could not be adequately cared for by his parents or relatives in his own country. It has never been the intention of the Rules that a child should be admitted here due to the wish of or for the benefit of other relatives in this country. This approach is entirely consistent with the internationally accepted principle that a child should first and foremost be cared for by his natural parent(s) or, if this is not possible, by his natural relatives in the country in which he lives. Only if the parent(s) or relative(s) in his own country cannot care for him should consideration be given to him joining relatives in another country. It is also consistent with the provisions of the European Convention on Human Rights, and the resolution on the harmonization of family reunification agreed by EU Ministers in June 1993.

The degree to which these considerations should be taken into account, and whether they should solely relate to the child or include those of the sponsor are determined by two factors, namely:

(a) whether the sponsor is a parent or other relative of the child; and
(b) whether or not the sponsor is settled here.

If the sponsor is not a parent but another relative (eg an aunt or grandparent), the factors which are to be considered relate only to the child and the circumstances in which he lives or lived prior to travelling to the UK. These circumstances should be exceptional in comparison with the ordinary circumstances of other children in his home country. It is not, for instance, sufficient to show he would be better off here by being able to attend a State school. The circumstances relating to the sponsors here (eg the fact that they are elderly or infirm and need caring for) are not taken into account.

If the sponsor in the UK is one of the child's parents, consideration needs to be given as to whether or not he or she is settled here or being admitted for settlement. If he or she is not, then the relevant circumstances relate solely to the child (as detailed above). But, if the child's sponsor is one of his parents and he or she is settled here (or being admitted for settlement), the considerations to be taken into account may relate either to the child and his circumstances in the country in which he lives or lived prior to travelling here, or to the parent who is settled here or being admitted for settlement. The circumstances surrounding the child must be exceptional in relation to those of other children living in that country, but in this case, circumstances relating to the parent here, both of an emotional and of a physical nature, may be taken into account. Such circumstances may include illness or infirmity which requires assistance.

> **Example**
>
> Marlene is the mother of Dora, who is aged 14. Both are citizens of Barbados. Marlene is divorced from Dora's father, who never contacts his daughter. When Dora was eight, Marlene came to the UK and left Dora in the care of her grandmother, who supports her granddaughter financially. She is now settled in the UK. She wishes to know whether Dora can now join her in the UK.
>
> Marlene cannot establish her sole responsibility for Dora, as she has not provided financial support for her from the UK. She must instead show that there are serious and compelling considerations which make Dora's exclusion undesirable (eg because Dora's grandmother is seriously ill, and incapable of looking after her). If this requirement is not met, Dora cannot be admitted for settlement in the UK.

14.15.5 Other requirements of para 297

Note that, by para 297(i)(f) of the Immigration Rules, the child's sponsor may, in such limited circumstances, be a relative.

Even if the child is under 18, he will not be allowed to settle with parents in the UK under para 297 if he is married, or has formed an independent family unit, or is leading an independent life. It must also be shown that the child can and will be maintained and accommodated adequately, without recourse to public funds in accommodation which the parents own or occupy exclusively. The BIA summarises that, to qualify under the Rules at the time of application and decision, a child must:

(a) be unmarried and not a civil partner, and not at any previous time have been married or in a civil partnership;

(b) not currently be in or have previously formed a relationship with another person (such as a common-law or homosexual relationship) which could be said to be the equivalent of being married, except for name and legal recognition;

(c) still be living with his parent(s) and any brothers and sisters who are living with their parent(s) (except where he is at boarding school as part of his full-time education);

(d) not be employed full time or for a significant number of hours per week (although the obtaining of a 'Saturday' job or a temporary job during his school holidays should not be counted against him); and

(e) be wholly or mainly dependent upon his parent(s), (or relative other than parents, if appropriate), for both his financial and emotional support.

What is 'adequate' accommodation for these purposes? In the case of *Loresco* (1999) INLP 18, the Tribunal relied on the statutory overcrowding test set out in the HA 1985 (the details of which can be found at **14.9.3** (Example 4)). In that case, three teenage children (one girl and two boys) sought to join their mother in the UK. Was the sponsor's two-bedroomed flat (with a living room that was also available as sleeping accommodation) too small for her, her husband, their 1-year-old child and the three teenagers? The Tribunal said 'Yes'. Three rooms were available to sleep in. There was one room for the sponsor and her husband, one room for the girl over 10, and the third room for the two boys over 10. However, under the so-called 'room number' yardstick, with only three available rooms, the permitted number of persons was five, but now the child aged 1 counted as half a person, and so that meant the total complement of the household would be five and a half persons. Despite the appellants' solicitors' argument that the flat would only be 'technically' overcrowded, the Tribunal insisted that it would be statutorily overcrowded.

Entry clearance must be obtained as the child of a settled parent.

Children of 18 and over must generally qualify for settlement in their own right. They may, however, be admitted as 'other relatives' under para 318 (see **14.16.5**).

14.15.6 Children of persons with limited leave

Children under 18 of students, fiancé(e)s, persons coming for employment, and businessmen may be admitted under paras 80, 303A, 198 and 244 respectively, with requirements similar to those applying to children entering for settlement. In each case, it must be shown that the child will not stay in the UK beyond the period of leave granted to his parents.

14.15.7 Children born in the UK

A child born in the UK after 1982 acquires British citizenship if a parent was a British citizen, or settled in the UK (see **12.2.3**). Otherwise, if he is under 18 and unmarried, paras 304–309 apply. The child is subject to immigration control, and requires leave to re-enter if he departs from the UK. On application while in the UK, leave to remain will generally be given for the same period as for his parents.

If one of the child's parents becomes settled in the UK before the child attains 18, or the child remains in the UK until the age of 10, the child has a right to register as a British citizen (BNA 1981, s 1(3), (4): see **12.2.7**).

14.15.8 Switching

If a child has entered the UK in another capacity (eg as a visitor) he can apply to remain for settlement with a parent, subject to requirements similar to those applying on entry. It is not necessary for the child to have obtained a visa for this purpose before entry, but if he has not, he must be under 18 at the date of application for leave to remain.

Switching to stay with a parent is not possible under the Rules for children of some categories of parents with limited leave unless entry clearance as a child was obtained before entry. These categories include trainees, work permit employees and businessmen.

14.15.9 Adopted children

Special provision is made in paras 309A–316F for adopted children. There are no rules dealing with children who come to the UK for adoption. The Home Office deals with such cases on an exceptional leave basis, outside the Rules. For further details, see the specialist practitioners' texts listed at **11.2.1**.

14.16 Parents and other relatives

14.16.1 Introduction

The Immigration Rules dealing with parents and other relatives will apply only if the entrant is not relying on a separate ground for entry, such as a right of abode or residence, or another category in the Immigration Rules.

> **Example 1**
>
> Jahangir is a citizen of Pakistan, settled in the UK. His mother, Begum, who lives in Pakistan, wishes to visit him.
>
> She should apply to enter as a visitor rather than as a parent. However, she must provide evidence that she intends to leave the UK at the end of the visit (eg by showing that she has strong family ties in Pakistan). The entry clearance officer may refuse a visa if he suspects that the real motive is to remain in the UK (eg because she is recently widowed and her son is her closest relative). If she does wish to settle she should apply for leave as the parent of someone settled in the UK.
>
> **Example 2**
>
> Bashir is a British citizen. He went to live and work in Dublin for six months. While there he was joined by his mother, Amina (who is financially dependent on him and therefore his family member under EC law). He wishes to know whether she can return with him to live in the UK.
>
> He may seek to rely on *Surinder Singh* and reg 9 of the I(EEA) Regs 2006 (see **13.9.12**) to show that he has the right to bring his mother with him on his return to the UK. If Bashir had not worked in another EC country, Amina would have to satisfy the requirements of the Rules for entry as a parent.

14.16.2 Requirements

Parents and other qualifying relatives (including children over 18) of persons present and settled in the UK may be permitted to join the settled person under para 318.

The following relatives qualify, as defined by para 317:

(a) a parent or grandparent who is a widow(er) aged 65 or over;

(b) parents or grandparents travelling together of whom at least one is aged 65 or over;

(c) a parent or grandparent aged 65 or over who has remarried or entered into a civil partnership but cannot look to the spouse, or civil partner or children of the second relationship for support; and the person settled in the UK is able and willing to maintain the parent or grandparent and any spouse, or civil partner or child of the second relationship who would be admissible as a dependant;

(d) a parent or grandparent under the age of 65, or a child, sister, brother, uncle or aunt, over 18 and living alone outside the UK in the most exceptional compassionate circumstances, and mainly dependent financially on relatives settled in the UK.

Under para 317, a qualifying relative may be admitted to the UK provided that he:

(a) is financially wholly or mainly dependent on the settled relative;

(b) can and will be maintained and accommodated adequately, together with dependants, without recourse to public funds in accommodation which the sponsor owns or occupies exclusively;

(c) has no other close relatives in his own country to whom he could turn for financial support.

Entry clearance in this capacity is required where the applicant is seeking leave to enter.

14.16.3 Parents and grandparents

The main difficulty encountered by parents seeking to join children settled in the UK will be the need to prove financial dependency. They will have to show that they were dependent on the settled child (known as the 'sponsor') before the application for entry clearance.

How does the overseas parent demonstrate that he is financially dependent upon the child who is present and settled in the UK? Evidence should be obtained of money remitted to the applicant by the sponsor, and of any other support the sponsor may provide. The evidence should normally be in the form of international money orders or a letter from the bank confirming that money is transferred on a regular basis. Other support may be a house provided by the sponsor or rent from land or property owned by him. This will be compared by the BIA with any other financial support available to the applicant from other sources, including money given to him by other relatives not in the UK and any income received from land, property or a pension. Consideration is also given as to whether or not the payments from the sponsor are essential to help the applicant achieve a reasonable lifestyle.

In addition, the overseas applicant will have to demonstrate that he has no other close relatives to turn to in his own country. If there is a relative in the applicant's own country who is able and willing to support him, it would not be unreasonable to expect him to turn to that relative for support, even if the sponsor in the UK is financially in a better position to do so. Close relatives may be sons, daughters, brothers, sisters, grandchildren, uncles, aunts, and possibly nephews, nieces, or in-laws. However, it should be noted that this will largely depend on their culture. For example, in the Indian sub-continent, married women are unlikely to be able to provide support. Alternatively, if there are several close relatives, there is no reason why it cannot be a collective ability among them to support the applicant. Although the onus is on the applicant to demonstrate that he has no close relative to turn to, BIA guidance is that any refusal on this basis should be usually backed up with sound evidence that this is not the case, such that, on occasions, it may be necessary to make local enquiries.

Applications from married couples are not refused solely on the basis that they have each other to turn to. Account is to be taken of the age and health of the applicants, as well as the ability of other relatives to visit them regularly.

Further, the applicant needs to show that he will be maintained and accommodated together with any dependants, by the sponsor, without recourse to public funds. The sponsor must have the means to maintain and accommodate the applicant and BIA guidance is that in the case of elderly dependent relatives he should be requested to complete the sponsorship declaration attached to the prescribed application form. The DfWP can then take action to claim back from the sponsor any benefits which may be claimed by the applicant (under the Social Security Administration Act 1992 (SSAA 1992), s 106).

In many cases, parents must also satisfy the 'exceptional compassionate circumstances' test, which applies to other relatives. This will be so if the parent is divorced, unless he or she is over 65, and has remarried but cannot look to the children of the second marriage for support. It will also apply to parents under 65. What are 'exceptional compassionate circumstances'? The BIA guidance states:

> each application must be considered on the individual merits of the case, it is therefore not possible to list every possible circumstance which may arise, however, illness, incapacity, isolation and poverty are all compassionate circumstances which should be considered.

In the case of *Nessa v Chief Adjudication Officer* [1999] 1 WLR 1937, the Tribunal held that being a relative, being financially dependent, and living alone, are conditions that must be met before the most exceptional compassionate circumstances can be considered, and such do not form part of those circumstances. A comparison should be made between the applicant's position and that of other people who are dependent upon relatives in the UK and who are living alone.

The Rules apply to grandparents in the same way as to parents.

14.16.4 Examples

Example 1

Sayana is a widow aged 72, and a citizen of Bangladesh. Her only son, Abdul, is settled in the UK, and she wishes to join him. He has been sending her money for many years, and could support her in the UK. The evidence presented to the entry clearance officer shows that she is living in her son's home in Bangladesh, and has brothers living in the same area who are fairly well off and would look after her if necessary. Does she meet the requirements of para 318?

She does not need to meet the 'exceptional compassionate circumstances' test, as she is a widow aged 72. She is financially dependent on her son. However, the Home Office may argue that she has close relatives in Bangladesh, to whom she could turn if necessary for financial support. Sayana cannot argue in reply that her brothers could not give the emotional support which her only son could provide. This argument was available under former Immigration Rules (see *R v Immigration Appeal Tribunal, ex p Sayana Khatun* [1989] Imm AR 482) but the current Rules make financial support the crucial issue. She does not meet the requirements of para 318.

Example 2

Agnes is a US citizen, aged 60. She is a divorcee. Her son, Bruce, is settled in the UK. Agnes is fairly wealthy, but is suffering from terminal cancer and wishes to spend her last years with her son in the UK. She has no close relatives in the USA. Does she meet the requirements of the Rules?

As a divorcee, she would have to meet the 'exceptional compassionate circumstances' test, and in the circumstances might well do so. However, she does not appear to be financially dependent on her son at all. She does not meet the requirements of the Rules, and would have to seek leave outside them.

14.16.5 Children over 18

If a child is over 18 at the time of an application to join a parent settled in the UK, he must qualify under para 318, in the same way as other relatives. The 'exceptional compassionate circumstances' test will apply (ie over and above the basic injustice of wrongly separating a family for many years). The BIA guidance is that:

> such applications will have to be decided on the individual merits of the case. As the majority of such applications will be from persons who are over the age of 18, but not necessarily old and frail, the compassionate circumstances will need to be very strong. The circumstances will have to be such that the applicant cannot function (either because of illness or disability) without the help and support of friends or relatives and that no such help or support is available to them in the country where they are living.

If the applicant is a young single or divorced woman living in a country where it is claimed that it is socially unacceptable for her to live alone, this may be taken into account by the BIA when considering whether there are sufficient exceptional compassionate circumstances, but such a situation is not, on its own, a sufficiently compelling reason to grant leave to enter or remain. These guidelines have been interpreted as meaning that the adult child must be 'necessarily' dependent on his parents, rather than by 'choice'. It also appears that 23 years of age is about the cut-off point.

> **Example**
>
> Alice is a citizen of Sri Lanka. Her father who is a widower is settled in the UK as a result of his recent marriage to a British citizen. Alice was 17 at the time of his marriage, but chose to stay in Sri Lanka to marry. She is now 22 and is divorced. Her former husband is not supporting her, and she relies entirely on money remitted by her father. She has no other relatives in Sri Lanka who would support her.
>
> Alice can only be admitted to the UK if she satisfies the 'exceptional compassionate circumstances' test. In assessing this, the entry clearance officer is entitled to take into account that, as a result of money remitted by her father, she is not in immediate financial need (see *Begum v Immigration Appeal Tribunal* [1994] Imm AR 381). Other relevant factors would be the fact that she has lived independently since attaining 18, her likely future earning capacity, and her prospects of remarriage. She will find it difficult to satisfy the test.

14.16.6 Human rights

Does the 'exceptional compassionate circumstances' test contravene Article 8 of the ECHR (the right to respect for private and family life) by imposing a disproportionate obstacle on the enjoyment of family life for those applicants who are subject to it? 'No', said Burnton J in the case of *R (Sayania) v Immigration Appeal Tribunal* (2001) LTL, 9 April.

14.17 Asylum-seekers and refugees

14.17.1 Introduction

Claims for asylum in the UK are considered in accordance with the UK's obligations under the 1951 United Nations Convention Relating to the Status of Refugees and the 1967 Protocol. A person who fulfils the criteria set out in the 1951 Convention or 1967 Protocol is a refugee. The UK, in granting asylum, is recognising the refugee's status and extending the protection required under its international obligations. Part 11 of the Immigration Rules deals with asylum claims. In particular see para 334.

Article 1 of the United Nations Convention Relating to the Status of Refugees 1951 and Protocol of 1967 (the Geneva Convention) defines the term 'refugee' in international law. The main part of the definition refers to a person who 'owing to a well founded fear of being persecuted for reasons of race, religion, nationality, membership of a particular social group, or political opinion, is outside his country of nationality and is unable, or owing to such fear, unwilling to avail himself of the protection of that country'.

Useful guidance on the interpretation of this definition is given in the *Handbook on Procedures and Criteria for Determining Refugee Status* published by the Office of the United Nations High Commissioner for Refugees. This is widely used, both by practitioners and by the Home Office.

Council Directive 2004/83/EC sets out minimum standards for the qualification and status of third country nationals or stateless persons as refugees, or as persons who otherwise need international protection. This Directive has been implemented by the Refugee or Person in Need of International Protection (Qualification) Regulations 2006 (SI 2006/2525) ('the Qualification Regulations 2006'). See **Appendix 12** to this Part of the book.

When considering whether a person is entitled to be treated as a refugee, it is important to consider each section of the Geneva Convention definition carefully.

14.17.2 'Well founded fear of persecution'

The claimant must be in fear of persecution, but his claim can be rejected if there is no reasonable likelihood of persecution (*R v Secretary of State for the Home Department, ex p Sivakumaran and conjoined appeals (UN High Commissioner for Refugees Intervening)* [1988] 1 All ER 193). The main issue will be the credibility of the claimant's testimony that he has a genuine fear (the subjective test), but the Home Office may rely on evidence of conditions in the country from which he is fleeing to show that there is insufficient basis for the fear (the objective test). The Home Office Country of Origin Information Service has produced assessments of certain countries that produce a significant number of asylum claims, including Afghanistan, Angola, Turkey and Uganda. These are used for background purposes by caseworkers. They are available on the Home Office website: www.homeoffice.gov.uk/rds/country-reports.html.

Obviously, the applicant may find it difficult to provide evidence of events in his home country and many statements may be unsupported. According to the UNHCR *Handbook*, statements should not necessarily be rejected for that reason: 'If the applicant's account appears credible, he should, unless there are good reasons to the contrary, be given the benefit of the doubt' (para 196). Unsupported statements need not, however, be accepted if they are inconsistent with the general account put forward by the applicant (para 197).

'Persecution' is not defined in the Geneva Convention on refugees. The UNHCR *Handbook* suggests that while it will often involve a threat to life or liberty, it could extend to other threats. Discrimination against a particular group does not of itself amount to persecution; but it may do so if serious, for example if it stops someone practising his religion, or earning a livelihood. 'Persecution' does not mean 'punishment'. A person who fears punishment for commission of a common-law crime will not normally be regarded as a refugee, unless, for example, the law under which he is to be punished is seriously discriminatory.

Further examples of persecution are listed in reg 5(2) of the Qualification Regulations 2006. These include an act of physical or mental violence, including an act of sexual violence; a legal, administrative, police, or judicial measure which in itself is discriminatory, or which is implemented in a discriminatory manner; and prosecution or punishment which is disproportionate or discriminatory.

In *R (Sivakumar) v Secretary of State for the Home Department* [2003] 2 All ER 1097, the House of Lords held that it is the severity of the treatment inflicted on the applicant that has a logical bearing on the issues. Excessive or arbitrary punishment can amount to persecution.

Regulation 5(1) of the Qualification Regulations 2006 provides that an act of persecution must be sufficiently serious by its nature or repetition as to constitute a severe violation of a basic human right, in particular a right from which derogation cannot be made under Article 15 of the ECHR. The basic human rights from which derogation cannot be made under the ECHR include Article 2 (right to life – save that derogation is permitted in respect of deaths resulting from lawful acts of war); Article 3 (prohibition of torture, inhuman or degrading treatment or punishment); Article 4(1) (prohibition of slavery) and Article 7 (no punishment without law). Alternatively, persecution may arise from an accumulation of various measures, including a violation of a human right which is sufficiently severe as to affect an individual in this manner.

A person does not have to be singled out for adverse treatment in order to be said to be persecuted (see *R v Secretary of State for the Home Department, ex p Jeyakumaran (Selladurai)* [1994] Imm AR 45). Discrimination may amount to persecution – this accords with the Tribunal decision of *Padhu* (12318), concerning the inability to work and deprivation of State benefits due to ethnic origin. What if the persecution feared comes from non-State actors? In the case of *Gashi and Nikshiqi v Secretary of State for the Home Department (United Nations High Commissioner for Refugees Intervening)* [1997] INLR 96, the Tribunal held that persecution includes the failure of a State to protect:

(a) those rights which are non-derogative even in times of compelling national emergency (the right to life; prohibition against torture and cruel, inhumane or degrading treatment);

(b) those rights which are derogative during an officially recognised life-threatening public emergency (freedom from arbitrary arrest and detention; fair trial);

(c) some aspects of those rights which require States to take steps to the maximum of their available resources to realise rights progressively in a non-discriminatory manner (the right to earn a livelihood; the right to a basic education; the right to food, housing and medical care).

Whilst there must be a current fear of persecution for a Convention reason upon return (see *Adan v Secretary of State for the Home Department* [1999] 1 AC 293), persecution suffered in the past is relevant to whether a person has a current, well-founded fear of persecution. This is recognised by para 339K of the Immigration Rules. It provides that the fact that a person has already been subject to persecution, or to direct threats of such persecution, will be regarded as a serious indication of the person's well-founded fear of persecution, unless there are good reasons to consider that such persecution will not be repeated. Equally, whilst a past history of no persecution is not determinative of future risks, unless circumstances in an asylum-seeker's return country have deteriorated or some other special factor is present, it is inevitable that an asylum-seeker will have difficulty in showing future risk in the absence of any finding of past persecution: see *Becerikil v Secretary of State for the Home Department* [2006] EWCA Civ 693.

The applicable law as to persecution by non-State actors is the House of Lords' decision in *Horvath v Secretary of State for the Home Department* [2001] 1 AC 489. This established that persecution implied a failure by the State to make protection available against the ill-treatment or violence which had been suffered at the hands of the persecutors. In such a case, the failure of the State to provide protection was an essential element, and accordingly the person claiming refugee status had to show that the feared persecution consisted of acts of violence against which the State was unable or unwilling to provide protection. Such a conclusion was consistent with the principle of surrogacy which underpinned the Convention, namely that the protection afforded by the Convention was activated only upon the failure of protection by the home State. Moreover, the application of that principle rested upon the assumption that the home State was not expected to achieve complete protection against random and isolated attacks. Accordingly, in determining whether the protection afforded by the applicant's home country was sufficient for the purposes of the Convention, the court had to apply a practical standard which took proper account of the duty owed by a State to all its nationals, rather than a standard which eliminated all risk. Thus, the sufficiency of State protection was to be measured not by the existence of a real risk of an abuse of human rights but by the availability of a system for the protection of the citizen and a reasonable willingness to operate that system.

Can an attack upon an applicant's spouse or close family member amount to persecution of the applicant for the purposes of an asylum claim, even though there was no direct threat to the applicant himself? 'Yes', said the Court of Appeal in *Frantisek Katrinak v Secretary of State for the Home Department* [2001] INLR 499. As Schiemann LJ said:

> If I return with my wife to a country where there is a reasonable degree of likelihood that she will be subjected to further grave physical abuse for racial reasons, that puts me in a situation where there is a reasonable degree of risk that I will be persecuted. It is possible to persecute a husband or a member of a family by what you do to other members of his immediate family. The essential task for the decision taker in these sort of circumstances is to consider what is reasonably likely to happen to the wife and whether that is reasonably likely to affect the husband in such a way as to amount to persecution of him.

Example 1
Bela has fled from his own country which is engaged in civil war. His farm has been destroyed in a battle, and he has no other means of earning his living.

The Home Office may argue that Bela is a displaced person rather than a refugee, unless he can show, for example, that he is likely to suffer persecution because he is identified with one of the sides in the civil war.

Example 2
Chaka has left his country because high taxes and an economic crisis have caused his business to fail.

The Home Office may argue that he is an economic migrant rather than a refugee, unless he can show, for example, that the tax measures were directed at a particular ethnic group of which he is a member, designed to destroy their economic position.

14.17.3 'For reasons of race, religion, nationality, membership of a particular social group or political opinion'

The term 'nationality' here is used in a broad sense, covering ethnic or linguistic groups, whether or not they have a distinct citizenship.

Over recent years, the courts have given much consideration as to what is meant by the expression 'particular social group'. In the joint cases of *Islam (Shahana) v Secretary of State for the Home Department; R v Immigration Appeal Tribunal and Secretary of State for the Home Department, ex p Syeda Shah* [1999] INLR 144, the House of Lords had to decide if two Pakistani women, who had fled Pakistan after false allegations of adultery, and violence by their husbands, were part of such a group. The House held that a 'particular social group' consists of a group of persons who share a common, immutable characteristic that either is beyond the power of an individual to change, or is so fundamental to the individual's identity or conscience that he ought not to be required to change it. Thus, as gender is an immutable characteristic that is beyond the power of the individual to change and as discrimination against women is prevalent in Pakistan, in violation of fundamental rights and freedoms, women in Pakistan constitute a particular social group.

In the *Islam* and *Shah* appeals, Lord Hoffmann asked:

> What is the reason for the persecution which the appellants fear? Here it is important to notice that it is made up of two elements. First, there is the threat of violence to Mrs Islam by her husband and his political friends and to Mrs Shah by her husband. This is a personal affair, directed against them as individuals. Secondly, there is the inability or unwillingness of the State to do anything to protect them. There is nothing personal about this. The evidence was that the State would not assist them because they were women. It denied them a protection against violence which it would have given to men. These two elements have to be combined to constitute persecution within the meaning of the Convention.

See also *RG (Ethiopia) v Secretary of State for the Home Department* [2006] EWCA Civ 339, where it was held that women and girls in Ethiopia constitute a particular social group. The Court found institutionalised discrimination, since the penal law in Ethiopia legitimises the marriage of abducted and raped girls to their violators, which marriage then exempts the latter from punishment. This, and the evidence of a lack of protection of women against sexual abuse and serious discrimination, shows a degree of complicity by the State in the treatment of women in Ethiopia, sufficient to conclude that women constitute a particular social group.

Regulation 6(1)(d) of the Qualification Regulations 2006, as interpreted in *K v Secretary of State for the Home Department; Fornah v Secretary of State for the Home Department* [2006] UKHL 45, [2007] 1 All ER 671, provides two useful guidelines defining a particular social group. First, where members of that group share an innate characteristic, or a common background that cannot be changed, or share a characteristic or belief that is so fundamental to identity or conscience that a person should not be forced to renounce it. Secondly, where the group has a distinct identity in the relevant country, because it is perceived as being different by the surrounding society.

To show persecution on grounds of political opinion, it is not enough for the claimant to establish that he holds opinions which his government opposes. He must show that they will not tolerate his opinions, and that they are aware that he holds them. Where the claimant has committed criminal offences in the course of political opposition, he cannot base a claim to refugee status on fear of his country's normal punishment for that offence.

Example

Enrico is a member of a minority linguistic group, and of the political party which represents it. The party is campaigning for language rights, for example in regional schools, and its political activities are permitted. His national government will not concede these rights and pursues discriminatory policies. Enrico has fled the country after setting fire to a school which refused to use the minority language.

The Home Office may argue that Enrico does not fear persecution on grounds of his political opinions, but rather punishment for an ordinary criminal offence. However, he may be able to show that his punishment would be excessive or arbitrary, which would amount to persecution. The discriminatory measures in themselves may not be sufficiently serious to amount to persecution on grounds of nationality.

In what circumstances may a person who objects to carrying out compulsory military service be granted asylum? In *Sepet v Secretary of State for the Home Department* [2003] 3 All ER 304, the House of Lords held that refugee status should be accorded to a person who refuses to undertake compulsory military service on the grounds that such service would or might require him to commit atrocities or gross human rights abuses, or participate in a conflict condemned by the international community, or where refusal to serve would earn grossly excessive or disproportionate punishment.

Even if a claimant does not hold political views which his government opposes, it may well be that the government believes that he does. So a person to whom a political opinion is imputed may qualify for refugee status: see *Sivakumar v Secretary of State for the Home Department* [2002] INLR 310.

> **Example**
> Adolf has fled from his own country because his brother has been imprisoned for political activities.
> The Home Office may argue that Adolf's fear is not well founded, unless he can show that persecution is for an imputed political opinion or extends to the social group associated with the political activity.

As to the meaning of the word 'religion' see *Omoruyi v Secretary of State for the Home Department* [2001] INLR 33. In the case the applicant was a Nigerian Christian persecuted by a group described variously as 'a secret cult ... associated with idol worshipping to the extent of drinking blood', 'a mafia organisation involving criminal acts', and a 'devil cult' carrying out 'rituals', namely 'the sacrificing of animals to a graven image'. The court held that the persecution was not for a Convention reason (ie it was not related to the applicant's beliefs but to the fact that he had failed to comply with certain demands made by the cult) and therefore his application for asylum failed.

Note that reg 6(1)(b) of the Qualification Regulations 2006 provides that the concept of religion includes, for example, the holding of theistic, non-theistic and atheistic beliefs; the participation in, or abstention from, formal worship in private or in public, either alone or in community with others; other religious acts or expressions of view, or forms of personal or communal conduct based on or mandated by any religious belief.

14.17.4 'Is outside the country of his nationality'

No one can claim to be a refugee until he has left the country of which he is a citizen. This means that a claimant cannot normally obtain a visa from a UK entry clearance officer in his country, clearing him to enter the UK as a refugee. He must (somehow) find his way to the UK and make the claim on arrival. This may be difficult, as airlines are fined for carrying people without correct travel documents (Immigration (Carriers' Liability) Act 1987).

14.17.4.1 The internal flight alternative or internal relocation

The claimant must be outside his country owing to fear of persecution there. What if the persecution is to be feared in only part of the country? Paragraph 339O of the Immigration Rules provides that the Secretary of State will not grant asylum if in part of the country of origin a person would not have a well-founded fear of being persecuted, and the person can reasonably be expected to stay in that part of the country. So if someone would be safe only if he lived in a remote village, separated from his family, his flight from the country can still be said to be based on a fear of persecution there (see *R v Immigration Appeal Tribunal, ex p Jonah* [1985] Imm AR 7).

The House of Lords, in *Januzi v Secretary of State for the Home Department* [2006] UKHL 5, gave further guidance on this issue. Lord Hope of Craighead said (paras 47–49):

> The question where the issue of internal relocation is raised can, then, be defined quite simply. As Linden JA put it in *Thirunavukkarasu v Canada (Minister of Employment and Immigration)* (1993) 109 DLR (4th) 682, 687, it is whether it would be unduly harsh to expect a claimant who is being persecuted for a Convention reason in one part of his country to move to a less hostile part before seeking refugee status abroad. The words 'unduly harsh' set the standard that must be met for this to be regarded as unreasonable. If the claimant can live a relatively normal life there judged by the standards that prevail in his country of nationality generally, and if he can reach the less hostile part without undue hardship or undue difficulty, it will not be unreasonable to expect him to move there.
>
> Care must, of course, be taken not to allow the argument that there is an internal relocation option to defeat the basic purposes of the Convention. That is why there is a further question that must be considered where the claimant has a well-founded fear of persecution for a Convention reason which is due to action taken, or threatened to be taken, against him by the state or by state agents within the country of his nationality and it is suggested that he could reasonably be expected to live in a place of relocation there. The dangers of a return to a country where the state is in full control of events and its agents of persecution are active everywhere within its borders are obvious. It hardly needs to be said that in such a case internal relocation is not an option that is available. Remoteness of the suggested place of relocation from the place of origin will provide no answer to the claimant's assertion that he has a well-founded fear of persecution throughout the country of his nationality.
>
> On the other hand control of events by the state may be so fragmented, or its activities may be being conducted in such a way, that it will be possible to identify places within its territory where there are no grounds for thinking that persecution by the state or its agents of the claimant for a Convention reason will be resorted to. A civil war may take that pattern where the extent of it is localised. So too may the process of ethnic cleansing affecting people of the claimant's ethnicity which is in progress in one area but not in others. The state may be ruthless in its attempts to move people of a given ethnicity out of one area. But it may be benign in its treatment of them when they reach an area which it regards as appropriate for people of that ethnicity. Of course, one kind of brutality may lead to another. Those who object to the state's policy may be treated differently from those who do not, wherever they happen to be for the time being. And those who move to a safe area may be at risk of being forced to move back again. The situation in the country of the claimant's nationality may be so unstable, or the persecution which the state condones in one place may be so difficult to limit to a given area, that it would be quite unreasonable to expect the claimant to relocate anywhere within its territory.

14.17.5 'And is unable, or, owing to such fear, is unwilling to avail himself of the protection of that country'

A claimant would be unable to avail himself of his country's protection if, for example, it refused entry to him, or refused to issue him with a passport. A claimant who fears persecution will normally be unwilling to accept his government's protection, and it is inconsistent with his claim to refugee status if, for example, he wishes to retain his national passport.

14.17.6 Exclusion from refugee status

Article 1F of the Geneva Convention excludes the following claimants from asylum because they are considered not to be deserving of international protection. This is because there are serious reasons for considering that they:

(a) have committed a crime against peace, a war crime or a crime against humanity; or

(b) have committed a serious non-political crime outside the country of refuge prior to admission into that country; or

(c) are guilty of acts contrary to the purposes and principles of the United Nations.

Note that reg 7(2) of the Qualification Regulations 2006 interprets the meaning of Article 1F(b) as follows:

> The reference to 'serious non-political crime' includes a particularly cruel action, even if it is committed with an allegedly political objective. The reference to the crime being committed outside the country of refuge prior to his admission as a refugee shall mean the time up to and including the day on which a residence permit [signifying the grant of refugee status] is issued.

Also note that s 54 of the IANA 2006 interprets the meaning of Article 1F(c). It provides that acts of committing, preparing or instigating terrorism, or encouraging or inducing others to do so, are included within the meaning of what constitutes 'acts contrary to the purposes and principles of the United Nations'.

Example

Danilow fled from his country after being imprisoned for distributing political leaflets. In order to finance his escape he commits an armed robbery.

Whether the armed robbery amounts to a serious non-political crime depends on whether it has been committed for political motives, or for personal reasons or gain, and whether the act was proportionate to the alleged objective. The Home Office may well argue that Danilow's criminal character outweighs his character as a bona fide refugee (see *T v Secretary of State for the Home Department* (1996) *The Times*, 23 May).

14.17.7 What is an 'asylum claim'?

Paragraph 327 of the Immigration Rules defines an 'asylum claim' as a claim that it would be contrary to the UK's obligations under the Convention to remove the claimant or require him to leave. This refers in particular to Article 33 of the Geneva Convention on refugees, which prohibits expulsion or return ('*refoulement*') of a refugee to the frontiers of territories where his life or freedom would be threatened on account of his race, religion, nationality, membership of a particular social group or political opinion. However, Article 33 does not apply where the refugee has been convicted of a particularly serious crime and is a danger to the community. See NIAA 2002, s 72 and the NIAA 2002 (Specification of Particularly Serious Crimes) Order 2004 (SI 2004/1910).

14.17.7.1 Safe third country exception (AI(TC)A 2004, Sch 3)

There will be no breach of obligation if the UK returns the refugee to a 'safe country' which itself has an obligation to grant him asylum, and which could be expected to fulfil the requirements of the Geneva Convention on refugees. The general principle operated by governments is that a refugee should seek asylum in the first 'safe country' he reaches.

Under EC Council Regulation 343/2003 ('the Regulation') or the Dublin Convention, the UK may return an asylum seeker to the EU Member State which has responsibility for the asylum claim under the terms of the Geneva Convention on refugees (eg because that State granted him a visa, or he first entered that State as an illegal entrant). The Home Office will not remove the asylum seeker until the State receiving him has accepted its responsibility under the Regulation or the Dublin Convention. Once that has happened, the Home Office will assume that the receiving State will itself consider the claim and grant refugee status if the claim is well founded.

In these cases, it is possible for someone who meets the Geneva Convention on refugees' definition of 'refugee' to claim asylum in the UK, but for his claim, on examination by the Home Office, to fall outside the statutory definition of an asylum claim in the UK. Because return is to a 'safe country', the Home Office may refuse these claims 'without substantive consideration', that is without looking at other aspects of the claimant's case, such as whether he fears persecution in his home country (Immigration Rules, para 345).

Schedule 3 to the AI(TC)A 2004 (which replaced earlier similar provisions) is intended to deal with the fact that many Regulation or Dublin Convention cases were, in the Government's opinion, subject to unnecessary and lengthy delay as a result of judicial review applications which challenged the safety of the transfer. The Schedule sets out in Parts 2 to 5 a graduated approach to the 'safety' of third countries for the purposes of the Geneva Convention on refugees and the ECHR. Broadly, these are as follows.

Part 2 of Sch 3 deals with countries that are deemed safe for Geneva Convention on refugees' purposes and for claims that onward removal from the State would breach the ECHR. All other human rights claims against removal will be certified by the Secretary of State as clearly unfounded unless he is satisfied that they are not. The countries listed at para 2 of Part 2 are those which are subject to or have agreed to be bound by the Dublin Convention, currently the members of the EU (see **13.7.1** and **Appendix 5** to this Part of the book) together with Norway and Iceland.

Paragraph 4 of Part 2 disapplies s 77 of the NIAA 2002 (which prevents removal while an asylum claim is pending) where the Secretary of State certifies that a person is to be removed to a listed State and he is not a national or citizen of that State. Paragraph 5 of Part 2 prevents a person being removed from bringing an appeal within the UK on the basis that the country is not safe for Geneva Convention on refugees' purposes or ECHR purposes in terms of onward removal. Paragraph 5 provides that where a human rights claim made on another basis is certified as clearly unfounded, a person being removed is similarly prevented from bringing an appeal within the UK. Lastly, para 5 provides that any human rights claim against removal (other than on the basis of onward removal) will be certified by the Secretary of State as clearly unfounded unless he is satisfied that it is not.

14.17.7.2 Human rights and removal in breach of UK's obligations

In the case of *R (Ullah) v Special Adjudicator; Do v Secretary of State for the Home Department* [2004] UKHL 26, the House of Lords had to consider this question: to what extent does the Human Rights Act 1998 inhibit the UK from expelling asylum-seekers who fall short of demonstrating a well-founded fear of persecution? The House held that removal may in exceptional circumstances give rise to an issue under Articles 2 to 9 of the ECHR, and hence engage the responsibility of the UK under the Convention. Substantial grounds will have been shown for believing that the person concerned, if removed, faces a near certainty of death, or a real risk of being subjected to torture or to inhuman or degrading treatment or punishment etc in the country to which he is being removed. See in particular the summary of Lord Bingham at para 24. Also see *R (Razgar) v Secretary of State for the Home Department* [2004] UKHL 27 and *Huang v Secretary of State for the Home Department* [2007] UKHL 11, for a more detailed discussion of Article 8.

Specific country guidance given by the AIT may assist, eg *Eritrea CG* [2005] UKIAT 00106 provides that persons who would be perceived as draft evaders or deserters face a real risk of persecution and ill-treatment on being returned to Eritrea.

Ever since the ECtHR held in *D v United Kingdom* (1997) 24 EHRR 423 that the expulsion of an AIDS sufferer to St Kitts would breach Article 3 of the ECHR, the Strasbourg court has sought to distinguish that case. In the case of *D*, the court extended the reach of Article 3. The court noted that Contracting States have the right, as a matter of well-established international law and subject to their treaty obligations including the ECHR, to control the entry, residence and expulsion of aliens. The court applied Article 3 in what it described as the 'very exceptional circumstances' of that case, namely that the applicant was in the final stage of a terminal illness, AIDS, and had no prospect of medical care or family support on expulsion to St Kitts. In *N(FC) v Secretary of State for the Home Department* [2005] UKHL 31, [2005] 2 WLR 1124, the House of Lords was not persuaded to extend Article 3 any further. The House held that it must be shown that the applicant's medical condition has reached such a critical state that there are compelling humanitarian grounds for not removing him or her to a place which lacks the medical and social services which he or she would need to prevent acute suffering.

Caution needs to be taken when considering an Article 3 argument. In *R v Secretary of State for the Home Department, ex p Bagdanavicius* [2005] UKHL 38, [2005] 2 WLR 1359, Lord Brown of Eaton-under-Heywood gave the judgment of the House, and stressed at para 30: 'Certainly your Lordships should state for the guidance of practitioners and tribunals generally that in the great majority of cases an article 3 claim to avoid expulsion will add little if anything to an asylum claim.' His Lordship indicated that different tests apply to acts by the State as opposed to non-state actors:

> The plain fact is that the argument throughout has been bedevilled by a failure to grasp the distinction in non-state agent cases between on the one hand the risk of serious harm and on the other hand the risk of treatment contrary to article 3. In cases where the risk 'emanates from intentionally inflicted acts of the public authorities in the receiving country' (the language of para 49 of *D v United Kingdom* 24 EHRR 423, 447) one can use those terms interchangeably: the intentionally inflicted acts would without more constitute the proscribed treatment. Where, however, the risk emanates from non-state bodies, that is not so: any harm inflicted by non-state agents will not constitute article 3 ill-treatment unless in addition the state has failed to provide reasonable protection. If someone is beaten up and

seriously injured by a criminal gang, the member state will not be in breach of article 3 unless it has failed in its positive duty to provide reasonable protection against such criminal acts ... Non-state agents do not subject people to torture or the other proscribed forms of ill-treatment, however violently they treat them: what, however, would transform such violent treatment into article 3 ill-treatment would be the state's failure to provide reasonable protection against it (para 24).

14.17.8 Successful claimants

By accepting an asylum claim, the Home Office undertakes to confer on the refugee the protection to which he is entitled under the Geneva Convention on refugees. The refugee has full rights to live and work and claim benefits in the UK, and to be joined by his dependants, whether or not they also qualify as refugees. The refugee will be given leave to remain for five years. Thereafter an application can be made for indefinite leave to remain in the UK. The refugee is entitled to a Convention Travel Document, which replaces his national passport, and his five years' limited leave is indorsed on a residence permit.

14.17.9 Making an asylum claim

Anyone in the UK can make an asylum claim, whatever his immigration status. He may be someone who has arrived without a visa or with forged documents, or someone who has obtained limited leave to enter for a different reason (eg as a visitor), an overstayer, or even an illegal entrant. The claim can be made on entry or after entry to the UK.

In April 2007 the Home Office introduced a 'New Asylum Model' (NAM), which aims to render a decision on an asylum claim within one month of the claim being made. To act so quickly, the Home Office official responsible for the case, known as 'the case owner' conducts the claim from start to finish to a strict timetable. The case owner should also work closely with the claimant's representative.

On the day a claim is made, the claimant has a screening interview to establish his identity and nationality. At this point fingerprints and photographs are also taken. A few basic questions about the claim are asked. The claim is then transferred to a NAM centre at Glasgow, Cardiff, Leeds, Liverpool, Solihull, Central London or West London. The claimant meets the case owner within three working days. By the tenth working day, the representative should submit the claimant's statement and any supporting evidence. In the following days, the case owner and representative discuss the case to work out what parts of the claim are accepted and what further evidence is needed. On the fifteenth working day, the claimant has an interview. Following any further discussion between the case owner and the representative, the case owner's decision, whether to grant or refuse asylum, is given by the twentieth working day.

14.17.10 The Home Office decision

In deciding the case, the Home Office is obliged to apply the Geneva Convention on refugees. An adviser must ensure that the claimant provides all the evidence he has which would help to establish his refugee status. As explained above, there are subjective and objective criteria.

The main issue on the question of 'well founded fear of persecution' will often be the credibility of the claimant. He will damage his case if he makes inconsistent statements, or if his story is confused. An adviser can help by taking him through his story chronologically, ensuring that he has the details clear in his own mind.

If the Home Office has evidence of conditions in the claimant's country which suggests that his fear is not well founded, this will be disclosed to the claimant. This will be difficult to contest, but organisations such as Amnesty International or the Refugee Legal Centre may provide helpful evidence.

14.17.11 Consideration of cases

The Immigration Rules (paras 339I–339N) list some factors which are taken into account. These start by imposing a duty on the claimant to submit to the Secretary of State, as soon as possible, all material factors needed to substantiate the asylum claim. These material factors include the claimant's statement of the reasons for making an asylum claim; all documentation at the claimant's disposal regarding his age, background, identity, nationality(ies), country(ies) and place(s) of previous residence, previous asylum applications, and travel routes; and identity and travel documents.

It is further the duty of the claimant to substantiate the claim. Paragraph 339L of the Immigration Rules provides that where aspects of the claimant's statements are not supported by documentary or other evidence, those aspects will not need confirmation when *all* of the following conditions are met:

(a) the claimant has made a genuine effort to substantiate his asylum claim;

(b) all material factors at the claimant's disposal have been submitted, and a satisfactory explanation regarding any lack of other relevant material has been given;

(c) the claimant's statements are found to be coherent and plausible, and do not run counter to available specific and general information relevant to his case;

(d) the claimant has made an asylum claim at the earliest possible time, unless he can demonstrate good reason for not having done so; and

(e) the general credibility of the claimant has been established.

Paragraph 339M of the Immigration Rules provides that the Secretary of State may consider that a person has not substantiated his asylum claim if he fails, without reasonable explanation, to make a prompt and full disclosure of material facts, either orally or in writing, or otherwise to assist the Secretary of State in establishing the facts of the case. This includes, for example, a failure to attend an interview, failure to report to a designated place to be fingerprinted, failure to complete an asylum questionnaire or failure to comply with a requirement to report to an immigration officer for examination.

Section 8(1) of the AI(TC)A 2004 includes similar guidelines for assessing the credibility of the claimant. Any behaviour by a claimant that is designed or likely to conceal information or to mislead, or which obstructs or delays the handling or resolution of the claim or the taking of a decision, may be said to damage credibility.

By s 8(2) the following kinds of behaviour are to be treated as designed or likely to conceal information or to mislead:

(a) the failure without reasonable explanation to produce a passport on request to an immigration officer or to the Secretary of State (see also **13.5.8**);

(b) the production of a document which is not a valid passport as if it were;

(c) the destruction, alteration or disposal, in each case without reasonable explanation, of a passport;

(d) the destruction, alteration or disposal, in each case without reasonable explanation, of a ticket or other document connected with travel;

(e) the failure without reasonable explanation to answer a question asked by a deciding authority.

This section also applies to a failure by the claimant to take advantage of a reasonable opportunity to make an asylum claim or human rights claim while in any EEA country, or failure to make an asylum claim or human rights claim before being notified of an immigration decision, unless the claim relies wholly on matters arising after the notification.

14.17.12 Dangers of making an unsuccessful claim

In many cases, an entrant may feel that he has nothing to lose in making an asylum claim. However, his adviser should consider whether he has any other basis for remaining in the UK, which might be prejudiced by an unsuccessful claim. If an applicant already has limited leave, the Home Office may, having refused asylum, proceed to consider whether he still meets the requirements of the Rules under which he was admitted to the UK. If he does not, his existing leave can be 'curtailed' (under AIAA 1993, s 7) and he may then be removed from the UK.

Example

Manuel was admitted to the UK as a student with 12 months' leave. Three months later he claims asylum. The Home Office refuses the claim. The Home Office may argue that he no longer meets the requirements of para 57 of the Immigration Rules (see **14.2**), for example because he does not intend to leave the UK at the end of his studies. His leave can be curtailed (see **13.6.7**) so that he is required to leave his course before it ends.

14.17.13 Humanitarian protection and discretionary leave

Where the Home Office does not grant an asylum application it may nevertheless grant humanitarian protection (previously known as exceptional leave to remain), outside the Immigration Rules. Humanitarian protection is granted to anyone who is unable to demonstrate a claim for asylum but who will face a serious risk to life or person arising from the death penalty or unlawful killing or torture, inhuman or degrading treatment or punishment. Serious criminals, including war criminals, terrorists or others who raise a threat to national security and anyone who is considered to be of bad character, conduct or associations, are excluded. Protection is usually granted for up to five years. If at the end of that period, following a review, it is decided that further protection is needed, a claimant is usually granted settled status. If protection is no longer needed and a person has no other basis of stay in the UK, he is expected to leave.

What if humanitarian protection is refused? Discretionary leave may still be granted for a limited number of specific reasons. These people will either not be considered to be in need of international protection, or will have been excluded from such protection. It may be granted, say, to an applicant who has an Article 8 claim or an Article 3 claim only on medical grounds or extreme humanitarian cases, or who is able to demonstrate particularly compelling reasons why removal would not be appropriate. An individual grant of discretionary leave should not be made for more than three years. After the period has expired the claimant's situation is reviewed, with further leave granted if appropriate. A person on this type of leave will normally become eligible to apply for settlement after six years. However, a person who has been excluded from asylum and/or humanitarian protection but granted discretionary leave is excluded from settlement under these provisions. He will be able to apply for settlement only under the long-residence rules (see **13.6.5**), and even then he may be excluded. A person who no longer qualifies for leave is expected to depart from the UK.

In the case of *Holub and Holub v Secretary of State for the Home Department* [2001] INLR 219, the 11-year-old daughter of a failed asylum seeker sought exceptional leave to remain on the basis that she had a right to education in the UK under Protocol 1, Article 2 of the ECHR. The Court of Appeal upheld the Secretary of State's refusal. The court said that a child's right to education whilst in the UK did not carry with it the right to remain.

14.17.14 Asylum checklist

Consider questions (a) to (f) below when deciding if a client might be granted asylum. If asylum is refused, consider question (g). Also, do not overlook any right of appeal against refusal (see **Chapter 16**).

(a) Does the safe third country exception apply? (see **14.17.7.1**);

(b) Might it be argued that the client is not afraid of availing himself of the protection of the whole of the country of his nationality because of the *internal flight alternative*? (See **14.17.4.1**);

(c) Is what the client fears *persecution*?

(d) Is the reason for the fear of persecution a *Convention reason*?

(e) Is that fear of persecution for a Convention reason well founded?

(f) Is the client excluded?

(g) What human rights arguments, if any, can be made?

Chapter 15

Deportation and Administrative Removal

15.1	Deportation	307
15.2	Administrative removal	310
15.3	Enforcement action in cases involving spouses	312
15.4	Enforcement action involving children or parents	315

15.1 Deportation

15.1.1 General

Under s 5 of the IA 1971, the Home Secretary has powers to make deportation orders. A deportation order requires a person to leave the UK and prohibits him from re-entering while the order is in force. It also invalidates any leave to enter or remain.

British citizens and others with the right of abode in the UK cannot be deported. Some Commonwealth and Irish citizens are exempt from deportation (see **15.1.5**). A person who is settled in the UK is liable to deportation. See, for example, *Samaroo and Sezek v Secretary of State for the Home Department* [2001] UKHRR 1150.

15.1.2 Grounds for deportation and its effects

The Home Secretary may deport only on alternative grounds specified in s 3(5)(b) and (6) of the IA 1971. These are as follows:

(a) the Home Secretary deems deportation to be conducive to the public good;
(b) a person is a member of the family of a deportee;
(c) a court has recommended deportation, in the case of a person aged 17 or more, convicted of an offence punishable with imprisonment.

What are the effects of a deportation order? A person may not legally enter the UK whilst an order is in force (see **15.1.8** as to revoking an order). By para 320(2) of the Immigration Rules, entry clearance and leave to enter will be refused to such a person.

15.1.3 Relevant factors

The fact that a person is liable to be deported does not mean that he will be deported. The matter is one of discretion for the Home Secretary. However, the Immigration Rules, para 364 makes it clear that where a person is liable to deportation then the presumption shall be that the public interest requires deportation. It will only be in exceptional circumstances that the public interest in deportation will be outweighed, in a case where it would not be contrary to the ECHR and the Refugee Convention to deport.

Many deportations are based on previous convictions. In the case of *Aramide v Secretary of State for the Home Department* (2000) LTL, 24 July, the Court of Appeal held that in considering whether to deport a person pursuant to the provisions of s 3(5)(b) of the IA 1971, where that person had been convicted of a criminal offence, the seriousness of the offence on the one hand (which could often usefully be gauged by the length of the sentence) had to be carefully balanced against the family ties on the other. And what about EC law and the ECHR? In the case of *B v Secretary of State for the Home Department* [2000] Imm AR 478, B was born in Sicily in 1955. He settled in the UK when he was 7 years old. His family were largely based in the UK. He was convicted of assaulting his infant son and was given a suspended sentence of one year's imprisonment. He was later convicted on a number of counts of gross indecency and indecent assault upon his daughter, for which he received a sentence totalling five years' imprisonment. Prior to his release from prison, the Home Secretary notified him that he was considering deportation, which in due course was ordered. B appealed against that order. The Tribunal upheld the Home Secretary's decision, holding that there were exceptional cases in which past conduct justified deportation of an EU citizen and that, in the instant case, B displayed a propensity to act in a manner contrary to public policy.

The Court of Appeal allowed B's appeal. It held that, whilst interference with free movement was one thing, interference with private and family life was another. Even where both arise from the same deportation, they enhanced the private interests against which public policy was to be set and to which deportation had to be a proportionate response. In the instant case, what rendered deportation a disproportionate response to B's offending, serious as it was, and to his propensity to offend, such as it may now be, was the fact that it would take him from the country in which he had grown up, had lived his whole adult life and had such social relationships as he possessed. It would negate both his freedom of movement and respect for his private life in the one place where these had real meaning for him. In relation to Article 39 EC this was self-evident; in relation to Article 8 of the ECHR, it was because the jurisprudence of the Strasbourg court had carried the notion of private life beyond simple autonomy and to a certain degree into the right to establish and develop relationships with other human beings. What was proposed in the instant case was, although in law, deportation, more akin to exile. In order to ensure that the reason for deportation was one recognised by the ECHR, questions of propensity were likely to be engaged rather than of past conduct. If so, deportation in the instant case, which turned chiefly on the gravity of past conduct, would become that much harder to justify.

15.1.4 Deportation of family members

This can be a controversial ground for deportation, as someone who is deported as the family member of another may have committed no breach of immigration law. It is particularly used where the family member has settled status, and so cannot be removed from the UK by a refusal of leave to remain. However, it cannot be used to deport anyone who has the right of abode (eg as a British citizen).

Where a spouse is being deported, the other spouse and the children under 18 of either of them can also be deported as family members. However, no family deportation can be made once eight weeks have elapsed since the other family member was deported (see IA 1971, s 5).

> **Example**
>
> Svetlana, a citizen of Russia, obtains settlement in the UK as the spouse of a British citizen. She divorces and remarries Boris, also a citizen of Russia. He is also given settlement in the UK and they have a child, Ivan, born in London.
>
> Boris is convicted of serious drugs offences and recommended for deportation by the court. Can Svetlana and Ivan be deported?
>
> Svetlana is liable to deportation as the spouse of Boris. Ivan is not liable to deportation as he is a British citizen (born in the UK after 1982 to a settled parent). However, if his

parents are deported he may still be 'expected to leave' with them. They could not use his British citizenship alone as a reason to resist their own deportation.

In these cases, compassionate grounds are obviously important and the Home Office has issued guidelines covering some family cases (see **15.3** and **15.4**).

15.1.5 Exemption from deportation

The main exemptions from deportation are dealt with in s 7(1)(b) and (c) of the IA 1971. They apply only to Commonwealth or Irish citizens who had that citizenship at 1 January 1973 and were then ordinarily resident in the UK. Such persons are exempt from deportation on any ground if they have been ordinarily resident in the UK and Islands 'for the last five years' ending with the date of the Home Secretary's decision to deport, or court conviction in the case of deportation on the recommendation of a court.

The term 'ordinary residence' is considered in **13.2.5**. However, s 7(2) provides that, for the purpose of this exemption, if a person has at any time acquired ordinary residence in the UK, he does not lose it by remaining in breach of immigration laws. This means that a person who has overstayed, or broken conditions of entry, may nevertheless qualify for exemption.

15.1.6 Procedure

The general procedure is described in paras 381, 382 and 384 of the Immigration Rules. Initially, the Home Office takes a decision to deport. Notice of this is then normally given to the deportee. He may then exercise his rights of appeal. If he fails to appeal, or loses his appeal, the Home Secretary may then sign the deportation order. Under Sch 3 to the IA 1971, the deportee may then be removed to the country of which he is a national, or to another country which is likely to receive him. He may also be detained following the decision to deport, or court recommendation.

This procedure under para 381 does not apply to deportation following a court recommendation. In this case, no order will be made until rights of appeal against conviction or sentence have been exhausted. The normal practice is to make the order when the sentence has been served.

Rights of appeal against deportation are dealt with in **Chapter 16**.

15.1.7 Voluntary and supervised removal

What if a person is subject to enforcement action but a deportation order has not yet been signed? As an order cannot be made against a person who is not in the UK, it is open to the person to leave the UK voluntarily. Enforcement action will cease if it is known that a person has embarked. Alternatively, a person subject to deportation may be allowed to leave by supervised departure without a deportation order being made against him. This generally occurs where the person agrees to leave immediately on detection and signs a waiver regarding his appeal rights. Supervised departure may either be at the person's own expense or paid from public funds.

Are there any advantages to these types of departures? Yes, as a person who is subject to enforcement action and who makes a voluntary or supervised departure is not subsequently debarred from re-entering the UK (although he must, of course, satisfy the requirements of the Immigration Rules for which he is seeking entry in the normal way).

15.1.8 Revoking a deportation order

Paragraph 390 of the Immigration Rules sets out the basic guidelines when an application is made to revoke a deportation order. Further, where the order was made following a criminal conviction, BIA guidance is that it will not be usual to revoke it for at least 10 years after the person's departure where he was convicted of serious offences such as murder, manslaughter, grievous and actual bodily harm, sexual offences against children, rape, procurement, pornography, burglary, robbery, theft, blackmail, counterfeiting, forgery (including trafficking in forged passports), trafficking in dangerous drugs, public order, riot, affray, etc.

15.2 Administrative removal

15.2.1 Grounds for removal

Removal from the UK is often described as 'administrative removal', as that is what it is in reality, namely an administrative step. For ease of reference, we will call it 'removal'. Under s 10 of the IAA 1999, the following people may be removed from the UK:

(a) anyone who has failed to observe the conditions attached to their leave;
(b) overstayers;
(c) anyone who has obtained leave to remain by deception, or who sought to obtain such leave by deception;
(d) the family members of such people.

The most common grounds for removal will be that a person has remained beyond the period specified in his limited leave, or has broken a condition attached to it. For example, a person's leave to enter or remain will often either prohibit or restrict the freedom to take employment and the person is liable to administrative removal procedures if he is found to be working without authority. The BIA guidance is that there must be firm and recent (within six months) evidence of working in breach. The immigration officer will look for at least an admission by the offender under caution of working in breach; or a statement by the employer; or pay slips or the offender's details on the payroll; or visual observation, by the immigration officer, of the applicant working.

As explained in **13.6.2**, a person who wishes to extend his stay should apply for a variation before his leave expires. He commits a criminal offence under s 24(1)(b) of the IA 1971 if he knowingly overstays or fails to observe a condition of the leave. Note that it is not usual practice for a prosecution to occur. Removal does not require a knowing breach and so that is more common.

In addition, illegal entrants (see **15.2.2**) may be removed from the UK.

15.2.2 Definition of illegal entrant

An illegal entrant is a person who unlawfully enters or seeks to enter in breach of a deportation order or of the immigration laws. This includes a person who has so entered.

A person who, contrary to the IA 1971, knowingly enters the UK in breach of a deportation order or without leave commits a criminal offence under s 24(1)(a). However, it is possible to be an illegal entrant without having committed any criminal offence, for instance, where a person obtains leave by producing false documents, without knowing them to be false (*R v Immigration Officer, ex p Chan* [1992] 1 WLR 541).

A person will be an illegal entrant if he obtains leave to enter by deception, although mere non-disclosure of material facts will not amount to deception, as the entrant has no positive duty to reveal facts if a relevant question is not asked. It is for the Home Office to prove the deception (*R v Secretary of State for the Home Department, ex p Khawaja* [1984] AC 74).

For an example, see **14.9.6.3**.

15.2.3 Relevant factors

Before deciding to remove an individual, para 395C of the Immigration Rules requires the Secretary of State to have regard to the following factors:

(a) *Age*

Generally speaking, a person will be considered for removal *in his own right* if he is aged between 16 and 65, but the younger or older a person is, the more weight might be attached to age as a compassionate factor.

(b) *Length of residence in the United Kingdom*

Generally speaking, a person will be considered for removal *in his own right* if the period of stay is less than 14 years. However, removal may nonetheless be considered where the length of residence exceeds 14 years if, for example, there are factors known to the person's detriment such as a poor immigration history or a concerted effort to avoid detection.

(c) *Strength of connections with the United Kingdom*

Caseworkers will examine issues such as family ties and other connections such as business or employment interests.

(d) *Personal history*

Personal history will include character, conduct and employment record. This is self-explanatory and will be a balance between a person's known history whilst in the United Kingdom against the public interest in taking enforcement action.

(e) *Domestic circumstances*

There is considerable overlap here with 'strength of connections', but physical domestic circumstances, such as housing, as well as whether the person has anyone who relies on him for support, whether physically, financially or emotionally, will be taken into account.

(f) *Previous criminal record and the nature of any offence of which the person has been convicted*

A previous unspent conviction will be considered irrespective of the section of the Act under which enforcement action is being pursued. However, the seriousness of the offence is balanced against any mitigating factors.

(g) *Compassionate circumstances*

Any compelling or compassionate circumstances will be considered, with the gravity of the circumstances being given due weight.

(h) *Any representations received on the person's behalf*

This is self-explanatory.

15.2.4 Procedure

If a person is to be removed, he will have no in-country right of appeal against that decision (save on asylum and human rights grounds), although the matter may be challenged by way of judicial review (see **Chapters 16** and **17** for full details). However, in considering whether or not to remove a person, the Home Office is expected to apply the same guidelines on compassionate factors affecting spouses and children, where relevant, as in deportation cases (see **15.3** and **15.4**).

If, after consideration of all the relevant facts, the BIA decides that administrative removal is the correct course of action, a notice of liability to administrative removal is served. The immigration officer normally serves the notice in person. It still remains open to the person who is subject to enforcement action to leave the UK voluntarily. Otherwise the immigration officer will set removal directions. The costs of complying with removal directions (so far as reasonably incurred) are met by the Secretary of State. Directions for removal of a person given under s 10 of the 1999 Act invalidate any leave to enter or remain in the UK.

15.2.5 Effects of removal

Unlike someone who has been deported, a person who is subject to administrative removal does not need to have the decision to remove him rescinded before he may return to the UK (provided that he otherwise qualifies for admission under the Immigration Rules).

15.3 Enforcement action in cases involving spouses

The Home Office has issued important guidelines on deportation and removal of people from the UK where the deportee or person to be removed has married someone settled in the UK (including a Commonwealth citizen with the right of abode and a British citizen) (DP 3/96 – see *Butterworths Immigration Law Service* D67–81).

The Home Office will not normally deport or remove a spouse if:

(a) he or she has a genuine and subsisting marriage with someone settled here and the couple have lived together continuously since their marriage for at least two years before the commencement of enforcement action; and

(b) it is unreasonable to expect the settled spouse to accompany his or her spouse on removal.

Deportation and Administrative Removal

The flowchart below (part of the Home Office guidance) sets out the position:

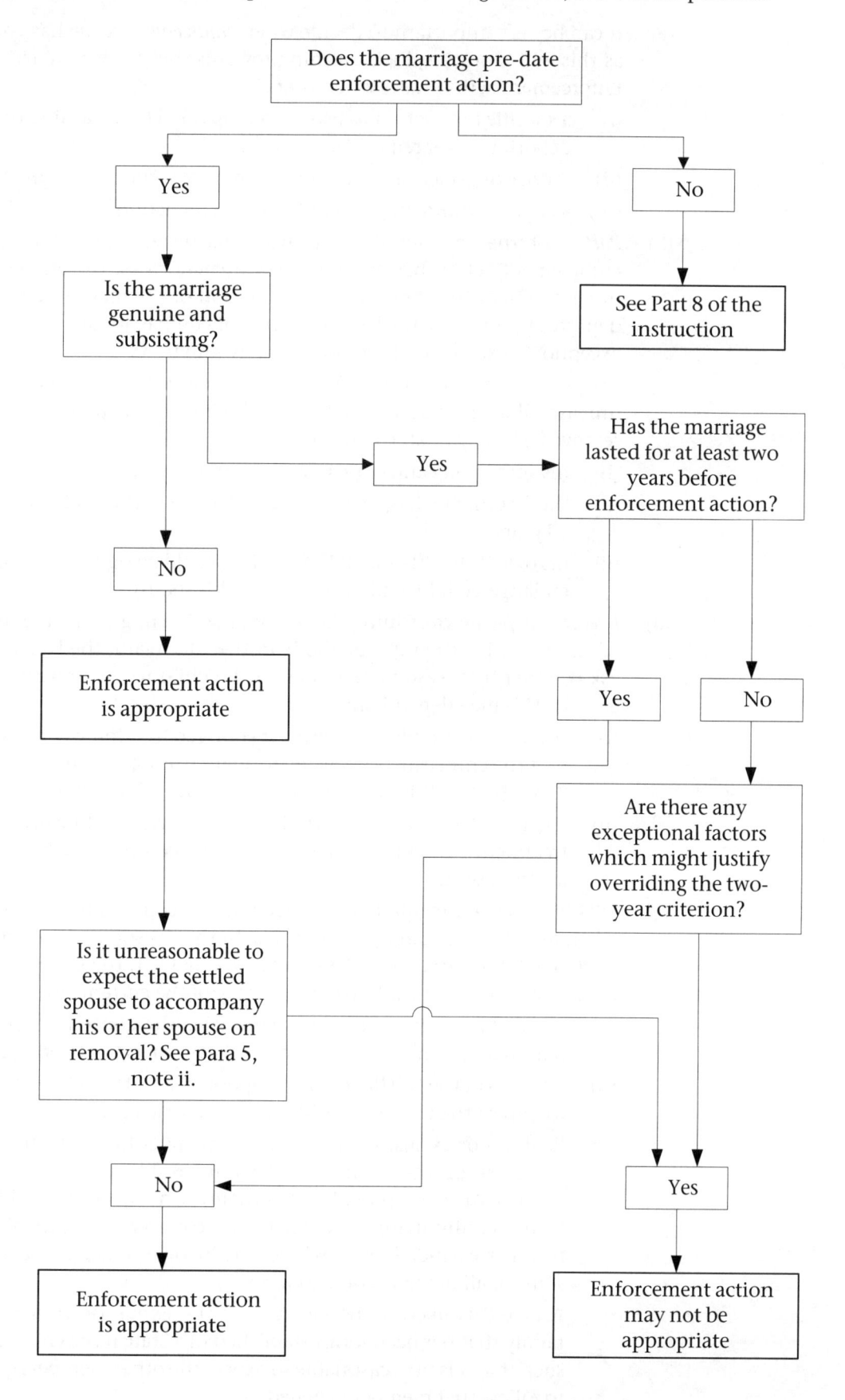

```
                    Does the marriage pre-date
                        enforcement action?
                       /                  \
                     Yes                   No
                      |                    |
           Is the marriage          See Part 8 of the
           genuine and                 instruction
           subsisting?
            /        \
          No         Yes ──→  Has the marriage
           |                  lasted for at least two
           |                  years before
           |                  enforcement action?
           |                       /         \
           |                     Yes          No
           |                      |            |
           |                      |    Are there any
           |                      |    exceptional factors
           |                      |    which might justify
           |                      |    overriding the two-
           |                      |    year criterion?
           ↓                      |         /       \
   Enforcement action             |        No       Yes
   is appropriate                 ↓         ↓        ↓
                        Is it unreasonable to
                        expect the settled
                        spouse to accompany
                        his or her spouse on
                        removal? See para 5,
                        note ii.
                         /        \
                       No          Yes
                        ↓           ↓
                Enforcement action   Enforcement action
                is appropriate       may not be
                                     appropriate
```

Notes

(a) It can be very important to decide when *enforcement action* has commenced, as this will 'stop the clock' running towards the two-year marriage period. Enforcement action starts when there is:
 (i) a specific instruction to leave, accompanied by a warning of liability to deportation (or removal);
 (ii) service of notice of intention to deport or service of removal papers;
 (iii) a court recommendation following a conviction.

(b) *Part 8* of the instruction deals with marriages which take place after enforcement action has commenced. In these cases, the Home Office will not even check the genuineness or duration of the marriage. It is up to the deportee to convince the Home Office that compassionate factors justify the exceptional exercise of discretion to allow him to stay.

(c) *Paragraph 5, note ii* requires the settled spouse to show that it would be unreasonable to expect him to live abroad, if his spouse is deported or removed. He may be able to rely on:
 (i) his very strong and close family ties in the UK;
 (ii) the fact that he has been settled and living in the UK for at least the last 10 years;
 (iii) his own ill-health – such that his life would be significantly impaired or endangered if he had to accompany his spouse.

(d) *Exceptional factors* overriding the two-year period might include the presence of children with the right of abode in the UK. Again, the Home Office will ask whether it is reasonable to expect the child to accompany the parents abroad. This may depend on:
 (i) the age of the child – if 7 years or younger, the Home Office will assume that the child can be expected to adapt (the age was reduced from 10 to 7 by a Home Office press notice issued on 1 March 1999);
 (ii) whether the child is suffering from serious ill-health, for which treatment would not be available in the country to which his parents are to be sent.

(e) DP3/96 has been regularly challenged in the courts but upheld, including when tested on human rights grounds. In the case of *R v Secretary of State for the Home Department, ex p Mahmood* [2001] INLR 1, the Court of Appeal (at pp 22 and 23) gave the following summary of the current law:
 (i) A State has a right under international law to control the entry of non-nationals into its territory, subject always to its treaty obligations.
 (ii) Article 8 of the ECHR does not impose on a State any general obligation to respect the choice of residence of a married couple.
 (iii) Removal or exclusion of one family member from a State where other members of the family are lawfully resident will not necessarily infringe Article 8, provided that there are no insurmountable obstacles to the family living together in the country of origin of the family member excluded, even where this involves a degree of hardship for some or all members of the family.
 (iv) Article 8 is likely to be violated by the expulsion of a member of a family that has been long established in a State if the circumstances are such that it is not reasonable to expect the other members of the family to follow that member expelled.

(v) Knowledge on the part of one spouse at the time of marriage that rights of residence of the other were precarious militates against a finding that an order excluding the latter spouse violates Article 8.

(vi) Whether interference with family rights is justified in the interests of controlling immigration will depend on the facts of the particular case and the circumstances prevailing in the State whose action is impugned.

Example 1

Helen entered the UK to visit relatives in the UK. She overstayed. Without contacting the Home Office to apply for an extension, she married Gary, a British citizen, who has always been resident in the UK. They had been married for six months when Helen decided to regularise her immigration position in order to get a job. She applied to the Home Office for leave to remain as a spouse. The Home Office replied by letter refusing the application and stating that as an overstayer she did not meet the requirements of para 284, was liable to removal and must leave the UK immediately. They have taken no further action as yet. Can Helen rely on compassionate grounds under DP 3/96?

As the marriage does pre-date enforcement action, the Home Office will still consider whether Helen's marriage gives compassionate grounds for a decision not to deport her. However, the Home Office letter has 'stopped the clock' running towards the two-year period. Even so, Helen can still submit evidence of exceptional factors which might justify overriding the two-year criterion, and the Home Office will consider this before deciding to remove her.

Example 2

As Example 1, but Helen married after receiving a notice of intention to remove her.

The Home Office will not take the marriage into account unless Helen can convince them that they should do so on an exceptional basis.

Example 3

Alan is a citizen of the USA who entered the UK as the husband of Beth, a British citizen. The marriage broke down within his 12-month period of leave as a spouse. He did not apply for settlement, but remained in the UK. Three months after expiry of his leave, he married Carol, a citizen of Jamaica who had been settled in the UK for two years. She already had, living with her, a 3-year-old son, David, by an earlier marriage. He has settled status but not the right of abode. Alan has not been in contact with the Home Office since his divorce. He has now been married to Carol for two years.

As no enforcement action has yet been commenced against Alan, and his present marriage has lasted for two years, any Home Office decision on whether to remove him as an overstayer will depend on whether it is reasonable to expect Carol to accompany him abroad (see the flow chart and note (c) above). As Carol has not been settled in the UK for 10 years the key issue may be whether she has 'close family ties' in the UK. If David is close to his father and his father's family this may be enough.

15.4 Enforcement action involving children or parents

The Home Office has also issued separate guidance on cases involving children or affecting the parent–child relationship (DP 4/96 and DP 5/96 – see *Butterworths Immigration Law Service* D83–87). These apply in addition to DP 3/96 (see **15.3**), dealing with marriage policy, in cases where a deportation or removal would affect both spouse and children. They will apply on their own in a case where, for example, a single parent is to be deported or removed but has a child in the UK.

The main principles are as follows:

(a) There is no age bar to deportation or removal of a child. However, the child must be liable to removal, for example as a family member of a parent who is to be deported or removed (see **15.1.4** and **15.2**).

(b) A child who is under age 16 and on his own in the UK will not normally be removed as an overstayer.

(c) Enforcement action may be abandoned where there is evidence that the care arrangements in the country to which he is to be sent are seriously inadequate.

(d) When considering deportation or removal of a parent, the Home Office must take into account the presence of children in the UK.

(e) Whether it is the child or the parent who is being deported or removed, the Home Office will look at the length of time the child has spent in the UK; but will assume that if it is less than seven years, the child will be able to adapt to life abroad. However, the Home Office may still consider that enforcement action is appropriate despite the lengthy residence of a child, for example in cases where the parents have a particularly poor immigration history and have deliberately seriously delayed consideration of their case. In all cases the following factors are relevant in reaching a judgement on whether enforcement action should proceed:

  (i) the length of the parents' residence without leave; whether removal has been delayed through protracted (and often repetitive) representations or by the parents going to ground;

  (ii) the age of the children and whether the children were conceived at a time when either of the parents had leave to remain;

  (iii) whether return to the parents' country of origin would cause extreme hardship for the children or put their health seriously at risk;

  (iv) whether either of the parents has a history of criminal behaviour or deception.

(f) A divorced or separated parent may be deported or removed even where there is a child in the UK and he has access rights to the child. The Immigration Rules (paras 246–248) allow parents to be admitted to the UK for the purpose of access to children. So a parent may be deported or removed and then be expected to apply for access from abroad. The Home Office has received legal advice that deportation or removal of a parent in these circumstances is unlikely to involve breach of Article 8 of the ECHR (respect for family life), as family life has already broken down as a result of the divorce.

(g) The Home Office may (through the Treasury Solicitor) intervene in various court proceedings involving children (eg adoption, wardship) if it thinks that the proceedings are designed purely to enable the child or parent to evade immigration control. (Even though in such proceedings the welfare of the child is supposed to be paramount under the Children Act 1989, a court must still consider whether the purpose of an application is to evade the operation of immigration law (*Findlay v Matondo* [1993] Imm AR 541). The Home Office may intervene to argue the case.)

Example 1

Bina is a citizen of India. She married Nilkanth, a British citizen and was granted 12 months' leave to remain as his spouse. The couple had a son, born in the UK, now aged 2. Subsequently the marriage broke down, and she did not apply for settled status. As a result she became an overstayer. Nilkanth has not sought rights of access (contact) to the child, and Bina has custody (residence).

The Home Office may well decide to remove Bina in these circumstances. She has no claim to remain with Nilkanth on compassionate grounds, as their marriage is no longer subsisting. The issue is whether it is reasonable to expect her son (who is a British citizen) to accompany her abroad. As the child is under 7, the Home Office may conclude that he could reasonably be expected to adapt to life abroad. He does not have close ties with his father, who will remain in the UK. They are therefore likely to deport Bina. She is likely to take her child with her, although as a British citizen he cannot be deported or removed.

The Home Office argues that removal in this type of case does not breach Art 8 of the ECHR (respect for family life) as family life has already broken down (see *R v Secretary of State for the Home Department, ex p Patel* [1995] Imm AR 223).

Example 2

Assume that the facts are similar to Example 1 but the husband Nilkanth is the overstayer. After the divorce Bina, a British citizen, has custody but Nilkanth retains rights of access to his child.

Nilkanth appears to have no compassionate grounds to argue against removal. Under (f) above he would be expected to apply from abroad to exercise his access rights.

Chapter 16
Immigration Appeals

16.1	Appeals: the general rule	319
16.2	Decisions against which there is a right of appeal	319
16.3	Grounds of appeal	320
16.4	Appeal rights exercisable in the UK	320
16.5	The 'one stop' process	321
16.6	The appeals system	322
16.7	Pending and abandoned appeals	323
16.8	Ineligible appeals	324
16.9	Visitors or students without entry clearance	324
16.10	Family visitor refused entry clearance	324
16.11	Student	325
16.12	National security and similar matters	325
16.13	'Public good' exclusion	325
16.14	EEA nationals	326
16.15	Asylum appeals: 'third country' removal	326
16.16	Unfounded human rights or asylum claims	326
16.17	Deprivation of citizenship orders	327
16.18	Immigration, Asylum and Nationality Act 2006	327

16.1 Appeals: the general rule

The NIAA 2002 sets out a revised system of appeals, including a system for a 'one stop' comprehensive appeal following refusal of leave to enter or remain. It replaces all rights of appeal established in earlier legislation. The Act establishes the principle that there is one right of appeal against any of the listed 'immigration decisions' (see **16.2**). Where multiple decisions would result in multiple rights of appeal these are subsumed into one appeal. All appealable grounds can and should be raised in an appeal (see **16.5**). Most, but not all, appeal rights can be exercised in the UK (see **16.4**). Exceptions and limitations restrict rights of appeal in certain circumstances (see **16.8** onwards).

16.2 Decisions against which there is a right of appeal

By s 82(2) an appeal can be made against an 'immigration decision', namely:

(a) refusal of leave to enter the UK;

(b) refusal of entry clearance;

(c) refusal of a certificate of entitlement of the right of abode (see **12.3.3**);

(d) refusal to vary a person's leave to enter or remain in the UK if the result of the refusal is that the person has no leave to enter or remain;

(e) variation of a person's leave to enter or remain in the UK if when the variation takes effect the person has no leave to enter or remain;

(f) revocation of indefinite leave to enter or remain in the UK;

(g) a decision that a person is to be removed from the UK by way of directions under s 10 of the IAA 1999 (see **Chapter 15**);

(h) a decision that an illegal entrant is to be removed from the UK by way of directions under Sch 2 to the IA 1971 (see **Chapter 15**);

(i) a decision to make a deportation order under s 5(1) of that Act; and

(j) refusal to revoke a deportation order under s 5(2) of that Act.

Note that a variation or revocation of the kind referred to in (e) or (f) above does not have effect while an appeal could be brought (ignoring any possibility of an appeal out of time with permission) or is pending.

These rights of appeal are subject to exceptions and limitations (see **16.8** onwards).

16.3 Grounds of appeal

By s 84, an appeal against an immigration decision (see **16.2**) must be brought on one or more of the following grounds:

(a) that the decision is not in accordance with Immigration Rules;

(b) that the decision is unlawful by virtue of s 19B of the Race Relations Act 1976 (ie discrimination by public authorities);

(c) that the decision is unlawful under s 6 of the Human Rights Act 1998 as being incompatible with the appellant's ECHR rights;

(d) that the appellant is an EEA national or a member of the family of an EEA national and the decision breaches the appellant's rights under the Community Treaties in respect of entry to or residence in the UK;

(e) that the decision is otherwise not in accordance with the law;

(f) that the person taking the decision should have exercised differently a discretion conferred by Immigration Rules;

(g) that removal of the appellant from the UK in consequence of the immigration decision would breach the UK's obligations under the Geneva Convention on refugees, or would be unlawful under s 6 of the Human Rights Act 1998 as being incompatible with the appellant's Convention rights.

Any number of grounds can be set out but such will constitute one appeal (see **16.5**).

16.4 Appeal rights exercisable in the UK

By s 92, an appeal right is not exercisable whilst the appellant is in the UK unless:

(a) the appeal is against an immigration decision of the kind specified in s 82(2)(c), (d), (e), (f) and (j) (see **16.2**);

(b) the appeal is against refusal of leave to enter where at the time of the refusal the appellant is in the UK and he has either entry clearance or a work permit;

(c) the appeal is against an immigration decision and the appellant has made an asylum claim, or a human rights claim, while in the UK, or is an EEA national or a member of the family of an EEA national and makes a claim to the Secretary of State that the decision breaches the appellant's rights under the Community Treaties in respect of entry to or residence in the UK.

All other appeal rights can be exercised only from abroad.

Note that by s 113, a 'human rights claim' is defined as a claim made by a person to the Secretary of State at a place designated by the Secretary of State that to remove the person from or require him to leave the UK would be unlawful under s 6 of the Human Rights Act 1998. An 'asylum claim' means a claim made by a person to the Secretary of State at a place designated by the Secretary of State that to remove the person from or require him to leave the UK would breach the UK's obligations under the Geneva Convention on refugees.

16.5 The 'one stop' process

16.5.1 Notice of appealable decision

The Immigration (Notices) Regulations 2003 (SI 2003/658) provide that a decision-maker (eg entry clearance officer, immigration officer, Secretary of State) must give written notice to a person of any immigration decision taken in respect of him which is appealable. The notice must include or be accompanied by a statement of the reasons for the decision to which it relates and if it relates to an immigration decision specified in s 82(2)(a), (g), (h), (i) or (j) of the 2002 Act, state the country or territory to which it is proposed to remove the person.

The notice must also include, or be accompanied by, a statement which advises the person of his right of appeal and the statutory provision on which his right of appeal is based; whether or not such an appeal may be brought while in the UK; the grounds on which such an appeal may be brought; and the facilities available for advice and assistance in connection with such an appeal. It must also be accompanied by a notice which indicates the time limit for bringing the appeal (see **16.6.3**), the address to which it should be sent or may be taken by hand and a fax number for service by fax. Where the exercise of the appeal right is restricted by an exception or limitation (see **16.8** onwards), the notice must also include or be accompanied by a statement which refers to the provision limiting or restricting the right of appeal.

Further, by s 120 if a person has made an application to enter or remain in the UK, or an immigration decision (see **16.2**) has been taken or may be taken in respect of him, then the Secretary of State or an immigration officer may by notice in writing require him to state:

(a) his reasons for wishing to enter or remain in the UK;
(b) any grounds on which he should be permitted to enter or remain in the UK; and
(c) any grounds on which he should not be removed from or required to leave the UK.

16.5.2 Consequences of failing to disclose all grounds of appeal

What if a s 120 notice is not answered? Any attempt to raise such grounds later on may lead to certification under s 96 with the effect that there can be no appeal against the decision, or that those grounds cannot be raised in connection with a further appeal.

16.5.3 Other certificates under s 96

Certificates can be issued under s 96 otherwise than in relation to s 120 notices (see **16.5.2**).

Note that no appeal can be brought on any ground against an otherwise appealable decision if the Secretary of State or immigration officer certifies that the person was notified of a right of appeal against another decision (whether or not any appeal was lodged or completed) *and* that in his opinion the person made the claim or application in order to delay removal, or the removal of a family member, *and* that in his opinion the person had no other legitimate purpose for making the claim or application. If an appeal has already been brought, the appeal may not be continued if a certificate is issued.

Further s 96 prevents an appeal being brought if the Secretary of State or immigration officer certifies that a new decision relates to a ground which was raised on an earlier appeal or could have been raised at an appeal had the applicant chosen to exercise a right of appeal. If an appeal has already been brought, the appeal may not be continued if a certificate is issued.

Finally, where a further appeal right does arise, the Secretary of State or immigration officer may certify that certain grounds of appeal were already considered in an earlier appeal. The appellant is not then allowed to rely on those grounds.

16.6 The appeals system

16.6.1 The Asylum and Immigration Tribunal (AIT)

A right of appeal lies to the AIT under s 82 of the NIAA 2002, against an immigration decision (see **16.2**); in certain circumstances, against a decision to reject an asylum claim (see **14.17**); and under s 40A of the BNA 1981, against a decision to make an order depriving a person of a British citizenship status (see **12.2.9**).

The titles of the legally qualified members of the AIT are Immigration Judges, Designated Immigration Judges and Senior Immigration Judges. The President of the AIT may allocate cases to specified classes of AIT member under Sch 4 to the 2002 Act. Sometimes a particular class of judge must deal with a specific type of application, for example, applications for permission to appeal from the AIT to the Court of Appeal must be determined by a Senior Immigration Judge (see further below).

An appeal to the AIT may only be started by giving notice of appeal on a prescribed form in accordance with the Asylum and Immigration Tribunal (Procedure) Rules 2005 (SI 2005/230). Practitioners must also be familiar with the AIT Practice Directions. Normally there is a case management review hearing. This will determine the issues in dispute and the evidence necessary to deal with them. Directions are usually given as to the filing of evidence etc.

At the appeal hearing the Immigration Judges determine whether or not to uphold the original decision. If the determination is made by only one or two Immigration Judges, then an application can be made asking the AIT to reconsider its determination. The application is dealt with by a Senior Immigration Judge without a hearing, and by reference only to the applicant's written submissions and the documents filed with the application notice. It will only be granted if it is considered that the AIT may have made an error of law and there is a real possibility that the AIT would decide the appeal differently on reconsideration.

If a reconsideration hearing takes place, a differently constituted AIT must decide if the original AIT made a material error of law. If it decides that the original AIT did so, it must substitute a fresh decision to allow or dismiss the appeal.

If a reconsideration is refused, appeal lies to the Administrative Court. The Court may either dismiss it, refer it to the Court of Appeal, or direct the AIT to reconsider the appeal (see Civil Procedure Rules 1998, r 54.33).

Appeal on a point of law from a reconsideration hearing or a first hearing that was conducted by a panel of three Immigration Judges lies to the Court of Appeal. It is necessary to obtain that court's permission first.

All appeals are heard in various appeal centres across the UK. The main centres are: London, Belfast, Birmingham, Bradford, Bromley, Cardiff, Croydon, Glasgow, Harmondsworth and Manchester. There are also a number of satellite courts across the country where hearings take place.

16.6.2 Appeals to the Court of Appeal

The Court of Appeal has the power to give any decision which might have been given by the AIT. It can also remit the matter for rehearing and determination by the AIT and then may offer the AIT its opinion and make directions with which the AIT must comply.

16.6.3 The appeals timetable

An appellant appealing in the UK must give notice of appeal not later than 10 days after receiving the decision. However, if the appeal is being made from outside the UK he must give notice of appeal within 28 days after receiving notice of the decision or, if later, within 28 days of leaving the UK.

An appellant seeking a reconsideration of a determination must apply for such if he is in the UK no later than five working days after receiving the determination or within 28 days after receiving it if he is outside the UK.

An application to the AIT for leave to appeal to the Court of Appeal must be made within 10 days of receipt of the AIT's determination.

Appeals are expedited or 'fast tracked' if the appellant is in detention. For details see the AIT (Fast Track Procedure) Rules 2005 (SI 2005/560).

16.7 Pending and abandoned appeals

Section 104 sets out when an appeal is pending and when it ends: it clarifies that an appeal ceases to be pending when it is 'abandoned'. An appeal may be treated as abandoned because the appellant leaves the UK, is granted leave to enter or remain, or a deportation order is made against him. However, an appeal continues to be pending so long as a further appeal may be brought and until such further appeal is finally determined.

As a general rule, while an appeal is pending, the leave to which the appeal relates and any conditions subject to which it was granted continue to have effect. Hence, the person has a right to remain in the UK whilst pursuing the appeal. But what does 'the leave to which the appeal relates' mean? It is referring to the leave that the appellant had when he made the application that has been refused. It does not mean the leave for which the appellant applied.

By s 77, while a person's claim for asylum is pending he may not be removed from or required to leave the UK in accordance with a provision of the Immigration Acts.

However, this does not prevent the giving of a direction for the claimant's removal from the UK, the making of a deportation order in respect of the claimant, or the taking of any other interim or preparatory action.

By s 78, while a person's appeal under s 82 is pending he may not be removed from or required to leave the UK in accordance with a provision of the Immigration Acts. However, this does not prevent the giving of a direction for the appellant's removal from the UK, the making of a deportation order in respect of the appellant (subject to s 79: see below), or the taking of any other interim or preparatory action.

Section 78 only applies to an appeal brought while the appellant is in the UK in accordance with s 92 (see **16.4**).

By s 79 a deportation order may not be made in respect of a person while an appeal under s 82 against the decision to make the order could be brought (ignoring any possibility of an appeal out of time with permission), or is pending.

Note that s 99 provides that where a certificate is issued under s 96 (see **16.5.2**) or ss 97 or 98 (see **16.12** and **16.13**) in respect of a pending appeal, then that appeal lapses.

16.8 Ineligible appeals

Section 88 applies to an immigration decision of the kind referred to in s 82(2)(a), (b), (d) or (e). These are detailed at **16.2**. A person may not appeal under s 82 against such an immigration decision which is taken on the grounds that he or a person of whom he is a dependant:

(a) does not satisfy a requirement as to age, nationality or citizenship specified in immigration rules;

(b) does not have an immigration document of a particular kind (or any immigration document);

(c) is seeking to be in the UK for a period greater than that permitted in his case by immigration rules; or

(d) is seeking to enter or remain in the UK for a purpose other than one for which entry or remaining is permitted in accordance with immigration rules.

For the purposes of (b) above an 'immigration document' means either entry clearance, a passport, a work permit or other immigration employment document, or a document which relates to a national of a country other than the UK and which is designed to serve the same purpose as a passport.

An appeal may nevertheless be brought on asylum, human rights or race discrimination grounds.

16.9 Visitors or students without entry clearance

Section 89 applies to a person who seeks leave to enter the UK:

(a) as a visitor;

(b) in order to follow a course of study for which he has been accepted and which will not last more than six months;

(c) in order to study but without having been accepted for a course; or

(d) as the dependant of such a person.

Any such person may not appeal under s 82 against refusal of leave to enter the UK if at the time of the refusal he does not have entry clearance. An appeal may nevertheless be brought on asylum, human rights or race discrimination grounds.

16.10 Family visitor refused entry clearance

By s 90, a person who applies for entry clearance for the purpose of entering the UK as a visitor may appeal under s 82 against refusal of entry clearance only if the application was made for the purpose of visiting a member of the applicant's family.

The Immigration Appeals (Family Visitor) Regulations 2003 (SI 2003/518) define a member of the applicant's family for the purposes of s 90 as any of the following persons:

(a) the applicant's spouse, father, mother, son, daughter, grandfather, grandmother, grandson, granddaughter, brother, sister, uncle, aunt, nephew, niece or first cousin (the latter is the son or daughter of his uncle or aunt);

(b) the father, mother, brother or sister of the applicant's spouse;

(c) the spouse of the applicant's son or daughter;

(d) the applicant's stepfather, stepmother, stepson, stepdaughter, stepbrother or stepsister; or

(e) a person with whom the applicant has lived as a member of an unmarried couple for at least two of the three years before the day on which his application for entry clearance was made.

16.11 Student

By s 91 a person may not appeal under s 82 against refusal of entry clearance if he seeks it:

(a) in order to follow a course of study for which he has been accepted and which will not last more than six months;

(b) in order to study but without having been accepted for a course; or

(c) as the dependant of such a person.

An appeal may nevertheless be brought on asylum, human rights or race discrimination grounds.

16.12 National security and similar matters

Section 97 provides that an appeal under s 82 cannot be made or continued where the Secretary of State certifies that a decision was taken to exclude or remove a person from the UK:

(a) in the interests of national security;

(b) in the interests of the relationship between the UK and another country; or

(c) otherwise in the public interest.

However, under the Special Immigration Appeals Commission Act 1997 an appeal can be made to the Special Immigration Appeals Commission (SIAC). This body was set up specifically to deal with appeals where national security and other sensitive matters are a consideration. The proceedings of the SIAC are governed by the Special Immigration Appeals Commission (Procedure) Rules 2003 (SI 2003/1034).

16.13 'Public good' exclusion

Section 98 provides that an appeal cannot be made or continued against a refusal of leave to enter or refusal of entry clearance if the Secretary of State has certified that the person's exclusion from the UK is conducive to the public good, or directed that the person be refused on that ground. However, this does not prevent the person appealing on human rights or race discrimination grounds, or from appealing refusal of leave to enter on asylum grounds.

16.14 EEA nationals

The I(EEA) Regs 2006 give rights of appeal which have been prescribed under EU law for EEA nationals, members of their family and certain non-EEA nationals who are members of a UK national's family (see **13.9**). There are also additional categories of persons who are entitled to similar rights under agreements to which the UK is a party or by which it is bound. The rights of appeal cover decisions relating to admission, residence and the issue or withdrawal of relevant documentation. Appeals against decisions will be heard by the AIT or, where appropriate, by the SIAC. A copy of the Regulations can be found at **Appendix 7** to this Part of the book.

16.15 Asylum appeals: 'third country' removal

By s 93, a person may not appeal under s 82 while he is in the UK if a certificate has been issued in relation to him (see **14.7.7.1**). However, if the appellant has made a human rights claim and the Secretary of State has not certified that in his opinion that human rights claim is clearly unfounded (see **16.16**), then the appeal can be pursued in the UK.

16.16 Unfounded human rights or asylum claims

Section 94 applies to an appeal made under s 82 where the appellant has made an asylum claim and/or a human rights claim as defined by s 113 (see **16.4**). A person may not pursue the appeal whilst in the UK if the Secretary of State certifies that the claim is or claims are clearly unfounded.

Note that if the Secretary of State is satisfied that an asylum claimant or human rights claimant is entitled to reside in a State listed in s 94(4), he *must* certify the claim unless he is satisfied that it is not clearly unfounded. The s 94(4) States considered to be generally safe in the context of asylum and human rights claims are:

(a) the Republic of Albania;
(b) Serbia and Montenegro;
(c) Jamaica;
(d) Macedonia;
(e) the Republic of Moldova;
(f) India;
(g) Bolivia;
(h) Brazil;
(i) Ecuador;
(j) South Africa;
(k) Ukraine;
(l) Mongolia;
(m) Ghana (in respect of men);
(n) Nigeria (in respect of men).

Further, a person may not bring an appeal if the Secretary of State certifies that it is proposed to remove the person to a country of which he is not a national or citizen, and there is no reason to believe that the person's rights under the ECHR will be breached in that country. In determining whether a person in relation to whom such a certificate has been issued may be removed from the UK, the country specified in the certificate is to be regarded as a place where a person's life and liberty is not threatened by reason of his race, religion, nationality, membership of a particular social group, or political opinion, and a place from which a person will not be sent to another country otherwise than in accordance with the Geneva Convention on refugees.

A certificate can be challenged by way of judicial review (see **Chapter 17**).

16.17 Deprivation of citizenship orders

By s 40A of the BNA 1981, a person given notice of a decision to make an order depriving him of his British citizenship (see **12.2.9**) has a right of appeal to the AIT. Where, however, the Secretary of State has certified that the decision to deprive was based wholly or partly in reliance on information which he believes should not be made public, the appeal at first instance will instead be heard by the SIAC.

16.18 Immigration, Asylum and Nationality Act 2006

When in force the Act will make the following changes to the matters discussed in **16.9** and **16.10**. All appeals against refusal of entry clearance will be limited to human rights and race discrimination grounds, with the exception of family visitors and people wishing to join dependants in the UK (new s 88A(1)). Provision is also made for regulations, which will define in detail the relationships, degree of dependency and circumstances which count for these categories.

Chapter 17
Judicial Review

17.1	General	329
17.2	Availability of judicial review	329
17.3	Prompt action	330
17.4	Statutory review under NIAA 2002, s 101	330
17.5	Habeas corpus	330

17.1 General

Decisions adverse to a client may sometimes be challenged by means of an application for judicial review. The application will usually be for a quashing order in respect of a decision of the Home Secretary or the AIT. The court may, in addition, remit the case to the Home Secretary, or AIT, with a direction to reconsider according to the findings of the court.

Before an application is made to the court, the judicial review pre-action protocol should be consulted. This is on the Ministry of Justice website (www.justice. gov.uk/civil/procrules_fin/index.htm). The protocol sets out a code of good practice and contains the steps which parties should generally follow before making a claim for judicial review.

An application for judicial review is expensive and time-consuming, usually involving preparation of a considerable amount of documentary evidence. It is governed by Part 54 of the Civil Procedure Rules 1998 (SI 1998/3132) (CPR 1998). Counsel will usually be instructed. The judicial review procedure has the unusual feature of two separate stages. First, the claimant must lodge a CPR 1998, Part 8 claim form and permission to proceed with it must be granted. Secondly, after the parties have filed various documents, a full judicial review hearing takes place. As to the first stage, by r 54.5 of the CPR 1998 the permission of the Administrative Court is required before a claim can proceed, whether it was started under Part 54 or transferred to that court. This hurdle is intended to eliminate at the outset frivolous or obviously untenable claims. Where the claim is proceeding in the Administrative Court in London, documents must be filed at the Administrative Court Office, the Royal Courts of Justice, Strand, London, WC2A 2LL. Grounds of challenge are grouped under the three heads of illegality (eg an error in interpreting the Immigration Acts or Rules), irrationality (including failure to consider factors relevant to a decision), and procedural impropriety (usually involving a failure to give a fair hearing). Permission may be refused, for example, if the application does not show sufficient grounds, or if there has been undue delay. Whilst it is beyond the scope of Part II of this book to deal in detail with judicial review, the need for prompt action requires particular emphasis, and the topic is covered separately in **17.3**.

17.2 Availability of judicial review

Judicial review will be refused if an alternative remedy is more appropriate. In particular, leave will be refused where the applicant has failed to use a right of appeal, unless he can show that the circumstances are exceptional (*R v Secretary of State for the Home Department, ex p Swati* [1986] 1 All ER 717). It is not enough to show that the right of appeal is a less convenient remedy, for instance, because it must be conducted from abroad (*Soon Ok Ryoo v Secretary of State for the Home Department* [1992] Imm AR 59). However, if it would be practically impossible to conduct the appeal from abroad, leave may be given (*R v Chief Immigration Officer, Gatwick Airport, ex p Kharrazi* [1980] 1 WLR 1396 and *R v Secretary of State for the Home Department and Immigration Officer, Waterloo International Station, ex p Canbolat* [1997] INLR 198).

Where there is no right of appeal, for example in removal cases, judicial review may be the only available remedy (but see **17.5**).

Similarly, where rights of appeal have been exhausted, the last resort may be to apply for review of an AIT decision.

17.3 Prompt action

An application for permission to apply for judicial review must be made promptly and in any event within three months from the date when grounds for the application first arose. The court may extend the period if there is good reason for the delay, but delay may still result in refusal of a remedy at the final hearing (*R (Lichfield Securities Ltd) v Lichfield District Council* (2001) *The Times,* 30 March).

17.4 Statutory review under NIAA 2002, s 101

Section 101 of the NIAA 2002 replaces judicial review of an AIT decision to refuse leave to appeal. It also allows any party to challenge an AIT decision to grant leave to appeal. The procedure is governed by Part 54 of the CPR 1998. The application is determined by a single judge without a hearing.

17.5 Habeas corpus

Habeas corpus is used to obtain an immediate decision on the legality of a detention. In immigration cases, it can be used to challenge the validity of detention pending removal from the UK. It has the advantage over an application for judicial review that initial permission to proceed is not needed. However, where detention is based on an underlying exercise of discretion, it cannot be used to challenge the underlying decision, for example, on the ground of irrationality. It can be used where the applicant alleges that a factual condition for the exercise of a power of detention has not been met, for example, where he disputes a finding that he is an illegal entrant (*R v Secretary of State for the Home Department, ex p Khawaja* [1984] AC 74). In these cases, it is for the Home Office to prove the facts which give rise to the power of detention. In cases of refusal of entry, however, it is usually for the applicant to show that a discretion has been improperly exercised, and the appropriate procedure is to apply for judicial review, rather than habeas corpus (*R v Secretary of State for the Home Department, ex p Muboyayi* [1991] 3 WLR 442).

Chapter 18
Advising the Client

18.1	Personal details	331
18.2	Immigration status	331
18.3	The disputed decision	331
18.4	Reasons for disputed decision	332
18.5	Time limits	332
18.6	Client's objectives	332
18.7	Available options	332

This chapter cannot attempt to deal with the full range of difficulties which a client may have with the immigration authorities, but it does aim to give some general guidance. The *Immigration, Nationality and Refugee Law Handbook*, published by the Joint Council for the Welfare of Immigrants, provides comprehensive coverage. However, most cases will involve checking the following points.

18.1 Personal details

Obtain the following information about the client:

(a) name;
(b) nationality;
(c) date of birth;
(d) marital status;
(e) details of close family, including nationality, immigration status and current whereabouts.

Check these facts with the client's passport if possible.

Further information may be needed for advice on the requirements of particular rules. In many cases, evidence of means of the entrant or any sponsor will have to be obtained.

18.2 Immigration status

If the client is in the UK and does not have the right of abode, ask for:

(a) date of entry;
(b) port of entry;
(c) details of journey to UK and previous visits;
(d) immigration reference number;
(e) evidence of entry clearance and leave to enter.

These details should again be checked with the client's passport and any other relevant documents. It will be necessary to decipher any stamps in the passport.

18.3 The disputed decision

Often the client will consult a solicitor only when he has received an adverse decision from the immigration authorities. Check whether it is, for example:

(a) refusal of entry clearance;
(b) refusal of entry;
(c) refusal of an extension of stay;
(d) notice of intention to deport;
(e) removal.

Ask for documentary evidence of the decision.

18.4 Reasons for disputed decision

Reasons for the decision may be given in the notice of the decision, but in any event, the client should be asked what he has been told by the immigration authorities, and what he has said to them.

18.5 Time limits

Check whether urgent action is required because time limits are about to expire. In particular, check the time limit on leave to enter or remain by consulting the passport. Notice of an adverse decision may state the time limits for appeal.

18.6 Client's objectives

Try to get a clear picture of both short-term and long-term objectives. Check in particular:

(a) whether the client has made previous statements to the immigration authorities which are inconsistent with his present objectives;

(b) when advising a sponsor, whether the proposed entrant has the same intentions as the sponsor (eg whether elderly parents really wish to settle with children in the UK, or whether they would be content with frequent lengthy visits).

18.7 Available options

In giving advice the basic rule is to 'advise the whole client'. The adviser should consider immigration status as a whole and not simply the immediate objectives or current status of the client. For example, a Commonwealth citizen who wishes to remain in the UK to take employment, or to marry, may have a claim to the right of abode, by virtue of parental connection with the UK (see **12.3**). If so, leave to remain will not be needed. A foreign national seeking entry as the spouse of a British citizen may rely on rights under EC law, instead of the Immigration Rules, if the couple have previously lived and worked in another EU country (see **13.9.3**). Consider all possible options.

Remember also that in many cases the application of the Immigration Rules is a matter of judgement. Immigration officers may have to take decisions based on their view of whether the entrant's story is credible, and many decisions involve the exercise of discretion. If a client is in difficulties on arrival in the UK, there may be scope for negotiation, or 'appeal' to a superior officer before a final decision is taken.

If the client's port reference number includes '/RLE/', a final decision to refuse leave has been taken and the remedy is a formal appeal (see **Chapter 16**).

When advising on applications (eg for an extension of stay), much of the information to be supplied to the immigration authorities will be routine, but usually the applicant will be required to explain his reasons for the application. These reasons should be drafted with the relevant provisions of the Rules in mind, but the adviser should allow the client to tell his own story. Even if it is badly written, the client's account of emotional and family ties may be more credible and persuasive than one expressed more formally.

APPENDICES TO PART II

		Page
Appendix 1	Statement of Changes in Immigration Rules 1994 (HC 395)	337
Appendix 2	Commonwealth Citizens	491
Appendix 3	British Overseas Territories	493
Appendix 4	Visa Nationals	495
Appendix 5	The European Union and Associated States	497
Appendix 6	Directive 2004/38/EC	499
Appendix 7	Immigration (European Economic Area) Regulations 2006	513
Appendix 8	Work Permits (UK) Shortage Occupation List, May 2007	537
Appendix 9	Extracts from the European Convention on Human Rights	541
Appendix 10	Income Categories: Highly Skilled Migrants over 28	545
Appendix 11	MBA Eligible Programmes	547
Appendix 12	Refugee or Person in Need of International Protection (Qualification) Regulations 2006	549

Appendix 1

Statement of Changes in Immigration Rules 1994 (HC 395)

Laid before Parliament on 23 May 1994 under Section 3(2) of the Immigration Act 1971
Ordered by the House of Commons to be printed 23 May 1994
Includes all statements of changes up to and including Cm 7075, April 2007

CONTENTS	Paragraphs
Introduction	1–3
Implementation and transitional provisions	4
Application	5
Interpretation	6

Part 1: General provisions regarding leave to enter or remain in the United Kingdom

Leave to enter the United Kingdom	7–9
Exercise of the power to refuse leave to enter the United Kingdom or to cancel leave to enter or remain which is in force	10
Suspension of leave to enter or remain in the United Kingdom	10A
Cancellation of leave to enter or remain in the United Kingdom	10B
Requirement for persons arriving in the United Kingdom or seeking entry through the Channel Tunnel to produce evidence of identity and nationality	11
Requirement for a person not requiring leave to enter the United Kingdom to prove that he has the right of abode	12–14
Common Travel Area	15
Admission for certain British passport holders	16–17
Persons outside the United Kingdom	17A–17B
Returning residents	18–20
Non-lapsing leave	20A
Holders of restricted travel documents and passports	21–23
Leave to enter granted on arrival in the United Kingdom	23A–23B
Entry clearance	24–30C
Variation of leave to enter or remain in the United Kingdom	31–33A
Knowledge of language and life in the United Kingdom	33B–33F
Withdrawn applications for variation of leave to enter or remain in the United Kingdom	34
Undertakings	35
Medical	36–39
Students	39A

Part 2: Persons seeking to enter or remain in the United Kingdom for visits

Visitors	40–46
Child visitors	46A–46F
Visitors in transit	47–50
Visitors seeking to enter or remain for private medical treatment	51–56

CONTENTS	Paragraphs
Parent of a child at school	56A–56C
Visitors seeking to enter for the purposes of marriage or civil partnership	56D–56F
Visitors seeking leave to enter under the Approved Destination Status (ADS) Agreement with China	56G–56J
Student visitors	56K–56M

Part 3: Persons seeking to enter or remain in the United Kingdom for studies

Students	57–62
Student nurses	63–69
Re-sits of examinations	69A–69F
Writing up a thesis	69G–69L
Requirements for leave to enter as an overseas qualified nurse or midwife	69M–69R
Postgraduate doctors, dentists and trainee general practitioners	70–75M
Spouses or civil partners of students or prospective students	76–78
Children of students or prospective students	79–81
Prospective students	82–87
Students' union sabbatical officers	87A–87F

Part 4: Persons seeking to enter or remain in the United Kingdom in an 'au pair' placement, as a working holidaymaker or for training or work experience

Au pair placements	88–94
Working holidaymakers	95–97
Children of working holidaymakers	101–103
Seasonal agricultural workers	104–109
Requirements for leave to enter as a teacher or language assistant under an approved exchange scheme	110–115
Home Office approved training or work experience	116–121
Spouses or civil partners of persons with limited leave to enter or remain under paragraphs 110–121	122–124
Children of persons admitted or allowed to enter or remain under paragraphs 110–121	125–127

Part 5: Persons seeking to enter or remain in the United Kingdom for employment

Work permit employment	128–135
Highly skilled migrants	135A–135HA
Sectors-Based Scheme	135I–135N
International Graduates Scheme	135O–135T
Representatives of overseas newspapers, news agencies and broadcasting organisations	136–143
Requirements for leave to enter the United Kingdom as a Fresh Talent: Working in Scotland scheme participant	143A–143F
Representatives of overseas firms which have no branch, subsidiary or other representative in the United Kingdom (sole representatives)	144–151
Private servants in diplomatic households	152–159
Domestic workers in private households	159A–159H
Overseas government employees	160–169
Requirements for leave to enter as a minister of religion, missionary, or member of a religious order	170–177G
Airport based operational ground staff of overseas-owned airlines	178–185

CONTENTS	Paragraphs
Persons with United Kingdom ancestry	186–193
Spouses or civil partners of persons who have or have had limited leave to enter or remain under paragraphs 128–193 (but not paragraphs 135I–135K)	194–196F
Children of persons with limited leave to enter or remain in the United Kingdom under paragraphs 128–193 (but not paragraphs 135I–135K)	197–199
Multiple Entry work permit employment	199A–199C

Part 6: Persons seeking to enter or remain in the United Kingdom as a businessman, self-employed person, investor, writer, composer or artist

Persons intending to establish themselves in business	200–210
Innovators	210A–210H
Persons intending to establish themselves in business under provisions of EC Association Agreements	222–223A
Requirements for leave to enter the United Kingdom as an investor	224–231
Writers, composers and artists	232–239
Spouses or civil partners of persons with limited leave to enter or remain under paragraphs 200–239	240–242F
Children of persons with limited leave to enter or remain under paragraphs 200–239	243–245

Part 7: Other categories

Persons exercising rights of access to a child resident in the United Kingdom	246–248F
EEA nationals and their families	255–257E
Retired persons of independent means	263–270
Spouses or civil partners of persons with limited leave to enter or remain in the United Kingdom as retired persons of independent means	271–273F
Children of persons with limited leave to enter or remain in the United Kingdom as retired persons of independent means	274–276
Long residence	276A–276D
HM Forces	276E–276AI

Part 8: Family Members

Spouses and civil partners	277–289
Victims of domestic violence	289A–289C
Fiancé(e)s and proposed civil partners	289AA–295
Unmarried or same-sex partners	295AA–295O
Children	296–316F
Parents, grandparents and other dependent relatives	317–319

Part 9: General grounds for the refusal of entry clearance, leave to enter or variation of leave to enter or remain in the United Kingdom

Refusal of entry clearance or leave to enter the United Kingdom	320
Refusal of leave to enter in relation to a person in possession of an entry clearance	321–321A
Refusal of variation of leave to enter or remain or curtailment of leave	322–323
Crew members	324

Part 10: Registration with the police	325–326

CONTENTS	Paragraphs
Part 11: Asylum	327–352G
Part 11A: Temporary protection	354–356B
Part 11B: Asylum	357–361
Part 12: Procedure and rights of appeal	353
Part 13: Deportation	362–395F

Appendix 1: Visa requirements for the United Kingdom

Appendix 2: Countries or territories whose nationals or citizens are relevant foreign nationals for the purposes of Part 10 of these Rules

Appendix 3: List of countries participating in the working holidaymaker scheme

Appendix 4: Points criteria needed to succeed under paragraph 135D(ii) of these Rules

Appendix 5: Documents referred to in paragraph 135D(ii) and 135D(iii)b

Introduction

1. The Home Secretary has made changes in the Rules laid down by him as to the practice to be followed in the administration of the Immigration Acts for regulating entry into and the stay of persons in the United Kingdom and contained in the statement laid before Parliament on 23 March 1990 (HC 251) (as amended). This statement contains the Rules as changed and replaces the provisions of HC 251 (as amended).

2. Immigration Officers, Entry Clearance Officers and all staff of the Home Office Immigration and Nationality Directorate will carry out their duties without regard to the race, colour or religion of persons seeking to enter or remain in the United Kingdom and in compliance with the provisions of the Human Rights Act 1998.

3. In these Rules words importing the masculine gender include the feminine unless the contrary intention appears.

Implementation and transitional provisions

4. These Rules come into effect on 1 October 1994 and will apply to all decisions taken on or after that date save that any application made before 1 October 1994 for entry clearance, leave to enter or remain or variation of leave to enter or remain other than an application for leave by a person seeking asylum shall be decided under the provisions of HC 251, as amended, as if these Rules had not been made.

Application

5. Save where expressly indicated, these Rules do not apply to those persons who are entitled to enter or remain in the United Kingdom by virtue of the provisions of the 2006 EEA Regulations. But any person who is not entitled to rely on the provisions of those Regulations is covered by these Rules.

Interpretation

6. In these Rules the following interpretations apply:

'the Immigration Acts' mean the Immigration Act 1971 and the Immigration Act 1988.

'the 1993 Act' is the Asylum and Immigration Appeals Act 1993.

'the 1996 Act' is the Asylum and Immigration Act 1996

'the 2006 EEA Regulations' are the Immigration (European Economic Area) Regulations 2006.

'adoption' unless the contrary intention appears, includes a de facto adoption in accordance with the requirements of paragraph 309A of these Rules, and 'adopted' and 'adoptive parent' should be construed accordingly.

'Approved Destination Status Agreement with China' means the Memorandum of Understanding on visa and related issues concerning tourist groups from the People's Republic of China to the United Kingdom as a approved destination, signed on 21 January 2005.

'*a bona fide* private education institution' is a private education institution which:

(a) maintains satisfactory records of enrolment and attendance of students, and supplies these to the Border and Immigration Agency when requested;

(b) provides courses which involve a minimum of 15 hours organised daytime study per week;

(c) ensures a suitably qualified tutor is present during the hours of study to offer teaching and instruction to the students;

(d) offers courses leading to qualifications recognised by the appropriate accreditation bodies;

(e) employs suitably qualified staff to provide teaching, guidance and support to the students;

(f) provides adequate accommodation, facilities, staffing levels and equipment to support the numbers of students enrolled at the institution; and

(g) if it offers tuition support to external students at degree level, ensures that such students are registered with the UK degree awarding body.

'civil partner' means a civil partnership which exists under or by virtue of the Civil Partnership Act 2004 (and any reference to a civil partner is to be read accordingly);

'degree level study' means a course which leads to a recognised United Kingdom degree at bachelor's level or above, or an equivalent qualification at level 6 or above of the revised National Qualifications Framework, or levels 9 or above of the Scottish Credit and Qualifications Framework.

'EEA national' has the meaning given in regulation 2(1) of the 2006 EEA Regulations.

'an external student' is a student studying for a degree from a UK degree awarding body without any requirement to attend the UK degree awarding body's premises or a UK Listed Body's premises for lectures and tutorials.

'United Kingdom passport' bears the meaning it has in the Immigration Act 1971.

'a UK Bachelors degree' means—

(a) A programme of study or research which leads to the award, by or on behalf of a university, college or other body which is authorised by Royal Charter or by or under an Act of Parliament to grant degrees, of a qualification designated by the awarding institution to be of Bachelors degree level; or

(b) A programme of study or research, which leads to a recognised award for the purposes of section 214(2)(c) of the Education Reform Act 1988, of a qualification designated by the awarding institution to be of Bachelors degree level.

'Immigration Officer' includes a Customs Officer acting as an Immigration Officer.

'Multiple Entry work permit employment' is work permit employment where the person concerned does not intend to spend a continuous period in the United Kingdom in work permit employment.

'public funds' means

(a) housing under Part VI or VII of the Housing Act 1996 and under Part II of the Housing Act 1985, Part I or II of the Housing (Scotland) Act 1987, Part II of the Housing (Northern Ireland) Order 1981 or Part II of the Housing (Northern Ireland) Order 1988;

(b) attendance allowance, severe disablement allowance, carer's allowance and disability living allowance under Part III of the Social Security Contribution and Benefits Act 1992;, income support, council tax benefit and housing benefit under Part VII of that Act; a social fund payment under Part VIII of that Act; child benefit under Part IX of that Act; income based jobseeker's allowance under the Jobseekers Act 1995, state pension credit under the State Pension Credit Act 2002; or child tax credit and working tax credit under Part 1 of the Tax Credits Act 2002.

(c) attendance allowance, severe disablement allowance, carer's allowance and disability living allowance under Part III of the Social Security Contribution and Benefits (Northern Ireland) Act 1992;, income support, council tax benefit, housing benefit under Part VII of that Act; a social fund payment under Part VIII of that Act; child benefit under Part IX of that Act; or income based jobseeker's allowance under the Jobseekers (Northern Ireland) Order 1995.

'settled in the United Kingdom' means that the person concerned:

(a) is free from any restriction on the period for which he may remain save that a person entitled to an exemption under Section 8 of the Immigration Act 1971 (otherwise than as a member of the home forces) is not to be regarded as settled in the United Kingdom except in so far as Section 8(5A) so provides; and

(b) is either:
   (i) ordinarily resident in the United Kingdom without having entered or remained in breach of the immigration laws; or
   (ii) despite having entered or remained in breach of the immigration laws, has subsequently entered lawfully or has been granted leave to remain and is ordinarily resident.

'a parent' includes

(a) the stepfather of a child whose father is dead (and the reference to stepfather includes a relationship arising through civil partnership);

(b) the stepmother of a child whose mother is dead (and the reference to stepmother includes a relationship arising through civil partnership);

(c) the father as well as the mother of an illegitimate child where he is proved to be the father;

(d) an adoptive parent, where a child was adopted in accordance with a decision taken by the competent administrative authority or court in a country whose adoption orders are recognised by the United Kingdom or where a child is the subject of a de facto adoption in accordance with the requirements of paragraph 309A of these Rules (except that an adopted child or a child who is the subject of a de facto adoption may not make an application for leave to enter or remain in order to accompany, join or remain with an adoptive parent under paragraphs 297–303);

(e) in the case of a child born in the United Kingdom who is not a British citizen, a person to whom there has been a genuine transfer of parental responsibility on the ground of the original parent(s)' inability to care for the child.

'intention to live permanently with the other' means an intention to live together, evidenced by a clear commitment from both parties that they will live together permanently in the United Kingdom immediately following the outcome of the application in question or as soon as circumstances permit thereafter, and 'intends to live permanently with the other' shall be construed accordingly.

'present and settled' means that the person concerned is settled in the United Kingdom, and, at the time that an application under these Rules is made, is physically present here or is coming here with or to join the applicant and intends to make the United Kingdom their home with the applicant if their application is successful.

'sponsor' means the person in relation to whom an applicant is seeking leave to enter or remain as their spouse, fiancé, civil partner, proposed civil partner, unmarried partner, same-sex partner or dependent relative, as the case may be, under paragraphs 277 to 295O or 317 to 319.

'visa nationals' are the persons specified in Appendix 1 to these Rules who need a visa for the United Kingdom.

'non-visa nationals' are persons who are not specified in Appendix 1 to these Rules.

'employment' unless the contrary intention appears, includes paid and unpaid employment, self employment and engaging in business or any professional activity.

'the Human Rights Convention' means the Convention for the Protection of Human Rights and Fundamental Freedoms, agreed by the Council of Europe at Rome on 4th November 1950 as it has effect for the time being in relation to the United Kingdom.

'Immigration employment document' means a work permit or any other document which relates to employment and is issued for the purpose of these Rules or in connection with leave to enter or remain in the United Kingdom.

6A. For the purpose of these Rules, a person is not to be regarded as having (or potentially having) recourse to public funds merely because he is (or will be) reliant in whole or in part on public funds provided to his sponsor, unless, as a result of his presence in the United Kingdom, the sponsor is (or would be) entitled to increased or additional public funds.

6B. A person shall not be regarded as having recourse to public funds if he is a person who is not excluded from specified benefits under section 115 of the Immigration and Asylum Act 1999 by virtue of regulations made under sub-sections (3) and (4) of that section or section 42 of the Tax Credits Act 2002.

Part 1: General provisions regarding leave to enter or remain in the United Kingdom

Leave to enter the United Kingdom

7. A person who is neither a British citizen nor a Commonwealth citizen with the right of abode nor a person who is entitled to enter or remain in the United Kingdom by virtue of the provisions of the 2006 EEA Regulations requires leave to enter the United Kingdom.

8. Under Sections 3 and 4 of the Immigration Act 1971 an Immigration Officer when admitting to the United Kingdom a person subject to immigration control under that Act may give leave to enter for a limited period and, if he does, may impose all or any of the following conditions:

   (i) a condition restricting employment or occupation in the United Kingdom;

   (ii) a condition requiring the person to maintain and accommodate himself, and any dependants of his, without recourse to public funds; and

   (iii) a condition requiring the person to register with the police.

   He may also require him to report to the appropriate Medical Officer of Environmental Health. Under Section 24 of the 1971 Act it is an offence knowingly to remain beyond the time limit or fail to comply with such a condition or requirement.

9. The time limit and any conditions attached will be made known to the person concerned either:

   (i) by written notice given to him or endorsed by the Immigration Officer in his passport or travel document; or

(ii) in any other manner permitted by the Immigration (Leave to Enter and Remain) Order 2000.

Exercise of the power to refuse leave to enter the United Kingdom or to cancel leave to enter or remain which is in force

10. The power to refuse leave to enter the United Kingdom or to cancel leave to enter or remain which is already in force is not to be exercised by an Immigration Officer acting on his own. The authority of a Chief Immigration Officer or of an Immigration Inspector must always be obtained.

Suspension of leave to enter or remain in the United Kingdom

10A. Where a person has arrived in the United Kingdom with leave to enter or remain which is in force but which was given to him before his arrival he may be examined by an Immigration Officer under paragraph 2A of Schedule 2 to the Immigration Act 1971. An Immigration Officer examining a person under paragraph 2A may suspend that person's leave to enter or remain in the United Kingdom until the examination is completed.

Cancellation of leave to enter or remain in the United Kingdom

10B. Where a person arrives in the United Kingdom with leave to enter or remain in the United Kingdom which is already in force, an Immigration Officer may cancel that leave.

Requirement for persons arriving in the United Kingdom or seeking entry through the Channel Tunnel to produce evidence of identity and nationality

11. A person must, on arrival in the United Kingdom or when seeking entry through the Channel Tunnel, produce on request by the Immigration Officer:
    (i) a valid national passport or other document satisfactorily establishing his identity and nationality; and
    (ii) such information as may be required to establish whether he requires leave to enter the United Kingdom and, if so, whether and on what terms leave to enter should be given.

Requirement for a person not requiring leave to enter the United Kingdom to prove that he has the right of abode

12. A person claiming to be a British citizen must prove that he has the right of abode in the United Kingdom by producing either:
    (i) a United Kingdom passport describing him as a British citizen or as a citizen of the United Kingdom and Colonies having the right of abode in the United Kingdom; or
    (ii) a certificate of entitlement duly issued by or on behalf of the Government of the United Kingdom certifying that he has the right of abode.

13. A person claiming to be a Commonwealth citizen with the right of abode in the United Kingdom must prove that he has the right of abode by producing a certificate of entitlement duly issued to him by or on behalf of the Government of the United Kingdom certifying that he has the right of abode.

14. A Commonwealth citizen who has been given limited leave to enter the United Kingdom may later claim to have the right of abode. The time limit on his stay may be removed if he is able to establish a claim to the right of abode, for example by showing that:
    (i) immediately before the commencement of the British Nationality Act 1981 he was a Commonwealth citizen born to or legally adopted by a parent who at the time of the birth had citizenship of the United Kingdom and Colonies by his birth in the United Kingdom or any of the Islands; and
    (ii) he has not ceased to be a Commonwealth citizen in the meanwhile.

Common Travel Area

15. The United Kingdom, the Channel Islands, the Isle of Man and the Republic of Ireland collectively form a common travel area. A person who has been examined for the purpose of immigration control at the point at which he entered the area does not normally require leave to enter any other part of it. However certain persons subject to the Immigration (Control of Entry through the Republic of Ireland) Order 1972 (as amended) who enter the United Kingdom through the Republic of Ireland do require leave to enter. This includes:
    (i) those who merely passed through the Republic of Ireland;
    (ii) persons requiring visas;
    (iii) persons who entered the Republic of Ireland unlawfully;
    (iv) persons who are subject to directions given by the Secretary of State for their exclusion from the United Kingdom on the ground that their exclusion is conducive to the public good;
    (v) persons who entered the Republic from the United Kingdom and Islands after entering there unlawfully or overstaying their leave.

Admission of certain British passport holders

16. A person in any of the following categories may be admitted freely to the United Kingdom on production of a United Kingdom passport issued in the United Kingdom and Islands or the Republic of Ireland prior to 1 January 1973, unless his passport has been endorsed to show that he was subject to immigration control:
    (i) a British Dependent Territories citizen;
    (ii) a British National (Overseas);
    (iii) a British Overseas citizen;
    (iv) a British protected person;
    (v) a British subject by virtue of Section 30(a) of the British Nationality Act 1981, (who, immediately before the commencement of the 1981 Act would have been a British subject not possessing citizenship of the United Kingdom and Colonies or the citizenship of any other Commonwealth country or territory).

17. British Overseas citizens who hold United Kingdom passports wherever issued and who satisfy the Immigration Officer that they have, since 1 March 1968, been given indefinite leave to enter or remain in the United Kingdom may be given indefinite leave to enter.

Persons outside the United Kingdom

17A. Where a person is outside the United Kingdom but wishes to travel to the United Kingdom an Immigration Officer may give or refuse him leave to enter. An Immigration Officer may exercise these powers whether or not he is, himself, in the United Kingdom. However, an Immigration Officer is not obliged to consider an application for leave to enter from a person outside the United Kingdom.

17B. Where a person having left the common travel area, has leave to enter the United Kingdom which remains in force under article 13 of the Immigration (Leave to Enter and Remain) Order 2000, an Immigration Officer may cancel that leave. An Immigration Officer may exercise these powers whether or not he is, himself, in the United Kingdom. If a person outside the United Kingdom has leave to remain in the United Kingdom which is in force in this way, the Secretary of State may cancel that leave.

Returning residents

18. A person seeking leave to enter the United Kingdom as a returning resident may be admitted for settlement provided the Immigration Officer is satisfied that the person concerned:

(i) had indefinite leave to enter or remain in the United Kingdom when he last left; and
(ii) has not been away from the United Kingdom for more than 2 years; and
(iii) did not receive assistance from public funds towards the cost of leaving the United Kingdom; and
(iv) now seeks admission for the purpose of settlement.

19. A person who does not benefit from the preceding paragraph by reason only of having been away from the United Kingdom too long may nevertheless be admitted as a returning resident if, for example, he has lived here for most of his life.

19A. Where a person who has indefinite leave to enter or remain in the United Kingdom accompanies, on a tour of duty abroad, a spouse, civil partner, unmarried partner or same-sex partner who is a member of HM Forces serving overseas, or a permanent member of HM Diplomatic Service, or a comparable United Kingdom-based staff member of the British Council, or a staff member of the Department for International Development who is a British Citizen or is settled in the United Kingdom, sub-paragraphs (ii) and (iii) of paragraph 18 shall not apply.

20. The leave of a person whose stay in the United Kingdom is subject to a time limit lapses on his going to a country or territory outside the common travel area if the leave was given for a period of six months or less or conferred by a visit visa. In other cases, leave lapses on the holder remaining outside the United Kingdom for a continuous period of more than two years. A person whose leave has lapsed and who returns after a temporary absence abroad within the period of this earlier leave has no claim to admission as a returning resident. His application to re-enter the United Kingdom should be considered in the light of all the relevant circumstances. The same time limit and any conditions attached will normally be reimposed if he meets the requirements of these Rules, unless he is seeking admission in a different capacity from the one in which he was last given leave to enter or remain.

Non-lapsing leave

20A. Leave to enter or remain in the United Kingdom will usually lapse on the holder going to a country or territory outside the common travel area. However, under article 13 of the Immigration (Leave to Enter and Remain) Order 2000 such leave will not lapse where it was given for a period exceeding six months or where it was conferred by means of an entry clearance (other than a visit visa).

Holders of restricted travel documents and passports

21. The leave to enter or remain in the United Kingdom of the holder of a passport or travel document whose permission to enter another country has to be exercised before a given date may be restricted so as to terminate at least 2 months before that date.

22. If his passport or travel document is endorsed with a restriction on the period for which he may remain outside his country of normal residence, his leave to enter or remain in the United Kingdom may be limited so as not to extend beyond the period of authorised absence.

23. The holder of a travel document issued by the Home Office should not be given leave to enter or remain for a period extending beyond the validity of that document. This paragraph and paragraphs 21-22 do not apply to a person who is eligible for admission for settlement or to a spouse or civil partner who is eligible for admission under paragraph 282 or to a person who qualifies for the removal of the time limit on his stay.

Leave to enter granted on arrival in the United Kingdom

23A. A person who is not a visa national and who is seeking leave to enter on arrival in the United Kingdom for a period not exceeding 6 months for a purpose for which prior entry clearance is not required under these Rules may be granted such leave, for a period not exceeding 6 months.

This paragraph does not apply where the person is a British National (Overseas), a British overseas territories citizen, a British Overseas citizen, a British protected person, or a person who under the British Nationality Act 1981 is a British subject.

23B. A person who is a British National (Overseas), a British overseas territories citizen, a British Overseas citizen, a British protected person, or a person who under the British Nationality Act 1981 is a British subject, and who is seeking leave to enter on arrival in the United Kingdom for a purpose for which prior entry clearance is not required under these Rules may be granted such leave, irrespective of the period of time for which he seeks entry, for a period not exceeding 6 months.

Entry clearance

24. The following must produce to the Immigration Officer a valid passport or other identity document endorsed with a United Kingdom entry clearance issued to him for the purpose for which he seeks entry:
    (i) a visa national;
    (ii) any other person (other than British Nationals (Overseas), a British overseas territories citizen, a British Overseas citizen, a British protected person or a person who under the British Nationality Act 1981 is a British subject) who is seeking entry for a period exceeding six months or is seeking entry for a purpose for which prior entry clearance is required under these Rules.

    Such a person will be refused leave to enter if he has no such current entry clearance. Any other person who wishes to ascertain in advance whether he is eligible for admission to the United Kingdom may apply for the issue of an entry clearance.

25. Entry clearance takes the form of a visa (for visa nationals) or an entry certificate (for non visa nationals). These documents are to be taken as evidence of the holder's eligibility for entry into the United Kingdom, and accordingly accepted as 'entry clearances' within the meaning of the Immigration Act 1971.

25A. An entry clearance which satisfies the requirements set out in article 3 of the Immigration (Leave to Enter and Remain) Order 2000 will have effect as leave to enter the United Kingdom. The requirements are that the entry clearance must specify the purpose for which the holder wishes to enter the United Kingdom and should be endorsed with the conditions to which it is subject or wish a statement that it has effect as indefinite leave to enter the United Kingdom. The holder of such an entry clearance will not require leave to enter on arrival in the United Kingdom and, for the purposes of these Rules, will be treated as a person who has arrived in the United Kingdom with leave to enter the United Kingdom which is in force but which was given to him before his arrival.

26. An application for entry clearance will be considered in accordance with the provisions in these Rules governing the grant or refusal of leave to enter. Where appropriate, the term 'Entry Clearance Officer' should be substituted for 'Immigration Officer'.

27. An application for entry clearance is to be decided in the light of the circumstances existing at the time of the decision, except that an applicant will not be refused an entry clearance where entry is sought in one of the categories contained in paragraphs 296-316 solely on account of his attaining the age of 18 years between receipt of his application and the date of the decision on it.

28. An applicant for an entry clearance must be outside the United Kingdom and Islands at the time of the application. An applicant for an entry clearance who is seeking entry as a visitor must apply to a post designated by the Secretary of State to accept applications for entry clearance for that purpose and from that category of applicant. Any other application must be made to the post in the country or territory where the applicant is living which has been designated by the Secretary of State to accept applications for entry clearance for that purpose and from that category of applicant. Where there is no such post the applicant must apply to the appropriate designated post outside the country or territory where he is living.

29. For the purposes of paragraph 28 'post' means a British Diplomatic Mission, British Consular post or the office of any person outside the United Kingdom and Islands who has been authorised by the Secretary of State to accept applications for entry clearance. A list of designated posts is published by the Foreign and Commonwealth Office.

30. An application for an entry clearance is not made until any fee required to be paid under the Consular Fees Act 1980 (including any Regulations or Orders made under that Act) has been paid.

30A. An entry clearance may be revoked if the Entry Clearance Officer is satisfied that:
   (i) whether or not to the holder's knowledge, false representations were employed or material facts were not disclosed, either in writing or orally, for the purpose of obtaining the entry clearance; or
   (ii) a change of circumstances since the entry clearance was issued has removed the basis of the holder's claim to be admitted to the United Kingdom, except where the change of circumstances amounts solely to his exceeding the age for entry in one of the categories contained in paragraphs 296–316 of these Rules since the issue of the entry clearance; or
   (iii) the holder's exclusion from the United Kingdom would be conducive to the public good.

30B. An entry clearance shall cease to have effect where the entry clearance has effect as leave to enter and an Immigration Officer cancels that leave in accordance with paragraph 2A(8) of Schedule 2 to the Immigration Act 1971.

30C. An Immigration Officer may cancel an entry clearance which is capable of having effect as leave to enter if the holder arrives in the United Kingdom before the day on which the entry clearance becomes effective or if the holder seeks to enter the United Kingdom for a purpose other than the purpose specified in the entry clearance.

Variation of leave to enter or remain in the United Kingdom

31. Under Section 3(3) of the 1971 Act a limited leave to enter or remain in the United Kingdom may be varied by extending or restricting its duration, by adding, varying or revoking conditions or by removing the time limit (where upon any condition attached to the leave ceases to apply). When leave to enter or remain is varied an entry is to be made in the applicant's passport or travel document (and his registration certificate where appropriate) or the decision may be made known in writing in some other appropriate way.

31A. Where a person has arrived in the United Kingdom with leave to enter or remain in the United Kingdom which is in force but was given to him before his arrival, he may apply, on arrival at the port of entry in the United Kingdom, for variation of that leave. An Immigration Officer acting on behalf of the Secretary of State may vary the leave at the port of entry but is not obliged to consider an application for variation made at the port of entry. If an Immigration Officer acting on behalf of the Secretary of State has declined to consider an application for variation of leave at a port of entry but the leave has not been cancelled under paragraph 2A(8) of Schedule 2 to the Immigration Act 1971, the person seeking variation should apply to the Home office under paragraph 32.

32. After admission to the United Kingdom any application for an extension of the time limit on or variation of conditions attached to a person's stay in the United Kingdom must be made to the Home Office before the applicant's current leave to enter or remain expires. With the exception of applications made under paragraph 31A (applications at the port of entry), paragraph 33 (work permits), 33A (applications made outside the United Kingdom), paragraphs 255 to 257 (EEA nationals) and Part 11 (asylum) all applications for variation of leave to enter or remain must be made using the form prescribed for the purpose by the Secretary of State, which must be completed in the manner required by the form and be accompanied by the documents and photographs specified in the form. An application for such a variation made in any other way is not valid.

33. Where the application is in respect of employment for which a work permit or a permit for training or work experience is required or is in respect of the spouse or civil partner or child of a person who is making such an application, the application should be made direct to Work Permits (UK) at the Home Office.

33A. Where a person having left the common travel area, has leave to enter or remain in the United Kingdom which remains in force under article 13 of the Immigration (Leave to Enter and Remain) Order 2000., his leave may be varied (including any condition to which it is subject in such form and manner as permitted for the giving of leave to enter. However, the Secretary of State is not obliged to consider an application for variation of leave to enter or remain from a person outside the United Kingdom.

Knowledge of language and life in the United Kingdom

33B. A person has sufficient knowledge of the English language and sufficient knowledge about life in the United Kingdom for the purpose of an application for indefinite leave to remain under these rules if–

(a) he has attended a course which used teaching materials derived from the document entitled 'Citizenship Materials for ESOL Learners' (ISBN 1-84478-5424) and he has thereby attained a relevant accredited qualification; or

(b) he has passed the test known as the 'Life in the UK Test' administered by an educational institution or other person approved for this purpose by the Secretary of State; or

(c) in the case of a person who is the spouse or civil partner or unmarried or same sex partner of:

(i) a permanent member of HM Diplomatic Service; or

(ii) a comparable UK-based staff member of the British Council on a tour of duty abroad; or

(iii) a staff member of the Department for International Development who is a British citizen or is settled in the UK, a person designated by the Secretary of State certifies in writing that he has sufficient knowledge of the English language and sufficient knowledge about life in the United Kingdom for this purpose.

33C. In these rules, a 'relevant accredited qualification' is–

(a) an ESOL 'Skills for Life' qualification in speaking and listening at Entry Level approved by the Qualifications and Curriculum Authority; or

(b) two ESOL units at Access Level under the Scottish Credit and Qualifications Framework approved by the Scottish Qualifications Authority.

33D. If in the special circumstances of any particular case the Secretary of State thinks fit, he may waive the need to fulfil the requirement to have sufficient knowledge of the English language and sufficient knowledge about life in the United Kingdom if he considers that, because of the applicant's physical or mental condition, it would be unreasonable to expect him to fulfil that requirement.

33E. Where an applicant applies for indefinite leave to remain under these rules, and:

(i) is required by these rules to have sufficient knowledge of the English language and sufficient knowledge about life in the United Kingdom, and

(ii) meets all the other requirements for indefinite leave to remain for the category he has applied under with the exception of the requirement in (i) above, and

(iii) has not made any false representations or failed to disclose any material fact in his application, his application will automatically fall to be considered under the rules for an extension of stay in the same category in which he applied for indefinite leave to remain. This provision does not apply to applications for indefinite leave to remain made under paragraphs 222 to 223A of these rules.

33F. Where an application is considered under the rules for an extension of stay in accordance with paragraph 33E above, and the Secretary of State is satisfied that the applicant qualifies for a grant of limited leave, leave should be granted for the duration and subject to the conditions normally imposed on an extension of stay in the category under which the application is being considered.

Withdrawn applications for variation of leave to enter or remain in the United Kingdom

34. Where a person whose application for variation of leave to enter or remain is being considered requests the return of his passport for the purpose of travel outside the common travel area, the application for variation of leave shall, provided it has not already been determined, be treated as withdrawn as soon as the passport is returned in response to that request.

Undertakings

35. A sponsor of a person seeking leave to enter or variation of leave to enter or remain in the United Kingdom may be asked to give an undertaking in writing to be responsible for that person's maintenance and accommodation for the period of any leave granted, including any further variation. Under the Social Security Administration Act 1992 and the Social Security Administration (Northern Ireland) Act 1992, the Department of Social Security or, as the case may be, the Department of Health and Social Services in Northern Ireland, may seek to recover from the person giving such an undertaking any income support paid to meet the needs of the person in respect of whom the undertaking has been given. Under the Immigration and Asylum Act 1999 the Home Office may seek to recover from the person giving such an undertaking amounts attributable to any support provided under section 95 of the Immigration and Asylum Act 1999 (support for asylum seekers) to, or in respect of, the person in respect of whom the undertaking has been given. Failure by the sponsor to maintain that person in accordance with the undertaking, may also be an offence under section 105 of the Social Security Administration Act 1992 and/or under section 108 of the Immigration and Asylum Act 1999 if, as a consequence, asylum support and/or income support is provided to, or in respect of, that person.

Medical

36. A person who intends to remain in the United Kingdom for more than 6 months should normally be referred to the Medical Inspector for examination. If he produces a medical certificate he should be advised to hand it to the Medical Inspector. Any person seeking entry who mentions health or medical treatment as a reason for his visit, or who appears not to be in good mental or physical health, should also be referred to the Medical Inspector; and the Immigration Officer has discretion, which should be exercised sparingly, to refer for examination in any other case.

37. Where the Medical Inspector advises that a person seeking entry is suffering from a specified disease or condition which may interfere with his ability to support himself or his dependants, the Immigration Officer should take account of this, in conjunction with other factors, in deciding whether to admit that person. The Immigration Officer should also take account of the Medical Inspector's assessment of the likely course of treatment in deciding whether a person seeking entry for private medical treatment has sufficient means at his disposal.

38. A returning resident should not be refused leave to enter or have existing leave to enter or remain cancelled on medical grounds. But where a person would be refused leave to enter or have existing leave to enter or remain cancelled on medical grounds if he were not a returning resident or in any case where it is decided on compassionate grounds not to exercise the power to refuse leave to enter or to cancel existing leave to enter or remain, or in any other case where the Medical Inspector so recommends, the Immigration Officer should give the person

concerned a notice requiring him to report to the Medical Officer of Environmental Health designated by the Medical Inspector with a view to further examination and any necessary treatment.

39. The Entry Clearance Officer has the same discretion as an Immigration Officer to refer applicants for entry clearance for medical examination and the same principles will apply to the decision whether or not to issue an entry clearance.

Students

39A. An application for a variation of leave to enter or remain made by a student who is sponsored by a government or international sponsorship agency may be refused if the sponsor has not given written consent to the proposed variation.

Part 2: Persons seeking to enter or remain in the United Kingdom for visits

Visitors

Requirements for leave to enter as a visitor

40. For the purpose of paragraphs 41-46 a visitor includes a person living and working outside the United Kingdom who comes to the United Kingdom to transact business (such as attending meetings and briefings, fact finding, negotiating or making contracts with United Kingdom businesses to buy or sell goods or services). A visitor seeking leave to enter or remain for private medical treatment must meet the requirements of paragraphs 51 or 54.

    A visitor seeking leave to enter for the purposes of marriage must meet the requirements of paragraph 56D.

41. The requirements to be met by a person seeking leave to enter the United Kingdom as a visitor are that he:
    (i) is genuinely seeking entry as a visitor for a limited period as stated by him, not exceeding 6 months; and
    (ii) intends to leave the United Kingdom at the end of the period of the visit as stated by him; and
    (iii) does not intend to take employment in the United Kingdom; and
    (iv) does not intend to produce goods or provide services within the United Kingdom, including the selling of goods or services direct to members of the public; and
    (v) does not intend to undertake a course of study; and
    (vi) will maintain and accommodate himself and any dependants adequately out of resources available to him without recourse to public funds or taking employment; or will, with any dependants, be maintained and accommodated adequately by relatives or friends; and
    (vii) can meet the cost of the return or onward journey; and
    (viii) is not a child under the age of 18.

Leave to enter as a visitor

42. A person seeking leave to enter to the United Kingdom as a visitor may be admitted for a period not exceeding 6 months, subject to a condition prohibiting employment, provided the Immigration Officer is satisfied that each of the requirements of paragraph 41 is met.

Refusal of leave to enter as a visitor

43. Leave to enter as a visitor is to be refused if the Immigration Officer is not satisfied that each of the requirements of paragraph 41 is met.

Requirements for an extension of stay as a visitor

44. Six months is the maximum permitted leave which may be granted to a visitor. The requirements for an extension of stay as a visitor are that the applicant:
    (i) meets the requirements of paragraph 41(ii)–(vii); and
    (ii) has not already spent, or would not as a result of an extension of stay spend, more than 6 months in total in the United Kingdom as a visitor. Any periods spent as a seasonal agricultural worker and as a student visitor are to be counted as a period spent as a visitor; and
    (iii) was not last admitted to the United Kingdom under the Approved Destination Status Agreement with China.

Extension of stay as a visitor

45. An extension of stay as a visitor may be granted, subject to a condition prohibiting employment, provided the Secretary of State is satisfied that each of the requirements of paragraph 44 is met.

Refusal of extension of stay as a visitor

46. An extension of stay as a visitor is to be refused if the Secretary of State is not satisfied that each of the requirements of paragraph 44 is met.

Child visitors

Requirements for leave to enter as a child visitor

46A The requirements to be met by a person seeking leave to enter the United Kingdom as a child visitor are that he:
   (i) meets the requirements of paragraph 41(i)–(vii); and
   (ii) is under the age of 18; and
   (iii) can demonstrate that suitable arrangements have been made for his travel to, and reception and care in the United Kingdom; and
   (iv) has a parent or guardian in his home country or country of habitual residence who is responsible for his care; and
   (v) if a visa national:
       (a) holds a valid United Kingdom entry clearance for entry as an accompanied child visitor and is travelling in the company of the adult identified on his entry clearance, who is on the same occasion being admitted to the United Kingdom; or
       (b) holds a valid United Kingdom entry clearance for entry as an unaccompanied child visitor; and
   (vi) he has been accepted for a course of study, this is to be provided by an organisation which is included on the Department for Education and Skills' Register of Education and Training Providers, and which is outside the maintained sector.

Leave to enter as a child visitor

46B A person seeking leave to enter the United Kingdom as a child visitor may be admitted for a period not exceeding 6 months, subject to a condition prohibiting employment, providing that the Immigration Officer is satisfied that each of the requirements of paragraph 46A is met.

Refusal of leave to enter as a child visitor

46C Leave to enter as a child visitor is to be refused if the Immigration Officer is not satisfied that each of the requirements of paragraph 46A is met.

Requirements for an extension of stay as a child visitor

46D Six months is the maximum permitted leave which may be granted to a child visitor. The requirements for an extension of stay as a child visitor are that the applicant:
  (i)   meets the requirements of paragraph 41(ii) to (vii); and
  (ii) is under the age of 18; and
  (iii) can demonstrate that there are suitable arrangements for his care in the United Kingdom; and
  (iv) has a parent or guardian in his home country or country of habitual residence who is responsible for his care; and
  (v)   has not already spent, or would not as a result of an extension of stay spend, more than 6 months in total in the United Kingdom as a child visitor.

Extension of stay as a child visitor

46E An extension of stay as a child visitor may be granted, subject to a condition prohibiting employment, provided the Secretary of State is satisfied that each of the requirements of paragraph 46D is met.

Refusal of extension of stay as a child visitor

46F An extension of stay as a child visitor is to be refused if the Secretary of State is not satisfied that each of the requirements of paragraph 46D is met.

Visitors in transit

Requirements for admission as a visitor in transit to another country

47. The requirements to be met by a person (not being a member of the crew of a ship, aircraft, hovercraft, hydrofoil or train) seeking leave to enter the United Kingdom as a visitor in transit to another country are that he:
  (i)   is in transit to a country outside the common travel area; and
  (ii) has both the means and the intention of proceeding at once to another country; and
  (iii) is assured of entry there; and
  (iv) intends and is able to leave the United Kingdom within 48 hours.

Leave to enter as a visitor in transit

48. A person seeking leave to enter the United Kingdom as a visitor in transit may be admitted for a period not exceeding 48 hours with a prohibition on employment provided the Immigration Officer is satisfied that each of the requirements of paragraph 47 is met.

Refusal of leave to enter as a visitor in transit

49. Leave to enter as a visitor in transit is to be refused if the Immigration Officer is not satisfied that each of the requirements of paragraph 47 is met.

Extension of stay as a visitor in transit

50. The maximum permitted leave which may be granted to a visitor in transit is 48 hours. An application for an extension of stay beyond 48 hours from a person admitted in this category is to be refused.

Visitors seeking to enter or remain for private medical treatment

Requirements for leave to enter as a visitor for private medical treatment

51. The requirements to be met by a person seeking leave to enter the United Kingdom as a visitor for private medical treatment are that he:

(i) meets the requirements set out in paragraph 41(iii)–(vii) for entry as a visitor; and
(ii) in the case of a person suffering from a communicable disease, has satisfied the Medical Inspector that there is no danger to public health; and
(iii) can show, if required to do so, that any proposed course of treatment is of finite duration; and
(iv) intends to leave the United Kingdom at the end of his treatment; and
(v) can produce satisfactory evidence, if required to do so, of:
    (a) the medical condition requiring consultation or treatment; and
    (b) satisfactory arrangements for the necessary consultation or treatment at his own expense; and
    (c) the estimated costs of such consultation or treatment; and
    (d) the likely duration of his visit; and
    (e) sufficient funds available to him in the United Kingdom to meet the estimated costs and his undertaking to do so.

Leave to enter as a visitor for private medical treatment

52. A person seeking leave to enter the United Kingdom as a visitor for private medical treatment may be admitted for a period not exceeding 6 months, subject to a condition prohibiting employment, provided the Immigration Officer is satisfied that each of the requirements of paragraph 51 is met.

Refusal of leave to enter as a visitor for private medical treatment

53. Leave to enter as a visitor for private medical treatment is to be refused if the Immigration Officer is not satisfied that each of the requirements of paragraph 51 is met.

Requirements for an extension of stay as a visitor for private medical treatment

54. The requirements for an extension of stay as a visitor to undergo or continue private medical treatment are that the applicant:
(i) meets the requirements set out in paragraph 41(iii)–(vii) and paragraph 51(ii)–(v); and
(ii) has produced evidence from a registered medical practitioner who holds an NHS consultant post or who appears in the Specialist Register of the General Medical Council of satisfactory arrangements for private medical consultation or treatment and its likely duration; and, where treatment has already begun, evidence as to its progress; and
(iii) can show that he has met, out of the resources available to him, any costs and expenses incurred in relation to his treatment in the United Kingdom; and
(iv) has sufficient funds available to him in the United Kingdom to meet the likely costs of his treatment and intends to meet those costs; and
(v) was not last admitted to the United Kingdom under the Approved Destination Status Agreement with China.

Extension of stay as a visitor for private medical treatment

55. An extension of stay to undergo or continue private medical treatment may be granted, with a prohibition on employment, provided the Secretary of State is satisfied that each of the requirements of paragraph 54 is met.

Refusal of extension of stay as a visitor for private medical treatment

56. An extension of stay as a visitor to undergo or continue private medical treatment is to be refused if the Secretary of State is not satisfied that each of the requirements of paragraph 54 is met.

Parent of a child at school

Requirements for leave to enter or remain as the parent of a child at school

56A. The requirements to be met by a person seeking leave to enter or remain in the United Kingdom as the parent of a child at school are that:
(i) the parent meets the requirements set out in paragraph 41(ii)-(vii); and
(ii) the child is attending an independent fee paying day school and meets the requirements set out in paragraph 57(i)-(vii); and
(iii) the child is under 12 years of age; and
(iv) the parent can provide satisfactory evidence of adequate and reliable funds for maintaining a second home in the United Kingdom; and
(v) the parent is not seeking to make the United Kingdom his main home; and
(vi) the parent was not last admitted to the United Kingdom under the Approved Destination Status Agreement with China.

Leave to enter or remain as the parent of a child at school

56B. A person seeking leave to enter or remain in the United Kingdom as the parent of a child at school may be admitted or allowed to remain for a period not exceeding 12 months, subject to a condition prohibiting employment, provided the Immigration Officer or, in the case of an application for limited leave to remain, the Secretary of State is satisfied that each of the requirements of paragraph 56A is met.

Refusal of leave to enter or remain as the parent of a child at school

56C. Leave to enter or remain in the United Kingdom as the parent of a child at school is to be refused if the Immigration Officer or, in the case of an application for limited leave to remain, the Secretary of State is not satisfied that each of the requirements of paragraph 56A is met.

Visitors seeking to enter for the purposes of marriage or civil partnership

Requirements for leave to enter as a visitor for marriage or civil partnership

56D. The requirements to be met by a person seeking leave to enter the United Kingdom as a visitor for marriage or civil partnership are that he:
(i) meets the requirements set out in paragraph 41 for entry as a visitor; and
(ii) can show that he intends to give notice of marriage or civil partnership, or marry or form a civil partnership, in the United Kingdom within the period for which entry is sought; and
(iii) can produce satisfactory evidence, if required to do so, of the arrangements for giving notice of marriage or civil partnership, or for his wedding or civil partnership ceremony to take place, in the United Kingdom during the period for which entry is sought; and
(iv) holds a valid United Kingdom entry clearance for entry in this capacity.

Leave to enter as a visitor for marriage or civil partnership

56E. A person seeking leave to enter the United Kingdom as a visitor for marriage or civil partnership may be admitted for a period not exceeding 6 months, subject to a condition prohibiting employment, provided the Immigration Officer is satisfied that each of the requirements of paragraph 56D is met.

Refusal of leave to enter as a visitor for marriage or civil partnership

56F. Leave to enter as a visitor for marriage or civil partnership is to be refused if the Immigration Officer is not satisfied that each of the requirements of paragraph 56D is met.

Visitors seeking leave to enter under the Approved Destination Status (ADS) Agreement with China

Requirements for leave to enter as a visitor under the Approved Destination Status Agreement with China ('ADS Agreement')

56G The requirements to be met by a person seeking leave to enter the United Kingdom as a visitor under the ADS Agreement with China are that he:
   (i) meets the requirements set out in paragraph 41(ii)–(vii); and
   (ii) is a national of the People's Republic of China; and
   (iii) is genuinely seeking entry as a visitor for a limited period as stated by him, not exceeding 30 days; and
   (iv) intends to enter, leave and travel within the territory of the United Kingdom as a member of a tourist group under the ADS agreement; and
   (v) holds a valid ADS agreement visit visa.

Leave to enter as a visitor under the ADS Agreement with China

56H A person seeking leave to enter the United Kingdom as a visitor under the ADS Agreement may be admitted for a period not exceeding 30 days, subject to a condition prohibiting employment, provided they hold an ADS Agreement visit visa.

Refusal of leave to enter as a visitor under the ADS Agreement with China

56I Leave to enter as a visitor under the ADS Agreement with China is to be refused if the person does not hold an ADS Agreement visit visa.

Extension of stay as a visitor under the ADS Agreement with China

56J Any application for an extension of stay as a visitor under the ADS Agreement with China is to be refused.

Student visitors

Requirements for leave to enter as a student visitor

56K. The requirements to be met by a person seeking leave to enter the United Kingdom as a student visitor are that he:
   (i) is genuinely seeking entry as a student visitor for a limited period as stated by him, not exceeding six months; and
   (ii) has been accepted on a course of study which is to be provided by an organisation which is included on the Department for Education and Skills' Register of Education and Training Providers; and
   (iii) intends to leave the United Kingdom at the end of his visit as stated by him; and
   (iv) does not intend to take employment in the United Kingdom; and
   (v) does not intend to engage in business, to produce goods or provide services within the United Kingdom, including the selling of goods or services direct to members of the public; and
   (vi) does not intend to study at a maintained school; and
   (vii) will maintain and accommodate himself and any dependants adequately out of resources available to him without recourse to public funds or taking employment; or will, with any dependants, be maintained and accommodated adequately by relatives or friends; and
   (viii) can meet the cost of the return or onward journey; and
   (ix) is not a child under the age of 18.

Leave to enter as a student visitor

56L. A person seeking leave to enter to the United Kingdom as a student visitor may be admitted for a period not exceeding 6 months, subject to a condition prohibiting employment, provided the Immigration Officer is satisfied that each of the requirements of paragraph 56K is met.

Refusal of leave to enter as a student visitor

56M. Leave to enter as a student visitor is to be refused if the Immigration Officer is not satisfied that each of the requirements of paragraph 56K is met.

Part 3: Persons seeking to enter or remain in the United Kingdom for studies

Students

Requirements for leave to enter as a student

57. The requirements to be met by a person seeking leave to enter the United Kingdom as a student are that he:
    (i) has been accepted for a course of study which is to be provided by an organisation which is included on the Department for Education and Skills' Register of Education and Training Providers, and is at either:
        (a) a publicly funded institution of further or higher education which maintains satisfactory records of enrolment and attendance of students and supplies these to the Border and Immigration Agency when requested; or
        (b) a *bona fide* private education institution; or
        (c) an independent fee paying school outside the maintained sector which maintains satisfactory records of enrolment and attendance of students and supplies these to the Border and Immigration Agency when requested; and
    (ii) is able and intends to follow either:
        (a) a recognised full time degree course at a publicly funded institution of further or higher education; or
        (b) a weekday full time course involving attendance at a single institution for a minimum of 15 hours organised daytime study per week of a single subject, or directly related subjects; or
        (c) a full time course of study at an independent fee paying school; and
    (iii) if under the age of 16 years is enrolled at an independent fee paying school on a full time course of studies which meets the requirements of the Education Act 1944; and
    (iv) if he has been accepted to study externally for a degree at a private education institution, he is also registered as an external student with the UK degree awarding body; and
    (v) intends to leave the United Kingdom at the end of his studies; and
    (vi) does not intend to engage in business or to take employment, except part time or vacation work undertaken with the consent of the Secretary of State; and
    (vii) is able to meet the costs of his course and accommodation and the maintenance of himself and any dependants without taking employment or engaging in business or having recourse to public funds; and
    (viii) holds a valid United Kingdom entry clearance for entry in this capacity.

Leave to enter as a student

58. A person seeking leave to enter the United Kingdom as a student may be admitted for an appropriate period depending on the length of his course of study and his means, and with a condition restricting his freedom to take employment, provided he is able to produce to the Immigration Officer on arrival a valid United Kingdom entry clearance for entry in this capacity.

Refusal of leave to enter as a student

59. Leave to enter as a student is to be refused if the Immigration Officer is not satisfied that each of the requirements of paragraph 57 is met.

Requirements for an extension of stay as a student

60. The requirements for an extension of stay as a student are that the applicant:
    (i) (a) was last admitted to the United Kingdom in possession of a valid student entry clearance in accordance with paragraphs 57–62 or valid prospective student entry clearance in accordance with paragraphs 82–87 of these Rules; or

    (b) has previously been granted leave to enter or remain in the United Kingdom to re-sit an examination in accordance with paragraphs 69A–69F of these Rules; or

    (c) if he has been accepted on a course of study at degree level or above, has previously been granted leave to enter or remain in the United Kingdom in accordance with paragraphs 87A–87F, 128–135, 135O–135T and143A–143F of these Rules; or

    (d) has valid leave as a student in accordance with paragraphs 57–62 of these Rules; and

    (ii) meets the requirements for admission as a student set out in paragraph 57(i)–(vii); and

    (iii) has produced evidence of his enrolment on a course which meets the requirements of paragraph 57; and

    (iv) can produce satisfactory evidence of regular attendance during any course which he has already begun; or any other course for which he has been enrolled in the past; and

    (v) can show evidence of satisfactory progress in his course of study including the taking and passing of any relevant examinations; and

    (vi) would not, as a result of an extension of stay, spend more than 2 years on short courses below degree level (ie courses of less than 1 years duration, or longer courses broken off before completion); and

    (vii) has not come to the end of a period of government or international scholarship agency sponsorship, or has the written consent of his official sponsor for a further period of study in the United Kingdom and satisfactory evidence that sufficient sponsorship funding is available.

Extension of stay as a student

61. An extension of stay as a student may be granted, subject to a restriction on his freedom to take employment, provided the Secretary of State is satisfied that the applicant meets each of the requirements of paragraph 60.

Refusal of extension of stay as a student

62. An extension of stay as a student is to be refused if the Secretary of State is not satisfied that each of the requirements of paragraph 60 is met.

Student nurses

Definition of student nurse

63. For the purposes of these Rules the term student nurse means a person accepted for training as a student nurse or midwife leading to a registered nursing qualification.

Requirements for leave to enter as a student nurse

64. The requirements to be met by a person seeking leave to enter the United Kingdom as a student nurse are that the person:
    (i) comes within the definition set out in paragraph 63 above; and
    (ii) has been accepted for a course of study in a recognised nursing educational establishment offering nursing training which meets the requirements of the Nursing and Midwifery Council; and
    (iii) did not obtain acceptance on the course of study referred to in (ii) above by misrepresentation; and
    (iv) is able and intends to follow the course; and
    (v) does not intend to engage in business or take employment except in connection with the training course; and
    (vi) intends to leave the United Kingdom at the end of the course; and
    (vii) has sufficient funds available for accommodation and maintenance for himself and any dependants without engaging in business or taking employment (except in connection with the training course) or having recourse to public funds. The possession of a Department of Health bursary may be taken into account in assessing whether the student meets the maintenance requirement.

Leave to enter the United Kingdom as a student nurse

65. A person seeking leave to enter the United Kingdom as a student nurse may be admitted for the duration of the course, with a restriction on his freedom to take employment, provided the Immigration Officer is satisfied that each of the requirements of paragraph 64 is met.

Refusal of leave to enter as a student nurse

66. Leave to enter as a student nurse is to be refused if the Immigration Officer is not satisfied that each of the requirements of paragraph 64 is met.

Requirements for an extension of stay as a student nurse

67. The requirements for an extension of stay as a student nurse are that the applicant:
    (i) was last admitted to the United Kingdom in possession of a valid student entry clearance, or valid prospective student entry clearance in accordance with paragraphs 82 to 87 of these Rules, if he is a person specified in Appendix 1 to these Rules; and
    (ii) meets the requirements set out in paragraph 64(i)–(vii); and
    (iii) has produced evidence of enrolment at a recognised nursing educational establishment; and
    (iv) can provide satisfactory evidence of regular attendance during any course which he has already begun; or any other course for which he has been enrolled in the past; and
    (v) would not, as a result of an extension of stay, spend more than 4 years in obtaining the relevant qualification; and
    (vi) has not come to the end of a period of government or international scholarship agency sponsorship, or has the written consent of his official sponsor for a further period of study in the United Kingdom and evidence that sufficient sponsorship funding is available.

Extension of stay as a student nurse

68. An extension of stay as a student nurse may be granted, subject to a restriction on his freedom to take employment, provided the Secretary of State is satisfied that the applicant meets each of the requirements of paragraph 67.

Refusal of extension of stay as a student nurse

69. An extension of stay as a student nurse is to be refused if the Secretary of State is not satisfied that each of the requirements of paragraph 67 is met.

Re-sits of examinations

Requirements for leave to enter to re-sit an examination

69A. The requirements to be met by a person seeking leave to enter the United Kingdom in order to re-sit an examination are that the applicant:
  - (i) (a) meets the requirements for admission as a student set out in paragraph 57(i)–(vii); or
       (b) met the requirements for admission as a student set out in paragraph 57(i)–(iii) in the previous academic year and continues to meet the requirements of paragraph 57(iv)–(vii); and
  - (ii) has produced written confirmation from the education institution or independent fee paying school which he attends or attended in the previous academic year that he is required to re-sit an examination; and
  - (iii) can provide satisfactory evidence of regular attendance during any course which he has already begun; or any other course for which he has been enrolled in the past; and
  - (iv) has not come to the end of a period of government or international scholarship agency sponsorship, or has the written consent of his official sponsor for a further period of study in the United Kingdom and satisfactory evidence that sufficient sponsorship funding is available; and
  - (v) has not previously been granted leave to re-sit the examination.

Leave to enter to re-sit an examination

69B. A person seeking leave to enter the United Kingdom in order to re-sit an examination may be admitted for a period sufficient to enable him to re-sit the examination at the first available opportunity with a condition restricting his freedom to take employment, provided the Immigration Officer is satisfied that each of the requirements of paragraph 69A is met.

Refusal of leave to enter to re-sit an examination

69C. Leave to enter to re-sit an examination is to be refused if the Immigration Officer is not satisfied that each of the requirements of paragraph 69A is met.

Requirements for an extension of stay to re-sit an examination

69D. The requirements for an extension of stay to re-sit an examination are that the applicant:
  - (i) was admitted to the United Kingdom with a valid student entry clearance if he was then a visa national; and
  - (ii) meets the requirements set out in paragraph 69A(i)–(v).

Extension of stay to re-sit an examination

69E. An extension of stay to re-sit an examination may be granted for a period sufficient to enable the applicant to re-sit the examination at the first available opportunity, subject to a restriction on his freedom to take employment, provided the Secretary of State is satisfied that the applicant meets each of the requirements of paragraph 69D.

Refusal of extension of stay to re-sit an examination

69F. An extension of stay to re-sit an examination is to be refused if the Secretary of State is not satisfied that each of the requirements of paragraph 69D is met.

Writing up a thesis

Requirements for leave to enter to write up a thesis

69G. The requirements to be met by a person seeking leave to enter the United Kingdom in order to write up a thesis are that the applicant:
- (i)
  - (a) meets the requirements for admission as a student set out in paragraph 57(i)–(vii); or
  - (b) met the requirements for admission as a student set out in paragraph 57(i)–(iii) in the previous academic year and continues to meet the requirements of paragraph 57(iv)–(vii); and
- (ii) can provide satisfactory evidence that he is a postgraduate student enrolled at an education institution as either a full time, part time or writing up student; and
- (iii) can demonstrate that his application is supported by the education institution; and
- (iv) has not come to the end of a period of government or international scholarship agency sponsorship, or has the written consent of his official sponsor for a further period of study in the United Kingdom and satisfactory evidence that sufficient sponsorship funding is available; and
- (v) has not previously been granted 12 months leave to write up the same thesis.

Leave to enter to write up a thesis

69H. A person seeking leave to enter the United Kingdom in order to write up a thesis may be admitted for 12 months with a condition restricting his freedom to take employment, provided the Immigration Officer is satisfied that each of the requirements of paragraph 69G is met.

Refusal of leave to enter to write up a thesis

69I. Leave to enter to write up a thesis is to be refused if the Immigration Officer is not satisfied that each of the requirements of paragraph 69G is met.

Requirements for an extension of stay to write up a thesis

69J. The requirements for an extension of stay to write up a thesis are that the applicant:
- (i) was admitted to the United Kingdom with a valid student entry clearance if he was then a visa national; and
- (ii) meets the requirements set out in paragraph 69G(i)–(v).

Extension of stay to write up a thesis

69K. An extension of stay to write up a thesis may be granted for 12 months subject to a restriction on his freedom to take employment, provided the Secretary of State is satisfied that the applicant meets each of the requirements of paragraph 69J.

Refusal of extension of stay to write up a thesis

69L. An extension of stay to write up a thesis is to be refused if the Secretary of State is not satisfied that each of the requirements of paragraph 69J is met.

Requirements for leave to enter as an overseas qualified nurse or midwife

69M. The requirements to be met by a person seeking leave to enter as an overseas qualified nurse or midwife are that the applicant:

(i) has obtained confirmation from the Nursing and Midwifery Council that he is eligible:
  (a) for admission to the Overseas Nurses Programme; or
  (b) to undertake a period of supervised practice; or
  (c) to undertake an adaptation programme leading to registration as a midwife; and
(ii) has been offered:
  (a) a supervised practice placement through an education provider that is recognised by the Nursing and Midwifery Council; or
  (b) a supervised practice placement in a setting approved by the Nursing and Midwifery Council; or
  (c) a midwifery adaptation programme placement in a setting approved by the Nursing and Midwifery Council; and
(iii) did not obtain acceptance of the offer referred to in paragraph 69(ii) by misrepresentation; and
(iv) is able and intends to undertake the supervised practice placement or midwife adaptation programme; and
(v) does not intend to engage in business or take employment, except:
  (a) in connection with the supervised practice placement or midwife adaptation programme; or
  (b) part-time work of a similar nature to the work undertaken on the supervised practice placement or midwife adaptation programme; and
(vi) is able to maintain and accommodate himself and any dependants without recourse to public funds.

Leave to enter the United Kingdom as an overseas qualified nurse or midwife

69N. Leave to enter the United Kingdom as an overseas qualified nurse or midwife may be granted for a period not exceeding 18 months, provided the Immigration Officer is satisfied that each of the requirements of paragraph 69M is met.

Refusal of leave to enter as an overseas qualified nurse or midwife

69O. Leave to enter the United Kingdom as an overseas qualified nurse or midwife is to be refused if the Immigration Officer is not satisfied that each of the requirements of paragraph 69M is met.

Requirements for an extension of stay as an overseas qualified nurse or midwife

69P. The requirements to be met by a person seeking an extension of stay as an overseas qualified nurse or midwife are that the applicant:
(i) has leave to enter or remain in the United Kingdom as a prospective student in accordance with paragraphs 82–87 of these Rules; or
(ii) has leave to enter or remain in the United Kingdom as a student in accordance with paragraphs 57 to 69L of these Rules; or
(iii) has leave to enter or remain in the United Kingdom as a working holidaymaker in accordance with paragraphs 95 to 97 of these Rules and has spent more than 12 months in total in the UK in this capacity; or
(iii)(a) has leave to enter or remain in the United Kingdom as a work permit holder in accordance with paragraphs 128 to 135 of these Rules; or
(iv) has leave to enter or remain as an overseas qualified nurse or midwife in accordance with paragraphs 69M–69R of these Rules; and
(v) meets the requirements set out in paragraph 69M(i)–(vi); and
(vi) can provide satisfactory evidence of regular attendance during any previous period of supervised practice or midwife adaptation course; and

(vii) if he has previously been granted leave:
  (a) as an overseas qualified nurse or midwife under paragraphs 69M–69R of these Rules, or
  (b) to undertake an adaptation course as a student nurse under paragraphs 63–69 of these Rules;

  is not seeking an extension of stay in this category which, when amalgamated with those previous periods of leave, would total more than 18 months; and

(viii) if his previous studies, supervised practice placement or midwife adaptation programme placement were sponsored by a government or international scholarship agency, he has the written consent of his official sponsor to remain in the United Kingdom as an overseas qualified nurse or midwife.

Extension of stay as an overseas qualified nurse or midwife

69Q. An extension of stay as an overseas qualified nurse or midwife may be granted for a period not exceeding 18 months, provided that the Secretary of State is satisfied that each of the requirements of paragraph 69P is met.

Refusal of extension of stay as an overseas qualified nurse or midwife

69R. An extension of stay as an overseas qualified nurse or midwife is to be refused if the Secretary of State is not satisfied that each of the requirements of paragraph 69P is met.

Postgraduate doctors, dentists and trainee general practitioners

Requirements for leave to enter the United Kingdom as a postgraduate doctor or dentist

70. The requirements to be met by a person seeking leave to enter the UK as a postgraduate doctor or dentist are that the applicant:
  (i) has successfully completed and obtained a recognised UK degree in medicine or dentistry from either:
    (a) a UK publicly funded institution of further or higher education; or
    (b) a UK bona fide private education institution which maintains satisfactory records of enrolment and attendance; and
  (ii) has previously been granted leave:
    (a) in accordance with paragraphs 57 to 69L of these Rules for the final academic year of the studies referred to in (i) above; and
    (b) as a student under paragraphs 57 to 62 of these Rules for at least one other academic year (aside from the final year) of the studies referred to in (i) above; and
  (iii) holds a letter from the Postgraduate Dean confirming he has a full-time place on a recognised Foundation Programme; and
  (iv) intends to train full time in his post on the Foundation Programme; and
  (v) is able to maintain and accommodate himself and any dependants without recourse to public funds; and
  (vi) intends to leave the United Kingdom if, on expiry of his leave under this paragraph, he has not been granted leave to remain in the United Kingdom as:
    (a) a doctor or dentist undertaking a period of clinical attachment or a dental observer post in accordance with paragraphs 75G to 75M of these Rules; or
    (b) a work permit holder in accordance with paragraphs 128 to 135 of these Rules; or
    (c) a highly skilled migrant in accordance with paragraphs 135A to 135H of these Rules; or

(d) a person intending to establish themselves in business in accordance with paragraphs 200 to 210 of these Rules; or

(e) an innovator in accordance with paragraphs 210A to 210H of these Rules; and

(vii) if his study at medical school or dental school, or any subsequent studies he has undertaken, were sponsored by a government or international scholarship agency, he has the written consent of his sponsor to enter or remain in the United Kingdom as a postgraduate doctor or dentist; and

(viii) has completed his medical or dental degree in the 12 months preceding this application; and

(ix) if he has previously been granted leave as a postgraduate doctor or dentist, is not seeking leave to enter to a date beyond 3 years from that date on which he was first granted leave to enter or remain in this category; and

(x) holds a valid entry clearance for entry in this capacity except where he is a British National (Overseas), a British overseas territories citizen, a British Overseas citizen, a British protected person or a person who under the British Nationality Act 1981 is a British subject.

Leave to enter as a postgraduate doctor or dentist

71. Leave to enter the United Kingdom as a postgraduate doctor or dentist may be granted for the duration of the Foundation Programme, for a period not exceeding 26 months, provided the Immigration Officer is satisfied that each of the requirements of paragraph 70 is met.

Refusal of leave to enter as a postgraduate doctor or dentist

72. Leave to enter as a postgraduate doctor or dentist is to be refused if the Immigration Officer is not satisfied that each of the requirements of paragraph 70 is met.

Requirements for an extension of stay as a postgraduate doctor or dentist

73. The requirements to be met by a person seeking an extension of stay as a postgraduate doctor or dentist are that the applicant:

(i) meets the requirements of paragraph 70(i) to (vii); and

(ii) has leave to enter or remain in the United Kingdom as either:

(a) a student in accordance with paragraphs 57 to 69L of these Rules; or

(b) as a postgraduate doctor or dentist in accordance with paragraphs 70 to 75 of these Rules; or

(c) as a doctor or dentist undertaking a period of clinical attachment or a dental observer post in accordance with paragraphs 75G to 75M of these Rules.

(iii) if he has not previously been granted leave in this category, has completed his medical or dental degree in the last 12 months;

(iv) would not, as a result of an extension of stay, remain in the United Kingdom as a postgraduate doctor or dentist to a date beyond 3 years from the date on which he was first given leave to enter or remain in this capacity.

Extension of stay as a postgraduate doctor or dentist

74. An extension of stay as a postgraduate doctor or dentist may be granted for the duration of the Foundation Programme, for a period not exceeding 3 years, provided the Secretary of State is satisfied that each of the requirements of paragraph 73 is met.

Refusal of an extension of stay as a postgraduate doctor or dentist

75. An extension of stay as a postgraduate doctor or dentist is to be refused if the Secretary of State is not satisfied that each of the requirements of paragraph 73 is met.

Requirements for leave to enter the United Kingdom to take the PLAB Test

75A. The requirements to be met by a person seeking leave to enter in order to take the PLAB Test are that the applicant:
   (i) is a graduate from a medical school and intends to take the PLAB Test in the United Kingdom; and
   (ii) can provide documentary evidence of a confirmed test date or of his eligibility to take the PLAB Test; and
   (iii) meets the requirements of paragraph 41(iii)–(vii) for entry as a visitor; and
   (iv) intends to leave the United Kingdom at the end of his leave granted under this paragraph unless he is successful in the PLAB Test and granted leave to remain:
      (a) as a postgraduate doctor or trainee general practitioner in accordance with paragraphs 70 to 75; or
      (b) to undertake a clinical attachment in accordance with paragraphs 75G to 75M of these Rules; or
      (c) as a work permit holder for employment in the United Kingdom as a doctor in accordance with paragraphs 128 to 135; or
      (d) as a doctor under the highly skilled migrant programme in accordance with paragraphs 135A to 135H.

Leave to enter to take the PLAB Test

75B. A person seeking leave to enter the United Kingdom to take the PLAB Test may be admitted for a period not exceeding 6 months, provided the Immigration Officer is satisfied that each of the requirements of paragraph 75A is met.

Refusal of leave to enter to take the PLAB Test

75C. Leave to enter the United Kingdom to take the PLAB Test is to be refused if the Immigration Officer is not satisfied that each of the requirements of paragraph 75A is met.

Requirements for an extension of stay in order to take the PLAB Test

75D. The requirements for an extension of stay in the United Kingdom in order to take the PLAB Test are that the applicant:
   (i) was given leave to enter the United Kingdom for the purposes of taking the PLAB Test in accordance with paragraph 75B of these Rules; and
   (ii) intends to take the PLAB Test and can provide documentary evidence of a confirmed test date; and
   (iii) meets the requirements set out in paragraph 41(iii)–(vii); and
   (iv) intends to leave the United Kingdom at the end of his leave granted under this paragraph unless he is successful in the PLAB Test and granted leave to remain:
      (a) as a postgraduate doctor or trainee general practitioner in accordance with paragraphs 70 to 75; or
      (b) to undertake a clinical attachment in accordance with paragraphs 75G to 75M of these Rules; or
      (c) as a work permit holder for employment in the United Kingdom as a doctor in accordance with paragraphs 128 to 135; or
      (d) as a doctor under the highly skilled migrant programme in accordance with paragraphs 135A to 135H; and
   (v) would not as a result of an extension of stay spend more than 18 months in the United Kingdom for the purpose of taking the PLAB Test.

Extension of stay to take the PLAB Test

75E. A person seeking leave to remain in the United Kingdom to take the PLAB Test may be granted an extension of stay for a period not exceeding 6 months, provided the Secretary of State is satisfied that each of the requirements of paragraph 75D is met.

Refusal of extension of stay to take the PLAB Test

75F. Leave to remain in the United Kingdom to take the PLAB Test is to be refused if the Secretary of State is not satisfied that each of the requirements of paragraph 75D is met.

Requirements for leave to enter to undertake a clinical attachment or dental observer post

75G. The requirements to be met by a person seeking leave to enter to undertake a clinical attachment or dental observer post are that the applicant:
    (i)   is a graduate from a medical or dental school and intends to undertake a clinical attachment or dental observer post in the United Kingdom; and
    (ii)   can provide documentary evidence of the clinical attachment or dental observer post which will:
        (a)   be unpaid; and
        (b)   only involve observation, not treatment, of patients; and
    (iii)   meets the requirements of paragraph 41(iii)–(vii) of these Rules; and
    (iv)   intends to leave the United Kingdom at the end of his leave granted under this paragraph unless he is granted leave to remain:
        (a)   as a postgraduate doctor, dentist or trainee general practitioner in accordance with paragraphs 70 to 75;
        (b)   as a work permit holder for employment in the United Kingdom as a doctor or dentist in accordance with paragraphs 128 to 135; or
        (c)   as a General Practitioner under the highly skilled migrant programme in accordance with paragraphs 135A to 135H; and
    (v)   if he has previously been granted leave in this category, is not seeking leave to enter which, when amalgamated with those previous periods of leave, would total more than 6 months.

Leave to enter to undertake a clinical attachment or dental observer post

75H. A person seeking leave to enter the United Kingdom to undertake a clinical attachment or dental observer post may be admitted for the period of the clinical attachment or dental observer post, up to a maximum of 6 weeks at a time or 6 months in total in this category, provided the Immigration Officer is satisfied that each of the requirements of paragraph 75G is met.

Refusal of leave to enter to undertake a clinical attachment or dental observer post

75J. Leave to enter the United Kingdom to undertake a clinical attachment or dental observer post is to be refused if the Immigration Officer is not satisfied that each of the requirements of paragraph 75G is met.

Requirements for an extension of stay in order to undertake a clinical attachment or dental observer post

75K. The requirements to be met by a person seeking an extension of stay to undertake a clinical attachment or dental observer post are that the applicant:
    (i) was given leave to enter or remain in the United Kingdom to undertake a clinical attachment or dental observer post or:
        (a)   for the purposes of taking the PLAB Test in accordance with paragraphs 75A to 75F and has passed both parts of the PLAB Test;

(b) as a postgraduate doctor, dentist or trainee general practitioner in accordance with paragraphs 70 to 75; or

(c) as a work permit holder for employment in the UK as a doctor or dentist in accordance with paragraphs 128 to 135; and

(ii) is a graduate from a medical or dental school and intends to undertake a clinical attachment or dental observer post in the United Kingdom; and

(iii) can provide documentary evidence of the clinical attachment or dental observer post which will:

(a) be unpaid; and

(b) only involve observation, not treatment, of patients; and

(iv) intends to leave the United Kingdom at the end of his period of leave granted under this paragraph unless he is granted leave to remain:

(a) as a postgraduate doctor, dentist or trainee general practitioner in accordance with paragraphs 70 to 75; or

(b) as a work permit holder for employment in the United Kingdom as a doctor or dentist in accordance with paragraphs 128 to 135; or

(c) as a General Practitioner under the highly skilled migrant programme in accordance with paragraphs 135A to 135H.; and

(v) meets the requirements of paragraph 41(iii)–(vii) of these Rules; and

(vi) if he has previously been granted leave in this category, is not seeking an extension of stay which, when amalgamated with those previous periods of leave, would total more than 6 months.

Extension of stay to undertake a clinical attachment or dental observer post

75L. A person seeking leave to remain in the United Kingdom to undertake a clinical attachment or dental observer post may be granted an extension of stay for the period of their clinical attachment or dental observer post up to a maximum of 6 weeks at a time or 6 months in total in this category, provided that the Secretary of State is satisfied that each of the requirements of paragraph 75K is met.

Refusal of extension of stay to undertake a clinical attachment or dental observer post

75M. Leave to remain in the United Kingdom to undertake a clinical attachment or dental observer post is to be refused if the Secretary of State is not satisfied that each of the requirements of paragraph 75K is met.

Spouses or civil partners of students or prospective students

Requirements for leave to enter or remain as the spouse or civil partner of a student or prospective student

76. The requirements to be met by a person seeking leave to enter or remain in the United Kingdom as the spouse or civil partner of a student or a prospective student are that:

(i) the applicant is married to or the civil partner of a person admitted to or allowed to remain in the United Kingdom under paragraphs 57–75 or 82–87; and

(ii) each of the parties intends to live with the other as his or her spouse or civil partner during the applicant's stay and the marriage or civil partnership is subsisting; and

(iii) there will be adequate accommodation for the parties and any dependants without recourse to public funds; and

(iv) the parties will be able to maintain themselves and any dependants adequately without recourse to public funds; and

(v) the applicant does not intend to take employment except as permitted under paragraph 77 below; and

(vi) the applicant intends to leave the United Kingdom at the end of any period of leave granted to him.

Leave to enter or remain as the spouse or civil partner of a student or prospective student

77. A person seeking leave to enter or remain in the United Kingdom as the spouse or civil partner of a student or a prospective student may be admitted or allowed to remain for a period not in excess of that granted to the student or prospective student provided the Immigration Officer or, in the case of an application for limited leave to remain, the Secretary of State is satisfied that each of the requirements of paragraph 76 is met. Employment may be permitted where the period of leave granted to the student or prospective student is, or was, 12 months or more.

Refusal of leave to enter or remain as the spouse or civil partner of a student or prospective student

78. Leave to enter or remain as the spouse or civil partner of a student or prospective student is to be refused if the Immigration Officer or, in the case of an application for limited leave to remain, the Secretary of State is not satisfied that each of the requirements of paragraph 76 is met.

Children of students or prospective students

Requirements for leave to enter or remain as the child of a student or prospective student

79. The requirements to be met by a person seeking leave to enter or remain in the United Kingdom as the child of a student or prospective student are that he:
    (i) is the child of a parent admitted to or allowed to remain in the United Kingdom as a student or prospective student under paragraphs 57–75 or 82–87; and
    (ii) is under the age of 18 or has current leave to enter or remain in this capacity; and
    (iii) is unmarried, has not formed an independent family unit and is not leading an independent life; and
    (iv) can, and will, be maintained and accommodated adequately without recourse to public funds; and
    (v) will not stay in the United Kingdom beyond any period of leave granted to his parent.

Leave to enter or remain as the child of a student or prospective student

80. A person seeking leave to enter or remain in the United Kingdom as the child of a student or prospective student may be admitted or allowed to remain for a period not in excess of that granted to the student or prospective student provided the Immigration Officer or, in the case of an application for limited leave to remain, the Secretary of State is satisfied that each of the requirements of paragraph 79 is met. Employment may be permitted where the period of leave granted to the student or prospective student is, or was, 12 months or more.

Refusal of leave to enter or remain as the child of a student or prospective student

81. Leave to enter or remain in the United Kingdom as the child of a student or prospective student is to be refused if the Immigration Officer or, in the case of an

application for limited leave to remain, the Secretary of State, is not satisfied that each of the requirements of paragraph 79 is met.

Prospective students

Requirements for leave to enter as a prospective student

82. The requirements to be met by a person seeking leave to enter the United Kingdom as a prospective student are that he:
    (i) can demonstrate a genuine and realistic intention of undertaking, within 6 months of his date of entry:
        (a) a course of study which would meet the requirements for an extension of stay as a student under paragraphs 60 to 67 of these Rules; or
        (b) a supervised practice placement or midwife adaptation course which would meet the requirements for an extension of stay as an overseas qualified nurse or midwife under paragraphs 69P to 69R of these Rules; and
    (ii) intends to leave the United Kingdom on completion of his studies or on the expiry of his leave to enter if he is not able to meet the requirements for an extension of stay:
        (a) as a student in accordance with paragraph 60 or 67 of these Rules; or
        (b) as an overseas qualified nurse or midwife in accordance with paragraph 69P of these Rules; and
    (iii) is able without working or recourse to public funds to meet the costs of his intended course and accommodation and the maintenance of himself and any dependants while making arrangements to study and during the course of his studies; and
    (iv) holds a valid United Kingdom entry clearance for entry in this capacity.

Leave to enter as a prospective student

83. A person seeking leave to enter the United Kingdom as a prospective student may be admitted for a period not exceeding 6 months with a condition prohibiting employment, provided he is able to produce to the Immigration Officer on arrival a valid United Kingdom entry clearance for entry in this capacity.

Refusal of leave to enter as a prospective student

84. Leave to enter as a prospective student is to be refused if the Immigration Officer is not satisfied that each of the requirements of paragraph 82 is met.

Requirements for extension of stay as a prospective student

85. Six months is the maximum permitted leave which may be granted to a prospective student. The requirements for an extension of stay as a prospective student are that the applicant:
    (i) was admitted to the United Kingdom with a valid prospective student entry clearance; and
    (ii) meets the requirements of paragraph 82; and
    (iii) would not, as a result of an extension of stay, spend more than 6 months in the United Kingdom.

Extension of stay as a prospective student

86. An extension of stay as a prospective student may be granted, with a prohibition on employment, provided the Secretary of State is satisfied that each of the requirements of paragraph 85 is met.

Refusal of extension of stay as a prospective student

87. An extension of stay as a prospective student is to be refused if the Secretary of State is not satisfied that each of the requirements of paragraph 85 is met.

Students' unions sabbatical officers

Requirements for leave to enter as a sabbatical officer

87A. The requirements to be met by a person seeking leave to enter the United Kingdom as a sabbatical officer are that the person:
   (i) has been elected to a full-time salaried post as a sabbatical officer at an educational establishment at which he is registered as a student;
   (ii) meets the requirements set out in paragraph 57(i)–(ii) or met the requirements set out in paragraph 57(i)–(ii) in the academic year prior to the one in which he took up or intends to take up sabbatical office; and
   (iii) does not intend to engage in business or take employment except in connection with his sabbatical post; and
   (iv) is able to maintain and accommodate himself and any dependants adequately without recourse to public funds; and
   (v) at the end of the sabbatical post he intends to:
       (a) complete a course of study which he has already begun; or
       (b) take up a further course of study which has been deferred to enable the applicant to take up the sabbatical post; or
       (c) leave the United Kingdom; and
   (vi) has not come to the end of a period of government or international scholarship agency sponsorship, or has the written consent of his official sponsor to take up a sabbatical post in the United Kingdom; and
   (vii) has not already completed 2 years as a sabbatical officer.

Leave to enter the United Kingdom as a sabbatical officer

87B. A person seeking leave to enter the United Kingdom as a sabbatical officer may be admitted for a period not exceeding 12 months on conditions specifying his employment provided the Immigration Officer is satisfied that each of the requirements of paragraph 87A is met.

Refusal of leave to enter the United Kingdom as a sabbatical officer

87C. Leave to enter as a sabbatical officer is to be refused if the Immigration Officer is not satisfied that each of the requirements of paragraph 87A is met.

Requirements for an extension of stay as a sabbatical officer

87D. The requirements for an extension of stay as a sabbatical officer are that the applicant:
   (i) was admitted to the United Kingdom with a valid student entry clearance if he was then a visa national; and
   (ii) meets the requirements set out in paragraph 87A(i)–(vi); and
   (iii) would not, as a result of an extension of stay, remain in the United Kingdom as a sabbatical officer to a date beyond 2 years from the date on which he was first given leave to enter the United Kingdom in this capacity.

Extension of stay as a sabbatical officer

87E. An extension of stay as a sabbatical officer may be granted for a period not exceeding 12 months on conditions specifying his employment provided the Secretary of State is satisfied that the applicant meets each of the requirements of paragraph 87D.

Refusal of extension of stay as a sabbatical officer

87F. An extension of stay as a sabbatical officer is to be refused if the Secretary of State is not satisfied that each of the requirements of paragraph 87D is met.

Part 4: Persons seeking to enter or remain in the United Kingdom in an 'au pair' placement, as a working holidaymaker or for training or work experience

'Au pair' placements

Definition of an 'au pair' placement

88. For the purposes of these Rules an 'au pair' placement is an arrangement whereby a young person:

   (a) comes to the United Kingdom for the purpose of learning the English language; and

   (b) lives for a time as a member of an English speaking family with appropriate opportunities for study; and

   (c) helps in the home for a maximum of 5 hours per day in return for a reasonable allowance and with two free days per week.

Requirements for leave to enter as an 'au pair'

89. The requirements to be met by a person seeking leave to enter the United Kingdom as an 'au pair' are that he:

   (i) is seeking entry for the purpose of taking up an arranged placement which can be shown to fall within the definition set out in paragraph 88; and

   (ii) is aged between 17–27 inclusive or was so aged when first given leave to enter in this capacity; and

   (iii) is unmarried and is not a civil partner; and

   (iv) is without dependants; and

   (v) is a national of one of the following countries: Andorra, Bosnia-Herzegovina, Croatia, The Faroes, Greenland, Macedonia, Monaco, San Marino or Turkey; and

   (vi) does not intend to stay in the United Kingdom for more than 2 years as an 'au pair'; and

   (vii) intends to leave the United Kingdom on completion of his stay as an 'au pair'; and

   (viii) if he has previously spent time in the United Kingdom as an 'au pair', is not seeking leave to enter to a date beyond 2 years from the date on which he was first given leave to enter the United Kingdom in this capacity; and

   (ix) is able to maintain and accommodate himself without recourse to public funds.

Leave to enter as an 'au pair'

90. A person seeking leave to enter the United Kingdom as an 'au pair' may be admitted for a period not exceeding 2 years with a prohibition on employment except as an 'au pair' provided the Immigration Officer is satisfied that each of the requirements of paragraph 89 is met. (A non visa national who wishes to ascertain in advance whether a proposed 'au pair' placement is likely to meet the requirements of paragraph 89 is advised to obtain an entry clearance before travelling to the United Kingdom).

Refusal of leave to enter as an 'au pair'

91. An application for leave to enter as an 'au pair' is to be refused if the Immigration Officer is not satisfied that each of the requirements of paragraph 89 is met.

Requirements for an extension of stay as an 'au pair'

92. The requirements for an extension of stay as an 'au pair' are that the applicant:
    (i) was given leave to enter the United Kingdom as an 'au pair' under paragraph 90; and
    (ii) is undertaking an arranged 'au pair' placement which can be shown to fall within the definition set out in paragraph 88; and
    (iii) meets the requirements of paragraph 89(ii)–(ix); and
    (iv) would not, as a result of an extension of stay, remain in the United Kingdom as an 'au pair' to a date beyond 2 years from the date on which he was first given leave to enter the United Kingdom in this capacity.

Extension of stay as an 'au pair'

93. An extension of stay as an 'au pair' may be granted with a prohibition on employment except as an 'au pair' provided the Secretary of State is satisfied that each of the requirements of paragraph 92 is met.

Refusal of extension of stay as an 'au pair'

94. An extension of stay as an 'au pair' is to be refused if the Secretary of State is not satisfied that each of the requirements of paragraph 92 is met.

Working holidaymakers

Requirements for leave to enter as a working holidaymaker

95. The requirements to be met by a person seeking leave to enter the United Kingdom as a working holidaymaker are that he:
    (i) is a national or citizen of a country listed in Appendix 3 of these Rules, or a British Overseas Citizen; a British Overseas Territories Citizen; or a British National (Overseas); and
    (ii) is aged between 17 and 30 inclusive or was so aged at the date of his application for leave to enter; and
    (iii) (a) is unmarried and is not a civil partner, or
    (b) is married to, or the civil partner of, a person who meets the requirements of this paragraph and the parties to the marriage or civil partnership intend to take a working holiday together; and
    (iv) has the means to pay for his return or onward journey; and
    (v) is able and intends to maintain and accommodate himself without recourse to public funds; and
    (vi) is intending only to take employment incidental to a holiday, and not to engage in business, or to provide services as a professional sportsperson, and in any event not to work for more than 12 months during his stay; and
    (vii) does not have dependent children any of whom are 5 years of age or over or who will reach 5 years of age before the applicant completes his working holiday; and
    (viii) intends to leave the UK at the end of his working holiday: and
    (ix) has not spent time in the United Kingdom on a previous working holidaymaker entry clearance; and
    (x) holds a valid United Kingdom entry clearance, granted for a limited period not exceeding 2 years, for entry in this capacity.

Leave to enter as a working holidaymaker

96. A person seeking to enter the United Kingdom as a working holidaymaker may be admitted provided he is able to produce on arrival a valid United Kingdom entry clearance granted for a period not exceeding 2 years for entry in this capacity.

Refusal of leave to enter as a working holidaymaker

97. Leave to enter as a working holidaymaker is to be refused if a valid United Kingdom entry clearance for entry in this capacity is not produced to the Immigration Officer on arrival.

Children of working holidaymakers

Requirements for leave to enter or remain as the child of a working holidaymaker

101. The requirements to be met by a person seeking leave to enter or remain in the United Kingdom as the child of a working holidaymaker are that:
     (i) he is the child of a parent admitted to, and currently present in, the United Kingdom as a working holidaymaker; and
     (ii) he is under the age of 5 and will leave the United Kingdom before reaching that age; and
     (iii) he can and will be maintained and accommodated adequately without recourse to public funds or without his parent(s) engaging in employment except as provided by paragraph 95 above; and
     (iv) both parents are being or have been admitted to the United Kingdom, save where:
          (a) the parent he is accompanying or joining is his sole surviving parent; or
          (b) the parent he is accompanying or joining has had sole responsibility for his upbringing; or
          (c) there are serious and compelling family or other considerations which make exclusion from the United Kingdom undesirable and suitable arrangements have been made for his care; and
     (v) he holds a valid United Kingdom entry clearance for entry in this capacity or, if seeking leave to remain, was admitted with a valid United Kingdom entry clearance for entry in this capacity, and is seeking leave to a date not beyond the date to which his parent(s) have leave to enter in the working holidaymaker category.

Leave to enter or remain as the child of a working holidaymaker

102. A person seeking to enter the United Kingdom as the child of working holidaymaker/s must be able to produce on arrival a valid United Kingdom entry clearance for entry in this capacity.

Refusal of leave to enter or remain as the child of a working holidaymaker

103. Leave to enter or remain in the United Kingdom as the child of a working holidaymaker is to be refused if, in relation to an application for leave to enter, a valid United Kingdom entry clearance for entry in this capacity is not produced to the Immigration Officer on arrival or, in the case of an application for leave to remain, the applicant was not admitted with a valid United Kingdom entry clearance for entry in this capacity or is unable to satisfy the Secretary of State that each of the requirements of paragraph 101(i)–(iv) is met.

Seasonal agricultural workers

Requirements for leave to enter as a seasonal agricultural worker

104. The requirements to be met by a person seeking leave to enter the United Kingdom as a seasonal agricultural worker are that he:
     (i) is a student in full time education aged 18 or over; and

(ii) holds an immigration employment document in the form of a valid Home Office work card issued by the operator of a scheme approved by the Secretary of State; and

(iii) intends to leave the United Kingdom at the end of his period of leave as a seasonal worker; and

(iv) does not intend to take employment except as permitted by his work card and within the terms of this paragraph; and

(v) is not seeking leave to enter on a date less than 3 months from the date on which an earlier period of leave to enter or remain granted to him in this capacity expired; and

(vi) is able to maintain and accommodate himself without recourse to public funds.

Leave to enter as a seasonal agricultural worker

105. A person seeking leave to enter the United Kingdom as a seasonal agricultural worker may be admitted with a condition restricting his freedom to take employment for a period not exceeding 6 months providing the Immigration Officer is satisfied that each of the requirements of paragraph 104 is met.

Refusal of leave to enter as a seasonal agricultural worker

106. Leave to enter the United Kingdom as a seasonal agricultural worker is to be refused if the Immigration Officer is not satisfied that each of the requirements of paragraph 104 is met.

Requirements for extension of stay as a seasonal agricultural worker

107. The requirements for an extension of stay as a seasonal agricultural worker are that the applicant:

(i) entered the United Kingdom as a seasonal agricultural worker under paragraph 105; and

(ii) meets the requirements of paragraph 104(iii)–(vi); and

(iii) would not, as a result of an extension of stay sought, remain in the United Kingdom as a seasonal agricultural worker beyond 6 months from the date on which he was given leave to enter the United Kingdom on this occasion in this capacity.

Extension of stay as a seasonal agricultural worker

108. An extension of stay as a seasonal agricultural worker may be granted with a condition restricting his freedom to take employment for a period which does not extend beyond 6 months from the date on which he was given leave to enter the United Kingdom on this occasion in this capacity, provided the Secretary of State is satisfied that the applicant meets each of the requirements of paragraph 107.

Refusal of extension of stay as a seasonal worker

109. An extension of stay as a seasonal worker is to be refused if the Secretary of State is not satisfied that each of the requirements of paragraph 107 is met.

Requirements for leave to enter as a teacher or language assistant under an approved exchange scheme

110. The requirements to be met by a person seeking leave to enter the United Kingdom as a teacher or language assistant on an approved exchange scheme are that he:

(i) is coming to an educational establishment in the United Kingdom under an exchange scheme approved by the Department for Education and Skills, the Scottish or Welsh Office of Education or the Department of Education, Northern Ireland, or administered by the British Council's Education and

Training Group or the League for the Exchange of Commonwealth Teachers; and

(ii) intends to leave the United Kingdom at the end of his exchange period; and

(iii) does not intend to take employment except in the terms of this paragraph; and

(iv) is able to maintain and accommodate himself and any dependants without recourse to public funds; and

(v) holds a valid United Kingdom entry clearance for entry in this capacity.

Leave to enter as a teacher or language assistant under an exchange scheme

111. A person seeking leave to enter the United Kingdom as a teacher or language assistant under an approved exchange scheme may be given leave to enter for a period not exceeding 12 months provided he is able to produce to the Immigration Officer, on arrival, a valid United Kingdom entry clearance for entry in this capacity.

Refusal of leave to enter as a teacher or language assistant under an approved exchange scheme

112. Leave to enter the United Kingdom as a teacher or language assistant under an approved exchange scheme is to be refused if a valid United Kingdom entry clearance for entry in this capacity is not produced to the Immigration Officer on arrival.

Requirements for extension of stay as a teacher or language assistant under an approved exchange scheme

113. The requirements for an extension of stay as a teacher or language assistant under an approved exchange scheme are that the applicant:

(i) entered the United Kingdom with a valid United Kingdom entry clearance as a teacher or language assistant; and

(ii) is still engaged in the employment for which his entry clearance was granted; and

(iii) is still required for the employment in question, as certified by the employer; and

(iv) meets the requirements of paragraph 110(ii)–(iv); and

(v) would not, as a result of an extension of stay, remain in the United Kingdom as an exchange teacher or language assistant for more than 2 years from the date on which he was first given leave to enter the United Kingdom in this capacity.

Extension of stay as a teacher or language assistant under an approved exchange scheme

114. An extension of stay as a teacher or language assistant under an approved exchange scheme may be granted for a further period not exceeding 12 months provided the Secretary of State is satisfied that each of the requirements of paragraph 113 is met.

Refusal of extension of stay as a teacher or language assistant under an approved exchange scheme

115. An extension of stay as a teacher or language assistant under an approved exchange scheme is to be refused if the Secretary of State is not satisfied that each of the requirements of paragraph 113 is met.

Home Office approved training or work experience

Requirements for leave to enter for Home Office approved training or work experience

116. The requirements to be met by a person seeking leave to enter the United Kingdom for Home Office approved training or work experience are that he:
    (i) holds a valid work permit from the Home Office issued under the Training and Work Experience Scheme; and
    (ii) DELETED
    (iii) is capable of undertaking the training or work experience as specified in his work permit; and
    (iv) intends to leave the United Kingdom on the completion of his training or work experience; and
    (v) does not intend to take employment except as specified in his work permit; and
    (vi) is able to maintain and accommodate himself and any dependants adequately without recourse to public funds; and
    (vii) holds a valid United Kingdom entry clearance for entry in this capacity except where he holds a work permit valid for 6 months or less or he is a British National (Overseas), a British overseas territories citizen, a British Overseas citizen, a British protected person or a person who under the British Nationality Act 1981 is a British subject.

Leave to enter for Home Office approved training or work experience

117. A person seeking leave to enter the United Kingdom for the purpose of approved training or approved work experience under the Training or Work Experience Scheme may be admitted to the United Kingdom for a period not exceeding the period of training or work experience approved by the Home Office for this purpose(as specified in his work permit), subject to a condition restricting him to that approved employment, provided he is able to produce to the Immigration Officer, on arrival, a valid United Kingdom entry clearance for entry in this capacity or, where entry clearance is not required, provided the Immigration Officer is satisfied that each of the requirements of paragraph 116(i)–(vi) is met.

Refusal of leave to enter for Home Office approved training or work experience

118. Leave to enter the United Kingdom for Home Office approved training or work experience under the Training and Work Experience scheme is to be refused if a valid United Kingdom entry clearance for entry in this capacity is not produced to the Immigration Officer on arrival or, where entry clearance is not required, if the Immigration Officer is not satisfied that each of the requirements of paragraph 116(i)–(vi) is met.

Requirements for extension of stay for Home Office approved training or work experience

119. The requirements for an extension of stay for Home Office approved training or work experience are that the applicant:
    (i) entered the United Kingdom with a valid work permit under paragraph 117 or was admitted or allowed to remain in the United Kingdom as a student; and
    (ii) has written approval from the Home Office for an extension of stay in this category; and
    (iii) meets the requirements of paragraph 116(ii)–(vi).

Extension of stay for Home Office approved training or work experience

120. An extension of stay for approved training or approved work experience under the Training and Work Experience scheme may be granted for a further period not exceeding the extended period of training or work experience approved by the Home Office for this purpose (as specified in his work permit), provided that in each case the Secretary of State is satisfied that the requirements of paragraph 119 are met. An extension of stay is to be subject to a condition permitting the applicant to take or change employment only with the permission of the Home Office.

Refusal of extension of stay for Home Office approved training or work experience

121. An extension of stay for approved training or approved work experience under the Training and Work Experience scheme is to be refused if the Secretary of State is not satisfied that each of the requirements of paragraph 119 is met.

Spouses or civil partners of persons with limited leave to enter or remain under paragraphs 110–121

Requirements for leave to enter or remain as the spouse or civil partner of a person with limited leave to enter or remain in the United Kingdom under paragraphs 110–121

122. The requirements to be met by a person seeking leave to enter or remain in the United Kingdom as the spouse or civil partner of a person with limited leave to enter or remain in the United Kingdom under paragraphs 110–121 are that:
    (i) the applicant is married to or the civil partner of a person with limited leave to enter or remain in the United Kingdom under paragraphs 110–121; and
    (ii) each of the parties intends to live with the other as his or her spouse or civil partner during the applicant's stay and the marriage or civil partnership is subsisting; and
    (iii) there will be adequate accommodation for the parties and any dependants without recourse to public funds in accommodation which they own or occupy exclusively; and
    (iv) the parties will be able to maintain themselves and any dependants adequately without recourse to public funds; and
    (v) the applicant does not intend to stay in the United Kingdom beyond any period of leave granted to his spouse or civil partner; and
    (vi) if seeking leave to enter, the applicant holds a valid United Kingdom entry clearance for entry in this capacity or, if seeking leave to remain, was admitted with a valid United Kingdom entry clearance for entry in this capacity.

Leave to enter or remain as the spouse or civil partner of a person with limited leave to enter or remain in the United Kingdom under paragraphs 110–121

123. A person seeking leave to enter or remain in the United Kingdom as the spouse or civil partner of a person with limited leave to enter or remain in the United Kingdom under paragraphs 110–121 may be given leave to enter or remain in the United Kingdom for a period of leave not in excess of that granted to the person with limited leave to enter or remain under paragraphs 110–121 provided that, in relation to an application for leave to enter, he is able, on arrival, to produce to the Immigration Officer a valid United Kingdom entry clearance for entry in this capacity or, in the case of an application for limited leave to remain, was admitted with a valid United Kingdom entry clearance for entry in this capacity and he is able to satisfy the Secretary of State that each of the requirements of paragraph 122(i)–(v) is met.

Refusal of leave to enter or remain as the spouse or civil partner of a person with limited leave to enter or remain in the United Kingdom under paragraphs 110–121

124. Leave to enter or remain in the United Kingdom as the spouse or civil partner of a person with limited leave to enter or remain in the United Kingdom under paragraphs 110–121 is to be refused if, in relation to an application for leave to enter, a valid United Kingdom entry clearance for entry in this capacity is not produced to the Immigration Officer on arrival or, in the case of an application for limited leave to remain, if the applicant was not admitted with a valid United Kingdom entry clearance for entry in this capacity or is unable to satisfy the Secretary of State that each of the requirements of paragraph 122(i)–(v) is met.

Children of persons admitted or allowed to remain under paragraphs 110–121

Requirements for leave to enter or remain as the child of a person with limited leave to enter or remain in the United Kingdom under paragraphs 110–121

125. The requirements to be met by a person seeking leave to enter or remain in the United Kingdom as the child of a person with limited leave to enter or remain in the United Kingdom under paragraphs 110–121 are that:
    (i) he is the child of a parent who has limited leave to enter or remain in the United Kingdom under paragraphs 110–121; and
    (ii) he is under the age of 18 or has current leave to enter or remain in this capacity; and
    (iii) he is unmarried and is not a civil partner, has not formed an independent family unit and is not leading an independent life; and
    (iv) he can, and will, be maintained and accommodated adequately without recourse to public funds in accommodation which his parent(s) own or occupy exclusively; and
    (v) he will not stay in the United Kingdom beyond any period of leave granted to his parent(s); and
    (vi) both parents are being or have been admitted to or allowed to remain in the United Kingdom save where:
        (a) the parent he is accompanying or joining is his sole surviving parent; or
        (b) the parent he is accompanying or joining has had sole responsibility for his upbringing; or
        (c) there are serious and compelling family or other considerations which make exclusion from the United Kingdom undesirable and suitable arrangements have been made for his care; and
    (vii) if seeking leave to enter, he holds a valid United Kingdom entry clearance for entry in this capacity or, if seeking leave to remain, was admitted with a valid United Kingdom entry clearance for entry in this capacity.

Leave to enter or remain as the child of a person with limited leave to enter or remain in the United Kingdom under paragraphs 110–121

126. A person seeking leave to enter or remain in the United Kingdom as the child of a person with limited leave to enter or remain in the United Kingdom under paragraphs 110–121 may be given leave to enter or remain in the United Kingdom for a period of leave not in excess of that granted to the person with limited leave to enter or remain under paragraphs 110–121 provided that, in relation to an application for leave to enter, he is able, on arrival, to produce to the Immigration Officer a valid United Kingdom entry clearance for entry in this capacity or, in the case of an application for limited leave to remain, he was admitted with a valid

United Kingdom entry clearance for entry in this capacity and is able to satisfy the Secretary of State that each of the requirements of paragraph 125(i)–(vi) is met.

Refusal of leave to enter or remain as the child of a person with limited leave to enter or remain in the United Kingdom under paragraphs 110–121

127. Leave to enter or remain in the United Kingdom as the child of a person with limited leave to enter or remain in the United Kingdom under paragraphs 110–121 is to be refused if, in relation to an application for leave to enter, a valid United Kingdom entry clearance for entry in this capacity is not produced to the Immigration Officer on arrival, or, in the case of an application for limited leave to remain, if the applicant was not admitted with a valid United Kingdom entry clearance for entry in this capacity or is unable to satisfy the Secretary of State that each of the requirements of paragraph 125(i)–(vi) is met.

Part 5: Persons seeking to enter or remain in the United Kingdom for employment

Section 1

Work permit employment

Requirements for leave to enter the United Kingdom for work permit employment

128. The requirements to be met by a person coming to the United Kingdom to seek or take employment (unless he is otherwise eligible for admission for employment under these Rules or is eligible for admission as a seaman under contract to join a ship due to leave British waters) are that he:
    (i) holds a valid Home Office work permit; and
    (ii) is not of an age which puts him outside the limits for employment; and
    (iii) is capable of undertaking the employment specified in the work permit; and
    (iv) does not intend to take employment except as specified in his work permit; and
    (v) is able to maintain and accommodate himself and any dependants adequately without recourse to public funds; and
    (vi) in the case of a person in possession of a work permit which is valid for a period of 12 months or less, intends to leave the United Kingdom at the end of his approved employment; and
    (vii) holds a valid United Kingdom entry clearance for entry in this capacity except where he holds a work permit valid for 6 months or less or he is a British National (Overseas), a British overseas territories citizen, a British Overseas citizen, a British protected person or a person who under the British Nationality Act 1981 is a British subject.

Leave to enter for work permit employment

129. A person seeking leave to enter the United Kingdom for the purpose of work permit employment may be admitted for a period not exceeding the period of employment approved by the Home Office (as specified in his work permit), subject to a condition restricting him to that approved employment, provided he is able to produce to the Immigration Officer, on arrival, a valid United Kingdom entry clearance for entry in this capacity or, where entry clearance is not required, provided the Immigration Officer is satisfied that each of the requirements of paragraph 128(i)–(vi) is met.

Refusal of leave to enter for employment

130. Leave to enter for the purpose of work permit employment is to be refused if a valid United Kingdom entry clearance for entry in this capacity is not produced to the Immigration Officer on arrival or, where entry clearance is not required, if the Immigration Officer is not satisfied that each of the requirements of paragraph 128(i)–(vi) is met.

Requirements for an extension of stay for work permit employment

131. The requirements for an extension of stay to seek or take employment (unless the applicant is otherwise eligible for an extension of stay for employment under these Rules) are that the applicant:

    (i) entered the United Kingdom with a valid work permit under paragraph 129; and

    (ii) has written approval from the Home Office for the continuation of his employment; and

    (iii) meets the requirements of paragraph 128(ii)–(v).

131A. The requirements for an extension of stay to take employment (unless the applicant is otherwise eligible for an extension of stay for employment under these Rules) for a student are that the applicant:

    (i) entered the United Kingdom or was given leave to remain as a student in accordance with paragraphs 57 to 62 of these Rules; and

    (ii) has obtained a degree qualification on a recognised degree course at either a United Kingdom publicly funded further or higher education institution or a bona fide United Kingdom private education institution which maintains satisfactory records of enrolment and attendance; and

    (iii) holds a valid Home Office immigration employment document for employment; and

    (iv) has the written consent of his official sponsor to such employment if he is a member of a government or international scholarship agency sponsorship and that sponsorship is either ongoing or has recently come to an end at the time of the requested extension; and

    (v) meets each of the requirements of paragraph 128(ii) to (vi).

131B. The requirements for an extension of stay to take employment (unless the applicant is otherwise eligible for an extension of stay for employment under these Rules) for a student nurse, overseas qualified nurse or midwife, postgraduate doctor or postgraduate dentist are that the applicant:

    (i) entered the United Kingdom or was given leave to remain as a student nurse in accordance with paragraphs 63 to 69 of these Rules; or

    (ia) entered the United Kingdom or was given leave to remain as an overseas qualified nurse or midwife in accordance with paragraphs 69M to 69R of these Rules; and

    (ii) entered the United Kingdom or was given leave to remain as a postgraduate doctor or a postgraduate dentist in accordance with paragraphs 70 to 75 of these Rules; and

    (iii) holds a valid Home Office immigration employment document for employment as a nurse, doctor or dentist; and

    (iv) has the written consent of his official sponsor to such employment if he is a member of a government or international scholarship agency sponsorship and that sponsorship is either ongoing or has recently come to an end at the time of the requested extension; and

    (v) meets each of the requirements of paragraph 128(ii) to (vi).

131C The requirements for an extension of stay to take employment for a Science and Engineering Graduate Scheme or International Graduates Scheme participant are that the applicant:

(i) entered the United Kingdom or was given leave to remain as a Science and Engineering Graduate Scheme or International Graduates Scheme participant in accordance with paragraphs 135O to 135T of these Rules; and

(ii) holds a valid Home Office immigration employment document for employment; and

(iii) meets each of the requirements of paragraph 128(ii) to (vi).

131D. The requirements for an extension of stay to take employment (unless the applicant is otherwise eligible for an extension of stay for employment under these Rules) for a working holidaymaker are that the applicant:

(i) entered the United Kingdom as a working holidaymaker in accordance with paragraphs 95 to 96 of these Rules; and

(ii) he has spent more than 12 months in total in the UK in this capacity; and

(iii) holds a valid Home Office immigration employment document for employment in an occupation listed on the Work Permits (UK) shortage occupations list; and

(iv) meets each of the requirements of paragraph 128(ii) to (vi).

131E. The requirements for an extension of stay to take employment for a highly skilled migrant are that the applicant:

(i) entered the United Kingdom or was given leave to remain as a highly skilled migrant in accordance with paragraphs 135A to 135E of these Rules; and

(ii) holds a valid work permit; and

(iii) meets each of the requirements of paragraph 128(ii) to (vi).

131F. The requirements for an extension of stay to take employment (unless the applicant is otherwise eligible for an extension of stay for employment under these Rules) for an Innovator are that the applicant:

(i) entered the United Kingdom or was given leave to remain as an Innovator in accordance with paragraphs 210A to 210E of these Rules; and

(ii) holds a valid Home Office immigration employment document for employment; and

(iii) meets each of the requirements of paragraph 128(ii) to (vi).

131G. The requirements for an extension of stay to take employment (unless the applicant is otherwise eligible for an extension of stay for employment under these Rules) for an individual who has leave to enter or leave to remain in the United Kingdom to take the PLAB Test or to undertake a clinical attachment or dental observer post are that the applicant:

(i) entered the United Kingdom or was given leave to remain for the purposes of taking the PLAB Test in accordance with paragraphs 75A to 75F of these Rules; or

(ii) entered the United Kingdom or was given leave to remain to undertake a clinical attachment or dental observer post in accordance with paragraphs 75G to 75M of these Rules; and

(iii) holds a valid Home Office immigration employment document for employment as a doctor or dentist; and

(iv) meets each of the requirements of paragraph 128(ii) to (vi).

131H. The requirements for an extension of stay to take employment (unless the applicant is otherwise eligible for an extension of stay for employment under these Rules) in the case of a person who has leave to enter or remain as a Fresh Talent: Working in Scotland scheme participant are that the applicant:

(i) entered the United Kingdom or was given leave to remain as a Fresh Talent: Working in Scotland scheme participant in accordance with paragraphs 143A to 143F of these Rules; and

(ii) holds a valid Home Office immigration employment document for employment in Scotland; and

(iii) has the written consent of his official sponsor to such employment if the studies which led to him being granted leave under the Fresh Talent: Working in Scotland scheme in accordance with paragraphs 143A to 143F of these Rules, or any studies he has subsequently undertaken, were sponsored by a government or international scholarship agency; and

(iv) meets each of the requirements of paragraph 128(ii) to (vi).

Extension of stay for work permit employment

132. An extension of stay for work permit employment may be granted for a period not exceeding the period of approved employment recommended by the Home Office provided the Secretary of State is satisfied that each of the requirements of paragraphs 131, 131A, 131B, 131C, 131D, 131E, 131F, 131G or 131H is met. An extension of stay is to be subject to a condition restricting the applicant to employment approved by the Home Office.

Refusal of extension of stay for employment

133. An extension of stay for employment is to be refused if the Secretary of State is not satisfied that each of the requirements of paragraphs 131, 131A, 131B, 131C, 131D, 131E, 131F, 131G or 131H is met (unless the applicant is otherwise eligible for an extension of stay for employment under these Rules).

Indefinite leave to remain for a work permit holder

134. Indefinite leave to remain may be granted, on application, to a person admitted as a work permit holder provided:
(i) he has spent a continuous period of 5 years in the United Kingdom in this capacity; and
(ii) he has met the requirements of paragraph 128(i) to (v) throughout the 5 year period; and
(iii) he is still required for the employment in question, as certified by his employer; and
(iv) he has sufficient knowledge of the English language and sufficient knowledge about life in the United Kingdom, unless he is under the age of 18 or aged 65 or over at the time he makes his application.

Refusal of indefinite leave to remain for a work permit holder

135. Indefinite leave to remain in the United Kingdom for a work permit holder is to be refused if the Secretary of State is not satisfied that each of the requirements of paragraph 134 is met.

Highly skilled migrants

Requirements for leave to enter the United Kingdom as a highly skilled migrant

135A. The requirements to be met by a person seeking leave to enter as a highly skilled migrant are that the applicant:
(i) must produce a valid document issued by the Home Office confirming that he meets, at the time of the issue of that document, the criteria specified by the Secretary of State for entry to the United Kingdom under the Highly Skilled Migrant Programme; and
(ii) intends to make the United Kingdom his main home; and
(iii) is able to maintain and accommodate himself and any dependants adequately without recourse to public funds; and
(iv) holds a valid United Kingdom entry clearance for entry in this capacity.

Leave to enter as a highly skilled migrant

135B. A person seeking leave to enter the United Kingdom as a highly skilled migrant may be admitted for a period not exceeding 2 years, provided the Immigration Officer is satisfied that each of the requirements of paragraph 135A is met and that the application does not fall for refusal under paragraph 135HA.

Refusal of leave to enter as a highly skilled migrant

135C. Leave to enter as a highly skilled migrant is to be refused if the Immigration Officer is not satisfied that each of the requirements of paragraph 135A is met or if the application falls for refusal under paragraph 135HA.

Requirements for an extension of stay as a highly skilled migrant

135D. The requirements for an extension of stay as a highly skilled migrant for a person who has previously been granted entry clearance or leave in this capacity, are that the applicant:

　(i)　entered the United Kingdom with a valid United Kingdom entry clearance as a highly skilled migrant, or has previously been granted leave in accordance with paragraphs 135DA–135DH of these Rules; and

　(ii)　has achieved at least 75 points in accordance with the criteria specified in Appendix 4 of these Rules, having provided all the documents which are set out in Appendix 5 (Part I) of these Rules which correspond to the points which he is claiming; and

　(iii)　(a)　has produced an International English Language Testing System certificate issued to him to certify that he has achieved at least band 6 competence in English; or

　　　(b)　has demonstrated that he holds a qualification which was taught in English and which is of an equivalent level to a UK Bachelors degree by providing both documents which are set out in Appendix 5 (Part II) of these Rules; and

　(iv)　meets the requirements of paragraph 135A(ii)–(iii).

135DA. The requirements for an extension of stay as a highly skilled migrant for a work permit holder are that the applicant:

　(i)　entered the United Kingdom or was given leave to remain as a work permit holder in accordance with paragraphs 128 to 132 of these Rules; and

　(ii)　meets the requirements of paragraph 135A(i)–(iii).

135DB. The requirements for an extension of stay as a highly skilled migrant for a student are that the applicant:

　(i)　entered the United Kingdom or was given leave to remain as a student in accordance with paragraphs 57 to 62 of these Rules; and

　(ii)　has obtained a degree qualification on a recognised degree course at either a United Kingdom publicly funded further or higher education institution or a bona fide United Kingdom private education institution which maintains satisfactory records of enrolment and attendance; and

　(iii)　has the written consent of his official sponsor to remain as a highly skilled migrant if he is a member of a government or international scholarship agency sponsorship and that sponsorship is either ongoing or has recently come to an end at the time of the requested extension; and

　(iv)　meets the requirements of paragraph 135A(i)–(iii).

135DC. The requirements for an extension of stay as a highly skilled migrant for a postgraduate doctor or postgraduate dentist are that the applicant:

　(i)　entered the United Kingdom or was given leave to remain as a postgraduate doctor or a postgraduate dentist in accordance with paragraphs 70 to 75 of these Rules; and

　(ii)　has the written consent of his official sponsor to such employment if he is a member of a government or international scholarship agency sponsorship and that sponsorship is either ongoing or has recently come to an end at the time of the requested extension; and

(iii) meets the requirements of paragraph 135A(i)–(iii).

135DD. The requirements for an extension of stay as a highly skilled migrant for a working holidaymaker are that the applicant:

(i) entered the United Kingdom as a working holidaymaker in accordance with paragraphs 95 to 96 of these Rules; and

(ii) meets the requirements of paragraph 135A(i)–(iii).

135DE. The requirements for an extension of stay as a highly skilled migrant for a participant in the Science and Engineering Graduates Scheme or International Graduates Scheme are that the applicant:

(i) entered the United Kingdom or was given leave to remain as a participant in the Science and Engineering Graduates Scheme or International Graduates Scheme in accordance with paragraphs 135O to 135T of these Rules; and

(ii) meets the requirements of paragraph 135A(i)–(iii).

135DF. The requirements for an extension of stay as a highly skilled migrant for an innovator are that the applicant:

(i) entered the United Kingdom or was given leave to remain as an innovator in accordance with paragraphs 210A to 210E of these Rules; and

(ii) meets the requirements of paragraph 135A(i)–(iii).

135DH. The requirements for an extension of stay as a highly skilled migrant for a participant in the Fresh Talent: Working in Scotland scheme are that the applicant:

(i) entered the United Kingdom or was given leave to remain as a Fresh Talent: Working in Scotland scheme participant in accordance with paragraphs 143A to 143F of these Rules; and

(ii) has the written consent of his official sponsor to such employment if the studies which led to him being granted leave under the Fresh Talent: Working in Scotland scheme in accordance with paragraphs 143A to 143F of these Rules, or any studies he has subsequently undertaken, were sponsored by a government or international scholarship agency; and

(iii) meets the requirements of paragraph 135A(i)–(iii).

Extension of stay as a highly skilled migrant

135E. An extension of stay as a highly skilled migrant may be granted for a period not exceeding 3 years, provided that the Secretary of State is satisfied that each of the requirements of paragraph 135D, 135DA, 135DB, 135DC, 135DD, 135DE, 135DF or 135DH is met and that the application does not fall for refusal under paragraph 135HA.

Refusal of extension of stay as a highly skilled migrant

135F. An extension of stay as a highly skilled migrant is to be refused if the Secretary of State is not satisfied that each of the requirements of paragraph 135D, 135DA, 135DB, 135DC, 135DD, 135DE, 135DF or 135DH is met or if the application falls for refusal under paragraph 135HA.

Requirements for indefinite leave to remain as a highly skilled migrant

135G. The requirements for indefinite leave to remain for a person who has been granted leave as a highly skilled migrant are that the applicant:

(i) has spent a continuous period of 5 years lawfully in the United Kingdom, of which the most recent period must have been spent with leave as a highly skilled migrant (in accordance with paragraphs 135A to 135F of these Rules), and the remainder must be made up of leave as a highly skilled migrant, leave as a work permit holder (under paragraphs 128 to 133 of these Rules), or leave as an Innovator (under paragraphs 210A to 210F of these Rules); and

(ii) throughout the five years spent in the United Kingdom has been able to maintain and accommodate himself and any dependants adequately without recourse to public funds; and

(iii) is lawfully economically active in the United Kingdom in employment, self-employment or a combination of both; and

(iv) has sufficient knowledge of the English language and sufficient knowledge about life in the United Kingdom, unless he is under the age of 18 or aged 65 or over at the time he makes his application.

Indefinite leave to remain as a highly skilled migrant

135GA. Indefinite leave to remain may be granted provided that the Secretary of State is satisfied that each of the requirements of paragraph 135G is met and that the application does not fall for refusal under paragraph 135HA.

Refusal of indefinite leave to remain as a highly skilled migrant

135H. Indefinite leave to remain in the United Kingdom is to be refused if the Secretary of State is not satisfied that each of the requirements of paragraph 135G is met or if the application falls for refusal under paragraph 135HA.

Additional grounds for refusal for highly skilled migrants

135HA. An application under paragraphs 135A–135H of these Rules is to be refused, even if the applicant meets all the requirements of those paragraphs, if:

(i) the applicant submits any document which, whether or not it is material to his application, is forged or not genuine, unless the Immigration Officer or Secretary of State is satisfied that the applicant is unaware that the document is forged or not genuine; or

(ii) the Immigration Officer or Secretary of State has cause to doubt the genuineness of any document submitted by the applicant and, having taken reasonable steps to verify the document, has been unable to verify that it is genuine.

Sectors-Based Scheme

Requirements for leave to enter the United Kingdom for the purpose of employment under the Sectors-Based Scheme

135I. The requirements to be met by a person seeking leave to enter the United Kingdom for the purpose of employment under the Sectors-Based Scheme are that he:

(i) holds a valid Home Office immigration employment document issued under the Sectors-Based Scheme; and

(ii) is aged between 18 and 30 inclusive or was so aged at the date of his application for leave to enter; and

(iii) is capable of undertaking the employment specified in the immigration employment document; and

(iv) does not intend to take employment except as specified in his immigration employment document; and

(v) is able to maintain and accommodate himself adequately without recourse to public funds; and

(vi) intends to leave the United Kingdom at the end of his approved employment; and

(vii) holds a valid United Kingdom entry clearance for entry in this capacity.

Leave to enter for the purpose of employment under the Sectors-Based Scheme

135J. A person seeking leave to enter the United Kingdom for the purpose of employment under the Sectors-Based Scheme may be admitted for a period not exceeding 12 months (normally as specified in his work permit), subject to a condition restricting him to employment approved by the Home Office, provided the Immigration Officer is satisfied that each of the requirements of paragraph 135I is met.

Refusal of leave to enter for the purpose of employment under the Sectors-Based Scheme

135K. Leave to enter the United Kingdom for the purpose of employment under the Sectors-Based Scheme is to be refused if the Immigration Officer is not satisfied that each of the requirements of paragraph 135I is met.

Requirements for an extension of stay for Sector-Based employment

135L. The requirements for an extension of stay for Sector-Based employment are that the applicant:
  (i) entered the United Kingdom with a valid Home Office immigration employment document issued under the sectors-Based Scheme and;
  (ii) has written approval from the Home Office for the continuation of his employment under the Sectors-Based Scheme; and
  (iii) meets the requirements of paragraph 135I(ii) to (vi); and
  (iv) would not, as a result of the extension of stay sought, remain in the United Kingdom for Sector-Based Scheme employment to a date beyond 12 months from the date on which he was given leave to enter the United Kingdom on this occasion in this capacity.

Extension of stay for Sectors-Based Scheme employment

135M. An extension of stay for Sectors-Based Scheme employment may be granted for a period not exceeding the period of approved employment recommended by the Home Office provided the Secretary of State is satisfied that each of the requirements of paragraph 135L are met. An extension of stay is to be subject to a condition restricting the applicant to employment approved by the Home Office.

Refusal of extension of stay for Sectors-Based Scheme employment

135N. An extension of stay for Sector-Based Scheme employment is to be refused if the Secretary of State is not satisfied that each of the requirements of paragraph 135L is met.

International Graduates Scheme

Requirements for leave to enter as a participant in the International Graduates Scheme

135O. The requirements to be met by a person seeking leave to enter as a participant in the International Graduates Scheme are that he:
  (i) has successfully completed and obtained either:
     (a) a recognised UK degree (with second class honours or above) in a subject approved by the Department for Education and Skills for the purposes of the Science and Engineering Graduates scheme, completed before 1 May 2007; or
     (b) a recognised UK degree, Master's degree, or PhD in any subject completed on or after 1 May 2007;or
     (c) a postgraduate certificate or postgraduate diploma in any subject completed on or after 1 May 2007;
     at a UK education institution which is a recognised or listed body;
  (ii) intends to seek and take work during the period for which leave is granted in this capacity;
  (iii) can maintain and accommodate himself and any dependants without recourse to public funds;

(iv) completed his degree, Master's degree, PhD or postgraduate certificate or diploma, in the last 12 months;

(v) if he has previously spent time in the UK as a participant in the Science and Engineering Graduates Scheme or International Graduates Scheme, is not seeking leave to enter to a date beyond 12 months from the date he was first given leave to enter or remain under the Science and Engineering Graduates Scheme or the International Graduates Scheme;

(vi) intends to leave the United Kingdom if, on expiry of his leave under this scheme, he has not been granted leave to remain in the United Kingdom in accordance with paragraphs 57–62, 128–135H or 200–210H of these Rules;

(vii) has the written consent of his official sponsor to enter or remain in the United Kingdom under the Science and Engineering Graduates Scheme or International Graduates Scheme if his approved studies, or any studies he has subsequently undertaken, were sponsored by a government or international scholarship agency; and

(viii) holds a valid entry clearance for entry in this capacity except where he is a British National (Overseas),a British overseas territories citizen, a British Overseas citizen, a British protected person or a person who under the British Nationality Act 1981 is a British subject.

Leave to enter as a participant in the International Graduates Scheme

135P. A person seeking leave to enter the United Kingdom as a participant in the International Graduates Scheme may be admitted for a period not exceeding 12 months provided he is able to produce to the Immigration Officer, on arrival, a valid United Kingdom entry clearance for entry in this capacity.

Refusal of leave to enter as a participant in the International Graduates Scheme

135Q. Leave to enter as a participant in the International Graduates Scheme is to be refused if the Immigration Officer is not satisfied that each of the requirements of paragraph 135O is met.

Requirements for leave to remain as a participant in the International Graduates Scheme

135R. The requirements to be met by a person seeking leave to remain as a participant in the International Graduates Scheme are that he:

(i) meets the requirements of paragraph 135O(i) to (vii); and

(ii) has leave to enter or remain as a student or as a participant in the Science and Engineering Graduates Scheme or International Graduates Scheme in accordance with paragraphs 57–69L or 135O–135T of these Rules;

(iii) would not, as a result of an extension of stay, remain in the United Kingdom as a participant in the International Graduates Scheme to a date beyond 12 months from the date on which he was first given leave to enter or remain in this capacity or under the Science and Engineering Graduates Scheme.

Leave to remain as a participant in the International Graduates Scheme

135S. Leave to remain as a participant in the International Graduates Scheme may be granted if the Secretary of State is satisfied that the applicant meets each of the requirements of paragraph 135R.

Refusal of leave to remain as a participant in the International Graduates Scheme

135T. Leave to remain as a participant in the International Graduates Scheme is to be refused if the Secretary of State is not satisfied that each of the requirements of paragraph 135R is met.

Representatives of overseas newspapers, news agencies and broadcasting organisations

Requirements for leave to enter as a representative of an overseas newspaper, news agency or broadcasting organisation

136. The requirements to be met by a person seeking leave to enter the United Kingdom as a representative of an overseas newspaper, news agency or broadcasting organisation are that he:
    (i) has been engaged by that organisation outside the United Kingdom and is being posted to the United Kingdom on a long term assignment as a representative; and
    (ii) intends to work full time as a representative of that overseas newspaper, news agency or broadcasting organisation; and
    (iii) does not intend to take employment except within the terms of this paragraph; and
    (iv) can maintain and accommodate himself and any dependants adequately without recourse to public funds; and
    (v) holds a valid United Kingdom entry clearance for entry in this capacity.

Leave to enter as a representative of an overseas newspaper, newsagency or broadcasting organisation

137. A person seeking leave to enter the United Kingdom as a representative of an overseas newspaper, news agency or broadcasting organisation may be admitted for a period not exceeding 2 years provided he is able to produce to the Immigration Officer, on arrival, a valid United Kingdom entry clearance for entry in this capacity.

Refusal of leave to enter as a representative of an overseas newspaper, news agency or broadcasting organisation

138. Leave to enter as a representative of an overseas newspaper, news agency or broadcasting organisation is to be refused if a valid United Kingdom entry clearance for entry in this capacity is not produced to the Immigration Officer on arrival.

Requirements for an extension of stay as a representative of an overseas newspaper, news agency or broadcasting organisation

139. The requirements for an extension of stay as a representative of an overseas newspaper, news agency or broadcasting organisation are that the applicant:
    (i) entered the United Kingdom with a valid United Kingdom entry clearance as a representative of an overseas newspaper, news agency or broadcasting organisation; and
    (ii) is still engaged in the employment for which his entry clearance was granted; and
    (iii) is still required for the employment in question, as certified by his employer; and
    (iv) meets the requirements of paragraph 136(ii)–(iv).

Extension of stay as a representative of an overseas newspaper, news agency or broadcasting organisation

140. An extension of stay as a representative of an overseas newspaper, news agency or broadcasting organisation may be granted for a period not exceeding 3 years provided the Secretary of State is satisfied that each of the requirements of paragraph 139 is met.

Refusal of extension of stay as a representative of an overseas newspaper, news agency or broadcasting organisation

141. An extension of stay as a representative of an overseas newspaper, news agency or broadcasting organisation is to be refused if the Secretary of State is not satisfied that each of the requirements of paragraph 139 is met.

Indefinite leave to remain for a representative of an overseas newspaper, news agency or broadcasting organisation

142. Indefinite leave to remain may be granted, on application, to a representative of an overseas newspaper, news agency or broadcasting organisation provided:
    (i) he has spent a continuous period of 5 years in the United Kingdom in this capacity; and
    (ii) he has met the requirements of paragraph 139 throughout the 5-year period; and
    (iii) he is still required for the employment in question, as certified by his employer; and
    (iv) he has sufficient knowledge of the English language and sufficient knowledge about life in the United Kingdom, unless he is under the age of 18 or aged 65 or over at the time he makes his application.

Refusal of indefinite leave to remain for a representative of an overseas newspaper, news agency or broadcasting organisation

143. Indefinite leave to remain in the United Kingdom for a representative of an overseas newspaper, news agency or broadcasting organisation is to be refused if the Secretary of State is not satisfied that each of the requirements of paragraph 142 is met.

Requirements for leave to enter the United Kingdom as a Fresh Talent: Working in Scotland scheme participant

143A. The requirements to be met by a person seeking leave to enter as a Fresh Talent: Working in Scotland scheme participant are that the applicant:
    (i) has been awarded:
        (a) a HND, by a Scottish publicly funded institution of further or higher education, or a Scottish bona fide private education institution; or
        (b) a recognised UK undergraduate degree, Master's degree or PhD or postgraduate certificate or diploma, by a Scottish education institution which is a recognised or listed body; and
    (ii) has lived in Scotland for an appropriate period of time whilst studying for the HND, undergraduate degree, Master's degree, PhD or postgraduate certificate or diploma referred to in (i) above; and
    (iii) intends to seek and take employment in Scotland during the period of leave granted under this paragraph; and
    (iv) is able to maintain and accommodate himself and any dependants adequately without recourse to public funds; and
    (v) has completed the HND, undergraduate degree, Master's degree, PhD or postgraduate certificate or diploma referred to in (i) above in the last 12 months; and
    (vi) intends to leave the United Kingdom if, on expiry of his leave under this paragraph, he has not been granted leave to remain in the United Kingdom as:
        (a) a work permit holder in accordance with paragraphs 128–135 of these Rules; or

(b) under the highly skilled migrant programme in accordance with paragraphs 135A–135H of these Rules; or

(c) a person intending to establish themselves in business in accordance with paragraphs 200–210 of these Rules; or

(d) an innovator in accordance with paragraphs 210A–210H of these Rules; and

(vii) has the written consent of his official sponsor to enter or remain in the United Kingdom as a Fresh Talent: Working in Scotland scheme participant, if the studies which led to his qualification under (i) above (or any studies he has subsequently undertaken) were sponsored by a government or international scholarship agency; and

(viii) if he has previously been granted leave as either:

(a) a Fresh Talent: Working in Scotland scheme participant in accordance with this paragraph; and/or

(b) a participant in the Science and Engineering Graduates Scheme or International Graduates Scheme in accordance with paragraphs 135O–135T of these Rules is not seeking leave to enter under this paragraph which, when amalgamated with any previous periods of leave granted in either of these two categories, would total more than 24 months; and

(ix) holds a valid entry clearance for entry in this capacity except where he is a British National (Overseas), a British overseas territories citizen, a British Overseas citizen, a British protected person or a person who under the British Nationality Act 1981 is a British subject.

Leave to enter as a Fresh Talent: Working in Scotland scheme participant

143B. A person seeking leave to enter the United Kingdom as a Fresh Talent: Working in Scotland scheme participant may be admitted for a period not exceeding 24 months provided the Immigration Officer is satisfied that each of the requirements of paragraph 143A is met.

Refusal of leave to enter as a Fresh Talent: Working in Scotland scheme participant

143C. Leave to enter as a Fresh Talent: Working in Scotland scheme participant is to be refused if the Immigration Officer is not satisfied that each of the requirements of paragraph 143A is met.

Requirements for an extension of stay as a Fresh Talent: Working in Scotland scheme participant

143D. The requirements to be met by a person seeking an extension of stay as a Fresh Talent: Working in Scotland scheme participant are that the applicant:

(i) meets the requirements of paragraph 143A(i) to (vii); and

(ii) has leave to enter or remain in the United Kingdom as either:

(a) a student in accordance with paragraphs 57–69L of these Rules; or

(b) a participant in the Science and Engineering Graduates Scheme or International Graduates Scheme in accordance with paragraphs 135O–135T of these Rules; or

(c) a Fresh Talent: Working in Scotland scheme participant in accordance with paragraphs 143A–143F of these Rules; and

(iii) if he has previously been granted leave as either:

(a) a Fresh Talent: Working in Scotland scheme participant in accordance with paragraphs 143A–143F of these Rules; and/or

(b) a Science and Engineering Graduates Scheme or International Graduates Scheme participant in accordance with paragraphs 135O–135T of these Rules is not seeking leave to remain under this paragraph which, when amalgamated with any previous periods of leave granted in either of these two categories, would total more than 24 months.

Extension of stay as a Fresh Talent: Working in Scotland scheme participant

143E. An extension of stay as a Fresh Talent: Working in Scotland scheme participant may be granted for a period not exceeding 24 months if the Secretary of State is satisfied that each of the requirements of paragraph 143D is met.

Refusal of an extension of stay as a Fresh Talent: Working in Scotland scheme participant

143F. An extension of stay as a Fresh Talent: Working in Scotland scheme participant is to be refused if the Secretary of State is not satisfied that each of the requirements of paragraph 143D is met.

Representatives of overseas firms which have no branch, subsidiary or other representative in the United Kingdom (sole representatives)

Requirements for leave to enter as a sole representative

144. The requirements to be met by a person seeking leave to enter the United Kingdom as a sole representative are that he:
    (i) has been recruited and taken on as an employee outside the United Kingdom as a representative of a firm which has its headquarters and principal place of business outside the United Kingdom and which has no branch, subsidiary or other representative in the United Kingdom; and
    (ii) seeks entry to the United Kingdom as a senior employee with full authority to take operational decisions on behalf of the overseas firm for the purpose of representing it in the United Kingdom by establishing and operating a registered branch or wholly owned subsidiary of that overseas firm; and
    (iii) intends to be employed full time as a representative of that overseas firm; and
    (iv) is not a majority shareholder in that overseas firm; and
    (v) does not intend to take employment except within the terms of this paragraph; and
    (vi) can maintain and accommodate himself and any dependants adequately without recourse to public funds; and
    (vii) holds a valid United Kingdom entry clearance for entry in this capacity.

Leave to enter as a sole representative

145. A person seeking leave to enter the United Kingdom as a sole representative may be admitted for a period not exceeding 2 years provided he is able to produce to the Immigration Officer, on arrival, a valid United Kingdom entry clearance for entry in this capacity.

Refusal of leave to enter as a sole representative

146. Leave to enter as a sole representative is to be refused if a valid United Kingdom entry clearance for entry in this capacity is not produced to the Immigration Officer on arrival.

Requirements for an extension of stay as a sole representative

147. The requirements for an extension of stay as a sole representative are that the applicant:
    (i) entered the United Kingdom with a valid United Kingdom entry clearance as a sole representative of an overseas firm; and

(ii) can show that the overseas firm still has its headquarters and principal place of business outside the United Kingdom; and

(iii) is employed full time as a representative of that overseas firm and has established and is in charge of its registered branch or wholly owned subsidiary; and

(iv) is still required for the employment in question, as certified by his employer; and

(v) meets the requirements of paragraph 144(iii)–(vi).

Extension of stay as a sole representative

148. An extension of stay not exceeding 3 years as a sole representative may be granted provided the Secretary of State is satisfied that each of the requirements of paragraph 147 is met.

Refusal of extension of stay as a sole representative

149. An extension of stay as a sole representative is to be refused if the Secretary of State is not satisfied that each of the requirements of paragraph 147 is met.

Indefinite leave to remain for a sole representative

150. Indefinite leave to remain may be granted, on application, to a sole representative provided:

(i) he has spent a continuous period of 5 years in the United Kingdom in this capacity; and

(ii) he has met the requirements of paragraph 147 throughout the 5 year period; and

(iii) he is still required for the employment in question, as certified by his employer; and

(iv) he has sufficient knowledge of the English language and sufficient knowledge about life in the United Kingdom, unless he is under the age of 18 or aged 65 or over at the time he makes his application.

Refusal of indefinite leave to remain for a sole representative

151. Indefinite leave to remain in the United Kingdom for a sole representative is to be refused if the Secretary of State is not satisfied that each of the requirements of paragraph 150 is met.

Private servants in diplomatic households

Requirements for leave to enter as a private servant in a diplomatic household

152. The requirements to be met by a person seeking leave to enter the United Kingdom as a private servant in a diplomatic household are that he:

(i) is aged 18 or over; and

(ii) is employed as a private servant in the household of a member of staff of a diplomatic or consular mission who enjoys diplomatic privileges and immunity within the meaning of the Vienna Convention on Diplomatic and Consular Relations or a member of the family forming part of the household of such a person; and

(iii) intends to work full time as a private servant within the terms of this paragraph; and

(iv) does not intend to take employment except within the terms of this paragraph; and

(v) can maintain and accommodate himself and any dependants adequately without recourse to public funds; and

(vi) holds a valid United Kingdom entry clearance for entry in this capacity.

Leave to enter as a private servant in a diplomatic household

153. A person seeking leave to enter the United Kingdom as a private servant in a diplomatic household may be given leave to enter for a period not exceeding 12 months provided he is able to produce to the Immigration Officer, on arrival, a valid United Kingdom entry clearance for entry in this capacity.

Refusal of leave to enter as a private servant in a diplomatic household

154. Leave to enter as a private servant in a diplomatic household is to be refused if a valid United Kingdom entry clearance for entry in this capacity is not produced to the Immigration Officer on arrival.

Requirements for an extension of stay as a private servant in a diplomatic household

155. The requirements for an extension of stay as a private servant in a diplomatic household are that the applicant:
    (i) entered the United Kingdom with a valid United Kingdom entry clearance as a private servant in a diplomatic household; and
    (ii) is still engaged in the employment for which his entry clearance was granted; and
    (iii) is still required for the employment in question, as certified by the employer; and
    (iv) meets the requirements of paragraph 152(iii)–(v).

Extension of stay as a private servant in a diplomatic household

156. An extension of stay as a private servant in a diplomatic household may be granted for a period not exceeding 12 months at a time provided the Secretary of State is satisfied that each of the requirements of paragraph 155 is met.

Refusal of extension of stay as a private servant in a diplomatic household

157. An extension of stay as a private servant in a diplomatic household is to be refused if the Secretary of State is not satisfied that each of the requirements of paragraph 155 is met.

Indefinite leave to remain for a servant in a diplomatic household

158. Indefinite leave to remain may be granted, on application, to a private servant in a diplomatic household provided:
    (i) he has spent a continuous period of 5 years in the United Kingdom in this capacity; and
    (ii) he has met the requirements of paragraph 155 throughout the 5-year period; and
    (iii) he is still required for the employment in question, as certified by his employer; and
    (iv) he has sufficient knowledge of the English language and sufficient knowledge about life in the United Kingdom, unless he is under the age of 18 or aged 65 or over at the time he makes his application.

Refusal of indefinite leave to remain for a servant in a diplomatic household

159. Indefinite leave to remain in the United Kingdom for a private servant in a diplomatic household is to be refused if the Secretary of State is not satisfied that each of the requirements of paragraph 158 is met.

Section 2

Domestic workers in private households

Requirements for leave to enter as a domestic worker in a private household

159A. The requirements to be met by a person seeking leave to enter the United Kingdom as a domestic worker in a private household are that he:
  (i) is aged 18–65 inclusive;
  (ii) has been employed as a domestic worker for one year or more immediately prior to application for entry clearance under the same roof as his employer or in a household that the employer uses for himself on a regular basis and where there is evidence that there is a connection between employer and employee;
  (iii) that he intends to travel to the United Kingdom in the company of his employer, his employer's spouse or civil partner or his employer's minor child;
  (iv) intends to work full time as a domestic worker under the same roof as his employer or in a household that the employer uses for himself on a regular basis and where there is evidence that there is a connection between employer and employee;
  (v) does not intend to take employment except within the terms of this paragraph; and
  (vi) can maintain and accommodate himself adequately without recourse to public funds; and
  (vii) holds a valid United Kingdom entry clearance for entry in this capacity.

Leave to enter as a domestic worker in a private household

159B. A person seeking leave to enter the United Kingdom as a domestic worker in a private household may be given leave to enter for that purpose for a period not exceeding 12 months provided he is able to produce to the Immigration Officer, on arrival, a valid United Kingdom entry clearance for entry in this capacity.

Refusal of leave to enter as a domestic worker in a private household

159C. Leave to enter as a domestic worker in a private household is to be refused if a valid United Kingdom entry clearance for entry in this capacity is not produced to the Immigration Officer on arrival.

Requirements for extension of stay as a domestic worker in a private household

159D. The requirements for an extension of stay as a domestic worker in a private household are that the applicant:
  (i) entered the United Kingdom with a valid United Kingdom entry clearance as a domestic worker in a private household; and
  (ii) has continued to be employed for the duration of his leave as a domestic worker in a private household; and
  (iii) continues to be required for employment for the period of the extension sought as a domestic worker in a private household within the terms of paragraph 159A as certified by his current employer; and
  (iv) meets each of the requirements of paragraph 159A(i) to (vi).

Extension of stay as a domestic worker in a private household

159E. An extension of stay as a domestic worker in a private household may be granted for a period not exceeding 12 months at a time provided the Secretary of State is satisfied that each of the requirements of paragraph 159D is met.

Refusal of extension of stay as a domestic worker in a private household.

159F. An extension of stay as a domestic worker may be refused if the Secretary of State is not satisfied that each of the requirements of paragraph 159D is met.

Indefinite leave to remain for a domestic worker in a private household.

159G. Indefinite leave to remain may be granted, on application, to a domestic worker in a private household provided that:
  (i) he has spent a continuous period of 5 years in the United Kingdom employed in this capacity; and
  (ii) he has met the requirements of paragraph 159A throughout the 5-year period; and
  (iii) he is still required for employment as a domestic worker in a private household, as certified by the current employer; and
  (iv) he has sufficient knowledge of the English language and sufficient knowledge about life in the United Kingdom, unless he is under the age of 18 or aged 65 or over at the time he makes his application.

Refusal of indefinite leave to remain for a domestic worker in a private household

159H. Indefinite leave to remain in the United Kingdom for a domestic worker in a private household is to be refused if the Secretary of State is not satisfied that each of the requirements of paragraph 159G is met.

Overseas government employees

Requirements for leave to enter as an overseas government employee

160. For the purposes of these Rules an overseas government employee means a person coming for employment by an overseas government or employed by the United Nations Organisation or other international organisation of which the United Kingdom is a member.

161. The requirements to be met by a person seeking leave to enter the United Kingdom as an overseas government employee are that he:
  (i) is able to produce either a valid United Kingdom entry clearance for entry in this capacity or satisfactory documentary evidence of his status as an overseas government employee; and
  (ii) intends to work full time for the government or organisation concerned; and
  (iii) does not intend to take employment except within the terms of this paragraph; and
  (iv) can maintain and accommodate himself and any dependants adequately without recourse to public funds.

Leave to enter as an overseas government employee

162. A person seeking leave to enter the United Kingdom as an overseas government employee may be given leave to enter for a period not exceeding 2 years, provided he is able, on arrival, to produce to the Immigration Officer a valid United Kingdom entry clearance for entry in this capacity or satisfy the Immigration Officer that each of the requirements of paragraph 161 is met.

Refusal of leave to enter as an overseas government employee

163. Leave to enter as an overseas government employee is to be refused if a valid United Kingdom entry clearance for entry in this capacity is not produced to the Immigration Officer on arrival or if the Immigration Officer is not satisfied that each of the requirements of paragraph 161 is met.

Requirements for an extension of stay as an overseas government employee

164. The requirements to be met by a person seeking an extension of stay as an overseas government employee are that the applicant:
    (i) was given leave to enter the United Kingdom under paragraph 162 as an overseas government employee; and
    (ii) is still engaged in the employment in question; and
    (iii) is still required for the employment in question, as certified by the employer; and
    (iv) meets the requirements of paragraph 161 (ii)–(iv).

Extension of stay as an overseas government employee

165. An extension of stay as an overseas government employee may be granted for a period not exceeding 3 years provided the Secretary of State is satisfied that each of the requirements of paragraph 164 is met.

Refusal of extension of stay as an overseas government employee

166. An extension of stay as an overseas government employee is to be refused if the Secretary of State is not satisfied that each of the requirements of paragraph 164 is met.

Indefinite leave to remain for an overseas government employee

167. Indefinite leave to remain may be granted, on application, to an overseas government employee provided:
    (i) he has spent a continuous period of 5 years in the United Kingdom in this capacity; and
    (ii) he has met the requirements of paragraph 164 throughout the 5-year period; and
    (iii) he is still required for the employment in question, as certified by his employer; and
    (iv) he has sufficient knowledge of the English language and sufficient knowledge about life in the United Kingdom, unless he is under the age of 18 or aged 65 or over at the time he makes his application.

Refusal of indefinite leave to remain for an overseas government employee

168. Indefinite leave to remain in the United Kingdom for an overseas government employee is to be refused if the Secretary of State is not satisfied that each of the requirements of paragraph 167 is met.

169. For the purposes of these Rules:
    (i) a minister of religion means a religious functionary whose main regular duties comprise the leading of a congregation in performing the rites and rituals of the faith and in preaching the essentials of the creed;
    (ii) a missionary means a person who is directly engaged in spreading a religious doctrine and whose work is not in essence administrative or clerical;
    (iii) a member of a religious order means a person who is coming to live in a community run by that order.

Requirements for leave to enter as a minister of religion, missionary, or member of a religious order

170. The requirements to be met by a person seeking leave to enter the United Kingdom as a minister of religion, missionary or member of a religious order are that he:

(i) (a) if seeking leave to enter as a minister of religion has either been working for at least one year as a minister of religion in any of the 5 years immediately prior to the date on which the applicaton is made or, where ordination is prescribed by a religious faith as the sole means of entering the ministry, has been ordained as a minister of religion following at least one year's full time or two years' part time training for the ministry; or

(b) if seeking leave to enter as a missionary has been trained as a missionary or has worked as a missionary and is being sent to the United Kingdom by an overseas organisation; or

(c) if seeking leave to enter as a member of a religious order is coming to live in a community maintained by the religious order of which he is a member and, if intending to teach, does not intend to do so save at an establishment maintained by his order; and

(ii) intends to work full time as a minister of religion, missionary or for the religious order of which he is a member; and

(iii) does not intend to take employment except within the terms of this paragraph; and

(iv) can maintain and accommodate himself and any dependants adequately without recourse to public funds; and

(iva) if seeking leave as a minister of religion can produce an International English Language Testing System certificate issued to him to certify that he has achieved level 6 competence in spoken and written English and that is dated not more than two years prior to the date on which the application is made.

(v) holds a valid United Kingdom entry clearance for entry in this capacity.

Leave to enter as a minister of religion, missionary, or member of a religious order

171. A person seeking leave to enter the United Kingdom as a minister of religion, missionary or member of a religious order may be admitted for a period not exceeding 2 years provided he is able to produce to the Immigration Officer, on arrival, a valid United Kingdom entry clearance for entry in this capacity.

Refusal of leave to enter as a minister of religion, missionary or member of a religious order

172. Leave to enter as a minister of religion, missionary or member of a religious order is to be refused if a valid United Kingdom entry clearance for entry in this capacity is not produced to the Immigration Officer on arrival.

Requirements for an extension of stay as a minister of religion where entry to the United Kingdom was granted in that capacity

173. The requirements for an extension of stay as a minister of religion, where entry to the United Kingdom was granted in that capacity, missionary or member of a religious order are that the applicant:

(i) entered the United Kingdom with a valid United Kingdom entry clearance as a minister of religion, missionary or member of a religious order; and

(ii) is still engaged in the employment for which his entry clearance was granted; and

(iii) is still required for the employment in question as certified by the leadership of his congregation, his employer or the head of his religious order; and

(iv) (a) if he entered the United Kingdom as a minister of religion, missionary or member of a religious order in accordance with sub paragraph (i) prior to 23 August 2004 meets the requirements of paragraph 170(ii)–(iv); or

(b) if he entered the United Kingdom as a minister of religion, missionary or member of a religious order in accordance with sub paragraph (i), on or after 23 August 2004 but prior to 19 April 2007, or was granted leave to remain in accordance with paragraph 174B between those dates, meets the requirements of paragraph 170(ii)–(iv), and if a minister of religion met the requirement to produce an International English Language Testing System certificate certifying that he achieved level 4 competence in spoken English at the time he was first granted leave in this capacity; or

(c) if he entered the United Kingdom as a minister of religion, missionary or member of a religious order in accordance with sub paragraph (i) on or after 19 April 2007, or was granted leave to remain in accordance with paragraph 174B on or after that date, meets the requirements of paragraph 170(ii)–(iv), and if a minister of religion met the requirement to produce an International English Language Testing System certificate certifying that he achieved level 6 competence in spoken and written English at the time he was first granted leave in this capacity.

Extension of stay as a minister of religion, missionary or member of a religious order

174. An extension of stay as a minister of religion, missionary or member of a religious order may be granted for a period not exceeding 3 years provided the Secretary of State is satisfied that each of the requirements of paragraph 173 is met.

Requirements for an extension of stay as a minister of religion where entry to the United Kingdom was not granted in that capacity

174A. The requirements for an extension of stay as a minister of religion for an applicant who did not enter the United Kingdom in that capacity are that he:

(i) entered the United Kingdom, or was given an extension of stay, in accordance with these Rules, except as a minister of religion or as a visitor under paragraphs 40–56 of these Rules, and has spent a continuous period of at least 12 months here pursuant to that leave immediately prior to the application being made; and

(ii) has either been working for at least one year as a minister of religion in any of the 5 years immediately prior to the date on which the application is made (provided that, when doing so, he was not in breach of a condition of any subsisting leave to enter or remain) or, where ordination is prescribed by a religious faith as the sole means of entering the ministry, has been ordained as a minister of religion following at least one year's full-time or two years part-time training for the ministry; and

(iii) is imminently to be appointed, or has been appointed, to a position as a minister of religion in the United Kingdom and is suitable for such a position, as certified by the leadership of his prospective congregation; and

(iv) meets the requirements of paragraph 170(ii)–(iva)

Extension of stay as a minister of religion where leave to enter was not granted in that capacity

174B. An extension of stay as a minister of religion may be granted for a period not exceeding 3 years at a time provided the Secretary of State is satisfied that each of the requirements of paragraph 174A is met.

Refusal of extension of stay as a minister of religion, missionary or member of a religious order

175. An extension of stay as a minister of religion, missionary or member of a religious order is to be refused if the Secretary of State is not satisfied that each of the requirements of paragraph 173 or 174A is met.

Indefinite leave to remain for a minister of religion, missionary or member of a religious order

176. Indefinite leave to remain may be granted, on application, to a person admitted as a minister of religion, missionary or member of a religious order provided:

    (i) he has spent a continuous period of 5 years in the United Kingdom in this capacity; and

    (ii) he has met the requirements of paragraph 173 or 174A throughout the 5-year period; and

    (iii) he is still required for the employment in question as certified by the leadership of his congregation, his employer or the head of the religious order to which he belongs; and

    (iv) he has sufficient knowledge of the English language and sufficient knowledge about life in the United Kingdom, unless he is under the age of 18 or aged 65 or over at the time he makes his application.

Refusal of indefinite leave to remain for a minister of religion, missionary or member of a religious order

177. Indefinite leave to remain in the United Kingdom for a minister of religion, missionary or member of a religious order is to be refused if the Secretary of State is not satisfied that each of the requirements of paragraph 176 is met.

177A. For the purposes of these Rules:

    (i) a visiting religious worker means a person coming to the UK for a short period to perform religious duties at one or more locations in the UK;

    (ii) a religious worker in a non-pastoral role means a person employed in the UK by the faith he is coming here to work for, whose duties include performing religious rites within the religious community, but not preaching to a congregation.

Requirements for leave to enter the United Kingdom as a visiting religious worker or a religious worker in a non-pastoral role

177B. The requirements to be met by a person seeking leave to enter as a visiting religious worker or a religious worker in a non-pastoral role are that the applicant:

    (i) (a) if seeking leave to enter as a visiting religious worker:

        (i) is an established religious worker based overseas; and

        (ii) submits a letter(s) from a senior member or senior representative of one or more local religious communities in the UK confirming that he is invited to perform religious duties as a visiting religious worker at one or more locations in the UK and confirming the expected duration of that employment; and

        (iii) if he has been granted leave as a visiting religious worker in the last 12 months, is not seeking leave to enter which, when amalgamated with his previous periods of leave in this category in the last 12 months, would total more than 6 months; or

    (b) if seeking leave to enter as a religious worker in a non-pastoral role:

        (i) has at least one year of full time training or work experience, or a period of part time training or work experience equivalent to one year full time training or work experience, accrued in the five years preceding the application in the faith with which he has employment in the UK; and

        (ii) can show that, at the time of his application, at least one full-time member of staff of the local religious community which the applicant is applying to join in the UK has a sufficient knowledge of English; and

(iii) submits a letter from a senior member or senior representative of the local religious community which has invited him to the UK, confirming that he has been offered employment as religious worker in a non-pastoral role in that religious community, and confirming the duration of that employment; and

(ii) does not intend to take employment except as a visiting religious worker or religious worker in a non-pastoral role, whichever is the basis of his application; and

(iii) does not intend to undertake employment as a Minister of Religion, Missionary or Member of a Religious Order, as described in paragraphs 169–177 of these Rules; and

(iv) is able to maintain and accommodate himself and any dependants without recourse to public funds, or will, with any dependants, be maintained and accommodated adequately by the religious community employing him; and

(v) intends to leave the UK at the end of his leave in this category; and

(vi) holds a valid entry clearance for entry in this capacity except where he is a British National (Overseas), a British overseas territories citizen, a British Overseas citizen, a British protected person or a person who under the British Nationality Act 1981 is a British subject.

Leave to enter as a visiting religious worker or a religious worker in a non-pastoral role

177C. Leave to enter the United Kingdom as a visiting religious worker or a religious worker in a non-pastoral role may be granted:

(a) as a visiting religious worker, for a period not exceeding 6 months; or

(b) as a religious worker in a non-pastoral role, for a period not exceeding 12 months; provided the Immigration Officer is satisfied that each of the requirements of paragraph 177B is met.

Refusal of leave to enter as a visiting religious worker or a religious worker in a non-pastoral role

177D. Leave to enter as a visiting religious worker or a religious worker in a non pastoral role is to be refused if the Immigration Officer is not satisfied that each of the requirements of paragraph 177B is met.

Requirements for an extension of stay as a visiting religious worker or a religious worker in a non pastoral role

177E. The requirements to be met by a person seeking an extension of stay as a visiting religious worker or a religious worker in a non-pastoral role are that the applicant:

(i) entered the United Kingdom with a valid entry clearance in this capacity or was given leave to enter as a visiting religious worker or a religious worker in a non-pastoral role; and

(ii) intends to continue employment as a visiting religious worker or a religious worker in a nonpastoral role; and

(iii) if seeking an extension of stay as a visiting religious worker:

(a) meets the requirement of paragraph 177B(i)(a)(i) above; and

(b) submits a letter from a senior member or senior representative of one or more local religious communities in the UK confirming that he is still wanted to perform religious duties as a visiting religious worker at one or more locations in the UK and confirming the expected duration of that employment; and

(c) would not, as the result of an extension of stay, be granted leave as a visiting religious worker which, when amalgamated with his previous periods of leave in this category in the last 12 months, would total more than 6 months; or

(iv) if seeking an extension of stay as a religious worker in a non-pastoral role:
   (a) meets the requirements of paragraph 177B(i)(b)(i) and (ii); and
   (b) submits a letter from a senior member or senior representative of the local religious community for which he works in the UK confirming that his employment as a religious worker in a non-pastoral role in that religious community will continue, and confirming the duration of that employment; and
   (c) would not, as the result of an extension of stay, remain in the UK for a period of more than 24 months as a religious worker in a non-pastoral role; and
(v) meets the requirements of paragraph 177B(ii) to (v); and

Extension of stay as a visiting religious worker or a religious worker in a non-pastoral role

177F. An extension of stay as a visiting religious worker or a religious worker in a non-pastoral role may be granted:
   (a) as a visiting religious worker, for a period not exceeding 6 months; or
   (b) as a religious worker in a non-pastoral role, for a period not exceeding 24 months;
   if the Secretary of State is satisfied that each of the requirements of paragraph 177E is met.

Refusal of an extension of stay as a visiting religious worker or a religious worker in a non pastoral role

177G. An extension of stay as a visiting religious worker or a religious worker in a non-pastoral role is to be refused if the Secretary of State is not satisfied that each of the requirements of paragraph 177E is met.

Section 3

Airport based operational ground staff of overseas-owned airlines

Requirements for leave to enter the United Kingdom as a member of the operational ground staff of an overseas-owned airline

178. The requirements to be met by a person seeking leave to enter the United Kingdom as a member of the operational ground staff of an overseas owned airline are that he:
   (i) has been transferred to the United Kingdom by an overseas-owned airline operating services to and from the United Kingdom to take up duty at an international airport as station manager, security manager or technical manager; and
   (ii) intends to work full time for the airline concerned; and
   (iii) does not intend to take employment except within the terms of this paragraph; and
   (iv) can maintain and accommodate himself and any dependants without recourse to public funds; and
   (v) holds a valid United Kingdom entry clearance for entry in this capacity.

Leave to enter as a member of the operational ground staff of an overseas owned airline

179. A person seeking leave to enter the United Kingdom as a member of the operational ground staff of an overseas owned airline may be given leave to enter for a period not exceeding 2 years, provided he is able to produce to the Immigration Officer, on arrival, a valid United Kingdom entry clearance for entry in this capacity.

Refusal of leave to enter as a member of the operational ground staff of an overseas owned airline

180. Leave to enter as a member of the operational ground staff of an overseas owned airline is to be refused if a valid United Kingdom entry clearance for entry in this capacity is not produced to the Immigration Officer on arrival.

Requirements for an extension of stay as a member of the operational ground staff of an overseas owned airline

181. The requirements to be met by a person seeking an extension of stay as a member of the operational ground staff of an overseas owned airline are that the applicant:
    (i) entered the United Kingdom with a valid United Kingdom entry clearance as a member of the operational ground staff of an overseas owned airline; and
    (ii) is still engaged in the employment for which entry was granted; and
    (iii) is still required for the employment in question, as certified by the employer; and
    (iv) meets the requirements of paragraph 178(ii)–(iv).

Extension of stay as a member of the operational ground staff of an overseas owned airline

182. An extension of stay as a member of the operational ground staff of an overseas owned airline may be granted for a period not exceeding 3 years, provided the Secretary of State is satisfied that each of the requirements of paragraph 181 is met.

Refusal of extension of stay as a member of the operational ground staff of an overseas owned airline

183. An extension of stay as a member of the operational ground staff of an overseas owned airline is to be refused if the Secretary of State is not satisfied that each of the requirements of paragraph 181 is met.

Indefinite leave to remain for a member of the operational ground staff of an overseas owned airline

184. Indefinite leave to remain may be granted, on application, to a member of the operational ground staff of an overseas-owned airline provided:
    (i) he has spent a continuous period of 5 years in the United Kingdom in this capacity; and
    (ii) he has met the requirements of paragraph 181 throughout the 5-year period; and
    (iii) he is still required for the employment in question as certified by the employer; and
    (iv) he has sufficient knowledge of the English language and sufficient knowledge about life in the United Kingdom, unless he is under the age of 18 or aged 65 or over at the time he makes his application.

Refusal of indefinite leave to remain for a member of the operational ground staff of an overseas owned airline

185. Indefinite leave to remain in the United Kingdom for a member of the operational ground staff of an overseas owned airline is to be refused if the Secretary of State is not satisfied that each of the requirements of paragraph 184 is met.

Persons with United Kingdom ancestry

Requirements for leave to enter on the grounds of United Kingdom ancestry

186. The requirements to be met by a person seeking leave to enter the United Kingdom on the grounds of his United Kingdom ancestry are that he:
    (i) is a Commonwealth citizen; and
    (ii) is aged 17 or over; and
    (iii) is able to provide proof that one of his grandparents was born in the United Kingdom and Islands and that any such grandparent is the applicant's blood grandparent or grandparent by reason of an adoption recognised by the laws of the United Kingdom relating to adoption; and
    (iv) is able to work and intends to take or seek employment in the United Kingdom; and
    (v) will be able to maintain and accommodate himself and any dependants adequately without recourse to public funds; and
    (vi) holds a valid United Kingdom entry clearance for entry in this capacity.

Leave to enter the United Kingdom on the grounds of United Kingdom ancestry

187. A person seeking leave to enter the United Kingdom on the grounds of his United Kingdom ancestry may be given leave to enter for a period not exceeding 2 years provided he is able to produce to the Immigration Officer, on arrival, a valid United Kingdom entry clearance for entry in this capacity.

Refusal of leave to enter on the grounds of United Kingdom ancestry

188. Leave to enter the United Kingdom on the grounds of United Kingdom ancestry is to be refused if a valid United Kingdom entry clearance for entry in this capacity is not produced to the Immigration Officer on arrival.

Requirements for an extension of stay on the grounds of United Kingdom ancestry

189. The requirements to be met by a person seeking an extension of stay on the grounds of United Kingdom ancestry are that:
    (i) he is able to meet each of the requirements of paragraph 186(i)–(v); and
    (ii) he was admitted to the United Kindom on the grounds of United Kingdom ancestry in accordance with paragraphs 186 to 188 or has been granted an extension of stay in this capacity.

Extension of stay on the grounds of United Kingdom ancestry

190. An extension of stay on the grounds of United Kingdom ancestry may be granted for a period not exceeding 3 years provided the Secretary of State is satisfied that each of the requirements of paragraph 189 is met.

Refusal of extension of stay on the grounds of United Kingdom ancestry

191. An extension of stay on the grounds of United Kingdom ancestry is to be refused if the Secretary of State is not satisfied that each of the requirements of paragraph 189 is met.

Indefinite leave to remain on the grounds of United Kingdom ancestry

192. Indefinite leave to remain may be granted, on application, to a Commonwealth citizen with a United Kingdom born grandparent provided:
    (i) he meets the requirements of paragraph 186(i)–(v); and
    (ii) he has spent a continuous period of 5 years in the United Kingdom in this capacity; and

(iii) he has sufficient knowledge of the English language and sufficient knowledge about life in the United Kingdom, unless he is under the age of 18 or aged 65 or over at the time he makes his application.

Refusal of indefinite leave to remain on the grounds of United Kingdom ancestry

193. Indefinite leave to remain in the United Kingdom on the grounds of a United Kingdom born grandparent is to be refused if the Secretary of State is not satisfied that each of the requirements of paragraph 192 is met.

Spouses or civil partners of persons who have or have had leave to enter or remain under paragraphs 128–193 (but not paragraphs 135I–135K)

Requirements for leave to enter as the spouse or civil partner of a person with limited leave to enter or remain in the United Kingdom under paragraphs 128–193 (but not paragraphs 135I–135K)

194. The requirements to be met by a person seeking leave to enter the United Kingdom as the spouse or civil partner of a person with limited leave to enter or remain in the United Kingdom under paragraphs 128–193 (but not paragraphs 135I–135K) are that:
 (i) the applicant is married to or a civil partner of a person with limited leave to enter in the United Kingdom under paragraphs 128-193 (but not paragraphs 135I–135K); and
 (ii) each of the parties intends to live with the other as his or her spouse or civil partner during the applicant's stay and the marriage or civil partnership is subsisting; and
 (iii) there will be adequate accommodation for the parties and any dependants without recourse to public funds in accommodation which they own or occupy exclusively; and
 (iv) the parties will be able to maintain themselves and any dependants adequately without recourse to public funds; and
 (v) the applicant does not intend to stay in the United Kingdom beyond any period of leave granted to his spouse; and
 (vi) the applicant holds a valid United Kingdom entry clearance for entry in this capacity.

Leave to enter as the spouse or civil partner of a person with limited leave to enter or remain in the United Kingdom under paragraphs 128–193 (but not paragraphs 135I–135K)

195. A person seeking leave to enter the United Kingdom as the spouse or civil partner of a person with limited leave to enter or remain in the United Kingdom under paragraphs 128–193 (but not paragraphs 135I–135K) may be given leave to enter for a period not in excess of that granted to the person with limited leave to enter or remain under paragraphs 128–193 (but not paragraphs 135I–135K) provided the Immigration Officer is satisfied that each of the requirements of paragraph 194 is met.

Refusal of leave to enter as the spouse or civil partners of a person with limited leave to enter or remain in the United Kingdom under paragraphs 128–193 (but not paragraphs 135I–135K)

196. Leave to enter the United Kingdom as the spouse or civil partner of a person with limited leave to enter or remain in the United Kingdom under paragraphs 128–193

(but not paragraphs 135I-135K) is to be refused if the Immigration Officer is not satisfied that each of the requirements of paragraph 194 is met.

Requirements for extension of stay as the spouse or civil partner of a person who has or has had leave to enter or remain in the United Kingdom under paragraphs 128–193 (but not paragraphs 135I–135K)

196A. The requirements to be met by a person seeking an extension of stay in the United Kingdom as the spouse or civil partner of a person who has or has had leave to enter or remain in the United Kingdom under paragraphs 128–193 (but not paragraphs 135I–135K) are that the applicant:

    (i) is married to or civil partner of a person with limited leave to enter or remain in the United Kingdom under paragraphs 128–193 (but not paragraphs 135I–135K); or

    (ii) is married to or civil partner of a person who has limited leave to enter or remain in the United Kingdom under paragraphs 128–193 (but not paragraphs 135I–135K) and who is being granted indefinite leave to remain at the same time; or

    (iii) is married to or a civil partner of a person who has indefinite leave to remain in the United Kingdom and who had limited leave to enter or remain in the United Kingdom under paragraphs 128–193 (but not paragraphs 135I–135K) immediately before being granted indefinite leave to remain; and

    (iv) meets the requirements of paragraph 194(ii)–(v); and

    (v) was admitted with a valid United Kingdom entry clearance for entry in this capacity.

Extension of stay as the spouse or civil partner of a person who has or has had leave to enter or remain in the United Kingdom under paragraphs 128–193 (but not paragraphs 135I–135K)

196B. An extension of stay in the United Kingdom as:

    (i) the spouse or civil partner of a person who has limited leave to enter or remain under paragraphs 128–193 (but not paragraphs 135I–135K) may be granted for a period not in excess of that granted to the person with limited leave to enter or remain; or

    (ii) the spouse or civil partner of a person who is being admitted at the same time for settlement, or the spouse or civil partner of a person who has indefinite leave to remain, may be granted for a period not exceeding 2 years, in both instances, provided the Secretary of State is satisfied that each of the requirements of paragraph 196A is met.

Refusal of extension of stay as the spouse or civil partner of a person who has or has had leave to enter or remain in the United Kingdom under paragraphs 128–193 (but not paragraphs 135I–135K)

196C. An extension of stay in the United Kingdom as the spouse or civil partner of a person who has or has had leave to enter or remain in the United Kingdom under paragraphs 128–193 (but not paragraphs 135I–135K) is to be refused if the Secretary of State is not satisfied that each of the requirements of paragraph 196A is met.

Requirements for indefinite leave to remain for the spouse or civil partner of a person who has or has had leave to enter or remain in the United Kingdom under paragraphs 128–193 (but not paragraphs 135I–135K)

196D. The requirements to be met by a person seeking indefinite leave to remain in the United Kingdom as the spouse or civil partner of a person who has or has had leave to enter or remain in the United Kingdom under paragraphs 128–193 (but not paragraphs 135I–135K) are that the applicant:

(i) is married to or civil partner of a person who has limited leave to enter or remain in the United Kingdom under paragraphs 128–193 (but not paragraphs 135I–135K) and who is being granted indefinite leave to remain at the same time; or

(ii) is married to or a civil partner of a person who has indefinite leave to remain in the United Kingdom and who had limited leave to enter or remain in the United Kingdom under paragraphs 128–193 (but not paragraphs 135I–135K) immediately before being granted indefinite leave to remain; and

(iii) meets the requirements of paragraph 194(ii)–(v); and

(iv) has sufficient knowledge of the English language and sufficient knowledge about life in the United Kingdom, unless he is under the age of 18 or aged 65 or over at the time he makes his application; and

(v) was admitted with a valid United Kingdom entry clearance for entry in this capacity.

Indefinite leave to remain as the spouse or civil partner of a person who has or has had leave to enter or remain in the United Kingdom under paragraphs 128–193 (but not paragraphs 135I–135K)

196E. Indefinite leave to remain in the United Kingdom for the spouse or civil partner of a person who has or has had leave to enter or remain in the United Kingdom under paragraphs 128–193 (but not paragraphs 135I–135K) may be granted provided the Secretary of State is satisfied that each of the requirements of paragraph 196D is met.

Refusal of indefinite leave to remain as the spouse or civil partner of a person who has or has had leave to enter or remain in the United Kingdom under paragraphs 128–193 (but not paragraphs 135I–135K)

196F. Indefinite leave to remain in the United Kingdom for the spouse or civil partner of a person who has or has had limited leave to enter or remain in the United Kingdom under paragraphs 128–193 (but not paragraphs 135I–135K) is to be refused if the Secretary of State is not satisfied that each of the requirements of paragraph 194D is met.

Children of persons with limited leave to enter or remain in the United Kingdom under paragraphs 128–193 (but not paragraphs 135I–135K)

Requirements for leave to enter or remain as the child of a person with limited leave to enter or remain in the United Kingdom under paragraphs 128–193 (but not paragraphs 135I–135K)

197. The requirements to be met by a person seeking leave to enter or remain in the United Kingdom as a child of a person with limited leave to enter or remain in the United Kingdom under paragraphs 128–193 (but not paragraphs 135I–135K) are that:

(i) he is the child of a parent with limited leave to enter or remain in the United Kingdom under paragraphs 128–193(but not paragraphs 135I–135K); and

(ii) he is under the age of 18 or has current leave to enter or remain in this capacity; and

(iii) he is unmarried and is not a civil partner, has not formed an independent family unit and is not leading an independent life; and

(iv) he can and will be maintained and accommodated adequately without recourse to public funds in accommodation which his parent(s) own or occupy exclusively; and

(v) he will not stay in the United Kingdom beyond any period of leave granted to his parent(s); and

(vi) both parents are being or have been admitted to or allowed to remain in the United Kingdom save where:

    (a) the parent he is accompanying or joining is his sole surviving parent; or

    (b) the parent he is accompanying or joining has had sole responsibility for his upbringing; or

    (c) there are serious and compelling family or other considerations which make exclusion from the United Kingdom undesirable and suitable arrangements have been made for his care; and

(vii) if seeking leave to enter, he holds a valid United Kingdom entry clearance for entry in this capacity or, if seeking leave to remain, was admitted with a valid United Kingdom entry clearance for entry in this capacity.

Leave to enter or remain as the child of a person with limited leave to enter or remain in the United Kingdom under paragraphs 128–193 (but not paragraphs 135I–135K)

198. A person seeking leave to enter or remain in the United Kingdom as the child of a person with limited leave to enter or remain in the United Kingdom under paragraphs 128–193 (but not paragraphs 135I–135K) may be given leave to enter or remain in the United Kingdom for a period of leave not in excess of that granted to the person with limited leave to enter or remain under paragraphs 128–193 (but not paragraphs 135I–135K) provided that, in relation to an application for leave to enter, he is able to produce to the Immigration Officer, on arrival, a valid United Kingdom entry clearance for entry in this capacity or, in the case of an application for limited leave to remain, he was admitted with a valid United Kingdom entry clearance for entry in this capacity and is able to satisfy the Secretary of State that each of the requirements of paragraph 197(i)–(vi) is met. An application for indefinite leave to remain in this category may be granted provided the applicant was admitted with a valid United Kingdom entry clearance for entry in this capacity and is able to satisfy the Secretary of State that each of the requirements of paragraph 197(i)–(vi) is met and provided indefinite leave to remain is, at the same time, being granted to the person with limited leave to enter or remain under paragraphs 128–193 (but not paragraphs 135I–135K).

Refusal of leave to enter or remain as the child of a person with limited leave to enter or remain in the United Kingdom under paragraphs 128–193 (but not paragraphs 135I–135K)

199. Leave to enter or remain in the United Kingdom as the child of a person with limited leave to enter or remain in the United Kingdom under paragraphs 128–193 (but not paragraphs 135I–135K) is to be refused if, in relation to an application for leave to enter, a valid United Kingdom entry clearance for entry in this capacity is not produced to the Immigration Officer on arrival or, in the case of an application for limited leave to remain, if the applicant was not admitted with a valid United Kingdom entry clearance for entry in this capacity or is unable to satisfy the Secretary of State that each of the requirements of paragraph 197(i)–(vi) is met. An application for indefinite leave to remain in this category is to be refused if the applicant was not admitted with a valid United Kingdom entry clearance for entry in this capacity or is unable to satisfy the Secretary of State that each of the requirements of paragraph 197(i)–(vi) is met or if indefinite leave to remain is not, at the same time, being granted to the person with limited leave to enter or remain under paragraphs 128–193 (but not paragraphs 135I–135K).

Multiple Entry work permit employment

Requirements for leave to enter for Multiple Entry work permit employment.

199A. The requirements to be met by a person coming to the United Kingdom to seek or take Multiple Entry work permit employment are that he:
  (i) holds a valid work permit;
  (ii) is not of an age which puts him outside the limits for employment;
  (iii) is capable of undertaking the employment specified in the work permit;
  (iv) does not intend to take employment except as specified in his work permit;
  (v) is able to maintain and accommodate himself adequately without recourse to public funds; and
  (vi) intends to leave the United Kingdom at the end of the employment covered by the Multiple Entry work permit and holds a valid United Kingdom Entry clearance for entry into this capacity excepts where he holds a work permit valid for 6 months or less or he is a British National (Overseas), a British overseas territories citizen, a British Overseas citizen, a British protected person or a person who under the British Nationality Act 1981 ia a British subject.

Leave to enter for Multiple Entry work permit employment

199B. A person seeking leave to enter the United Kingdom for the purpose of Multiple Entry work permit employment may be admitted for a period not exceeding 2 years provided that the Immigration Officer is satisfied that each of the requirements of paragraph 199A are met.

Refusal of leave to enter for Multiple Entry work permit employment

199C. Leave to enter for the purpose of Multiple Entry work permit employment is to be refused if the Immigration Officer is not satisfied that each of the requirements of paragraph 199A is met.

Part 6: Persons seeking to enter or remain in the United Kingdom as a businessman, self-employed person, investor, writer, composer or artist

Persons intending to establish themselves in business

Requirements for leave to enter the United Kingdom as a person intending to establish himself in business

200. For the purpose of paragraphs 201-210 a business means an enterprise as:
  - a sole trader; or
  - a partnership; or
  - a company registered in the United Kingdom.

201. The requirements to be met by a person seeking leave to enter the United Kingdom to establish himself in business are:
  (i) that he satisfies the requirements of either paragraph 202 or paragraph 203; and
  (ii) that he has not less than £200,000 of his own money under his control and disposable in the United Kingdom which is held in his own name and not by a trust or other investment vehicle and which he will be investing in the business in the United Kingdom; and
  (iii) that until his business provides him with an income he will have sufficient additional funds to maintain and accommodate himself and any dependants

without recourse to employment (other than his work for the business) or to public funds; and

(iv) that he will be actively involved full time in trading or providing services on his own account or in partnership, or in the promotion and management of the company as a director; and

(v) that his level of financial investment will be proportional to his interest in the business; and

(vi) that he will have either a controlling or equal interest in the business and that any partnership or directorship does not amount to disguised employment; and

(vii) that he will be able to bear his share of liabilities; and

(viii) that there is a genuine need for his investment and services in the United Kingdom; and

(ix) that his share of the profits of the business will be sufficient to maintain and accommodate himself and any dependants without recourse to employment (other than his work for the business) or to public funds; and

(x) that he does not intend to supplement his business activities by taking or seeking employment in the United Kingdom other than his work for the business; and

(xi) that he holds a valid United Kingdom entry clearance for entry in this capacity.

202. Where a person intends to take over or join as a partner or director an existing business in the United Kingdom he will need, in addition to meeting the requirements at paragraph 201, to produce:

(i) a written statement of the terms on which he is to take over or join the business; and

(ii) audited accounts for the business for previous years; and

(iii) evidence that his services and investment will result in a net increase in the employment provided by the business to persons settled here to the extent of creating at least 2 new full time jobs.

203. Where a person intends to establish a new business in the United Kingdom he will need, in addition to meeting the requirements at paragraph 201 above, to produce evidence:

(i) that he will be bringing into the country sufficient funds of his own to establish a business; and

(ii) that the business will create full time paid employment for at least 2 persons already settled in the United Kingdom.

Leave to enter the United Kingdom as a person seeking to establish himself in business

204. A person seeking leave to enter the United Kingdom to establish himself in business may be admitted for a period not exceeding 2 years with a condition restricting his freedom to take employment provided he is able to produce to the Immigration Officer, on arrival, a valid United Kingdom entry clearance for entry in this capacity.

Refusal of leave to enter the United Kingdom as a person seeking to establish himself in business

205. Leave to enter the United Kingdom as a person seeking to establish himself in business is to be refused if a valid United Kingdom entry clearance for entry in this capacity is not produced to the Immigration Officer on arrival.

Requirements for an extension of stay in order to remain in business

206. The requirements for an extension of stay in order to remain in business in the United Kingdom are that the applicant can show:

(i) that he entered the United Kingdom with a valid United Kingdom entry clearance as a businessman; and

(ii) audited accounts which show the precise financial position of the business and which confirm that he has invested not less than £200,000 of his own money directly into the business in the United Kingdom; and

(iii) that he is actively involved on a full time basis in trading or providing services on his own account or in partnership or in the promotion and management of the company as a director; and

(iv) that his level of financial investment is proportional to his interest in the business; and

(v) that he has either a controlling or equal interest in the business and that any partnership or directorship does not amount to disguised employment; and

(vi) that he is able to bear his share of any liability the business may incur; and

(vii) that there is a genuine need for his investment and services in the United Kingdom; and

(viii) (a) that where he has established a new business, new full time paid employment has been created in the business for at least 2 persons settled in the United Kingdom; or

(b) that where he has taken over or joined an existing business, his services and investment have resulted in a net increase in the employment provided by the business to persons settled here to the extent of creating at least 2 new full time jobs; and

(ix) that his share of the profits of the business is sufficient to maintain and accommodate him and any dependants without recourse to employment (other than his work for the business) or to public funds; and

(x) that he does not and will not have to supplement his business activities by taking or seeking employment in the United Kingdom other than his work for the business.

206A. The requirements for an extension of stay as a person intending to establish himself in business in the United Kingdom for a person who has leave to enter or remain for work permit employment are that the applicant:

(i) entered the United Kingdom or was given leave to remain as a work permit holder in accordance with paragraphs 128 to 133 of these Rules; and

(ii) meets each of the requirements of paragraph 201(i)-(x).

206B. The requirements for an extension of stay as a person intending to establish himself in business in the United Kingdom for a highly skilled migrant are that the applicant:

(i) entered the United Kingdom or was given leave to remain as a highly skilled migrant in accordance with paragraphs 135A to 135F of these Rules; and

(ii) meets each of the requirements of paragraph 201(i)-(x).

206C. The requirements for an extension of stay as a person intending to establish himself in business in the United Kingdom for a participant in the Science and Engineering Graduates Scheme or International Graduates Scheme are that the applicant:

(i) entered the United Kingdom or was given leave to remain as a participant in the Science and Engineering Graduates Scheme or International Graduates Scheme in accordance with paragraphs 135O to 135T of these Rules; and

(ii) meets each of the requirements of paragraph 201(i)-(x).

206D. The requirements for an extension of stay as a person intending to establish himself in business in the United Kingdom for an innovator are that the applicant:

(i) entered the United Kingdom or was given leave to remain as an innovator in accordance with paragraphs 210A to 210F of these Rules; and

(ii) meets each of the requirements of paragraph 201(i)-(x).

206E. The requirements for an extension of stay as a person intending to establish himself in business in the United Kingdom for a student are that the applicant:

(i) entered the United Kingdom or was given leave to remain as a student in accordance with paragraphs 57 to 62 of these Rules; and

(ii) has obtained a degree qualification on a recognised degree course at either a United Kingdom publicly funded further or higher education institution or a bona fide United Kingdom private education institution which maintains satisfactory records of enrolment and attendance; and

(iii) has the written consent of his official sponsor to such self employment if he is a member of a government or international scholarship agency sponsorship and that sponsorship is either ongoing or has recently come to an end at the time of the requested extension; and

(iv) meets each of the requirements of paragraph 201(i)-(x).

206F. The requirements for an extension of stay as a person intending to establish himself in business in the United Kingdom for a working holidaymaker are that the applicant:

(i) entered the United Kingdom or was given leave to remain as a working holidaymaker in accordance with paragraphs 95 to 100 of these Rules; and

(ii) has spent more than 12 months in total in the UK in this capacity; and

(iii) meets each of the requirements of paragraph 201(i)-(x).

206G. The requirements for an extension of stay as a person intending to establish himself in business in the United Kingdom in the case of a person who has leave to enter or remain as a Fresh Talent: Working in Scotland scheme participant are that the applicant:

(i) entered the United Kingdom or was given leave to remain as a Fresh Talent: Working in Scotland scheme participant in accordance with paragraphs 143A to 143F of these Rules; and

(ii) has the written consent of his official sponsor to such employment if the studies which led to him being granted leave under the Fresh Talent: Working in Scotland scheme in accordance with paragraphs 143A to 143F of these Rules, or any studies he has subsequently undertaken, were sponsored by a government or international scholarship agency; and

(iii) meets each of the requirements of paragraph 201(i)-(x).

206H. The requirements for an extension of stay as a person intending to establish himself in business in the United Kingdom for a Postgraduate Doctor or Dentist are that the applicant:

(i) entered the United Kingdom or was given leave to remain as a Postgraduate Doctor or Dentist in accordance with paragraphs 70 to 75 of these Rules; and

(ii) has the written consent of his official sponsor to such self employment if he is a member of a government or international scholarship agency sponsorship and that sponsorship is either ongoing or has recently come to an end at the time of the requested extension; and

(iii) meets each of the requirements of paragraph 201(i)-(x).

Extension of stay in order to remain in business

207. An extension of stay in order to remain in business with a condition restricting his freedom to take employment may be granted for a period not exceeding 3 years at a time provided the Secretary of State is satisfied that each of the requirements of paragraph 206, 206A, 206B, 206C, 206D, 206E, 206F, 206G or 206H is met.

Refusal of extension of stay in order to remain in business

208. An extension of stay in order to remain in business is to be refused if the Secretary of State is not satisfied that each of the requirements of paragraph 206, 206A, 206B, 206C, 206D,206E, 206F, 206G or 206H is met.

Indefinite leave to remain for a person established in business

209. Indefinite leave to remain may be granted, on application, to a person established in business provided he:
    (i) has spent a continuous period of 5 years in the United Kingdom in this capacity and is still engaged in the business in question; and
    (ii) has met the requirements of paragraph 206 throughout the 5-year period; and
    (iii) submits audited accounts for the first 5 years of trading and management accounts for the 5th year; and
    (iv) has sufficient knowledge of the English language and sufficient knowledge about life in the United Kingdom, unless he is under the age of 18 or aged 65 or over at the time he makes his application.

Refusal of indefinite leave to remain for a person established in business

210. Indefinite leave to remain in the United Kingdom for a person established in business is to be refused if the Secretary of State is not satisfied that each of the requirements of paragraph 209 is met.

Innovators

Requirements for leave to enter the United Kingdom as an innovator

210A. The requirements to be met by a person seeking leave to enter as an innovator are that the applicant:
    (i) is approved by the Home Office as a person who meets the criteria specified by the Secretary of State for entry under the innovator scheme at the time that approval is sought under that scheme;
    (ii) intends to set up a business that will create full-time paid employment for at least 2 persons already settled in the UK; and
    (iii) intends to maintain a minimum five per cent shareholding of the equity capital in that business, once it has been set up, throughout the period of his stay as an innovator; and
    (iv) will be able to maintain and accommodate himself and any dependants adequately without recourse to public funds or to other employment; and
    (v) holds a valid United Kingdom entry clearance for entry in this capacity.

Leave to enter as an innovator

210B. A person seeking leave to enter the United Kingdom as an innovator may be admitted for a period not exceeding 2 years, provided the Immigration Officer is satisfied that each of the requirements of paragraph 210A is met.

Refusal of leave to enter as an innovator

210C. Leave to enter as an innovator is to be refused if the Immigration Officer is not satisfied that each of the requirements of paragraph 210A are met.

Requirements for an extension of stay as an innovator

210D. The requirements for an extension of stay in the United Kingdom as an innovator, in the case of a person who was granted leave to enter under paragraph 210A, are that the applicant:
    (i) has established a viable trading business, by reference to the audited accounts and trading records of that business; and
    (ii) continues to meet the requirements of paragraph 210A(i) and (iv); and has set up a business that will create full-time paid employment for at least 2 persons already settled in the UK; and
    (iii) has maintained a minimum five per cent shareholding of the equity capital in that business, once it has been set up, throughout the period of his stay.

210DA. The requirements for an extension of stay in the United Kingdom as an innovator, in the case of a person who has leave for the purpose of work permit employment are that the applicant:

(i) entered the United Kingdom or was given leave to remain as a work permit holder in accordance with paragraphs 128 to 132 of these Rules; and

(ii) meets the requirements of paragraph 210A(i)–(iv).

210DB. The requirements for an extension of stay in the United Kingdom as an innovator in the case of a person who has leave as a student are that the applicant:

(i) entered the United Kingdom or was given leave to remain as a student in accordance with paragraphs 57 to 62 of these Rules; and

(ii) has obtained a degree qualification on a recognised degree course at either a United Kingdom publicly funded further or higher education institution or a bona fide United Kingdom private education institution which maintains satisfactory records of enrolment and attendance; and

(iii) has the written consent of his official sponsor to remain under the Innovator category if he is a member of a government or international scholarship agency sponsorship and that sponsorship is either ongoing or has recently come to an end at the time of the requested extension; and

(iv) meets the requirements of paragraph 210(i)–(iv).

210DC. The requirements to be met for an extension of stay as an innovator, for a person who has leave as a working holidaymaker are that the applicant:

(i) entered the United Kingdom as a working holidaymaker in accordance with paragraphs 95 to 96 of these Rules; and

(ii) meets the requirements of paragraph 210A(i)–(iv).

210DD. The requirements to be met for an extension of stay as an innovator, for a postgraduate doctor, postgraduate dentist or trainee general practitioner are that the applicant:

(i) entered the United Kingdom or was given leave to remain as a postgraduate doctor, postgraduate dentist or trainee general practitioner in accordance with paragraphs 70 to 75 of these Rules; and

(ii) has the written consent of his official sponsor to remain under the innovator category if he is a member of a government or international scholarship agency sponsorship and that sponsorship is either ongoing or has recently come to an end at the time of the requested extension; and

(iii) meets the requirements of paragraph 210(i)–(iv).

210DE. The requirements to be met for an extension of stay as an innovator, for a participant in the Science and Engineering Graduate Scheme or International Graduates Scheme are that the applicant:

(i) entered the United Kingdom or was given leave to remain as a participant in the Science and Engineering Graduate Scheme or International Graduates Scheme in accordance with paragraphs 135O to 135T of these Rules; and

(ii) meets the requirements of paragraph 210A(i)–(iv).

210DF. The requirements to be met for an extension of stay as an innovator, for a highly skilled migrant are that the applicant:

(i) entered the United Kingdom or was given leave to remain as a highly skilled migrant in accordance with paragraphs 135A to 135E of these Rules; and

(ii) meets the requirements of paragraph 210A(i)–(iv)

210DG. The requirements to be met for an extension of stay as an innovator, for a person in the United Kingdom to establish themselves or remain in business are that the applicant:

(i) entered the United Kingdom or was granted leave to remain as a person intending to establish themselves or remain in business in accordance with paragraphs 201–208 of these Rules; and

(ii) meets the requirements of paragraph 210(i)–(iv).'.

210DH. The requirements to be met for an extension of stay as an innovator, in the case of a person who has leave to enter or remain as a Fresh Talent: Working in Scotland scheme participant are that the applicant:
  (i) entered the United Kingdom or was given leave to remain as a Fresh Talent: Working in Scotland scheme participant in accordance with paragraphs 143A to 143F of these Rules; and
  (ii) has the written consent of his official sponsor to such employment if the studies which led to him being granted leave under the Fresh Talent: Working in Scotland scheme in accordance with paragraphs 143A to 143F of these Rules, or any studies he has subsequently undertaken, were sponsored by a government or international scholarship agency; and
  (iii) meets each of the requirements of paragraph 210(i)–(iv).

Extension of stay as an innovator

210E. An extension of stay as an innovator may be granted for a period not exceeding 3 years at a time provided the Secretary of State is satisfied that each of the requirements of paragraph 210D, 210DA, 210DB, 210DC, 210DD, 210DE, 210DF, 210DG or 210DH is met.

Refusal of extension of stay as an innovator

210F. An extension of stay as an innovator is to be refused if the Secretary of State is not satisfied that each of the requirements of paragraph 210D, 210DA, 210DB, 210DC, 210DD, 210DE, 210DF, 210DG or 210DH is met.

Indefinite leave to remain for an innovator

210G. Indefinite leave to remain may be granted, on application, to a person currently with leave as an innovator provided that he:
  (i) has spent a continuous period of at least 5 years in the United Kingdom in this capacity; and
  (ii) has met the requirements of paragraph 210D throughout the 5-year period; and
  (iii) he has sufficient knowledge of the English language and sufficient knowledge about life in the United Kingdom, unless he is under the age of 18 or aged 65 or over at the time he makes his application.

Refusal of indefinite leave to remain as an innovator

210H. Indefinite leave to remain in the United Kingdom as a person currently with leave as a innovator is to be refused if the Secretary of State is not satisfied that each of the requirements of paragraph 210G is met.

Persons intending to establish themselves in business under provisions of EC Association Agreements

Indefinite leave to remain for a person established in business under the provisions of an EC Association Agreement

222. Indefinite leave to remain may be granted, on application, to a person established in business provided he–
  (i) is a national of Bulgaria or Romania; and
  (ii) entered the United Kingdom with a valid United Kingdom entry clearance as a person intending to establish himself in business under the provisions of an EC Association Agreement; and
  (iii) was granted an extension of stay before 1st January 2007 in order to remain in business under the provisions of the Agreement; and

(iv) established himself in business in the United Kingdom, spent a continuous period of 5 years in the United Kingdom in this capacity and is still so engaged; and

(v) met the requirements of paragraph 222A throughout the period of 5 years; and

(vi) submits audited accounts for the first 4 years of trading and management accounts for the 5th year; and

(vii) he has sufficient knowledge of the English language and sufficient knowledge about life in the United Kingdom, unless he is under the age of 18 or aged 65 or over at the time he makes his application.

222A. The requirements mentioned in paragraph 222(v) are that throughout the period of 5 years–

(i) the applicant's share of the profits of the business has been sufficient to maintain and accommodate himself and any dependants without recourse to employment (other than his work for the business) or to public funds; and

(ii) he has not supplemented his business activities by taking or seeking employment in the United Kingdom (other than his work for the business); and

(iii) he has satisfied the requirements in paragraph 222B or 222C.

222B. Where the applicant has established himself in a company in the United Kingdom which he effectively controls, the requirements for the purpose of paragraph 222A(iii) are that–

(i) the applicant has been actively involved in the promotion and management of the company; and

(ii) he has had a controlling interest in the company; and

(iii) the company was registered in the United Kingdom and has been trading or providing services in the United Kingdom; and

(iv) the company owned the assets of the business.

222C. Where the applicant has established himself as a sole trader or in a partnership in the United Kingdom, the requirements for the purpose of paragraph 222A(iii) are that–

(i) the applicant has been actively involved in trading or providing services on his own account or in a partnership in the United Kingdom; and

(ii) the applicant owned, or together with his partners owned, the assets of the business; and

(iii) in the case of a partnership, the applicant's part in the business did not amount to disguised employment.

Refusal of indefinite leave to remain for a person established in business under the provisions of an EC Association Agreement

223. Indefinite leave to remain in the United Kingdom for a person established in business is to be refused if the Secretary of State is not satisfied that each of the requirements of paragraph 222 is met.

223A. Notwithstanding paragraph 5, paragraphs 222 to 223 shall apply to a person who is entitled to remain in the United Kingdom by virtue of the provisions of the 2006 EEA Regulations.

Requirements for leave to enter the United Kingdom as an investor

224. The requirements to be met by a person seeking leave to enter the United Kingdom as an investor are that he:

(i) (a) has money of his own under his control in the United Kingdom amounting to no less than £1 million; or

(b) (i) owns personal assets which, taking into account any liabilities to which he is subject, have a value exceeding £2 million; and

(ii) has money under his control in the United Kingdom amounting to no less than £1 million, which may include money loaned to him provided that it was loaned by a financial institution regulated by the Financial Services Authority; and

(ii) intends to invest not less than £750,000 of his capital in the United Kingdom by way of United Kingdom Government bonds, share capital or loan capital in active and trading United Kingdom registered companies (other than those principally engaged in property investment and excluding investment by the applicant by way of deposits with a bank, building society or other enterprise whose normal course of business includes the acceptance of deposits); and

(iii) intends to make the United Kingdom his main home; and

(iv) is able to maintain and accommodate himself and any dependants without taking employment (other than self employment or business) or recourse to public funds; and

(v) holds a valid United Kingdom entry clearance for entry in this capacity.

Leave to enter as an investor

225. A person seeking leave to enter the United Kingdom as an investor may be admitted for a period not exceeding 2 years with a restriction on his right to take employment, provided he is able to produce to the Immigration Officer, on arrival, a valid United Kingdom entry clearance for entry in this capacity.

Refusal of leave to enter as an investor

226. Leave to enter as an investor is to be refused if a valid United Kingdom entry clearance for entry in this capacity is not produced to the Immigration Officer on arrival.

Requirements for an extension of stay as an investor

227. The requirements for an extension of stay as an investor are that the applicant:
   (i) entered the United Kingdom with a valid United Kingdom entry clearance as an investor; and
   (ii) (a) has money of his own under his control in the United Kingdom amounting to no less than £1 million; or
       (b) (i) owns personal assets which, taking into account any liabilities to which he is subject, have a value exceeding £2 million; and
           (ii) has money under his control in the United Kingdom amounting to no less than £1 million, which may include money loaned to him provided that it was loaned by a financial institution regulated by the Financial Services Authority; and
   (iii) has invested not less than £750,000 of his capital in the United Kingdom on the terms set out in paragraph 224(ii) above and intends to maintain that investment on the terms set out in paragraph 224(ii); and
   (iv) has made the United Kingdom his main home; and
   (v) is able to maintain and accommodate himself and any dependants without taking employment (other than his self employment or business) or recourse to public funds.

227A. The requirements to be met for an extension of stay as an investor, for a person who has leave to enter or remain in the United Kingdom as a work permit holder are that the applicant:
   (i) entered the United Kingdom or was granted leave to remain as a work permit holder in accordance with paragraphs 128 to 133 of these Rules; and
   (ii) meets the requirements of paragraph 224(i)–(iv).

227B. The requirements to be met for an extension of stay as an investor, for a person in the United Kingdom as a highly skilled migrant are that the applicant:
   (i) entered the United Kingdom or was granted leave to remain as a highly skilled migrant in accordance with paragraphs 135A to 135F of these Rules; and
   (ii) meets the requirements of paragraph 224(i)–(iv).

227C. The requirements to be met for an extension of stay as an investor, for a person in the United Kingdom to establish themselves or remain in business are that the applicant:
   (i) entered the United Kingdom or was granted leave to remain as a person intending to establish themselves or remain in business in accordance with paragraphs 201 to 208 of these Rules; and
   (ii) meets the requirements of paragraph 224(i)–(iv).

227D. The requirements to be met for an extension of stay as an investor, for a person in the United Kingdom as an innovator are that the applicant:
   (i) entered the United Kingdom or was granted leave to remain as an innovator in accordance with paragraphs 210A to 210F of these Rules; and
   (ii) meets the requirements of paragraph 224(i)–(iv).

Extension of stay as an investor

228. An extension of stay as an investor, with a restriction on the taking of employment, may be granted for a period not exceeding 3 years at a time, provided the Secretary of State is satisfied that each of the requirements of paragraph 227, 227A, 227B, 227C or 227D is met.

Refusal of extension of stay as an investor

229. An extension of stay as an investor is to be refused if the Secretary of State is not satisfied that each of the requirements of paragraph 227, 227A, 227B, 227C or 227D is met.

Indefinite leave to remain for an investor

230. Indefinite leave to remain may be granted, on application, to a person admitted as an investor provided he:
   (i) has spent a continuous period of 5 years in the United Kingdom in this capacity; and
   (ii) has met the requirements of paragraph 227 throughout the 5-year period including the requirement as to the investment of £750,000 and continues to do so; and
   (iii) he has sufficient knowledge of the English language and sufficient knowledge about life in the United Kingdom, unless he is under the age of 18 or aged 65 or over at the time he makes his application.

Refusal of indefinite leave to remain for an investor

231. Indefinite leave to remain in the United Kingdom for an investor is to be refused if the Secretary of State is not satisfied that each of the requirements of paragraph 230 is met.

Writers, composers and artists

Requirements for leave to enter the United Kingdom as a writer, composer or artist

232. The requirements to be met by a person seeking leave to enter the United Kingdom as a writer, composer or artist are that he:
   (i) has established himself outside the United Kingdom as a writer, composer or artist primarily engaged in producing original work which has been

published (other than exclusively in newspapers or magazines), performed or exhibited for its literary, musical or artistic merit; and

(ii) does not intend to work except as related to his self employment as a writer, composer or artist; and

(iii) has for the preceding year been able to maintain and accommodate himself and any dependants from his own resources without working except as a writer, composer or artist; and

(iv) will be able to maintain and accommodate himself and any dependants from his own resources without working except as a writer, composer or artist and without recourse to public funds; and

(v) holds a valid United Kingdom entry clearance for entry in this capacity.

Leave to enter as a writer, composer or artist

233. A person seeking leave to enter the United Kingdom as a writer, composer or artist may be admitted for a period not exceeding 2 years, subject to a condition restricting his freedom to take employment, provided he is able to produce to the Immigration Officer, on arrival, a valid United Kingdom entry clearance for entry in this capacity.

Refusal of leave to enter as a writer, composer or artist

234. Leave to enter as a writer, composer or artist is to be refused if a valid United Kingdom entry clearance for entry in this capacity is not produced to the Immigration Officer on arrival.

Requirements for an extension of stay as a writer, composer or artist

235. The requirements for an extension of stay as a writer, composer or artist are that the applicant:

(i) entered the United Kingdom with a valid United Kingdom entry clearance as a writer, composer or artist; and

(ii) meets the requirements of paragraph 232(ii)–(iv).

Extension of stay as a writer, composer or artist

236. An extension of stay as a writer, composer or artist may be granted for a period not exceeding 3 years with a restriction on his freedom to take employment, provided the Secretary of State is satisfied that each of the requirements of paragraph 235 is met.

Refusal of extension of stay as a writer, composer or artist

237. An extension of stay as a writer, composer or artist is to be refused if the Secretary of State is not satisfied that each of the requirements of paragraph 235 is met.

Indefinite leave to remain for a writer, composer or artist

238. Indefinite leave to remain may be granted, on application, to a person admitted as a writer, composer or artist provided he:

(i) has spent a continuous period of 5 years in the United Kingdom in this capacity; and

(ii) has met the requirement of paragraph 235 throughout the 5-year period; and

(iii) he has sufficient knowledge of the English language and sufficient knowledge about life in the United Kingdom, unless he is under the age of 18 or aged 65 or over at the time he makes his application.

Refusal of indefinite leave to remain for a writer, composer or artist

239. Indefinite leave to remain for a writer, composer or artist is to be refused if the Secretary of State is not satisfied that each of the requirements of paragraph 238 is met.

Spouses or civil partners of persons with limited leave to enter or remain under paragraphs 200–239

Requirements for leave to enter as the spouse or civil partner of a person with limited leave to enter or remain under paragraphs 200–239

240. The requirements to be met by a person seeking leave to enter the United Kingdom as the spouse or civil partner of a person with limited leave to enter or remain in the United Kingdom under paragraphs 200–239 are that:
    (i) the applicant is married to or the civil partner of a person with limited leave to enter or remain in the United Kingdom under paragraphs 200–239; and
    (ii) each of the parties intends to live with the other as his or her spouse or civil partner during the applicant's stay and the marriage or civil partnership is subsisting; and
    (iii) there will be adequate accommodation for the parties and any dependants without recourse to public funds in accommodation which they own or occupy exclusively; and
    (iv) the parties will be able to maintain themselves and any dependants adequately without recourse to public funds; and
    (v) the applicant does not intend to stay in the United Kingdom beyond any period of leave granted to his spouse or civil partner; and
    (vi) the applicant holds a valid United Kingdom entry clearance for entry in this capacity.

Leave to enter as the spouse or civil partner of a person with limited leave to enter or remain in the United Kingdom under paragraphs 200–239

241. A person seeking limited leave to enter the United Kingdom as the spouse or civil partner of a person with limited leave to enter or remain in the United Kingdom under paragraphs 200–239 may be given leave to enter for a period not in excess of that granted to the person with limited leave to enter or remain under paragraphs 200–239 provided the Immigration Officer is satisfied that each of the requirements of paragraph 240 is met.

Refusal of leave to enter as the spouse or civil partner of a person with limited leave to enter or remain in the United Kingdom under paragraphs 200–239

242. Leave to enter the United Kingdom as the spouse or civil partner of a person with limited leave to enter or remain in the United Kingdom under paragraphs 200–239 is to be refused if the Immigration Officer is not satisfied that each of the requirements of paragraph 240 is met.

Requirements for extension of stay as the spouse or civil partner of a person who has or has had leave to enter or remain in the United Kingdom under paragraphs 200–239

242A. The requirements to be met by a person seeking an extension of stay in the United Kingdom as the spouse or civil partner of a person who has or has had leave to enter or remain under paragraphs 200–239 are that the applicant:
    (i) is married to or the civil partner of a person with limited leave to enter or remain in the United Kingdom under paragraphs 200–239; or
    (ii) is married to or civil partner of a person who has limited leave to enter or remain in the United Kingdom under paragraphs 200–239 and who is being granted indefinite leave to remain at the same time; or
    (iii) is married to or civil partner of a person who has indefinite leave to remain in the United Kingdom and who had limited leave to enter or remain in the

United Kingdom under paragraphs 200–239 immediately before being granted indefinite leave to remain; and

(iv) meets the requirements of paragraph 240(ii)–(v); and

(v) was admitted with a valid United Kingdom entry clearance for entry in this capacity.

Extension of stay as the spouse or civil partner of a person who has or has had leave to enter or remain in the United Kingdom under paragraphs 200–239

242B. An extension of stay in the United Kingdom as:

(i) the spouse or civil partner of a person who has limited leave to enter or remain under paragraphs 200–239 may be granted for a period not in excess of that granted to the person with limited to enter or remain; or

(ii) the spouse or civil partner of a person who is being admitted at the same time for settlement or the spouse or civil partner of a person who has indefinite leave to remain may be granted for a period not exceeding 2 years, in both instances, provided the Secretary of State is satisfied that each of the requirements of paragraph 242A is met.

Refusal of extension of stay as the spouse or civil partner of a person who has or has had leave to enter or remain in the United Kingdom under paragraphs 200–239

242C. An extension of stay in the United Kingdom as the spouse or civil partner of a person who has or has had leave to enter or remain under paragraphs 200–239 is to be refused if the Secretary of State is not satisfied that each of the requirements of paragraph 242A is met.

Requirements for indefinite leave to remain as the spouse or civil partner of a person who has or has had leave to enter or remain in the United Kingdom under paragraphs 200–239

242D. The requirements to be met by a person seeking indefinite leave to remain in the United Kingdom as the spouse or civil partner of a person who has or has had leave to enter or remain in the United Kingdom under paragraphs 200–239 are that the applicant:

(i) is married to or civil partner of a person who has limited leave to enter or remain in the United Kingdom under paragraphs 200–239 and who is being granted indefinite leave to remain at the same time; or

(ii) is married to or civil partner of a person who has indefinite leave to remain in the United Kingdom and who had limited leave to enter or remain under paragraphs 200–239 immediately before being granted indefinite leave to remain; and

(iii) meets the requirements of paragraph 240(ii) to (v);

(iv) has sufficient knowledge of the English language and sufficient knowledge about life in the United Kingdom, unless the applicant is under the age of 18 or aged 65 or over at the time he makes his application; and

(v) was admitted with a valid United Kingdom entry clearance for entry in this capacity.

Indefinite leave to remain as the spouse or civil partner of a person who has or has had leave to enter or remain in the United Kingdom under paragraphs 200–239

242E. Indefinite leave to remain in the United Kingdom as the spouse or civil partner of a person who has or has had limited leave to enter or remain in the United Kingdom under paragraphs 200–239 may be granted provided the Secretary of State is satisfied that each of the requirements of paragraph 242D is met.

Refusal of indefinite leave to remain as the spouse or civil partner of a person who has or has had leave to enter or remain in the United Kingdom under paragraphs 200–239

242F. Indefinite leave to remain in the United Kingdom as the spouse or civil partner of a person who has or has had limited leave to enter or remain in the United Kingdom under paragraphs 200–239 is to be refused if the Secretary of State is not satisfied that each of the requirements of paragraph 242D is met.

Children of persons with limited leave to enter or remain under paragraphs 200–239

Requirements for leave to enter or remain as the child of a person with limited leave to enter or remain in the United Kingdom under paragraphs 200–239

243. The requirements to be met by a person seeking leave to enter or remain in the United Kingdom as a child of a person with limited leave to enter or remain in the United Kingdom under paragraphs 200–239 are that:
    (i) he is the child of a parent who has leave to enter or remain in the United Kingdom under paragraphs 200–239; and
    (ii) he is under the age of 18 or has current leave to enter or remain in this capacity; and
    (iii) he is unmarried and is not a civil partner, has not formed an independent family unit and is not leading an independent life; and
    (iv) he can and will be maintained and accommodated adequately without recourse to public funds in accommodation which his parent(s) own or occupy exclusively; and
    (v) he will not stay in the United Kingdom beyond any period of leave granted to his parent(s); and
    (vi) both parents are being or have been admitted to or allowed to remain in the United Kingdom save where:
        (a) the parent he is accompanying or joining is his sole surviving parent; or
        (b) the parent he is accompanying or joining has had sole responsibility for his upbringing; or
        (c) there are serious and compelling family or other considerations which make exclusion from the United Kingdom undesirable and suitable arrangements have been made for his care; and
    (vii) if seeking leave to enter, he holds a valid United Kingdom entry clearance for entry in this capacity or, if seeking leave to remain, was admitted with a valid United Kingdom entry clearance for entry in this capacity.

Leave to enter or remain as the child of a person with limited leave to enter or remain in the United Kingdom under paragraphs 200–239

244. A person seeking leave to enter or remain in the United Kingdom as the child of a person with limited leave to enter or remain in the United Kingdom under paragraphs 200–239 may be admitted to or allowed to remain in the United Kingdom for the same period of leave as that granted to the person given limited leave to enter or remain under paragraphs 200–239 provided that, in relation to an application for leave to enter, he is able to produce to the Immigration Officer, on arrival, a valid United Kingdom entry clearance for entry in this capacity or, in the case of an application for limited leave to remain, he was admitted with a valid United Kingdom entry clearance for entry in this capacity and is able to satisfy the Secretary of State that each of the requirements of paragraph 243(i)–(vi) is met. An application for indefinite leave to remain in this category may be granted provided the applicant was admitted with a valid United Kingdom entry clearance for entry

in this capacity and is able to satisfy the Secretary of State that each of the requirements of paragraph 243(i)–(vi) is met and provided indefinite leave to remain is, at the same time, being granted to the person with limited leave to remain under paragraphs 200–239.

Refusal of leave to enter or remain as the child of a person with limited leave to enter or remain in the United Kingdom under paragraphs 200–239

245. Leave to enter or remain in the United Kingdom as the child of a person with limited leave to enter or remain in the United Kingdom under paragraphs 200–239 is to be refused if, in relation to an application for leave to enter, a valid United Kingdom entry clearance for entry in this capacity is not produced to the Immigration Officer on arrival or, in the case of an application for limited leave to remain, if the applicant was not admitted with a valid United Kingdom entry clearance for entry in this capacity and is unable to satisfy the Secretary of State that each of the requirements of paragraph 243(i)–(vi) is met. An application for indefinite leave to remain in this capacity is to be refused if the applicant was not admitted with a valid United Kingdom entry clearance for entry in this capacity or is unable to satisfy the Secretary of State that each of the requirements of paragraph 243(i)–(vi) is met or if indefinite leave to remain is not, at the same time, being granted to the person with limited leave to remain under paragraphs 200–239

Part 7: Other categories

Persons exercising rights of access to a child resident in the United Kingdom

Requirements for leave to enter the United Kingdom as a person exercising rights of access to a child resident in the United Kingdom

246. The requirements to be met by a person seeking leave to enter the United Kingdom to exercise access rights to a child resident in the United Kingdom are that:
    (i) the applicant is the parent of a child who is resident in the United Kingdom; and
    (ii) the parent or carer with whom the child permanently resides is resident in the United Kingdom; and
    (iii) the applicant produces evidence that he has access rights to the child in the form of:
        (a) a Residence Order or a Contact Order granted by a Court in the United Kingdom; or
        (b) a certificate issued by a district judge confirming the applicant's intention to maintain contact with the child; and
    (iv) the applicant intends to take an active role in the child's upbringing; and
    (v) the child is under the age of 18; and
    (vi) there will be adequate accommodation for the applicant and any dependants without recourse to public funds in accommodation which the applicant owns or occupies exclusively; and
    (vii) the applicant will be able to maintain himself and any dependants adequately without recourse to public funds; and
    (viii) the applicant holds a valid United Kingdom entry clearance for entry in this capacity.

Leave to enter the United Kingdom as a person exercising rights of access to a child resident in the United Kingdom

247. Leave to enter as a person exercising access rights to a child resident in the United Kingdom may be granted for 12 months in the first instance, provided that a valid United Kingdom entry clearance for entry in this capacity is produced to the Immigration Officer on arrival.

Refusal of leave to enter the United Kingdom as a person exercising rights of access to a child resident in the United Kingdom

248. Leave to enter as a person exercising rights of access to a child resident in the United Kingdom is to be refused if a valid United Kingdom entry clearance for entry in this capacity is not produced to the Immigration Officer on arrival.

Requirements for leave to remain in the United Kingdom as a person exercising rights of access to a child resident in the United Kingdom

248A. The requirements to be met by a person seeking leave to remain in the United Kingdom to exercise access rights to a child resident in the United Kingdom are that:

   (i) the applicant is the parent of a child who is resident in the United Kingdom; and

   (ii) the parent or carer with whom the child permanently resides is resident in the United Kingdom; and

   (iii) the applicant produces evidence that he has access rights to the child in the form of:

   (a) a Residence Order or a Contact Order granted by a Court in the United Kingdom; or

   (b) a certificate issued by a district judge confirming the applicant's intention to maintain contact with the child; or

   (c) a statement from the child's other parent (or, if contact is supervised, from the supervisor) that the applicant is maintaining contact with the child; and

   (iv) the applicant takes and intends to continue to take an active role in the child's upbringing; and

   (v) the child visits or stays with the applicant on a frequent and regular basis and the applicant intends this to continue; and

   (vi) the child is under the age of 18; and

   (vii) the applicant has limited leave to remain in the United Kingdom as the spouse, civil partner, unmarried partner or same-sex partner of a person present and settled in the United Kingdom who is the other parent of the child; and

   (viii) the applicant has not remained in breach of the immigration laws; and

   (ix) there will be adequate accommodation for the applicant and any dependants without recourse to public funds in accommodation which the applicant owns or occupies exclusively; and

   (x) the applicant will be able to maintain himself and any dependants adequately without recourse to public funds.

Leave to remain in the United Kingdom as a person exercising rights of access to a child resident in the United Kingdom

248B. Leave to remain as a person exercising access rights to a child resident in the United Kingdom may be granted for 12 months in the first instance, provided the Secretary of State is satisfied that each of the requirements of paragraph 248A is met.

Refusal of leave to remain in the United Kingdom as a person exercising rights of access to a child resident in the United Kingdom

248C. Leave to remain as a person exercising rights of access to a child resident in the United Kingdom is to be refused if the Secretary of State is not satisfied that each of the requirements of paragraph 248A is met.

Indefinite leave to remain in the United Kingdom as a person exercising rights of access to a child resident in the United Kingdom

248D. The requirements for indefinite leave to remain in the United Kingdom as a person exercising rights of access to a child resident in the United Kingdom are that:
- (i) the applicant was admitted to the United Kingdom or granted leave to remain in the United Kingdom for a period of 12 months as a person exercising rights of access to a child and has completed a period of 12 months as a person exercising rights of access to a child; and
- (ii) the applicant takes and intends to continue to take an active role in the child's upbringing; and
- (iii) the child visits or stays with the applicant on a frequent and regular basis and the applicant intends this to continue; and
- (iv) there will be adequate accommodation for the applicant and any dependants without recourse to public funds in accommodation which the applicant owns or occupies exclusively; and
- (v) the applicant will be able to maintain himself and any dependants adequately without recourse to public funds; and
- (vi) the child is under 18 years of age; and
- (vii) he has sufficient knowledge of the English language and sufficient knowledge about life in the United Kingdom, unless he is under the age of 18 or aged 65 or over at the time he makes his application.

Indefinite leave to remain as a person exercising rights of access to a child resident in the United Kingdom

248E. Indefinite leave to remain as a person exercising rights of access to a child may be granted provided the Secretary of State is satisfied that each of the requirements of paragraph 248D is met.

Refusal of indefinite leave to remain in the United Kingdom as a person exercising rights of access to a child resident in the United Kingdom

248F. Indefinite leave to remain as a person exercising rights of access to a child is to be refused if the Secretary of State is not satisfied that each of the requirements of paragraph 248D is met.

EEA nationals and their families

Note: Paragraphs 255 to 255B and 257A and 257B are deleted but shall continue to apply for the purpose of determining an application made before 30 April 2006.

Settlement

255. *Any person (other than a student) who under, either the Immigration (European Economic Area) Order 1994, or the 2000 EEA Regulations has been issued with a residence permit or residence document valid for 5 years, and who has remained in the United Kingdom in accordance with the provisions of that Order or those Regulations (as the case may be) for 5 years and continues to do so may, on application, have his residence permit or residence document (as the case may be) endorsed to show permission to remain in the United Kingdom indefinitely.*

255A. *This paragraph applies where a Swiss national has been issued with a residence permit under the 2000 EEA Regulations and, prior to 1st June 2002, remained in the United*

Kingdom in accordance with the provisions of these Rules and in a capacity which would have entitled that Swiss national to apply for indefinite leave to remain after a continuous period of 5 years in that capacity in the United Kingdom. Where this paragraph applies, the period during which the Swiss national remained in the United Kingdom prior to 1st June 2002 shall be treated as a period during which he remained in the United Kingdom in accordance with the 2000 EEA Regulations for the purpose of calculating the 5 year period referred to in paragraph 255.

255B. *This paragraph applies where an Accession State national has been issued with a residence permit under the 2000 EEA Regulations and, prior to 1st May 2004, remained in the United Kingdom in accordance with the provisions of these Rules and in a capacity which would have entitled that Accession State national to apply for indefinite leave to remain after a continuous period of 5 years in that capacity in the United Kingdom. Where this paragraph applies, the period during which the Accession State national remained in the United Kingdom prior to 1st May 2004 shall be treated as a period during which he remained in the United Kingdom in accordance with the 2000 EEA Regulations for the purpose of calculating the 5 year period referred to in paragraph 255.*

257A. *This paragraph applies where a Swiss national was admitted to the United Kingdom before 1st June 2002 for an initial period not exceeding 12 months pursuant to paragraph 282 and on or after that date became a qualified person or the family member of a qualified person under the 2000 EEA Regulations. Where this paragraph applies the Swiss national may, on application, have his residence permit endorsed to show permission to remain in the United Kingdom indefinitely if he meets the requirements set out in paragraph 287.*

257B. *This paragraph applies where an Accession State national was admitted to the United Kingdom before 1st May 2004 for an initial period not exceeding 12 months pursuant to paragraph 282 and on or after that date became a qualified person or the family member of a qualified person under the 2000 EEA Regulations. Where this paragraph applies the Accession State national may, on application, have his residence permit endorsedto show permission to remain in the United Kingdom indefinitely if he meets the requirements set out in paragraph 287.*

Requirements for leave to enter or remain as the primary carer or relative of an EEA national self-sufficient child

257C. The requirements to be met by a person seeking leave to enter or remain as the primary carer or relative of an EEA national self-sufficient child are that the applicant:

   (i) is:

   (a) the primary carer; or

   (b) the parent; or

   (c) the sibling,

   of an EEA national under the age of 18 who has a right of residence in the United Kingdom under the 2006 EEA Regulations as a self-sufficient person; and

   (ii) is living with the EEA national or is seeking entry to the United Kingdom in order to live with the EEA national; and

   (iii) in the case of a sibling of the EEA national:

   (a) is under the age of 18 or has current leave to enter or remain in this capacity; and

   (b) is unmarried and is not a civil partner, has not formed an independent family unit and is not leading an independent life; and

   (iv) can, and will, be maintained and accommodated without taking employment or having recourse to public funds; and

   (v) if seeking leave to enter, holds a valid United Kingdom entry clearance for entry in this capacity.

   In this paragraph, 'sibling', includes a half-brother or half-sister and a stepbrother or stepsister.

Leave to enter or remain as the primary carer or relative of an EEA national self-sufficient child

257D. Leave to enter or remain in the United Kingdom as the primary carer or relative of an EEA national self-sufficient child may be granted for a period not exceeding five years or the remaining period of validity of any residence permit held by the EEA national under the 2006 EEA Regulations, whichever is the shorter, provided that, in the case of an application for leave to enter, the applicant is able to produce to the Immigration Officer, on arrival a valid entry clearance for entry in this capacity or, in the case of an application for leave to remain, the applicant is able to satisfy the Secretary of State that each of the requirements of paragraph 257C(i) to (iv) is met. Leave to enter or remain is to be subject to a condition prohibiting employment and recourse to public funds.

Refusal of leave to enter or remain as the primary carer or relative of an EEA national self-sufficient child

257E. Leave to enter or remain in the United Kingdom as the primary carer or relative of an EEA national self-sufficient child is to be refused if, in the case of an application for leave to enter, the applicant is unable to produce to the Immigration Officer on arrival a valid United Kingdom entry clearance for entry in this capacity or, in the case of an application for leave to remain, if the applicant is unable to satisfy the Secretary of State that each of the requirements of paragraph 257C(i) to (iv) is met.

Retired persons of independent means

Requirements for leave to enter the United Kingdom as a retired person of independent means

263. The requirements to be met by a person seeking leave to enter the United Kingdom as a retired person of independent means are that he:
    (i) is at least 60 years old; and
    (ii) has under his control and disposable in the United Kingdom an income of his own of not less than £25,000 per annum; and
    (iii) is able and willing to maintain and accommodate himself and any dependants indefinitely in the United Kingdom from his own resources with no assistance from any other person and without taking employment or having recourse to public funds; and
    (iv) can demonstrate a close connection with the United Kingdom; and
    (v) intends to make the United Kingdom his main home; and
    (vi) holds a valid United Kingdom entry clearance for entry in this capacity.

Leave to enter as a retired person of independent means

264. A person seeking leave to enter the United Kingdom as a retired person of independent means may be admitted subject to a condition prohibiting employment for a period not exceeding 5 years, provided he is able to produce to the Immigration Officer, on arrival, a valid United Kingdom entry clearance for entry in this capacity.

Refusal of leave to enter as a retired person of independent means

265. Leave to enter as a retired person of independent means is to be refused if a valid United Kingdom entry clearance for entry in this capacity is not produced to the Immigration Officer on arrival.

Requirements for an extension of stay as a retired person of independent means

266. The requirements for an extension of stay as a retired person of independent means are that the applicant:

(i) entered the United Kingdom with a valid United Kingdom entry clearance as a retired person of independent means; and
(ii) meets the requirements of paragraph 263(ii)–(iv); and
(iii) has made the United Kingdom his main home.

266A. The requirements for an extension of stay as a retired person of independent means for a person in the United Kingdom as a work permit holder are that the applicant:
(i) entered the United Kingdom or was granted leave to remain as a work permit holder in accordance with paragraphs 128 to 133 of these Rules; and
(ii) meets the requirements of paragraph 263(i)–(v).

266B. The requirements for an extension of stay as a retired person of independent means for a person in the United Kingdom as a highly skilled migrant are that the applicant:
(i) entered the United Kingdom or was granted leave to remain as a highly skilled migrant in accordance with paragraphs 135A to 135F of these Rules; and
(ii) meets the requirements of paragraph 263(i)–(v).

266C. The requirements for an extension of stay as a retired person of independent means for a person in the United Kingdom to establish themselves or remain in business are that the applicant:
(i) entered the United Kingdom or was granted leave to remain as a person intending to establish themselves or remain in business in accordance with paragraphs 201 to 208 of these Rules; and
(ii) meets the requirements of paragraph 263(i)–(v).

266D. The requirements for an extension of stay as a retired person of independent means for a person in the United Kingdom as an innovator are that the applicant:
(i) entered the United Kingdom or was granted leave to remain as an innovator in accordance with paragraphs 210A to 210F of these Rules; and
(ii) meets the requirements of paragraph 263(i)–(v).

Extension of stay as a retired person of independent means

267. An extension of stay as a retired person of independent means, with a prohibition on the taking of employment, may be granted so as to bring the person's stay in this category up to a maximum of 5 years in aggregate, provided the Secretary of State is satisfied that each of the requirements of paragraph 266 is met. An extension of stay as a retired person of independent means, with a prohibition on the taking of employment, may be granted for a maximum period of 5 years, provided the Secretary of State is satisfied that each of the requirements of paragraph 266A, 266B, 266C or 266D is met.

Refusal of extension of stay as a retired person of independent means

268. An extension of stay as a retired person of independent means is to be refused if the Secretary of State is not satisfied that each of the requirements of paragraph 266, 266A, 266B, 266C or 266D is met.

Indefinite leave to remain for a retired person of independent means

269. Indefinite leave to remain may be granted, on application, to a person admitted as a retired person of independent means provided he:
(i) has spent a continuous period of 5 years in the United Kingdom in this capacity; and
(ii) has met the requirements of paragraph 266 throughout the 5-year period and continues to do so.

Refusal of indefinite leave to remain for a retired person of independent means

270. Indefinite leave to remain in the United Kingdom for a retired person of independent means is to be refused if the Secretary of State is not satisfied that each of the requirements of paragraph 269 is met.

Spouses or civil partners of persons with limited leave to enter or remain in the United Kingdom as retired persons of independent means

Requirements for leave to enter as the spouse or civil partner of a person with limited leave to enter or remain in the United Kingdom as a retired person of independent means

271. The requirements to be met by a person seeking leave to enter the United Kingdom as the spouse or civil partner of a person with limited leave to enter or remain in the United Kingdom as a retired person of independent means are that:
    (i) the applicant is married to or the civil partner of a person with limited leave to enter or remain in the United Kingdom as a retired person of independent means; and
    (ii) each of the parties intends to live with the other as his or her spouse or civil partners during the applicant's stay and the marriage or civil partnership is subsisting; and
    (iii) there will be adequate accommodation for the parties and any dependants without recourse to public funds in accommodation which they own or occupy exclusively; and
    (iv) the parties will be able to maintain themselves and any dependants adequately without recourse to public funds; and
    (v) the applicant does not intend to stay in the United Kingdom beyond any period of leave granted to his spouse or civil partner; and
    (vi) the applicant holds a valid United Kingdom entry clearance for entry in this capacity.

Leave to enter as the spouse or civil partner of a person with limited leave to enter or remain in the United Kingdom as a retired person of independent means

272. A person seeking leave to enter the United Kingdom as the spouse or civil partner of a person with limited leave to enter or remain in the United Kingdom as a retired person of independent means may be given leave to enter for a period not in excess of that granted to the person with limited leave to enter or remain as a retired person of independent means, provided the Immigration Officer is satisfied that each of the requirements of paragraph 271 is met.

Refusal of leave to enter as the spouse or civil partner of a person with limited leave to enter or remain in the United Kingdom as a retired person of independent means

273. Leave to enter as the spouse or civil partner of a person with limited leave to enter or remain in the United Kingdom as a retired person of independent means is to be refused if the Immigration Officer is not satisfied that each of the requirements of paragraph 271 is met.

Requirements for extension of stay as the spouse or civil partner of a person who has or has had leave to enter or remain in the United Kingdom as a retired person of independent means

273A. The requirements to be met by a person seeking an extension of stay in the United Kingdom as the spouse or civil partner of a person who has or has had leave to enter or remain in the United Kingdom as a retired person of independent means are that the applicant:
    (i) is married to or the civil partner of a person with limited leave to enter or remain in the United Kingdom as a retired person of independent means; or

(ii) is married to or the civil partner of a person who has limited leave to enter or remain in the United Kingdom as a retired person of independent means and who is being granted indefinite leave to remain at the same time; or

(iii) is married to or the civil partner of a person who has indefinite leave to remain in the United Kingdom and who had limited leave to enter or remain as a retired person of independent means immediately before being granted indefinite leave to remain; and

(iv) meets the requirements of paragraph 271(ii)-(v); and

(v) was admitted with a valid United Kingdom entry clearance for entry in this capacity.

Extension of stay as the spouse or civil partner of a person who has or has had leave to enter or remain in the United Kingdom as a retired person of independent means

273B. An extension of stay in the United Kingdom as:

(i) the spouse or civil partner of a person who has limited leave to enter or remain as a retired person of independent means may be granted for a period not in excess of that granted to the person with limited leave to enter or remain; or

(ii) the spouse or civil partner of a person who is being admitted at the same time for settlement or the spouse or civil partner of a person who has indefinite leave to remain may be granted for a period not exceeding 2 years, in both instances, provided the Secretary of State is satisfied that each of the requirements of paragraph 273A is met.

Refusal of extension of stay as the spouse or civil partner of a person who has or has had leave to enter or remain in the United Kingdom as a retired person of independent means

273C. An extension of stay in the United Kingdom as the spouse or civil partner of a person who has or has had leave to enter or remain in the United Kingdom as a retired person of independent means is to be refused if the Secretary of State is not satisfied that each of the requirements of paragraph 273A is met.

Requirements for indefinite leave to remain for the spouse or civil partner of a person who has or has had leave to enter or remain in the United Kingdom as a retired person of independent means

273D. The requirements to be met by a person seeking indefinite leave to remain in the United Kingdom as the spouse or civil partner of a person who has or has had leave to enter or remain in the United Kingdom as a retired person of independent means are that the applicant:

(i) is married to or the civil partner of a person who has limited leave to enter or remain in the United Kingdom as a retired person of independent means and who is being granted indefinite leave to remain at the same time; or

(ii) is married to or the civil partner of a person who has indefinite leave to remain in the United Kingdom and who had limited leave to enter or remain as a retired person of independent means immediately before being granted indefinite leave to remain; and

(iii) meets the requirements of paragraph 271(ii)-(v); and

(iv) has sufficient knowledge of the English language and sufficient knowledge about life in the United Kingdom, unless he is under the age of 18 or aged 65 or over at the time he makes his application; and

(v) was admitted with a valid United Kingdom entry clearance for entry in this capacity.

Indefinite leave to remain as the spouse or civil partner of a person who has or has had leave to enter or remain in the United Kingdom as a retired person of independent means

273E. Indefinite leave to remain in the United Kingdom for the spouse or civil partner of a person who has or has had leave to enter or remain in the United Kingdom as a retired person of independent means may be granted provided the Secretary of State is satisfied that each of the requirements of paragraph 273D is met.

Refusal of indefinite leave to remain as the spouse or civil partner of a person who has or has had leave to enter or remain in the United Kingdom as a retired person of independent means

273F. Indefinite leave to remain in the United Kingdom for the spouse or civil partner of a person who has or has had leave to enter or remain in the United Kingdom as a retired person of independent means is to be refused if the Secretary of State is not satisfied that each of the requirements of paragraph 273D is met.

Children of persons with limited leave to enter or remain in the United Kingdom as retired persons of independent means

Requirements for leave to enter or remain as the child of a person with limited leave to enter or remain in the United Kingdom as a retired person of independent means

274. The requirements to be met by a person seeking leave to enter or remain in the United Kingdom as the child of a person with limited leave to enter or remain in the United Kingdom as a retired person of independent means are that:

   (i) he is the child of a parent who has been admitted to or allowed to remain in the United Kingdom as a retired person of independent means; and

   (ii) he is under the age of 18 or has current leave to enter or remain in this capacity; and

   (iii) he is unmarried, has not formed an independent family unit and is not leading an independent life; and

   (iv) he can, and will, be maintained and accommodated adequately without recourse to public funds in accommodation which his parent(s) own or occupy exclusively; and

   (v) he will not stay in the United Kingdom beyond any period of leave granted to his parent(s); and

   (vi) both parents are being or have been admitted to or allowed to remain in the United Kingdom save where:

       (a) the parent he is accompanying or joining is his sole surviving parent; or

       (b) the parent he is accompanying or joining has had sole responsibility for his upbringing; or

       (c) there are serious and compelling family or other considerations which make exclusion from the United Kingdom undesirable and suitable arrangements have been made for his care; and

   (vii) if seeking leave to enter, he holds a valid United Kingdom entry clearance for entry in this capacity or, if seeking leave to remain, was admitted with a valid United Kingdom entry clearance for entry in this capacity.

Leave to enter or remain as the child of a person with limited leave to enter or remain in the United Kingdom as a retired person of independent means

275. A person seeking leave to enter or remain in the United Kingdom as the child of a person with limited leave to enter or remain in the United Kingdom as a retired

person of independent means may be given leave to enter or remain in the United Kingdom for a period of leave not in excess of that granted to the person with limited leave to enter or remain as a retired person of independent means provided that, in relation to an application for leave to enter, he is able to produce to the Immigration Officer, on arrival, a valid United Kingdom entry clearance for entry in this capacity or, in the case of an application for limited leave to remain, he was admitted with a valid United Kingdom entry clearance for entry in this capacity and is able to satisfy the Secretary of State that each of the requirements of paragraph 274(i)–(vi) is met. An application for indefinite leave to remain in this category may be granted provided the applicant was admitted to the United Kingdom with a valid United Kingdom entry clearance for entry in this capacity and is able to satisfy the Secretary of State that each of the requirements of paragraph 274(i)–(vi) is met and provided indefinite leave to remain is, at the same time, being granted to the person with limited leave to enter or remain as a retired person of independent means. Leave to enter or remain is to be subject to a condition prohibiting employment except in relation to the grant of indefinite leave to remain.

Refusal of leave to enter or remain as the child of a person with limited leave to enter or remain in the United Kingdom as a retired person of independent means

276. Leave to enter or remain in the United Kingdom as the child of a person with limited leave to enter or remain in the United Kingdom as a retired person of independent means is to be refused if, in relation to an application for leave to enter, a valid United Kingdom entry clearance for entry in this capacity is not produced to the Immigration Officer on arrival, or in the case of an application for limited leave to remain, if the applicant was not admitted with a valid United Kingdom entry clearance for entry in this capacity or is unable to satisfy the Secretary of State that each of the requirements of paragraph 274(i)–(vi) is met. An application for indefinite leave to remain in this category is to be refused if the applicant was not admitted with a valid United Kingdom entry clearance for entry in this capacity or is unable to satisfy the Secretary of State that each of the requirements of paragraph 274(i)–(vi) is met or if indefinite leave to remain is not, at the same time, being granted to the person with limited leave to enter or remain as a retired person of independent means.

Long residence

Long residence in the United Kingdom

276A. For the purposes of paragraphs 276B to 276D:
  (a) 'continuous residence' means residence in the United Kingdom for an unbroken period, and for these purposes a period shall not be considered to have been broken where an applicant is absent from the United Kingdom for a period of 6 months or less at any one time, provided that the applicant in question has existing limited leave to enter or remain upon their departure and return, but shall be considered to have been broken if the applicant:
    (i) has been removed under Schedule 2 of the 1971 Act, section 10 of the 1999 Act, has been deported or has left the United Kingdom having been refused leave to enter or remain here; or
    (ii) has left the United Kingdom and, on doing so, evidenced a clear intention not to return; or
    (iii) left the United Kingdom in circumstances in which he could have had no reasonable expectation at the time of leaving that he would lawfully be able to return; or
    (iv) has been convicted of an offence and was sentenced to a period of imprisonment or was directed to be detained in an institution other

than a prison (including, in particular, a hospital or an institution for young offenders), provided that the sentence in question was not a suspended sentence; or

(v) has spent a total of more than 18 months absent from the United Kingdom during the period in question.

(b) 'lawful residence' means residence which is continuous residence pursuant to:
(i) existing leave to enter or remain; or
(ii) temporary admission within section 11 of the 1971 Act where leave to enter or remain is subsequently granted; or
(iii) an exemption from immigration control, including where an exemption ceases to apply if it is immediately followed by a grant of leave to enter or remain.

Requirements for an extension of stay on the ground of long residence in the United Kingdom

276A1. The requirement to be met by a person seeking an extension of stay on the ground of long residence in the United Kingdom is that the applicant meets all the requirements in paragraph 276B of these rules, except the requirement to have sufficient knowledge of the English language and sufficient knowledge about life in the United Kingdom contained in paragraph 276B(iii).

Extension of stay on the ground of long residence in the United Kingdom

276A2. An extension of stay on the ground of long residence in the United Kingdom may be granted for a period not exceeding 2 years provided that the Secretary of State is satisfied that the requirement in paragraph 276A1 is met.

Conditions to be attached to extension of stay on the ground of long residence in the United Kingdom

276A3. Where an extension of stay is granted under paragraph 276A2:
(i) if the applicant has spent less than 14 years in the UK, the grant of leave should be subject to the same conditions attached to his last period of lawful leave, or
(ii) if the applicant has spent 14 years or more in the UK, the grant of leave should not contain any restriction on employment.

Refusal of extension of stay on the ground of long residence in the United Kingdom

276A4. An extension of stay on the ground of long residence in the United Kingdom is to be refused if the Secretary of State is not satisfied that the requirement in paragraph 276A1 is met.

Requirements for indefinite leave to remain on the ground of long residence in the United Kingdom

276B. The requirements to be met by an applicant for indefinite leave to remain on the ground of long residence in the United Kingdom are that:
(i) (a) he has had at least 10 years continuous lawful residence in the United Kingdom; or
(b) he has had at least 14 years continuous residence in the United Kingdom, excluding any period spent in the United Kingdom following service of notice of liability to removal or notice of a decision to remove by way of directions under paragraphs 8 to 10A, or 12 to 14, of Schedule 2 to the Immigration Act 1971 or section 10 of the Immigration and Asylum Act 1999 Act, or of a notice of intention to deport him from the United Kingdom; and

(ii) having regard to the public interest there are no reasons why it would be undesirable for him to be given indefinite leave to remain on the ground of long residence, taking into account his:
   (a) age; and
   (b) strength of connections in the United Kingdom; and
   (c) personal history, including character, conduct, associations and employment record; and
   (d) domestic circumstances; and
   (e) previous criminal record and the nature of any offence of which the person has been convicted; and
   (f) compassionate circumstances; and
   (g) any representations received on the person's behalf; and
(iii) he has sufficient knowledge of the English language and sufficient knowledge about life in the United Kingdom, unless he is under the age of 18 or aged 65 or over at the time he makes his application.

Indefinite leave to remain on the ground of long residence in the United Kingdom

276C. Indefinite leave to remain on the ground of long residence in the United Kingdom may be granted provided that the Secretary of State is satisfied that each of the requirements of paragraph 276B is met.

Refusal of indefinite leave to remain on the ground of long residence in the United Kingdom

276D. Indefinite leave to remain on the ground of long residence in the United Kingdom is to be refused if the Secretary of State is not satisfied that each of the requirements of paragraph 276B is met.

HM Forces

Definition of Gurkha

276E. For the purposes of these Rules the term 'Gurkha' means a citizen or national of Nepal who has served in the Brigade of Gurkhas of the British Army under the Brigade of Gurkhas' terms and conditions of service.

Leave to enter or remain in the United Kingdom as a Gurkha discharged from the British Army

Requirements for indefinite leave to enter the United Kingdom as a Gurkha discharged from the British Army

276F. The requirements for indefinite leave to enter the United Kingdom as a Gurkha discharged from the British Army are that:
   (i) the applicant has completed at least four years' service as a Gurkha with the British Army; and
   (ii) was discharged from the British Army in Nepal on completion of engagement on or after 1 July 1997; and
   (iii) was not discharged from the British Army more than 2 years prior to the date on which the application is made; and
   (iv) holds a valid United Kingdom entry clearance for entry in this capacity.

Indefinite leave to enter the United Kingdom as a Gurkha discharged from the British Army

276G. A person seeking indefinite leave to enter the United Kingdom as a Gurkha discharged from the British Army may be granted indefinite leave to enter provided a valid United Kingdom entry clearance for entry in this capacity is produced to the Immigration Officer on arrival.

Refusal of indefinite leave to enter the United Kingdom as a Gurkha discharged from the British Army

276H. Indefinite leave to enter the United Kingdom as a Gurkha discharged from the British Army is to be refused if a valid United Kingdom entry clearance for entry in this capacity is not produced to the Immigration Officer on arrival.

Requirements for indefinite leave to remain in the United Kingdom as a Gurkha discharged from the British Army

276I. The requirements for indefinite leave to remain in the United Kingdom as a Gurkha discharged from the British Army are that:
- (i) the applicant has completed at least four years' service as a Gurkha with the British Army; and
- (ii) was discharged from the British Army in Nepal on completion of engagement on or after 1 July 1997; and
- (iii) was not discharged from the British Army more than 2 years prior to the date on which the application is made; and
- (iv) on the date of application has leave to enter or remain in the United Kingdom.

Indefinite leave to remain in the United Kingdom as a Gurkha discharged from the British Army

276J. A person seeking indefinite leave to remain in the United Kingdom as a Gurkha discharged from the British Army may be granted indefinite leave to remain provided the Secretary of State is satisfied that each of the requirements of paragraph 276I is met.

Refusal of indefinite leave to remain in the United Kingdom as a Gurkha discharged from the British Army

276K. Indefinite leave to remain in the United Kingdom as a Gurkha discharged from the British Army is to be refused if the Secretary of State is not satisfied that each of the requirements of paragraph 276I is met.

Leave to enter or remain in the United Kingdom as a foreign or Commonwealth citizen discharged from HM Forces

Requirements for indefinite leave to enter the United Kingdom as a foreign or Commonwealth citizen discharged from HM Forces

276L. The requirements for indefinite leave to enter the United Kingdom as a foreign or Commonwealth citizen discharged from HM Forces are that:
- (i) the applicant has completed at least four years' service with HM Forces; and
- (ii) was discharged from HM Forces on completion of engagement; and
- (iii) was not discharged from HM Forces more than 2 years prior to the date on which the application is made; and
- (iv) holds a valid United Kingdom entry clearance for entry in this capacity.

Indefinite leave to enter the United Kingdom as a foreign or Commonwealth citizen discharged from HM Forces

276M. A person seeking indefinite leave to enter the United Kingdom as a foreign or Commonwealth citizen discharged from HM Forces may be granted indefinite leave to enter provided a valid United Kingdom entry clearance for entry in this capacity is produced to the Immigration Officer on arrival.

Refusal of indefinite leave to enter the United Kingdom as a foreign or Commonwealth citizen discharged from HM Forces

276N. Indefinite leave to enter the United Kingdom as a foreign or Commonwealth citizen discharged from HM Forces is to be refused if a valid United Kingdom entry clearance for entry in this capacity is not produced to the Immigration Officer on arrival.

Requirements for indefinite leave to remain in the United Kingdom as a foreign or Commonwealth citizen discharged from HM Forces

276O. The requirements for indefinite leave to remain in the United Kingdom as a foreign or Commonwealth citizen discharged from HM Forces are that:
   (i) the applicant has completed at least four years' service with HM Forces; and
   (ii) was discharged from HM Forces on completion of engagement; and
   (iii) was not discharged from HM Forces more than 2 years prior to the date on which the application is made; and
   (iv) on the date of application has leave to enter or remain in the United Kingdom.

Indefinite leave to remain in the United Kingdom as a foreign or Commonwealth citizen discharged from HM Forces

276P. A person seeking indefinite leave to remain in the United Kingdom as a foreign or Commonwealth citizen discharged from HM Forces may be granted indefinite leave to remain provided the Secretary of State is satisfied that each of the requirements of paragraph 276O is met.

Refusal of indefinite leave to remain in the United Kingdom as a foreign or Commonwealth citizen discharged from HM Forces

276Q. Indefinite leave to remain in the United Kingdom as a foreign or Commonwealth citizen discharged from HM Forces is to be refused if the Secretary of State is not satisfied that each of the requirements of paragraph 276O is met.

Spouses or civil partners of persons settled or seeking settlement in the United Kingdom in accordance with paragraphs 276E to 276Q (HM Forces rules)

Leave to enter or remain in the UK as the spouse or civil partner of a person present and settled in the United Kingdom or being granted settlement on the same occasion in accordance with paragraphs 276E to 276Q

Requirements for indefinite leave to enter the United Kingdom as the spouse or civil partner of a person present and settled in the United Kingdom or being admitted on the same occasion for settlement under paragraphs 276E to 276Q

276R. The requirements to be met by a person seeking indefinite leave to enter the United Kingdom as the spouse or civil partner of a person present and settled in the United Kingdom or being admitted on the same occasion for settlement in accordance with paragraphs 276E to 276Q are that:
   (i) the applicant is married to or the civil partner of a person present and settled in the United Kingdom or who is being admitted on the same occasion for settlement in accordance with paragraphs 276E to 276Q; and
   (ii) the parties to the marriage or civil partnership have met; and
   (iii) the parties were married or formed a civil partnership at least 2 years ago; and

(iv) each of the parties intends to live permanently with the other as his or her spouse or civil partner; and
(v) the marriage or civil partnership is subsisting; and
(vi) the applicant holds a valid United Kingdom entry clearance for entry in this capacity.

Indefinite leave to enter the United Kingdom as the spouse or civil partner of a person present and settled in the United Kingdom or being admitted on the same occasion for settlement in accordance with paragraphs 276E to 276Q

276S. A person seeking leave to enter the United Kingdom as the spouse or civil partner of a person present and settled in the United Kingdom or being admitted on the same occasion for settlement in accordance with paragraphs 276E to 276Q may be granted indefinite leave to enter provided a valid United Kingdom entry clearance for entry in this capacity is produced to the Immigration Officer on arrival.

Refusal of indefinite leave to enter the United Kingdom as the spouse or civil partner of a person present and settled in the UK or being admitted on the same occasion for settlement in accordance with paragraphs 276E to 276Q

276T. Leave to enter the United Kingdom as the spouse or civil partner of a person present and settled in the United Kingdom or being admitted on the same occasion for settlement in accordance with paragraphs 276E to 276Q is to be refused if a valid United Kingdom entry clearance for entry in this capacity is not produced to the Immigration Officer on arrival.

Requirements for indefinite leave to remain in the United Kingdom as the spouse or civil partner of a person present and settled in the United Kingdom or being granted settlement on the same occasion in accordance with paragraphs 276E to 276Q

276U. The requirements to be met by a person seeking indefinite leave to remain in the United Kingdom as the spouse or civil partner of a person present and settled in the United Kingdom or being granted settlement on the same occasion in accordance with paragraphs 276E to 276Q are that:
(i) the applicant is married to or the civil partner of a person present and settled in the United Kingdom or being granted settlement on the same occasion in accordance with paragraphs 276E to 276Q; and
(ii) the parties to the marriage or civil partnership have met; and
(iii) the parties were married or formed a civil partnership at least 2 years ago; and
(iv) each of the parties intends to live permanently with the other as his or her spouse or civil partner; and
(v) the marriage or civil partnership is subsisting; and
(vi) has leave to enter or remain in the United Kingdom.

Indefinite leave to remain in the United Kingdom as the spouse or civil partner of a person present and settled in the United Kingdom or being granted settlement on the same occasion in accordance with paragraphs 276E to 276Q

276V. Indefinite leave to remain in the United Kingdom as the spouse or civil partner of a person present and settled in the United Kingdom or being granted settlement on the same occasion in accordance with paragraphs 276E to 276Q may be granted provided the Secretary of State is satisfied that each of the requirements of paragraph 276U is met.

Refusal of indefinite leave to remain in the United Kingdom as the spouse or civil partner of a person present and settled in the United Kingdom or being granted settlement on the same occasion in accordance with paragraphs 276E to 276Q

276W. Indefinite leave to remain in the United Kingdom as the spouse or civil partner of a person present and settled in the United Kingdom or being granted settlement on the same occasion in accordance with paragraphs 276E to 276Q is to be refused if the Secretary of State is not satisfied that each of the requirements of paragraph 276U is met.

Children of a parent, parents or a relative settled or seeking settlement in the United Kingdom under paragraphs 276E to 276Q (HM Forces rules)

Leave to enter or remain in the United Kingdom as the child of a parent, parents or a relative present and settled in the United Kingdom or being granted settlement on the same occasion in accordance with paragraphs 276E to 276Q

Requirements for indefinite leave to enter the United Kingdom as the child of a parent, parents or a relative present and settled in the United Kingdom or being admitted for settlement on the same occasion in accordance with paragraphs 276E to 276Q

276X. The requirements to be met by a person seeking indefinite leave to enter the United Kingdom as the child of a parent, parents or a relative present and settled in the United Kingdom or being admitted for settlement on the same occasion in accordance with paragraphs 276E to 276Q are that:
  (i) the applicant is seeking indefinite leave to enter to accompany or join a parent, parents or a relative in one of the following circumstances:
    (a) both parents are present and settled in the United Kingdom; or
    (b) both parents are being admitted on the same occasion for settlement; or
    (c) one parent is present and settled in the United Kingdom and the other is being admitted on the same occasion for settlement; or
    (d) one parent is present and settled in the United Kingdom or being admitted on the same occasion for settlement and the other parent is dead; or
    (e) one parent is present and settled in the United Kingdom or being admitted on the same occasion for settlement and has had sole responsibility for the child's upbringing; or
    (f) one parent or a relative is present and settled in the United Kingdom or being admitted on the same occasion for settlement and there are serious and compelling family or other considerations which make exclusion of the child undesirable and suitable arrangements have been made for the child's care; and
  (ii) is under the age of 18; and
  (iii) is not leading an independent life, is unmarried and is not a civil partner, and has not formed an independent family unit; and
  (iv) holds a valid United Kingdom entry clearance for entry in this capacity.

Indefinite leave to enter the United Kingdom as the child of a parent, parents or a relative present and settled in the United Kingdom or being admitted for settlement on the same occasion in accordance with paragraphs 276E to 276Q

276Y. Indefinite leave to enter the United Kingdom as the child of a parent, parents or a relative present and settled in the United Kingdom or being admitted for settlement on the same occasion in accordance with paragraphs 276E to 276Q may be granted provided a valid United Kingdom entry clearance for entry in this capacity is produced to the Immigration Officer on arrival.

Refusal of indefinite leave to enter the United Kingdom as the child of a parent, parents or a relative present and settled in the United Kingdom or being admitted for settlement on the same occasion in accordance with paragraphs 276E to 276Q

276Z. Indefinite leave to enter the United Kingdom as the child of a parent, parents, or a relative present and settled in the United Kingdom or being admitted for settlement on the same occasion in accordance with paragraphs 276E to 276Q is to be refused if a valid United Kingdom entry clearance for entry in this capacity is not produced to the Immigration Officer on arrival.

Requirements for indefinite leave to remain in the United Kingdom as the child of a parent, parents or a relative present and settled in the United Kingdom or being granted settlement on the same occasion in accordance with paragraphs 276E to 276Q

276AA The requirements to be met by a person seeking indefinite leave to remain in the United Kingdom as the child of a parent, parents or a relative present and settled in the United Kingdom or being granted settlement on the same occasion in accordance with paragraphs 276E to 276Q are that:
  (i)   the applicant is seeking indefinite leave to remain with a parent, parents or a relative in one of the following circumstances:
    (a) both parents are present and settled in the United Kingdom or being granted settlement on the same occasion; or
    (b) one parent is present and settled in the United Kingdom or being granted settlement on the same occasion and the other parent is dead; or
    (c) one parent is present and settled in the United Kingdom or being granted settlement on the same occasion and has had sole responsibility for the child's upbringing; or
    (d) one parent or a relative is present and settled in the United Kingdom or being granted settlement on the same occasion and there are serious and compelling family or other considerations which make exclusion of the child undesirable and suitable arrangements have been made for the child's care; and
  (ii) is under the age of 18; and
  (iii) is not leading an independent life, is unmarried and is not a civil partner, and has not formed an independent family unit; and
  (iv) has leave to enter or remain in the United Kingdom.

Indefinite leave to remain in the United Kingdom as the child of a parent, parents or a relative present and settled in the United Kingdom or being granted settlement on the same occasion in accordance with paragraphs 276E to 276Q

276AB. Indefinite leave to remain in the United Kingdom as the child of a parent, parents or a relative present and settled in the United Kingdom or being granted settlement on the same occasion in accordance with paragraphs 276E to 276Q may be granted if the Secretary of State is satisfied that each of the requirements of paragraph 276AA is met.

Refusal of indefinite leave to remain in the United Kingdom as the child of a parent, parents or a relative present and settled in the United Kingdom or being granted settlement on the same occasion in accordance with paragraphs 276E to 276Q

276AC. Indefinite leave to remain in the United Kingdom as the child of a parent, parents or a relative present and settled in the United Kingdom or being granted settlement on the same occasion in accordance with paragraphs 276E to 276Q is to be refused if the Secretary of State is not satisfied that each of the requirements of paragraph 276AA is met.

Spouses or civil partners of armed forces members who are exempt from immigration control under section 8(4) of the Immigration Act 1971

Requirements for leave to enter or remain as the spouse or civil partner of an armed forces member who is exempt from immigration control under section 8(4) of the Immigration Act 1971

276AD. The requirements to be met by a person seeking leave to enter or remain in the United Kingdom as the spouse or civil partner of an armed forces member who is exempt from immigration control under section 8(4) of the Immigration Act 1971 are that:
  (i) the applicant is married to or the civil partner of an armed forces member who is exempt from immigration control under section 8(4) of the Immigration Act 1971; and
  (ii) each of the parties intends to live with the other as his or her spouse or civil partner during the applicant's stay and the marriage or civil partnership is subsisting; and
  (iii) there will be adequate accommodation for the parties and any dependants without recourse to public funds in accommodation which they own or occupy exclusively; and
  (iv) the parties will be able to maintain themselves and any dependants adequately without recourse to public funds; and
  (v) the applicant does not intend to stay in the United Kingdom beyond his or her spouse's or civil partner's enlistment in the home forces, or period of posting or training in the United Kingdom.

Leave to enter or remain as the spouse or civil partner of an armed forces member who is exempt from immigration control under section 8(4) of the Immigration Act 1971

276AE. A person seeking leave to enter or remain in the United Kingdom as the spouse or civil partner of an armed forces member who is exempt from immigration control under section 8(4) of the Immigration Act 1971 may be given leave to enter or remain in the United Kingdom for a period not exceeding 4 years or the duration of the enlistment, posting or training of his or her spouse or civil partner, whichever is shorter, provided that the Immigration Officer, or in the case of an application for leave to remain, the Secretary of State, is satisfied that each of the requirements of paragraph 276AD(i)–(v) is met.

Refusal of leave to enter or remain as the spouse or civil partner of an armed forces member who is exempt from immigration control under section 8(4) of the Immigration Act 1971

276AF. Leave to enter or remain in the United Kingdom as the spouse or civil partner an armed forces member who is exempt from immigration control under section 8(4) of the Immigration Act 1971 is to be refused if the Immigration Officer, or in the case of an application for leave to remain, the Secretary of State, is not satisfied that each of the requirements of paragraph 276AD(i)–(v) is met.

Children of armed forces members who are exempt from immigration control under section 8(4) of the Immigration Act 1971

Requirements for leave to enter or remain as the child of an armed forces member exempt from immigration control under section 8(4) of the Immigration Act 1971

276AG. The requirements to be met by a person seeking leave to enter or remain in the United Kingdom as the child of an armed forces member exempt from immigration control under section 8(4) of the Immigration Act 1971 are that:

(i) he is the child of a parent who is an armed forces member exempt from immigration control under section 8(4) of the Immigration Act 1971; and

(ii) he is under the age of 18 or has current leave to enter or remain in this capacity; and

(iii) he is unmarried and is not a civil partner, has not formed an independent family unit and is not leading an independent life; and

(iv) he can and will be maintained and accommodated adequately without recourse to public funds in accommodation which his parent(s) own or occupy exclusively; and

(v) he will not stay in the United Kingdom beyond the period of his parent's enlistment in the home forces, or posting or training in the United Kingdom; and

(vi) his other parent is being or has been admitted to or allowed to remain in the United Kingdom save where:

(a) the parent he is accompanying or joining is his sole surviving parent; or

(b) the parent he is accompanying or joining has had sole responsibility for his upbringing; or

(c) there are serious and compelling family or other considerations which make exclusion from the United Kingdom undesirable and suitable arrangements have been made for his care.

Leave to enter or remain as the child of an armed forces member exempt from immigration control under section 8(4) of the Immigration Act 1971

276AH. A person seeking leave to enter or remain in the United Kingdom as the child of an armed forces member exempt from immigration control under section 8(4) of the Immigration Act 1971 may be given leave to enter or remain in the United Kingdom for a period not exceeding 4 years or the duration of the enlistment, posting or training of his parent, whichever is the shorter, provided that the Immigration Officer, or in the case of an application for leave to remain, the Secretary of State, is satisfied that each of the requirements of 276AG(i)–(vi) is met.

Refusal of leave to enter or remain as the child of an armed forces member exempt from immigration control under section 8(4) of the Immigration Act 1971

276AI. Leave to enter or remain in the United Kingdom as the child of an armed forces member exempt from immigration control under section 8(4) of the Immigration

Act 1971 is to be refused if the Immigration Officer, or in the case of an application for leave to remain, the Secretary of State, is not satisfied that each of the requirements of paragraph 276AG(i)–(vi) is met.

Part 8: Family members

Section 1

Spouses and civil partners

277. Nothing in these Rules shall be construed as permitting a person to be granted entry clearance, leave to enter, leave to remain or variation of leave as a spouse or civil partner of another if either the applicant or the sponsor will be aged under 18 on the date of arrival in the United Kingdom or (as the case may be) on the date on which the leave to remain or variation of leave would be granted.

278. Nothing in these Rules shall be construed as allowing a person to be granted entry clearance, leave to enter, leave to remain or variation of leave as the spouse of a man or woman (the sponsor) if:

  (i) his or her marriage or civil partnership to the sponsor is polygamous; and

  (ii) there is another person living who is the husband or wife of the sponsor and who:

  (a) is, or at any time since his or her marriage or civil partnership to the sponsor has been, in the United Kingdom; or

  (b) has been granted a certificate of entitlement in respect of the right of abode mentioned in Section 2(1)(a) of the Immigration Act 1988 or an entry clearance to enter the United Kingdom as the husband or wife of the sponsor.

  For the purpose of this paragraph a marriage or civil partnership may be polygamous although at its inception neither party had any other spouse or civil partner.

279. Paragraph 278 does not apply to any person who seeks entry clearance, leave to enter, leave to remain or variation of leave where:

  (i) he or she has been in the United Kingdom before 1 August 1988 having been admitted for the purpose of settlement as the husband or wife of the sponsor; or

  (ii) he or she has, since their marriage or civil partnership to the sponsor, been in the United Kingdom at any time when there was no such other spouse or civil partner living as is mentioned in paragraph 278(ii).

  But where a person claims that paragraph 278 does not apply to them because they have been in the United Kingdom in circumstances which cause them to fall within sub paragraphs (i) or (ii) of that paragraph it shall be for them to prove that fact.

280. For the purposes of paragraphs 278 and 279 the presence of any wife or husband in the United Kingdom in any of the following circumstances shall be disregarded:

  (i) as a visitor; or

  (ii) an illegal entrant; or

  (iii) in circumstances whereby a person is deemed by Section 11(1) of the Immigration Act 1971 not to have entered the United Kingdom.

Spouses or civil partners of persons present and settled in the United Kingdom or being admitted on the same occasion for settlement

Requirements for leave to enter the United Kingdom with a view to settlement as the spouse or civil partner of a person present and settled in the United Kingdom or being admitted on the same occasion for settlement

281. The requirements to be met by a person seeking leave to enter the United Kingdom with a view to settlement as the spouse or civil partner of a person present and settled in the United Kingdom or who is on the same occasion being admitted for settlement are that:
    - (i) (a) the applicant is married to or the civil partner of a person present and settled in the United Kingdom or who is on the same occasion being admitted for settlement; or
        - (b) (i) the applicant is married to or the civil partner of a person who has a right of abode in the United Kingdom or indefinite leave to enter or remain in the United Kingdom and is on the same occasion seeking admission to the United Kingdom for the purposes of settlement and the parties were married or formed a civil partnership at least 4 years ago, since which time they have been living together outside the United Kingdom; and
            - (ii) the applicant has sufficient knowledge of the English language and sufficient knowledge about life in the United Kingdom, unless he is under the age of 18 or aged 65 or over at the time he makes his application; and
    - (ii) the parties to the marriage or civil partnership have met; and
    - (iii) each of the parties intends to live permanently with the other as his or her spouse or civil partner and the marriage or civil partnership is subsisting; and
    - (iv) there will be adequate accommodation for the parties and any dependants without recourse to public funds in accommodation which they own or occupy exclusively; and
    - (v) the parties will be able to maintain themselves and any dependants adequately without recourse to public funds; and
    - (vi) the applicant holds a valid United Kingdom entry clearance for entry in this capacity.

    For the purposes of this paragraph and paragraphs 282–289 a member of HM Forces serving overseas, or a permanent member of HM Diplomatic Service or a comparable UK-based staff member of the British Council on a tour of duty abroad, or a staff member of the Department for International Development who is a British Citizen or is settled in the United Kingdom, is to be regarded as present and settled in the United Kingdom.

Leave to enter as the spouse or civil partner of a person present and settled in the United Kingdom or being admitted for settlement on the same occasion

282. A person seeking leave to enter the United Kingdom as the spouse or civil partner of a person present and settled in the United Kingdom or who is on the same occasion being admitted for settlement may:
    - (a) in the case of a person within paragraph 281(i)(a), be admitted for an initial period not exceeding 2 years, or
    - (b) in the case of a person who meets both of the requirements in paragraph 281(i)(b), be granted indefinite leave to enter, or

(c) in the case of a person who meets the requirement in paragraph 281(i)(b)(i), but not the requirement in paragraph 281(i)(b)(ii) to have sufficient knowledge of the English language and about life in the United Kingdom, be admitted for an initial period not exceeding 2 years, in all cases provided the Immigration Officer is satisfied that each of the relevant requirements of paragraph 281 is met.

Refusal of leave to enter as the spouse or civil partner of a person present and settled in the United Kingdom or being admitted on the same occasion for settlement

283. Leave to enter the United Kingdom as the spouse or civil partner of a person present and settled in the United Kingdom or who is on the same occasion being admitted for settlement is to be refused if the Immigration Officer is not satisfied that each of the requirements of paragraph 281 is met.

Requirements for an extension of stay as the spouse or civil partner of a person present and settled in the United Kingdom

284. The requirements for an extension of stay as the spouse or civil partner of a person present and settled in the United Kingdom are that:

(i) the applicant has limited leave to enter or remain in the United Kingdom which was given in accordance with any of the provisions of these Rules, other than where as a result of that leave he would not have been in the United Kingdom beyond 6 months from the date on which he was admitted to the United Kingdom on this occasion in accordance with these Rules, unless the leave in question is limited leave to enter as a fiancé or proposed civil partner; and

(ii) is married to a person present and settled in the United Kingdom; and

(iii) the parties to the marriage or civil partnership have met; and

(iv) the applicant has not remained in breach of the immigration laws; and

(v) the marriage or civil partnership has not taken place after a decision has been made to deport the applicant or he has been recommended for deportation or been given notice under Section 6(2) of the Immigration Act 1971; and

(vi) each of the parties intends to live permanently with the other as his or her spouse or civil partner and the marriage or civil partnership is subsisting; and

(vii) there will be adequate accommodation for the parties and any dependants without recourse to public funds in accommodation which they own or occupy exclusively; and

(viii) the parties will be able to maintain themselves and any dependants adequately without recourse to public funds.

Extension of stay as the spouse or civil partner of a person present and settled in the United Kingdom

285. An extension of stay as the spouse or civil partner of a person present and settled in the United Kingdom may be granted for a period of 2 years in the first instance, provided the Secretary of State is satisfied that each of the requirements of paragraph 284 is met.

Refusal of extension of stay as the spouse or civil partner of a person present and settled in the United Kingdom

286. An extension of stay as the spouse of a person present and settled in the United Kingdom is to be refused if the Secretary of State is not satisfied that each of the requirements of paragraph 284 is met.

Requirements for indefinite leave to remain for the spouse or civil partner of a person present and settled in the United Kingdom

287. (a) The requirements for indefinite leave to remain for the spouse or civil partner of a person present and settled in the United Kingdom are that:

 (i) (a) the applicant was admitted to the United Kingdom or given an extension of stay for a period of 2 years in accordance with paragraphs 281 to 286 of these Rules and has completed a period of 2 years as the spouse of a person present and settled in the United Kingdom; or

 (b) the applicant was admitted to the United Kingdom or given an extension of stay for a period of 2 years in accordance with paragraphs 295AA to 295F of these Rules and during that 2 year period married or formed a civil partnership with the person whom he or she was admitted or granted an extension of stay to join and has completed a period of 2 years as the unmarried or same-sex partner and then the spouse or civil partner of a person present and settled in the United Kingdom; or

 (c) was admitted to the United Kingdom in accordance with leave granted under paragraph 282(c) of these rules; and

 (ii) the applicant is still the spouse or civil partner of the person he or she was admitted or granted an extension of stay to join and the marriage or civil partnership is subsisting; and

 (iii) each of the parties intends to live permanently with the other as his or her spouse or civil partner; and

 (iv) there will be adequate accommodation for the parties and any dependants without recourse to public funds in accommodation which they own or occupy exclusively; and

 (v) the parties will be able to maintain themselves and any dependants adequately without recourse to public funds; and

 (vi) he has sufficient knowledge of the English language and sufficient knowledge about life in the United Kingdom, unless he is under the age of 18 or aged 65 or over at the time he makes his application.

(b) The requirements for indefinite leave to remain for the bereaved spouse or civil partner of a person who was present and settled in the United Kingdom are that:

 (i) (a) the applicant was admitted to the United Kingdom or given an extension of stay for a period of 2 years as the spouse of a person present and settled in the United Kingdom in accordance with paragraphs 281 to 286 of these Rules; or

 (b) the applicant was admitted to the United Kingdom or given an extension of stay for a period of 2 years as the unmarried partner of a person present and settled in the United Kingdom in accordance with paragraphs 295AA to 295F of these Rules and during that 2 year period married the person whom he or she was admitted or granted an extension of stay to join; and

 (ii) the person whom the applicant was admitted or granted an extension of stay to join died during that 2 year period; and

 (iii) the applicant was still the spouse or civil partner of the person he or she was admitted or granted an extension of stay to join at the time of the death; and

 (iv) each of the parties intended to live permanently with the other as his or her spouse or civil partner and the marriage or civil partnership was subsisting at the time of the death.

Indefinite leave to remain for the spouse or civil partner of a person present and settled in the United Kingdom

288. Indefinite leave to remain for the spouse or civil partner of a person present and settled in the United Kingdom may be granted provided the Secretary of State is satisfied that each of the requirements of paragraph 287 is met.

Refusal of indefinite leave to remain for the spouse or civil partner of a person present and settled in the United Kingdom

289. Indefinite leave to remain for the spouse or civil partner of a person present and settled in the United Kingdom is to be refused if the Secretary of State is not satisfied that each of the requirements of paragraph 287 is met.

Refusal of indefinite leave to remain in the United Kingdom as the victim of domestic violence

289A. The requirements to be met by a person who is the victim of domestic violence and who is seeking indefinite leave to remain in the United Kingdom are that the applicant:

(i) was admitted to the United Kingdom or given an extension of stay for a period of 2 years as the spouse or civil partner of a person present and settled here; or

(ii) was admitted to the United Kingdom or given an extension of stay for a period of 2 years as the unmarried or same-sex partner of a person present and settled here; and

(iii) the relationship with their spouse, civil partner, unmarried partner or same-sex partner, as appropriate, was subsisting at the beginning of the relevant period of leave or extension of stay referred to in (i) or (ii) above; and

(iv) is able to produce such evidence as may be required by the Secretary of State to establish that the relationship was caused to permanently break down before the end of that period as a result of domestic violence.

Indefinite leave to remain as the victim of domestic violence

289B. Indefinite leave to remain as the victim of domestic violence may be granted provided the Secretary of State is satisfied that each of the requirements of paragraph 289A is met.

Refusal of indefinite leave to remain as the victim of domestic violence

289C. Indefinite leave to remain as the victim of domestic violence is to be refused if the Secretary of State is not satisfied that each of the requirements of paragraph 289A is met.

Fiancé(e)s and proposed civil partners

289AA. Nothing in these Rules shall be construed as permitting a person to be granted entry clearance, leave to enter or variation of leave as a fiancé(e) or proposed civil partner if either the applicant or the sponsor will aged under 18 on the date of arrival of the applicant in the United Kingdom or (as the case may be) on the date on which the leave to enter or variation of leave would be granted.

Requirements for leave to enter the United Kingdom as a fiancé(e) or proposed civil partner (ie with a view to marriage or civil partnership and permanent settlement in the United Kingdom)

290. The requirements to be met by a person seeking leave to enter the United Kingdom as a fiancé(e) or proposed civil partner are that:

(i) the applicant is seeking leave to enter the United Kingdom for marriage to a person present and settled in the United Kingdom or who is on the same occasion being admitted for settlement; and

(ii) the parties to the proposed marriage have met; and
(iii) each of the parties intends to live permanently with the other as his or her spouse or civil partner after the marriage or civil partnership; and
(iv) adequate maintenance and accommodation without recourse to public funds will be available for the applicant until the date of the marriage or civil partnership; and
(v) there will, after the marriage or civil partnership, be adequate accommodation for the parties and any dependants without recourse to public funds in accommodation which they own or occupy exclusively; and
(vi) the parties will be able after the marriage or civil partnership to maintain themselves and any dependants adequately without recourse to public funds; and
(vii) the applicant holds a valid United Kingdom entry clearance for entry in this capacity.

290A. For the purposes of paragraph 290 and paragraphs 291-295, an EEA national who holds a registration certificate or a document certifying permanent residence issued under the 2006 EEA Regulations (including an EEA national who holds a residence permit issued under the Immigration (European Economic Area) Regulations 2000 which is treated as if it were such a certificate or document by virtue of Schedule 4 to the 2006 EEA Regulations) is to be regarded as present and settled in the United Kingdom.

Leave to enter as a fiancé(e) or proposed civil partner

291. A person seeking leave to enter the United Kingdom as a fiancé(e) or proposed civil partner may be admitted, with a prohibition on employment, for a period not exceeding 6 months to enable the marriage or civil partnership to take place provided a valid United Kingdom entry clearance for entry in this capacity is produced to the Immigration Officer on arrival.

Refusal of leave to enter as a fiancé(e) or proposed civil partner

292. Leave to enter the United Kingdom as a fiancé(e) or proposed civil partner is to be refused if a valid United Kingdom entry clearance for entry in this capacity is not produced to the Immigration Officer on arrival.

Requirements for an extension of stay as a fiancé(e) or proposed civil partner

293. The requirements for an extension of stay as a fiancé(e) or proposed civil partner are that:
(i) the applicant was admitted to the United Kingdom with a valid United Kingdom entry clearance as a fiancé(e) or proposed civil partner; and
(ii) good cause is shown why the marriage or civil partnership did not take place within the initial period of leave granted under paragraph 291; and
(iii) there is satisfactory evidence that the marriage or civil partnership will take place at an early date; and
(iv) the requirements of paragraph 290(ii)-(vi) are met.

Extension of stay as a fiancé(e) or proposed civil partner

294. An extension of stay as a fiancé(e) or proposed civil partner may be granted for an appropriate period with a prohibition on employment to enable the marriage or civil partnership to take place provided the Secretary of State is satisfied that each of the requirements of paragraph 293 is met.

Refusal of extension of stay as a fiancé(e) or proposed civil partner

295. An extension of stay is to be refused if the Secretary of State is not satisfied that each of the requirements of paragraph 293 is met.

Leave to enter as the unmarried or same-sex partner of a person present and settled in the United Kingdom or being admitted on the same occasion for settlement

295AA. Nothing in these Rules shall be construed as permitting a person to be granted entry clearance, leave to enter or variation of leave as an unmarried or same-sex partner if either the applicant or the sponsor will aged under 18 on the date of arrival of the applicant in the United Kingdom or (as the case may be) on the date on which the leave to enter or variation of leave would be granted.

Requirements for leave to enter the United Kingdom with a view to settlement as the unmarried or same-sex partner of a person present and settled in the United Kingdom or being admitted on the same occasion for settlement

295A. The requirements to be met by a person seeking leave to enter the United Kingdom with a view to settlement as the unmarried or same-sex partner of a person present and settled in the United Kingdom or being admitted on the same occasion for settlement, are that:

(i)   (a)   the applicant is the unmarried or same-sex partner of a person present and settled in the United Kingdom or who is on the same occasion being admitted for settlement and the parties have been living together in a relationship akin to marriage or civil partnership which has subsisted for two years or more; or

       (b)   (i)   the applicant is the unmarried or same-sex partner of a person who has a right of abode in the United Kingdom or indefinite leave to enter or remain in the United Kingdom and is on the same occasion seeking admission to the United Kingdom for the purposes of settlement and the parties have been living together outside the United Kingdom in a relationship akin to marriage which has subsisted for 4 years or more; and

                (ii)   the applicant has sufficient knowledge of the English language and sufficient knowledge about life in the United Kingdom, unless he is under the age of 18 or aged 65 or over at the time he makes his application; and

(ii)   any previous marriage or civil partnership (or similar relationship) by either partner has permanently broken down; and

(iii)   the parties are not involved in a consanguineous relationship with one another; and

(iv)   DELETED

(v)   there will be adequate accommodation for the parties and any dependants without recourse to public funds in accommodation which they own or occupy exclusively; and

(vi)   the parties will be able to maintain themselves and any dependants adequately without recourse to public funds; and

(vii)   the parties intend to live together permanently; and

(viii)   the applicant holds a valid United Kingdom entry clearance for entry in this capacity.

For the purposes of this paragraph and paragraphs 295B–295I, a member of HM Forces serving overseas, or a permanent member of HM Diplomatic Service or a comparable UK-based staff member of the British Council on a tour of duty abroad, or a staff member of the Department for International Development who is a British Citizen or is settled in the United Kingdom, is to be regarded as present and settled in the United Kingdom.

Leave to enter the United Kingdom with a view to settlement as the unmarried or same-sex partner of a person present and settled in the United Kingdom or being admitted on the same occasion for settlement

295B. A person seeking leave to enter the United Kingdom as the unmarried or same-sex partner of a person present and settled in the United Kingdom or who is on the same occasion being admitted for settlement may:

    (a) in the case of a person within paragraph 295A(i)(a), be admitted for an initial period not exceeding 2 years, or

    (b) in the case of a person who meets both of the requirements in paragraph 295A(i)(b), be granted indefinite leave to enter, or

    (c) in the case of a person who meets the requirement in paragraph 295A(i)(b)(i), but not the requirement in paragraph 295A(i)(b)(ii) to have sufficient knowledge of the English language and about life in the United Kingdom, be admitted for an initial period not exceeding 2 years, in all cases provided the Immigration Officer is satisfied that each of the relevant requirements of paragraph 295A is met.

Refusal of leave to enter the United Kingdom with a view to settlement as the unmarried or same-sex partner of a person present and settled in the United Kingdom or being admitted on the same occasion for settlement

295C. Leave to enter the United Kingdom with a view to settlement as the unmarried or same-sex partner of a person present and settled in the United Kingdom or being admitted on the same occasion for settlement, is to be refused if the Immigration Officer is not satisfied that each of the requirements of paragraph 295A is met.

Leave to remain as the unmarried or same-sex partner of a person present and settled in the United Kingdom

Requirements for leave to remain as the unmarried or same-sex partner of a person present and settled in the United Kingdom

295D. The requirements to be met by a person seeking leave to remain as the unmarried or same-sex partner of a person present and settled in the United Kingdom are that:

    (i) the applicant has limited leave to remain in the United Kingdom which was given in accordance with any of the provisions of these Rules; and

    (ii) any previous marriage or civil partnership (or similar relationship) by either partner has permanently broken down; and

    (iii) the applicant is the unmarried or same-sex partner of a person who is present and settled in the United Kingdom; and

    (iv) the applicant has not remained in breach of the immigration laws; and

    (v) the parties are not involved in a consanguineous relationship with one another; and

    (vi) the parties have been living together in a relationship akin to marriage or civil partnership which has subsisted for two years or more; and

    (vii) the parties' relationship pre-dates any decision to deport the applicant, recommend him for deportation, give him notice under Section 6(2) of the Immigration Act 1971, or give directions for his removal under section 10 of the Immigration and Asylum Act 1999; and

    (viii) there will be adequate accommodation for the parties and any dependants without recourse to public funds in accommodation which they own or occupy exclusively; and

    (ix) the parties will be able to maintain themselves and any dependants adequately without recourse to public funds; and

    (x) the parties intend to live together permanently.

Leave to remain as the unmarried or same-sex partner of a person present and settled in the United Kingdom

295E. Leave to remain as the unmarried or same-sex partner of a person present and settled in the United Kingdom may be granted for a period of 2 years in the first instance provided that the Secretary of State is satisfied that each of the requirements of paragraph 295D are met.

Refusal of leave to remain as the unmarried or same-sex partner of a person present and settled in the United Kingdom

295F. Leave to remain as the unmarried or same-sex partner of a person present and settled in the United Kingdom is to be refused if the Secretary of State is not satisfied that each of the requirements of paragraph 295D is met.

Indefinite leave to remain as the unmarried or same-sex partner of a person present and settled in the United Kingdom

Requirements for indefinite leave to remain as the unmarried or same-sex partner of a person present and settled in the United Kingdom

295G. The requirements to be met by a person seeking indefinite leave to remain as the unmarried or same-sex partner of a person present and settled in the United Kingdom are that:

(i) the applicant was admitted to the United Kingdom or given an extension of stay for a period of 2 years in accordance with paragraphs 295AA to 295F of these Rules and has completed a period of 2 years as the unmarried or same-sex partner of a person present and settled here; or

(i) (a) was admitted to the United Kingdom in accordance with leave granted under paragraph 295B(c) of these rules; and

(ii) the applicant is still the unmarried or same-sex partner of the person he was admitted or granted an extension of stay to join and the relationship is still subsisting; and

(iii) each of the parties intends to live permanently with the other as his partner; and

(iv) there will be adequate accommodation for the parties and any dependants without recourse to public funds in accommodation which they own or occupy exclusively; and

(v) the parties will be able to maintain themselves and any dependants adequately without recourse to public funds; and

(vi) he has sufficient knowledge of the English language and sufficient knowledge about life in the United Kingdom, unless he is under the age of 18 or aged 65 or over at the time he makes his application.

Indefinite leave to remain as the unmarried or same-sex partner of a person present and settled in the United Kingdom

295H. Indefinite leave to remain as the unmarried or same-sex partner of a person present and settled in the United Kingdom may be granted provided that the Secretary of State is satisfied that each of the requirements of paragraph 295G is met.

Refusal of indefinite leave to remain as the unmarried or same-sex partner of a person present and settled in the United Kingdom

295I. Indefinite leave to remain as the unmarried or same-sex partner of a person present and settled in the United Kingdom is to be refused if the Secretary of State is not satisfied that each of the requirements of paragraph 295G is met.

Leave to enter or remain as the unmarried or same-sex partner of a person with limited leave to enter or remain in the United Kingdom under paragraphs 128–193; 200–239; or 263–270

Requirements for leave to enter or remain as the unmarried or same-sex partner of a person with limited leave to enter or remain in the United Kingdom under paragraphs 128–193; 200–239; or 263–270

295J. The requirements to be met by a person seeking leave to enter or remain as the unmarried or same-sex partner of a person with limited leave to enter or remain in the United Kingdom under paragraphs 128–193; 200–239; or 263–270; are that:
  (i) the applicant is the unmarried or same-sex partner of a person who has limited leave to enter or remain in the United Kingdom under paragraphs 128–193; 200–239; or 263–270; and
  (ii) any previous marriage or civil partnership (or similar relationship) by either partner has permanently broken down; and
  (iii) the parties are not involved in a consanguineous relationship with one another; and
  (iv) the parties have been living together in a relationship akin to marriage which has subsisted for 2 years or more; and
  (v) each of the parties intends to live with the other as his partner during the applicant's stay; and
  (vi) there will be adequate accommodation for the parties and any dependants without recourse to public funds in accommodation which they own or occupy exclusively; and
  (vii) the parties will be able to maintain themselves and any dependants adequately without recourse to public funds; and
  (viii) the applicant does not intend to stay in the United Kingdom beyond any period of leave granted to his partner; and
  (ix) if seeking leave to enter, the applicant holds a valid United Kingdom entry clearance for entry in this capacity or, if seeking leave to remain, was admitted with a valid United Kingdom entry clearance for entry in this capacity.

Leave to enter or remain as the unmarried or same-sex partner of a person with limited leave to enter or remain in the United Kingdom under paragraphs 128–193; 200–239; or 263–270

295K. Leave to enter as the unmarried or same-sex partner of a person with limited leave to enter or remain in the United Kingdom under paragraphs 128–193; 200–239; or 263–270; may be granted provided that a valid United Kingdom entry clearance for entry in this capacity is produced to the Immigration Officer on arrival. Leave to remain as the unmarried or same-sex partner of a person with limited leave to enter or remain in the United Kingdom under paragraphs 128–193; 200–239; or 263–270; may be granted provided that the Secretary of State is satisfied that each of the requirements of paragraph 295J is met.

Refusal of leave to enter or remain as the unmarried or same-sex partner of a person with limited leave to enter or remain in the United Kingdom under paragraphs 128–193; 200–239; or 263–270

295L. Leave to enter as the unmarried or same-sex partner of a person with limited leave to enter or remain in the United Kingdom under paragraphs 128–193; 200–239; or 263–270; is to be refused if a valid United Kingdom entry clearance for entry in this capacity is not produced to the Immigration Officer on arrival. Leave to remain as the unmarried or same-sex partner of a person with limited leave to enter or remain in the United Kingdom under paragraphs 128–193; 200–239; or 263–270; is to be refused if the Secretary of State is not satisfied that each of the requirements of paragraph 295J is met.

Indefinite leave to remain for the bereaved unmarried or same-sex partner of a person present and settled in the United Kingdom

Requirements for indefinite leave to remain for the bereaved unmarried or same-sex partner of a person present and settled in the United Kingdom

295M. The requirements to be met by a person seeking indefinite leave to remain as the bereaved unmarried or same-sex partner of a person present and settled in the United Kingdom, are that:

  (i) the applicant was admitted to the United Kingdom or given an extension of stay for a period of 2 years in accordance with paragraphs 295AA to 295F of these Rules as the unmarried or same-sex partner of a person present and settled in the United Kingdom; and

  (ii) the person whom the applicant was admitted or granted an extension of stay to join died during that 2 year period; and

  (iii) the applicant was still the unmarried or same-sex partner of the person he was admitted or granted an extension of stay to join at the time of the death; and

  (iv) each of the parties intended to live permanently with the other as his partner and the relationship was subsisting at the time of the death.

Indefinite leave to remain for the bereaved unmarried or same-sex partner of a person present and settled in the United Kingdom

295N. Indefinite leave to remain for the bereaved unmarried or same-sex partner of a person present and settled in the United Kingdom, may be granted provided that the Secretary of State is satisfied that each of the requirements of paragraph 295M is met.

Refusal of indefinite leave to remain for the bereaved unmarried or same-sex partner of a person present and settled in the United Kingdom

295O. Indefinite leave to remain for the bereaved unmarried or same-sex partner of a person present and settled in the United Kingdom, is to be refused if the Secretary of State is not satisfied that each of the requirements of paragraph 295M is met.

Section 2

Children

296. Nothing in these Rules shall be construed as permitting a child to be granted entry clearance, leave to enter or remain, or variation of leave where his parent is party to a polygamous marriage and any application by that parent for admission or leave to remain for settlement or with a view to settlement would be refused pursuant to paragraphs 278 or 278A.

Leave to enter or remain in the United Kingdom as the child of a parent, parents or a relative present and settled or being admitted for settlement in the United Kingdom

Requirements for indefinite leave to enter the United Kingdom as the child of a parent, parents or a relative present and settled or being admitted for settlement in the United Kingdom

297. The requirements to be met by a person seeking indefinite leave to enter the United Kingdom as the child of a parent, parents or a relative present and settled or being admitted for settlement in the United Kingdom are that he:

  (i) is seeking leave to enter to accompany or join a parent, parents or a relative in one of the following circumstances:

(a) both parents are present and settled in the United Kingdom; or
(b) both parents are being admitted on the same occasion for settlement; or
(c) one parent is present and settled in the United Kingdom and the other is being admitted on the same occasion for settlement; or
(d) one parent is present and settled in the United Kingdom or being admitted on the same occasion for settlement and the other parent is dead; or
(e) one parent is present and settled in the United Kingdom or being admitted on the same occasion for settlement and has had sole responsibility for the child's upbringing; or
(f) one parent or a relative is present and settled in the United Kingdom or being admitted on the same occasion for settlement and there are serious and compelling family or other considerations which make exclusion of the child undesirable and suitable arrangements have been made for the child's care; and

(ii) is under the age of 18; and
(iii) is not leading an independent life, is unmarried and is not a civil partner, and has not formed an independent family unit; and
(iv) can, and will, be accommodated adequately by the parent, parents or relative the child is seeking to join without recourse to public funds in accommodation which the parent, parents or relative the child is seeking to join, own or occupy exclusively; and
(v) can, and will, be maintained adequately by the parent, parents, or relative the child is seeking to join, without recourse to public funds; and
(vi) holds a valid United Kingdom entry clearance for entry in this capacity.

Requirements for indefinite leave to remain in the United Kingdom as the child of a parent, parents or a relative present and settled or being admitted for settlement in the United Kingdom

298. The requirements to be met by a person seeking indefinite leave to remain in the United Kingdom as the child of a parent, parents or a relative present and settled in the United Kingdom are that he:

(i) is seeking to remain with a parent, parents or a relative in one of the following circumstances:
(a) both parents are present and settled in the United Kingdom; or
(b) one parent is present and settled in the United Kingdom and the other parent is dead; or
(c) one parent is present and settled in the United Kingdom and has had sole responsibility for the child's upbringing; or
(d) one parent or a relative is present and settled in the United Kingdom and there are serious and compelling family or other considerations which make exclusion of the child undesirable and suitable arrangements have been made for the child's care; and

(ii) has limited leave to enter or remain in the United Kingdom, and
(a) is under the age of 18; or
(b) was given leave to enter or remain with a view to settlement under paragraph 302; and

(iii) is not leading an independent life, is unmarried and is not a civil partner, and has not formed an independent family unit; and
(iv) can, and will, be accommodated adequately by the parent, parents or relative the child was admitted to join, without recourse to public funds in accommodation which the parent, parents or relative the child was admitted to join, own or occupy exclusively; and

(v) can, and will, be maintained adequately by the parent, parents or relative the child was admitted to join, without recourse to public funds.

Indefinite leave to enter or remain in the United Kingdom as the child of a parent, parents or a relative present and settled or being admitted for settlement in the United Kingdom

299. Indefinite leave to enter the United Kingdom as the child of a parent, parents or a relative present and settled or being admitted for settlement in the United Kingdom may be granted provided a valid United Kingdom entry clearance for entry in this capacity is produced to the Immigration Officer on arrival. Indefinite leave to remain in the United Kingdom as the child of a parent, parents or a relative present and settled in the United Kingdom may be granted provided the Secretary of State is satisfied that each of the requirements of paragraph 298 is met.

Refusal of indefinite leave to enter or remain in the United Kingdom as the child of a parent, parents or a relative present and settled or being admitted for settlement in the United Kingdom

300. Indefinite leave to enter the United Kingdom as the child of a parent, parents or a relative present and settled or being admitted for settlement in the United Kingdom is to be refused if a valid United Kingdom entry clearance for entry in this capacity is not produced to the Immigration Officer on arrival. Indefinite leave to remain in the United Kingdom as the child of a parent, parents or a relative present and settled in the United Kingdom is to be refused if the Secretary of State is not satisfied that each of the requirements of paragraph 298 is met.

Requirements for limited leave to enter or remain in the United Kingdom with a view to settlement as the child of a parent or parents given limited leave to enter or remain in the United Kingdom with a view to settlement

301. The requirements to be met by a person seeking limited leave to enter or remain in the United Kingdom with a view to settlement as the child of a parent or parents given limited leave to enter or remain in the United Kingdom with a view to settlement are that he:
    (i) is seeking leave to enter to accompany or join or remain with a parent or parents in one of the following circumstances:
        (a) one parent is present and settled in the United Kingdom or being admitted on the same occasion for settlement and the other parent is being or has been given limited leave to enter or remain in the United Kingdom with a view to settlement; or
        (b) one parent is being or has been given limited leave to enter or remain in the United Kingdom with a view to settlement and has had sole responsibility for the child's upbringing; or
        (c) one parent is being or has been given limited leave to enter or remain in the United Kingdom with a view to settlement and there are serious and compelling family or other considerations which make exclusion of the child undesirable and suitable arrangements have been made for the child's care; and
    (ii) is under the age of 18; and
    (iii) is not leading an independent life, is unmarried and is not a civil partner, and has not formed an independent family unit; and
    (iv) can, and will, be accommodated adequately without recourse to public funds, in accommodation which the parent or parents own or occupy exclusively; and
    (iva) can, and will, be maintained adequately by the parent or parents without recourse to public funds; and

(v) (where an application is made for limited leave to remain with a view to settlement) has limited leave to enter or remain in the United Kingdom; and

(vi) if seeking leave to enter, holds a valid United Kingdom entry clearance for entry in this capacity or, if seeking leave to remain, was admitted with a valid United Kingdom entry clearance for entry in this capacity.

Limited leave to enter or remain in the United Kingdom with a view to settlement as the child of a parent or parents given limited leave to enter or remain in the United Kingdom with a view to settlement

302. A person seeking limited leave to enter the United Kingdom with a view to settlement as the child of a parent or parents given limited leave to enter or remain in the United Kingdom with a view to settlement may be admitted for a period not exceeding 24 months provided he is able, on arrival, to produce to the Immigration Officer a valid United Kingdom entry clearance for entry in this capacity. A person seeking limited leave to remain in the United Kingdom with a view to settlement as the child of a parent or parents given limited leave to enter or remain in the United Kingdom with a view to settlement may be given limited leave to remain for a period not exceeding 24 months provided the Secretary of State is satisfied that each of the requirements of paragraph 301(i)–(v) is met.

Refusal of limited leave to enter or remain in the United Kingdom with a view to settlement as the child of a parent or parents given limited leave to enter or remain in the United Kingdom with a view to settlement

303. Limited leave to enter the United Kingdom with a view to settlement as the child of a parent or parents given limited leave to enter or remain in the United Kingdom with a view to settlement is to be refused if a valid United Kingdom entry clearance for entry in this capacity is not produced to the Immigration Officer on arrival. Limited leave to remain in the United Kingdom with a view to settlement as the child of a parent or parents given limited leave to enter or remain in the United Kingdom with a view to settlement is to be refused if the Secretary of State is not satisfied that each of the requirements of paragraph 301(i)–(v) is met.

Leave to enter and extension of stay in the United Kingdom as the child of a parent who is being, or has been admitted to the United Kingdom as a fiancé(e) or proposed civil partner

Requirements for limited leave to enter the United Kingdom as the child of a fiancé(e) or proposed civil partner

303A. The requirements to be met by a person seeking limited leave to enter the United Kingdom as the child of a fiancé(e) or proposed civil partner, are that:

(i) he is seeking to accompany or join a parent who is, on the same occasion that the child seeks admission, being admitted as a fiancé(e) or proposed civil partner, or who has been admitted as a fiancé(e) or proposed civil partner; and

(ii) he is under the age of 18; and

(iii) he is not leading an independent life, is unmarried and is not a civil partner, and has not formed an independent family unit; and

(iv) he can and will be maintained and accommodated adequately without recourse to public funds with the parent admitted or being admitted as a fiancé(e) or proposed civil partner; and

(v) there are serious and compelling family or other considerations which make the child's exclusion undesirable, that suitable arrangements have been made for his care in the United Kingdom, and there is no other person outside the United Kingdom who could reasonably be expected to care for him; and

(vi) he holds a valid United Kingdom entry clearance for entry in this capacity.

Limited leave to enter the United Kingdom as the child of a parent who is being, or has been admitted to the United Kingdom as a fiancé(e) or proposed civil partner

303B. A person seeking limited leave to enter the United Kingdom as the child of a fiancé(e) or proposed civil partner, may be granted limited leave to enter the United Kingdom for a period not in excess of that granted to the fiancé(e) or proposed civil partner, provided that a valid United Kingdom entry clearance for entry in this capacity is produced to the Immigration Officer on arrival. Where the period of limited leave granted to a fiancé(e) or proposed civil partner will expire in more than 6 months, a person seeking limited leave to enter as the child of the fiancé(e) or proposed civil partner should be granted leave for a period not exceeding six months.

Refusal of limited leave to enter the United Kingdom as the child of a parent who is being, or has been admitted to the United Kingdom as a fiancé(e) or proposed civil partner

303C. Limited leave to enter the United Kingdom as the child of a fiancé(e) or proposed civil partner, is to be refused if a valid United Kingdom entry clearance for entry in this capacity is not produced to the Immigration Officer on arrival.

Requirements for an extension of stay in the United Kingdom as the child of a fiancé(e) or proposed civil partner

303D. The requirements to be met by a person seeking an extension of stay in the United Kingdom as the child of a fiancé(e) or proposed civil partner are that:
  (i) the applicant was admitted with a valid United Kingdom entry clearance as the child of a fiancé(e) or proposed civil partner; and
  (ii) the applicant is the child of a parent who has been granted limited leave to enter, or an extension of stay, as a fiancé(e) or proposed civil partner; and
  (iii) the requirements of paragraph 303A(ii)–(v) are met.

Extension of stay in the United Kingdom as the child of a fiancé(e) or proposed civil partner

303E. An extension of stay as the child of a fiancé(e) or proposed civil partner may be granted provided that the Secretary of State is satisfied that each of the requirements of paragraph 303D is met.

Refusal of an extension of stay in the United Kingdom as the child of a fiancé(e) or proposed civil partner

303F. An extension of stay as the child of a fiancé(e) or proposed civil partner is to be refused if the Secretary of State is not satisfied that each of the requirements of paragraph 303D is met.

Children born in the United Kingdom who are not British citizens

304. This paragraph and paragraphs 305–309 apply only to dependent children under 18 years of age who are unmarried and are not civil partners and who were born in the United Kingdom on or after 1 January 1983 (when the British Nationality Act 1981 came into force) but who, because neither of their parents was a British Citizen or settled in the United Kingdom at the time of their birth, are not British Citizens and are therefore subject to immigration control. Such a child requires leave to enter where admission to the United Kingdom is sought, and leave to remain where permission is sought for the child to be allowed to stay in the United Kingdom. If he qualifies for entry clearance, leave to enter or leave to remain under any other part of these Rules, a child who was born in the United Kingdom but is not a British

Citizen may be granted entry clearance, leave to enter or leave to remain in accordance with the provisions of that other part.

Requirements for leave to enter or remain in the United Kingdom as the child of a parent or parents given leave to enter or remain in the United Kingdom

305. The requirements to be met by a child born in the United Kingdom who is not a British Citizen who seeks leave to enter or remain in the United Kingdom as the child of a parent or parents given leave to enter or remain in the United Kingdom are that he:
    (i) (a) is accompanying or seeking to join or remain with a parent or parents who have, or are given, leave to enter or remain in the United Kingdom; or
        (b) is accompanying or seeking to join or remain with a parent or parents one of whom is a British Citizen or has the right of abode in the United Kingdom; or
        (c) is a child in respect of whom the parental rights and duties are vested solely in a local authority; and
    (ii) is under the age of 18; and
    (iii) was born in the United Kingdom; and
    (iv) is not leading an independent life, is unmarried and is not a civil partner, and has not formed an independent family unit; and
    (v) (where an application is made for leave to enter) has not been away from the United Kingdom for more than 2 years.

Leave to enter or remain in the United Kingdom

306. A child born in the United Kingdom who is not a British Citizen and who requires leave to enter or remain in the circumstances set out in paragraph 304 may be given leave to enter for the same period as his parent or parents where paragraph 305(i)(a) applies, provided the Immigration Officer is satisfied that each of the requirements of paragraph 305(ii)–(v) is met. Where leave to remain is sought, the child may be granted leave to remain for the same period as his parent or parents where paragraph 305(i)(a) applies, provided the Secretary of State is satisfied that each of the requirements of paragraph 305(ii)–(iv) is met. Where the parent or parents have or are given periods of leave of different duration, the child may be given leave to whichever period is longer except that if the parents are living apart the child should be given leave for the same period as the parent who has day to day responsibility for him.

307. If a child does not qualify for leave to enter or remain because neither of his parents has a current leave, (and neither of them is a British Citizen or has the right of abode), he will normally be refused leave to enter or remain, even if each of the requirements of paragraph 305(ii)–(v) has been satisfied. However, he may be granted leave to enter or remain for a period not exceeding 3 months if both of his parents are in the United Kingdom and it appears unlikely that they will be removed in the immediate future, and there is no other person outside the United Kingdom who could reasonably be expected to care for him.

308. A child born in the United Kingdom who is not a British Citizen and who requires leave to enter or remain in the United Kingdom in the circumstances set out in paragraph 304 may be given indefinite leave to enter where paragraph 305(i)(b) or (i)(c) applies provided the Immigration Officer is satisfied that each of the requirements of paragraph 305(ii)–(v) is met. Where an application is for leave to remain, such a child may be granted indefinite leave to remain where paragraph 305(i)(b) or (i)(c) applies, provided the Secretary of State is satisfied that each of the requirements of paragraph 305(ii)–(iv) is met.

Refusal of leave to enter or remain in the United Kingdom

309. Leave to enter the United Kingdom where the circumstances set out in paragraph 304 apply is to be refused if the Immigration Officer is not satisfied that each of the requirements of paragraph 305 is met. Leave to remain for such a child is to be refused if the Secretary of State is not satisfied that each of the requirements of paragraph 305(i)–(iv) is met.

Adopted children

309A. For the purposes of adoption under paragraphs 310–316C a de facto adoption shall be regarded as having taken place if:
   (a) at the time immediately preceding the making of the application for entry clearance under these Rules the adoptive parent or parents have been living abroad (in applications involving two parents both must have lived abroad together) for at least a period of time equal to the first period mentioned in sub-paragraph (b)(i) and must have cared for the child for at least a period of time equal to the second period material in that sub-paragraph; and
   (b) during their time abroad, the adoptive parent or parents have:
      (i) lived together for a minimum period of 18 months, of which the 12 months immediately preceding the application for entry clearance must have been spent living together with the child; and
      (ii) have assumed the role of the child's parents, since the beginning of the 18 month period, so that there has been a genuine transfer of parental responsibility.

Requirements for indefinite leave to enter the United Kingdom as the adopted child of a parent or parents present and settled or being admitted for settlement in the United Kingdom

310. The requirements to be met in the case of a child seeking indefinite leave to enter the United Kingdom as the adopted child of a parent or parents present and settled or being admitted for settlement in the United Kingdom are that he:
   (i) is seeking leave to enter to accompany or join an adoptive parent or parents in one of the following circumstances;
      (a) both parents are present and settled in the United Kingdom; or
      (b) both parents are being admitted on the same occasion for settlement; or
      (c) one parent is present and settled in the United Kingdom and the other is being admitted on the same occasion for settlement; or
      (d) one parent is present and settled in the United Kingdom or being admitted on the same occasion for settlement and the other parent is dead; or
      (e) one parent is present and settled in the United Kingdom or being admitted on the same occasion for settlement and has had sole responsibility for the child's upbringing; or
      (f) one parent is present and settled in the United Kingdom or being admitted on the same occasion for settlement and there are serious and compelling family or other considerations which make exclusion of the child undesirable and suitable arrangements have been made for the child's care; or
      (g) in the case of a de facto adoption one parent has a right of abode in the United Kingdom or indefinite leave to enter or remain in the United Kingdom and is seeking admission to the United Kingdom on the same occasion for the purposes of settlement; and
   (ii) is under the age of 18; and

(iii) is not leading an independent life, is unmarried and is not a civil partner, and has not formed an independent family unit; and

(iv) can, and will, be accommodated and maintained adequately without recourse to public funds in accommodation which the adoptive parent or parents own or occupy exclusively; and

(v) DELETED

(vi) (a) was adopted in accordance with a decision taken by the competent administrative authority or court in his country of origin or the country in which he is resident, being a country whose adoption orders are recognised by the United Kingdom; or

(b) is the subject of a de facto adoption; and

(vii) was adopted at a time when:

(a) both adoptive parents were resident together abroad; or

(b) either or both adoptive parents were settled in the United Kingdom; and

(viii) has the same rights and obligations as any other child of the adoptive parent's or parents' family; and

(ix) was adopted due to the inability of the original parent(s) or current carer(s) to care for him and there has been a genuine transfer of parental responsibility to the adoptive parents; and

(x) has lost or broken his ties with his family of origin; and

(xi) was adopted, but the adoption is not one of convenience arranged to facilitate his admission to or remaining in the United Kingdom; and

(xii) holds a valid United Kingdom entry clearance for entry in this capacity.

Requirements for indefinite leave to remain in the United Kingdom as the adopted child of a parent or parents present and settled in the United Kingdom

311. The requirements to be met in the case of a child seeking indefinite leave to remain in the United Kingdom as the adopted child of a parent or parents present and settled in the United Kingdom are that he:

(i) is seeking to remain with an adoptive parent or parents in one of the following circumstances:

(a) both parents are present and settled in the United Kingdom; or

(b) one parent is present and settled in the United Kingdom and the other parent is dead; or

(c) one parent is present and settled in the United Kingdom and has had sole responsibility for the child's upbringing; or

(d) one parent is present and settled in the United Kingdom and there are serious and compelling family or other considerations which make exclusion of the child undesirable and suitable arrangements have been made for the child's care; or

(e) in the case of a de facto adoption one parent has a right of abode in the United Kingdom or indefinite leave to enter or remain in the United Kingdom and is seeking admission to the United Kingdom on the same occasion for the purpose of settlement; and

(ii) has limited leave to enter or remain in the United Kingdom, and

(a) is under the age of 18; or

(b) was given leave to enter or remain with a view to settlement under paragraph 315 or paragraph 316B; and

(iii) is not leading an independent life, is unmarried, and has not formed an independent family unit; and

(iv) can, and will, be accommodated and maintained adequately without recourse to public funds in accommodation which the adoptive parent or parents own or occupy exclusively; and
(v) DELETED
(vi) (a) was adopted in accordance with a decision taken by the competent administrative authority or court in his country of origin or the country in which he is resident, being a country whose adoption orders are recognised by the United Kingdom; or
(b) is the subject of a de facto adoption; and
(vii) was adopted at a time when:
(a) both adoptive parents were resident together abroad; or
(b) either or both adoptive parents were settled in the United Kingdom; and
(viii) has the same rights and obligations as any other child of the adoptive parent's or parents' family; and
(ix) was adopted due to the inability of the original parent(s) or current carer(s) to care for him and there has been a genuine transfer of parental responsibility to the adoptive parents; and
(x) has lost or broken his ties with his family of origin; and
(xi) was adopted, but the adoption is not one of convenience arranged to facilitate his admission to or remaining in the United Kingdom.

Section 3

Indefinite leave to enter or remain in the United Kingdom as the adopted child of a parent or parents present and settled or being admitted for settlement in the United Kingdom

312. Indefinite leave to enter the United Kingdom as the adopted child of a parent or parents present and settled or being admitted for settlement in the United Kingdom may be granted provided a valid United Kingdom entry clearance for entry in this capacity is produced to the Immigration Officer on arrival. Indefinite leave to remain in the United Kingdom as the adopted child of a parent or parents present and settled in the United Kingdom may be granted provided the Secretary of State is satisfied that each of the requirements of paragraph 311 is met.

Refusal of indefinite leave to enter or remain in the United Kingdom as the adopted child of a parent or parents present and settled or being admitted for settlement in the United Kingdom

313. Indefinite leave to enter the United Kingdom as the adopted child of a parent or parents present and settled or being admitted for settlement in the United Kingdom is to be refused if a valid United Kingdom entry clearance for entry in this capacity is not produced to the Immigration Officer on arrival. Indefinite leave to remain in the United Kingdom as the adopted child of a parent or parents present and settled in the United Kingdom is to be refused if the Secretary of State is not satisfied that each of the requirements of paragraph 311 is met.

Requirements for limited leave to enter or remain in the United Kingdom with a view to settlement as the adopted child of a parent or parents given limited leave to enter or remain in the United Kingdom with a view to settlement

314. The requirements to be met in the case of a child seeking limited leave to enter or remain in the United Kingdom with a view to settlement as the adopted child of a parent or parents given limited leave to enter or remain in the United Kingdom with a view to settlement are that he:

(i) is seeking leave to enter to accompany or join or remain with a parent or parents in one of the following circumstances:
   (a) one parent is present and settled in the United Kingdom or being admitted on the same occasion for settlement and the other parent is being or has been given limited leave to enter or remain in the United Kingdom with a view to settlement; or
   (b) one parent is being or has been given limited leave to enter or remain in the United Kingdom with a view to settlement and has had sole responsibility for the child's upbringing; or
   (c) one parent is being or has been given limited leave to enter or remain in the United Kingdom with a view to settlement and there are serious and compelling family or other considerations which make exclusion of the child undesirable and suitable arrangements have been made for the child's care; or
   (d) in the case of a de facto adoption one parent has a right of abode in the United Kingdom or indefinite leave to enter or remain in the United Kingdom and is seeking admission to the United Kingdom on the same occasion for the purpose of settlement; and
(ii) is under the age of 18; and
(iii) is not leading an independent life, is unmarried, and has not formed an independent family unit; and
(iv) can, and will, be accommodated and maintained adequately without recourse to public funds in accommodation which the adoptive parent or parents own or occupy exclusively; and
(v) (a) was adopted in accordance with a decision taken by the competent administrative authority or court in his country of origin or the country in which he is resident, being a country whose adoption orders are recognised by the United Kingdom; or
   (b) is the subject of a de facto adoption; and
(vi) was adopted at a time when:
   (a) both adoptive parents were resident together abroad; or
   (b) either or both adoptive parents were settled in the United Kingdom; and
(vii) has the same rights and obligations as any other child of the adoptive parent's or parents' family; and
(viii) was adopted due to the inability of the original parent(s) or current carer(s) to care for him and there has been a genuine transfer of parental responsibility to the adoptive parents; and
(ix) has lost or broken his ties with his family of origin; and
(x) was adopted, but the adoption is not one of convenience arranged to facilitate his admission to the United Kingdom; and
(xi) (where an application is made for limited leave to remain with a view to settlement) has limited leave to enter or remain in the United Kingdom; and
(xii) if seeking leave to enter, holds a valid United Kingdom entry clearance for entry in this capacity.

Limited leave to enter or remain in the United Kingdom with a view to settlement as the adopted child of a parent or parents given limited leave to enter or remain in the United Kingdom with a view to settlement

315. A person seeking limited leave to enter the United Kingdom with a view to settlement as the adopted child of a parent or parents given limited leave to enter or remain in the United Kingdom with a view to settlement may be admitted for a period not exceeding 12 months provided he is able, on arrival, to produce to the Immigration Officer a valid United Kingdom entry clearance for entry in this

capacity. A person seeking limited leave to remain in the United Kingdom with a view to settlement as the adopted child of a parent or parents given limited leave to enter or remain in the United Kingdom with a view to settlement may be granted limited leave for a period not exceeding 12 months provided the Secretary of State is satisfied that each of the requirements of paragraph 314(i)–(xi) is met.

Refusal of limited leave to enter or remain in the United Kingdom with a view to settlement as the adopted child of a parent or parents given limited leave to enter or remain in the United Kingdom with a view to settlement

316. Limited leave to enter the United Kingdom with a view to settlement as the adopted child of a parent or parents given limited leave to enter or remain in the United Kingdom with a view to settlement is to be refused if a valid United Kingdom entry clearance for entry in this capacity is not produced to the Immigration Officer on arrival. Limited leave to remain in the United Kingdom with a view to settlement as the adopted child of a parent or parents given limited leave to enter or remain in the United Kingdom with a view to settlement is to be refused if the Secretary of State is not satisfied that each of the requirements of paragraph 314(i)–(xi) is met.

Requirements for limited leave to enter the United Kingdom with a view to settlement as a child for adoption

316A. The requirements to be satisfied in the case of a child seeking limited leave to enter the United Kingdom for the purpose of being adopted (which, for the avoidance of doubt, does not include a de facto adoption) in the United Kingdom are that he:

  (i) is seeking limited leave to enter to accompany or join a person or persons who wish to adopt him in the United Kingdom (the 'prospective parent(s)'), in one of the following circumstances:

   (a) both prospective parents are present and settled in the United Kingdom; or

   (b) both prospective parents are being admitted for settlement on the same occasion that the child is seeking admission; or

   (c) one prospective parent is present and settled in the United Kingdom and the other is being admitted for settlement on the same occasion that the child is seeking admission; or

   (d) one prospective parent is present and settled in the United Kingdom and the other is being given limited leave to enter or remain in the United Kingdom with a view to settlement on the same occasion that the child is seeking admission, or has previously been given such leave; or

   (e) one prospective parent is being admitted for settlement on the same occasion that the other is being granted limited leave to enter with a view to settlement, which is also on the same occasion that the child is seeking admission; or

   (f) one prospective parent is present and settled in the United Kingdom or is being admitted for settlement on the same occasion that the child is seeking admission, and has had sole responsibility for the child's upbringing; or

   (g) one prospective parent is present and settled in the United Kingdom or is being admitted for settlement on the same occasion that the child is seeking admission, and there are serious and compelling family or other considerations which would make the child's exclusion undesirable, and suitable arrangements have been made for the child's care; and

  (ii) is under the age of 18; and

(iii) is not leading an independent life, is unmarried and is not a civil partner, and has not formed an independent family unit; and

(iv) can, and will, be maintained and accommodated adequately without recourse to public funds in accommodation which the prospective parent or parents own or occupy exclusively; and

(v) will have the same rights and obligations as any other child of the marriage or civil partnership; and

(vi) is being adopted due to the inability of the original parent(s) or current carer(s) (or those looking after him immediately prior to him being physically transferred to his prospective parent or parents) to care for him, and there has been a genuine transfer of parental responsibility to the prospective parent or parents; and

(vii) has lost or broken or intends to lose or break his ties with his family of origin; and

(viii) will be adopted in the United Kingdom by his prospective parent or parents in accordance with the law relating to adoption in the United Kingdom, but the proposed adoption is not one of convenience arranged to facilitate his admission to the United Kingdom.

Limited leave to enter the United Kingdom with a view to settlement as a child for adoption

316B. A person seeking limited leave to enter the United Kingdom with a view to settlement as a child for adoption may be admitted for a period not exceeding 24 months provided he is able, on arrival, to produce to the Immigration Officer a valid United Kingdom entry clearance for entry in this capacity.

Refusal of limited leave to enter the United Kingdom with a view to settlement as a child for adoption

316C. Limited leave to enter the United Kingdom with a view to settlement as a child for adoption is to be refused if a valid United Kingdom entry clearance for entry in this capacity is not produced to the Immigration Officer on arrival.

Requirements for limited leave to enter the United Kingdom with a view to settlement as a child for adoption under the Hague Convention

316D. The requirements to be satisfied in the case of a child seeking limited leave to enter the United Kingdom for the purpose of being adopted in the United Kingdom under the Hague Convention are that he:

(i) is seeking limited leave to enter to accompany one or two people each of whom are habitually resident in the United Kingdom and who wish to adopt him under the Hague Convention ('the prospective parents');

(ii) is the subject of an agreement made under Article 17(c) of the Hague Convention; and

(iii) has been entrusted to the prospective parents by the competent administrative authority of the country from which he is coming to the United Kingdom for adoption under the Hague Convention; and

(iv) is under the age of 18; and

(v) can, and will, be maintained and accommodated adequately without recourse to public funds in accommodation which the prospective parent or parents own or occupy exclusively; and

(vi) holds a valid United Kingdom entry clearance for entry in this capacity.

Limited leave to enter the United Kingdom with a view to settlement as a child for adoption under the Hague Convention

316E. A person seeking limited leave to enter the United Kingdom with a view to settlement as a child for adoption under the Hague Convention may be admitted for a period not exceeding 24 months provided he is able, on arrival, to produce to the Immigration Officer a valid United Kingdom entry clearance for entry in this capacity.

Refusal of limited leave to enter the United Kingdom with a view to settlement as a child for adoption under the Hague Convention

316F. Limited leave to enter the United Kingdom with a view to settlement as a child for adoption under the Hague Convention is to be refused if a valid United Kingdom entry clearance for entry in this capacity is not produced to the Immigration Officer on arrival.

Parents, grandparents and other dependent relatives of persons present and settled in the United Kingdom

Requirements for indefinite leave to enter or remain in the United Kingdom as the parent, grandparent or other dependent relative of a person present and settled in the United Kingdom

317. The requirements to be met by a person seeking indefinite leave to enter or remain in the United Kingdom as the parent, grandparent or other dependent relative of a person present and settled in the United Kingdom are that the person:
    (i) is related to a person present and settled in the United Kingdom in one of the following ways:
        (a) mother or grandmother who is a widow aged 65 years or over; or
        (b) father or grandfather who is a widower aged 65 years or over; or
        (c) parents or grandparents travelling together of whom at least one is aged 65 or over; or
        (d) a parent or grandparent aged 65 or over who has entered into a second relationship of marriage or civil partnership but cannot look to the spouse, civil partner or children of that second relationship for financial support; and where the person settled in the United Kingdom is able and willing to maintain the parent or grandparent and any spouse or civil partner or child of the second relationship who would be admissible as a dependant; or
        (e) parent or grandparent under the age of 65 if living alone outside the United Kingdom in the most exceptional compassionate circumstances and mainly dependent financially on relatives settled in the United Kingdom; or
        (f) the son, daughter, sister, brother, uncle or aunt over the age of 18 if living alone outside the United Kingdom in the most exceptional compassionate circumstances and mainly dependent financially on relatives settled in the United Kingdom; and
    (ii) is joining or accompanying a person who is present and settled in the United Kingdom or who is on the same occasion being admitted for settlement; and
    (iii) is financially wholly or mainly dependent on the relative present and settled in the United Kingdom; and
    (iv) can, and will, be accommodated adequately, together with any dependants, without recourse to public funds, in accommodation which the sponsor owns or occupies exclusively; and
    (iva) can, and will, be maintained adequately, together with any dependants, without recourse to public funds; and
    (v) has no other close relatives in his own country to whom he could turn for financial support; and
    (vi) if seeking leave to enter, holds a valid United Kingdom entry clearance for entry in this capacity.

Indefinite leave to enter or remain as the parent, grandparent or other dependent relative of a person present and settled in the United Kingdom

318. Indefinite leave to enter the United Kingdom as the parent, grandparent or other dependent relative of a person present and settled in the United Kingdom may be granted provided a valid United Kingdom entry clearance for entry in this capacity is produced to the Immigration Officer on arrival. Indefinite leave to remain in the United Kingdom as the parent, grandparent or other dependent relative of a person present and settled in the United Kingdom may be granted provided the Secretary of State is satisfied that each of the requirements of paragraph 317(i)–(v) is met.

Refusal of indefinite leave to enter or remain in the United Kingdom as the parent, grandparent or other dependent relative of a person present and settled in the United Kingdom

319. Indefinite leave to enter the United Kingdom as the parent, grandparent or other dependent relative of a person settled in the United Kingdom is to be refused if a valid United Kingdom entry clearance for entry in this capacity is not produced to the Immigration Officer on arrival. Indefinite leave to remain in the United Kingdom as the parent, grandparent or other dependent relative of a person present and settled in the United Kingdom is to be refused if the Secretary of State is not satisfied that each of the requirements of paragraph 317(i)–(v) is met.

Part 9: General grounds for the refusal of entry clearance, leave to enter or variation of leave to enter or remain in the United Kingdom

Refusal of entry clearance or leave to enter the United Kingdom

320. In addition to the grounds of refusal of entry clearance or leave to enter set out in Parts 2–8 of these Rules, and subject to paragraph 321 below, the following grounds for the refusal of entry clearance or leave to enter apply:

Grounds on which entry clearance or leave to enter the United Kingdom is to be refused

(1) the fact that entry is being sought for a purpose not covered by these Rules;

(2) the fact that the person seeking entry to the United Kingdom is currently the subject of a deportation order;

(3) failure by the person seeking entry to the United Kingdom to produce to the Immigration Officer a valid national passport or other document satisfactorily establishing his identity and nationality;

(4) failure to satisfy the Immigration Officer, in the case of a person arriving in the United Kingdom or seeking entry through the Channel Tunnel with the intention of entering any other part of the common travel area, that he is acceptable to the immigration authorities there;

(5) failure, in the case of a visa national, to produce to the Immigration Officer a passport or other identity document endorsed with a valid and current United Kingdom entry clearance issued for the purpose for which entry is sought;

(6) where the Secretary of State has personally directed that the exclusion of a person from the United Kingdom is conducive to the public good;

(7) save in relation to a person settled in the United Kingdom or where the Immigration Officer is satisfied that there are strong compassionate reasons justifying admission, confirmation from the Medical Inspector that, for medical reasons, it is undesirable to admit a person seeking leave to enter the United Kingdom.

Grounds on which entry clearance or leave to enter the United Kingdom should normally be refused

(8) failure by a person arriving in the United Kingdom to furnish the Immigration Officer with such information as may be required for the purpose of deciding whether he requires leave to enter and, if so, whether and on what terms leave should be given;

(8A) where the person seeking leave is outside the United Kingdom, failure by him to supply any information, documents, copy documents or medical report requested by an Immigration Officer;

(9) failure by a person seeking leave to enter as a returning resident to satisfy the Immigration Officer that he meets the requirements of paragraph 18 of these Rules, or that he seeks leave to enter for the same purpose as that for which his earlier leave was granted;

(10) production by the person seeking leave to enter the United Kingdom of a national passport or travel document issued by a territorial entity or authority which is not recognised by Her Majesty's Government as a state or is not dealt with as a government by them, or which does not accept valid United Kingdom passports for the purpose of its own immigration control; or a passport or travel document which does not comply with international passport practice;

(11) failure to observe the time limit or conditions attached to any grant of leave to enter or remain in the United Kingdom;

(12) the obtaining of a previous leave to enter or remain by deception;

(13) failure, except by a person eligible for admission to the United Kingdom for settlement or a spouse or civil partner eligible for admission under paragraph 282, to satisfy the Immigration Officer that he will be admitted to another country after a stay in the United Kingdom;

(14) refusal by a sponsor of a person seeking leave to enter the United Kingdom to give, if requested to do so, an undertaking in writing to be responsible for that person's maintenance and accommodation for the period of any leave granted;

(15) whether or not to the holder's knowledge, the making of false representations or the failure to disclose any material fact for the purpose of obtaining an immigration employment document;

(16) failure, in the case of a child under the age of 18 years seeking leave to enter the United Kingdom otherwise than in conjunction with an application made by his parent(s) or legal guardian to provide the Immigration Officer, if required to do so, with written consent to the application from his parent(s) or legal guardian; save that the requirement as to written consent does not apply in the case of a child seeking admission to the United Kingdom as an asylum seeker;

(17) save in relation to a person settled in the United Kingdom, refusal to undergo a medical examination when required to do so by the Immigration Officer;

(18) save where the Immigration Officer is satisfied that admission would be justified for strong compassionate reasons, conviction in any country including the United Kingdom of an offence which, if committed in the United Kingdom, is punishable with imprisonment for a term of 12 months or any greater punishment or, if committed outside the United Kingdom, would be so punishable if the conduct constituting the offence had occurred in the United Kingdom;

(19) where, from information available to the Immigration Officer, it seems right to refuse leave to enter on the ground that exclusion from the United Kingdom is conducive to the public good; if, for example, in the light of the character, conduct or associations of the person seeking leave to enter it is undesirable to give him leave to enter;

(20) failure by a person seeking entry into the United Kingdom to comply with a requirement relating to the provision of physical data to which he is subject by regulations made under section 126 of the Nationality, Immigration and Asylum Act 2002;

(21) whether or not to the applicant's knowledge, the submission of a false document in support of an application.

Refusal of leave to enter in relation to a person in possession of an entry clearance

321. A person seeking leave to enter the United Kingdom who holds an entry clearance which was duly issued to him and is still current may be refused leave to enter only where the Immigration Officer is satisfied that:
    (i) whether or not to the holder's knowledge, false representations were employed or material facts were not disclosed, either in writing or orally, for the purpose of obtaining the entry clearance; or
    (ii) a change of circumstances since it was issued has removed the basis of the holder's claim to admission, except where the change of circumstances amounts solely to the person becoming over age for entry in one of the categories contained in paragraphs 296–316 of these Rules since the issue of the entry clearance; or
    (iii) refusal is justified on grounds of restricted return ability; on medical grounds; on grounds of criminal record; because the person seeking leave to enter is the subject of a deportation order or because exclusion would be conducive to the public good.

Grounds on which leave to enter or remain which is in force is to be cancelled at port or while the holder is outside the United Kingdom

321A. The following grounds for the cancellation of a person's leave to enter or remain which is in force on his arrival in, or whilst he is outside, the United Kingdom apply:
    (1) there has been such a change in the circumstances of that person's case since the leave was given, that it should be cancelled; or
    (2) the leave was obtained as a result of false information given by that person or by that person's failure to disclose material facts; or
    (3) save in relation to a person settled in the United Kingdom or where the Immigration Officer or the Secretary of State is satisfied that there are strong compassionate reasons justifying admission, where it is apparent that, for medical reasons, it is undesirable to admit that person to the United Kingdom; or
    (4) where the Secretary of State has personally directed that the exclusion of that person from the United Kingdom is conducive to the public good; or
    (5) where from information available to the Immigration Officer or the Secretary of State, it seems right to cancel leave on the ground that exclusion from the United Kingdom is conductive to the public good; if, for example, in the light of the character, conduct or associations of that person it is undesirable for him to have leave to enter the United Kingdom; or
    (6) where that person is outside the United Kingdom, failure by that person to supply any information, documents, copy documents or medical report requested by an Immigration Officer or the Secretary of State.

Refusal of variation of leave to enter or remain or curtailment of leave

322. In addition to the grounds for refusal of extension of stay set out in Parts 2–8 of these Rules, the following provisions apply in relation to the refusal of an application for variation of leave to enter or remain or, where appropriate, the curtailment of leave:

Grounds on which an application to vary leave to enter or remain in the United Kingdom is to be refused

(1) the fact that variation of leave to enter or remain is being sought for a purpose not covered by these Rules.

Grounds on which an application to vary leave to enter or remain in the United Kingdom should normally be refused

(2) the making of false representations or the failure to disclose any material fact for the purpose of obtaining leave to enter or a previous variation of leave;

(3) failure to comply with any conditions attached to the grant of leave to enter or remain;

(4) failure by the person concerned to maintain or accommodate himself and any dependants without recourse to public funds;

(5) the undesirability of permitting the person concerned to remain in the United Kingdom in the light of his character, conduct or associations or the fact that he represents a threat to national security;

(6) refusal by a sponsor of the person concerned to give, if requested to do so, an undertaking in writing to be responsible for his maintenance and accommodation in the United Kingdom or failure to honour such an undertaking once given;

(7) failure by the person concerned to honour any declaration or undertaking given orally or in writing as to the intended duration and/or purpose of his stay;

(8) failure, except by a person who qualifies for settlement in the United Kingdom or by the spouse or civil partner of a person settled in the United Kingdom, to satisfy the Secretary of State that he will be returnable to another country if allowed to remain in the United Kingdom for a further period;

(9) failure by an applicant to produce within a reasonable time information, documents or other evidence required by the Secretary of State to establish his claim to remain under these Rules;

(10) failure, without providing a reasonable explanation, to comply with a request made on behalf of the Secretary of State to attend for interview;

(11) failure, in the case of a child under the age of 18 years seeking a variation of his leave to enter or remain in the United Kingdom otherwise than in conjunction with an application by his parent(s) or legal guardian, to provide the Secretary of State, if required to do so, with written consent to the application from his parent(s) or legal guardian; save that the requirement as to written consent does not apply in the case of a child who has been admitted to the United Kingdom as an asylum seeker.

Grounds on which leave to enter or remain may be curtailed

323. A person's leave to enter or remain may be curtailed:
    (i) on any of the grounds set out in paragraph 322(2)–(5) above; or
    (ii) if he ceases to meet the requirements of the Rules under which his leave to enter or remain was granted; or
    (iii) if he is the dependant, or is seeking leave to remain as the dependant, of an asylum applicant whose claim has been refused and whose leave has been curtailed under section 7 of the 1993 Act, and he does not qualify for leave to remain in his own right;
    (iv) on any of the grounds set out in paragraph 339A(i)–(vi) and paragraph 339G(i)–(vi).

Crew members

324. A person who has been given leave to enter to join a ship, aircraft, hovercraft, hydrofoil or international train service as a member of its crew, or a crew member who has been given leave to enter for hospital treatment, repatriation or transfer to another ship, aircraft, hovercraft, hydrofoil or international train service in the

United Kingdom, is to be refused leave to remain unless an extension of stay is necessary to fulfil the purpose for which he was given leave to enter or unless he meets the requirements for an extension of stay as a spouse or civil partner in paragraph 284.

Part 10: Registration with the police

325. For the purposes of paragraph 326, a 'relevant foreign national' is a person aged 16 or over who is:
    (i) a national or citizen of a country or territory listed in Appendix 2 to these Rules;
    (ii) a stateless person; or
    (iii) a person holding a non-national travel document.

326. (1) Subject to sub-paragraph (2) below, a condition requiring registration with the police should normally be imposed on any relevant foreign national who is:
    (i) given limited leave to enter the United Kingdom for longer than six months; or
    (ii) given limited leave to remain which has the effect of allowing him to remain in the United Kingdom for longer than six months, reckoned from the date of his arrival (whether or not such a condition was imposed when he arrived).

    (2) Such a condition should not normally be imposed where the leave is given:
    (i) as a seasonal agricultural worker;
    (ii) as a private servant in a diplomatic household;
    (iii) as a minister of religion, missionary or member of a religious order;
    (iv) on the basis of marriage to or civil partnership with a person settled in the United Kingdom or as the unmarried or same-sex partner of a person settled in the United Kingdom;
    (v) as a person exercising access rights to a child resident in the United Kingdom;
    (vi) as the parent of a child at school; or
    (vii) following the grant of asylum.

    (3) Such a condition should also be imposed on any foreign national given limited leave to enter the United Kingdom where, exceptionally, the Immigration Officer considers it necessary to ensure that he complies with the terms of the leave.

Part 11: Asylum

Definition of asylum applicant

327. Under the Rules an asylum applicant is a person who makes a request to be recognised as a refugee under the Geneva Convention on the basis that it would be contrary to the United Kingdom's obligations under the Geneva Convention for him to be removed from or required to leave the United Kingdom.

Applications for asylum

328. All asylum applications will be determined by the Secretary of State in accordance with the United Kingdom's obligations under the Geneva Convention. Every asylum application made by a person at a port or airport in the United Kingdom will be referred by the Immigration Officer for determination by the Secretary of State in accordance with these Rules.

329. Until an asylum application has been determined by the Secretary of State or the Secretary of State has issued a certificate under Part 2, 3, 4 or 5 of Schedule 3 to the Asylum and Immigration (Treatment of Claimants, etc.) Act 2004 no action will be

taken to require the departure of the asylum applicant or his dependants from the United Kingdom.

330. If the Secretary of State decides to grant asylum and the person has not yet been given leave to enter, the Immigration Officer will grant limited leave to enter.

331. If a person seeking leave to enter is refused asylum, the Immigration Officer will consider whether or not he is in a position to decide to give or refuse leave to enter without interviewing the person further. If the Immigration Officer decides that a further interview is not required he may serve the notice giving or refusing leave to enter by post. If the Immigration Officer decides that a further interview is required, he will then resume his examination to determine whether or not to grant the person leave to enter under any other provision of these Rules. If the person fails at any time to comply with a requirement to report to an Immigration Officer for examination, the Immigration Officer may direct that the person's examination shall be treated as concluded at that time. The Immigration Officer will then consider any outstanding applications for entry on the basis of any evidence before him.

332. If a person who has been refused leave to enter applies for asylum and that application is refused, leave to enter will again be refused unless the applicant qualifies for admission under any other provision of these Rules.

Grant of asylum

334. An asylum applicant will be granted asylum in the United Kingdom if the Secretary of State is satisfied that:
    (i) he is in the United Kingdom or has arrived at a port of entry in the United Kingdom;
    (ii) he is a refugee, as defined in regulation 2 of the Refugee or Person in Need of International Protection (Qualification) Regulations 2006;
    (iii) there are no reasonable grounds for regarding him as a danger to the security of the United Kingdom;
    (iv) he does not, having been convicted by a final judgment of a particularly serious crime, constitute danger to the community of the United Kingdom; and
    (iii) refusing his application would result in him being required to go (whether immediately or after the time limited by any existing leave to enter or remain) in breach of the Geneva Convention, to a country in which his life or freedom would be threatened on account of his race, religion, nationality, political opinion or membership of a particular social group.

335. If the Secretary of State decides to grant asylum to a person who has been given leave to enter (whether or not the leave has expired) or to a person who has entered without leave, the Secretary of State will vary the existing leave or grant limited leave to remain.

Refusal of asylum

336. An application which does not meet the criteria set out in paragraph 334 will be refused.

338. When a person in the United Kingdom is notified that his asylum application has been refused he may, if he is liable to removal as an illegal entrant, removal under section 10 of the Immigration and Asylum Act 1999 or to deportation, at the same time be notified of removal directions, served with a notice of intention to make a deportation order, or served with a deportation order, as appropriate.

Revocation or refusal to renew a grant of asylum

339A. A person's grant of asylum under paragraph 334 will be revoked or not renewed if the Secretary of State is satisfied that:
    (i) he has voluntarily re-availed himself of the protection of the country of nationality;

(ii) having lost his nationality, he has voluntarily re-acquired it; or
(iii) he has acquired a new nationality, and enjoys the protection of the country of his new nationality;
(iv) he has voluntarily re-established himself in the country which he left or outside which he remained owing to a fear of persecution;
(v) he can no longer, because the circumstances in connection with which he has been recognised as a refugee have ceased to exist, continue to refuse to avail himself of the protection of the country of nationality;
(vi) being a stateless person with no nationality, he is able, because the circumstances in connection with which he has been recognised a refugee have ceased to exist, to return to the country of former habitual residence;
(vii) he should have been or is excluded from being a refugee in accordance with regulation 7 of The Refugee or Person in Need of International Protection (Qualification) Regulations 2006;
(viii) his misrepresentation or omission or facts, including the use of false documents, were decisive for the grant of asylum;
(ix) there are reasonable grounds for regarding him as a danger to the security of the United Kingdom; or
(x) having been convicted by a final judgment of a particularly serious crime he constitutes danger to the community of the United Kingdom.

In considering (v) and (vi), the Secretary of State shall have regard to whether the change of circumstances is of such a significant and non-temporary nature that the refugee's fear of persecution can no longer be regarded as well-founded.

Where an application for asylum was made on or after the 21st October 2004, the Secretary of State will revoke or refuse to renew a person's grant of asylum where he is satisfied that at least one of the provisions in sub-paragraph (i)–(vi) apply.

339B. When a person's grant of asylum is revoked or not renewed any limited leave which they have may be curtailed

Grant of humanitarian protection

339C. A person will be granted humanitarian protection in the United Kingdom if the Secretary of State is satisfied that:
(i) he is in the United Kingdom or has arrived at a port of entry in the United Kingdom;
(ii) he does not qualify as a refugee as defined in regulation 2 of The Refugee or Person in Need of International Protection (Qualification) Regulations 2006;
(iii) substantial grounds have been shown for believing that the person concerned, if he returned to the country of return, would face a real risk of suffering serious harm and is unable, or, owing to such risk, unwilling to avail himself of the protection of that country; and
(iv) he is not excluded from a grant of humanitarian protection. Serious harm consists of:
  (i) the death penalty or execution;
  (ii) unlawful killing;
  (iii) torture or inhuman or degrading treatment or punishment of a person in the country of return; or
  (iv) serious and individual threat to a civilian's life or person by reason of indiscriminate violence in situations of international or internal armed conflict.

Exclusion from humanitarian protection

339D. A person is excluded from a grant of humanitarian protection under paragraph 339C (iv) where the Secretary of State is satisfied that:

(i) there are serious reasons for considering that he has committed a crime against peace, a war crime, a crime against humanity, or any other serious crime or instigated or otherwise participated in such crimes;

(ii) there are serious reasons for considering that he is guilty of acts contrary to the purposes and principles of the United Nations or has committed, prepared or instigated such acts or encouraged or induced others to commit, prepare or instigate instigated such acts;

(iii) there are serious reasons for considering that he constitutes a danger to the community or to the security of the United Kingdom; and

(iv) prior to his admission to the United Kingdom the person committed a crime outside the scope of (i) and (ii) that would be punishable by imprisonment were it committed in the United Kingdom and the person left his country of origin solely in order to avoid sanctions resulting from the crime.

339E. If the Secretary of State decides to grant humanitarian protection and the person has not yet been given leave to enter, the Secretary of State or an Immigration Officer will grant limited leave to enter. If the Secretary of State decides to grant humanitarian protection to a person who has been given limited leave to enter (whether or not that leave has expired) or a person who has entered without leave, the Secretary of State will vary the existing leave or grant limited leave to remain.

Refusal of humanitarian protection

339F. Where the criteria set out in paragraph 339C is not met humanitarian protection will be refused.

Revocation of humanitarian protection

339G. A person's humanitarian protection granted under paragraph 339C will be revoked or not renewed if the Secretary of State is satisfied that at least one of the following applies:

(i) the circumstances which led to the grant of humanitarian protection have ceased to exist or have changed to such a degree that such protection is no longer required;

(ii) the person granted humanitarian protection should have been or is excluded from humanitarian protection because there are serious reasons for considering that he has committed a crime against peace, a war crime, a crime against humanity, or any other serious crime or instigated or otherwise participated in such crimes;

(iii) the person granted humanitarian protection should have been or is excluded from humanitarian protection because there are serious reasons for considering that he is guilty of acts contrary to the purposes and principles of the United Nations or has committed, prepared or instigated such acts or encouraged or induced others to commit, prepare or instigate such acts;

(iv) the person granted humanitarian protection should have been or is excluded from humanitarian protection because there are serious reasons for considering that he constitutes a danger to the community or to the security of the United Kingdom;

(v) the person granted humanitarian protection misrepresented or omitted facts, including the use of false documents, which were decisive to the grant of humanitarian protection; or

(vi) the person granted humanitarian protection should have been or is excluded from humanitarian protection because prior to his admission to the United Kingdom the person committed a crime outside the scope of (ii) and (iii) that would be punishable by imprisonment had it been committed in the United Kingdom and the person left his country of origin solely in order to avoid sanctions resulting from the crime.

In applying (i) the Secretary of State shall have regard to whether the change of circumstances is of such a significant and non-temporary nature that the person no longer faces a real risk of serious harm;

339H. When a person's humanitarian protection is revoked or not renewed any limited leave which they have may be curtailed.

Consideration of applications

339I. When the Secretary of State considers a person's asylum claim, eligibility for a grant of humanitarian protection or human rights claim it is the duty of the person to submit to the Secretary of State as soon as possible all material factors needed to substantiate the asylum claim or establish that he is a person eligible for humanitarian protection or substantiate the human rights claim, which the Secretary of State shall assess in cooperation with the person.

The material factors include:

(i) the person's statement on the reasons for making an asylum claim or on eligibility for a grant of humanitarian protection or for making a human rights claim;

(ii) all documentation at the person's disposal regarding the person's age, background (including background details of relevant relatives), identity, nationality(ies), country(ies) and place(s) of previous residence, previous asylum applications, travel routes; and

(iii) identity and travel documents.

339J. The assessment by the Secretary of State of an asylum claim, eligibility for a grant of humanitarian protection or a human rights claim will be carried out on an individual basis. This will include taking into account in particular:

(i) all relevant facts as they relate to the country of origin or country of return at the time of taking a decision on the grant; including laws and regulations of the country of origin or country of return and the manner in which they are applied;

(ii) relevant statements and documentation presented by the person including information on whether the person has been or may be subject to persecution or serious harm;

(iii) the individual position and personal circumstances of the person, including factors such as background, gender and age, so as to assess whether, on the basis of the person's personal circumstances, the acts to which the person has been or could be exposed would amount to persecution or serious harm;

(iv) whether the person's activities since leaving the country of origin or country of return were engaged in for the sole or main purpose of creating the necessary conditions for making an asylum claim or establishing that he is a person eligible for humanitarian protection or a human rights claim, so as to assess whether these activities will expose the person to persecution or serious harm if he returned to that country; and

(v) whether the person could reasonably be expected to avail himself of the protection of another country where he could assert citizenship.

339K. The fact that a person has already been subject to persecution or serious harm, or to direct threats of such persecution or such harm, will be regarded as a serious indication of the person's well-founded fear of persecution or real risk of suffering serious harm, unless there are good reasons to consider that such persecution or serious harm will not be repeated.

339L. It is the duty of the person to substantiate the asylum claim or establish that he is a person eligible humanitarian protection or substantiate his human rights claim. Where aspects of the person's statements are not supported by documentary or other evidence, those aspects will not need confirmation when all of the following conditions are met:

(i) the person has made a genuine effort to substantiate his asylum claim or establish that he is a person eligible humanitarian protection or substantiate his human rights claim;

(ii) all material factors at the person's disposal have been submitted, and a satisfactory explanation regarding any lack of other relevant material has been given;

(iii) the person's statements are found to be coherent and plausible and do not run counter to available specific and general information relevant to the person's case;

(iv) the person has made an asylum claim or sought to establish that he is a person eligible for humanitarian protection or made a human rights claim at the earliest possible time, unless the person can demonstrate good reason for not having done so; and

(v) the general credibility of the person has been established.

339M. The Secretary of State may consider that a person has not substantiated his asylum claim or established that he is a person eligible for humanitarian protection or substantiated his human rights claim if he fails, without reasonable explanation, to make a prompt and full disclosure of material facts, either orally or in writing, or otherwise to assist the Secretary of State in establishing the facts of the case; this includes, for example, a failure to attend an interview, failure to report to a designated place to be fingerprinted, failure to complete an asylum questionnaire or failure to comply with a requirement to report to an immigration officer for examination.

339N. In determining whether the general credibility of the person has been established the Secretary of State will apply the provisions in s 8 of the Asylum and Immigration (Treatment of Claimants, etc.) Act 2004.

Internal relocation

339O (i) The Secretary of State will not make:

(a) a grant of asylum if in part of the country of origin a person would not have a well founded fear of being persecuted, and the person can reasonably be expected to stay in that part of the country; or

(b) a grant of humanitarian protection if in part of the country of return a person would not face a real risk of suffering serious harm, and the person can reasonably be expected to stay in that part of the country.

(ii) In examining whether a part of the country of origin or country of return meets the requirements in (i) the Secretary of State, when making his decision on whether to grant asylum or humanitarian protection, will have regard to the general circumstances prevailing in that part of the country and to the personal circumstances of the person.

(iii) (i) applies notwithstanding technical obstacles to return to the country of origin or country of return

Sur place **claims**

339P. A person may have a well-founded fear of being persecuted or a real risk of suffering serious harm based on events which have taken place since the person left the country of origin or country of return and/or activates which have been engaged in by a person since he left he country of origin or country of return, in particular where it is established that the activities relied upon constitute the expression and continuation of convictions or orientations held in the country of origin or country of return.

Residence Permits

339Q (i) The Secretary of State will issue to a person granted asylum in the United Kingdom a United Kingdom Residence Permit (UKRP) as soon as possible after the grant of asylum. The UKRP will be valid for five years and renewable, unless compelling reasons of national security or public order otherwise require or where there are reasonable grounds for considering that the applicant is a danger to the security of the UK or having been convicted by a final judgment of a particularly serious crime, the applicant constitutes a danger to the community of the UK.

(ii) The Secretary of State will issue to a person granted humanitarian protection in the United Kingdom a UKRP as soon as possible after the grant of humanitarian protection. The UKRP will be valid for five years and renewable, unless compelling reasons of national security or public order otherwise require or where there are reasonable grounds for considering that the person granted humanitarian protection is a danger to the security of the UK or having been convicted by a final judgment of a serious crime, this person constitutes a danger to the community of the UK.

(iii) The Secretary of State will issue a UKRP to a family member of a person granted asylum or humanitarian protection where the family member does not qualify for such status. A UKRP will be granted for a period of five years. The UKRP is renewable on the terms set out in (i) and (ii) respectively.

(iv) The Secretary of State may revoke or refuse to renew a person's UKRP where their grant of asylum or humanitarian protection is revoked under the provisions in the immigration rules.

Consideration of asylum applications and human rights claims

342. The actions of anyone acting as an agent of the asylum applicant or human rights claimant may also be taken into account in regard to the matters set out in paragraphs 340 and 341.

Travel documents

344A. (i) After having received a complete application for a travel document, the Secretary of State will issue to a person granted asylum in the United Kingdom and their family members travel documents, in the form set out in the Schedule to the Geneva Convention, for the purpose of travel outside the United Kingdom, unless compelling reasons of national security or public order otherwise require.

(ii) After having received a complete application for a travel document, the Secretary of State will issue travel documents to a person granted humanitarian protection in the United Kingdom where that person is unable to obtain a national passport or other identity documents which enable him to travel, unless compelling reasons of national security or public order otherwise require.

(iii) Where the person referred to in (ii) can obtain a national passport or identity documents but has not done so, the Secretary of State will issue that person with a travel document where he can show that he has made reasonable attempts to obtain a national passport or identity document and there are serious humanitarian reasons for travel.

Access to Employment

344B. The Secretary of State will not impose conditions restricting the employment or occupation in the United Kingdom of a person granted asylum or humanitarian protection.

Information

344C. A person who is granted asylum or humanitarian protection will be provided with access to information in a language that they may reasonably be supposed to understand which sets out the rights and obligations relating to that status. The Secretary of State will provide the information as soon as possible after the grant of asylum or humanitarian protection.

Third country cases

345. (1) In a case where the Secretary of State is satisfied that the conditions set out in Paragraphs 4 and 5(1), 9 and 10(1), 14 and 15(1) or 17 of Schedule 3 to the Asylum and Immigration (Treatment of Claimants, etc.) Act 2004 are fulfilled, he will normally decline to examine the asylum application substantively and issue a certificate under Part 2, 3, 4 or 5 of Schedule 3 to the Asylum and Immigration (Treatment of Claimants, etc.) Act 2004 as appropriate.

(2) The Secretary of State shall not issue a certificate under Part 2, 3, 4 or 5 of Schedule 3 to the Asylum and Immigration (Treatment of Claimants, etc.) Act 2004 unless:

  (i) the asylum applicant has not arrived in the United Kingdom directly from the country in which he claims to fear persecution and has had an opportunity at the border or within the third country or territory to make contact with the authorities of that third country or territory in order to seek their protection; or

  (ii) there is other clear evidence of his admissibility to a third country or territory.

Provided that he is satisfied that a case meets these criteria, the Secretary of State is under no obligation to consult the authorities of the third country or territory before the removal of an asylum applicant to that country or territory.

(3) Where a certificate is issued under Part 2, 3, 4 or 5 of Schedule 3 to the Asylum and Immigration (Treatment of Claimants, etc.) Act 2004 in relation to the asylum claim and the person is seeking leave to enter the Immigration Officer will consider whether or not he is in a position to decide to give or refuse leave to enter without interviewing the person further. If the Immigration Officer decides that a further interview is not required he may serve the notice giving or refusing leave to enter by post. If the Immigration Officer decides that a further interview is required, he will then resume his examination to determine whether or not to grant the person leave to enter under any other provision of these Rules. If the person fails at any time to comply with a requirement to report to an Immigration Officer for examination, the Immigration Officer may direct that the person's examination shall be treated as concluded at that time. The Immigration Officer will then consider any outstanding applications for entry on the basis of any evidence before him.

(4) Where a certificate is issued under Part 2, 3, 4 or 5 of Schedule 3 to the Asylum and Immigration (Treatment of Claimants, etc.) Act 2004 the person may, if liable to removal as an illegal entrant, or removal under section 10 of the Immigration and Asylum Act 1999 or to deportation, at the same time be notified of removal directions, served with a notice of intention to make a deportation order, or served with a deportation order, as appropriate.

Dependants

349. A spouse, civil partner, unmarried or same-sex partner, or minor child accompanying a principal applicant may be included in his application for asylum as his dependant. A spouse, civil partner, unmarried or same-sex partner, or minor child may also claim asylum in his own right. If the principal applicant is granted asylum and leave to enter or remain any spouse, civil partner, unmarried or same-sex partner, or minor child will be granted leave to enter or remain for the same duration. The case of any dependant who claims asylum in his own right will be considered individually in accordance with paragraph 334 above. An applicant under this paragraph, including an accompanied child, may be interviewed where he makes a claim as a dependant or in his own right.

If the spouse, civil partner, unmarried or same-sex partner, or minor child in question has a claim in his own right, that claim should be made at the earliest opportunity. Any failure to do so will be taken into account and may damage credibility if no reasonable explanation for it is given. Where an asylum application is unsuccessful, at the same time that asylum is refused the applicant may be notified of removal directions or served with a notice of the Secretary of State's intention to deport him, as appropriate. In this paragraph and paragraphs 350–352 a child means a person who is under 18 years of age or who, in the absence of documentary evidence establishing age, appears to be under that age. An unmarried or same sex partner for the purposes of this paragraph, is a person who has been living together with the principal applicant in a subsisting relationship akin to marriage or a civil partnership for two years or more.

Unaccompanied children

350. Unaccompanied children may also apply for asylum and, in view of their potential vulnerability, particular priority and care is to be given to the handling of their cases.

351. A person of any age may qualify for refugee status under the Convention and the criteria in paragraph 334 apply to all cases. However, account should be taken of the applicant's maturity and in assessing the claim of a child more weight should be given to objective indications of risk than to the child's state of mind and understanding of his situation. An asylum application made on behalf of a child should not be refused solely because the child is too young to understand his situation or to have formed a well founded fear of persecution. Close attention should be given to the welfare of the child at all times.

352. An accompanied or unaccompanied child who has claimed asylum in his own right may be interviewed about the substance of his claim or to determine his age and identity. When an interview is necessary it should be conducted in the presence of a parent, guardian, representative or another adult who for the time being takes responsibility for the child and is not an Immigration Officer, an officer of the Secretary of State or a police officer. The interviewer should have particular regard to the possibility that a child will feel inhibited or alarmed. The child should be allowed to express himself in his own way and at his own speed. If he appears tired or distressed, the interview should be stopped.

352A. The requirements to be met by a person seeking leave to enter or remain in the United Kingdom as the spouse or civil partner of a refugee are that:

(i) the applicant is married to or the civil partner of a person granted asylum in the United Kingdom; and

(ii) the marriage or civil partnership did not take place after the person granted asylum left the country of his former habitual residence in order to seek asylum; and

(iii) the applicant would not be excluded from protection by virtue of article 1F of the United Nations Convention and Protocol relating to the Status of Refugees if he were to seek asylum in his own right; and

(iv) each of the parties intends to live permanently with the other as his or her spouse or civil partner and the marriage or civil partnership is subsisting; and

(v) if seeking leave to enter, the applicant holds a valid United Kingdom entry clearance for entry in this capacity.

352AA. The requirements to be met by a person seeking leave to enter or remain in the United Kingdom as the unmarried or the same-sex partner of a refugee are that:

(i) the applicant is the unmarried or same-sex partner of a person granted asylum in the UK on or after 9th October 2006; and

(ii) the parties have been living together in a relationship akin to either a marriage or a civil partnership which has subsisted for two years or more; and

(iii) the relationship existed before the person granted asylum left the country of his former habitual residence in order to seek asylum; and

(iv) the applicant would not be excluded from protection by virtue of paragraph 334(iii) or

(iv) of these Rules or article 1F of the Geneva Convention if he were to seek asylum in his own right; and

(v) each of the parties intends to live permanently with the other as his or her unmarried or same-sex partner and the relationship is subsisting; and

(vi) if seeking leave to enter, the applicant holds a valid United Kingdom entry clearance for entry in this capacity

352B. Limited leave to enter the United Kingdom as the spouse or civil partner of a refugee may be granted provided a valid United Kingdom entry clearance for entry in this capacity is produced to the Immigration Officer on arrival. Limited leave to remain in the United Kingdom as the spouse or civil partner of a refugee may be granted provided the Secretary of State is satisfied that each of the requirements of paragraph 352A(i)–(iii) are met.

352BA. Limited leave to enter the United Kingdom as the unmarried or same-sex partner of a refugee may be granted provided a valid United Kingdom entry clearance for entry in this capacity is produced to the Immigration Officer on arrival. Limited leave to remain in the United Kingdom as the unmarried or same sex partner of a refugee may be granted provided the Secretary of State is satisfied that each of the requirements of paragraph 352AA(i)–(v) are met.

352C. Limited leave to enter the United Kingdom as the spouse or civil partner of a refugee is to be refused if a valid United Kingdom entry clearance for entry in this capacity is not produced to the Immigration Officer on arrival. Limited leave to remain as the spouse or civil partner of a refugee is to be refused if the Secretary of State is not satisfied that each of the requirements of paragraph 352A(i)–(iii) are met.

352CA. Limited leave to enter the United Kingdom as the unmarried or same-sex partner of a refugee is to be refused if a valid United Kingdom entry clearance for entry in this capacity is not produced to the Immigration Officer on arrival. Limited leave to remain as the unmarried or same sex partner of a refugee is to be refused if the Secretary of State is not satisfied that each of the requirements of paragraph 352AA(i)–(v) are met.

352D. The requirements to be met by a person seeking leave to enter or remain in the United Kingdom in order to join or remain with the parent who has been granted asylum in the United Kingdom are that the applicant:

(i) is the child of a parent who has been granted asylum in the United Kingdom; and

(ii) is under the age of 18; and

(iii) is not leading an independent life, is unmarried and is not a civil partner, and has not formed an independent family unit; and

(iv) was part of the family unit of the person granted asylum at the time that the person granted asylum left the country of his habitual residence in order to seek asylum; and

(v) would not be excluded from protection by virtue of article 1F of the United Nations Convention and Protocol relating to the Status of Refugees if he were to seek asylum in his own right; and

(vi) if seeking leave to enter, holds a valid United Kingdom entry clearance for entry in this capacity.

352E. Limited leave to enter the United Kingdom as the child of a refugee may be granted provided a valid United Kingdom entry clearance for entry in this capacity is produced to the Immigration Officer on arrival. Limited leave to remain in the United Kingdom as the child of a refugee may be granted provided the Secretary of State is satisfied that each of the requirements of paragraph 352D(i)–(v) are met.

352F. Limited leave to enter the United Kingdom as the child of a refugee is to be refused if a valid United Kingdom entry clearance for entry in this capacity is not produced to the Immigration Officer on arrival. Limited leave to remain as the child of a refugee is to be refused if the Secretary of State is not satisfied that each of the requirements of paragraph 352D(i)–(v) are met.

Interpretation

352G. For the purposes of this Part:
- (a) 'Geneva Convention' means the United Nations Convention and Protocol relating to the Status of Refugees;
- (b) 'Country of return' means a country or territory listed in paragraph 8(c) of Schedule 2 of the Immigration Act 1971;
- (c) 'Country of origin' means the country or countries of nationality or, for a stateless person, or former habitual residence.

Part 11A: Temporary protection

Definition of Temporary Protection Directive

354. For the purposes of paragraphs 355 to 356B, 'Temporary Protection Directive' means Council Directive 2001/55/EC of 20 July 2001 regarding the giving of temporary protection by Member States in the event of a mass influx of displaced persons.

Grant of temporary protection

355. An applicant for temporary protection will be granted temporary protection if the Secretary of State is satisfied that:
- (i) the applicant is in the United Kingdom or has arrived at a port of entry in the United Kingdom; and
- (ii) the applicant is a person entitled to temporary protection as defined by, and in accordance with, the Temporary Protection Directive; and
- (iii) the applicant does not hold an extant grant of temporary protection entitling him to reside in another Member State of the European Union. This requirement is subject to the provisions relating to dependants set out in paragraphs 356 to 356B and to any agreement to the contrary with the Member State in question; and
- (iv) the applicant is not excluded from temporary protection under the provisions in paragraph 355A.

355A. An applicant or a dependant may be excluded from temporary protection if:
- (i) there are serious reasons for considering that:
  - (a) he has committed a crime against peace, a war crime, or a crime against humanity, as defined in the international instruments drawn up to make provision in respect of such crimes; or
  - (b) he has committed a serious non-political crime outside the United Kingdom prior to his application for temporary protection; or
  - (c) he has committed acts contrary to the purposes and principles of the United Nations; or
- (ii) there are reasonable grounds for regarding the applicant as a danger to the security of the United Kingdom or, having been convicted by a final judgment of a particularly serious crime, to be a danger to the community of the United Kingdom.

Consideration under this paragraph shall be based solely on the personal conduct of the applicant concerned. Exclusion decisions or measures shall be based on the principle of proportionality.

355B. If temporary protection is granted to a person who has been given leave to enter or remain (whether or not the leave has expired) or to a person who has entered without leave, the Secretary of State will vary the existing leave or grant limited leave to remain.

355C. A person to whom temporary protection is granted will be granted limited leave to enter or remain, which is not to be subject to a condition prohibiting employment, for a period not exceeding 12 months. On the expiry of this period, he will be entitled to apply for an extension of this limited leave for successive periods of 6 months thereafter.

355D. A person to whom temporary protection is granted will be permitted to return to the United Kingdom from another Member State of the European Union during the period of a mass influx of displaced persons as established by the Council of the European Union pursuant to Article 5 of the Temporary Protection Directive.

355E. A person to whom temporary protection is granted will be provided with a document in a language likely to be understood by him in which the provisions relating to temporary protection and which are relevant to him are set out. A person with temporary protection will also be provided with a document setting out his temporary protection status.

355F. The Secretary of State will establish and maintain a register of those granted temporary protection. The register will record the name, nationality, date and place of birth and marital status of those granted temporary protection and their family relationship to any other person who has been granted temporary protection.

355G. If a person who makes an asylum application is also eligible for temporary protection, the Secretary of State may decide not to consider the asylum application until the applicant ceases to be entitled to temporary protection.

Dependants

356. In this part:

    'dependant' means a family member or a close relative.

    'family member' means:

    (i) the spouse or civil partner of an applicant for, or a person who has been granted, temporary protection; or

    (ii) the unmarried or same-sex partner of an applicant for, or a person who has been granted, temporary protection where the parties have been living together in a relationship akin to marriage or civil partnership which has subsisted for 2 years or more; or

    (iii) the minor child (who is unmarried and not a civil partner) of an applicant for, or a person who has been granted, temporary protection or his spouse,

    who lived with the principal applicant as part of the family unit in the country of origin immediately prior to the mass influx.

    'close relative' means:

    (i) the adult child (who is unmarried and not a civil partner), parent or grandparent of an applicant for, or person who has been granted, temporary protection; or

    (ii) the sibling (who is unmarried and not a civil partner) or the uncle or aunt of an applicant for, or person who has been granted, temporary protection, who lived with the principal applicant as part of the family unit in the country of origin immediately prior to the mass influx and was wholly or mainly dependent upon the principal applicant at that time, and would face extreme hardship if reunification with the principal applicant did not take place.

356A. A dependant may apply for temporary protection. Where the dependant falls within paragraph 356 and does not fall to be excluded under paragraph 355A, he will be granted temporary protection for the same duration and under the same conditions as the principal applicant.

356B. When considering any application by a dependant child, the Secretary of State shall take into consideration the best interests of that child.

Part 11B: Asylum

Reception conditions for non-EU asylum applicants

357. Part 11B only applies to asylum applicants (within the meaning of these Rules) who are not nationals of a member State.

Information to be provided to asylum applicants

358. The Secretary of State shall inform asylum applicants within a reasonable time not exceeding fifteen days after their claim for asylum has been recorded of the benefits and services that they may be eligible to receive and of the rules and procedures with which they must comply relating to them. The Secretary of State shall also provide information on non-governmental organisations and persons that provide legal assistance to asylum applicants and which may be able to help asylum applicants or provide information on available benefits and services.

358A. The Secretary of State shall ensure that the information referred to in paragraph 358 is available in writing and, to the extent possible, will provide the information in a language that asylum applicants may reasonably be supposed to understand. Where appropriate, the Secretary of State may also arrange for this information to be supplied orally.

Information to be provided by asylum applicants

358B. An asylum applicant must notify the Secretary of State of his current address and of any change to his address or residential status. If not notified beforehand, any change must be notified to the Secretary of State without delay after it occurs.

Documentation

359. The Secretary of State shall ensure that, within three working days of recording an asylum application, a document is made available to that asylum applicant, issued in his own name, certifying his status as an asylum applicant or testifying that he is allowed to remain in the United Kingdom while his asylum application is pending. For the avoidance of doubt, in cases where the Secretary of State declines to examine an application it will no longer be pending for the purposes of this rule.

359A. The obligation in paragraph 359 above shall not apply where the asylum applicant is detained under the Immigration Acts, the Immigration and Asylum Act 1999 or the Nationality, Immigration and Asylum Act 2002.

359B. A document issued to an asylum applicant under paragraph 359 does not constitute evidence of the asylum applicant's identity.

359C. In specific cases the Secretary of State or an Immigration Officer may provide an asylum applicant with evidence equivalent to that provided under rule 359. This might be, for example, in circumstances in which it is only possible or desirable to issue a time-limited document.

Right to request permission to take up employment

360. An asylum applicant may apply to the Secretary of State for permission to take up employment which shall not include permission to become self employed or to engage in a business or professional activity if a decision at first instance has not been taken on the applicant's asylum application within one year of the date on which it was recorded. The Secretary of State shall only consider such an application if, in his opinion, any delay in reaching a decision at first instance cannot be attributed to the applicant.

360A. If an asylum applicant is granted permission to take up employment under rule 360 this shall only be until such time as his asylum application has been finally determined.

Interpretation

361. For the purposes of this Part—
   (a) 'working day' means any day other than a Saturday or Sunday, a bank holiday, Christmas day or Good Friday;
   (b) 'member State' has the same meaning as in Schedule 1 to the European Communities Act 1972.

Part 12: Procedure

Fresh claims

353. When a human rights or asylum claim has been refused and any appeal relating to that claim is no longer pending, the decision maker will consider any further submissions and, if rejected, will then determine whether they amount to a fresh claim. The submissions will amount to a fresh claim if they are significantly different from the material that has previously been considered. The submissions will only be significantly different if the content:
    (i) had not already been considered; and
    (ii) taken together with the previously considered material, created a realistic prospect of success,notwithstanding its rejection.

    This paragraph does not apply to claims made overseas.

Part 13: Deportation

A deportation order

362. A deportation order requires the subject to leave the United Kingdom and authorises his detention until he is removed. It also prohibits him from re-entering the country for as long as it is in force and invalidates any leave to enter or remain in the United Kingdom given him before the Order is made or while it is in force.

363. The circumstances in which a person is liable to deportation include:
    (i) where the Secretary of State deems the person's deportation to be conducive to the public good;
    (ii) where the person is the spouse, civil partner or child under 18 of a person ordered to be deported; and
    (iii) where a court recommends deportation in the case of a person over the age of 17 who has been convicted of an offence punishable with imprisonment.

363A. Prior to 2 October 2000, a person would have been liable to deportation in certain circumstances in which he is now liable to administrative removal. These circumstances are listed in paragraph 394B below. However, such a person remains liable to deportation, rather than administrative removal where:
    (i) a decision to make a deportation order against him was taken before 2 October 2000; or
    (ii) the person has made a valid application under the Immigration (Regularisation Period for Overstayers) Regulations 2000.

364. Subject to paragraph 380, while each case will be considered on its merits, where a person is liable to deportation the presumption shall be that the public interest requires deportation. The Secretary of State will consider all relevant factors in considering whether the presumption is outweighed in any particular case, although it will only be in exceptional circumstances that the public interest in deportation will be outweighed in a case where it would not be contrary to the Human Rights Convention and the Convention and Protocol relating to the Status of Refugees to deport. The aim is an exercise of the power of deportation which is consistent and fair as between one person and another, although one case will rarely be identical with another in all material respects. In the cases detailed in paragraph 363A deportation will normally be the proper course where a person has failed to comply with or has contravened a condition or has remained without authority.

Deportation of family members

365. Section 5 of the Immigration Act 1971 gives the Secretary of State power in certain circumstances to make a deportation order against the spouse, civil partner or child of a person against whom a deportation order has been made. The Secretary of State will not normally decide to deport the spouse or civil partner of a deportee where:

(i) he has qualified for settlement in his own right; or
(ii) he has been living apart from the deportee.

366. The Secretary of State will not normally decide to deport the child of a deportee where:
   (i) he and his mother or father are living apart from the deportee; or
   (ii) he has left home and established himself on an independent basis; or
   (iii) he married or formed a civil partnership before deportation came into prospect.

367. In considering whether to require a spouse or child to leave with the deportee the Secretary of State will take account of all relevant factors, including:
   (i) the ability of the spouse or civil partner to maintain himself and any children in the United Kingdom, or to be maintained by relatives or friends without charge to public funds, not merely for a short period but for the foreseeable future; and
   (ii) in the case of a child of school age, the effect of removal on his education; and
   (iii) the practicality of any plans for a child's care and maintenance in this country if one or both of his parents were deported; and
   (iv) any representations made on behalf of the spouse or civil partner or child.

368. Where the Secretary of State decides that it would be appropriate to deport a member of a family as such, the decision, and the right of appeal, will be notified and it will at the same time be explained that it is open to the member of the family to leave the country voluntarily if he does not wish to appeal or if he appeals and his appeal is dismissed.

Hearing of appeals

378. A deportation order may not be made while it is still open to the person to appeal against the Secretary of State's decision, or while an appeal is pending. There is no appeal within the immigration appeal system against the making of a deportation order on the recommendation of a court; but there is a right of appeal to a higher court against the recommendation itself. A deportation order may not be made while it is still open to the person to appeal against the relevant conviction, sentence or recommendation, or while such an appeal is pending.

Persons who have claimed asylum

380. A deportation order will not be made against any person if his removal in pursuance of the order would be contrary to the United Kingdom's obligations under the Convention and Protocol relating to the Status of Refugees or the Human Rights Convention.

Procedure

381. When a decision to make a deportation order has been taken (otherwise than on the recommendation of a court) a notice will be given to the person concerned informing him of the decision and of his right of appeal.

382. Following the issue of such a notice the Secretary of State may authorise detention or make an order restricting a person as to residence, employment or occupation and requiring him to report to the police, pending the making of a deportation order.

384. If a notice of appeal is given within the period allowed, a summary of the facts of the case on the basis of which the decision was taken will be sent to the appropriate appellate authorities, who will notify the appellant of the arrangements for the appeal to be heard.

Arrangements for removal

385. A person against whom a deportation order has been made will normally be removed from the United Kingdom. The power is to be exercised so as to secure the person's return to the country of which he is a national, or which has most recently provided him with a travel document, unless he can show that another country will receive him. In considering any departure from the normal arrangements, regard will be had to the public interest generally, and to any additional expense that may fall on public funds.

386. The person will not be removed as the subject of a deportation order while an appeal may be brought against the removal directions or such an appeal is pending.

Returned deportees

388. Where a person returns to this country when a deportation order is in force against him, he may be deported under the original order. The Secretary of State will consider every such case in the light of all the relevant circumstances before deciding whether to enforce the order.

Returned family members

389. Persons deported in the circumstances set out in paragraphs 365–368 above (deportation of family members) may be able to seek re-admission to the United Kingdom under the Immigration Rules where:
    (i) a child reaches 18 (when he ceases to be subject to the deportation order); or
    (ii) in the case of a spouse or civil partner, the marriage or civil partnership comes to an end.

Revocation of deportation order

390. An application for revocation of a deportation order will be considered in the light of all the circumstances including the following:
    (i) the grounds on which the order was made;
    (ii) any representations made in support of revocation;
    (iii) the interests of the community, including the maintenance of an effective immigration control;
    (iv) the interests of the applicant, including any compassionate circumstances.

391. In the case of an applicant with a serious criminal record continued exclusion for a long term of years will normally be the proper course. In other cases revocation of the order will not normally be authorised unless the situation has been materially altered, either by a change of circumstances since the order was made, or by fresh information coming to light which was not before the court which made the recommendation or the appellate authorities or the Secretary of State. The passage of time since the person was deported may also in itself amount to such a change of circumstances as to warrant revocation of the order. However, save in the most exceptional circumstances, the Secretary of State will not revoke the order unless the person has been absent from the United Kingdom for a period of at least 3 years since it was made.

392. Revocation of a deportation order does not entitle the person concerned to re-enter the United Kingdom; it renders him eligible to apply for admission under the Immigration Rules. Application for revocation of the order may be made to the Entry Clearance Officer or direct to the Home Office.

Rights of appeal in relation to a decision not to revoke a deportation order

395. There may be a right of appeal against refusal to revoke a deportation order. Where an appeal does lie the right of appeal will be notified at the same time as the decision to refuse to revoke the order.

Administrative removal

395A. A person is now liable to administrative removal in certain circumstances in which he would, prior to 2 October 2000, have been liable to deportation.

395B. These circumstances are set out in section 10 of the 1999 Act. They are:
(i) failure to comply with a condition attached to his leave to enter or remain, or remaining beyond the time limited by the leave;
(ii) where the person has obtained leave to remain by deception; and
(iii) where the person is the spouse, civil partner or child under 18 of someone in respect of whom directions for removal have been given under section 10.

395C. Before a decision to remove under section 10 is given, regard will be had to all the relevant factors known to the Secretary of State, including:
(i) age;
(ii) length of residence in the United Kingdom;
(iii) strength of connections with the United Kingdom;
(iv) personal history, including character, conduct and employment record;
(v) domestic circumstances;
(vi) previous criminal record and the nature of any offence of which the person has been convicted;
(vii) compassionate circumstances;
(viii) any representations received on the person's behalf.

In the case of family members, the factors listed in paragraphs 365-368 must also be taken into account.

395D. No one shall be removed under section 10 if his removal would be contrary to the United Kingdom's obligations under the Convention and Protocol relating to the Status of Refugees or under the Human Rights Convention.

Procedure

395E. When a decision that a person is to be removed under section 10 has been given, a notice will be given to the person concerned informing him of the decision and of any right of appeal.

395F. Following the issue of such a notice an Immigration Officer may authorise detention or make an order restricting a person as to residence, employment or occupation and requiring him to report to the police, pending the removal.

Appendix 1: Visa requirements for the United Kingdom

1. Subject to paragraph 2 below the following persons need a visa for the United Kingdom:
   (a) Nationals or citizens of the following countries or territorial entities:

Afghanistan	Burma	Djibouti
Albania	Burundi	Dominican Republic
Algeria	Cambodia	Ecuador
Angola	Cameroon	Egypt
Armenia	Cape Verde	Equatorial Guinea
Azerbaijan	Central African Republic	Eritrea
Bahrain	Chad	Ethiopia
Bangladesh	Colombia	Fiji
Belarus	Comoros	Gabon
Benin	Congo	Gambia
Bhutan	Cuba	Georgia
Bosnia Herzegovina	Democratic Republic of the Congo	Ghana
Burkina Faso		Guinea

Guinea Bissau	Moldova	Sudan
Guyana	Mongolia	Surinam
Haiti	Morocco	Syria
India	Mozambique	Taiwan
Indonesia	Nepal	Tajikistan
Iran	Niger	Tanzania
Iraq	Nigeria	Thailand
Ivory Coast	Oman	Togo
Jamaica	Pakistan	Tunisia
Jordan	People's Republic of China (except those referred to in sub-paragraphs 2(d) and (e) of this Appendix)	Turkey
Kazakhstan		Turkmenistan
Kenya		Uganda
Korea (North)		Ukraine
Kuwait	Peru	United Arab Emirates
Kyrgyzstan	Philippines	Uzbekistan
Laos	Qatar	Vietnam
Lebanon	Russia	Yemen
Liberia	Rwanda	Zambia
Libya	São Tomé e Príncipe	Zimbabwe
Macedonia	Saudi Arabia	The territories formerly comprising the socialist Federal Republic of Yugoslavia
Madagascar	Senegal	
Malawi	Sierra Leone	
Mali	Somalia	
Mauritania	Sri Lanka	

    (b)   Persons who hold passports or travel documents issued by the former Soviet Union or by the former Socialist Federal Republic of Yugoslavia.

    (c)   Stateless persons.

    (d)   Persons who hold non-national documents.

2.   The following persons do not need a visa for the United Kingdom:

    (a)   those who qualify for admission to the United Kingdom as returning residents in accordance with paragraph 18;

    (b)   those who seek leave to enter the United Kingdom within the period of their earlier leave and for the same purpose as that for which that leave was granted, unless it

        (i)   was for a period of six months or less; or

        (ii)   was extended by statutory instrument or by section 3C of the Immigration Act 1971 (inserted by section 3 of the Immigration and Asylum Act 1999);

    (c)   DELETED

    (d)   those nationals or citizens of the People's Republic of China holding passports issued by Hong Kong Special Administrative Region; or

    (e)   those nationals or citizens of the People's Republic of China holding passports issued by Macao Special Administrative Region.

    (f)   those who arrive in the United Kingdom with leave to enter which is in force but which was given before arrival so long as those in question arrive within the period of their earlier leave and for the same purpose as that for which leave was granted, unless that leave—

        (i)   was for a period of six months or less, or

        (ii)   was extended by statutory instrument or by section 3C of the Immigration Act 1971 (inserted by section 3 of the Immigration and Asylum Act 1999).

Appendix 2: Countries or territories whose nationals or citizens are relevant foreign nationals for the purposes of Part 10 of these Rules

(Registration with the police)

Afghanistan	Iran	Peru
Algeria	Iraq	Qatar
Argentina	Israel	Russia
Armenia	Jordan	Saudi Arabia
Azerbaijan	Kazakhstan	Sudan
Bahrain	Kuwait	Syria
Belarus	Kyrgyzstan	Tajikistan
Bolivia	Lebanon	Tunisia
Brazil	Libya	Turkey
China	Moldova	Turkmenistan
Colombia	Morocco	United Arab Emirates
Cuba	North Korea	Ukraine
Egypt	Oman	Uzbekistan
Georgia	Palestine	Yemen

Appendix 3: List of countries participating in the working holidaymaker scheme

Antigua and Barbuda,	Kenya,	Seychelles,
Australia,	Kiribati,	Sierra Leone,
The Bahamas,	Malawi,	Singapore,
Bangladesh,	Malaysia,	Solomon Islands,
Barbados,	Maldives,	South Africa,
Belize,	Mauritius,	Sri Lanka,
Botswana,	Mozambique,	Swaziland,
Brunei Darussalam,	Namibia,	Tanzania, United Republic of,
Canada,	Nauru,	Tonga,
Cameroon,	New Zealand,	Trinidad and Tobago,
Dominica,	Nigeria,	Tuvalu,
Fiji Islands,	Pakistan,	Uganda,
The Gambia,	Papua New Guinea,	Vanuatu,
Ghana,	Saint Christopher and Nevis,	Western Samoa,
Grenada,	Saint Lucia,	Zambia,
Guyana,	Saint Vincent and the Grenadines,	Zimbabwe.
India,		
Jamaica,		

Appendix 4: Points criteria needed to succeed under paragraph 135D(ii) of these Rules

QUALIFICATIONS	
Points	Qualifications (can include equivalent level professional qualifications) Applicants may claim points for only one qualification.
50	PhD
35	Masters degree
30	Bachelors degree
PREVIOUS EARNINGS	
Points	Applicants whose previous grant of leave to enter/remain under HSMP was for a period of more than 12 months: Previous Earnings from 12 out of the 15 months preceding the application.
5	16–17,999 Pounds Sterling (£)
10	18–19,999
15	20–22,999
20	23–25,999
25	26–28,999
30	29–31,999
35	32–34,999
40	35–39,999
45	40+
Points	Applicants whose previous grant of leave to enter/remain under HSMP was for a period of 12 months or less: Previous Earnings from 8 out of the 12 months preceding the application.
5	10,650–11,999 Pounds Sterling (£)
10	12,000–13,299
15	13,300–15,299
20	15,300–17,299
25	17,300–19,299
30	19,300–21,299
35	21,300–23,299
40	23,300–26,499
45	26,500+
UK EXPERIENCE	
Points 5	Applicants whose previous grant of leave to enter/remain under HSMP was for a period of more than 12 months: At least £16,000 of the past earnings for which points have been claimed under the previous points scoring section, have been earned in the United Kingdom.
Points 5	Applicants whose previous grant of leave to enter/remain under HSMP was for a period of 12 months or less: At least £10,650 of the past earnings for which points have been claimed under the previous points scoring section, have been earned in the United Kingdom.
AGE	
Points	Age (as at date of posting of application)
20	29 or under
10	30 or 31
5	32 or 33

Appendix 5: Documents referred to in paragraph 135D(ii) and 135D(iii)b

Part I: Qualifications – if achieved after initial HSMP grant

Required evidence for those with an academic qualification
Original academic certificate showing: • Title of the award; • Date of award; • Institution; • Name of applicant.
Required evidence for those with a professional/vocational qualification
Original award certificate showing: • Title of award; • Date of award; • Institution; • Name of applicant; and Letter from UK professional body confirming qualification's equivalence to UK academic level showing: • Name of award including country and awarding body; • Equivalence of award to UK academic levels.
Required evidence for those who have just graduated
Letter from institution on headed paper showing: • Name of applicant; • Qualification awarded; • Date of award; • Date certificate will be issued; and Academic transcript showing: • Name of applicant; • Institution; • Course details; • Confirmation of award.
Previous Earnings
Required evidence for those who have been in salaried employment
Both the following covering the full period claimed for: • Income tax returns; • Wage slips.
Required evidence for those who worked in a country with no tax system
Any two of the following three to cover the full period claimed for: • Bank statements; • Wage slips; • Letter from employer stating salary.
Required evidence for independent contractors
All of the following to cover the full period claimed for: • Income tax return; • Copies of contracts from employers covering the total amount of earnings claimed; • Invoices covering the full amount claimed; and • Bank statements showing incoming payments covering the full amount claimed.

Required evidence for those who have been self employed
Both the following to cover the full period claimed for: • Applicant's individual personal income tax return; and • Applicant's personal bank statements; Plus one of the following combinations of documents covering the full period claimed for: • Company audited accounts PLUS Company Tax return (one of these documents must confirm the total payment claimed by the applicant); OR • Unaudited business/management accounts confirming the total payment claimed by the applicant PLUS either • Business bank statements AND a business tax return; OR • Copies of contracts totalling the full amount payable to the individual AND corroborating invoices.

UK Experience
Required evidence for those claiming points for previous earnings Evidence will be assessed for that sent in to qualify for Previous Earnings criteria. No additional documents required.

Age assessment
Required evidence for those claiming points under the age assessment The original passport or travel document.

Part II: English Language

Required evidence for those claiming a degree taught in English to fulfil criteria

Both of the following:
• Original degree certificate; and
• Original letter on headed paper from the institution confirming the degree was taught in English showing:
  – Name;
  – Qualification awarded;
  – Date awarded.

Appendix 2

Commonwealth Citizens

Citizens of the following countries are currently Commonwealth citizens according to Sch 3 to the British Nationality Act 1981 (as amended).

Antigua and Barbuda	Mozambique
Australia	Namibia
The Bahamas	Nauru
Bangladesh	New Zealand
Barbados	Nigeria
Belize	Pakistan
Botswana	Papua New Guinea
Brunei	Saint Christopher and Nevis
Cameroon	Saint Lucia
Canada	Saint Vincent and the Grenadines
Republic of Cyprus	Seychelles
Dominica	Sierra Leone
Fiji	Singapore
The Gambia	Solomon Islands
Ghana	South Africa
Grenada	Sri Lanka
Guyana	Swaziland
India	Tanzania
Jamaica	Tonga
Kenya	Trinidad and Tobago
Kiribati	Tuvalu
Lesotho	Uganda
Malawi	Vanuatu
Malaysia	Western Samoa
Maldives	Zambia
Malta	Zimbabwe
Mauritius	

Note that British citizens, and some other categories of British Nationals (including British dependent territories citizens and British overseas citizens) are Commonwealth citizens by virtue of s 37 of the 1981 Act.

It is important to note that as Cameroon, Mozambique, Namibia, Pakistan and South Africa were not members of the Commonwealth on 31 December 1982, then nationals of those countries cannot take advantage of the provisions dealt with at **12.3**.

Appendix 3

British Overseas Territories

The following are currently British Overseas Territories according to Sch 6 to the British Nationality Act 1981 (as amended).

Anguilla
Bermuda
British Antarctic Territory
British Indian Ocean Territory
Cayman Islands
Gibraltar
Montserrat
Pitcairn, Henderson, Ducie and Oeno Islands
St Helena and Dependencies
South Georgia
South Sandwich Islands
The Sovereign Base Areas of Akrotiri and Dhekelia
Turks and Caicos Islands
Virgin Islands

Note that people from the Falkland Islands were made into full British citizens under the British Nationality (Falkland Islands) Act 1983.

Appendix 4

Visa Nationals

Citizens of the following countries generally need a visa to enter the UK unless, for example, they are returning residents (Appendix 1 to Immigration Rules):

Afghanistan	Ivory Coast
Albania	Jamaica
Algeria	Jordan
Angola	Kazakhstan
Armenia	Kenya
Azerbaijan	Kirgizstan
Bahrain	Korea (North)
Bangladesh	Kuwait
Belarus	Laos
Benin	Lebanon
Bhutan	Liberia
Bosnia-Herzogovina	Libya
Burkina Faso	Macedonia
Burma	Madagascar
Burundi	Malawi
Cambodia	Maldives
Cameroon	Mali
Cape Verde	Mauritania
Central African Republic	Mauritius
Chad	Moldova
China	Mongolia
Colombia	Morocco
Comoros	Mozambique
Congo	Nepal
Cuba	Niger
Djibouti	Nigeria
Dominican Republic	Oman
Ecuador	Pakistan
Egypt	Papua New Guinea
Equatorial Guinea	Peru
Entrea	Philippines, The
Ethiopia	Qatar
Fiji	Russia
Gabon	Rwanda
Gambia	São Tomé e Principe
Georgia	Saudi Arabia
Ghana	Senegal
Guinea	Sierra Leone
Guinea-Bissau	Somalia
Guyana	Sri Lanka
Haiti	Sudan
India	Surinam
Indonesia	Syria
Iran	Taiwan
Iraq	Tajikistan

Tanzania
Thailand
Togo
Tunisia
Turkey
Turkmenistan
Uganda
Ukraine

United Arab Emirates
Uzbekistan
Vietnam
Yemen
Zaire
Zambia
Zimbabwe
The territories formerly comprising the Socialist Federal Republic of Yugoslavia

Appendix 5

The European Union and Associated States

Member States of the European Union (see Chapter 13)

Austria	Latvia
Belgium	Lithuania
Bulgaria	Luxembourg
Cyprus	Malta
Czech Republic	The Netherlands
Denmark	Poland
Estonia	Portugal
Finland	Romania
France	Slovakia
Germany	Slovenia
Greece	Spain
Hungary	Sweden
Republic of Ireland	United Kingdom
Italy	

Other Members of the European Economic Area (see Chapter 13)

Iceland	Liechtenstein
Norway	(As to Switzerland, see **13.7.1**)

Appendix 6

Directive 2004/58/EC

CHAPTER I – GENERAL PROVISIONS

Article 1 – Subject

This Directive lays down:

(a) the conditions governing the exercise of the right of free movement and residence within the territory of the Member States by Union citizens and their family members;

(b) the right of permanent residence in the territory of the Member States for Union citizens and their family members;

(c) the limits placed on the rights set out in (a) and (b) on grounds of public policy, public security or public health.

Article 2 – Definitions

For the purposes of this Directive:
1. 'Union citizen' means any person having the nationality of a Member State;
2. 'family member' means:
    (a) the spouse;
    (b) the partner with whom the Union citizen has contracted a registered partnership, on the basis of the legislation of a Member State, if the legislation of the host Member State treats registered partnerships as equivalent to marriage and in accordance with the conditions laid down in the relevant legislation of the host Member State;
    (c) the direct descendants who are under the age of 21 or are dependants and those of the spouse or partner as defined in point (b);
    (d) the dependent direct relatives in the ascending line and those of the spouse or partner as defined in point (b);
3. 'host Member State' means the Member State to which a Union citizen moves in order to exercise his/her right of free movement and residence.

Article 3 – Beneficiaries

1. This Directive shall apply to all Union citizens who move to or reside in a Member State other than that of which they are a national, and to their family members as defined in point 2 of Article 2 who accompany or join them.
2. Without prejudice to any right to free movement and residence the persons concerned may have in their own right, the host Member State shall, in accordance with its national legislation, facilitate entry and residence for the following persons:
    (a) any other family members, irrespective of their nationality, not falling under the definition in point 2 of Article 2 who, in the country from which they have come, are dependants or members of the household of the Union citizen having the primary right of residence, or where serious health grounds strictly require the personal care of the family member by the Union citizen;
    (b) the partner with whom the Union citizen has a durable relationship, duly attested.

The host Member State shall undertake an extensive examination of the personal circumstances and shall justify any denial of entry or residence to these people.

CHAPTER II – RIGHT OF EXIT AND ENTRY

Article 4 – Right of exit

1. Without prejudice to the provisions on travel documents applicable to national border controls, all Union citizens with a valid identity card or passport and their family members who are not nationals of a Member State and who hold a valid passport shall have the right to leave the territory of a Member State to travel to another Member State.
2. No exit visa or equivalent formality may be imposed on the persons to whom paragraph 1 applies.
3. Member States shall, acting in accordance with their laws, issue to their own nationals, and renew, an identity card or passport stating their nationality.
4. The passport shall be valid at least for all Member States and for countries through which the holder must pass when travelling between Member States. Where the law of a Member State does not provide for identity cards to be issued, the period of validity of any passport on being issued or renewed shall be not less than five years.

Article 5 – Right of entry

1. Without prejudice to the provisions on travel documents applicable to national border controls, Member States shall grant Union citizens leave to enter their territory with a valid identity card or passport and shall grant family members who are not nationals of a Member State leave to enter their territory with a valid passport.

   No entry visa or equivalent formality may be imposed on Union citizens.
2. Family members who are not nationals of a Member State shall only be required to have an entry visa in accordance with Regulation (EC) No 539/2001 or, where appropriate, with national law. For the purposes of this Directive, possession of the valid residence card referred to in Article 10 shall exempt such family members from the visa requirement.

   Member States shall grant such persons every facility to obtain the necessary visas. Such visas shall be issued free of charge as soon as possible and on the basis of an accelerated procedure.
3. The host Member State shall not place an entry or exit stamp in the passport of family members who are not nationals of a Member State provided that they present the residence card provided for in Article 10.
4. Where a Union citizen, or a family member who is not a national of a Member State, does not have the necessary travel documents or, if required, the necessary visas, the Member State concerned shall, before turning them back, give such persons every reasonable opportunity to obtain the necessary documents or have them brought to them within a reasonable period of time or to corroborate or prove by other means that they are covered by the right of free movement and residence.
5. The Member State may require the person concerned to report his/her presence within its territory within a reasonable and non-discriminatory period of time. Failure to comply with this requirement may make the person concerned liable to proportionate and non-discriminatory sanctions.

CHAPTER III – RIGHT OF RESIDENCE

Article 6 – Right of residence for up to three months

1. Union citizens shall have the right of residence on the territory of another Member State for a period of up to three months without any conditions or any formalities other than the requirement to hold a valid identity card or passport.

2. The provisions of paragraph 1 shall also apply to family members in possession of a valid passport who are not nationals of a Member State, accompanying or joining the Union citizen.

Article 7 – Right of residence for more than three months

1. All Union citizens shall have the right of residence on the territory of another Member State for a period of longer than three months if they:
    (a) are workers or self-employed persons in the host Member State; or
    (b) have sufficient resources for themselves and their family members not to become a burden on the social assistance system of the host Member State during their period of residence and have comprehensive sickness insurance cover in the host Member State; or
    (c) — are enrolled at a private or public establishment, accredited or financed by the host Member State on the basis of its legislation or administrative practice, for the principal purpose of following a course of study, including vocational training; and
    — have comprehensive sickness insurance cover in the host Member State and assure the relevant national authority, by means of a declaration or by such equivalent means as they may choose, that they have sufficient resources for themselves and their family members not to become a burden on the social assistance system of the host Member State during their period of residence; or
    (d) are family members accompanying or joining a Union citizen who satisfies the conditions referred to in points (a), (b) or (c).
2. The right of residence provided for in paragraph 1 shall extend to family members who are not nationals of a Member State, accompanying or joining the Union citizen in the host Member State, provided that such Union citizen satisfies the conditions referred to in paragraph 1(a), (b) or (c).
3. For the purposes of paragraph 1(a), a Union citizen who is no longer a worker or self-employed person shall retain the status of worker or self-employed person in the following circumstances:
    (a) he/she is temporarily unable to work as the result of an illness or accident;
    (b) he/she is in duly recorded involuntary unemployment after having been employed for more than one year and has registered as a job-seeker with the relevant employment office;
    (c) he/she is in duly recorded involuntary unemployment after completing a fixed-term employment contract of less than a year or after having become involuntarily unemployed during the first twelve months and has registered as a job-seeker with the relevant employment office. In this case, the status of worker shall be retained for no less than six months;
    (d) he/she embarks on vocational training. Unless he/she is involuntarily unemployed, the retention of the status of worker shall require the training to be related to the previous employment.
4. By way of derogation from paragraphs 1(d) and 2 above, only the spouse, the registered partner provided for in Article 2(2)(b) and dependent children shall have the right of residence as family members of a Union citizen meeting the conditions under 1(c) above. Article 3(2) shall apply to his/her dependent direct relatives in the ascending lines and those of his/her spouse or registered partner.

Article 8 – Administrative formalities for Union citizens

1. Without prejudice to Article 5(5), for periods of residence longer than three months, the host Member State may require Union citizens to register with the relevant authorities.

2. The deadline for registration may not be less than three months from the date of arrival. A registration certificate shall be issued immediately, stating the name and address of the person registering and the date of the registration. Failure to comply with the registration requirement may render the person concerned liable to proportionate and non-discriminatory sanctions.

3. For the registration certificate to be issued, Member States may only require that

— Union citizens to whom point (a) of Article 7(1) applies present a valid identity card or passport, a confirmation of engagement from the employer or a certificate of employment, or proof that they are self-employed persons,

— Union citizens to whom point (b) of Article 7(1) applies present a valid identity card or passport and provide proof that they satisfy the conditions laid down therein,

— Union citizens to whom point (c) of Article 7(1) applies present a valid identity card or passport, provide proof of enrolment at an accredited establishment and of comprehensive sickness insurance cover and the declaration or equivalent means referred to in point (c) of Article 7(1). Member States may not require this declaration to refer to any specific amount of resources.

4. Member States may not lay down a fixed amount which they regard as 'sufficient resources', but they must take into account the personal situation of the person concerned. In all cases this amount shall not be higher than the threshold below which nationals of the host Member State become eligible for social assistance, or, where this criterion is not applicable, higher than the minimum social security pension paid by the host Member State.

5. For the registration certificate to be issued to family members of Union citizens, who are themselves Union citizens, Member States may require the following documents to be presented:

(a) a valid identity card or passport;

(b) a document attesting to the existence of a family relationship or of a registered partnership;

(c) where appropriate, the registration certificate of the Union citizen whom they are accompanying or joining;

(d) in cases falling under points (c) and (d) of Article 2(2), documentary evidence that the conditions laid down therein are met;

(e) in cases falling under Article 3(2)(a), a document issued by the relevant authority in the country of origin or country from which they are arriving certifying that they are dependants or members of the household of the Union citizen, or proof of the existence of serious health grounds which strictly require the personal care of the family member by the Union citizen;

(f) in cases falling under Article 3(2)(b), proof of the existence of a durable relationship with the Union citizen.

Article 9 – Administrative formalities for family members who are not nationals of a Member State

1. Member States shall issue a residence card to family members of a Union citizen who are not nationals of a Member State, where the planned period of residence is for more than three months.

2. The deadline for submitting the residence card application may not be less than three months from the date of arrival.

3. Failure to comply with the requirement to apply for a residence card may make the person concerned liable to proportionate and non-discriminatory sanctions.

Article 10 – Issue of residence cards

1. The right of residence of family members of a Union citizen who are not nationals of a Member State shall be evidenced by the issuing of a document called 'Residence card of a family member of a Union citizen' no later than six months from the date on which they submit the application. A certificate of application for the residence card shall be issued immediately.
2. For the residence card to be issued, Member States shall require presentation of the following documents:
   (a) a valid passport;
   (b) a document attesting to the existence of a family relationship or of a registered partnership;
   (c) the registration certificate or, in the absence of a registration system, any other proof of residence in the host MemberState of the Union citizen whom they are accompanying or joining;
   (d) in cases falling under points (c) and (d) of Article 2(2), documentary evidence that the conditions laid down therein are met;
   (e) in cases falling under Article 3(2)(a), a document issued by the relevant authority in the country of origin or country from which they are arriving certifying that they are dependants or members of the household of the Union citizen, or proof of the existence of serious health grounds which strictly require the personal care of the family member by the Union citizen;
   (f) in cases falling under Article 3(2)(b), proof of the existence of a durable relationship with the Union citizen.

Article 11 – Validity of the residence card

1. The residence card provided for by Article 10(1) shall be valid for five years from the date of issue or for the envisaged period of residence of the Union citizen, if this period is less than five years.
2. The validity of the residence card shall not be affected by temporary absences not exceeding six months a year, or by absences of a longer duration for compulsory military service or by one absence of a maximum of 12 consecutive months for important reasons such as pregnancy and childbirth, serious illness, study or vocational training, or a posting in another Member State or a third country.

Article 12 – Retention of the right of residence by family members in the event of death or departure of the Union citizen

1. Without prejudice to the second subparagraph, the Union citizen's death or departure from the host Member State shall not affect the right of residence of his/her family members who are nationals of a Member State.

   Before acquiring the right of permanent residence, the persons concerned must meet the conditions laid down in points (a), (b), (c) or (d) of Article 7(1).

2. Without prejudice to the second subparagraph, the Union citizen's death shall not entail loss of the right of residence of his/her family members who are not nationals of a Member State and who have been residing in the host Member State as family members for at least one year before the Union citizen's death.

   Before acquiring the right of permanent residence, the right of residence of the persons concerned shall remain subject to the requirement that they are able to show that they are workers or self-employed persons or that they have sufficient resources for themselves and their family members not to become a burden on the social assistance system of the host Member State during their period of residence and have comprehensive sickness insurance cover in the host Member State, or that they are members of the family, already constituted in the host Member State, of a person satisfying these requirements. 'Sufficient resources' shall be as defined in Article 8(4).

Such family members shall retain their right of residence exclusively on a personal basis.

3. The Union citizen's departure from the host Member State or his/her death shall not entail loss of the right of residence of his/her children or of the parent who has actual custody of the children, irrespective of nationality, if the children reside in the host Member State and are enrolled at an educational establishment, for the purpose of studying there, until the completion of their studies.

Article 13 – Retention of the right of residence by family members in the event of divorce, annulment of marriage or termination of registered partnership

1. Without prejudice to the second subparagraph, divorce, annulment of the Union citizen's marriage or termination of his/her registered partnership, as referred to in point 2(b) of Article 2 shall not affect the right of residence of his/her family members who are nationals of a Member State.

    Before acquiring the right of permanent residence, the persons concerned must meet the conditions laid down in points (a), (b), (c) or (d) of Article 7(1).

2. Without prejudice to the second subparagraph, divorce, annulment of marriage or termination of the registered partnership referred to in point 2(b) of Article 2 shall not entail loss of the right of residence of a Union citizen's family members who are not nationals of a Member State where:

    (a) prior to initiation of the divorce or annulment proceedings or termination of the registered partnership referred to in point 2(b) of Article 2, the marriage or registered partnership has lasted at least three years, including one year in the host Member State; or

    (b) by agreement between the spouses or the partners referred to in point 2(b) of Article 2 or by court order, the spouse or partner who is not a national of a Member State has custody of the Union citizen's children; or

    (c) this is warranted by particularly difficult circumstances, such as having been a victim of domestic violence while the marriage or registered partnership was subsisting; or

    (d) by agreement between the spouses or partners referred to in point 2(b) of Article 2 or by court order, the spouse or partner who is not a national of a Member State has the right of access to a minor child, provided that the court has ruled that such access must be in the host Member State, and for as long as is required.

    Before acquiring the right of permanent residence, the right of residence of the persons concerned shall remain subject to the requirement that they are able to show that they are workers or self-employed persons or that they have sufficient resources for themselves and their family members not to become a burden on the social assistance system of the host Member State during their period of residence and have comprehensive sickness insurance cover in the host Member State, or that they are members of the family, already constituted in the host Member State, of a person satisfying these requirements. 'Sufficient resources' shall be as defined in Article 8(4).

    Such family members shall retain their right of residence exclusively on personal basis.

Article 14 – Retention of the right of residence

1. Union citizens and their family members shall have the right of residence provided for in Article 6, as long as they do not become an unreasonable burden on the social assistance system of the host Member State.

2. Union citizens and their family members shall have the right of residence provided for in Articles 7, 12 and 13 as long as they meet the conditions set out therein.

In specific cases where there is a reasonable doubt as to whether a Union citizen or his/her family members satisfies the conditions set out in Articles 7, 12 and 13, Member States may verify if these conditions are fulfilled. This verification shall not be carried out systematically.

3. An expulsion measure shall not be the automatic consequence of a Union citizen's or his or her family member's recourse to the social assistance system of the host Member State.

4. By way of derogation from paragraphs 1 and 2 and without prejudice to the provisions of Chapter VI, an expulsion measure may in no case be adopted against Union citizens or their family members if:

(a) the Union citizens are workers or self-employed persons, or

(b) the Union citizens entered the territory of the host Member State in order to seek employment. In this case, the Union citizens and their family members may not be expelled for as long as the Union citizens can provide evidence that they are continuing to seek employment and that they have a genuine chance of being engaged.

Article 15 – Procedural safeguards

1. The procedures provided for by Articles 30 and 31 shall apply by analogy to all decisions restricting free movement of Union citizens and their family members on grounds other than public policy, public security or public health.

2. Expiry of the identity card or passport on the basis of which the person concerned entered the host Member State and was issued with a registration certificate or residence card shall not constitute a ground for expulsion from the host Member State.

3. The host Member State may not impose a ban on entry in the context of an expulsion decision to which paragraph 1 applies.

CHAPTER IV – RIGHT OF PERMANENT RESIDENCE

Section I – Eligibility

Article 16 – General rule for Union citizens and their family members

1. Union citizens who have resided legally for a continuous period of five years in the host Member State shall have the right of permanent residence there. This right shall not be subject to the conditions provided for in Chapter III.

2. Paragraph 1 shall apply also to family members who are not nationals of a Member State and have legally resided with the Union citizen in the host Member State for a continuous period of five years.

3. Continuity of residence shall not be affected by temporary absences not exceeding a total of six months a year, or by absences of a longer duration for compulsory military service, or by one absence of a maximum of 12 consecutive months for important reasons such as pregnancy and childbirth, serious illness, study or vocational training, or a posting in another Member State or a third country.

4. Once acquired, the right of permanent residence shall be lost only through absence from the host Member State for a period exceeding two consecutive years.

Article 17 – Exemptions for persons no longer working in the host Member State and their family members

1. By way of derogation from Article 16, the right of permanent residence in the host Member State shall be enjoyed before completion of a continuous period of five years of residence by:

    (a) workers or self-employed persons who, at the time they stop working, have reached the age laid down by the law of that Member State for entitlement to an old age pension or workers who cease paid employment to take early retirement, provided that they have been working in that Member State for at least the preceding twelve months and have resided there continuously for more than three years.

    If the law of the host Member State does not grant the right to an old age pension to certain categories of self-employed persons, the age condition shall be deemed to have been met once the person concerned has reached the age of 60;

    (b) workers or self-employed persons who have resided continuously in the host Member State for more than two years and stop working there as a result of permanent incapacity to work.

    If such incapacity is the result of an accident at work or an occupational disease entitling the person concerned to a benefit payable in full or in part by an institution in the host Member State, no condition shall be imposed as to length of residence;

    (c) workers or self-employed persons who, after three years of continuous employment and residence in the host Member State, work in an employed or self-employed capacity in another Member State, while retaining their place of residence in the host Member State, to which they return, as a rule, each day or at least once a week.

    For the purposes of entitlement to the rights referred to in points (a) and (b), periods of employment spent in the Member State in which the person concerned is working shall be regarded as having been spent in the host Member State.

    Periods of involuntary unemployment duly recorded by the relevant employment office, periods not worked for reasons not of the person's own making and absences from work or cessation of work due to illness or accident shall be regarded as periods of employment.

2. The conditions as to length of residence and employment laid down in point (a) of paragraph 1 and the condition as to length of residence laid down in point (b) of paragraph 1 shall not apply if the worker's or the self-employed person's spouse or partner as referred to in point 2(b) of Article 2 is a national of the host Member State or has lost the nationality of that Member State by marriage to that worker or self-employed person.

3. Irrespective of nationality, the family members of a worker or a self-employed person who are residing with him in the territory of the host Member State shall have the right of permanent residence in that Member State, if the worker or self-employed person has acquired himself the right of permanent residence in that Member State on the basis of paragraph 1.

4. If, however, the worker or self-employed person dies while still working but before acquiring permanent residence status in the host Member State on the basis of paragraph 1, his family members who are residing with him in the host Member State shall acquire the right of permanent residence there, on condition that:

    (a) the worker or self-employed person had, at the time of death, resided continuously on the territory of that Member State for two years; or

    (b) the death resulted from an accident at work or an occupational disease; or

    (c) the surviving spouse lost the nationality of that Member State following marriage to the worker or self-employed person.

Article 18 – Acquisition of the right of permanent residence by certain family members who are not nationals of a Member State

Without prejudice to Article 17, the family members of a Union citizen to whom Articles 12(2) and 13(2) apply, who satisfy the conditions laid down therein, shall acquire the right of permanent residence after residing legally for a period of five consecutive years in the host Member State.

Section II – Administrative formalities

Article 19 – Document certifying permanent residence for Union citizens

1. Upon application Member States shall issue Union citizens entitled to permanent residence, after having verified duration of residence, with a document certifying permanent residence.
2. The document certifying permanent residence shall be issued as soon as possible.

Article 20 – Permanent residence card for family members who are not nationals of a Member State

1. Member States shall issue family members who are not nationals of a Member State entitled to permanent residence with a permanent residence card within six months of the submission of the application. The permanent residence card shall be renewable automatically every 10 years.
2. The application for a permanent residence card shall be submitted before the residence card expires. Failure to comply with the requirement to apply for a permanent residence card may render the person concerned liable to proportionate and non-discriminatory sanctions.
3. Interruption in residence not exceeding two consecutive years shall not affect the validity of the permanent residence card.

Article 21 – Continuity of residence

For the purposes of this Directive, continuity of residence may be attested by any means of proof in use in the host Member State. Continuity of residence is broken by any expulsion decision duly enforced against the person concerned.

CHAPTER V – PROVISIONS COMMON TO THE RIGHT OF RESIDENCE AND THE RIGHT OF PERMANENT RESIDENCE

Article 22 – Territorial scope

The right of residence and the right of permanent residence shall cover the whole territory of the host Member State. Member States may impose territorial restrictions on the right of residence and the right of permanent residence only where the same restrictions apply to their own nationals.

Article 23 – Related rights

Irrespective of nationality, the family members of a Union citizen who have the right of residence or the right of permanent residence in a Member State shall be entitled to take up employment or self-employment there.

Article 24 – Equal treatment

1. Subject to such specific provisions as are expressly provided for in the Treaty and secondary law, all Union citizens residing on the basis of this Directive in the territory of the host Member State shall enjoy equal treatment with the nationals of that Member State within the scope of the Treaty. The benefit of this right shall be extended to family members who are not nationals of a Member State and who have the right of residence or permanent residence.

2. By way of derogation from paragraph 1, the host Member State shall not be obliged to confer entitlement to social assistance during the first three months of residence or, where appropriate, the longer period provided for in Article 14(4)(b), nor shall it be obliged, prior to acquisition of the right of permanent residence, to grant maintenance aid for studies, including vocational training, consisting in student grants or student loans to persons other than workers, self-employed persons, persons who retain such status and members of their families.

Article 25 – General provisions concerning residence documents

1. Possession of a registration certificate as referred to in Article 8, of a document certifying permanent residence, of a certificate attesting submission of an application for a family member residence card, of a residence card or of a permanent residence card, may under no circumstances be made a precondition for the exercise of a right or the completion of an administrative formality, as entitlement to rights may be attested by any other means of proof.

2. All documents mentioned in paragraph 1 shall be issued free of charge or for a charge not exceeding that imposed on nationals for the issuing of similar documents.

Article 26 – Checks

Member States may carry out checks on compliance with any requirement deriving from their national legislation for non-nationals always to carry their registration certificate or residence card, provided that the same requirement applies to their own nationals as regards their identity card. In the event of failure to comply with this requirement, Member States may impose the same sanctions as those imposed on their own nationals for failure to carry their identity card.

CHAPTER VI – RESTRICTIONS ON THE RIGHT OF ENTRY AND THE RIGHT OF RESIDENCE ON GROUNDS OF PUBLIC POLICY, PUBLIC SECURITY OR PUBLIC HEALTH

Article 27 – General principles

1. Subject to the provisions of this Chapter, Member States may restrict the freedom of movement and residence of Union citizens and their family members, irrespective of nationality, on grounds of public policy, public security or public health. These grounds shall not be invoked to serve economic ends.

2. Measures taken on grounds of public policy or public security shall comply with the principle of proportionality and shall be based exclusively on the personal conduct of the individual concerned. Previous criminal convictions shall not in themselves constitute grounds for taking such measures.

    The personal conduct of the individual concerned must represent a genuine, present and sufficiently serious threat affecting one of the fundamental interests of society. Justifications that are isolated from the particulars of the case or that rely on considerations of general prevention shall not be accepted.

3. In order to ascertain whether the person concerned represents a danger for public policy or public security, when issuing the registration certificate or, in the absence

of a registration system, not later than three months from the date of arrival of the person concerned on its territory or from the date of reporting his/her presence within the territory, as provided for in Article 5(5), or when issuing the residence card, the host Member State may, should it consider this essential, request the Member State of origin and, if need be, other Member States to provide information concerning any previous police record the person concerned may have. Such enquiries shall not be made as a matter of routine. The Member State consulted shall give its reply within two months.

4. The Member State which issued the passport or identity card shall allow the holder of the document who has been expelled on grounds of public policy, public security, or public health from another Member State to re-enter its territory without any formality even if the document is no longer valid or the nationality of the holder is in dispute.

Article 28 – Protection against expulsion

1. Before taking an expulsion decision on grounds of public policy or public security, the host Member State shall take account of considerations such as how long the individual concerned has resided on its territory, his/her age, state of health, family and economic situation, social and cultural integration into the host Member State and the extent of his/her links with the country of origin.
2. The host Member State may not take an expulsion decision against Union citizens or their family members, irrespective of nationality, who have the right of permanent residence on its territory, except on serious grounds of public policy or public security.
3. An expulsion decision may not be taken against Union citizens, except if the decision is based on imperative grounds of public security, as defined by Member States, if they:
    (a) have resided in the host Member State for the previous 10 years; or
    (b) are a minor, except if the expulsion is necessary for the best interests of the child, as provided for in the United Nations Convention on the Rights of the Child of 20 November 1989.

Article 29 – Public health

1. The only diseases justifying measures restricting freedom of movement shall be the diseases with epidemic potential as defined by the relevant instruments of the World Health Organisation and other infectious diseases or contagious parasitic diseases if they are the subject of protection provisions applying to nationals of the host Member State.
2. Diseases occurring after a three-month period from the date of arrival shall not constitute grounds for expulsion from the territory.
3. Where there are serious indications that it is necessary, Member States may, within three months of the date of arrival, require persons entitled to the right of residence to undergo, free of charge, a medical examination to certify that they are not suffering from any of the conditions referred to in paragraph 1. Such medical examinations may not be required as a matter of routine.

Article 30 – Notification of decisions

1. The persons concerned shall be notified in writing of any decision taken under Article 27(1), in such a way that they are able to comprehend its content and the implications for them.
2. The persons concerned shall be informed, precisely and in full, of the public policy, public security or public health grounds on which the decision taken in their case is based, unless this is contrary to the interests of State security.

3. The notification shall specify the court or administrative authority with which the person concerned may lodge an appeal, the time limit for the appeal and, where applicable, the time allowed for the person to leave the territory of the Member State. Save in duly substantiated cases of urgency, the time allowed to leave the territory shall be not less than one month from the date of notification.

Article 31 – Procedural safeguards

1. The persons concerned shall have access to judicial and, where appropriate, administrative redress procedures in the host Member State to appeal against or seek review of any decision taken against them on the grounds of public policy, public security or public health.
2. Where the application for appeal against or judicial review of the expulsion decision is accompanied by an application for an interim order to suspend enforcement of that decision, actual removal from the territory may not take place until such time as the decision on the interim order has been taken, except:
   — where the expulsion decision is based on a previous judicial decision; or
   — where the persons concerned have had previous access to judicial review; or
   — where the expulsion decision is based on imperative grounds of public security under Article 28(3).
3. The redress procedures shall allow for an examination of the legality of the decision, as well as of the facts and circumstances on which the proposed measure is based. They shall ensure that the decision is not disproportionate, particularly in view of the requirements laid down in Article 28.
4. Member States may exclude the individual concerned from their territory pending the redress procedure, but they may not prevent the individual from submitting his/her defence in person, except when his/her appearance may cause serious troubles to public policy or public security or when the appeal or judicial review concerns a denial of entry to the territory.

Article 32 – Duration of exclusion orders

1. Persons excluded on grounds of public policy or public security may submit an application for lifting of the exclusion order after a reasonable period, depending on the circumstances, and in any event after three years from enforcement of the final exclusion order which has been validly adopted in accordance with Community law, by putting forward arguments to establish that there has been a material change in the circumstances which justified the decision ordering their exclusion.

   The Member State concerned shall reach a decision on this application within six months of its submission.
2. The persons referred to in paragraph 1 shall have no right of entry to the territory of the Member State concerned while their application is being considered.

Article 33 – Expulsion as a penalty or legal consequence

1. Expulsion orders may not be issued by the host Member State as a penalty or legal consequence of a custodial penalty, unless they conform to the requirements of Articles 27, 28 and 29.
2. If an expulsion order, as provided for in paragraph 1, is enforced more than two years after it was issued, the Member State shall check that the individual concerned is currently and genuinely a threat to public policy or public security and shall assess whether there has been any material change in the circumstances since the expulsion order was issued.

CHAPTER VII – FINAL PROVISIONS

Article 34 – Publicity

Member States shall disseminate information concerning the rights and obligations of Union citizens and their family members on the subjects covered by this Directive, particularly by means of awareness-raising campaigns conducted through national and local media and other means of communication.

Article 35 – Abuse of rights

Member States may adopt the necessary measures to refuse, terminate or withdraw any right conferred by this Directive in the case of abuse of rights or fraud, such as marriages of convenience. Any such measure shall be proportionate and subject to the procedural safeguards provided for in Articles 30 and 31.

Article 36 – Sanctions

Member States shall lay down provisions on the sanctions applicable to breaches of national rules adopted for the implementation of this Directive and shall take the measures required for their application. The sanctions laid down shall be effective and proportionate. Member States shall notify the Commission of these provisions not later than 30 April 2006 and as promptly as possible in the case of any subsequent changes.

Article 37 – More favourable national provisions

The provisions of this Directive shall not affect any laws, regulations or administrative provisions laid down by a Member State which would be more favourable to the persons covered by this Directive.

Article 38 – Repeals

1. Articles 10 and 11 of Regulation (EEC) No 1612/68 shall be repealed with effect from 30 April 2006.
2. Directives 64/221/EEC, 68/360/EEC, 72/194/EEC, 73/148/EEC, 75/34/EEC, 75/35/EEC, 90/364/EEC, 90/365/EEC and 93/96/EEC shall be repealed with effect from 30 April 2006.
3. References made to the repealed provisions and Directives shall be construed as being made to this Directive.

Article 39 – Report

No later than 30 April 2006 the Commission shall submit a report on the application of this Directive to the European Parliament and the Council, together with any necessary proposals, notably on the opportunity to extend the period of time during which Union citizens and their family members may reside in the territory of the host Member State without any conditions. The Member States shall provide the Commission with the information needed to produce the report.

Article 40 – Transposition

1. Member States shall bring into force the laws, regulations and administrative provisions necessary to comply with this Directive by 30 April 2006.

    When Member States adopt those measures, they shall contain a reference to this Directive or shall be accompanied by such a reference on the occasion of their official publication. The methods of making such reference shall be laid down by the Member States.

2. Member States shall communicate to the Commission the text of the provisions of national law which they adopt in the field covered by this Directive together with a table showing how the provisions of this Directive correspond to the national provisions adopted.

Article 41 – Entry into force

This Directive shall enter into force on the day of its publication in the *Official Journal of the European Union*.

Article 42 – Addressees

This Directive is addressed to the Member States.

Done at Strasbourg, 29 April 2004.

Appendix 7

Immigration (European Economic Area) Regulations 2006

SI 2006/1003
PART I
INTERPRETATION ETC

1. **Citation and commencement**

These Regulations may be cited as the Immigration (European Economic Area) Regulations 2006 and shall come into force on 30th April 2006.

2. **General interpretation**

(1) In these Regulations—

'the 1971 Act' means the Immigration Act 1971;

'the 1999 Act' means the Immigration and Asylum Act 1999;

'the 2002 Act' means the Nationality, Immigration and Asylum Act 2002;

'civil partner' does not include a party to a civil partnership of convenience;

'decision maker' means the Secretary of State, an immigration officer or an entry clearance officer (as the case may be);

'document certifying permanent residence' means a document issued to an EEA national, in accordance with regulation 18, as proof of the holder's permanent right of residence under regulation 15 as at the date of issue;

'EEA decision' means a decision under these Regulations that concerns a person's—

(a) entitlement to be admitted to the United Kingdom;

(b) entitlement to be issued with or have renewed, or not to have revoked, a registration certificate, residence card, document certifying permanent residence or permanent residence card; or

(c) removal from the United Kingdom;

'EEA family permit' means a document issued to a person, in accordance with regulation 12, in connection with his admission to the United Kingdom;

'EEA national' means a national of an EEA State;

'EEA State' means—

(a) a member State, other than the United Kingdom;

(b) Norway, Iceland or Liechtenstein; or

(c) Switzerland;

'entry clearance' has the meaning given in section 33(1) of the 1971 Act;

'entry clearance officer' means a person responsible for the grant or refusal of entry clearance;

'immigration rules' has the meaning given in section 33(1) of the 1971 Act;

'military service' means service in the armed forces of an EEA State;

'permanent residence card' means a card issued to a person who is not an EEA national, in accordance with regulation 18, as proof of the holder's permanent right of residence under regulation 15 as at the date of issue;

'registration certificate' means a certificate issued to an EEA national, in accordance with regulation 16, as proof of the holder's right of residence in the United Kingdom as at the date of issue;

'relevant EEA national' in relation to an extended family member has the meaning given in regulation 8(6);

'residence card' means a card issued to a person who is not an EEA national, in accordance with regulation 17, as proof of the holder's right of residence in the United Kingdom as at the date of issue;

'spouse' does not include a party to a marriage of convenience;

'United Kingdom national' means a person who falls to be treated as a national of the United Kingdom for the purposes of the Community Treaties.

(2) Paragraph (1) is subject to paragraph 1(a) of Schedule 4 (transitional provisions).

3. Continuity of residence

(1) This regulation applies for the purpose of calculating periods of continuous residence in the United Kingdom under regulation 5(1) and regulation 15.

(2) Continuity of residence is not affected by—

(a) periods of absence from the United Kingdom which do not exceed six months in total in any year;

(b) periods of absence from the United Kingdom on military service; or

(c) any one absence from the United Kingdom not exceeding twelve months for an important reason such as pregnancy and childbirth, serious illness, study or vocational training or an overseas posting.

(3) But continuity of residence is broken if a person is removed from the United Kingdom under regulation 19(3).

4. 'Worker', 'self-employed person', 'self-sufficient person' and 'student'

(1) In these Regulations —

(a) 'worker' means a worker within the meaning of Article 39 of the Treaty establishing the European Community;

(b) 'self-employed person' means a person who establishes himself in order to pursue activity as a self-employed person in accordance with Article 43 of the Treaty establishing the European Community;

(c) 'self-sufficient person' means a person who has—

(i) sufficient resources not to become a burden on the social assistance system of the United Kingdom during his period of residence; and

(ii) comprehensive sickness insurance cover in the United Kingdom;

(d) 'student' means a person who—

(i) is enrolled at a private or public establishment, included on the Department for Education and Skills' Register of Education and Training Providers or financed from public funds, for the principal purpose of following a course of study, including vocational training;

(ii) has comprehensive sickness insurance cover in the United Kingdom; and

(iii) assures the Secretary of State, by means of a declaration, or by such equivalent means as the person may choose, that he has sufficient resources not to become a burden on the social assistance system of the United Kingdom during his period of residence.

(2) For the purposes of paragraph (1)(c), where family members of the person concerned reside in the United Kingdom and their right to reside is dependent upon their being family members of that person—

(a) the requirement for that person to have sufficient resources not to become a burden on the social assistance system of the United Kingdom during his period of residence shall only be satisfied if his resources and those of the family members are sufficient to avoid him and the family members becoming such a burden;

(b) the requirement for that person to have comprehensive sickness insurance cover in the United Kingdom shall only be satisfied if he and his family members have such cover.

(3) For the purposes of paragraph (1)(d), where family members of the person concerned reside in the United Kingdom and their right to reside is dependent upon their being family members of that person, the requirement for that person to assure the Secretary of State that he has sufficient resources not to become a burden on the social assistance system of the United Kingdom during his period of residence shall only be satisfied if he assures the Secretary of State that his resources and those of the family members are sufficient to avoid him and the family members becoming such a burden.

(4) For the purposes of paragraphs (1)(c) and (d) and paragraphs (2) and (3), the resources of the person concerned and, where applicable, any family members, are to be regarded as sufficient if they exceed the maximum level of resources which a United Kingdom national and his family members may possess if he is to become eligible for social assistance under the United Kingdom benefit system.

5. **'Worker or self-employed person who has ceased activity'**

(1) In these Regulations, 'worker or self-employed person who has ceased activity' means an EEA national who satisfies the conditions in paragraph (2), (3), (4) or (5).

(2) A person satisfies the conditions in this paragraph if he—
  (a) terminates his activity as a worker or self-employed person and—
    (i) has reached the age at which he is entitled to a state pension on the date on which he terminates his activity; or
    (ii) in the case of a worker, ceases working to take early retirement;
  (b) pursued his activity as a worker or self-employed person in the United Kingdom for at least twelve months prior to the termination; and
  (c) resided in the United Kingdom continuously for more than three years prior to the termination.

(3) A person satisfies the conditions in this paragraph if—
  (a) he terminates his activity in the United Kingdom as a worker or self-employed person as a result of a permanent incapacity to work; and
  (b) either—
    (i) he resided in the United Kingdom continuously for more than two years prior to the termination; or
    (ii) the incapacity is the result of an accident at work or an occupational disease that entitles him to a pension payable in full or in part by an institution in the United Kingdom.

(4) A person satisfies the conditions in this paragraph if—
  (a) he is active as a worker or self-employed person in an EEA State but retains his place of residence in the United Kingdom, to which he returns as a rule at least once a week; and
  (b) prior to becoming so active in that EEA State, he had been continuously resident and continuously active as a worker or self-employed person in the United Kingdom for at least three years.

(5) A person who satisfies the condition in paragraph (4)(a) but not the condition in paragraph (4)(b) shall, for the purposes of paragraphs (2) and (3), be treated as being active and resident in the United Kingdom during any period in which he is working or self-employed in the EEA State.

(6) The conditions in paragraphs (2) and (3) as to length of residence and activity as a worker or self-euloyed person shall not apply in relation to a person whose spouse or civil partner is a United Kingdom national.

(7) For the purposes of this regulation—

(a) periods of inactivity for reasons not of the person's own making;
(b) periods of inactivity due to illness or accident; and
(c) in the case of a worker, periods of involuntary unemployment duly recorded by the relevant employment office,

shall be treated as periods of activity as a worker or self-employed person, as the case may be.

6. **'Qualified person'**

(1) In these Regulations, 'qualified person' means a person who is an EEA national and in the United Kingdom as—
  (a) a jobseeker;
  (b) a worker;
  (c) a self-employed person;
  (d) a self-sufficient person; or
  (e) a student.

(2) A person who is no longer working shall not cease to be treated as a worker for the purpose of paragraph (1)(b) if—
  (a) he is temporarily unable to work as the result of an illness or accident;
  (b) he is in duly recorded involuntary unemployment after having been employed in the United Kingdom, provided that he has registered as a jobseeker with the relevant employment office and—
    (i) he was employed for one year or more before becoming unemployed;
    (ii) he has been unemployed for no more than six months; or
    (iii) he can provide evidence that he is seeking employment in the United Kingdom and has a genuine chance of being engaged;
  (c) he is involuntarily unemployed and has embarked on vocational training; or
  (d) he has voluntarily ceased working and embarked on vocational training that is related to his previous employment.

(3) A person who is no longer in self-employment shall not cease to be treated as a self-employed person for the purpose of paragraph (1)(c) if he is temporarily unable to pursue his activity as a self-employed person as the result of an illness or accident.

(4) For the purpose of paragraph (1)(a), 'jobseeker' means a person who enters the United Kingdom in order to seek employment and can provide evidence that he is seeking employment and has a genuine chance of being engaged.

7. **Family member**

(1) Subject to paragraph (2), for the purposes of these Regulations the following persons shall be treated as the family members of another person—
  (a) his spouse or his civil partner;
  (b) direct descendants of his, his spouse or his civil partner who are—
    (i) under 21; or
    (ii) dependants of his, his spouse or his civil partner;
  (c) dependent direct relatives in his ascending line or that of his spouse or his civil partner;
  (d) a person who is to be treated as the family member of that other person under paragraph (3).

(2) A person shall not be treated under paragraph (1)(b) or (c) as the family member of a student residing in the United Kingdom after the period of three months beginning on the date on which the student is admitted to the United Kingdom unless—

(a) in the case of paragraph (b), the person is the dependent child of the student or of his spouse or civil partner; or

(b) the student also falls within one of the other categories of qualified persons mentioned in regulation 6(1).

(3) Subject to paragraph (4), a person who is an extended family member and has been issued with an EEA family permit, a registration certificate or a residence card shall be treated as the family member of the relevant EEA national for as long as he continues to satisfy the conditions in regulation 8(2), (3), (4) or (5) in relation to that EEA national and the permit, certificate or card has not ceased to be valid or been revoked.

(4) Where the relevant EEA national is a student, the extended family member shall only be treated as the family member of that national under paragraph (3) if either the EEA family permit was issued under regulation 12(2), the registration certificate was issued under regulation 16(5) or the residence card was issued under regulation 17(4).

8. **'Extended family member'**

    (1) In these Regulations 'extended family member" means a person who is not a family member of an EEA national under regulation 7(1)(a), (b) or (c) and who satisfies the conditions in paragraph (2), (3), (4) or (5).

    (2) A person satisfies the condition in this paragraph if the person is a relative of an EEA national, his spouse or his civil partner and—

    (a) the person is residing in an EEA State in which the EEA national also resides and is dependent upon the EEA national or is a member of his household;

    (b) the person satisfied the condition in paragraph (a) and is accompanying the EEA national to the United Kingdom or wishes to join him there; or

    (c) the person satisfied the condition in paragraph (a), has joined the EEA national in the United Kingdom and continues to be dependent upon him or to be a member of his household.

    (3) A person satisfies the condition in this paragraph if the person is a relative of an EEA national or his spouse or his civil partner and, on serious health grounds, strictly requires the personal care of the EEA national his spouse or his civil partner.

    (4) A person satisfies the condition in this paragraph if the person is a relative of an EEA national and would meet the requirements in the immigration rules (other than those relating to entry clearance) for indefinite leave to enter or remain in the United Kingdom as a dependent relative of the EEA national were the EEA national a person present and settled in the United Kingdom.

    (5) A person satisfies the condition in this paragraph if the person is the partner of an EEA national (other than a civil partner) and can prove to the decision maker that he is in a durable relationship with the EEA national.

    (6) In these Regulations 'relevant EEA national' means, in relation to an extended family member, the EEA national who is or whose spouse or civil partner is the relative of the extended family member for the purpose of paragraph (2), (3) or (4) or the EEA national who is the partner of the extended family member for the purpose of paragraph (5).

9. **Family members of United Kingdom nationals**

    (1) If the conditions in paragraph (2) are satisfied, these Regulations apply to a person who is the family member of a United Kingdom national as if the United Kingdom national were an EEA national.

    (2) The conditions are that—

(a) the United Kingdom national is residing in an EEA State as a worker or self-employed person or was so residing before returning to the United Kingdom; and

(b) if the family member of the United Kingdom national is his spouse or civil partner, the parties are living together in the EEA State or had entered into the marriage or civil partnership and were living together in that State before the United Kingdom national returned to the United Kingdom.

(3) Where these Regulations apply to the family member of a United Kingdom national the United Kingdom national shall be treated as holding a valid passport issued by an EEA State for the purpose of the application of regulation 13 to that family member.

10. **'Family member who has retained the right of residence'**

(1) In these Regulations, 'family member who has retained the right of residence' means, subject to paragraph (8), a person who satisfies the conditions in paragraph (2), (3), (4) or (5).

(2) A person satisfies the conditions in this paragraph if—

(a) he was a family member of a qualified person when the qualified person died;

(b) he resided in the United Kingdom in accordance with these Regulations for at least the year immediately before the death of the qualified person; and

(c) he satisfies the condition in paragraph (6).

(3) A person satisfies the conditions in this paragraph if—

(a) he is the direct descendant of—

(i) a qualified person who has died;

(ii) a person who ceased to be a qualified person on ceasing to reside in the United Kingdom; or

(iii) the person who was the spouse or civil partner of the qualified person mentioned in sub-paragraph (i) when he died or is the spouse or civil partner of the person mentioned in sub-paragraph (ii); and

(b) he was attending an educational course in the United Kingdom immediately before the qualified person died or ceased to be a qualified person and continues to attend such a course.

(4) A person satisfies the conditions in this paragraph if the person is the parent with actual custody of a child who satisfies the condition in paragraph (3).

(5) A person satisfies the conditions in this paragraph if—

(a) he ceased to be a family member of a qualified person on the termination of the marriage or civil partnership of the qualified person;

(b) he was residing in the United Kingdom in accordance with these Regulations at the date of the termination;

(c) he satisfies the condition in paragraph (6); and

(d) either—

(i) prior to the initiation of the proceedings for the termination of the marriage or the civil partnership the marriage or civil partnership had lasted for at least three years and the parties to the marriage or civil partnership had resided in the United Kingdom for at least one year during its duration;

(ii) the former spouse or civil partner of the qualified person has custody of a child of the qualified person;

(iii) the former spouse or civil partner of the qualified person has the right of access to a child of the qualified person under the age of 18 and a court has ordered that such access must take place in the United Kingdom; or

(iv) the continued right of residence in the United Kingdom of the person is warranted by particularly difficult circumstances, such as he or another family member having been a victim of domestic violence while the marriage or civil partnership was subsisting.

(6) The condition in this paragraph is that the person—

(a) is not an EEA national but would, if he were an EEA national, be a worker, a self-employed person or a self-sufficient person under regulation 6; or

(b) is the family member of a person who falls within paragraph (a).

(7) In this regulation, 'educational course' means a course within the scope of Article 12 of Council Regulation (EEC) No. 1612/68 on freedom of movement for workers.

(8) A person with a permanent right of residence under regulation 15 shall not become a family member who has retained the right of residence on the death or departure from the United Kingdom of the qualified person or the termination of the marriage or civil partnership, as the case may be, and a family member who has retained the right of residence shall cease to have that status on acquiring a permanent right of residence under regulation 15.

PART 2
EEA RIGHTS

11. Right of admission to the United Kingdom

(1) An EEA national must be admitted to the United Kingdom if he produces on arrival a valid national identity card or passport issued by an EEA State.

(2) A person who is not an EEA national must be admitted to the United Kingdom if he is a family member of an EEA national, a family member who has retained the right of residence or a person with a permanent right of residence under regulation 15 and produces on arrival—

(a) a valid passport; and

(b) an EEA family permit, a residence card or a permanent residence card.

(3) An immigration officer may not place a stamp in the passport of a person admitted to the United Kingdom under this regulation who is not an EEA national if the person produces a residence card or permanent residence card.

(4) Before an immigration officer refuses admission to the United Kingdom to a person under this regulation because the person does not produce on arrival a document mentioned in paragraph (1) or (2), the immigration officer must give the person every reasonable opportunity to obtain the document or have it brought to him within a reasonable period of time or to prove by other means that he is—

(a) an EEA national;

(b) a family member of an EEA national with a right to accompany that national or join him in the United Kingdom; or

(c) a family member who has retained the right of residence or a person with a permanent right of residence under regulation 15.

(5) But this regulation is subject to regulations 19(1) and (2).

12. Issue of EEA family permit

(1) An entry clearance officer must issue an EEA family permit to a person who applies for one if the person is a family member of an EEA national and—

(a) the EEA national—

(i) is residing in the UK in accordance with these Regulations; or

(ii) will be travelling to the United Kingdom within six months of the date of the application and will be an EEA national residing in the United Kingdom in accordance with these Regulations on arrival in the United Kingdom; and

(b) the family member will be accompanying the EEA national to the United Kingdom or joining him there and—

(i) is lawfully resident in an EEA State; or

(ii) would meet the requirements in the immigration rules (other than those relating to entry clearance) for leave to enter the United Kingdom as the family member of the EEA national or, in the case of direct descendants or dependent direct relatives in the ascending line of his spouse or his civil partner, as the family member of his spouse or his civil partner, were the EEA national or the spouse or civil partner a person present and settled in the United Kingdom.

(2) An entry clearance officer may issue an EEA family permit to an extended family member of an EEA national who applies for one if—

(a) the relevant EEA national satisfies the condition in paragraph (1)(a);

(b) the extended family member wishes to accompany the relevant EEA national to the United Kingdom or to join him there; and

(c) in all the circumstances, it appears to the entry clearance officer appropriate to issue the EEA family permit.

(3) Where an entry clearance officer receives an application under paragraph (2) he shall undertake an extensive examination of the personal circumstances of the applicant and if he refuses the application shall give reasons justifying the refusal unless this is contrary to the interests of national security.

(4) An EEA family permit issued under this regulation shall be issued free of charge and as soon as possible.

(5) But an EEA family permit shall not be issued under this regulation if the applicant or the EEA national concerned falls to be excluded from the United Kingdom on grounds of public policy, public security or public health in accordance with regulation 21.

13. **Initial right of residence**

(1) An EEA national is entitled to reside in the United Kingdom for a period not exceeding three months beginning on the date on which he is admitted to the United Kingdom provided that he holds a valid national identity card or passport issued by an EEA State.

(2) A family member of an EEA national residing in the United Kingdom under paragraph (1) who is not himself an EEA national is entitled to reside in the United Kingdom provided that he holds a valid passport.

(3) But—

(a) this regulation is subject to regulation 19(3)(b); and

(b) an EEA national or his family member who becomes an unreasonable burden on the social assistance system of the United Kingdom shall cease to have the right to reside under this regulation.

14. **Extended right of residence**

(1) A qualified person is entitled to reside in the United Kingdom for so long as he remains a qualified person.

(2) A family member of a qualified person residing in the United Kingdom under paragraph (1) or of an EEA national with a permanent right of residence under regulation 15 is entitled to reside in the United Kingdom for so long as he remains the family member of the qualified person or EEA national.

(3) A family member who has retained the right of residence is entitled to reside in the United Kingdom for so long as he remains a family member who has retained the right of residence.

(4) A right to reside under this regulation is in addition to any right a person may have to reside in the United Kingdom under regulation 13 or 15.

(5) But this regulation is subject to regulation 19(3)(b).

15. Permanent right of residence

(1) The following persons shall acquire the right to reside in the United Kingdom permanently—

   (a) an EEA national who has resided in the United Kingdom in accordance with these Regulations for a continuous period of five years;

   (b) a family member of an EEA national who is not himself an EEA national but who has resided in the United Kingdom with the EEA national in accordance with these Regulations for a continuous period of five years;

   (c) a worker or self-employed person who has ceased activity;

   (d) the family member of a worker or self-employed person who has ceased activity;

   (e) a person who was the family member of a worker or self-employed person where—

      (i) the worker or self-employed person has died;

      (ii) the family member resided with him immediately before his death; and

      (iii) the worker or self-employed person had resided continuously in the United Kingdom for at least the two years immediately before his death or the death was the result of an accident at work or an occupational disease;

   (f) a person who—

      (i) has resided in the United Kingdom in accordance with these Regulations for a continuous period of five years; and

      (ii) was, at the end of that period, a family member who has retained the right of residence.

(2) Once acquired, the right of permanent residence under this regulation shall be lost only through absence from the United Kingdom for a period exceeding two consecutive years.

(3) But this regulation is subject to regulation 19(3)(b).

PART 3
RESIDENCE DOCUMENTATION

16. Issue of registration certificate

(1) The Secretary of State must issue a registration certificate to a qualified person immediately on application and production of—

   (a) a valid identity card or passport issued by an EEA State;

   (b) proof that he is a qualified person.

(2) In the case of a worker, confirmation of the worker's engagement from his employer or a certificate of employment is sufficient proof for the purposes of paragraph (1)(b).

(3) The Secretary of State must issue a registration certificate to an EEA national who is the family member of a qualified person or of an EEA national with a permanent right of residence under regulation 15 immediately on application and production of—

   (a) a valid identity card or passport issued by an EEA State; and

   (b) proof that the applicant is such a family member.

(4) The Secretary of State must issue a registration certificate to an EEA national who is a family member who has retained the right of residence on application and production of—
(a) a valid identity card or passport; and
(b) proof that the applicant is a family member who has retained the right of residence.

(5) The Secretary of State may issue a registration certificate to an extended family member not falling within regulation 7(3) who is an EEA national on application if—
(a) the relevant EEA national in relation to the extended family member is a qualified person or an EEA national with a permanent right of residence under regulation 15; and
(b) in all the circumstances it appears to the Secretary of State appropriate to issue the registration certificate.

(6) Where the Secretary of State receives an application under paragraph (5) he shall undertake an extensive examination of the personal circumstances of the applicant and if he refuses the application shall give reasons justifying the refusal unless this is contrary to the interests of national security.

(7) A registration certificate issued under this regulation shall state the name and address of the person registering and the date of registration and shall be issued free of charge.

(8) But this regulation is subject to regulation 20(1).

17. **Issue of residence card**

(1) The Secretary of State must issue a residence card to a person who is not an EEA national and is the family member of a qualified person or of an EEA national with a permanent right of residence under regulation 15 on application and production of—
(a) a valid passport; and
(b) proof that the applicant is such a family member.

(2) The Secretary of State must issue a residence card to a person who is not an EEA national but who is a family member who has retained the right of residence on application and production of—
(a) a valid passport; and
(b) proof that the applicant is a family member who has retained the right of residence.

(3) On receipt of an application under paragraph (1) or (2) and the documents that are required to accompany the application the Secretary of State shall immediately issue the applicant with a certificate of application for the residence card and the residence card shall be issued no later than six months after the date on which the application and documents are received.

(4) The Secretary of State may issue a residence card to an extended family member not falling within regulation 7(3) who is not an EEA national on application if—
(a) the relevant EEA national in relation to the extended family member is a qualified person or an EEA national with a permanent right of residence under regulation 15; and
(b) in all the circumstances it appears to the Secretary of State appropriate to issue the residence card.

(5) Where the Secretary of State receives an application under paragraph (4) he shall undertake an extensive examination of the personal circumstances of the applicant and if he refuses the application shall give reasons justifying the refusal unless this is contrary to the interests of national security.

(6) A residence card issued under this regulation may take the form of a stamp in the applicant's passport and shall be entitled 'Residence card of a family member of an EEA national' and be valid for—

    (a) five years from the date of issue; or

    (b) in the case of a residence card issued to the family member or extended family member of a qualified person, the envisaged period of residence in the United Kingdom of the qualified person,

whichever is the shorter.

(7) A residence card issued under this regulation shall be issued free of charge.

(8) But this regulation is subject to regulation 20(1).

18. Issue of a document certifying permanent residence and a permanent residence card

(1) The Secretary of State must issue an EEA national with a permanent right of residence under regulation 15 with a document certifying permanent residence as soon as possible after an application for such a document and proof that the EEA national has such a right is submitted to the Secretary of State.

(2) The Secretary of State must issue a person who is not an EEA national who has a permanent right of residence under regulation 15 with a permanent residence card no later than six months after the date on which an application for a permanent residence card and proof that the person has such a right is submitted to the Secretary of State.

(3) Subject to paragraph (5) and regulation 20(3), a permanent residence card shall be valid for ten years from the date of issue and must be renewed on application.

(4) A document certifying permanent residence and a permanent residence card shall be issued free of charge.

(5) A document certifying permanent residence and a permanent residence card shall cease to be valid if the holder ceases to have a right of permanent residence under regulation 15.

PART 4
REFUSAL OF ADMISSION AND REMOVAL ETC

19. Exclusion and removal from the United Kingdom

(1) A person is not entitled to be admitted to the United Kingdom by virtue of regulation 11 if his exclusion is justified on grounds of public policy, public security or public health in accordance with regulation 21.

(2) A person is not entitled to be admitted to the United Kingdom as the family member of an EEA national under regulation 11(2) unless, at the time of his arrival—

    (a) he is accompanying the EEA national or joining him in the United Kingdom; and

    (b) the EEA national has a right to reside in the United Kingdom under these Regulations.

(3) Subject to paragraphs (4) and (5), a person who has been admitted to, or acquired a right to reside in, the United Kingdom under these Regulations may be removed from the United Kingdom if—

    (a) he does not have or ceases to have a right to reside under these Regulations; or

    (b) he would otherwise be entitled to reside in the United Kingdom under these Regulations but the Secretary of State has decided that his removal is justified on the grounds of public policy, public security or public health in accordance with regulation 21.

(4) A person must not be removed under paragraph (3) as the automatic consequence of having recourse to the social assistance system of the United Kingdom.

(5) A person must not be removed under paragraph (3) if he has a right to remain in the United Kingdom by virtue of leave granted under the 1971 Act unless his removal is justified on the grounds of public policy, public security or public health in accordance with regulation 21.

20. **Refusal to issue or renew and revocation of residence documentation**

    (1) The Secretary of State may refuse to issue, revoke or refuse to renew a registration certificate, a residence card, a document certifying permanent residence or a permanent residence card if the refusal or revocation is justified on grounds of public policy, public security or public health.

    (2) The Secretary of State may revoke a registration certificate or a residence card or refuse to renew a residence card if the holder of the certificate or card has ceased to have a right to reside under these Regulations.

    (3) The Secretary of State may revoke a document certifying permanent residence or a permanent residence card or refuse to renew a permanent residence card if the holder of the certificate or card has ceased to have a right of permanent residence under regulation 15.

    (4) An immigration officer may, at the time of a person's arrival in the United Kingdom—

    (a) revoke that person's residence card if he is not at that time the family member of a qualified person or of an EEA national who has a right of permanent residence under regulation 15, a family member who has retained the right of residence or a person with a right of permanent residence under regulation 15;

    (b) revoke that person's permanent residence card if he is not at that time a person with a right of permanent residence under regulation 15.

    (5) An immigration officer may, at the time of a person's arrival in the United Kingdom, revoke that person's EEA family permit if—

    (a) the revocation is justified on grounds of public policy, public security or public health; or

    (b) the person is not at that time the family member of an EEA national with the right to reside in the United Kingdom under these Regulations or is not accompanying that national or joining him in the United Kingdom.

    (6) Any action taken under this regulation on grounds of public policy, public security or public health shall be in accordance with regulation 21.

21. **Decisions taken on public policy, public security and public health grounds**

    (1) In this regulation a 'relevant decision' means an EEA decision taken on the grounds of public policy, public security or public health.

    (2) A relevant decision may not be taken to serve economic ends.

    (3) A relevant decision may not be taken in respect of a person with a permanent right of residence under regulation 15 except on serious grounds of public policy or public security.

    (4) A relevant decision may not be taken except on imperative grounds of public security in respect of an EEA national who—

    (a) has resided in the United Kingdom for a continuous period of at least ten years prior to the relevant decision; or

    (b) is under the age of 18, unless the relevant decision is necessary in his best interests, as provided for in the Convention on the Rights of the Child adopted by the General Assembly of the United Nations on 20th November 1989.

(5) Where a relevant decision is taken on grounds of public policy or public security it shall, in addition to complying with the preceding paragraphs of this regulation, be taken in accordance with the following principles—
  (a) the decision must comply with the principle of proportionality;
  (b) the decision must be based exclusively on the personal conduct of the person concerned;
  (c) the personal conduct of the person concerned must represent a genuine, present and sufficiently serious threat affecting one of the fundamental interests of society;
  (d) matters isolated from the particulars of the case or which relate to considerations of general prevention do not justify the decision;
  (e) a person's previous criminal convictions do not in themselves justify the decision.

(6) Before taking a relevant decision on the grounds of public policy or public security in relation to a person who is resident in the United Kingdom the decision maker must take account of considerations such as the age, state of health, family and economic situation of the person, the person's length of residence in the United Kingdom, the person's social and cultural integration into the United Kingdom and the extent of the person's links with his country of origin.

(7) In the case of a relevant decision taken on grounds of public health—
  (a) a disease that does not have epidemic potential as defined by the relevant instruments of the World Health Organisation or is not a disease to which section 38 of the Public Health (Control of Disease) Act 1984 applies (detention in hospital of a person with a notifiable disease) shall not constitute grounds for the decision; and
  (b) if the person concerned is in the United Kingdom, diseases occurring after the three month period beginning on the date on which he arrived in the United Kingdom shall not constitute grounds for the decision.

PART 5
PROCEDURE IN RELATION TO EEA DECISIONS

22. **Person claiming right of admission**

(1) This regulation applies to a person who claims a right of admission to the United Kingdom under regulation 11 as—
  (a) a person, not being an EEA national, who is a family member of an EEA national, a family member who has retained the right of residence or a person with a permanent right of residence under regulation 15; or
  (b) an EEA national, where there is reason to believe that he may fall to be excluded from the United Kingdom on grounds of public policy, public security or public health.

(2) A person to whom this regulation applies is to be treated as if he were a person seeking leave to enter the United Kingdom under the 1971 Act for the purposes of paragraphs 2, 3, 4, 7, 16 to 18 and 21 to 24 of Schedule 2 to the 1971 Act (administrative provisions as to control on entry etc), except that—
  (a) the reference in paragraph 2(1) to the purpose for which the immigration officer may examine any persons who have arrived in the United Kingdom is to be read as a reference to the purpose of determining whether he is a person who is to be granted admission under these Regulations;
  (b) the references in paragraphs 4(2A), 7 and 16(1) to a person who is, or may be, given leave to enter are to be read as references to a person who is, or may be, granted admission under these Regulations; and

(c) a medical examination is not be carried out under paragraph 2 or paragraph 7 as a matter of routine and may only be carried out within three months of a person's arrival in the United Kingdom.

(3) For so long as a person to whom this regulation applies is detained, or temporarily admitted or released while liable to detention, under the powers conferred by Schedule 2 to the 1971 Act, he is deemed not to have been admitted to the United Kingdom.

23. **Person refused admission**

    (1) This regulation applies to a person who is in the United Kingdom and has been refused admission to the United Kingdom—

    (a) because he does not meet the requirement of regulation 11 (including where he does not meet those requirements because his EEA family permit, residence card or permanent residence card has been revoked by an immigration officer in accordance with regulation 20); or

    (b) in accordance with regulation 19(1) or (2).

    (2) A person to whom this regulation applies, is to be treated as if he were a person refused leave to enter under the 1971 Act for the purpose of paragraphs 8, 10, 10A, 11, 16 to 19 and 21 to 24 of Schedule 2 to the 1971 Act, except that the reference in paragraph 19 to a certificate of entitlement, entry clearance or work permit is to be read as a reference to an EEA family permit, residence card or a permanent residence card.

24. **Person subject to removal**

    (1) This regulation applies to a person whom it has been decided to remove from the United Kingdom in accordance with regulation 19(3).

    (2) Where the decision is under regulation 19(3)(a), the person is to be treated as if he were a person to whom section 10(1)(a) of the 1999 Act applied, and section 10 of that Act (removal of certain persons unlawfully in the United Kingdom) is to apply accordingly.

    (3) Where the decision is under regulation l9(3)(b), the person is to be treated as if he were a person to whom section 3(5)(a) of the 1971 Act (liability to deportation) applied, and section 5 of that Act (procedure for deportation) and Schedule 3 to that Act (supplementary provision as to deportation) are to apply accordingly.

    (4) A person who enters or seeks to enter the United Kingdom in breach of a deportation order made against him pursuant to paragraph (3) shall be removable as an illegal entrant under Schedule 2 to the 1971 Act and the provisions of that Schedule shall apply accordingly.

    (5) Where such a deportation order is made against a person but he is not removed under the order during the two year period beginning on the date on which the order is made, the Secretary of State shall only take action to remove the person under the order after the end of that period if, having assessed whether there has been any material change in circumstances since the deportation order was made, he considers that the removal continues to be justified on the grounds of public policy, public security or public health.

    (6) A person to whom this regulation applies shall be allowed one month to leave the United Kingdom, beginning on the date on which he is notified of the decision to remove him, before being removed pursuant to that decision except—

    (a) in duly substantiated cases of urgency;

    (b) where the person is detained pursuant to the sentence or order of any court;

    (c) where a person is a person to whom regulation 24(4) applies.

PART 6
APPEALS UNDER THESE REGULATIONS

25. **Interpretation of Part 6**

    (1) In this Part—

    'Asylum and Immigration Tribunal' has the same meaning as in the 2002 Act;

    'Commission' has the same meaning as in the Special Immigration Appeals Commission Act 1997;

    'the Human Rights Convention' has the same meaning as 'the Convention' in the Human Rights Act 1998; and

    'the Refugee Convention' means the Convention relating to the Status of Refugees done at Geneva on 28th July 1951 and the Protocol relating to the Status of Refugees done at New York on 31st January 1967.

    (2) For the purposes of this Part, and subject to paragraphs (3) and (4), an appeal is to be treated as pending during the period when notice of appeal is given and ending when the appeal is finally determined, withdrawn or abandoned.

    (3) An appeal is not to be treated as finally determined while a further appeal may be brought; and, if such a further appeal is brought, the original appeal is not to be treated as finally determined until the further appeal is determined, withdrawn or abandoned.

    (4) A pending appeal is not to be treated as abandoned solely because the appellant leaves the United Kingdom.

26. **Appeal rights**

    (1) Subject to the following paragraphs of this regulation, a person may appeal under these Regulations against an EEA decision.

    (2) If a person claims to be an EEA national, he may not appeal under these Regulations unless he produces a valid national identity card or passport issued by an EEA State.

    (3) If a person claims to be the family member or relative of an EEA national he may not appeal under these Regulations unless he produces—

    (a) an EEA family permit; or

    (b) other proof that he is related as claimed to an EEA national.

    (4) A person may not bring an appeal under these Regulations on a ground certified under paragraph (5) or rely on such a ground in an appeal brought under these Regulations.

    (5) The Secretary of State or an immigration officer may certify a ground for the purposes of paragraph (4) if it has been considered in a previous appeal brought under these Regulations or under section 82(1) of the 2002 Act.

    (6) Except where an appeal lies to the Commission, an appeal under these Regulations lies to the Asylum and Immigration Tribunal.

    (7) The provisions of or made under the 2002 Act referred to in Schedule 1 shall have effect for the purposes of an appeal under these Regulations to the Asylum and Immigration Tribunal in accordance with that Schedule.

27. **Out of country appeals**

    (1) Subject to paragraphs (2) and (3), a person may not appeal under regulation 26 whilst he is in the United Kingdom against an EEA decision—

    (a) to refuse to admit him to the United Kingdom;

    (b) to refuse to revoke a deportation order made against him;

    (c) to refuse to issue him with an EEA family permit; or

    (d) to remove him from the United Kingdom after he has entered or sought to enter the United Kingdom in breach of a deportation order.

    (2) Paragraph (1)(a) does not apply where—

(a) the person held an EEA family permit, a registration certificate, a residence card, a document certifying permanent residence or a permanent residence card on his arrival in the United Kingdom or can otherwise prove that he is resident in the United Kingdom;

(b) the person is deemed not to have been admitted to the United Kingdom under regulation 22(3) but at the date on which notice of the decision to refuse to admit him is given he has been in the United Kingdom for at least 3 months;

(c) the person is in the United Kingdom and a ground of the appeal is that, in taking the decision, the decision maker acted in breach of his rights under the Human Rights Convention or the Refugee Convention, unless the Secretary of State certifies that that ground of appeal is clearly unfounded.

(3) Paragraph (1)(d) does not apply where a ground of the appeal is that, in taking the decision, the decision maker acted in breach of the appellant's rights under the Human Rights Convention or the Refugee Convention, unless the Secretary of State certifies that that ground of appeal is clearly unfounded.

28. Appeals to the Commission

(1) An appeal against an EEA decision lies to the Commission where paragraph (2) or (4) applies.

(2) This paragraph applies if the Secretary of State certifies that the EEA decision was taken—

(a) by the Secretary of State wholly or partly on a ground listed in paragraph (3); or

(b) in accordance with a direction of the Secretary of State which identifies the person to whom the decision relates and which is given wholly or partly on a ground listed in paragraph (3).

(3) The grounds mentioned in paragraph (2) are that the person's exclusion or removal from the United Kingdom is—

(a) in the interests of national security; or

(b) in the interests of the relationship between the United Kingdom and another country.

(4) This paragraph applies if the Secretary of State certifies that the EEA decision was taken wholly or partly in reliance on information which in his opinion should not be made public—

(a) in the interests of national security;

(b) in the interests of the relationship between the United Kingdom and another country; or

(c) otherwise in the public interest.

(5) In paragraphs (2) and (4) a reference to the Secretary of State is to the Secretary of State acting in person.

(6) Where a certificate is issued under paragraph (2) or (4) in respect of a pending appeal to the Asylum and Immigration Tribunal the appeal shall lapse.

(7) An appeal against an EEA decision lies to the Commission where an appeal lapses by virtue of paragraph (6).

(8) The Special Immigration Appeals Commission Act 1997 shall apply to an appeal to the Commission under these Regulations as it applies to an appeal under section 2 of that Act to which subsection (2) of that section applies (appeals against an immigration decision) but paragraph (i) of that subsection shall not apply in relation to such an appeal.

29. Effect of appeals to the Asylum and Immigration Tribunal

(1) This Regulation applies to appeals under these Regulations made to the Asylum and Immigration Tribunal.

(2) If a person in the United Kingdom appeals against an EEA decision to refuse to admit him to the United Kingdom, any directions for his removal from the United Kingdom previously given by virtue of the refusal cease to have effect, except in so far as they have already been carried out, and no directions may be so given while the appeal is pending.

(3) If a person in the United Kingdom appeals against an EEA decision to remove him from the United Kingdom, any directions given under section 10 of the 1999 Act or Schedule 3 to the 1971 Act for his removal from the United Kingdom are to have no effect, except in so far as they have already been carried out, while the appeal is pending.

(4) But the provisions of Part I of Schedule 2, or as the case may be, Schedule 3 to the 1971 Act with respect to detention and persons liable to detention apply to a person appealing against a refusal to admit him or a decision to remove him as if there were in force directions for his removal from the United Kingdom, except that he may not be detained on board a ship or aircraft so as to compel him to leave the United Kingdom while the appeal is pending.

(5) In calculating the period of two months limited by paragraph 8(2) of Schedule 2 to the 1971 Act for—

(a) the giving of directions under that paragraph for the removal of a person from the United Kingdom; and

(b) the giving of a notice of intention to give such directions,

any period during which there is pending an appeal by him under is to be disregarded.

(6) If a person in the United Kingdom appeals against an EEA decision to remove him from the United Kingdom, a deportation order is not to be made against him under section 5 of the 1971 Act while the appeal is pending.

(7) Paragraph 29 of Schedule 2 to the 1971 Act (grant of bail pending appeal) applies to a person who has an appeal pending under these Regulations as it applies to a person who has an appeal pending under section 82(1) of the 2002 Act.

PART 7
GENERAL

30. Effect on other legislation

Schedule 2 (effect on other legislation) shall have effect.

31. Revocations, transitional provisions and consequential amendments

(1) The Regulations listed in column 1 of the table in Part 1 of Schedule 3 are revoked to the extent set out in column 3 of that table, subject to Part 2 of that Schedule and to Schedule 4.

(2) Schedule 4 (transitional provisions) and Schedule 5 (consequential amendments) shall have effect.

Regulation 26(7)

SCHEDULE 1
APPEALS TO THE ASYLUM AND IMMIGRATION TRIBUNAL

The following provisions of, or made under, the 2002 Act have effect in relation to an appeal under these Regulations to the Asylum and Immigration Tribunal as if it were an appeal against an immigration decision under section 82(1) of that Act:

section 84(1), except paragraphs (a) and (f);

sections 85 to 87;

sections 103A to 103E;

section 105 and any regulations made under that section; and

section 106 and any rules made under that section.

SCHEDULE 2 Regulation 30
EFFECT ON OTHER LEGISLATION

1. **Leave under the 1971 Act**

    (1) In accordance with section 7 of the Immigration Act 1988, a person who is admitted to or acquires a right to reside in the United Kingdom under these Regulations shall not require leave to remain in the United Kingdom under the 1971 Act during any period in which he has a right to reside under these Regulations but such a person shall require leave to remain under the 1971 Act during any period in which he does not have such a right.

    (2) Where a person has leave to enter or remain under the 1971 Act which is subject to conditions and that person also has a right to reside under these Regulations, those conditions shall not have effect for as long as the person has that right to reside.

2. **Persons not subject to restriction on the period for which they may remain**

    (1) For the purposes of the 1971 Act and the British Nationality Act 1981, a person who has a permanent right of residence under regulation 15 shall be regarded as a person who is in the United Kingdom without being subject under the immigration laws to any restriction on the period for which he may remain.

    (2) But a qualified person, the family member of a qualified person and a family member who has retained the right of residence shall not, by virtue of that status, be so regarded for those purposes.

3. **Carriers' liability under the 1999 Act**

    For the purposes of satisfying a requirement to produce a visa under section 40(1)(b) of the 1999 Act (charges in respect of passenger without proper documents), 'a visa of the required kind' includes an EEA family permit, a residence card or a permanent residence card required for admission under regulation 11(2).

4. **Appeals under the 2002 Act and previous immigration Acts**

    (1) The following EEA decisions shall not be treated as immigration decisions for the purpose of section 82(2) of the 2002 Act (right of appeal against an immigration decision)—

    (a) a decision that a person is to be removed under regulation 19(3)(a) by way of a direction under section 10(1)(a) of the 1999 Act (as provided for by regulation 24(2));

    (b) a decision to remove a person under regulation 19(3)(b) by making a deportation order under section 5(1) of the 1971 Act (as provided for by regulation 24(3));

    (c) a decision to remove a person mentioned in regulation 24(4) by way of directions under paragraphs 8 to 10 of Schedule 2 to the 1971 Act.

    (2) A person who has been issued with a registration certificate, residence card, a document certifying permanent residence or a permanent residence card under these Regulations or a registration certificate under the Accession (Immigration and Worker Registration) Regulations 2004, or a person whose passport has been stamped with a family member residence stamp, shall have no right of appeal under section 2 of the Special Immigration Appeals Commission Act 1997 or section 82(1) of the 2002 Act. Any existing appeal under those sections of those Acts or under the Asylum and Immigration Appeals Act 1993, the Asylum and Immigration Act 1996 or the 1999 Act shall be treated as abandoned.

    (3) Subject to paragraph (4), a person may appeal to the Asylum and Immigration Tribunal under section 83(2) of the 2002 Act against the rejection of his asylum claim where—

    (a) that claim has been rejected, but

    (b) he has a right to reside in the United Kingdom under these Regulations.

(4) Paragraph (3) shall not apply if the person is an EEA national and the Secretary of State certifies that the asylum claim is clearly unfounded.

(5) The Secretary of State shall certify the claim under paragraph (4) unless satisfied that it is not clearly unfounded.

(6) In addition to the national of a State which is a contracting party to the Agreement referred to in section 84(2) of the 2002 Act, a Swiss national shall also be treated as an EEA national for the purposes of section 84(1)(d) of that Act.

(7) An appeal under these Regulations against an EEA decision (including an appeal made on or after 1st April 2003 which is treated as an appeal under these Regulations under Schedule 4 but not an appeal made before that date) shall be treated as an appeal under section 82(1) of the 2002 Act against an immigration decision for the purposes of section 96(1)(a) of the 2002 Act.

(8) Section 120 of the 2002 Act shall apply to a person if an EEA decision has been taken or may be taken in respect of him and, accordingly, the Secretary of State or an immigration officer may by notice require a statement from that person under subsection (2) of that section and that notice shall have effect for the purpose of section 96(2) of the 2002 Act.

(9) In sub-paragraph (1), 'family member residence stamp' means a stamp in the passport of a family member of an EEA national confirming that he is the family member of an accession State worker requiring registration with a right of residence under these Regulations as the family member of that worker; and in this sub-paragraph 'accession State worker requiring registration' has the same meaning as in regulation 2 of the Accession (Immigration and Worker Registration) Regulations 2004.

SCHEDULE 3
REVOCATIONS AND SAVINGS

Regulation 31(2)

PART 1
TABLE OF REVOCATIONS

(1)	(2)	(3)
Regulations revoked	*References*	*Extent of revocation*
The Immigration (European Economic Area) Regulations 2000	SI 2000/2326	The whole Regulations
The Immigration (European Economic Area) (Amendment) Regulations 2001	SI 2001/865	The whole Regulations
The Immigration (Swiss Free Movement of Persons) (No. 3) Regulations 2002	SI 2002/1241	The whole Regulations
The Immigration (European Economic Area) (Amendment) Regulations 2003	SI 2003/549	The whole Regulations
The Immigration (European Economic Area) (Amendment No. 2) Regulations 2003	SI 2003/3188	The whole Regulations
The Accession (Immigration and Worker Registration) Regulations 2004	SI 2004/12 19	Regulations 3 and 6
The Immigration (European Economic Area) and Accession (Amendment) Regulations 2004	SI 2004/1236	Regulation 2
The Immigration (European Economic Area) (Amendment) Regulations 2005	SI 2005/47	The whole Regulations
The Immigration (European Economic Area) (Amendment) (No. 2) Regulations 2005	SI 2005/671	The whole Regulations

PART 2
SAVINGS

1. The—
   (a) Immigration (Swiss Free Movement of Persons) (No. 3) Regulations 2002 are not revoked insofar as they apply the 2000 Regulations to posted workers; and
   (b) the 2000 Regulations and the Regulations amending the 2000 Regulations are not revoked insofar as they are so applied to posted workers;

   and, accordingly, the 2000 Regulations, as amended, shall continue to apply to posted workers in accordance with the Immigration (Swiss Free Movement of Persons) (No. 3) Regulations 2002.

2. In paragraph 1, 'the 2000 Regulations' means the Immigration (European Economic Area) Regulations 2000 and 'posted worker' has the meaning given in regulation 2(4)(b) of the Immigration (Swiss Free Movement of Persons) (No. 3) Regulations 2002.

SCHEDULE 4
Regulation 31(2)
TRANSITIONAL PROVISIONS

1. **Interpretation**

   In this Schedule—
   (a) the '2000 Regulations' means the Immigration (European Economic Area) Regulations 2000 and expressions used in relation to documents issued or applied for under those Regulations shall have the meaning given in regulation 2 of those Regulations;
   (b) the 'Accession Regulations' means the Accession (Immigration and Worker Registration) Regulations 2004.

2. **Existing documents**

   (1) An EEA family permit issued under the 2000 Regulations shall, after 29th April 2006, be treated as if it were an EEA family permit issued under these Regulations.

   (2) Subject to paragraph (4), a residence permit issued under the 2000 Regulations shall, after 2th April 2006, be treated as if it were a registration certificate issued under these Regulations.

   (3) Subject to paragraph (5), a residence document issued under the 2000 Regulations shall, after 29th April 2006, be treated as if it were a residence card issued under these Regulations.

   (4) Where a residence permit issued under the 2000 Regulations has been endorsed under the immigration rules to show permission to remain in the United Kingdom indefinitely it shall, after 29th April 2006, be treated as if it were a document certifying permanent residence issued under these Regulations and the holder of the permit shall be treated as a person with a permanent right of residence under regulation 15.

   (5) Where a residence document issued under the 2000 Regulations has been endorsed under the immigration rules to show permission to remain in the United Kingdom indefinitely it shall, after 29th April 2006, be treated as if it were a permanent residence card issued under these Regulations and the holder of the permit shall be treated as a person with a permanent right of residence under regulation 15.

   (6) Paragraphs (4) and (5) shall also apply to a residence permit or residence document which is endorsed under the immigration rules on or after 30th April 2006 to show permission to remain in the United Kingdom indefinitely pursuant to an application for such an endorsement made before that date.

3. **Outstanding applications**
   (1) An application for an EEA family permit, a residence permit or a residence document made but not determined under the 2000 Regulations before 30 April 2006 shall be treated as an application under these Regulations for an EEA family permit, a registration certificate or a residence card, respectively.
   (2) But the following provisions of these Regulations shall not apply to the determination of an application mentioned in sub-paragraph (1)—
      (a) the requirement to issue a registration certificate immediately under regulation 16(1); and
      (b) the requirement to issue a certificate of application for a residence card under regulation 17(3).

4. **Decisions to remove under the 2000 Regulations**
   (1) A decision to remove a person under regulation 21(3)(a) of the 2000 Regulations shall, after 29th April 2006, be treated as a decision to remove that person under regulation 19(3)(a) of these Regulations.
   (2) A decision to remove a person under regulation 21(3)(b) of the 2000 Regulations, including a decision which is treated as a decision to remove a person under that regulation by virtue of regulation 6(3)(a) of the Accession Regulations, shall, after 29th April 2006, be treated as a decision to remove that person under regulation 19(3)(b) of these Regulations.
   (3) A deportation order made under section 5 of the 1971 Act by virtue of regulation 26(3) of the 2000 Regulations shall, after 29th April 2006, be treated as a deportation made under section 5 of the 1971 Act by virtue of regulation 24(3) of these Regulations.

5. **Appeals**
   (1) Where an appeal against an EEA decision under the 2000 Regulations is pending immediately before 30th April 2006 that appeal shall be treated as a pending appeal against the corresponding EEA Decision under these Regulations.
   (2) Where an appeal against an EEA decision under the 2000 Regulations has been determined, withdrawn or abandoned it shall, on and after 30th April 2006, be treated as an appeal against the corresponding EEA decision under these Regulations which has been determined, withdrawn or abandoned, respectively.
   (3) For the purpose of this paragraph—
      (a) a decision to refuse to admit a person under these Regulations corresponds to a decision to refuse to admit that person under the 2000 Regulations;
      (b) a decision to remove a person under regulation 19(3)(a) of these Regulations corresponds to a decision to remove that person under regulation 21(3)(a) of the 2000 Regulations;
      (c) a decision to remove a person under regulation 19(3)(b) of these Regulations corresponds to a decision to remove that person under regulation 21(3)(b) of the 2000 Regulations, including a decision which is treated as a decision to remove a person under regulation 21(3)(b) of the 2000 Regulations by virtue of regulation 6(3)(a) of the Accession Regulations;
      (d) a decision to refuse to revoke a deportation order made against a person under these Regulations corresponds to a decision to refuse to revoke a deportation order made against that person under the 2000 Regulations, including a decision which is treated as a decision to refuse to revoke a deportation order under the 2000 Regulations by virtue of regulation 6(3)(b) of the Accession Regulations;

(e) a decision not to issue or renew or to revoke an EEA family permit, a registration certificate or a residence card under these Regulations corresponds to a decision not to issue or renew or to revoke an EEA family permit, a residence permit or a residence document under the 2000 Regulations, respectively.

6. **Periods of residence under the 2000 Regulations**

(1) Any period during which a person carried out an activity or was resident in the United Kingdom in accordance with the 2000 Regulations shall be treated as a period during which the person carried out that activity or was resident in the United Kingdom in accordance with these Regulations for the purpose of calculating periods of activity and residence under these Regulations.

SCHEDULE 5 Regulation 31(2)
CONSEQUENTIAL AMENDMENTS
Statutory Instruments
The Channel Tunnel (International Arrangements) Order 1993

1. (1) The Channel Tunnel (International Arrangements) Order 1993 is amended as follows.

(2) In Schedule 4, in paragraph 5—

(a) at the beginning of the paragraph, for 'the Immigration (European Economic Area) Regulations 2000' there is substituted 'the Immigration (European Economic Area) Regulations 2006';

(b) in sub-paragraph (a), for 'regulation 12(2)' there is substituted 'regulation 11(2)' and for 'residence document or document proving family membership' there is substituted 'residence card or permanent residence card';

(c) for sub-paragraph (b) there is substituted—

'(b) in regulations 11(4) and 19(2) after the word 'arrival' and in regulations 20(4) and (5) after the words 'United Kingdom' insert 'or the time of his production of the required documents in a control zone or a supplementary control zone'.'

The Travel Restriction Order (Prescribed Removal Powers) Order 2002

2. (1) The Travel Restriction Order (Prescribed Removal Powers) Order 2002 is amended as follows.

(2) In the Schedule, for 'Immigration (European Economic Area) Regulations 2000 (2000/2326)' in the first column of the table there is substituted 'Immigration (European Economic Area) Regulations 2006' and for 'Regulation 21(3)' in the corresponding row in the second column of the table there is substituted 'Regulation 19(3)'.

The Immigration (Notices) Regulations 2003

3. (1) The Immigration (Notices) Regulations 2003 are amended as follows.

(2) In regulation 2, in the definition of 'EEA decision'—

(a) at the end of paragraph (b), 'or' is omitted;

(b) in paragraph (c), after 'residence document;', there is inserted 'or'; and

(c) after paragraph (c), there is inserted—

'(d) on or after 30th April 2006, entitlement to be issued with or have renewed, or not to have revoked, a registration certificate, residence card, document certifying permanent residence or permanent residence card;'

The Nationality, Immigration and Asylum Act 2002 (Juxtaposed Controls) Order 2003

4. (1) The Nationality, Immigration and Asylum Act 2002 (Juxtaposed Controls) Order 2003 is amended as follows.

(2) In article 11(1), for sub-paragraph (e) there is substituted—

'(e) the Immigration (European Economic Area) Regulations 2006.'.

(3) In Schedule 2, in paragraph 5—

  (a) at the beginning of the paragraph, for 'the Immigration (European Economic Area) Regulations 2000' there is substituted 'the Immigration (European Economic Area) Regulations 2006';

  (b) in sub-paragraph (a), for 'in regulation 2, at the beginning insert' there is substituted 'in regulation 2(1), after the definition of 'civil partner' insert';

  (c) in sub-paragraph (b), for 'regulation 12(2)' there is substituted 'regulation 11(2)' and for 'residence document or document proving family membership' there is substituted 'residence card or permanent residence card';

  (d) for sub-paragraph (c) there is substituted—

    '(c) in regulations 11(4) and 19(2) after the word 'arrival' and in regulations 20(4) and (5) after the words 'United Kingdom' insert 'or the time of his production of the required documents in a Control Zone'.

The Immigration and Asylum Act 1999 (Part V Exemption: Relevant Employers) Order 2003

5. (1) The Immigration and Asylum Act 1999 (Part V Exemption: Relevant Employers) Order 2003 is amended as follows.

  (2) In Article 2, in the definition of 'EEA national' and 'family member of an EEA national', for 'Immigration (European Economic Area) Regulations 2000' there is substituted 'Immigration (European Economic Area) Regulations 2006'.

The Immigration (Restrictions on Employment) Order 2004

6. (1) The Immigration (Restrictions on Employment) Order 2004 is amended as follows.

  (2) In Part 1 of the Schedule (descriptions of documents for the purpose of article 4(2)(a) of the Order)–

    (a) for paragraph 4 there is substituted—

      '4. A registration certificate or document certifying permanent residence within the meaning of regulation 2 of the Immigration (European Economic Area) Regulations 2006, including a document which is treated as a registration certificate or document certifying permanent residence by virtue of Schedule 4 to those Regulations.';

    (b) for paragraph 5 there is substituted—

      '5. A residence card or a permanent residence card within the meaning of regulation 2 of the Immigration (European Economic Area) Regulations 2006, including a document which is treated as a residence card or a permanent residence card by virtue of Schedule 4 to those Regulations'.

The Accession (Immigration and Worker Registration) Regulations 2004

7. (1) The Accession (Immigration and Worker Registration) Regulations 2004 are amended as follows.

  (2) In regulation 1(2) (interpretation)—

    (a) after paragraph (b) there is inserted—

      '(ba)'the 2006 Regulations' means the Immigration (European Economic Area) Regulations 2006;';

    (b) in paragraph (j), for 'regulation 3 of the 2000 Regulations' these is substituted 'reguration 4 of the 2006 Regulations'.

  (3) In regulation 2 ('accession State worker requiring registration')—

    (a) for paragraph (6)(b) there is substituted—

'(b) a family member of a Swiss or EEA national (other than an accession State worker requiring registration) who has a right to reside in the United Kingdom under regulation 14(1) or 15 of the 2006 Regulations;';

(b) paragraph (9)(a) is omitted;

(c) for paragraph (9)(c) there is substituted—

'(c) 'family member' has the same meaning as in regulation 7 of the 2006 Regulations.'

(4) In regulation 4 (right of residence of work seekers and workers from relevant acceding States during the accession period)—

(a) in paragraph (1), before 'Council Directive' there is inserted 'Council Directive 2004/38/EC of the European Parliament and of the Council on the right of citizens of the Union and their family members to move and reside freely within the territory of the Member States, insofar as it takes over provisions of';

(b) in paragraph (3), for '2000 Regulations' there is substituted '2006 Regulations';

(c) in paragraph (4), for 'An' there is substituted 'A national of a relevant accession State who is seeking employment and an' and for '2000 Regulations' there is substituted '2006 Regulations'.

(5) For regulation 5 (application of 2000 Regulations in relation to accession State worker requiring registration) there is substituted—

'**Application of 2006 Regulations in relation to accession State worker requiring registration**

5. (1) The 2006 Regulations shall apply in relation to a national of a relevant accession State subject to the modifications set out in this regulation.

(2) A national of a relevant accession State who is seeking employment in the United Kingdom shall not be treated as a jobseeker for the purpose of the definition of 'qualified person' in regulation 6(1) of the 2006 Regulations and an accession State worker requiring registration shall be treated as a worker for the purpose of that definition only during a period in which he is working in the United Kingdom for an authorised employer.

(3) Subject to paragraph (4), regulation 6(2) of the 2006 Regulations shall not apply to an accession State worker requiring registration who ceases to work.

(4) Where an accession State worker requiring registration ceases working for an authorised employer in the circumstances mentioned in regulation 6(2) of the 2006 Regulations during the one month period beginning on the date on which the work begins, that regulation shall apply to that worker during the remainder of that one month period.

(5) An accession State worker requiring registration shall not be treated as a qualified person for the purpose of regulations 16 and 17 of the 2006 Regulations (issue of registration certificates and residence cards).'

The Asylum and Immigration Tribunal (Procedure) Rules 2005

8. (1) The Asylum and Immigration Tribunal (Procedure) Rules 2005 are amended as follows.

(2) In regulation 18(1)(b), after '('the 2000 Regulations')' there is inserted 'or, on or after 30th April 2006, paragraph 4(2) of Schedule 2 to the Immigration (European Economic Area) Regulations 2006 ('the 2006 Regulations')'.

(3) In regulation 18(2), after '2000 Regulations' there is inserted 'or paragraph 4(2) of Schedule 2 to the 2006 Regulations'.

Appendix 8

Work Permits (UK) Shortage Occupation List
May 2007

Engineering occupations

Transportation and highways engineers

Engineers who are required to have a transport-related degree, or a degree and at least 2 years' relevant experience from a civil background in the following specialisms:

Traffic Engineer or Transport Planner
Highways Design Engineer or Highways Planning Engineer

Ground engineering

Ground engineering occupations relate solely to the construction sector and not to oil/gas extraction:

Geoenvironmental Engineer
Geotechnical Engineer
Geological Advisor
Geological Analyst
Geological Associate
Geological Engineer
Geologist/Hydrogeologist
Geology/Reservoir Engineer
Geomechanics Engineer
Geophysical Specialist
Geophysicist
Geoscientist
Geosupport Engineer
Engineering Geologist
Ground Engineer
Contaminated Land Specialist

Other engineering

CAA Licensed Aircraft Engineer
Overhead Electricity Linesworker
Chartered Quantity Surveyor

Healthcare occupations

Doctors

Salaried GPs

Dentists

Consultants in Dental Specialities

Consultant posts in the following specialist areas

Accident and Emergency
Additional Dental Specialities
Anaesthetics
Cardiology
Cardiothoracic Surgery

Chemical Pathology
Child and Adolescent Psychiatry
Clinical Neurophysiology
Clinical Oncology
Clinical Radiology
Dermatology
Endocrinology and Diabetes Mellitus
Endodentics
Forensic Psychiatry
Gastroenterology
General Adult Psychiatry
General Internal Medicine
General Surgery
Genito-urinary medicine
Geriatric Medicine
Haematology
Histopathology
Immunology
Infectious Diseases
Intensive Care Medicine
Medical Microbiology & Virology
Medical Oncology
Neurology
Neurosurgery
Nuclear Medicine
Obstetrics and Gynaecology
Occupational Health
Old Age Psychiatry
Ophthalmology
Oral & Maxillo-facial Surgery
Orthodontics
Otolaryngology
Paediatric Cardiology
Paediatrics
Palliative Medicine
Plastic Surgery
Psychotherapy
Public Health Medicine
Rehabilitation Medicine
Renal Medicine
Respiratory Medicine
Rheumatology
Trauma and Orthopaedic Surgery
Urology

General
Audiologist
Audiological scientist
Clinical Psychologist
Dietician
Occupational Therapist
Pharmacists
Pharmacy Technician Higher Level (Band 5 and above)

Pre-Registration Cytogeneticists
Speech and Language Therapist
Social Worker
State Registered Scientists in Cytogenetics
Biomedical Scientist/Medical Laboratory Scientific Officer (MLSO)
Qualified HPC Registered Diagnostic and Therapeutic Radiographers, including Ultrasonographers

Nurses

Midwives

Registered Nurse employed or engaged at Band 7 or Band 8 of Agenda for Change or their Independent sector equivalents

Registered Nurse employed or engaged in the following specialities:
- Audiology
- Sleep/respiratory physiology
- Neurophysiology
- Cardiac physiology
- Operating theatre nursing
- Clinical radiology
- Pathology
- Critical care (nurses working in wards with a Level 2 or Level 3 classification)

Other occupations

Teachers – All posts in England and Scotland covering compulsory schooling
Veterinary Surgeon

Appendix 9

Extracts from the European Convention on Human Rights

Article 2 – right to life

1. Everyone's right to life shall be protected by law. No one shall be deprived of his life intentionally save in the execution of a sentence of a court following his conviction of a crime for which this penalty is provided by law.
2. Deprivation of life shall not be regarded as inflicted in contravention of this Article when it results from the use of force which is no more than absolutely necessary:

Article 3 – prohibition of torture

No one shall be subjected to torture or to inhuman or degrading treatment or punishment.

Article 5 – right to liberty and security

1. Everyone has the right to liberty and security of person. No one shall be deprived of his liberty save in the following cases and in accordance with a procedure prescribed by law:
    (a) the lawful detention of a person after conviction by a competent court;
    (b) the lawful arrest or detention of a person for non-compliance with the lawful order of a court or in order to secure the fulfilment of any obligation prescribed by law;
    (c) the lawful arrest or detention of a person effected for the purpose of bringing him before the competent legal authority on reasonable suspicion of having committed an offence or when it is reasonably considered necessary to prevent his committing an offence or fleeing after having done so;
    (d) the detention of a minor by lawful order for the purpose of educational supervision or his lawful detention for the purpose of bringing him before the competent legal authority;
    (e) the lawful detention of persons for the prevention of the spreading of infectious diseases, of persons of unsound mind, alcoholics or drug addicts or vagrants;
    (f) the lawful arrest or detention of a person to prevent his effecting an unauthorised entry into the country or of a person against whom action is being taken with a view to deportation or extradition.
2. Everyone who is arrested shall be informed promptly, in a language which he understands, of the reasons for his arrest and of any charge against him.
3. Everyone arrested or detained in accordance with the provisions of paragraph 1(c) of this Article shall be brought promptly before a judge or other officer authorised by law to exercise judicial power and shall be entitled to trial within a reasonable time or to release pending trial. Release may be conditioned by guarantees to appear for trial.
4. Everyone who is deprived of his liberty by arrest or detention shall be entitled to take proceedings by which the lawfulness of his detention shall be decided speedily by a court and his release ordered if the detention is not lawful.
5. Everyone who has been the victim of arrest or detention in contravention of the provisions of this Article shall have an enforceable right to compensation.

Article 6 – right to a fair trial

1. In the determination of his civil rights and obligations or of any criminal charge against him, everyone is entitled to a fair and public hearing within a reasonable time by an independent and impartial tribunal established by law. Judgment shall be pronounced publicly but the press and public may be excluded from all or part of the trial in the interest of morals, public order or national security in a democratic society, where the interests of juveniles or the protection of the private life of the parties so require, or to the extent strictly necessary in the opinion of the court in special circumstances where publicity would prejudice the interests of justice.
2. Everyone charged with a criminal offence shall be presumed innocent until proved guilty according to law.
3. Everyone charged with a criminal offence has the following minimum rights:
    (a) to be informed promptly, in a language which he understands and in detail, of the nature and cause of the accusation against him;
    (b) to have adequate time and facilities for the preparation of his defence;
    (c) to defend himself in person or through legal assistance of his own choosing or, if he has not sufficient means to pay for legal assistance, to be given it free when the interests of justice so require;
    (d) to examine or have examined witnesses against him and to obtain the attendance and examination of witnesses on his behalf under the same conditions as witnesses against him;
    (e) to have the free assistance of an interpreter if he cannot understand or speak the language used in court.

Article 8 – right to respect for private and family life

1. Everyone has the right to respect for his private and family life, his home and his correspondence.
2. There shall be no interference by a public authority with the exercise of this right except such as is in accordance with the law and is necessary in a democratic society in the interests of national security, public safety or the economic well-being of the country, for the prevention of disorder or crime, for the protection of health or morals, or for the protection of the rights and freedoms of others.

Article 9 – freedom of thought, conscience and religion

1. Everyone has the right to freedom of thought, conscience and religion; this right includes freedom to change his religion or belief and freedom, either alone or in community with others and in public or private, to manifest his religion or belief, in worship, teaching, practice and observance.
2. Freedom to manifest one's religion or beliefs shall be subject only to such limitations as are prescribed by law and are necessary in a democratic society in the interests of public safety, for the protection of public order, health or morals, or for the protection of the rights and freedoms of others.

Article 10 – freedom of expression

1. Everyone has the right to freedom of expression. This right shall include freedom to hold opinions and to receive and impart information and ideas without interference by public authority and regardless of frontiers. This Article shall not prevent States from requiring the licensing of broadcasting, television or cinema enterprises.
2. The exercise of these freedoms, since it carries with it duties and responsibilities, may be subject to such formalities, conditions, restrictions or penalties as are prescribed by law and are necessary in a democratic society, in the interests of national security, territorial integrity or public safety, for the prevention of disorder

or crime, for the protection of health or morals, for the protection of the reputation or rights of others, for preventing the disclosure of information received in confidence, or for maintaining the authority and impartiality of the judiciary.

Article 11 – freedom of assembly and association

1. Everyone has the right to freedom of peaceful assembly and to freedom of association with others, including the right to form and to join trade unions for the protection of his interests.
2. No restrictions shall be placed on the exercise of these rights other than such as are prescribed by law and are necessary in a democratic society in the interests of national security or public safety, for the prevention of disorder or crime, for the protection of health or morals or for the protection of the rights and freedoms of others. This Article shall not prevent the imposition of lawful restrictions on the exercise of these rights by members of the armed forces, of the police or of the administration of the State.

Article 12 – right to marry

Men and women of marriageable age have the right to marry and to found a family, according to the national laws governing the exercise of this right.

Article 14 – prohibition of discrimination

The enjoyment of the rights and freedoms set forth in this Convention shall be secured without discrimination on any ground such as sex, race, colour, language, religion, political or other opinion, national or social origin, association with a national minority, property, birth or other status.

The First Protocol, Article 1 – protection of property

Every natural or legal person is entitled to the peaceful enjoyment of his possessions. No one shall be deprived of his possessions except in the public interest and subject to the conditions provided for by law and by the general principles of international law.

The preceding provisions shall not, however, in any way impair the right of a State to enforce such laws as it deems necessary to control the use of property in accordance with the general interest or to secure the payment of taxes or other contributions or penalties.

Appendix 10

Income Categories: Highly Skilled Migrants

The income bands required demonstrating the Previous Salary Criteria are:

Code A countries

Andorra; Aruba; Australia; Austria; Belgium; Bermuda; Canada; Cayman Islands; Channel Islands; Denmark; Finland; France; French Polynesia; Germany; Gibraltar; Guam; Hong Kong (Province of China); Iceland; Ireland; Italy; Japan; Kuwait; Liechtenstein; Luxembourg; Monaco; Netherlands; Norway; Qatar; San Marino; Singapore; Sweden; Switzerland; United Arab Emirates; United Kingdom; United States of America; Vatican.

Previous earnings (£) points scores				
5 pts	10 pts	15 pts	20 pts	25 pts
16,000+	18,000+	20,000+	23,000+	26,000+
30 pts	35 pts	40 pts	45 pts	
29,000+	32,000+	35,000+	40,000+	

Code B countries

American Samoa; Antigua and Barbuda; Argentina; Bahamas; Bahrain; Barbados; Botswana; Brunei Darussalam; Chile; Costa Rica; Croatia; Cyprus; Czech Republic; Estonia; Faroe Islands; Greece; Greenland; Grenada; Hungary; Israel; Korea (South); Latvia; Lebanon; Libya; Macao, (Province of China); Malaysia; Malta; Mauritius; Mexico; Netherlands Antilles; New Caledonia; New Zealand; Northern Mariana Islands; Oman; Palau; Panama; Poland; Portugal; Puerto Rico; Saudi Arabia; Seychelles; Slovak Republic; Slovenia; Spain; St Kitts and Nevis; St Lucia; Taiwan (Province of China); Trinidad and Tobago; Uruguay; Venezuela; Virgin Islands.

Previous earnings (£) points scores				
5 pts	10 pts	15 pts	20 pts	25 pts
7,000+	8,000+	9,000+	10,000+	11,500+
30 pts	35 pts	40 pts	45 pts	
12,500+	14,000+	15,500	17,500+	

Code C countries

Albania; Algeria; Belarus; Belize; Bolivia; Bosnia & Herzegovina; Brazil; Bulgaria; Cape Verde; China (Peoples Republic of); Colombia; Dominica; Dominican Republic; Ecuador; Egypt; El Salvador; Fiji; Gabon; Guatemala; Honduras; Iran; Jamaica; Jordan; Kazakhstan; Lithuania; Macedonia; Maldives; Marshall Islands; Micronesia; Morocco; Namibia; Nauru; Paraguay; Peru; Philippines; Romania; Russian Federation; Samoa; South Africa; St Vincent & The Grenadines; Suriname; Swaziland; Syrian Arab Republic; Thailand; Tonga; Tunisia; Turkey; Turkmenistan; Vanuatu; West Bank and Gaza.

Previous earnings (£) points scores				
5 pts	10 pts	15 pts	20 pts	25 pts
5,000+	5,600+	6,300+	7,200+	8,100+
30 pts	35 pts	40 pts	45 pts	
9,100+	10,000+	11,000+	12,500+	

Code D countries

Angola; Armenia; Azerbaijan; Bangladesh; Benin; Bhutan; Cameroon; Comoros; Congo (Republic of); Cote d'Ivoire; Cuba; Djibouti; Equatorial Guinea; Gambia; Georgia; Guinea; Guyana; Haiti; India; Indonesia; Iraq; Kenya; Kiribati; Lesotho; Mauritania; Moldova; Mongolia; Montenegro; Myanmar; Nicaragua; Pakistan; Papua New Guinea; Senegal; Serbia; Solomon Islands; Sri Lanka; Sudan; Timor L'Este (East Timor); Ukraine; Uzbekistan; Vietnam; Yemen; Zambia; Zimbabwe.

Previous earnings (£) points scores				
5 pts	10 pts	15 pts	20 pts	25 pts
3,000+	3,400+	3,800+	4,300+	4,900+
30 pts	35 pts	40 pts	45 pts	
5,500+	6,000+	6,600+	7,500+	

Code E countries

Afghanistan; Burkina Faso; Burundi; Cambodia; Central African Republic; Congo, (Democratic Republic of); Chad; Eritrea; Ethiopia; Ghana; Guinea-Bissau; Korea (North); Kygyz Republic; Lao; Liberia; Madagascar; Malawi; Mali; Mayotte; Mozambique; Nepal; Niger; Nigeria; Rwanda; Sao Tome and Principe; Sierra Leone; Somalia; Tajikistan; Tanzania; Togo; Uganda.

Previous earnings (£) points scores				
5 pts	10 pts	15 pts	20 pts	25 pts
1,400+	1,600+	1,800+	2,000+	2,300+
30 pts	35 pts	40 pts	45 pts	
2,550+	2,800+	3,100+	3,500+	

Appendix 11

MBA Eligible Programmes

The 50 eligible schools are listed below in alphabetical order:
Ashridge (UK)
Australian Graduate School of Management (AUS)
Babson College: Olin (USA)
Boston University School of Management (USA)
Bradford School of Management/Nimbas (UK/NTH/GER
Carnegie Mellon University (USA)
Ceibs (CHN)
City University: Cass (UK)
Columbia Business School (USA)
Cornell University: Johnson (USA)
Cranfield School of Management (UK)
Dartmouth College: Tuck (USA)
Duke University: Fuqua (USA)
Emory University: Goizueta (USA)
Georgetown University: McDonough (USA)
Harvard Business School (USA)
IMD (SWI)
Insead (FR/Sing)
Instituto de Empresa (SP)
London Business School (UK)
Manchester Business School (UK)
Melbourne Business School (AUS)
MIT: Sloan (USA)
New York University: Stern (US)
North Western: Kellogg (USA)
Rice University: Jones (USA)
Rotterdam School of Management (Neth)
SDA Bocconi (IT)
Stanford University (USA)
UC Berkeley: Haas (USA)
UCLA: Anderson (USA)
Universiteit Nyenrode (NTH)
University College Dublin: Smurfit (IRE)
University of Cambridge: Judge (UK)
University of Chicago (USA)
University of Maryland: Smith (USA)
University of Michigan (USA)
University of North Carolina: Kenan-Flagler (USA)
University of Oxford: Said (UK)
University of Pennsylvania: Wharton (USA)
University of Rochester: Simon (USA)
University of Southern California: Marshall (USA)
University of Strathclyde (UK)

University of Toronto: Rothman (CAN)
University of Virginia: Darden (USA)
University of Western Ontario: Ivey (USA)
Vanderbilt University: Owen (USA)
Warwick Business School (UK)
Yale School of Management (USA)

Appendix 12

Refugee or Person in Need of International Protection (Qualification) Regulations 2006

SI 2006/2525

1. **Citation and commencement**

    (1) These Regulations may be cited as The Refugee or Person in Need of International Protection (Qualification) Regulations 2006 and shall come into force on 9th October 2006.

    (2) These Regulations apply to any application for asylum which has not been decided and any immigration appeal brought under the Immigration Acts (as defined in section 64(2) of the Immigration, Asylum and Nationality Act 2006) which has not been finally determined.

2. **Interpretation**

    In these Regulations—

    'application for asylum' means the request of a person to be recognised as a refugee under the Geneva Convention;

    'Geneva Convention' means the Convention Relating to the Status of Refugees done at Geneva on 28 July 1951 and the New York Protocol of 31 January 1967;

    'immigration rules' means rules made under section 3(2) of the Immigration Act 1971;

    'persecution' means an act of persecution within the meaning of Article 1(A) of the Geneva Convention;

    'person eligible for humanitarian protection' means a person who is eligible for a grant of humanitarian protection under the immigration rules;

    'refugee' means a person who falls within Article 1(A) of the Geneva Convention and to whom regulation 7 does not apply;

    'residence permit' means a document confirming that a person has leave to enter or remain in the United Kingdom whether limited or indefinite;

    'serious harm' means serious harm as defined in the immigration rules;

    'person' means any person who is not a British citizen.

3. **Actors of persecution or serious harm**

    In deciding whether a person is a refugee or a person eligible for humanitarian protection, persecution or serious harm can be committed by:

    (a) the State;

    (b) any party or organisation controlling the State or a substantial part of the territory of the State;

    (c) any non-State actor if it can be demonstrated that the actors mentioned in paragraphs (a) and (b), including any international organisation, are unable or unwilling to provide protection against persecution or serious harm.

4. **Actors of protection**

    (1) In deciding whether a person is a refugee or a person eligible for humanitarian protection, protection from persecution or serious harm can be provided by:

    (a) the State; or

    (b) any party or organisation, including any international organisation, controlling the State or a substantial part of the territory of the State.

    (2) Protection shall be regarded as generally provided when the actors mentioned in paragraph (1)(a) and (b) take reasonable steps to prevent the persecution or suffering of serious harm by operating an effective legal system for the detection, prosecution and punishment of acts constituting persecution or

serious harm, and the person mentioned in paragraph (1) has access to such protection.

(3) In deciding whether a person is a refugee or a person eligible for humanitarian protection the Secretary of State may assess whether an international organisation controls a State or a substantial part of its territory and provides protection as described in paragraph (2).

5. **Act of persecution**

    (1) In deciding whether a person is a refugee an act of persecution must be:

    (a) sufficiently serious by its nature or repetition as to constitute a severe violation of a basic human right, in particular a right from which derogation cannot be made under Article 15 of the Convention for the Protection of Human Rights and Fundamental Freedoms; or

    (b) an accumulation of various measures, including a violation of a human right which is sufficiently severe as to affect an individual in a similar manner as specified in (a).

    (2) An act of persecution may, for example, take the form of:

    (a) an act of physical or mental violence, including an act of sexual violence;

    (b) a legal, administrative, police, or judicial measure which in itself is discriminatory or which is implemented in a discriminatory manner;

    (c) prosecution or punishment, which is disproportionate or discriminatory;

    (d) denial of judicial redress resulting in a disproportionate or discriminatory punishment;

    (e) prosecution or punishment for refusal to perform military service in a conflict, where performing military service would include crimes or acts falling under regulation 7.

    (3) An act of persecution must be committed for at least one of the reasons in Article 1(A) of the Geneva Convention.

6. **Reasons for persecution**

    (1) In deciding whether a person is a refugee:

    (a) the concept of race shall include consideration of, for example, colour, descent, or membership of a particular ethnic group;

    (b) the concept of religion shall include, for example, the holding of theistic, non-theistic and atheistic beliefs, the participation in, or abstention from, formal worship in private or in public, either alone or in community with others, other religious acts or expressions of view, or forms of personal or communal conduct based on or mandated by any religious belief;

    (c) the concept of nationality shall not be confined to citizenship or lack thereof but shall include, for example, membership of a group determined by its cultural, ethnic, or linguistic identity, common geographical or political origins or its relationship with the population of another State;

    (d) a group shall be considered to form a particular social group where, for example:

    (i) members of that group share an innate characteristic, or a common background that cannot be changed, or share a characteristic or belief that is so fundamental to identity or conscience that a person should not be forced to renounce it, and

    (ii) that group has a distinct identity in the relevant country, because it is perceived as being different by the surrounding society;

    (e) a particular social group might include a group based on a common characteristic of sexual orientation but sexual orientation cannot be understood to include acts considered to be criminal in accordance with national law of the United Kingdom;

(f) the concept of political opinion shall include the holding of an opinion, thought or belief on a matter related to the potential actors of persecution mentioned in regulation 3 and to their policies or methods, whether or not that opinion, thought or belief has been acted upon by the person.

(2) In deciding whether a person has a well-founded fear of being persecuted, it is immaterial whether he actually possesses the racial, religious, national, social or political characteristic which attracts the persecution, provided that such a characteristic is attributed to him by the actor of persecution.

7. **Exclusion**

(1) A person is not a refugee, if he falls within the scope of Article 1D, 1E or 1F of the Geneva Convention.

(2) In the construction and application of Article 1F(b) of the Geneva Convention:

(a) the reference to serious non-political crime includes a particularly cruel action, even if it is committed with an allegedly political objective;

(b) the reference to the crime being committed outside the country of refuge prior to his admission as a refugee shall be taken to mean the time up to and including the day on which a residence permit is issued.

(3) Article 1F(a) and (b) of the Geneva Convention shall apply to a person who instigates or otherwise participates in the commission of the crimes or acts specified in those provisions.

Index

abbreviations *xxix–xxx*
accommodation
   children 289
   civil partners 276-8
   fiancé(e)s of settled person 283
   proposed civil partners 283
   room number yardstick 289
   spouses 276-8
administration of benefits
   appeals 12-13
   backdating 9-11
   carer's allowance 92
   child benefit 90
   claiming 8-9, 33-4
   council tax benefit 140
   housing benefit 138
   incapacity benefit 54-5
   judicial review 12
   local authority benefits 134
   payment 14
   revision of decision 11
   statutory sick pay 53
   supersession 11-12
   written reasons 11
Administrative Court
   immigration judicial review 329
administrative removal
   age 311
   compassionate circumstances 311
   connections in UK 311
   domestic circumstances 311
   effects of removal 312
   enforcement action
      children 315-17
      parents 315-17
      spouses 312-15
   grounds 310
   illegal entrant 310-11
   length of residence 311
   personal history 311
   previous criminal record 311
   procedure 311-12
   relevant factors 311
   representations received 311
adopted children 290
adult dependant increase
   carer's allowance 31, 92
   earnings of dependant 32
   earnings replacement benefit and 32
   incapacity benefit 31, 55
   jobseeker's allowance 45
   maternity allowance 31, 89
   non means-tested benefit 31-2
   State pension 31, 76
   statutory sick pay 53
aliens 222

allowances *see individual types eg attendance allowance*
Amnesty International 304
appeals 7
   asylum claims 301-2, 326
   immigration *see* **immigration appeals**
   welfare benefits
      Court of Appeal and above 13
      human rights 13
      procedure 12-13
      Social Security Commissioners 13
      tribunal procedure 12-13
applicable amount
   means-tested benefits 104
asylum claims
   appeals 301-2, 326
   attack on spouse or close family 296
   checklist 306
   claimant's duty to substantiate 304
   consideration of cases 304-5
   damage to credibility 305
   discretionary leave 306
   discrimination 295
   Dublin Convention 301
   excessive or arbitrary punishment 295
   failure to produce passport 305
   fear of persecution 294-7
   Geneva Convention 294, 304
   Home Office decision 303-4
   human rights 302-3
   humanitarian protection 305-6
   meaning 300-1
   medical conditions 302
   New Asylum Model 303
   persecution 294-7
      fear of 294-7
      nationality 297
      political opinion 298
      social group 297-8
   procedure 303
   Refugee or Person in Need of International Protection (Qualification) Regulations 2006 547-9
   safe third country exception 301-2
   successful claimants 303
   third country removal 326
   unfounded 326-7
   unsuccessful claims 305
Asylum and Immigration Appeal Tribunal 210-11, 322-3
asylum seekers
   benefits system and 183
attendance allowance 5, 48
   backdating 11
   claimant profile 74
   DLA care component compared 66
   pension credit and 79

attendance allowance – *continued*
  residence requirement 171-2

backdating of benefit 9-11
  appointee 9
  time limits for claim 9
  see also individual benefits
benefits system
  administration *see* **administration of benefits**
  asylum seekers 183
  checklists 16-17
  civil partnerships 19-20, 76
  claimant profiling *see* **claimant profiles**
  claimant's partner 19-20
  Common Travel Area 175
  contributory benefits 3-4, 21, 169, 182
  deductions 114-15
  earnings replacement 5
  EEA nationals claiming 183
  fact analysis 17
  human rights 13, 18-19
  immigrants into UK 167-9
  immigration and public funds 181-2
  international aspects *see* **international aspects of benefits**
  means-tested benefits 5-6, 95-165
  non means-tested benefits 4-5, 21-34
  non-contributory benefits 5, 21, 47, 55-6, 74, 169-71, 174
  Northern Ireland 175
  overview 3-6
  reciprocal benefits 168-9, 203
  statutory benefits 4, 22
  types of benefit 3
  urgent cases payments 183
  see also individual benefits eg **jobseeker's allowance**
bereavement
  retirement pensions and 77
bereavement allowance 81, 82
  claimant profile 83
  pension credit and 79
bereavement benefits 4
  backdating 9
  bereavement allowance *see* **bereavement allowance**
  child tax credit and 82
  claimant profile 83
  contribution conditions 29-30, 31
  council tax benefit and 82
  housing benefit and 82
  income support and 82
  jobseeker's allowance, income-based 82
  lump sum payment 82
  other benefits and 82
  pension credit and 82
  widowed parent's allowance 77, 79, 81, 82, 83
  working tax credit and 82
boarders
  means-tested benefits 103-4
Border and Immigration Agency 210

British Overseas Citizens (BOCs) 222
British Overseas Territories 493
British Overseas Territories Citizens (BOTCs) 222
budgeting loans 162
businessmen
  business plan 268
  creation of new jobs 268
  definition of business 266
  entry 269
  extension of stay 269
  free movement, EC right of 236
  immigration status 258-9, 266-9
  initial investment 269
  partnerships 266
  requirements 266-9
  switching categories 269

capital
  actual 96
  available on application 97
  diminishing notional capital rule 99
  disregarded 98
  income treated as 96
  limits 99
  means-tested benefits 96-9
  notional 96-8
  value of 98-9
carers
  contribution conditions 29
  of visitors to UK 250-1
carer's allowance 5
  administration of 92
  adult dependant increase 31, 92
  age requirement 91
  backdating 11
  caring week 91
  child tax credit and 92
  claimant profile 93
  council tax benefit and 92
  disability living allowance and 56
  full-time education 92
  gainful employment 92
  housing benefit and 92
  income support and 92
  jobseeker's allowance, income-based and 92
  NI contribution credit 25
  payment 92
  pension credit and 79, 92
  qualification for 91
  regularly and substantially engaged 91-2
  residence requirement 171-2
  severely disabled person 92
  statutory sick pay and 53
  working tax credit and 92
carer's premium 106
case law 7-8
  immigration 209
checklist of benefits
  low income 17
  physical or mental disability 17
  too ill to work 16

checklist of benefits – *continued*
   unemployed or working part time 17
child benefit 5, 89, 101
   administration of 90
   backdating 9
   child tax credit and 90
   claimant profile 93
   competing claims 90
   council tax benefit and 91
   housing benefit and 91
   incapacity benefit and 91
   income support and 91
   jobseeker's allowance and 91
   payment 90
   pension credit and 79
   qualifying child 89
      responsibility for 90
   qualifying young person 89-90
   residence requirement 172
   working tax credit and 90
child tax credit 6, 101, 133
   backdating 9
   being responsible for child 147
   bereavement benefits and 82
   calculation 148
   carer's allowance and 92
   child 147
   child benefit and 90
   claimant profiles 165
   council tax benefit and 160
   disability element 147
   disability living allowance and 56
   entitlement conditions 146-8
   family element 147
   housing benefit and 160
   incapacity benefit and 55
   income support and 131, 160
   individual element 147
   industrial disablement benefit and 73
   jobseeker's allowance and 44, 131, 160
   maternity allowance and 88
   maximum 147, 148
   pension credit and 79
   qualifying young persons 147
   residence requirement 172-3
   statutory maternity pay and 87
   statutory sick pay and 53
   tapering 156-7
   worked example 157
   see also **tax credits**
children
   administrative removal and 315-17
   deportation and 315-17
   disability living allowance
      care component 61
      mobility component 65
   immigration 285
      accommodation 289
      adopted 290
      born in UK 289
      conditions 288-9
      entering for settlement 286
      of limited leave persons 289

children – *continued*
      over 18 years 292-3
      serious and compelling reasons 287-8
      of settled parents 289
      sole responsibility 286-7
      sponsors 288
      switching 289-90
   NI contribution exempt 24
citizen of UK and colonies
   citizenship 220, 221
   right of abode 221
citizenship 213
   aliens 222
   appealing deprivation orders 327
   birth registered at consulates 215
   born outside UK
      after 1982 214
      before 1983 213-14
   born in UK
      after 1982 214
      before 1983 213
   British citizen 213-19, 221
   British Overseas Citizens (BOCs) 222
   British Overseas Territories Citizens
      (BOTCs) 222
   British subjects 220
   by descent 215
   change over time 220-2
   Commonwealth citizens 221, 491
      exclusions 220
      right of abode 219-20
   CUKC 220, 221
   deprivation of 217
      appeals 327
   European Union citizens 222
   Irish citizens 222
   naturalisation 215-17
      formalities 217
   otherwise than by descent 215
   patrials 221
   registration
      formalities 217
      right to register 217
   summary 218-19
civil partners, immigration 274
   accommodation 276-8, 283
   breakdown of civil partnership 281-2
   devotion 276
   EEA nationals 238
   entry clearance 275
   exempt groups 274-5
   intention to live together 276
   leave to enter 279
   maintenance 278-9
   permission to enter civil partnership 281
   of persons with limited leave 282
   polygamous civil partnership 282
   proposed
      accommodation 283
      maintenance 283
      of settled person 282-3
   public funds 276
   of settled persons 275-9

civil partners, immigration – *continued*
   settled status grant 279-80
   sham partnership 276
   switching status 281
   third-party support 278
   visitors 282
civil partnership
   breakdown 281-2
   with British citizen 216-17
   permission to enter 281
   polygamous 282
   sham 276
   State retirement pension 76
   visits 249-50
   welfare benefits and 19-20
claimant profiles 18
   attendance allowance 74
   bereavement allowance 83
   bereavement payment 83
   carer's allowance 93
   child benefit 93
   child tax credit 165
   constant attendance allowance 74
   council tax benefit 165
   disability living allowance
      care component 74
      mobility component 74
   housing benefit 165
   incapacity benefit 74
      non-contributory 74
   income support 131
   industrial disablement benefit 74
   jobseeker's allowance
      contribution-based 45
      income-based 131
   maternity allowance 93
   pension credit 83
   State retirement pension 82
   statutory maternity pay 93
   statutory sick pay 74
   widowed parent's allowance 83
   working tax credit 165
claiming benefits 8-9
   jobseeker's allowance 36
   more than one non means-tested benefits 33-4
   time limits 9
cohabitants
   akin to marriage 284
   immigration and 283-5
   living together meaning 284
   same-sex relationship 283, 284
   stable relationship 283
cold weather payments 161-2
Common Travel Area
   benefits system 175
   immigration 244-5
Commonwealth citizens 491
   right of abode
      acquired by marriage 219-20
      certificate of entitlement 220
      excluded nationals 220
      parental link 219

community care grants 162
conscientious objections
   jobseeker's allowance restrictions 40
constant attendance allowance
   claimant profile 74
   pension credit and 79
   rate of pay 73
continuous employment rule
   statutory maternity pay 86
contribution conditions
   benefit year 27
   bereavement benefit 29-30, 31
   carers 29
   contribution year 27
   home responsibilities protection 30-1
   incapacity benefit 28-9, 47
   jobseeker's allowance 27-8
   meaning 27
   retirement benefits 29-31
   statutory sick pay 29
   working life 27
contributory benefits 3-4
   EC and 169
   immigration law and 182
   non means-tested 21
   see also **contribution conditions;**
      National Insurance; *and individual*
      benefits eg **jobseeker's allowance**
council tax benefit 6, 8, 96, 133
   administration 140
   amount 140
   backdating 10-11
   bereavement benefits and 82
   calculation 140-1
   carer's allowance and 92
   child benefit and 91
   child tax credit and 160
   claimant profiles 165
   disability living allowance and 56
   exempt persons 139
   incapacity benefit and 55
   income support and 131, 136
   industrial disablement benefit and 73
   jobseeker's allowance and 45, 136
   lone parents 140
   maternity allowance and 89
   payment 14, 140
   pension credit and 136
   persons eligible 139
   residence requirement 173
   single occupiers 140
   special categories 140
   statutory maternity pay and 87
   statutory sick pay and 53
   working tax credit and 160
   see also **local authority benefits**
Court of Appeal
   immigration appeals to 323
***Crake* guidelines 109-11**
crisis loans 163

deductions from benefits 114-15

Department for Work and Pensions
  claiming benefits 8
deportation
  during appeal procedure 323-4
  effects of order 307
  enforcement action
    children 315-17
    parents 315-17
    spouses 312-15
  exemption from 309
  family members 308-9
  grounds 307
  Home Secretary powers 307
  human rights and 308
  ordinary residence 309
  previous convictions 301-2
  procedure 309
  relevant factors 307-8
  revocation of order 310
  spouses 312-15
  supervised removal 309
  voluntary removal 309
  see also **administrative removal**
detention
  habeas corpus 330
disability
  benefits 47-8
  incapacity for work compared 48
  prescribed degrees of disablement 197-9
  see also **attendance allowance; disability living allowance; industrial disablement benefit**
disability living allowance
  backdating 11
  care component 4, 47, 57-62
    attendance allowance compared 66
    bodily functions 57-9
    children under 16 years 61
    claimant profile 74
    continual daytime supervision 60
    cooking test 59
    entitlement conditions 57
    frequent daytime attention 60
    night-time attention 60-1
    night-time watching over 61
    rates of payment 59-61
    severity of disability 59-61
    significant portion of day 59
    summary 62
    terminally ill 61
    varying needs 61-2
  carer's allowance and 56
  child tax credit and 56
  council tax benefit and 56
  housing benefit and 56
  income support and 56
  jobseeker's allowance and 56
  mobility component 4, 48
    benefiting from enhanced facilities 65
    blind and deaf 64
    children under 16 years 65
    claimant profile 74
    double amputee 64

disability living allowance – *continued*
    entitlement conditions 62
    mental/behavioural problems 64
    rate of pay 63-5
    relevant age 65
    severity of disability 63-5
    summary 65-6
    unable to walk 63-4
  pension credit and 56, 79
  residence requirement 171-2
  visitor to UK 251
  working tax credit and 56
disability premium 107
disabled child premium 105
disablement
  claimant profiles 74
  industrial disablement benefit 5
  jobseeker's allowance 40
  New Deal 73
discretionary social fund 12, 162-3
Dublin Convention 301

earnings condition
  maternity allowance 88
  statutory maternity pay 87
  statutory sick pay 52
earnings factor
  NI contributions 23
earnings replacement benefits 5
EC Association Agreements
  countries which are parties to 495
EEA see **European Economic Area (EEA)**
employees
  NI contributions 23-4
employment condition
  maternity allowance 88
employment and support allowance 55
enhanced disability premium 106
enhanced pensioner premium 107
entertainers
  work-permits 265
entry clearance
  child of settled parents 289
  civil partners 275
  financial undertakings 227
  general rule 226-7
  spouses 275
  see also **leave to enter**
European Community law
  free movement
    British citizens in Europe 241-3
    businesses 236
    Directive 2004/58/EC 209, 244, 499-512
    family members 238-40
    self-employed persons 236
    service providers 236
    workers 235
  see also **European Union**
European Convention on Human Rights
  immigration law and 209-10
European Economic Area (EEA)
  Accession States 235

European Economic Area (EEA) – *continued*
  Directive 2004/58/EC 209, 244
    text 499-512
  Immigration Regulations 2006 236-44
    text 513-36
  industrial accident in 71
  member countries 234-5, 497
European Economic Area (EEA) nationals
  civil partners 238
  claiming benefits 183
  death of qualified person 241
  dependency test 239
  descendants 239
  Directive 2004/58/EC 209, 244, 499-512
  document certifying permanent residence 243
  exclusion from UK 243-4
  family members 237, 238-40, 243
    rights of admission 237
  glossary of terms 243
  habitual residence 177-8
  I(EEA) Regulations 2006 236-44
  immigration appeals 326
  immigration status 235
  jobseekers 237
  marriage of convenience 238
  national security ground 243
  permanent residence 240-1
    confirmation 241
    document certifying 243
  permanent residence card 243
  public health ground 244
  public policy ground 243
  qualified persons 237-8, 243
    death of 241
  registration certificate 243
  removal from UK 243-4
  residence card 240, 243
  residence documents 243
  rights of admission 237
    family members 237
  rights of residence
    beyond three months 237
    confirmation of 240
    initial three months 237
    permanent 240-1
  self-sufficient person 237
  settled status 217
  settlement in UK 225
  spouse 238
  students 237, 256
  travel documents 240
European Union
  citizens of 222
  immigration law 209
  Member States 497
  see also **European Community law**

fact analysis
  welfare benefits 17
family members
  civil partner 238

family members – *continued*
  death of qualified person 241
  dependency test 239
  deportation 308-9
  descendants 239
  EEA nationals 237, 243
  extended family 239
  family permit 240, 243
  free movement within EC 238-40
  residence card 240
  spouse 238
  students 254
  travel documents 240
  visitors to UK, immigration appeal 324-5
  work-permit holders 266
family permit 240, 243
fiancé(e)s of settled person
  accommodation 283
  maintenance test 283
free movement, EC right of
  British citizen in Europe 241-3
  businesses 236
  Directive 2004/58/EC 209, 244, 499-512
  family members 238-40
  self-employed persons 236
  service providers 236
  workers 235
free school meals 165
free school milk 164-5
funeral payments
  amount 161
  claimants 160-1
  resources taken into account 161

ground rent
  housing costs assistance 122

habeas corpus 330
habitual residence
  appreciable period 177
  centre of interest 176-7
  EEA nationals and families 177-8
  first-time entrants 178-9
  humanitarian protection 178
  refugees 178
  returning residents 179-81
  right to reside test 177
  settled intent 177
  test 176
hardship payments
  assessment of hardship 130
  claimants 129
  income support 129-30
  jobseeker's allowance 129-30
    disqualification 44
  passporting 130
  urgent cases payments 129
  vulnerable group 130
higher pensioner premium 107
highly skilled migrants 270-3
  age assessment 271-2
  education qualifications 271
  income categories 545

highly skilled migrants – *continued*
  language requirement 272
  past earnings 271
  UK experience 271
HM Revenue and Customs
  NI contributions 8
Home Office 208-9
  asylum claims decision 303-4
  Border and Immigration Agency 210
home responsibilities protection
  contribution conditions 30-1
  NI contribution credit 26
housing benefit 6, 8, 96, 133
  administration 138
  backdating 10-11
  bereavement benefits and 82
  calculation 139
  carer's allowance and 92
  child benefit and 91
  child tax credit and 160
  claimant profiles 165
  disability living allowance and 56
  incapacity benefit and 55
  income support and 131, 136
  industrial disablement benefit and 73
  jobseeker's allowance and 45, 136
  local housing allowance 138
  maternity allowance and 89
  payment 14, 138
  pension credit and 136
  people under 25 years 137
  persons entitled to 136
  rent 136
    allowable 138
    eligible 137-8
    people under 25 years 137
    reference 137
    relevant 137
  residence requirement 173
  restrictions on amount 136-8
  statutory maternity pay and 87
  statutory sick pay and 53
  working tax credit and 160
  see also **local authority benefits**
housing costs
  claimants for assistance 120
  excessive 123
  existing housing costs 123
  ground rent 122
  interest payments
    calculation and payment 123-5
    prescribed interest rate 124
  loan payments 120-1, 123
    maximum amounts 123
  meaning 120
  mortgage payments 120-1
  new housing costs 123-4
    treated as existing 124
  non-dependants 125
  repairs and improvements 121-2
  restrictions on 122-3
  service charges 122

human rights
  asylum claims 302-3
  benefits 18-19
  Convention text 541-3
  deportation 308
  discrimination 18-19
  immigration appeals 326-7
  immigration law and 209-10, 293
  welfare benefit appeals 13

Identity and Passport Service 210
illegal entrant 310-11
illegal working 266
immigration
  administrative removal *see* **administrative removal**
  advising the client *see* **immigration advice**
  appeals *see* **immigration appeals**
  asylum claim *see* **asylum claims**
  British Overseas Territories 492
  children
    accommodation 289
    adopted 290
    born in UK 289
    conditions 288-9
    entering for settlement 286
    of limited leave persons 289
    over 18 years 292-3
    serious and compelling reasons 287-8
    of settled parents 289
    sole responsibility 286-7
    sponsors 288
    switching 289-90
  citizenship *see* **citizenship**
  civil partners 274
    accommodation 276-8, 283
    breakdown of civil partnership 281-2
    devotion 276
    entry clearance 275
    exempt groups 274-5
    intention to live together 276
    leave to enter 279
    maintenance 278-9
    permission to enter civil partnership 281
    of persons with limited leave 282
    polygamous civil partnership 282
    proposed
      maintenance 283
      of settled person 282-3
    public funds 276
    of settled persons 275-9
    settled status grant 279-80
    sham partnership 276
    switching status 281
    third-party support 278
    visitors 282
  cohabitants 283-5
  Common Travel Area 244-5
  Commonwealth citizens 219-20, 491
  controls 226
  deportation *see* **deportation**

immigration – *continued*
  EC law *see* **European Community law**
  EEA nationals *see* **European Economic Area (EEA) nationals**
  employment 258-9
    Commonwealth citizens 262-3
    permit-free employment 259
    persons with UK ancestry 262-3
    sole representative of overseas firm 259-62
    work-permit 263-6
  entry clearance *see* **entry clearance**
  entry without passport 229-30
  fiancé(e)s of settled person 282-3
  financial undertakings 227
  highly skilled migrants 270-3, 545
  human rights 209-10, 293
  illegal entrant 310-11
  income support 181
  independent means 258
  industrial disablement benefit 182
  innovators 269-70
  investors 273-4
  jobseeker's allowance 182
  law *see* **immigration law**
  leave to enter *see* **leave to enter**
  long-residence rules 231-2
  marriage of convenience 238
  MBA eligible programmes 547-8
  nationality *see* **nationality**
  naturalisation *see* **naturalisation**
  non-contributory benefits and 169-71
  non-marital relationships 283-5
  parents and other relatives 290-3
    children over 18 years 292-3
    dependants of settled child 291
    exceptional compassionate circumstances 292, 293
    grandparents 292
    human rights 293
    qualifying relative 290-1
    requirements 290-1
    sponsor 291
  proposed civil partners
    accommodation 283
    maintenance 283
    of settled person 282-3
  public funds and 181-2
  refugees *see* **refugees**
  refusal of leave to enter 229
  right of abode *see* **right of abode**
  self-employed persons *see* **self-employed persons**
  settled status *see* **settlement**
  settlement *see* **settlement**
  social fund payments 183
  spouses 274
    accommodation 276-8
    certificate of approval of marriage 280
    devotion 276
    entry clearance 275
    exempt groups 274-5
    intention to live together 276

immigration – *continued*
  leave to enter 279
  maintenance 278-9
  marriage breakdown 281-2
  permission to marry 280-1
  of persons with limited leave 282
  polygamous marriage 282
  public funds 276
  of settled persons 275-9
  settled status grant 279-80
  sham marriage 276
  switching status 280-1
  third-party support 278
  statutory maternity pay 182
  statutory sick pay 182
  students *see* **students**
  Surinder Singh type cases 242
  switching categories of leave 231
  tax credits 181-2
  temporary admission 228
  trainees 257, 266
  urgent cases payments 183
  variation of leave 230-4
  visa national 493-4
  visitors *see* **visitors**
  work-permit *see* **work-permits**
  working holidaymakers 257-8, 266
  see also **residence requirement**
immigration advice
  available options 332-3
  client's objectives 332
  disputed decision 331-2
    reasons for 332
  immigration status 331
  passport 331
  personal details 331
  time limits 332
immigration appeals
  abandoned appeals 323-4
  asylum claims 301-2, 326-7
  Asylum and Immigration Appeal Tribunal 322-3
  certification under s 96 321-2
  Court of Appeal 323
  deprivation of citizenship 327
  EEA nationals 326
  family visitors 324-5
  general rule 319
  grounds 320
    failure to disclose all grounds 321
  human rights claims 320, 326-7
  ineligible appeals 324
  national security 325
  notice of appealable decision 321
  'one stop' process 321-2
  pending appeals 323-4
  public good exclusion 325-6
  right of appeal 319-20
  rights exercisable in UK 320
  Special Immigration Appeals Commission (SIAC) 325
  students 324, 325
  third country removal 326

immigration appeals – *continued*
  timetable 323
  visitors without entry clearance 324
  see also **judicial review**
Immigration, Asylum and Nationality Act 2006 327
immigration controls 211-12
Immigration (European Economic Area) Regulations 2006 236-44
immigration law
  case law 209
  EC law 209
  Home Office practices 208-9, 304
  Immigration Rules 208, 225
  institutions 210-11
  legislation 208
  practitioner texts 207
  sources 207-10
  Statement of Changes to Immigration Rules (HC 395) text 337-489
  websites 207-8
Immigration Rules 208, 225
  Statement of Changes to Immigration Rules (HC 395) text 337-489
immigration service 210
improvements
  housing cost assistance 121-2
incapacity benefit
  administration 54-5
  adult dependant increase 31, 55
  backdating 9
  child benefit and 91
  child tax credit and 55
  claimant profiles 74
  contribution conditions 28-9, 47
  contributory 4
  council tax benefit and 55
  employment and support allowance 55
  entitlement to 53-4
  housing benefit and 55
  income support and 55
  jobseeker's allowance and 45, 55
  linked periods of incapacity 54-5
  long-term benefit 54
  non-contributory 5, 47
    claimant profile 74
    entitlement conditions 55-6
    persons incapacitated in youth 55-6
  other benefits and 55
  other income and 54
  own occupation test 53
  payment 54-5
  pension credit and 55, 79
  personal capability assessment 53
  pregnancy and 52, 89
  prescribed pension payments and 54
  residence requirement 174
  retirement pension and 55
  short-term benefit 54
  statutory maternity pay and 55, 88
  statutory sick pay and 55
  working tax credit and 55

incapacity for work
  benefits 47
  deemed capacity 51-2
  disablement compared 48
  incapable of work meaning 48
  mental disability descriptors 50
  missed medicals 51
  own occupation test 48-9, 52
  personal capability assessment 49-51, 52
  physical activity descriptors 50
  pregnancy 52
  Social Security (Incapacity for Work) (General) Regulations 1995 text 191-5
  variable conditions 51
  see also **incapacity benefit; statutory sick pay**
income
  means-tested benefits
    earnings from employment 100
    earnings from self-employment 100
    maintenance 100
    meaning 99-100
    pensions 100
    tariff income 101
  tax credits 143-6
    employment income 145
    entitlement over tax year 146
    investment income 144
    notifying changes 146
    notional income 144-5
    overview 143-4
    pension income 144
    property income 144
    social security income 145
    trading income 145
    worked example 145-6
income support 6, 95
  backdating 9-10
  bereavement benefits and 82
  carer's allowance and 92
  child benefit and 91
  child tax credit and 131, 160
  claimant profiles 131
  claimants 119
  conditions of entitlement 117-18
  council tax benefit and 131, 136
  couples 181
  disability living allowance and 56
  hardship payments 129-30
  housing benefit and 131, 136
  housing costs *see* **housing costs**
  immigration law and 181
  incapacity benefit and 55
  industrial disablement benefit and 73
  interest payment *see* **housing costs**
  jobseeker's allowance and 45
  maternity allowance and 89
  own occupation test 48-9
  passport effect 128-9
  residence requirement 173
  statutory maternity pay and 87
  statutory sick pay and 53
  urgent cases payments 129, 130

income support – *continued*
  working tax credit and 131, 160
industrial accident 66-7
industrial disablement benefit 5, 48
  accident
    in Great Britain or EEA 71
    meaning 70-1
  backdating 9
  child tax credit and 73
  claimant profile 74
  council tax benefit and 73
  in course of employment
    case law 67
    contravention of regulations 67-8
    emergencies 69-70
    misconduct 70
    no evidence available 67
    rescuers 69
    statutory deeming provisions 67-70
    travelling 68-9
  degree of disability 72
  disablement 71
  employed earner's employment 70
  housing benefit and 73
  immigration law and 182
  income support and 73
  industrial accident 66-7
  jobseeker's allowance and 73
  loss of faculty 71
  meaning 66
  no-fault compensation 66
  pension credit and 79
  personal injury 67
  prescribed industrial diseases 71-2
  rate of benefit 73
  residence requirement 173-4
  waiting period 73
  working tax credit and 73
  see also **constant attendance allowance**
industrial disease 71-2
industrial disputes
  jobseeker's allowance disqualification 42
industrial injury benefit scheme 66
  see also **constant attendance allowance;**
  industrial disablement benefit
innovators 269-70
interest rates
  housing costs 124-5
  mortgage interest 124-5
  prescribed 124
international aspects of benefits
  contributory benefits and EC 169
  exclusionary rule 169-71
  immigrants into UK 167-9
  immigration status and 169-71
  reciprocal agreements 168-9, 203
  residence requirements 171-5
International Graduate Scheme 256
investors 273-4
Irish citizens 222

Jobcentre Plus 8
Jobseekers Act 1995 7

jobseeker's agreement
  challenging 37
  content 36-7
  form 36
  specimen 187-90
jobseeker's allowance
  actively seeking employment 40-1
  adult dependant increase and 45
  agreement *see* **jobseeker's agreement**
  available for work 38
  backdating 9-10
  bereavement benefits and 82
  charity workers 37
  claimant profile 45
  claiming 8, 36
  conditions of entitlement 36
  contribution-based 4, 35
    claimant profile 45
    contribution conditions 27-8
    immigration law and 182
    income-based compared 119
    pension credit and 79
    rates of payment 44
    residence requirement 174-5
    statutory maternity pay and 88
  deemed capable of work 51
  discretionary period sanctions 43
  disqualification
    grounds 41
    hardship payments 44
    industrial disputes 42
    missed appointments 41-2
    sanctions 43-4
    termination payments 42
  fixed-period sanctions 43
  hardship payments 44
  incapacity benefit and 55
  income-based 6, 35, 95
    carer's allowance and 92
    child benefit and 91
    child tax credit and 131, 160
    claimant profiles 131
    conditions of entitlement 117-18
    contribution-based compared 119
    council tax benefit and 131, 136
    couples 181
    disability living allowance and 56
    hardship payments 129-30
    housing benefit and 131, 136
    housing costs *see* **housing costs**
    immigration law 181
    industrial disablement benefit and 73
    joint claims 119
    passport effect 128-9
    payment of benefit 14
    residence requirement 173
    statutory maternity pay and 87
    statutory sick pay and 53
    urgent cases payments 129, 130
    working tax credit and 131, 160
  labour market conditions 38
  maternity allowance and 89
  meaning 35

jobseeker's allowance – *continued*
  New Deal 44
  NI contribution credit 25
  remunerative work 37-8
  restricting availability
    caring responsibilities 40
    conscientious objections 40
    disabilities 40
    during permitted period 39
    hours of work 39
    level of pay 39
    religious beliefs 40
  sanctions 43-4
  short-term illness 51
  treated as income 44-5
judicial review
  Administrative Court 329
  alternative remedy 329
  availability of 329-30
  habeas corpus 330
  hearing 329
  immigration claims 329-30
  permission to proceed 329
  prompt action 330
  statutory review 330
  welfare benefits 12

leave to enter
  civil partner of immigrant 279
  conditions 223-4
  curtailment of existing leave 234
  documentary evidence 228
  employment restrictions 224
  entry without passport 229-30
  general rule 227-8
  grant under general rule 228
  IAA 1999 229
  limited 223
  long-residence rules 231-2
  public funds, without recourse to 223
  refusal 229
  registration with police 224
  removal for illegal entry 234
  requirements 223-4
  spouse of immigrant 279
  switching categories 231
  temporary admission 228
  travel outside UK 228
  unlimited 223
  variation
    application for 230
    curtailment of existing leave 234
    general considerations 230-1
    procedure 232-4
living together as husband and wife
  children of relationship 110
  cohabitation 108-9
  Crake guidelines 109-11
  financial support 110
  membership of same household 110
  pooling of resources 110
  public image 110-11
  same household 108-9

living together as husband and wife – *continued*
  sexual relationship 110
  stability of relationship 110
loan payments
  housing cost assistance 120-1
  maximum amounts 123
local authority benefits 133
  administration 134
  applicable amount 135
  council tax benefit *see* **council tax benefit**
  housing benefit *see* **housing benefit**
  income 134-5
  income support and 136
  jobseeker's allowance and 136
  non-dependants 134
  overpayments 111-12
    automatic right of recovery 112
    no automatic right of recovery 111
  pension credit and 136
  tapering 135, 141-2
  worked examples 141-3
local housing allowance 138
lone parent family premium 106
lower earnings limits
  NI contributions 22

maintenance
  immigration and
    of civil partner 278-9
    of finance(e) 283
    proposed civil partners 283
    of spouse 278-9
  as income 100
marriage
  breakdown 281-2
  of convenience 238
  polygamous 282
  right of abode acquired by 219-20
  sham 276
  to British citizen 216-17
marriage visits 249-50, 282
maternity allowance 5, 85
  adult dependant increase 31, 89
  amount of benefit 88
  backdating 9
  child tax credit and 88
  claimant profile 93
  council tax benefit and 89
  earnings condition 88
  employment condition 88
  entitlement conditions 88
  housing benefit and 89
  income support and 89
  jobseeker's allowance and 45, 89
  key dates 86
  pension credit and 79, 80, 89
  period 88
  sick pay and 89
  threshold 86, 88
  working tax credit and 88

maternity benefits
  calculation of key dates 86
  children *see* **child benefit**
  expected week of childbirth 85
  incapacity benefit and 89
  maternity grant 89
  qualifying week 85
  terminology 85-6
  week, meaning 85
  see also **maternity allowance; maternity leave; maternity pay; statutory maternity pay**
maternity grant 89
maternity leave
  working tax credit and 150
maternity pay
  backdating 11
  jobseeker's allowance and 45
  period 87
  statutory *see* **statutory maternity pay**
MBA eligible programmes 547-8
means-tested benefits 5-6, 95-165
  aggregation of resources 102-3
  boarders 103-4
  capital
    actual 96
    available on application 97
    diminishing notional capital rule 99
    disregarded 98
    income treated as 96
    limits 99
    notional 96-8
    value of 98-9
  change of circumstances 128
  children of the family 102
  claimants benefits household 102-4
    persons not in 103
  claimant's partner 102
  common problems 108
  Common Travel Area 175
  comparison 108
  Crake guidelines 109-11
  deductions from benefits 114-15
  family meaning 102
  income
    earnings from employment 100
    earnings from self-employment 100
    maintenance 100
    meaning 99-100
    pensions 100
    tariff income 101
  income support *see* **income support**
  jobseeker's allowance *see* **jobseeker's allowance**
  living together as husband and wife 108-11
    children of relationship 110
    cohabitation 108-9
    Crake guidelines 109-11
    financial support 110
    membership of same household 110
    pooling of resources 110
    public image 110-11

means-tested benefits – *continued*
  same household 110
  sexual relationship 110
  local authorities *see* **council tax benefit; housing benefit; local authority benefits**
  means tests 96
  needs, applicable amount 104
  non-dependants 103
  overpayments
    automatic right of recovery 112, 114
    failure to disclose 113
    local authority benefits 111-12
    material fact 111
    mechanics of recovery 114
    misrepresentation 112-13
    no automatic right of recovery 111
    proof 113-14
    social security benefits 112-14
    tax credits 112-14
  passport effect 128-9
  personal allowances 104-5
  premiums
    carer's 106
    claiming together 107-8
    disability 107
    disabled child 105
    enhanced disability 106
    enhanced pensioner 107
    higher pensioner 107
    lone parent family 106
    pensioner 107
    severe disability 105
    standard rate family 105
  resources *see* capital; income
  reviews 128
  subtenants 103
  worked examples 125-8
  see also individual benefits
misrepresentation
  overpayments 112-13
missed appointments
  jobseeker's allowance disqualification 41-2
missed medicals
  incapacity for work 51
mortgages
  housing cost assistance 120-1
  interest 14

National Health Service benefits 134
  dental treatment 164
  fares to hospital 164
  glasses 164
  passport benefits 163
  prescriptions 163
  sight tests 164
National Insurance
  administration of contributions 8
  children 24
  Class 1 contribution 23-4
  Class 1 contributions, credits 25
  Class 2 contributions 24

National Insurance – *continued*
  Class 3 credits 26
  Class 3 voluntary contributions 26
  Class 4 contributions 24
  compulsory contributions 23-4
  contribution conditions
    benefit year 27
    bereavement benefit 29-30, 31
    carers 29
    contribution year 27
    home responsibilities protection 30-1
    incapacity benefit 28-9, 47
    jobseeker's allowance 27-8
    meaning 27
    retirement benefits 29-31
    statutory sick pay 29
    working life 27
  contributions 22-6
  earnings factor 23
  employees 23-4
  exempt persons 24
  home responsibilities protection 26
  liability to pay 23-4
  low-paid employees 25
  lower earnings limits 22
  primary contributions threshold 22
  retired persons 24
  retirement pension *see* **retirement pensions**
  secondary contribution threshold 22
  self-employed workers 24
  upper earnings limit 23
  young persons 26
national security
  immigration appeals 325
nationality
  British 213-19
  visa national 495-6
naturalisation
  civil partnership with British citizen 216-17
  EEA nationals 217
  formalities 217
  marriage to British citizen 216-17
  no civil partnership with British citizen 216
  no marriage to British citizen 216
needs
  means-tested benefits 104
New Asylum Model 303
New Deal 44
  jobseeker's allowance 44
  persons with disability 73
night-time attention 60-1
night-time watching over 61
non means-tested benefits
  adult dependant increase 31-2
  claiming more than one 33-4
  contributory 21
  incompatible 32-3
  NI contributions *see* **National Insurance**
  non-contributory 21
  overlapping 33

non means-tested benefits – *continued*
  statutory 22
non-contributory benefits
  immigration status and 169-71
  non means-tested 21
  see also **incapacity benefit**
Northern Ireland 175
notional capital 96-8
  diminishing notional capital rule 99

occupational pension 77
ordinarily resident 175-6
  deportation exemption 309
overpayment of benefits
  automatic right of recovery 112, 114
  failure to disclose 113
  local authority benefits 111-12
  material fact 111
  means-tested benefits 111-14
  mechanics of recovery 114
  misrepresentation 112-13
  no automatic right of recovery 111
  proof 113-14
  social security benefits 112-14
  tax credits 112-14
own occupation test
  incapacity benefit 53
  incapacity for work 48-9, 52
  income support 48-9
  statutory sick pay 49

parents and other relatives, immigration 290-3
  administrative removal and 315-17
  children over 18 years 292-3
  dependants of settled child 291
  deportation and 315-17
  exceptional compassionate circumstances 292, 293
  grandparents 292
  human rights 293
  qualifying relative 290-1
  requirements 290-1
  sponsor 291
passport
  entry without 229-30
  failure to produce 305
  immigration advice requirement 331
passport benefits
  council tax 128-9
  income-related benefits 6
  means-tested benefits 128-9
  NHS benefits 163
  school meals 165
  school milk 164-5
passporting
  hardship payments 130
payment of benefit 14
  carer's allowance 92
  child benefit 90
  constant attendance allowance 73
  council tax benefit 14, 140
  entrants to country 14

payment of benefit – *continued*
   exportation of benefits 14
   housing benefits 14, 138
   incapacity benefit 54-5
   industrial disablement benefit 73
   jobseeker's allowance 14
   mortgage interest 14
   overpayments *see* **overpayment of benefits**
   pension credit 80
   social fund payments 14
   statutory sick pay 53
   tax credits 160
pension credit 6
   attendance allowance and 79
   benefits counting as income 79
   bereavement allowance and 79
   carer's allowance and 79, 93
   child benefit and 79
   child tax credit and 79
   claimant profile 83
   constant attendance allowance and 79
   council tax benefit and 136
   disability living allowance and 56, 79
   elements 78-9
   entitlement conditions 78
   guarantee credit 78
   housing benefit and 136
   incapacity benefit and 55, 79
   income and 79-80
   industrial disablement benefit and 79
   jobseeker's allowance and 79
   maternity allowance and 79, 80, 89
   payment 81
   savings credit 78-80
   State pension and 79
   statutory maternity pay and 88
   statutory sick pay and 53
   widowed parent's allowance 79, 82
   worked examples 80
   working tax credit and 79, 80, 160
pensioner premium 107
pensions
   as income 100
   personal 77
   retirement 5
   stakeholder 77
   State pension 4, 9, 31, 75-7, 83
personal allowances
   means-tested benefits 104-5
personal capability assessment
   capability report 49
   deemed capacity for work 51-2
   exempt persons 52
   incapacity benefit 53
   incapacity report 49
   incapacity for work 49-51, 52
   mental disability descriptors 50
   physical activity descriptors 50
   variable conditions 51
personal injury
   industrial disablement benefit 67
personal pension 77

polygamous civil partnership 282
polygamous marriage 282
pregnancy
   incapacity for work 52
premiums
   carer's 106
   claiming together 107-8
   disability 107
   disabled child 105
   enhanced disability 106
   enhanced pensioner 107
   higher pensioner 107
   lone parent family 106
   pensioner 107
   severe disability 105
   standard rate family 105
prescribed industrial diseases 71-2
primary contributions threshold 22
public funds
   immigration and 181-2, 223, 276
   without recourse to 223, 254, 265
public good exclusion
   immigration appeals 325-6

reasons for decision 11
reciprocal benefits 168-9, 203
recovery of overpayments
   automatic right 112, 114
   mechanics of 114
   no automatic right 111
Refugee Legal Centre 304
refugees
   asylum claim *see* **asylum claims**
   attack on spouse or close family 296
   discrimination 295
   excessive or arbitrary punishment 295
   exclusion from status 300
   fear of persecution 294-7, 304
   Geneva Convention 294, 300, 301, 302, 304
   habitual residence 178
   internal flight/relocation alternative 299-300
   meaning of refugee 294
   outside country of nationality 299-300
   persecution 294-8
      nationality 296-7
      particular social group 297
      political opinion 297-8
      religion 298
   protection in own country 300
   Refugee or Person in Need of International Protection (Qualification) Regulations 2006 549-51
   safe third country exception 301-2
religious beliefs
   jobseeker's allowance restrictions 40
   persecution of refugees for 298-9
rent, housing benefit and 137-8
   allowable 138
   eligible 137-8
   people under 25 years 137
   reference 137

rent, housing benefit and – *continued*
   relevant 137
repairs
   housing cost assistance 121-2
residence
   EEA nationals and families 178
   habitual residence *see* habitual residence
   ordinarily resident 175-6
   ordinary 224, 226
   requirement for *see* residence requirement
   returning residents 179-81
residence requirement
   attendance allowance 171-2
   carer's allowance 171-2
   child benefit 172
   child tax credit 172-3
   council tax benefit 173
   disability living allowance 171-2
   housing benefit 173
   incapacity benefit 174
   income support 173
   industrial disablement benefit 173-4
   jobseeker's allowance
      contribution-based 174-5
      income-based 173
   statutory maternity pay 174
   statutory sick pay 174
   tax credits 172-3
   working tax credit 172-3
retired persons
   NI contribution exempt 24
retirement benefits
   claimant profile 83
   contribution conditions 29-31
   home responsibilities protection 30-1
retirement pensions 5, 24
   additional State pension scheme 77
   age over 80 years 77
   backdating 9
   bereaved persons 77
   bereavement after retirement age 77-8
   Category D pension 77
   deferring retirement 76
   dependent children 77
   earnings-related element 77
   incapacity benefit and 55
   jobseeker's allowance and 45
   occupational pension 77
   pension credit and 79
   personal pension 77
   retirement age 75-6
   stakeholder pension 77
   State pension 4, 9, 31, 75-7, 83
      adult dependant increase 31, 76
      civil partnerships 76
      couples 76
   see also pension credit
revision of decision 11
right of abode 213
   acquired by marriage 219-20
   certificate of entitlement 220
   Commonwealth citizens 219-20

right of abode – *continued*
   CUKCs 221
   deprivation 220
   parental link 219
right to reside test
   habitual residence 177

safe third country exception 301-2
savings credit 78-9
   qualifying income 79-80
secondary contribution threshold 22
self-employed persons
   business plan 268
   earnings from self-employment 100
   EC free movement right 236
   entry 269
   extensions 269
   higher-earning 24
   immigration status 258-9, 266-9
   initial investment 269
   NI contributions 24
   requirements 266-9
   switching categories 269
   types of business 266
service charges 122
settled status 224-5
settlement
   acquisition of status 225-6
   child of settled parents 289
   children entering for 286
   civil partner of settled person 275-9
   EEA nationals 225
   fiancé(e)s of settled person
      accommodation 283
      maintenance test 283
   grant to civil partner 279-80
   grant to spouse 279-80
   Immigration Rules 225
   ordinary residence 224, 226
   proposed civil partner
      accommodation 283
      maintenance test 283
   settled status 224-5
   spouse of settled person 275-9
   travel outside UK 228
severe disability element
   working tax credit 154
severe disability premium 105
short-term contracts
   statutory sick pay 53
sick pay
   backdating 11
   contribution conditions 29
   statutory *see* statutory sick pay
social fund 134
   budgeting loans 162
   cold weather payments 161-2
   community care grants 162
   crisis loans 163
   discretionary 12, 162-3
   funeral payments 160-1
   payments 14
      to immigrants 183

social fund – *continued*
  regulated 160
Social Security Administration Act 1992 7
Social Security Commissioners 7
  appeals to 13
Social Security (Contributions and Benefits) Act 1992 7
Special Immigration Appeals Commission (SIAC) 325
sportsmen
  work-permits 265
spouses, immigration 274
  accommodation 276-8
  certificate of approval of marriage 280
  devotion 276
  EEA nationals 238
  entry clearance 275
  exempt groups 274-5
  intention to live together 276
  leave to enter 279
  maintenance 278-9
  marriage breakdown 281-2
  permission to marry 280-1
  of persons with limited leave 282
  polygamous marriage 282
  public funds 276
  of settled persons 275-9
  settled status grant 279-80
  sham marriage 276
  switching status 280-1
  third-party support 278
stakeholder pension 77
standard rate family premium 105
state pension credit *see* **pension credit**
State Pension Credits Act 2002 7
Statement of Changes to Immigration Rules (HC 395)
  text 337-489
statutory benefits 4
  non means-tested 22
statutory instruments 7
statutory maternity pay 85, 101
  backdating 11
  child tax credit and 87
  claimant profile 93
  continuous employment rule 86
  council tax benefit and 87
  earnings condition 87
  housing benefit and 87
  immigration law and 182
  incapacity benefit and 55, 88
  income support and 87
  jobseeker's allowance and 45
    contribution-based 88
    income-based 87
  key dates
    calculation 86
    summary 87
  maternity pay period 87
  pension credit and 88
  qualifying conditions 86
  rate 87

statutory maternity pay – *continued*
  residence requirement 174
  sick pay and 88
  working tax credit and 87
  see also **maternity benefits**
statutory sick pay 47, 101
  administration 53
  adult dependant increase 53
  backdating 11
  carer's allowance and 53
  child tax credit and 53
  claimant profile 74
  contribution conditions 29
  council tax benefit and 53
  earnings condition 52
  entitlement conditions 52
  housing benefit and 53
  immigration law and 182
  incapacity benefit and 55
  income support and 53
  jobseeker's allowance and 45
    income-based 53
  maternity allowance and 89
  own occupation test 49
  payment 53
  pension credit and 53
  qualifying conditions 52
  residence requirement 174
  short-term contracts 53
  statutory maternity pay and 88
  working tax credit and 53, 150
students 266
  EEA nationals 238, 256
  entry 251-4
  extension of leave 255
  family members 254
  immigration appeals 324, 325
  immigration status 251-6
  independent fee-paying school 252-3
  International Graduate Scheme 256
  leaving country at end of studies 253
  length of leave 254
  part-time work 253-4
  recourse to public funds 254
  specified course 251-2
  specified institution 251
  switching category 255-6
  vacation work 253-4
  without entry clearance 324
subtenants
  means-tested benefits 103
supersession 11-12
Sure Start scheme
  maternity grant 89

tax credits
  age 143
  aims 143
  appeals 12
  backdating 9
  claim by couple 181-2
  employment income 145
  entitlement over tax year 146

tax credits – *continued*
  immigration requirements 143
  income 143-6
    overview 143-4
    worked example 145-6
  investment income 144
  judicial review 12
  notifying changes of income 146
  notional income 144-5
  overpayments 112-14
  payment 160
  pension income 144
  property income 144
  residence requirement 172-3
  social security income 145
  trading income 145
  worked examples 157-9
  see also **child tax credit; pension credit; working tax credit**
Tax Credits Act 2002 7
time limits
  benefit claim 9
  immigration advice 332

UKvisas 210
unemployment benefit *see* **jobseeker's allowance**
upper earnings limit
  NI contributions 23
urgent cases payments 129
  calculation of 130
  eligibility 130
  immigrants 183

visa national 495-6
visitors
  business visitor 248-9
  carers 250-1
  civil partnership visits 249-50, 282
  conditions 248
  extension of visit 250
  family members 324-5
  immigration appeals 324
  marriage visits 249-50, 282
  meaning of term 247
  switching category 251
  temporary purpose 256-8
  time limit 247, 249
vulnerable group 130

websites 15-16, 207-8
welfare benefits *see* **benefits system** *and individual benefits*
welfare law
  advisers' manuals 15
  benefits system *see* **benefits system**
  bibliography 14-15
  case law 7-8, 14
  commentary 14
  journals 15
  nature of 3
  sources 6-8
  statute 7, 14

welfare law – *continued*
  statutory instruments 7
  textbooks 15
Welfare Reform and Pensions Act 1999 7
widowed parent's allowance 81, 82
  claimant profile 83
  pension credit and 79
  retirement pension and 77
work-focused interviews 9
work-permits 263-6
  application 264-5
  duration 265-6
  entertainers 265
  entry requirements 265
  extensions 266
  family members 266
  illegal working 266
  no recourse to public funds 265
  professions 264
  qualification and skills criteria 263-4
  short supply list 537-9
  sportsmen 265
  switching categories 266
working holidaymakers 257-8, 266
working tax credit 6, 101, 133
  30-hour element 151-2
  50-plus element 154-5
  annual amounts 155-6
  backdating 9
  bereavement benefits and 82
  calculation 157
  carer's allowance and 92
  child benefit and 90
  child care element 152-4
  claimant profiles 165
  council tax credit and 160
  disability element 150-1
  disability living allowance and 56
  disability putting person at disadvantage 201-2
  entitlement conditions 148-9
  housing benefit and 160
  incapacity benefit and 55
  income support and 131, 160
  industrial disablement benefit and 73
  jobseeker's allowance and 44
    income-based 131, 160
  lone parent element 152
  maternity allowance and 88
  maternity leave and 150
  maximum 150-5
  pension credit and 79, 80, 160
  qualifying remunerative work 149-50
  residence requirement 172-3
  second adult element 152
  severe disability element 154
  statutory maternity pay and 87
  statutory sick pay and 53, 150
  tapering 156-7
  worked example 156, 157-8
  see also **tax credits**

young persons
  NI contribution credit 26